DATE DUE	
MAR 1 2 2014	
	PRINTED IN U.S.A.

Elgin Community College Library
Elgin, IL 60123

The Children of Eve

The Children of Eve

Population and Well-being in History

Louis P. Cain and Donald G. Paterson

A John Wiley & Sons, Ltd., Publication

This edition first published 2012
© 2012 Blackwell Publishing Ltd.

Blackwell Publishing was acquired by John Wiley & Sons in February 2007. Blackwell's publishing program has been merged with Wiley's global Scientific, Technical, and Medical business to form Wiley-Blackwell.

Registered Office
John Wiley & Sons Ltd, The Atrium, Southern Gate, Chichester, West Sussex, PO19 8SQ, UK

Editorial Offices
350 Main Street, Malden, MA 02148-5020, USA
9600 Garsington Road, Oxford, OX4 2DQ, UK
The Atrium, Southern Gate, Chichester, West Sussex, PO19 8SQ, UK

For details of our global editorial offices, for customer services, and for information about how to apply for permission to reuse the copyright material in this book please see our website at www.wiley.com/wiley-blackwell.

The right of Louis P. Cain and Donald G. Paterson to be identified as the authors of this work has been asserted in accordance with the UK Copyright, Designs and Patents Act 1988.

All rights reserved. No part of this publication may be reproduced, stored in a retrieval system, or transmitted, in any form or by any means, electronic, mechanical, photocopying, recording or otherwise, except as permitted by the UK Copyright, Designs and Patents Act 1988, without the prior permission of the publisher.

Wiley also publishes its books in a variety of electronic formats. Some content that appears in print may not be available in electronic books.

Designations used by companies to distinguish their products are often claimed as trademarks. All brand names and product names used in this book are trade names, service marks, trademarks or registered trademarks of their respective owners. The publisher is not associated with any product or vendor mentioned in this book. This publication is designed to provide accurate and authoritative information in regard to the subject matter covered. It is sold on the understanding that the publisher is not engaged in rendering professional services. If professional advice or other expert assistance is required, the services of a competent professional should be sought.

Library of Congress Cataloging-in-Publication Data

Cain, Louis P.
 The children of Eve : population and well-being in history / Louis P. Cain and Donald G. Paterson.
     p. cm.
 Includes bibliographical references and index.
   ISBN 978-1-4443-3689-4 (hardback) – ISBN 978-1-4443-3690-0 (paperback)
 1. Population–History. 2. Well-being–History. 3. Economic history. I. Paterson, Donald G., 1942– II. Title.
   HB871.C347 2012
   304.609–dc23
                                            2011032626

A catalogue record for this book is available from the British Library.

This book is published in the following electronic formats: ePDF [9781118169629]; ePub [9781118169636]; Mobi [9781118169643]

Set in 10/12.5pt Galliard by SPi Publisher Services, Pondicherry, India
Printed in Singapore by Ho Printing Singapore Pte Ltd

1 2012

For
Chelle, Elizabeth and the Fab Four

Contents

List of Figures, Tables, and Appendices	xi
Preface	xv
Acknowledgments	xviii

Part One   Initial Conditions   1

Chapter One   Overview   3

1.1	Introduction	3
1.2	Human Origins	7
1.3	The 40 000 Years to 10 000 BC	9
1.4	The Last 12 000 Years	11
1.5	A Few Fundamentals of Population Growth	14
1.6	The Quality and Quantity of Life	15
1.7	The English Parson, Thomas Malthus	17
1.8	Measurement and Inference	19
1.9	The Census	22
	A. A Nearly Modern Census	22
	B. Modern Censuses	24
	C. Some Problems of Early Modern Censuses	25
1.10	Models of Human Behavior	26
1.11	Outline	27

Chapter Two   The Historical Setting   31

2.1	Introduction	31
2.2	The Demographic Transition	31
2.3	Structural Transition of the Economy	33
2.4	Long-Run Changes in Economic Well-Being	36
2.5	Net Replacement	40
2.6	Dependency and Participation	43
2.7	How Does the Demographic Transition End or Does It?	45
2.8	Variation	50

2.9	Globalization, Macroeconomics and Population	52
2.10	Institutional Change and Externalities	56

Part Two   Growth and Dispersal of the Human Population   63

Chapter Three   Mortality: The Fourth Horseman   65

3.1	What Do People Die From?	65
3.2	Infant and Child Mortality	70
3.3	The Probability of Death and Life Expectancy	73
3.4	Seasonal Pattern of Death	82
3.5	Seasonality and Longevity	84
3.6	Urban Mortality	85
3.7	The Mortality Transition: Crude Death Rates	89

Chapter Four   The Fertility Transition   98

4.1	The Fertility Transition	98
4.2	The Queen and the Anabaptists	100
4.3	Strategic Choice	102
4.4	When to Marry	106
4.5	The "Never Married"	111
4.6	Illegitimacy	114
4.7	The Seasonal Pattern of Birth	115
4.8	Disruptions	117
4.9	The Fertility Transition: Crude Birth Rates	118
4.10	Farms and Towns	123

Chapter Five   Long Distance Migration   132

5.1	The Migratory Instinct	132
5.2	Who's In and Who's Out	136
5.3	Migration of the Unfree	138
	A. Slaves	138
	B. Convicts and Indentured Servants	141
	C. Child Migrants	144
5.4	The Atlantic: Waves of Immigration	145
5.5	Unbalanced Cargoes	150
5.6	Information and Advertising	152
5.7	Remittances: Then and Now	153
5.8	There and Back Again – Reverse Migrations	155
5.9	Diaspora	158
	A. The Chinese	158
	B. The Irish	162
	C. The Jews	164
5.10	The Barriers Go Up	166
5.11	The Walker Thesis, Displacement and Savings	168
5.12	A Final Word on Long Distance Migration	169

Chapter Six	**Regional Migration**	**181**
6.1	Introduction	181
6.2	The US Westward Movement and Other Frontiers	183
6.3	Urbanization and Industrial Change	188
6.4	The Rural-Urban Shift	191
6.5	Town and Farm and the Changing Economic Role of Children	195
6.6	The Great Black Migration in the US	195
6.7	Declining Regions: Dust Bowls and Yorkshire Coal Mines	198
6.8	Inter-Urban Migration	199
6.9	Migration: In the Neighborhood	200
	A. Scotland – England	200
	B. Canada – USA	201
6.10	The Undocumented	203
6.11	Convergence	205
6.12	Summary of Part Two – Putting It All Together	207

Part Three	**Choices and Their Consequences**	**217**
Chapter Seven	**The Changing Family**	**219**
7.1	Introduction	219
7.2	Courtship and Marriage	221
7.3	Household and Family Size	225
7.4	Child Labor	228
7.5	Family Connections: Networks	234
7.6	Marital Dissolution	236
7.7	Married Women's Property	240
7.8	Poverty: One-Parent Families and Elderly Females	242

Chapter Eight	**Health and Well-Being**	**255**
8.1	Introduction	255
8.2	Glasgow: Then and Now	256
8.3	Morbidity	257
8.4	Early Populations and Nutrition	262
8.5	Birth Weights	266
8.6	The Human Development Index	267
8.7	Obesity and the BMI	269
8.8	Household Space	274
8.9	Health and Hospital Care Systems	276

Chapter Nine	**Macroeconomic Effects of the Industrial Transition**	**286**
9.1	Introduction	286
9.2	Shocks and Echoes – the Baby Boom	287
9.3	Children and the Saving Shift	288
9.4	Intergenerational Contracts or Life Cycles: Pensions	291

9.5	The Work-Leisure Choice	297
9.6	Time Spent in Household Work	301
9.7	Education and Human Capital	305

Chapter Ten Population Catastrophes — 315

10.1	The Nature of Catastrophes	315
10.2	The Greenland Norse and the Easter Islanders	316
10.3	North American Native Indians	318
10.4	Famine	321
10.5	We All Fall Down! Plague	324
10.6	The HIV/AIDS Pandemic	333
10.7	When, Not If? But Not Now! Flu Pandemics	338
10.8	Summary	342

Part Four Conclusions — 351

Chapter Eleven Concluding Remarks — 353

General and Frequently Referenced Sources — 358

Index — 360

List of Figures, Tables, and Appendices

Figures

1.1	Eve and her Daughters, the mtDNA Pattern of Evolution	8
1.2	Logistic Growth	10
1.3	Model of Population Size Over 100 Years (compound rates of growth)	13
2.1	The Demographic Transition	32
2.2	Changing Composition of GDP by Sector during the Industrial Transition	35
2.3	Index of Real Earnings and Trend in England (and after 1707 Great Britain), 1264–2009	37
2.4	Real GDP Per Capita for the United States, Annually, 1791–2000	38
2.5	Kuznets Curve and Index of Income Inequality	39
2.6	Aging of the Populations of Selected OECD Countries, 1950–2050, Actual and Projected	43
2.7	Annual Average Labor Force Participation, United States, 1948–2005	45
2.8	Married Female Labor Force Participation in the US, 1880–2000	46
2.9	World Population Growth Rates, Actual and Projections, 1950–2050	50
3.1	Causes of Child (Under Five) Mortality World-Wide, 2000–2003	71
3.2	Infant Mortality Rate, United States, 1850–2000 – deaths of infants 0 to 5 years old per 1000 of live births	73
3.3	Probability of Dying for Selected Birth Cohorts, Canada, 1801–1940	75
3.4	Life Expectancy at Birth for Males, Canada, Sweden, United Kingdom and United States, 1750–2000	77
3.5	Life Expectancy at Birth of US Males and Females in the 20th Century	78
3.6	The Probability of Survival in History, 'Rectangularization'	81
3.7	Urban Mortality in London by Month, 1670 and 1800	83
3.8	Crude Death Rates in Western Europe and North America, 1750 to the Present	
	a Europe: Norway and Sweden	90
	b Europe: England (and Wales) and France	90
	c North America: The United States and Canada	91

4.1	Time Taken for Population Doubling With Different Growth Rates	100
4.2	Annual Age Specific (Nuptial) Fertility Rates for Dariusleut Hutterites, 1961–5 and 1981–5	101
4.3	Intergenerational Income Transfers and Implicit Pensions	103
4.4	Mean Age at First Marriage, England 1600–2003	107
4.5	Mean Age at First Marriage in the 20th Century, UK and US	109
4.6	Percentage of Marriages of First Married Couples by Age of Bride for England and Wales, 1991, 2001 and 2006	110
4.7	Percentage of the Native-Born Population (Aged 45–54) Which Never Married, 1850–2000	114
4.8	The Timing of Births: White and Black Births in Virginia, 1651–1744 and US Births (All Races), 1947–1976	116
4.9	Finnish CDRs and CBRs in the 19th century	118
4.10	The Fertility Decline: Two and a Half Centuries of Birth Rates from 1750	
	a Europe: Norway and Sweden	120
	b Europe: England (and Wales) and France	120
	c North America: The United States	121
	d North America: Quebec/Canada	121
5.1	Expected Wage Profiles by Location	134
5.2	Import of Black Slaves to the British West Indies, British North America and the US, 1630–1800	140
5.3	Annual Emigration of the British by Destination, 1825–1849	146
5.4	Emigration from Europe by Decade, 1851–1960	147
5.5	The Irish Population from the Great Famine to the Present	163
6.1	Probability of Entering the Migratory Stream by Age	183
6.2	Periods of Rapid Urbanization, England and Wales and the United States, 1750–2000	192
6.3	Percentage of the World's Population in Urban Areas, Actual and Projected, 1950–2050	193
6.4	The Percentage of the US White and Black Populations, Living in Urban Areas, 1880–1990	197
6.5	Real Income Per Capita Disparities: The Historic Regional Pattern	206
6.6	The Demographic Transition, 1750 to the Present	
	a Europe: Norway and Sweden	210
	b Europe: England and Wales	210
	c Europe: France	210
	d North America: United States	211
	e North America: Canada	211
7.1	Household Size by Decade in the United States from 1850 to 1990	226
7.2	Divorce in the United States and England and Wales, 1920–2007	240
7.3	Poverty Rates in United States, Canada and the United Kingdom, 1959–2007/8	243
8.1	Secular Trends in the Daily Calorific Supply Per Person in France and Great Britain, 1700–1989	263
8.2	The US Antebellum Height Puzzle	265

8.3	Historical Human Developments Indexes, Select Countries, 1755–1980	269
8.4	BMI and Relative Morbidity and Mortality	270
8.5	Percentage of the Population Obese, Selected Advanced Industrial Countries, 2007	271
8.6	Life Expectancy and Health Expenditure Per Capita, By Country, 2004	278
9.1	Shock and Echo Effects	287
9.2	Population Pyramids, Representations	289
9.3	Shift in the Saving Rate and Dependency in the 19th Century United States	291
9.4	Percentage of Inactive Population Aged 65 and Over to the Total Labor Force	292
10.1	A Catastrophe Path: Numeric Illustration of North American Indian Decline and Growth	319
10.2	Real Wages of Laborers in the Plague Centuries, Various Locations, 1300–1700	332
10.3	Female HIV Infection in the United States Rate by Race-Ethnicity, 2007	334
10.4	Estimated Number of People Living with HIV Globally, 1990–2009	336

Tables

1.1	Estimates of the World Population, 10 000 BC to 2050	14
2.1	Gross National Income Per Capita by World Region and Income Characteristics, 2003	39
2.2	Estimated and Projected Total Fertility: World, Development Areas and Regions, 1970–2050	42
2.3	Countries with the Lowest Current Rates of Population Growth, Net of Immigration and Emigration, 2007	42
3.1	Estimates of Death by Causes, World and Select Areas 2002	67
3.2	Human Disease, Its Origins and Conditions of Spread	68
3.3	Battle Connected Deaths in International Wars and Civil Wars, 1816–1980	69
3.4	Life Expectancy and Projections for England and Wales, 1841–2020	79
4.1	Age at (First) Marriage for Selected Western Countries, 19th Century	108
4.2	Age at Marriage for Several Locations in Colonial US, 17th and 18th Centuries	109
5.1	Region of Birth of the Foreign-Born Population of the United States: by Percentage, 1850 to 1930 and 1960 to 1990	137
5.2	Immigration into the US during the Colonial Period by Legal Status and Condition of Servitude	139
5.3	Remittances by Absolute Amount and Rank by Percentage of GDP, 2007	155

5.4	Italian Emigration by Destination, for Periods, 1876–1976	157
5.5	The Chinese Population of Singapore, 1824–1947	160
5.6	Countries Ranked by Size of Its Jewish Population, 2007	165
6.1	Regional Distribution of the US Population, 1790–1860	185
6.2	Percentage of the White US-Born Population, Residence by State of Birth, 1850–1990	194
6.3	Average Annual Rates of Natural Increases (CBR – CDR) Per 1000 By 25-Year Periods	208
7.1	Children in the Labor Force, Selected High Percentage Countries, Various Years	232
8.1	Disability Adjusted Life Years (DALYs) by Cause for the Year 2000	260
8.2	Morbidity Rates by Development Status, Current	261
8.3	Average Final Heights of Men Who Reached Maturity Between 1750 and 1975	265
8.4	The Costa-Steckel Human Development Index (HDI) and its Components for the United States, 1800–1970	268
8.5	BMI and Distributions Statistics for US White Males, 1890–2000	272
9.1	Estimates of the Average Hours Worked Per Day in US Manufacturing 1850–1919	297
9.2	Average Weekly Hours of Household Work, Various Countries, 1960s to Present	303
9.3	Average Weekly Hours Spent in Household Tasks, the US, 1965–2003	304
9.4	Average Number of Years of Schooling of the Adult Population (15 to 64 Years of Age) of Selected Countries, 1870–2010	307
10.1	Population of Selected European Countries, 1300–1700	329
10.2	Land Use in Southern England Before and After the Black Death	330
10.3	Selected National Death Rates Due to the Pandemic Influenza, 1918–1919	341
11.1	Actual and Predicted Population Growth Rates, 1950–2050	355

Appendices

2.1	Income Elasticities of Demand and Sector Shares	59
5.1	Net Present Value of Migration to the Individual	170
10.1	The Plague Transmission Cycle	344

Preface

This book explores contemporary population issues in an historical context. It is a wide-ranging economic history of demographic change with emphasis on the well-being of the population. The population story told here ranges broadly over time and space. By choosing a large canvas, we mean to emphasize the commonality of human experience: that different people, at different times, in varying circumstances, responded to similar economic forces in more or less the same way. Given the available historical evidence, we emphasize the formative population history of Europe and North America over the years since the Middle Ages. Asia and the southern hemisphere are discussed, but to a lesser extent. As economic historians, we are always hostage to the availability of evidence and, for some societies it is less abundant or unavailable in English or French. This necessarily shapes our treatment. We are creatures of our own historical interests, linguistic abilities, and prejudices with respect to both research and writing.

Even if we were capable of an encyclopedic treatment, we have resisted such a scope on the ground that the major themes would get lost in excess detail. Such a broad span involved some hard choices. For instance, when discussing the phenomenon of diaspora as part of long-distance migration (Chapter Five), we focus only on the historical cases of the Chinese, the Irish and the Jews. Other cases are compelling, the Scottish diaspora for instance, but these three are chosen because each offers different aspects of the phenomena. In addition, the Black diaspora is not treated as such, rather it is discussed throughout the narrative as part of the American and British stories.

About 50 years ago the Italian historian Carlo Cipolla wrote a splendid little book entitled *The Economic History of World Population*. His task was to confront the great gaps in knowledge and to draw together the fragmentary historical evidence of population growth. Fifty years on, with a virtual eruption of demographic scholarship in the intervening years, our task is different. It is to draw together the welter of evidence and make a coherent narrative. The lens through which we see history is that of modern economics. When Cipolla's book was published in 1962, the world's population stood at 3.2 billion. Today we are more than twice that number. By coincidence, as Cipolla wrote his book in the 1960s world population trend growth rates turned downward. So the issues we face today are:

- the world is very much larger;
- the growth rate of world population is declining;
- economic growth is uneven across the landscape of developing and mature economies;
- population is being redistributed across space due to migration;
- the world's people are aging (again at an uneven rate);
- the population is putting pressure on the world's resources and environment;
- the income derived from economic activity is distributed unevenly among the peoples of the earth.

We have written this book for a general audience who are curious about such issues. Obviously this includes students as we have spent our careers at universities. There are few courses that cover this material explicitly, but population issues have come to play a more and more important role in many university courses. In many cases, the population issues discussed in one course are not connected to those in another (e.g., there is seldom a tie between discussions of the demographic transition of developed countries and those countries' immigration policies). This book attempts to bridge that gap.

Organization of the Book

We address the economic history of these issues in three main parts.

Part One, *Initial Conditions* describes where we start. What are the pre-conditions of our history, and what assumptions do we make? It also considers some of the broad issues to be confronted by historical inquiry. It begins with a consideration of where the human race has come from and progresses to consider the evidence needed for a historical inquiry. Next, some of the major issues are highlighted. For this we have to develop a plan of attack – a method of analysis.

In Part Two, *Growth and Dispersal of the Human Population*, we analyze the growth and redistribution of the population. It may seem odd that this section begins with death. But that is the one thing that is certain in our history (apart from taxes as a wag once quipped); we all die, but the manner and timing of it is of deep historical significance. Furthermore, births, the second chapter of this part, are in some broad sense related to mortality rather than the other way around (again, noting the truism that one has to be born before dying). Next, we discuss the dispersal of the population around the world with particular attention to the story of the mass migrations of the 19th and 20th centuries. Once the phenomenon of geographic mobility becomes widespread, the movement of people within countries gives rise to one of the great population forces of modern history: the rural – urban shift.

In the next part of the book, Part Three, *Health and Well-Being*, our attention first turns to the larger picture of the family, its changing composition and function. This leads to a consideration of physical health and how it has changed, often (but not always) for the better. Families exist within a larger framework containing the aggregate economic forces that shaped their lives, and we examine those macroeconomic effects that contributed to the underlying growth of well-being. Last, there are the large, negative events that have affected us all throughout history. The population's reaction to these externally-imposed catastrophes tells the story of battles fought (and yet to be fought) against environmental change and the ravages of sudden disease: the plague, HIV/AIDS and influenza.

In the concluding section we offer a brief guide to how history has provided a map to build expectations for the future.

At the end of each chapter there is a bibliography of the works cited and other selected readings. There is one exception to this. Some books by their very nature make an appearance in multiple chapters; for example, Susan B. Carter, Scott Sigmund Gartner, Michael R. Haines, Alan L. Olmstead, Richard Sutch and Gavin Wright, editors (2006) *Historical Statistics of the United States: earliest times to the present* New York: Cambridge University Press. For such books, we have created a separate bibliography of frequently used titles and have adopted an abbreviated title in the text (*US Historical Statistics*).

Acknowledgments

There are many people to thank. In general, countless discussions with colleagues over the years have helped sharpen our understanding. University seminars and professional meeting presentations were often the formal start to what became an informative discussion elsewhere. At least one sentence in this book is a paraphrase of a luncheon comment in an Austin, Texas, barbecue joint.

In particular, among the many individuals we have to thank, first and foremost is our colleague Ron Shearer who read each chapter and consistently reminded us to keep to the straight and narrow. Anyone who reads this book will benefit from Ron's careful critiques. Joe Ferrie and Peter Ward also read the entire manuscript; we are very thankful for the views they offered. Others who made critical contributions to specific parts of the book include Martha Bailey, Hoyt Bleakley, Timothy Classen, Catherine Douglas, Mukesh Eswaren, David Haddock, Lorens Helmchen, Ashok Kotwal, Jacob Metzer, Joel Mokyr, and Marianne Wanamaker. Some readers from outside the academy also were very helpful by giving their perspectives; we particularly thank John Dennison, Gordon Gibson, Michael Ingham, Michael Catlif, Geoffrey Plant and Jamie Wright. We offer special thanks to Bob Allen for the use of his price and wage data, to Sam Williamson and Lawrence Officer for the use of the long-term GDP and wage data, and to Kimberly Fisher for authorization to use the Multinational Time Use Study data.

In the spring of 2005 Bob Fogel invited Cain to spend a year in the Center for Population Economics at the University of Chicago. That blossomed into a continuing association. We thank Bob for his continuing encouragement and friendship and for the right to use his copyrighted material. The notion of tying population economics and economic history was alive and well at the Center long before Cain and Paterson began their discussions. The weekly exposure to new material at the Center's workshop stimulated several sections of this book. Most importantly, this venture would have been impossible without the editorial assistance of the Center's Nat Grotte. Nat's attention to detail immensely improved the coherence of this book. We thank him.

George Lobell whom both of us worked with in the past recruited this book to Wiley-Blackwell. We also must thank Constance Adler. The Wiley-Blackwell team of

Nicole Benevenia and Steve Smith in Boston and Lisa Eaton and Hannah Rolls in Oxford shepherded the manuscript through its various stages. A. Britto Fleming Joe was in charge of the production process with Mariasusai Anithajohny. Dan Leissner was the very efficient copy editor. Katy Balcer provided an index (and much more) with speed and good humor. It is a pleasure to thank them all.

This book began in a "hot-tub" with a couple of gins. Some of Vancouver's justly famous liquid sunshine provided a contemplative ambiance. The conversation was about how we could more effectively integrate the history of population and that of the economy. What has emerged is a story of the interplay of forces that highlights two economic historians' view of what was important.

Louis P. Cain, Glenview, Illinois
Donald G. Paterson, Vancouver, British Columbia

Part One
Initial Conditions

Chapter One
Overview

1.1 Introduction

This book deals with human well-being in history: the growth of population and its economic welfare. For the most part it concerns itself with the economic and population changes of a part of the world that we would now consider long developed: Europe and North America. Only to a lesser extent does it deal with Asia and the southern hemisphere. Within this context it draws its evidence widely to emphasize the commonality of human experience. The aim of the book is to explore the relationships between the size of the population, the quality of life experienced and the economic circumstances that brought it about. It is an economic history of the human condition. It is not intended as a demographic history although many aspects of demographic change become part of the story. The book also focuses on the recent part of the human journey, since late medieval times to the present.

The entire history of human development is surprisingly short. Humans first migrated from their ancestral home in Africa about 50 000 years ago. This amounts to no more than about 2000 generations. The subsequent migrations have peopled the earth and, in the process, given rise to a wide variety of cultures, languages, economic, social and political arrangements. In these migratory wanderings, our human predecessors were continually faced with economic and social alternatives. Their goal was survival as individuals; survival as a species followed. So, throughout the centuries, humans have had to make choices. For example, should we continue to hunt here tomorrow or move to another (hopefully more plentiful) site? Each decision was constrained by factors that limited the range of available options. The outcome of their choices was uncertain and risky; some potential outcomes were undesirable. Collectively, the results of the decisions they made were themselves often modest, but of vital consequence. It is likely, however, that these small choices were systematic and

The Children of Eve: Population and Well-being in History, First Edition.
Louis P. Cain and Donald G. Paterson.
© 2012 Blackwell Publishing Ltd. Published 2012 by Blackwell Publishing Ltd.

that the daily wanderings turned into migrations that spanned the earth. In such a fashion, the cumulative effects of these small decisions were major.

Sometimes these choices were made by individuals, but often they were made collectively as part of a larger social group – a family, tribe or nation. Since the decisions concerned survival and material well-being at the basic level of the provision of food, shelter and clothing, the correct choices were often life-preserving. This history analyzes some of these key choices and the constraints under which they were made that enabled humans to grow in numbers and expand over the continents. It also examines the historical consequences, intended and unintended, of these choices.

The social and economic well-being of both individuals and whole populations was influenced by environmental conditions and events over which there was no, or little, human control. Nature could be bountiful or miserly. The local availability of plants and animals for sustenance was a fundamental requirement. Pre-historic migrations sought out such areas. Other early humans stayed near the oceans where shellfish and other marine resources were available. But, over time, nature could be capricious. Long-term climate change altered migration patterns and, in northern Europe and Asia, forced humans to adapt their lives for survival in cooler conditions. The last expansion of the North American ice cap, for instance, appears to have blocked the spread of the Clovis people (a prehistoric culture from which most native North and South Americans are descended) into North America until its late phases, about 13 000 years ago.[1] The end of the ice age also brought about desertification in Northern Africa and made that area inhospitable for all but the hardiest of individuals.

Many environmental events were not of such a long-lived nature, and some environmental change was relatively abrupt in geological time. After the so-called *warm late medieval period*, the mean temperature in northern Europe (where we have measurements) began to fall. The Greenland Viking colonies disappeared (see Chapter Ten). Crops such as vines ceased to grow where they once did. The general effect was a shift, of any given climate zone, south by 300 to 400 miles. The *Little Ice Age*, as this cooling in the northern hemisphere came to be known, lasted about 450 years, to about 1850, a relatively short period in climate history.[2] We might note that the agricultural and industrial revolutions of Europe are within this time envelope. Clearly, such environmental shifts required human adaptation. Fortunately, a key feature of modern human success was adaptability to environmental change, the ability to learn from, react to and occasionally manage the effects of some of these natural phenomena.

The most successful human adaptation to environmental change was the ability to cope with the annual climate cycle of the seasons. An early historical example is farming in the Nile Valley, which was only possible by learning how to use the river's annual flood cycle. At a more prosaic level was the necessity of storing and rationing foodstuffs between the harvests. The abundance of certain food for short periods of the year meant that from the outset humans were required by circumstances to plan out their consumption. Ultimately, if humans could not move to the seasonably available food supply, they had to invent methods of preservation: drying and salting fish; pickling cabbage (as in northern China and Korea); curing meats, to name a few.[3] Stocks of cereals not only had to be rationed over the yearly cycle but had to be stored and protected from rot and vermin requiring further adaptation in the technology of storage.

Some constraints limiting both the growth and improvement in the well-being of the human population were themselves of human origin. The summation of separate decisions determined how societies and their economies were organized. Each decision presumably was made for the greater good (in intent if not in practice), and these set limits on collective action. While the resulting societies undoubtedly met some sort of efficiency criteria (they would not have survived otherwise), they also constrained individual human action within them. Indeed, throughout most of human history, men and women were constrained to live much like their fathers and mothers had, occupied themselves with the same tasks and were assigned by birth to the same social rank. Systematic social and economic change is a condition of only the past few thousand years. Ubiquitous social and economic change is a product of only the past few hundred years. Yet, as noted earlier, humans proved to be adaptable, and occasionally individuals and societies managed to push against the constraints. Written and archaeological history is full of instances of discrete, permanent changes in the social, political and economic boundaries by human actions. Individuals departed from the norm – thought new thoughts, migrated to new areas and founded new societies. We would like to believe that these changes gave rise to greater individual well-being, but often they did not.

The natural environment also includes the constant human companions of microbes, both helpful and harmful.[4] Many of the helpful ones are essential to our well-being, such as those that we acquire in the first hours of life and which are necessary for our digestive tracts to function. Only very recently have we learned how to manipulate microbes to our advantage, expanding the role of the helpful ones and limiting the effects of the harmful ones. The harmful ones have occasionally given rise to catastrophic events and have had a profound effect on the growth and well-being of the human population. A disease may threaten a community or devastate a tribe. However, these diseases were often widespread, occasionally worldwide in their effects. In the 20th century alone there were three such events. First was a bubonic plague (or possibly its pneumonic variety) in southern Asia, especially India, in the late 19th and early 20th centuries. The death rate in India was thus kept higher than it otherwise would have been in the early 20th century, hovering in the range of the birth rate (about 45 per 1000 of population). Second, the great influenza pandemic of 1918–9 took a huge toll of the world's population, about 15 to 20%. Third, HIV/AIDS is a modern scourge currently endemic throughout the world but particularly severe in sub-Saharan Africa. In one of the countries most affected by the disease, South Africa, the life expectancy at birth is approximately one-half that in North America and Western Europe. Apart from sudden catastrophes there is also the ever-present endemic disease that may be survivable but debilitating to the affected individual. Disease is part of the human condition. It not only shortens life but reduces its quality.

In addition to the naturally occurring phenomena, there are human-inspired catastrophic events such as wars. Although they are preventable in some sense, to individuals caught up in them, these conflicts seem a force beyond their control. Stories of conflict between competing states and empires comprise some of our first written narratives. In times before such records, it is unlikely that human society was much different except in degree. Human conflict harms the individuals involved, but the greater toll is much wider. It comes in the form of the consequences of crops not planted, families reduced to slavery or penury, and a rise in the dependency ratio (the number of people supported by a worker). It is often noted that, before modern times, wars were limited in their negative effects. The Wars of the Roses in England (1455–85) lasted for about 30 years but only consisted of 13 weeks of campaigning and battles. Furthermore, it is argued of most wars prior to the modern period that the campaigns involved only a small part of the geography. Most areas were unaffected by the battles and the pillaging. But, if we account appropriately for all the indirect effects of these "limited" wars, the costs were likely much larger than that suggested by most historians. Farmers' absence from the land at critical times resulted in lost output, investment in war material that would otherwise have been directed to productive uses and so on. Even then, and in contrast, the major wars of the 19th and 20th centuries have been of a fundamentally different nature than those of earlier times in terms of the widespread scope of the conflict, the greater geography of the battlefield and the number of direct and indirect casualties.[5]

We can think of the well-being of individuals and groups having several distinct features. First is the basic standard of life in terms of food, clothing and housing or what we might call necessities. These necessities take a declining proportion of individual family budgets as personal income rises (i.e., they have a low income elasticity of demand). Second, economists argue that the increasing quantity and quality of goods consumed by individuals through time, is evidence of improved well-being. Through most of human history more consumption normally meant better lives. Improvements in well-being, and particularly the rise of nutritional standards, also led to the prolonging of life, the reduction of disease and suffering, and minimizing the amount of preventable death. These, and other matters of health, are generally the product of more affluent societies. One of the striking differences between modern advanced economies and historical ones is the cause of death. In economically advanced societies most people die as a result of aging. In earlier times trauma (violence, accident, starvation) and communicable disease were the main killers.

The increase in individual consumption was only achieved, however, at some social cost to society at large, the most obvious of which was environmental harm. From the beginning of the industrial revolution in the 18th century, this has been a persistent problem. It has proven to be difficult to solve because of a lack of incentives facing polluters, a lack of will on the part of the state (which often tends to undervalue the environmental degradation), and a lack of policy tools to control the pollution and minimize its damage. While the scale of modern pollution is a product of industrial growth it is not simply a modern problem – an upstream leather mill from pre-industrial times may pollute the water course and make use of the water downstream hazardous for drinking. Another major social cost in achieving higher rates of individual consumption is the over-exploitation of certain natural resources. For instance, we over-fish, causing the stock to decline leaving fewer fish for future harvests. Individuals are mortal, and, even though they may care for the future consumption of their grandchildren, today's consumption tends to be given greater weight.[6] This is a trade-off: more consumption today at the expense of that tomorrow. Society as a whole, however, may consider future well-being as being more important than does the individual. Today, in the mass consumption societies of Europe and

North America, there is the well-known revulsion to some aspects of individual consumption. Mass consumption means mass disposal of waste, which has, in turn, a deleterious environmental effect. While these are genuine concerns, they are also largely concerns of more recent times.

In tracing the human population and its well-being there are several overarching issues:

- What historical conditions gave rise to the growth of the human population?
- What were the consequences of population growth?
- What were the improvements in the human condition in terms of survival and length of life, and how were they connected to material well-being (consumption)?
- What brought about the restlessness of the human population that led to migration?

The consideration of these questions is the economic history of population change, of the human condition.

1.2 Human Origins

The general humanoid genus probably first appeared on the landscape about 1.5 million years ago in sub-Saharan Africa. Early humanoids gave way to the successful *homo erectus* about 0.5 million years ago, and this species spread from the African heartland to the Middle East, Asia and Europe. It then died out. Another variety, the Neanderthal humans, successfully populated Europe and Western Eurasia where they remained for many thousands of years. We, modern humans are a different branch of the same family called *homo sapiens* who also originated in sub-Saharan Africa but just more than 150–200 000 years ago. (There is some dispute about the exact dating.) There, *homo sapiens* remained until the relatively recent past, about 50 000 BC, as noted earlier. The migrations of our direct ancestors continued once they reached Eurasia. They then spread as far as Australia and through central Asia and China relatively rapidly. Others went westward into Europe, and yet others eastward over the Bering Sea land bridge into the Americas. When modern humans reached Europe in their migrations they were met by the earlier Neanderthal types – although the numbers involved must have been quite small. In Western Asia and Europe, Neanderthals and *homo sapiens* lived side by side for many generations, although eventually the Neanderthals disappeared and became somewhat of an anthropological mystery. Some may have inter-bred with humans but the evidence for this is meager. More than likely they died out in the competition with modern humans for the scarce food resources.[7]

Modern humans today display differences in language, culture, and society. Yet, despite superficial physical characteristics such as skin color, shape of eyes and others, we all carry basically the same genetic characteristics; all modern humans are, in more than a literal sense, cousins. Every person in the world alive today traces their origins to one particular woman who lived 80–160 000 years ago in Africa. Naturally, she is called "Eve."[8] This raises two issues. First, how do we know this to be so? Second, does

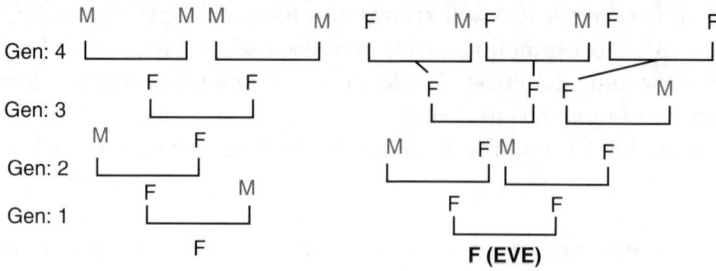

Figure 1.1 Eve and her Daughters, the mtDNA Pattern of Evolution.

this mean that the emergence of modern humans depended critically on just one person? We can answer both questions with the same explanation. Eve was indeed a real person, an early *homo sapien* woman. But in locating Eve historically we also find that she is a statistical construct. Our knowledge of Eve derives from human genetic sequences.

All women, but not men, pass on a substance called mitochondrial DNA [mtDNA].[9] This exists within the cell but is separate from the cell nucleus. As such, the mtDNA is passed only from the mother to her female offspring intact through the generations. The mtDNA is subject to very infrequent mutation, known as markers, which permit the identification of many generations of women. So how do all women today have the mtDNA that permit tracing back to a common type? Figure 1.1 helps explain this. There were probably several women who were candidates to be Eve, each with distinct mtDNA. Two are shown in Figure 1.1. Only Eve's mtDNA survives because only she had female children who survive her, and who, in turn, had female descendants that lived through the generations. Although the probability of a woman giving birth to a female child is approximately the same as that of giving birth to a male child (prob. = 0.5), in any one family there may be departures from this central tendency (as is the case for the third generation in the figure). The non-Eve female's mtDNA simply dies out in her branch of the family tree. Note that Eve's great grandson may marry (breed with) a woman with different mtDNA from his mother, but this has no effect on his female children as the only important relationship is the mother-daughter one.[10]

If we are all descended from Eve, was there an Adam? Anthropologists conjecture that there were about eight potential Eves and probably slightly more potential Adams. Sadly, however, Adam and Eve never knew each other as they lived many thousands of years apart. Tracking males into deep history is done by examining the Y chromosome, which is exclusively a male attribute and is passed intact from father to son. In this case, we can examine the nucleus of the DNA itself by the sequence of genetic codes. The male Y chromosome sequence is subject to more frequent and random mutations than the mtDNA also called markers. What is important for tracking the human population is that the genetic codes carry the history of all previous mutations. So for males, unlike the case for females, we can actually track human history over relatively short periods of time. If a marker distinguishes the central Asian male from, say, the east Asian male, we can determine which was closer to African roots.

Since we are all basically the same, it might be expected that we have common instincts and reactions, tempered of course by cultural and environmental differences. Racial distinctiveness, once thought to be an important attribute within the human species, is now argued, given the DNA evidence, to be the product of very recent history. It is probably in some large measure a local, slight evolutionary response to the physical environment, one that is continually changing. Not only does race not distinguish one human from another very well outside social markers, it is ephemeral. Certain characteristics appear among groups depending on where they originate in the genetic mutation sequence. For instance, the appearance of the HIV/AIDS blocker, itself a mutation, known as CCR5-delta 32, is only found subsequent to the appearance of the marker that separates Europeans from others, Europeans being very late arrivals. However, this is a result of random genetic mutations that do not depend on racial characteristics. It is simply a matter of geography and timing.

1.3 The 40 000 Years to 10 000 BC

Once out-of-Africa, the human population migrated in relatively small hunting and gathering groups. Animals were sought for their protein/fat value and the use of their pelts as clothing. Bone and antlers were made into fishhooks, scrapers, and needles for sewing and animal gut for binding. Foodstuff was also gathered from nature in the form of berries, edible plants and their roots. Recent evidence suggests that, since 26 000 BC in the Middle East, the harvests of kernels from wild grasses were ground to make a type of flour used for baking a type of flat bread. Nature also provided stone, especially flint, for the advanced tool making of arrows, axes and spearheads.[11] In fact, there is no point of historical observation when *homo sapiens* were not toolmakers. And for most of the period fire was mastered and used for warmth, light and cooking.

Modern humans were capable of abstract thought according to the evidence of petro-glyphs and cave painting, such as those at Lescaux. No such record is evident for the earlier Neanderthals. Abstract thought is a prerequisite for planning. That is, modern humans thought ahead about their activities of hunting and gathering rather than just being hostages to fortune. They saw opportunities and made choices. One inference is obvious: if *homo sapien* groups thought about the future, social groups were likely structured to be reasonably effective hunting/gathering units. Indeed, mankind was so successful at hunting that they were likely responsible for widespread extinction of some animal species, the easily pursued European woolly mammoth being one. Archaeological evidence also suggests that early mankind was a complex social being capable of compassion and a sense of community (or family). Skeletal remains of a severely physically malformed young woman dating back many tens of thousands of years have been found in Pakistan. The malformation was a condition of birth. This individual could not have survived without constant care and feeding. That she survived into young adulthood could only have been the result of extensive family nurturing.

Early human population growth was subject to the availability of edible vegetation and wild animal prey. In this sense, humans were no different from other animal

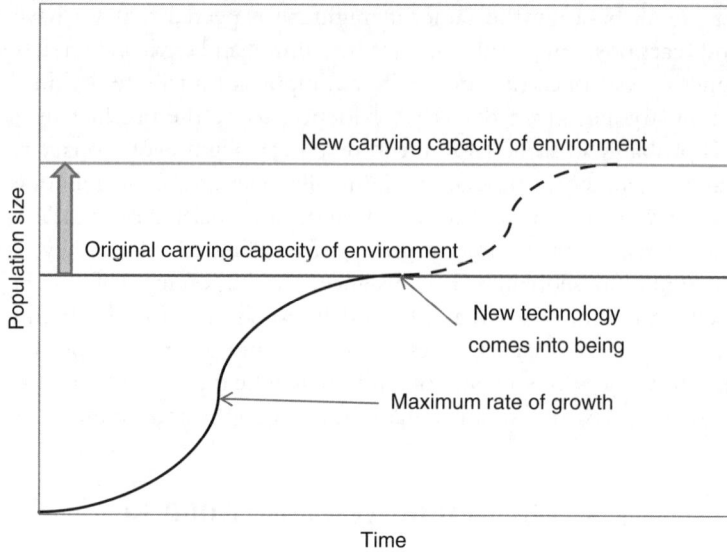

Figure 1.2 Logistic Growth.
Note: The carrying capacity of the environment is for a fixed technology. The upward shift indicated by the arrow illustrates the effect of a new technology or more available resources.

species although they were not systematically the prey of a superior predator. When a biological population is small, its growth is not very rapid, even when the environment can provide ample habitat and sustenance, as in Figure 1.2. (The growth, at any particular point in time, is taken as the slope of a tangent to the population curve.) At the other extreme, when the population of hunter/gatherers grows large, it is constrained by the carrying capacity of the environment – the availability of foodstuffs and clothing resources. From its small size the population grows and, as it does, it grows more rapidly. At some point, however, the growth will slow down as survival becomes more precarious for some individuals. On a per capita basis, the amount of food and necessities provided in a state of nature declines with the result that fewer progeny survive. At the theoretical limit, the environment cannot even absorb one more individual. At the maximum population carrying capacity of the environment, one individual has to die to make room for one new individual. The overall growth pattern that describes this growth is an "S" or logistic curve of population size over time. The carrying capacity is defined as a fixed technology. The upward shift indicated by the arrow illustrates the effects of a new and economically superior technology.

There is one main difference between humans and other biological species. It is likely that even in pre-history there were social limits to population growth when food and agreeable habitat were beginning to become scarce. Some family limitation (abstinence) was likely practiced by individual choice. Infanticide, if not common, was certainly a solution in extreme circumstances. Social proscriptions might also be enforced by the group – refusal of the right to marry (or its pre-history equivalent) and have children, ostracism from the tribe (likely leading to death), and establishing taboos, such as not marrying within the group, making procreation less easy or, in economists' terms, raising the *transaction cost* of family formation. Presumably the antipathies that arose out of competition among groups meant that the surplus males and females of any one group could not easily link with those of another. This limited procreation and family formation. Indeed, groups of humans might drive others beyond the local economic margin thereby eliminating them as competitors in the search for resources.

Over long periods of time, the resource constraint was not a fixed limit, but shifted up (or down) in terms of Figure 1.2. For instance, beneficial changes in climate, noted earlier, might improve the growth of the plant and animal resources on which humans directly depended. An upward movement of the resource constraint allowed the human population the scope to expand. The opposite might indeed be the case, and there is some evidence of climatic change that adversely affected human and other animal populations. At some stages in the 40 000 years after leaving Africa, the human population may have become extremely small, perhaps close to extinction. But the resource constraint might also change because of human inventiveness. Note that even in a hunter/gatherer society there is scope for one of humans' greatest abilities, the application of planning and the seeking of technological relief from the resource limit. For instance, some human groups engaged in systematic fishing and hunting techniques which were refined and made more efficient. Groups migrated regularly in an annual pattern to where resources were more plentiful at a particular time of the year. The local scarcity of nature was overcome.

In the course of this 40 000 or so years, the human population as a whole grew, but it was still small at the advent of arable agriculture. Despite local population pressure in areas such as the Middle East about 10 000 years ago, only about 5 million people lived on earth in the year 8000 BC (estimates of early populations are necessarily imperfect). The entire population of the earth was about the size of the Houston metropolitan area today. Or, put another way, today's population of Greater Shanghai is six times the number of people on the earth 10 000 years ago. The population of the world today is about 6.885 billion (2010).

1.4 The Last 12 000 Years

About 10 to 12 000 years ago, some hunter/gatherers gave up their nomadic way of life. They took to domesticating wild grasses and ruminant animals – the dog was already a human companion. Semi-nomadic at first, a sedentary population of farmers first appeared in the Euphrates-Tigris region (modern northern Iraq). Exactly what determined this shift from nomadic hunting/gathering to farming is not understood. Several conjectures have been made:

- The natural resources on which life depended were being depleted due to rising human numbers in that location (density of population).
- The weather pattern (northern hemisphere warming) precipitated the shift.
- Agriculture represented a superior alternative to hunting/gathering.

In Northern Iraq the first urban settlements emerged. One of the most ancient is the town of Ur, the reputed birthplace of the biblical Abraham. Undoubtedly the transition from a hunter/gathering society to a settled one took many generations, perhaps many hundreds of years. Nor did farming entirely displace the old activity of hunting and gathering. These continued, but now did so from a fixed base, presumably with decreasing success. With early agriculture there is the first evidence of writing and counting. As it turns out, literacy and numeracy are a response to the mundane need to count sheep and note quantities of grain.[12] Indeed, there were a whole range of economic specializations that emerged as the new farming villages provided a ready market for specific goods and services.

Some economic anthropologists argue that the switch from a peripatetic hunting/gathering society to a sedentary, agricultural one brought about a lowering of long-run material well-being. On farms and in the new village communities, disease (often the result of living close to domesticated animals) was more common. Humans became shorter in stature, a sign that there was a decline in nutritional standards. Life expectancy at birth probably declined somewhat. People, we presume, would not choose these outcomes either if they were aware of them or if there were alternatives to a lower standard of life. Of course, the decision that faced those who gave up hunting/gathering was not that of rejecting a plentiful nature for an agricultural alternative, but one of rejecting a way of life that was increasingly uncertain. The relatively greater nutritional certainty was responsible for a substantial, but unknown, growth of the population despite the increased hazards of a settled life.

Yet, the long-run rate of growth of the world's population until very recently was extremely low. From 8000 BC to 1 AD it was 0.0512% per year on average, only slightly more than the growth for the first 40 000 years (0.0351%).[13] Subsequently, for the next 1200 years, the growth rate was even lower. And it fell even further in the European medieval/Renaissance periods (c.1200–1650) and the Yuan and Ming dynasty periods in China (1271–1644). Long-run rates of growth can, however, be misleading because they do not account for shocks to the world's population. Earlier, we noted that the climate variations in the first 40 000 years probably wreaked havoc when they occurred. In the years from 1 AD to 1650 there were large shocks in the form of worldwide fatal diseases (pandemics). One of these occurred in the reign of the Roman Emperor Justinian (541 AD); it claimed a large, but unknown percentage of the people alive at that time. On slightly safer statistical grounds, the Black Death of the late 14th century took a toll of one-quarter to one-third of the entire world population (see Chapter Ten). Such instances, and many more that were less extensive in their effect, mean that the world's population was growing much more rapidly on a year to year basis than the low long-run rates suggest but that these shocks suddenly, and catastrophically, reduced the population. That is, there is much in human population history that suggests uneven growth.

From Figure 1.3 we can model how mortality shocks might affect population size over a 100 year period. First, the population is assumed to be 50 million and grows at a compound rate of 0.5%. Over 100 years the population grows to 82 million. However, with the same base population and over the same period, if the rate of growth was 0.75% then the terminal population would be 105 million. Now assume that the rate of growth is 0.75% but that in year 51 there is a mortality shock that kills 22.5% of the world population. The resulting population in year 100 is the same as it

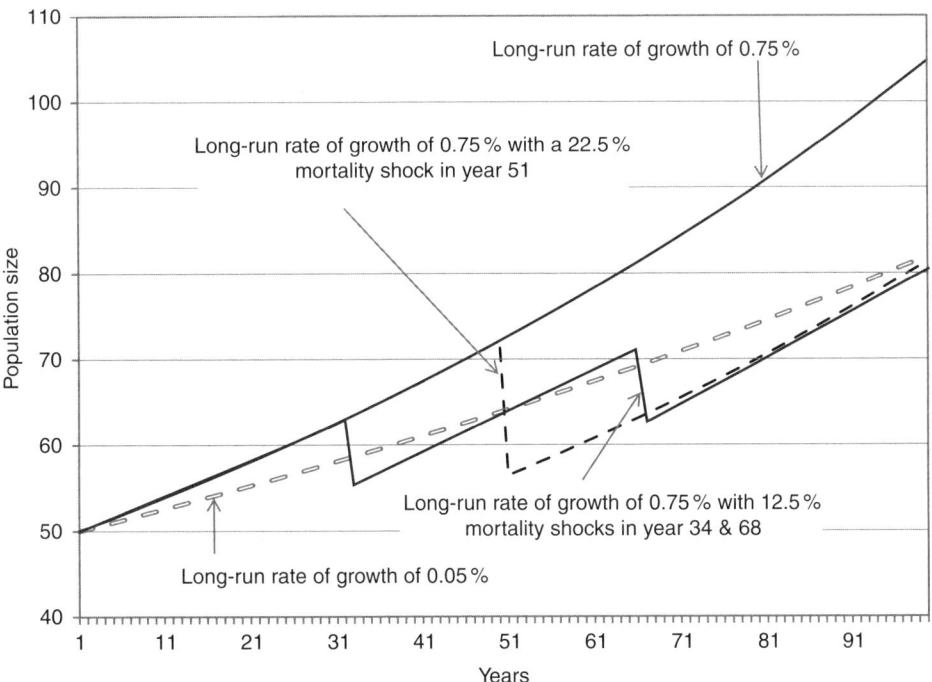

Figure 1.3 Model of Population Size Over 100 Years (compound rates of growth).

would have been with the lower growth rate with no mortality shocks. By similar modeling, a year-to-year growth of 0.75% but with two mortality shocks each of 12.5% of the population in years 34 and 68 produces the same result as the former case. Thus, in the three different cases the long-run measured rate of growth using the initial and terminal observations is 0.5%.[14]

The models in Figure 1.3 are necessarily quite simple. When confronted with the history of growth and population shocks some further questions have to be asked. For instance, does the growth of well-being (or income) expand at the same rate as the population? If it does not, who gains and who loses and how? Changes in income and its distribution might affect the overall rate of population growth. There are also modeling issues which, when accounted for, help provide greater reality. It is unlikely, for instance, that mortality shocks affected everyone in the same way. Vulnerable groups might include women, children and the elderly more than able-bodied males. It is unlikely then that we could assume that the immediate post-crisis population growth simply picked up at the same rate as existed before the mortality shock. We will return to this later.

From about 1650 the rate of growth of the world's population increased dramatically, at a multiple of the earlier rates – see the estimates of world population in Table 1.1. Although we cannot identify particular turning points from this evidence, after 1650 the rate of population growth was 0.465% (compared to 0.0240% in the previous 450 years). In a general way these changes in the rate of growth of the human

Table 1.1 Estimates of the World Population, 10 000 BC to 2050.

Year	Lower Bound Mills.	Upper Bound Mills.	Year	Lower Bound Mills.	Upper Bound Mills.
−10 000	1	10	1000	254	345
−8000	5		1100	301	320
−6500	5	1	1200	360	450
−5000	5	20	1250	400	416
−4000	7		1300	360	432
−3000	14		1340	443	
−2000	27		1400	350	374
−1000	50		1500	425	540
−500	100		1600	545	579
−400	162		1650	470	545
−200	150	231	1700	600	679
1	170	400	1750	629	961
200	190	256	1800	813	1125
400	190	206	1850	1128	1402
500	190	206	1900	1550	1762
600	200	206	1950	2400	2557
700	207	210	2000		6073
800	220	224	2050		9404
900	226	240			

Notes: Lower and Upper Bound estimates are the lowest and highest estimates from the literature noted. Where only one estimate is available it is listed as the lower bound one except for the recent period where the UN Population Division Medium estimates are the only ones and are consistent with the earlier upper bound estimates.

Sources: The table is constructed from material assembled by the US Census Bureau: US Census Bureau (2006), United Nations (1999) Table 1 and United Nations (current) *Population Prospects* – see General Sources.

population coincide, as noted earlier, with the coming of the agricultural revolution and, later, the industrial revolution in Northern Europe and the spread of these ideas beyond. In the 20th century the growth rate has yet again increased to 1.305% as a result of this spread into Africa and Asia. Carl Haub estimates that the number of people who have ever lived on earth totals about 106.486 billion. This means that 5.8% of everyone who has ever lived is alive today. If this unprecedented population growth of recent years was a product of i) an improvement in individual incomes; ii) technological advance; and iii) modern medicine, which came first?

1.5 A Few Fundamentals of Population Growth

For the world as a whole there is only one source of population growth, the net difference between births and deaths. However, for any country or region (or tribe or family) the net of births and deaths are supplemented by the addition of newcomers (immigrants) and diminished by the departures of existing members of the group (emigration). Thus, apart from the global counting, population change is the sum of the net natural increase and net migration:

$$\Delta \text{Population} = (\text{Births} - \text{Deaths}) + (\text{Immigration} - \text{Emigration})$$
$$= \text{Net natural increase} + \text{Net migration}$$

As indicated earlier, there is no requirement that these terms be positive or that population change be positive. The two basic net balances *may* reinforce one another by either increasing or declining together. They may also work in different directions. Later we will examine historical examples of all three possibilities. Not surprisingly, the two net balances are linked by more than arithmetic. Consider the cases of modern Canada and Australia, amongst other countries, whose net natural increase has been declining sharply in recent decades prompting governments to promote immigration. All of the components of population growth (right hand side of identity above) are influenced by the state of material well-being, although to different degrees and in different ways, as we shall see. Growth rates are also influenced by other external economic conditions. For instance, international migration has historically been governed by the cost of travel to and establishment in the country of destination – transaction costs again. Some of the forces that influence the four basic items of the population identity may be scientific (birth control), social (marriage prohibitions and taboos) or political in origin (the level of immigration). Despite their appearance, most of these effects can be analyzed within the framework of economic analysis because they involve "a choice among alternatives."

1.6   The Quality and Quantity of Life

The United Nations each year publishes a quality of life index for most countries. The Human Development Index is a construct that assigns numerical values to vastly different characteristics and then adds these values to produce an overall (weighed) index.[15] Countries are then ranked by the value of the index. The standard reaction of national governments is to point with pride to their high or rising position or to denounce the index as meaningless if their position in the rank ordering is low or falling. In addition, some of the individual characteristics that comprise the index are, by themselves, useful but separate measures of the quantity *and* quality of life and deserve attention.

It is only in very recent times that we have broad-based information about whole populations. These are referred to as *national aggregates*. Statistical profiles can also be defined for sub-groups within that population using census or large scale survey data – as seen in the following chapter. If there are difficulties measuring the quality of life today these difficulties are even greater when we try to measure it historically. As a general rule, the deeper we delve into history, the less complete our population and economic information becomes. There are some exceptions, but they are rare. There are two main types of comparability of the quantity and quality of life that are of interest.[16] First, were individuals (or groups or populations) better- or worse-off over time? This is referred to as *time series* analysis. How does the quality of life of textile workers in Lancashire change over the course of the 19th century? Often we are interested in comparisons, not over time, but between individuals or groups. For example, were tenant farmers worse-off than freehold farmers in colonial America of 1770? This involves looking at a *cross-section* of the population information, in this example, by the characteristic of land tenure. Such questions beg the issue of which individuals fall into our sample and raises problems of statistical comparability. Last, we may wish to combine the cross-section and time series analysis and look at the changing quality of life of comparison groups over time.

We take the "quantity of life" to mean the length of life. There are a variety of different perspectives on longevity – how long a person lives or how long an individual might be expected to live. The measure most commonly used is the expected life of an average person at the point of birth. In historical times, and today, women tended to have longer average lives than men, so we may wish to calculate the life expectancy separately by gender. A unisex life expectancy will *overstate* the length of time that males will live and *understate* how long females live. Nonetheless, calculating the quantity of an individual's life is, in theory, straightforward. The simple counting does, however, raise some perplexing issues. The most obvious of these is the question of how we deal with the instance of children dying at the point of being born. Should we think of this neo-natal mortality as being a short quantity of life for the poor unfortunates whose lives are only seconds or minutes long or should we think of it as a quality of life issue for the mother (or family) who loses the newborn child? It is both. The length of life and its quality are highly related. This is not at all surprising as both child and adult health, and therefore survival prospects, depend on nutritional levels and housing provision among other things. Even if life is not shortened by poor standards of material well-being, a life that is relatively free of disease and pain is of a higher quality than one in which disease and debilitation is common.

From a strictly economic point-of-view, a person crippled by a disease (or trauma) normally has a lower working productivity. National productivity (or national income growth) will be lower as a consequence. The individual affected will likely have a lower income. If pain and suffering lower the quality of life so too does psychological stress. A life where the uncertainty of minimal survival income is greater is a poorer quality life than that where there is less uncertainty. In general, we argue that the quality of an individual's life improves with the rise in consumption. This consumption comes about by the rise in income, which has to be measured in real, as opposed to nominal, terms in order to adjust for the movement in prices over time. A decline in prices with a constant nominal income will also produce a consumption gain. For instance, we can observe that the long-run nominal price of a bushel of wheat in the world's main commodity markets has changed very little over the past two hundred years giving rise to a much lower real price. Furthermore, the prices of basic grain and flour in far locations have tended to converge on those in the main commodity centers reducing these regional prices to an even greater extent – a benefit of globalization. *Private consumption* then increases with real income gains. But increases in the quality of life may also be attributed to increasing levels of *collectively consumed* goods and services, those parts of consumption from which no one can be arbitrarily excluded. This is the case of the "public goods."[17]

We are also better-off in some fundamental ways that capture the improved quality of our lives:

- *Freedom from bondage.* Slavery and serfdom of various forms have frequently been part of human society and individuals were denied the most basic of family, work and mobility rights. No country in the world now legally sanctions slavery.
- *A greater range of choice of both goods and services.* Not only does competition among suppliers tend to produce lower prices for a good of a certain quality, but it produces a range of quality and price alternatives.
- *Greater occupational and social mobility.* When individuals face fewer barriers to occupation status there is a greater likelihood that individual investment in education will pay off. Furthermore, since some of these barriers are arbitrary (such as limitations by gender, race and class) the reduction or elimination of them provides the incentive for educational investment.
- *Greater participation in society and its government.* Not only is this freedom an end in itself but it also gives individuals some advisory power, through the ballot, on the provision of public goods and appropriate taxing policy to pay for them.
- *Greater range of choice in social interactions.* In most countries today we are used to meeting many more people even in the course of a single day than our ancestors might have met in lifetime. We interact with many more. This gives us a richness of human experience from the casual to the more intimate, compared to our ancestors (perhaps as recently as our grandparents).

1.7 The English Parson, Thomas Malthus

In 1798, an English parson named Thomas Malthus published a pamphlet called *Essay on the Principle of Population*.[18] Expanded and reissued in 1803, it was the first systematic inquiry into the nature of population growth. It made Malthus an instant and controversial celebrity. The book conjectures that human breeding would, if left unchecked, expand at a geometric rate whereas the means to sustain the population would expand at only an arithmetic rate. At the limit, adjusting to the increased supply of labor, wages would provide an income that was below subsistence. The economy about which Malthus was thinking was principally an agricultural one. Malthus' observations were also a theory of class behavior as, in his view, it was the "working class" that had this tendency to unrestrained breeding. According to Malthus, they had not yet discovered alternative consumption; any extra income simply reduced the overall death rate, part of which was an increased survival rate of the very young. Since, again at the limit, the wages could not support the population, there would be a resulting increase in mortality. He referred to this mortality increase (famine and disease) as a *positive check* on population growth.[19]

The long-run (unstable) equilibrium, according to Malthus, was one where income in the form of wages always grew less rapidly than population. Over time the population size would oscillate around the subsistence wage, always driving the population back to the level supported by subsistence wages, always responding to unrestrained growth when the wage was above subsistence. This was a dismal view of human society with an urge to procreate that was quite animal in nature.

> *The Malthusian Cycle*: Population living below the subsistence wage → mortality and smaller population → increased real wages → improved living standards → increase in number of children → greater population → reduction of real wages.

The only solution lay in preventative checks. These were actions that reduced family fertility. Malthus himself thought that a rise in the age of marriage would be a powerful check. Of course, there would have to be a clear economic incentive for this if preventive checks were to be effective. The working class, he insisted, would have to become aware of the benefits that could accrue in a better-than-subsistence-wage world. Proscriptively, the working class had to be saved from their tendency of unrestrained breeding. Formal education might help awareness, but Malthus' main hope was that the workers would come to enjoy the extra consumption benefits possible from having fewer children to support. Should his hope not be realized, population growth would remain a problem. In some broad sense Malthus' solution to the population problem was for the working class to become more bourgeois in their tastes and attitude. While this was a paternalistic solution, Malthus was undoubtedly correct to observe that having children and increasing per capita consumption were, at the level of the family, competing interests. He was also right, although for the wrong reasons, that an increase in aggregate real income was not always matched by a similar increase in real income per worker.

The Malthusian scheme was undoubtedly wrong in its prediction that the rate of population growth would always outstrip the growth of wages (income). First, Malthus' conjecture was largely based on the behavior of the birth rate. Changes in the death rate played no significant role in his analysis except as a passive response to real wages and privation – a positive check. Furthermore, we might note, a decline in mortality does not automatically cause an increase in the supply of labor thereby depressing the real wage (it depends whose lives are saved). Second, while well aware of the industrial revolution that was happening all around him, Malthus was largely thinking of an economy with a fixed resource (land) base. Next, his theory of population was one without significant technical change (productivity growth) either in agriculture or the newly emerging activity of the industrial revolution – which in retrospect we know to be an on-going feature of industrial economies. Lastly, Malthus did not allow for factor substitution, that is he did not allow the factor proportions in production to vary over time. Economic history shows that the way in which factors are combined is fixed *only* in the short-run. In the long-run factor proportions are variable and tend to be employed in proportion to relative factor prices, one of which is the price (wage) of labor.

Unfortunately for Malthus' reputation, he is often misunderstood and misrepresented by historians who often refer to "Malthusian populations." In practice, there is little evidence that historical populations of any size have ever reached the Malthusian extremes. Most observation seems to support the view that, as Malthusian pressure exerted itself, human populations responded directly by limiting fertility, migrating or by indirectly finding other solutions in increased output. The crisis of the Malthusian limit was seldom, if ever, reached except during periods of sudden shocks such as a famine or an outbreak of disease.[20]

1.8 Measurement and Inference

Most of the evidence on the size and economic condition of the human population is indirect. The modern practice of taking a (large) population census dates from the late 18th century and was not refined to a reasonable standard of accuracy until the 19th century. To be sure at various times prior to this, there were occasional attempts at counting populations, but they were either very small populations or the counting was flawed. Few of these earlier attempts, for instance, include women or children. Thus, for most of history, our information about the size of the population is inferred from records that were gathered for other purposes such as taxation. We are similarly in difficulty measuring the well-being of any population. Knowing how much food a royal household consumed in ancient Egypt gives us very little information about the standard-of-living of ordinary folk; but it does give us some. For instance, we know that the nobles' diets likely defined the upper range of choice for that society. But, in general, most people and their standard-of-living in history have gone unobserved by the official records of their day.

Often it is reasonable to draw inferences about the population even when our evidence is selective or even biased. Let's imagine that we only know the number of males in a society and have evidence about their ages. The age distribution of these males is what we would expect of a well-balanced population. We also know that the historical gender ratio is 978/1000 males to females for populations in normal circumstances. Based on the assumption that the unobserved females would also have a well-balanced age distribution (but different from that of the males because of the longer life spans of women) we can infer that for every 978 males there were 1000 females. If the male population is 1 546 987, then the total population is estimated as 3 128 773, the difference being the unobserved females. Such a calculation is highly dependent on the assumptions about the unobserved females and the gender ratio.

Not only is the available historical evidence indirect, but it is usually a sample of the population. The sample varies from the representative to the biased with respect to the overall population. For instance, if we use information in the wills of farmers gathered from a probate court archive, the sample is biased in several ways. First, farmers represent only a proportion of the working population (which varies through time). This limits their broader applicability. Second, they are old. Wills are probated upon death when the farmer's estate generally was in a declining phase. Third, most farmers did not leave wills because their legacies were either too small or non-existent. Also, in most jurisdictions until fairly recently, married females had no, or few, inheritable rights. So we are restricted to the well-off males. Last, while the wealth left through the will represented the accumulated or *stock* of assets, it informs us about income *flow* only by inference.

Let us consider some of the historical records which contain selective, but still useful, information about the number of individuals and some aspects of their economic circumstances.

A. *Tax Records.* The functioning of a state always requires expenditures funded from revenue (or debt). This revenue can be gathered indirectly (as a tax upon goods) or directly (as a tax upon individuals, their consumption or income). From early records we gather information about taxes levied and the people who paid them. The first of these records go back 4500 years for the Middle East and are written in the ancient script of cuneiform. The Roman Empire was a great tax-gathering machine, but their records are very incomplete and only survive in fragmentary form. Modern governments use tax records, amongst other things, to monitor the migratory movements within the country during inter-censal periods.

B. *Probate Records.* These are documents that catalogue the transfer of assets on the death of an individual. Wills and supporting documents are the most common and are usually made legally effective by the judgment of a probate court. Since the state had an interest in the transfer for tax reasons, probate courts have a long history in many countries. But of course, only the wealthy had sufficient assets, so with these records we do not have a balanced view; most folk in history had so little, or nothing, to bequeath that a legal will was unnecessary.

C. *Military Records.* Organized armies, as opposed to hordes, normally have kept basic records on recruiting location (or birthplace), age, height and weight. Some of these records are extremely complete. Perhaps, the greatest set, prior to the 20th century, are those of the Union Army of the US Civil War era.[21] Veterans were eligible for benefits including medical care so we can track them through their lives as well as learn a great deal about their recruitment characteristics.

D. *Hospital, Charity and Institutional Records (Workhouses).* Important studies have often used these sources. For instance, the birth weights of infants over a century have been studied by the historian Peter Ward using the hospital admitting and birth records of many hospitals in North America and Europe – see Chapter Eight. Who were the Victorian-age poor of the English workhouses? Dickens alone will not do!

E. *Shipping Records.* Occasionally, we know a great deal about numbers and little that identifies the individual. From shipping records the volume of the 18th century slave trade has been quite well documented. But, in the mid-19th century many countries required shipping records of passengers, and so from that time on we can trace the movement of individual people to North America. Port of entry records in the United States, Australia, Canada and New Zealand recorded the landing of individuals from ships.

F. *Church Records.* In many jurisdictions, and at various times, the registration of baptisms, deaths and marriages was a church-related function. (The historical records of individual monasteries and nunneries also provide interesting detail of their small communities.)

Yet it is the parish records of baptism, marriages and deaths that have proven most historically useful. Even although they vary in completeness the parish registers are an invaluable source of these "vital statistics."[22] From them accurate pictures can be built up for specific locations for various periods in history. The reconstruction of family histories using the parish records, and their amalgamation, has been a popular and highly successful method of recovering the past. Our best understanding of the overall population change in England prior to the era of the modern census comes from the family re-construction work of the Cambridge Group led by E. (Tony) Wrigley and Roger Schofield.[23]

G. *Others.* Widely introduced in the 19th century were labor reports whose explicit task was to monitor the health and welfare of the ordinary citizens. These exist for many European and North American countries. Not surprisingly, the 19th century national statisticians often co-operated with one another so that one can find comparative data that are roughly similar in scope and reporting in several jurisdictions. The Bureau of Labor Statistics pioneered this work in the US. Modern governments have extended their concern to cover a great deal of labor market activity.

Demographers have often used sources in ingenious ways to collect information. Tombstones and obituaries are among those employed successfully. Archaeological evidence is particularly useful for gauging ancient populations. Genealogical records of family or clan histories can be very useful for estimating long-run demographic trends. In China where dynastic histories are sometimes very thorough and extensive in their coverage clan genealogies sometimes go back 2000 years.

H. *Other Modern Sources.* There are a great number of modern sources, usually governmental, that contain important information on certain subjects: the leisure surveys, discrimination in the workplace and so on. International agencies such as the OECD (Organization for Economic Co-operation and Development) and the various arms of the United Nations also collect and collate information on a broad international basis, sometimes a world-wide basis.[24]

Some Terms

Time series data: refers to information that appears in a regular, fixed-interval sequence. For instance: an annual measurement of the number of diphtheria cases in a certain location; the monthly price of wheat in a market for a given period; and so on.

Cross-sectional data: data that are from a fixed moment in time (such as the census) but vary by some other characteristic. For instance: the death rate by country; the ownership of indoor plumbing by income class; and so on.

Panel (combination of time series — cross-sectional) data: data that are both time series and cross-sectional are referred to as Panel Data. For instance: the average level of education (in years) in OECD countries for the period 1990–2006; the proportion of total land in farm by state for the census years 1850–1921; and so on.

Representative sample data: from a large population (or the entire data set) a sub-group is selected that is broadly representative. For instance, if we wish to calculate an average wage, we would not normally include children, but we would include women and men in proportion to their appearance in the labor force. This is often called *weighting the sample*. In this fashion, limited sample data are used to represent workers.

> Let us imagine that, in a historical study, we have a representative sample, say the average (real) wage of textile workers in 18th century England. If we want to draw inferences about the standard of living afforded by that wage as it changes over time, care must be exercised. Caution is needed because the historical actors age over time. Younger workers typically earn less than the average, and older workers earn more. For instance, if the reported wage is constant over time, our representative worker is getting better-off as he ages from a younger to older worker.
>
> *Cohort data*: when we take these life cycle effects into account we will often use a cohort analysis. For instance: the current occupational status of all those who graduated from Princeton University in 1963; the fertility of all females over time who first appeared in the census in 1801; and so on.

1.9 The Census

Of all the sources which inform us about population size only one was (is) direct. These are the censuses. Needless to say, the historical censuses were far from complete or accurate. Perhaps the most renowned of the early censuses was that conducted by William I, the Norman conqueror of Saxon England after his victory in 1066. The new king wanted a detailed list of the resources acquired with his new kingdom. Sometime later he commissioned the Domesday Book. This was a systematic recording, by districts in England, of all people of property along with their holdings of land, cattle and number of servants. Other details were also gathered. While never intended as an exact population count, nevertheless, it served as a count of those who could bear arms, a list of taxes collected and a reckoning of the assets under the ultimate control of the king.

A. A Nearly Modern Census

In 1665 the government of France took over direct control of the colony of New France, on the banks of the St. Lawrence River. Similar to the British colonies in North America, New France was first created and managed by a company of merchants. They brought traders and settlers to the new land. The New France colony became insolvent under company rule, and the government stepped into the administrative void. The civil servant sent out from France to take over control, known as the *Intendent*, recognized the first problem: how many people lived in the colony, what was their inventory of skills and what employment were they engaged in? Intendent Jean Talon immediately set out the rules for the census taking.

First he established the *de jure* principle of counting people where they lived. Second, he prescribed the recording of skills. Last, he had information taken systematically on the houses and farms. Talon's census was remarkably complete and showed that the colony's population was widely distributed geographically. For a small colony of only 3215 inhabitants it was serviced by a surprisingly broad array of tradesmen, administrators and church officials.[25] The most surprising fact, however,

Arrival of the Filles du Roi

A highly romantic 19th century pre-Raphaelite view of the mid-17th century event.
Source: Brickdale, Eleanor Fortescue (1871–1945), *Filles du Roi*, Courtesy of the Library and Archives of Canada/Bibliothèque et Archives Canada.

was the gender imbalance. The census recorded 2034 males and 1181 females. That is, in 1665 there were two males for every female (the ratio for ten years earlier may have been roughly 6:1). Talon immediately asked the French government to "recruit" marriageable aged young women for the colony. Between 1665 and 1673, 900 *filles du roi* – named "daughters of the king" because the royal exchequer financed their travel and paid each a dowry – arrived in New France. These were young women without prospects in France; orphans or those without families. Some young widows were included. The gender balance of near equality was quickly achieved and, because it was a young population, it was very fecund.[26] Many *filles du roi* married soldiers who were then urged to settle in the colony permanently.

A subsequent census in 1671 recorded 700 children born in that year, an incredibly high fertility rate. This surge of births was echoed and re-echoed for the next 100 years.

Mémoire de M. Talon adressé à Monseigneur Colbert
Fait à Québec, ce dixième Novembre 1670

"Monseigneur,... Toutes les filles venues cette année sont mariées à 15 près que j'ai fait distribuer dans des familles connues en attendant que les soldats qui les demandent aient formé quelque établissement et acquis de quoi les nourir. ..... Pour avancer le mariage de ces filles, je leur ai fait donner, ainsi que j'ai accoutumé de faire, outre quelques subsistances, la somme de 50 livres monnaie du Canada en denrées propres à leur ménage."

Source: *Mémoire de M. Talon, 1–118.*

'Filling Up the Census Paper'

Wife of his Bosom. "Upon my word, Mr. Peewitt! Is this the way you fill up your census? So you call yourself 'head of the family' – do you – and me a female!" The senior male in the household was designated 'head of family' in many modern-era censuses. A female could only be so designated if there were no adult males, what we call today a single-parent family. Otherwise, the female spouse was described as 'a female'.
Source: Punch, 1851. John Leech Archives, www. john-leech-archive.org.uk

B. Modern Censuses

The first national modern census in the US dates to late 18th century. In the new US, the Constitution extended suffrage to the free (male) population, and because representation in the Congress was related to population it was necessary to have an accurate count of voters by region. The 1790 census recorded little extra apart from a few characteristics such as age, place of birth and some rudimentary information about agriculture and industry. Each subsequent US Census was an improvement on the previous census. By 1851 the Census of Manufactures was added in such a way that it was consistent enough for later users to link it to later versions for time series analysis. Outside the US modern (usable) censuses appeared in many countries in the late 18th and 19th century: Denmark in 1769; United Kingdom in 1801; Canada in 1851/1871; New Zealand in 1851; Australia in 1841/1901, India in 1872; Germany in 1895 amongst others.

Census data are usually presented in aggregate form. They are snapshots of a population at a specific moment in time. Since censuses also include information on the households, they are extremely useful evidence (sometimes the only evidence) for vital public policy making. For instance, in the early 20th century censuses were used to track the electrification of households and the presence of indoor sanitation. This gave rise to targeted state or state-directed public investment. These aggregate data are then sub-divided by county or district, town or city. Indeed, there are a great variety of cross-sections that are presented.

The census data in aggregate form are compiled from the "census manuscripts." These are submitted by the census official known often as the enumerator. Census manuscripts are normally held secret for long lengths of time, typically one hundred years, because they record personal information about living individuals. Many countries are now releasing these documents from the 1901 and 1911 censuses. The task, however, is enormous and politically sensitive. In addition, they are often produced in digitized form, which makes them readily available for micro-historical purposes. Furthermore, databases can be linked to produce longitudinal studies, say tracking a particular family through the generations within a country or as they move from, say, England to Australia or Denmark to the US. Normally, the worksheets of the enumerators were prepared for each household and, by the mid-19th century, are rich in detail. In the US the 1850 Census reported the value of property held by the family (or head of household) and in the 1860 census, both annual income and property.[27] Generally, the census manuscripts varied tremendously in quality of reporting even in one year, and even within a country by where the data were gathered. The reliability of the data is dependent on the qualities of the enumerators. Enumerators were locals recruited for the task and were mostly known to the respondents. The conjecture is that as they moved from farm to farm in the American South, for instance, accepting a friendly glass of corn whisky at many of the stops, their recording skills slipped. Over time, the reliability of the information presented improved and the variation of reporting quality was reduced.

Of course, there are gaps between censuses, typically ten years. Partial censuses in more recent times have often been conducted in the middle of the inter-censal period after five years. They nonetheless provide essential checks of the otherwise estimated population size. They also provide an important residual calculation. If the total number of births and deaths are known and if we also know the number of arrivals from abroad, then the missing element of population change as reported in the census is the number of departures. Emigrants were seldom otherwise recorded. The difficulty with this calculation is that it tells nothing about the timing of their departures. Indeed, many researchers simply average the departures over the inter-censal gap. The history is usually different. Take Canada's emigration history of the 1880s. The Census show a large population decline over the decade but it is also clear from other evidence that this is accounted for by emigration and that the bulk of individuals who left departed in the last five years of the decade. Filling gaps seem to be one of our important historical tasks.

C. Some Problems of Early Modern Censuses

1. *Quality of enumeration (and enumerators)*: often questions were not well-defined or explained adequately to the respondent. The selection of enumerators was often haphazard and they themselves were, on occasion, barely literate and thus did not have the ability to question a patently incorrect response. Census questions and the quality of enumeration improved through time.
2. *Inaccuracies and misreading*: apart from incorrect transcriptions of the information there was ample scope for error.

3. *Coverage and thoroughness*: are determined by the resources devoted to the census gathering enterprise. Since the data are gathered on one particular day and because of noted errors, the ability to go back and find absentees and correct errors is critical to the veracity of the census. Indeed, some censuses were inadequately funded from the outset, forcing short-cuts.
4. *Representation of women (common to most historical censuses)*: The major omission has been the recording of female employment, work and income. Since women, historically, were not considered the main source of family income the question was often omitted or no declaration was given. This is undoubtedly due to the fact that women's incomes were often made in the informal labor market. These included: taking in washing, housekeeping, care of others' children for pay, piece work in the home and the like.

1.10 Models of Human Behavior

The human behavior of demographic change involves human decision-making at its most intimate. Few economists argue that individuals base their decisions on a fine economic calculus – yes, sensible economists do exist. It is helpful, nonetheless, to think of the *opportunity cost* of human actions. Thus, we might consider the price of a child to be the cost of opportunities foregone by having that child (e.g., the income of the mother if she takes uncompensated time away from the labor market, the cost of additional housing space, consumption of goods and services and so on). This raises an important issue, one that we find through history, of how we theorize about human responses to economic stimuli. Malthus laid out the territory. So far as possible we model human behavior with specific causal relationships in mind, state the assumptions from which we start and chart those to a conclusion. This suggests a fine degree of individual awareness and economic calculation. We know, however, that this is not how individual humans usually behave. Yet, when we examine the economic behavior of many individuals on average, or in aggregates, the responses often appear to conform to the theory *as if* individuals made these fine calculations. In practice, of course, there is a huge amount of individual variation. Our modeling of the process represents the tendencies in human decision-making, which turn out to be quite precise although not the exact reasoning of each participant.

Individual decision-making rests on individual preferences (or tastes) which when arranged are known as a "utility function." However, humans through all of their history have existed as part of families, and it is often families that are the decision-making units. The social dynamics of how these decisions are made varies both from family to family and with time. For instance, women quite frequently occupy the historical role as the main distributor of food within the family. They do not do so evenly: calories seem to be distributed in favor of those with the greater work (caloric) needs. So, family decision-making is not straightforward, as most families would attest. In general, we care about members of our families more intensely than we care about others. The historical evidence suggests that this is a very basic instinct and that it has always been present. In addition, there is nothing preventing individuals having preferences that are social in nature. The individual utility function may have "a taste" for a certain distribution of income and individuals exercise this taste by, say, voting for a more (or less) progressive tax structure.

In human decision-making we also demonstrate a concern for future generations. There are those who argue that we wish our genes to be passed on and to survive. Because we care about the fate of our children, grandchildren and those who follow, our time horizon is not limited to our natural life span. As a consequence, there are two distinct notions of accounting for time that enter into consideration, one that applies to each individually in a private context and that that applies in a social context with a broader viewpoint. These are:

- the discount rate or marginal rate of time preference; and
- the social rate of discount.

We can think of the discount rate as the return that individuals require in compensation for postponing the receipt of income or consumption today. Banks, for instance, induce private savings (the opposite of consumption) by offering a rate of return on the funds held. The higher the rate of return the greater is the inducement to save. This is the private discount rate. However, if we value something on societal grounds we are, in that valuation, applying a greater social rate of discount. For example, in order not to deplete a fishery too rapidly, a social benefit, we will reduce today's consumption in order to ensure an on-going stock of fish. That is, we have valued future consumption (preservation of the fish) and that of our children more highly in the future.

> the social rate of return = private rate of return + rate of net social benefits

The benefits to the individual (and to society) from any deliberate choice may be intrinsic. We call these the "psychic benefits". If an individual refuses a higher wage offered in a far location in order to remain at home, we have a ready appreciation of how much the individual values their current location, on balance. These intrinsic benefits will vary with each individual or family and indeed may be even be negative. As we see later on when discussing international migration, the vast majority of people do not enter into the flow of migrants. Our theory of migration then is limited; it is has little predictive value for the "non-movers." The psychic benefits (and costs) are the theory receptacles into which we place the social benefits (and costs), which are not directly quantifiable. Because of the inherent social nature of human society these are often large and persistent.

1.11 Outline

Population and its growth are at the heart of economic history. Indeed, they are so much part of the story that it is difficult to separate them from those other economic, social and political forces of history. Yet, with perhaps the exception of the most dedicated positivist, we simply cannot retain indifference to the human dimension. Capital, land, natural resources and labor may be functional inputs into production but most of us cheer for labor because it is the factor about which we all must make decisions. So with complex sets of events with complex historical outcomes, and with our human intuition, what is our analytic approach?

Throughout this history we separate the discussions into several useful economic groupings. Each focuses on the analysis of the population, both as an object and subject, from a different perspective. They are:

- *Aggregate economic performance (macro)*: the behavior of the economy-wide aggregates and indicators of performance including economic growth.
- *Individual and family (micro)*: the factors that influence the patterns of mortality, fertility and migratory behavior and the personal decision-making that determine these patterns.
- *Medical and epidemiology*: the advances in medical thinking that influence the health of the population, and the progress of disease and its influence.
- *Externalities*: the creation of social benefits and social costs that are not directly enjoyed or paid for by the economic agents engaged in an economic activity, such as production.
- *Catastrophes*: extraordinary (exogenous) events that cause large change in the population, its growth and behavior.
- *Institutional development*: the study of how society adapts to population change in terms of its institutional arrangements and property rights.
- *Education and technical change*: the influences that bear on investment in human capital.[28]

Naturally, these themes overlap one another. Migration is a case in point. It has micro foundations in individual decision-making, is influenced by macro events and has aggregate economic consequences. We begin, however, with the overview of the landscape of population and its macroeconomic history, the subject of the next chapter.

Endnotes

1. See Sykes (2001) and Wells (2007) for DNA version of spread. Also see Mann (2006).
2. It had two distinct phases: the cooling phase from about 1400 to 1650 and the cold phase to 1850 with substantial warming in the mid-19th century. There is no common agreement on the early dating because the effect was also local in character. Different locations of measurement from sediment, ice cores and seabeds yield slightly different dates. Most climate historians, however, agree that the Little Ice Age ended in the mid-19th century.
3. Modern forms of these techniques survive in Korean kimchi or Italian air-dried ham, prosciutto.
4. Diamond (1997).
5. This statement is often made of only 20th century conflicts. We include the Taiping Rebellion in mid-19th century China with its direct death toll of over 20 million and the US Civil War. The last phases of the US Civil War, especially the siege of Richmond, was very similar to the trench warfare of the 1914–1918 conflict.

6   This is the concept of the marginal rate of time preference.
7   Green *et al.* (2010).
8   See Dawkins (2004).
9   "DNA" stands for *deutro rhybo-nucleaic acid*.
10 Forster (2004), 255–64.
11 *Homo sapiens* were once thought to be unique as tool-makers. Evidence now suggests that other humanoids also made tools.
12 See Manguel (1996) and Mokyr (2002).
13 Calculated as the compound rate of growth necessary to predict the current observation from the base observation: $X_n = X_0 (1+r)^n$ where X is the population estimate, r is the rate of growth and n is the number of years between observations.
14 Indeed, the mortality shocks for this model have been cunningly calculated to produce exactly this result.
15 United Nations (current): http://hdr.undp.org/en/statistics/.
16 Even if we have complete information on whole populations there are statistical issues surrounding what is meant by comparability. These issues are explored later.
17 Private goods are those which when consumed are enjoyed by only the individual, e.g., a cup of coffee. A public good is one that is shared by others (they cannot be excluded). These collectively consumed goods include such items as police services. The fact that we cannot exclude others from enjoyment of these collectively consumed goods gives rise to the "free rider" problem, people who consume the good without paying their full share.
18 Hollander (1997) and Malthus (1798). Cambridge educated, Malthus went on to become Professor of Political Economy at the East India Company College in London.
19 Any increase in the supply of labor induced by the aggregate growth due to: i) new workers entering the labor market as the lowest wage at which they are willing to work is now met; or ii) net immigration has the potential to lower the real wage.
20 Despite its insertion into numerous contemporary histories.
21 These data have been collected by the Center for Population Economics at the University of Chicago under the direction of Prof. Robert W. Fogel (see http://www.cpe.uchicago.edu).
22 Parish (or the relevant church unit) records are also used for genealogical purposes. In most jurisdictions this function of registration has been taken over by the state. The Church of the Latter Day Saints (Mormons) have collected a huge number of these records world-wide, copied them, distributed them to many centers and make them available to the public on request.
23 Wrigley and Schofield (1981).
24 United Nations human statistics include those of: The World Bank, the World Health Organization (WHO), the International Labor Organization (ILO), United Nations Educational, Scientific and Cultural Organization (UNESCO) and others noted in this book.
25 Their occupations were: three notaries, three schoolmasters, three locksmiths, four bailiffs, five surgeons, five bakers, eight barrel makers, nine millers, 18 merchants, 27 joiners, and 36 carpenters, solders, farmers, fur traders, laborers, administrators, priests and other church officials (Censuses of Canada, 1665 to 1871 [1876]).
26 Fecundity is the capability of producing offspring in great numbers – see Chapter Three.
27 Only free individuals were covered although there was a separate enumeration of slaves.
28 Preston (1987), 619–44. Preston identifies the first three of these categories but adds a fourth, ethical and environmental considerations about the distribution of resources. We think, however, that the ethical dimension is best analyzed in the context of the social rate of discount and externalities and so include it in the categories noted above.

References

Dawkins, Richard (2004) *The Ancestor's Tale: A Pilgrimage To the Dawn of Evolution*, Boston: Houghton Mifflin.

Diamond, Jared M. (1997) *Guns, Germs, and Steel: The Fates of Human Societies*, W.W. Norton & Company: New York.

Durand, John D. (1974) "Historical Estimates of World Population: An Evaluation," University of Pennsylvania, *Population Center, Analytical and Technical Reports*, Number 10, table 2.

Forster, Peter (2004) "Ice Ages and the Mitochondrial DNA Chronology of Human Dispersals: A Review," *Philosophical Transactions: Biological Sciences, The Evolutionary Legacy of the Ice Ages*, 359, 1442, 255–64.

Green, Richard E. *et al.* (2010) "A Draft Sequence of the Neanderthal Genome", *Science*, 7 May, 328. 5979, 710–22.

Haub, Carl (1995) "How Many People Have Ever Lived on Earth?" *Population Today*, Feb., and Nov./Dec. 2002.

Hollander, Samuel (1997) *The Economics of Thomas Robert Malthus*, Toronto: University of Toronto Press.

Malthus, Thomas Robert (1798; 1965) *Essay On Population With Notes By James Bonar*, New York: A.M. Kelley.

Mann, Charles C. (2006) *1491, New Revelations of the Americas Before Columbus*, New York: Random House.

Manguel, Alberto (1996) *A History of Reading*, London: Harper Collins.

Mokyr, Joel (2002) *The Gifts Of Athena: Historical Origins Of The Knowledge Economy*, Princeton, N.J.: Princeton University Press.

Preston, Samuel H. (1987) "The Social Sciences and the Population Problem", *Sociological Forum*, **2**(4), 619–44.

Sykes, Brian (2001) *The Seven Daughters of Eve, The Science That Reveals Our Genetic Ancestry*, New York: W.W. Norton and Company.

United Nations (1973) "The Determinants and Consequences of Population Trends", *Population Studies*, 50, 10.

United States Census Bureau (USCB) (2006) "Total Midyear Population for the World: 1950–2050", Data updated 7-16-2007. http://www.census.gov/ipc/www/worldpop.html

United Nations (1999) *The World at Six Billion*, Table 1, "World Population From Year 0 to Stabilization", 5.
http://www.un.org/esa/population/publications/sixbillion/sixbilpart1.pdf

United Nations (2001) *World Population Prospects: The 2000 Revision*, United Nations: New York United Nations, and subsequent, annual revisions.

Wells, Spencer (2007) *Deep Ancestry; Inside the Genographic Project*, Washington: National Geographic.

Wrigley, E.A. and R.S. Schofield (1981) *The Population History of England, A Reconstruction*, London: Edward Arnold.

Chapter Two
The Historical Setting

2.1 Introduction

In most areas of the developed world today the population is growing more slowly than at any time during the last two centuries. No fewer than 29 countries are each currently projected to lose (net) over 200 000 of their population in the next 40 years.[1] Eight of those will lose over 4 million people each.[2] The world's population growth rate has been declining for the past 60 years. It is currently (2005–2010) 1.17% per year and estimated to become 0.36% by the period 2045–2050. Indeed, it is only due to extensive net migration that population decline has been avoided in many countries. What happened? This chapter analyzes the broad features of historical population change and economic development. It begins with the transforming events collectively known as the demographic transition. What causes mortality and then fertility to fall is the subject of later chapters.

2.2 The Demographic Transition

Slow or zero population growth results when the number of births is about the same as the number of deaths. This result has been observed throughout most of history – a slow growth of population. But the conditions of today are vastly different from those of deep history. Today, both birth and death rates are low. Before about 1700 – the dating is somewhat arbitrary – the number of people born was relatively high but so was the number of deaths, thus the resulting net increase of the population was also quite small – see Figure 2.1. The shift from a high birth and death rate regime to a low rate regime is known as the *demographic transition*. It is one of these historical processes that was, and is, universal. It is still underway in certain populations and has different timing in different countries. Yet, it is found everywhere. To be sure, there

The Children of Eve: Population and Well-being in History, First Edition.
Louis P. Cain and Donald G. Paterson.
© 2012 Blackwell Publishing Ltd. Published 2012 by Blackwell Publishing Ltd.

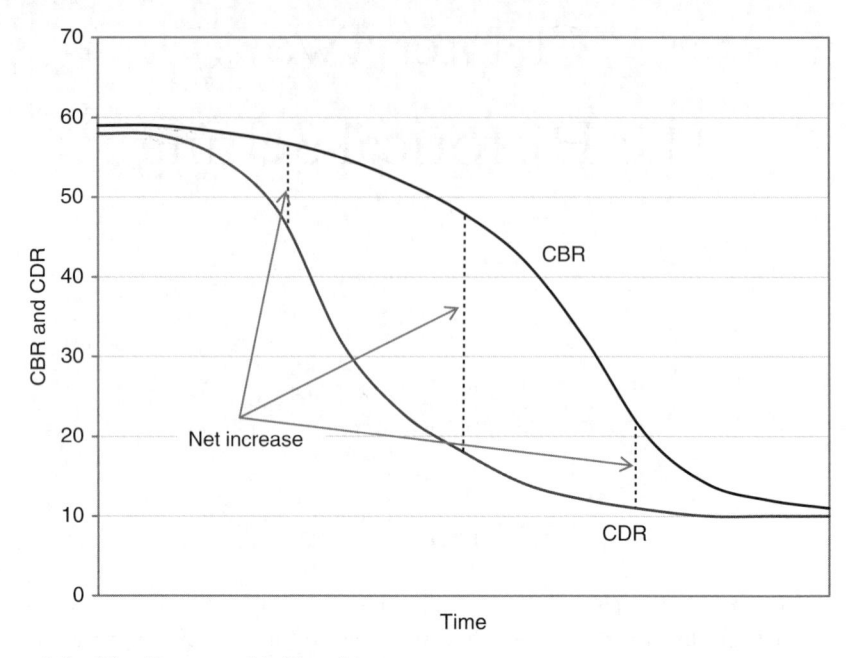

Figure 2.1 The Demographic Transition.

> ### Definitions
>
> CBR: Crude Birth Rate is the number of live births per 1000 of the population per year.
>
> CDR: Crude Death Rate is the number of deaths per 1000 of the population per year.
>
> Both measures are sensitive to the age structure of the population.

are local variants (later a distinction between Europe and China will be drawn). This is not surprising since the demographic transition was propelled by a large number of highly interrelated forces – economic, sociological, political, cultural and personal.

The demographic transition is marked by three main phases. First is the *traditional phase* with high fertility and high mortality associated with pre-industrial society. In general the birth rate was higher than the death rate but the gap was not great, as the slow rate of growth of the population testifies. Second, during the *transition phase*, the death rate began to decline slowly at first, picked up momentum and then declined very rapidly. However, fertility persisted at a high level. The growth of the population accelerated. Eventually, the birth rate also began to fall, and this slowed the rate of growth as the gap between births and deaths narrowed. The last major phase, the *modern phase*, is the new low birth and death rates found today in higher-income countries.

But this powerful model of demographic change overlooks several historical issues. First, is the transition complete? Even for today's higher-income countries, within the low birth and death rate regime, there are substantial variations in demographic outcomes. These reflect differences in underlying social and economic conditions. It is difficult to describe this as a post-transition equilibrium (a state of balance). What we observe today, in all the countries within the low birth and death rate regime, are differences that are the on-going process of adjustment with perhaps no settled outcome. Second, for any country, historical or contemporary, there are the effects of net migration (gross immigration minus gross emigration – the last two arguments in the basic population growth identity). The population is always changing due to these migratory patterns; the only issue is whether the effects are small or large. Third, many countries have not yet achieved a low birth and death rate regime, although all have progressed some way toward it. These countries are the less developed areas of the world. The fourth and final issue is the effect of technology and its spread. Technical change, in this context, has two dimensions: i) the technology of controlling the birth and death rate; and ii) the adoption, spread and application of technology that improves the income generating performance of economies. We will return to these themes in greater detail later.

How long it takes a country to undergo a demographic transition is a direct result of how long it takes that country to move from a traditional agricultural (primary) base to an advanced industrial (secondary) and services (tertiary) base.

2.3 Structural Transition of the Economy

It is difficult for any social scientist or historian to imagine that the demographic transition can ever be reversed in a major way. It is in the nature of a revolution. So too, systematic changes in the main sources of income are a largely irreversible shift in the economic structure of the economy. The demographic and economic transitions are intimately linked; they are both part of the same phenomenon, aggregate economic change, which in turn precipitated fundamental social and political change.

At the heart of the economic transformation is change in the *structure of the economy*, where structure is defined in terms of where the flow of income originates. These are the *shares* of national income (GDP) by sector. Structure may also be defined by the employment shares of each major sector, and, of course, there is a correspondence. Of the two measures, we usually find the *shares of GDP* change in advance of changes in the *shares of the labor force*. For any given economy, the marginal product of the expanding sector increases relative to that of the declining sector. Eventually, this will cause wages to be bid up in the expanding sector relative to those in the declining sector, but the labor market adjustment is not instantaneous.

As Nobel laureate Simon Kuznets observed, the major structural, long-term features of this economic development in terms of output (income) shares are:

- the decline of primary sector's share (agriculture, fishing, forestry and mining);
- the growth of the primary and secondary manufacturing share; and
- the growth of the tertiary or service shares.

Factory of Hotchkiss' Sons, Hardware Manufacturers

The factory, train and marine transport were hallmarks of the industrial transformation. Here the factory complex, idealized by the owners who commissioned the drawing, was located on the Connecticut side of Long Island Sound. The New York, New Haven and Hartford Rail Road is in foreground.
Source: Library of Congress, Prints and Photographs Division Washington.

National Income

Gross Domestic Product (GDP): is the flow of all income received *by anyone* from all activity in the domestic economy including payments to owners of capital. It is thus measured by either the sum of all factor payments or all expenditures on final goods or the sum of total value-added. It can also be measured net of depreciation (the amount reserved for replacement of capital that has reached the end of its economic cycle). As such, it is known as Net Domestic Product (NDP).

Gross National Product (GNP): is the flow of all income received *by all national residents* in the economy including payments to owners of capital. Thus, British (or US) GNP is the income received by all British residents (or US residents) from all sources domestic and foreign.

Throughout we will use the terms *national income* and *aggregate income* to mean GDP unless otherwise noted. Unfortunately, we have more historical estimates of GNP than GDP.

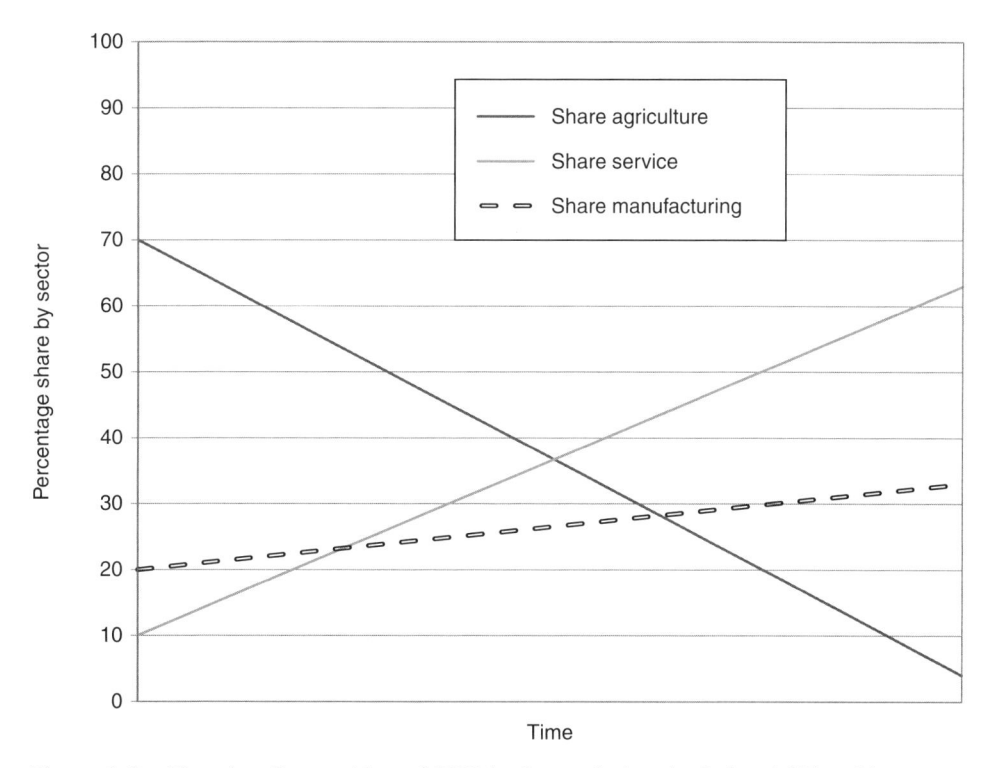

Figure 2.2 Changing Composition of GDP by Sector during the Industrial Transition.

Agriculture and other resource gathering such as hunting, mining and fishing have declined over the past several hundred years from about 70% to 80% to less than 5% in most modern economies. Manufacturing has grown over the same interval from about 20% to 30%. Although the growth is relatively modest in terms of shares this change from the modest blacksmith shop to the capital intensive, integrated multi-plant firm remain our abiding image of the industrial revolution. Yet, it is quantitatively eclipsed by the spectacular rise of the service sector. No less than 65% of all output (income) is generated in services in OECD economies. Since services also include such activities as construction and transportation, parts of the service sector actually have a high capital-output ratio; it is a sector that requires no less investment than manufacturing.[3] The importance of this economic transformation, seen in Figure 2.2, is that it gave rise to increases in per capita income – exactly how much and when are the subject of historical debate. It also governed the demand for labor, for particular types of labor, and it was directly responsible for the growth of urban areas at the expenses of rural ones as agglomeration effects exercised their influence. This was a transformation of peoples' lives in the most fundamental sense.

The rapidity with which a country moved through this historical industrial restructuring is a product of the existing and available technology as well as the country's endowment of resources. Some of the available technology is from those countries that embarked on the transformation earlier. The speed of transformation, therefore, depends on the chronological order; economies that started earlier took longer while those that started later took a shorter time. And, of course, many countries lacked the complementary conditions to progress very far in a transformation; some have made only modest progress. Although it should be noted that a technology, especially one associated with modern health care, is capable of being spread rapidly no matter what the receiving country's level of income can support – that it is not is one of the issues of our times.

Some of the relative change in the sectoral composition comes about because of efficiency gains. For instance, in traditional agriculture, a farmer may haul his produce to market; this would all be within the agricultural sector. With increased efficiency – greater output per unit of input – it may prove cost-reducing to hire a specialized haulage firm to move the crop to market. This would result in the shares being divided between the agricultural and service sectors. The farmer's marginal resources are freed for more crop cultivation. The relative factor shares have changed – services increased and agriculture has decreased – due only to the cost reductions brought about by a scale effect, the haulage firm's ability to move the crop for less. Note that both parties to the exchange, farmer and transport provider, gain by experiencing a per unit cost reduction. Provided there are co-operating resources in this example, the more farmers, the more the scale effects in transportation. The consumer also gains by a decline in price. There are many other examples: the building of logging roads (service) to exploit more forest timber is another where we might expect the same scale efficiencies. And, as a result, the composition of national income by source changes in relative importance.

2.4 Long-Run Changes in Economic Well-Being

Measures of well-being are difficult to construct even in modern, information-abundant societies. Our first, albeit crude, indicator is the average (or mean) income per capita, national income measured by Gross Domestic Product (GDP) divided by the population. Alternative indicators involve altering the denominator. If we use members of the labor force, we will get mean income per worker; if we use the number of households, we will find the mean income per family. Unfortunately, the numerator, national income, has been calculated only for the past three-quarters of a century or so. Throughout most of human history we must rely on estimates that are sometimes based on very little evidence.

The majority of individual income is derived from wages from the provision of labor services. In advanced modern societies, approximately 75% of all income goes to labor. The remainder is largely made up of payments to the owners of capital resources; this also includes individuals who received payments through the financial vehicles of pension plans, savings accounts of various types and returns on investment. Figure 2.3 shows the history of average earnings in England since 1264 (for the modern period they are British) in index form. Actual, or what are called nominal, earnings are adjusted for the change of prices creating a measure of real earnings. Real wages are the variable unit in determining real earnings and they increased from the point of first measurement in 1264 to roughly the end of the 15th century. This has been associated with two phenomena: the rise of trade in the late medieval period and, in the 14th century,

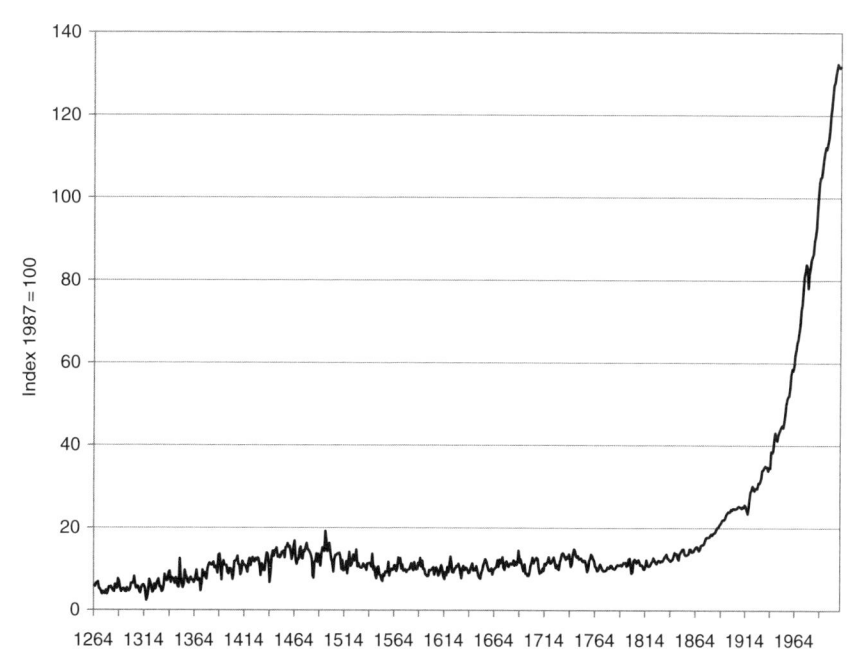

Figure 2.3 Index of Real Earnings and Trend in England (and after 1707 Great Britain), 1264–2009.
Source: Officer (current), http://www.en.net/nmit/ukearnpi/

the shortage of labor as a result of the widespread population loss due to the Black Death. There then followed a period of about 300 years during which the nominal wage rate rose, but rose more slowly than prices, resulting in a real earnings decline. This worsening took place despite the known advances in agricultural productivity and the beginnings of industrialization in 18th century Britain. Not until the 19th century was there a clear reversal. If this earnings history of England (UK) is a reasonable measure, it indicates that in the lives of ordinary people there were long, long periods when income levels did not improve. If this is true in relatively modern history, it is even more likely the case in the distant past. Improvement in the human condition, in terms of income levels, was often glacially slow and occasionally reversed. Persistent and improved standards of living have been the norm only over the past 200 years.

The United States is one economy for which we have reasonably good estimates of income over a long period of time, over 200 years. Since much of the information used to build measures of GDP come from population census information, the estimates are, until the 20th century, at ten-year intervals. There is fierce debate about whether or not these estimates of national income are consistent over short time periods. However, there is general agreement the estimates after 1860 are of better quality than those before that date. These concerns notwithstanding, we can look at the evidence with some reasonable assurances that they capture the main features of long-run income growth. There are several features of US national income growth evident in Figure 2.4. These are also likely to be the experience of other high-income countries.

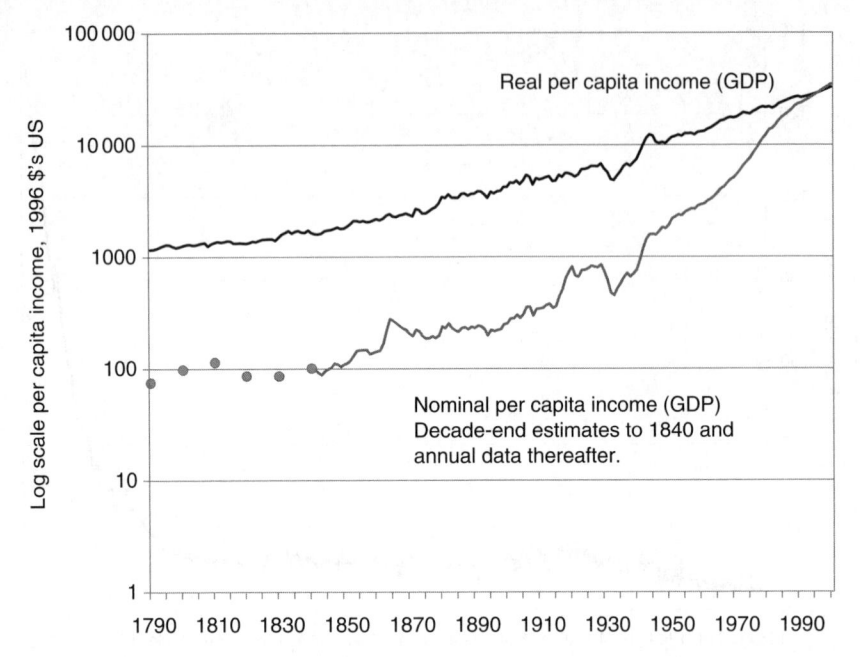

Figure 2.4 Real GDP per Capita for the United States, Annually, 1791–2000.
Source: Sutch (2006) *US Historical Statistics* and current estimates.

First, the short-run variation in *nominal* national income is greater than the variation in *real* national income. Second, the long-run rate of growth of real national income shows few particularly sudden shifts such as those exhibited in the nominal income series. Falling incomes were usually a sign of decreased aggregate demand but also of declining prices and *vice versa*. Third, real income per capita increased at a higher rate of growth in the more recent past, since about the mid- to late-19th century, than in the more distant past.

One problem with all these indicators is that they obscure the distribution of income (see David, 1996 for a discussion of the US distribution of income). A society where only a few individuals receive high income and the large majority receives low incomes is very different from one where income is distributed more evenly. Indeed we would expect that the aggregate demographic response to average income changes would be different in these two societies even if they both had the same mean income. We will return to this issue in greater detail later. For the moment we can simply note that mean values may not capture well the common experience.

Mean income levels in various regions of the world today are incredibly diverse. More than 2.73 billion people currently live at a level of income of less than $2US per day. While admitting that the equivalent of $2US buys more basic goods in rural India, for instance, than it does in New York City, it is nonetheless a depressingly low amount. In high-income countries, by contrast, the yearly per-capita income is about $29 000US as indicated in Table 2.1 converted to $US. Of course around such averages there are various distributions of incomes within regions or countries. Even

Table 2.1 Gross National Income Per Capita by World Region and Income Characteristics, 2003.

	GNI $US	PPP $ International
World	5500	8180
Low Income	450	2190
Middle Income	1920	6000
Lower middle income	1480	5510
Upper middle income	5340	9900
Low & middle income	1280	4320
East Asia & Pacific	1080	4680
Europe & Central Asia	2570	7570
Latin America & Caribbean	3260	7080
Middle East & North Africa	2250	5700
South Asia	510	2660
Sub-Saharan Africa	490	1,770
High income	28550	29450
European Monetary Union	22850	26260

Source: World Bank (current), *World Development Indicators*. http://www.worldbank.org/data
GNI is Gross National Income (Gross National Product) and converted to $US using current exchange rates. PPP is Purchasing Power Parity which is a conversion based on relative prices.

in very low-income per capita countries there are individuals whose incomes are high by any standard. And it follows that in high-income countries there are individuals whose yearly incomes are low by any standard. This raises a fundamental issue: does the distribution of income within an economy change as that economy grows?

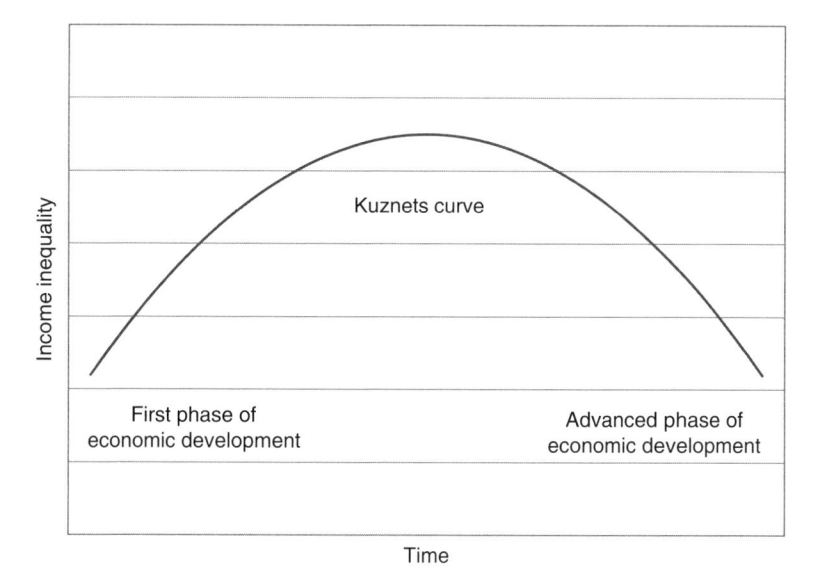

Figure 2.5 Kuznets Curve and Index of Income Inequality.

Economists have suggested that as a country begins to develop rapidly, as say in the early stages of its economic transition, the income distribution within that country widens.[4] That is, there is a rising degree of income inequality. This tendency continues for some unspecified time, and, as the economy moves into a phase of sustained growth, the income inequality begins to narrow, reversing the earlier trend. There is broad support for this proposition (named the *Kuznets Curve*) as a trend in the historical data, although each individual country's case is somewhat different. The inverted "U" shape is shown in Figure 2.5. There are similar trends within countries. Slow-growing parts of a national economy tend to have less income inequality than the faster growing parts. No doubt this is brought about by low levels of factor endowments in the low-income per capita sub-national regions. Thus when we observe the long run convergence of per capita incomes among regions, which is the key feature of regional development, it is linked to the redistribution of the population through both international and internal migration. Of course other forms of redistribution will also have an effect – the regional pattern of the national state's taxing and spending being an important one.[5]

In modern economies, individuals generally experience an increase in their incomes as they age. Wages (salaries) tend to increase as individual members of the labor force gain more experience. The tendency for this to occur varies both with the degree of formal education and with training levels. Whether this tendency was present in the past, or was widespread if present, is an open question. Certainly, there are obvious pre-industrial examples: the apprentice has a low wage but might look forward to higher wage compensation when a journeyman or master.[6] A young farming family member might move into a higher income range once the parents have surrendered their farming property rights to the younger generation. That is, the average income that we calculate is not necessarily the income the individual received at any specific age in the *life cycle*. In later chapters we will return and expand upon the economic concept of the individual life cycle of income.

2.5 Net Replacement

In the context of Figure 2.1 the net increase in the population (births minus deaths) first accelerates and then decelerates. Today most of the developed world has a birth rate that is near or below the death rate. Recall, from Chapter One, births minus deaths is the net natural increase of the population. In order to find out the implications of this demographers calculate a total fertility rate (TFR), which is defined below. The birth rate for every possible year of a woman's life is known as the age-specific birth rate. The TFR is then compared to the net replacement rate (NRR), also defined below, which informs us exactly how many children a woman must give birth to in order to replace herself and her male partner. If the TFR is less than the NRR, this means that the number of children being born plus those likely to be born is less than that necessary to keep the population of these countries from eventually falling. However, there are three reasons why the population will not necessarily decrease immediately. The first is a technical one. The TFR takes some

> *TFR*: The *total fertility rate* is the number of children a woman will give birth to, on average, over the course of her reproductive life. It is calculated from birth rates at each age and therefore is a projection based on the current pattern of fertility.
>
> *GRR*: The *gross reproduction rate* represents the average number of daughters born to a hypothetical cohort of 1000 women if they experienced the age-specific birth rates observed in a given year throughout their childbearing years (usually measured to age 49 but often only reported to age 45).
>
> *NRR*: The *net replacement rate* or net reproduction rate is the calculated number of children a woman must give birth to, on average, over the course of her reproductive life in order for her to exactly replace herself and her male partner. The number used by the UN Population Division is 2.1. This allows for the mortality of those under 16 years of age. In practice, where mortality is greater, the NRR is greater, and where it is less, the NRR is below 2.1. It is always greater than 2.0.

time to work its way through the population as the population ages. Second, the high-income countries that experience low TFR attract, and are deliberately seeking, international migrants. The immigrant numbers boost the population size over what it otherwise would have been. Third, these immigrants themselves tend to be young and continue to have a somewhat higher birth rate than the population of long residence.[7] Exactly how different fertility is among the immigrant population is a question of some debate as we will see later. The UN Population Division actually predicts a rise in the TFR by 2050 in some high-income countries, *although it will still be below the net replacement rate*. Nonetheless, the immigrants and their fertility forestall the drop in TFR somewhat.

Even the less developed parts of the world have experienced a substantial reduction in TFR in the past quarter century – see Table 2.2. The decline is such that the entire world is projected to be below the NRR by 2050, at 2.02% on average. We caution that this does *not* mean that the world's population will cease to grow after that date as it will take several decades for the TFR to have its full effect (even if the underlying assumptions of the projections prove correct). The worldwide decline in fertility, while anticipated by earlier forecasters, has come about much more rapidly than anyone imagined just a few years ago.[8]

As high(er) income countries experience below net replacement fertility there is a tendency for them to attract immigrants through the mechanisms of the labor market. This, as noted, boosts the populations in the receiving countries. Yet, this is not a once-and-for-all effect but an on-going one. Currently, the OECD countries as a group have substantially below-replacement NRRs. Europe, as a sub-group in the OECD, has by far the lowest TFR to date and is the receiver of large numbers of international migrants. Since these migrants come primarily from non-OECD Eastern

Table 2.2 Estimated and Projected Total Fertility: World, Development Areas and Regions, 1970–2050.

Major area	Total Fertility (average number of children per woman)		
	1970–1975	2005–2010	2045–2050
World	4.32	2.56	2.02
More developed regions*	2.17	1.64	1.80
Less developed regions	4.53	2.73	2.05
Least developed countries	6.74	4.39	2.41
Other less developed countries	4.97	2.46	1.93
Africa	6.69	4.61	2.40
Asia	4.76	2.35	1.90
Europe	2.19	1.50	1.80
Latin America and the Caribbean	5.01	2.26	1.82
Northern America	2.07	2.04	1.85
South America	4.64	2.18	1.80
Oceania	3.29	2.44	1.93

*The World Bank definition of development regions.
Note: Only countries and areas with populations greater than 100 000 in 2007 are included.
Source: Data from UN (2009), *World Population Prospects, The 2008 Revision*, http://esa.un.org/unpp/

Europe, it has lowered TFRs there and, combined with the exodus, their populations are declining. Table 2.3 lists the countries in the world with the lowest current rates of population growth, net of immigration and emigration. These rates of natural increase are, in fact, negative! If these trends continue, Russia's population will fall by 34.7 million in the next 40 years or so. Increasingly the flow of international migrants will be composed of citizens of countries in the less developed parts of the world.

Table 2.3 Countries with the Lowest Current Rates of Population Growth, Net of Immigration and Emigration, 2007.

Ukraine	−0.72
Bulgaria	−0.59
Russian Federation	−0.55
Belarus	−0.53
Latvia	−0.43
Hungary	−0.39
Estonia	−0.35
Lithuania	−0.32
Croatia	−0.31
Romania	−0.26

Note: Only countries or areas with 100 000 persons or more in 2007 are included.
Source: Data from UN (2009), *World Population Prospects, The 2008 Revision*, http://esa.un.org/unpp/

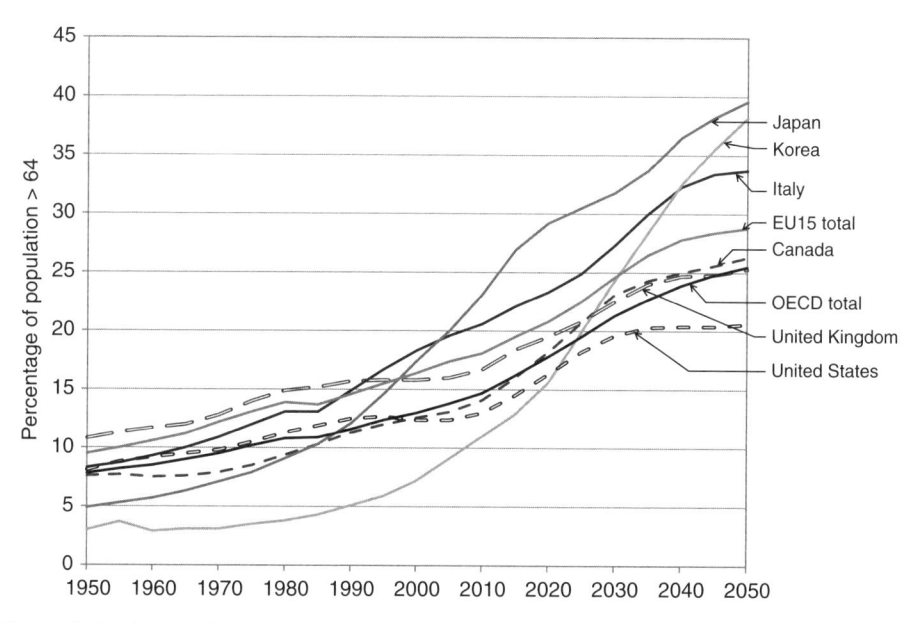

Figure 2.6 Aging of the Populations of Selected OECD Countries, 1950–2050, Actual and Projected.
Notes: EU 15 refers to Austria, Belgium, Denmark, Finland, France, Germany, Greece, Ireland, Italy, Luxembourg, the Netherlands, Portugal, Spain, Sweden and the United Kingdom.
Source: OECD (2007) *Factbook 2007*, http://www.oecd-ilibrary.org/statistics

2.6 Dependency and Participation

In the years before the demographic transition the population of most countries was, on average, quite young. Fertility was high but so was mortality among the young. Although we will explore this in detail in Chapter Three, it is pertinent to note that this causes a large dependent base of children and teenagers many of whom do not survive to reproductive age. After the demographic transition, the low fertility and mortality regimes produce a large dependent older population. In the long-run, this will be a stable proportion of the population. However, at present in the OECD (high-income) countries, a stable proportion has not been reached as net fertility is still adjusting. The result is population aging; as Figure 2.6 depicts, the proportion of the population over 64 years of age is rapidly growing in the OECD countries.

There are four countries of the OECD group that require special comment, three because of high aging rates and one because of a low rate (relative to the OECD average) – see Figure 2.6:

- *Japan and the Republic of Korea*: these countries experienced a post-1945 net fertility boom. The death rate simply fell away more rapidly than anticipated while fertility was much slower to adjust. The consequence, since neither country receives much net immigration, is that the population bulge is now aging and heading into retirement age, Japan in advance of Korea. The age group of 65 years of age and over is now predicted to be over 35% of the population by 2050. This prediction can be quite confidently stated as the scale of the elderly cohort is known – they've all been born. Only three unlikely demographic events could cause a reduction in the projected 2050 proportion: i) a large increase in senior age mortality at earlier ages than expected; ii) a very large and unexpected increase in fertility; and iii) a very large net immigration.[9] None of these events are likely. Of all countries, these two will have, in the near future, the world's largest elderly populations proportionally. Although not an OECD country, China is headed in the same direction.

- *Italy*: by any measure the fertility of the Italian population is currently extremely low. Although Italy does receive a stream of immigrants, it is not in such numbers that it increases the crude birth rate much at all. The issue is why have the Italians chosen this low-fertility option? The answer appears to be that more Italians, especially Italian women, have rejected the traditional form of marriage and traditional attitudes towards children. Indeed, this is true of all the European Mediterranean countries. We will explore this further in the next section.
- *United States*: currently it has the highest TFR among the OECD countries. By contrast, and as expected, it has the lowest proportion of elderly. But it is still higher than anything history records. One line of reasoning links the higher fertility to the large net immigration (legal and illegal).

The proportion of the population that is 65 years of age and over does not exactly equal the proportion of that group which is dependent since not all individuals retire or cease working at age 65. It does, nevertheless, set an upper limit. It is increasingly the case that individuals work beyond an arbitrary retirement age, usually 60 or 65 years of age. Mandatory retirement is no longer practiced in many jurisdictions; discrimination on the grounds of age is viewed by many as a violation of human rights. More prosaically, in order to cope with the dependency costs (pensions and old-age security schemes to

---

More Definitions

DR: *dependency rate* is the proportion of the population not working or seeking work.

LFP: *labor force participation* is the proportion of the population that is: i) employed; ii) self-employed; and iii) unemployed but actively seeking work.

$$LFP = 1 - DR$$

In the US and many other jurisdictions the LFP excludes "military personnel." Herein lies a further definitional problem when doing cross-country comparisons: some countries include certain types of activities within the "military" and others do not, such as contract personnel and coastal rescue services.

The LFP can also be defined for a large variety of subgroups. For instance, policy-makers may wish to know the effectiveness of certain labor market initiatives: what proportion of married women with dependent children participates in the labor force?

Figure 2.7 Annual Average Labor Force Participation, United States, 1948–2005.
Note: Civilian labor force only.
Source: BLS, Series Id: LNS11300000

name the most common), countries, particularly in Europe, have adopted policies that raise the age of pension eligibility (the problems of aging are discussed in Chapter Eight).

What is the size of the active labor force in the population? The labor force participation rate (LFP) gives this information. It is exactly equal to one minus the dependency rate (DR) *if all the information is known about the young and elderly age groups*. In addition, we would also have to know about other non-participants in the labor market, those physically or mentally unable to work, spouses (whose work in the home is excluded), and so on. Since in practice this information is extremely difficult to collect and assess, we calculate an explicit LFP. As it turns out, the explicit LFP can be manipulated to provide other useful policy-related information.

Above, in Figure 2.7, is the overall labor force participation rate for the US for the past half century. It mirrors the effects of the post-1945 boom in fertility as that cohort: i) first reduced dependency in the 1960s and raised the LFP; ii) as the leading edge entered retirement, stalled the growth of the LFP in the late 1990s; and iii) as the number of older-age dependents started to grow has caused a recent decline in the LFP, a decline which will continue for some time.

2.7 How Does the Demographic Transition End or Does It?

Economic development brought about a revolution in women's work. Women have always worked, of course, and worked hard.[10] Caring for the family, helping on the farm, and, for working-class women in the cities, doing the domestic chores of others for pay or taking on piece work were usually not counted as "in the workplace." The LFP simply measures women in the *formal* workplace. Raquel Fernandez has recently calculated,

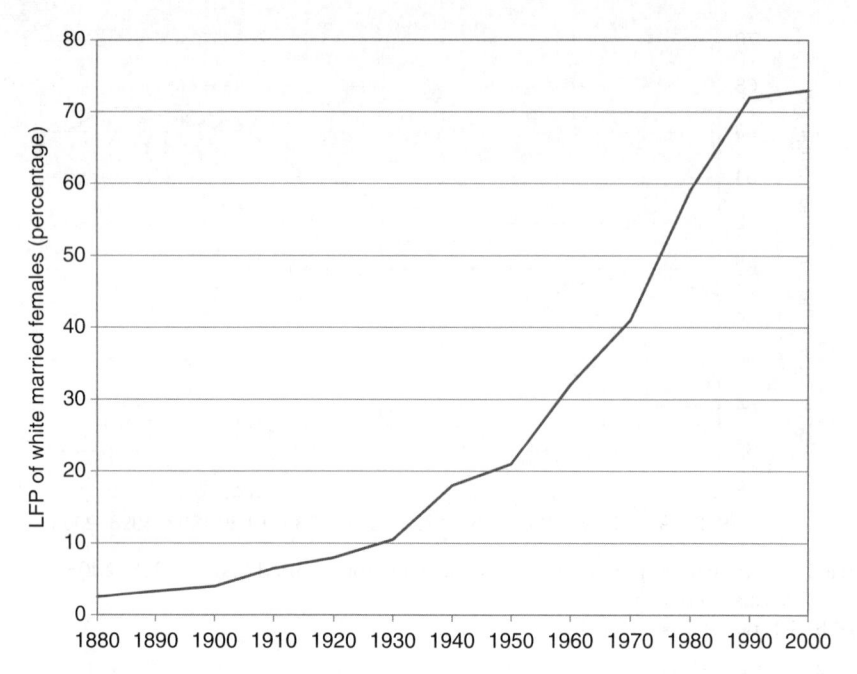

Figure 2.8 Married Female Labor Force Participation in the US, 1880–2000.
Note: White, married (spouse present) women born in the US, 25–44 years of age, who report being in the labor force. Data for 1890 are interpolated.
Source: Data from the US Census, 1880–2000 after Fernandez (2007), Figure 2.

using US Census data, that the LFP for white, married women was only 2% in 1880; it grew to 73% by 2000 – see Figure 2.8. It was undoubtedly higher for black women in the US – although their contributions cannot be so easily measured over the same time period.[11] In most developed countries, and in many less developed countries, the increased female participation in the labor market had direct consequences for fertility.

The decline in the total fertility rate (TFR) to below net replacement was not foreseen by the theory of the demographic transition – although it is not ruled out as a possibility. It has come about in a remarkably short period of time and been much more widespread than ever anticipated. This led Ron Lesthaeghe and David van de Kaa and some other observers to propose a "Second Demographic Transition" as an explanatory device.[12] The thrust of their argument is that society in general, and women in particular, have a new set of attitudes towards work, sex, marriage, families and children, all of which are fertility reducing. First, it recognizes the role of women in the workplace. Female participation rates have risen everywhere, especially with the removal of many of the discriminatory barriers that women faced in the past. This means that not only is work remunerative but more and lengthy careers are possible. So not only is the cost of having children going up (part of which is the reduced or compromised earnings of women) but careers are valued for their own sakes (i.e., they have utility). This is the economic analogue of social/political empowerment. The birth and subsequent care of children competes directly with labor market participation in a wholly new way. (It also is highly sensitive to the institutional arrangements of countries for the provision of support services for women and children.) Thus we

Women at Work, the 1890s

The growth of light manufacturing and the service industries drew more women into the regular workforce. Here women are employed at the Kodak Factory in Harrow, England processing photographic plates.
Source: From the Kodak Archive, Online Gallery, *The British Library*.

find in Western Europe behavior that supports this new labor market role: increased non-married cohabitation of individuals, increased divorce rates, greater proportions of single parent families by choice and delay of the birth of the first child. The social consequences of the post-1960s birth control technology brought about new attitudes to the family and its role and formed one of the threads of modernity. In Western Europe the decline in religiosity is said to be part (cause or symptom?) of this revolution in social attitudes. Among the high-income countries, however, there are clear distinctions about how they react in the second demographic transition.[13]

The second demographic transition with its low fertility raises some interesting issues. First, there was no sharp divide that separates the first and second demographic transitions. We prefer to think of it as a descriptive device used to highlight social issues in a low fertility – low mortality regime. Next, the second demographic transition was originally thought of as a phenomenon special to Western Europe. However, as more and more evidence becomes available, it is clear that it is much more widely spread. To be sure, the social characteristics of individual countries take on cultural dimensions that are unique, but the processes and outcomes are perfectly general.

- Is there a gap between the *desired* number of children and *actual* number of children? The implication is that the very low fertility levels are not desired and are just temporary. There is a fertility gap. Or, are we simply examining a process that seeks a new equilibrium at the low fertility levels? The jury is out!

- Japan and Korea are exceptional, as noted earlier in this chapter. Yet, some of the social characteristics of the second demographic transition, common in Western Europe, are not found in these societies such as the non-married cohabitation. But there are many points of similarity. A relatively strong patriarchal tradition is decaying in East Asia and in the countries of Southern (Mediterranean) Europe as women are empowered by education and the new birth control technology. Many educated women ignore the traditional concepts of family and children, by not participating, hence the low fertility. We can measure this shift in attitudes by changes in the marriage rate and the age at marriage. Postponing marriage generally reduces the number of children born within that marriage.
- Americans in general also do *not appear* to share some of the social characteristics common to the Western Europeans. For instance, the high rate of teenage pregnancies in the US is a modern example of the differences.[14] Yet, what is true about the US, as a whole, is not always (ever) true of its regions. For instance, the increase in religiosity affects demographic outcomes mainly in the South and mid-West. Of course depth of religious feeling may be inversely correlated with income and positively with other variables, and its effects alone are difficult to quantify. On the other hand, regions such as New England, New York State (and others areas including the major cities) display attitudes quite similar to Western Europe. They also display the same fertility outcomes.
- It is argued by Sara McLanahan that there is a growing gap in material resources for children, for the US as a whole, associated with rising income inequality. Her analysis suggests that the education of the parents is the root cause of this divergence.[15] Low levels produce greater fertility. This is probably true elsewhere although offset by specific policy measures to alleviate child poverty in other OECD countries. Income supplements directed at female-led single parent families are a policy thrust in many countries.
- Some observers note that, as the second demographic transition occurs with its extraordinary low fertility, a fundamental change takes place in society, a third demographic transition.[16] The ethnic composition of many countries, particularly in Western Europe, North America, Australia and New Zealand will change substantially as the net replacement gap is filled by immigrants who increasingly will be from non-traditional sources.[17] The long history of international migration in the 18th, 19th and early 20th centuries provide some lessons here – see Chapter Five. There are two over-riding economic concerns: immigrant fertility and labor force participation. Will the immigrants bring with them the fertility behavior of their home country (although, since a worldwide convergence is underway, this may be slight)? While there were, and are, exceptions for certain groups, most immigrants tend towards the norm of the country they enter. The second issue is the ease with which immigrants are absorbed into the labor force. Both immigrant fertility behavior and employment options depend on the level of education, and that is one of the key determinants of the speed of immigrant absorption into the economic mainstream. In a historical context, we must also consider levels of non-conventional human capital which are not a product of formal education which aids individual's participation.

For many countries in the less-developed world the main phases of the demographic transition have either ended abruptly or not ended at all. In the People's Republic of China, one of the world's most populous countries, it has been claimed that low fertility regime was accelerated by policy. The Chinese Government instituted the "one child per family" policy. The reasoning behind this policy has never been clearly stated.[18] It was broadly justified by the Government in 1978/1980 simply as necessary to contain the growth of the population. The policy was enforced with draconian measures, including forced abortions and sterilizations. However, the enforcement varied in its thoroughness by location. It tended to be more weakly enforced in the provinces and more rigorously in the urban areas. This one child per family policy continues to be the principal population policy in China, although the penalties for non-observance have been moderated considerably in recent years.[19] In 1970–1975 the TFR was 4.86, more than twice that of Canada, UK and the US. Twenty-five years later, China's TFR is below that of the other three countries. The result is that China's population is currently growing at a substantially lower rate than that of Canada and the US (and just greater than that of the UK).[20]

It is unlikely, however, that this dramatic change in China's TFR was entirely the product of the "one-child" policy. Before the policy initiative China had seen increases in the average age of first marriage, a fertility limiting family strategy. Marital fertility in every age group was also declining throughout the period from the early 1960s onward.[21] Thus, the question becomes: how much of the decline in TFR was due to the underlying trends that were fertility limiting and how much was due to the policy change? Both operated so as to reduce the TFR. (The reasoning of economic history is: *what is* contrasted with *what might have been*, the next most reasonable alternative.) Perhaps, China has been displaying more Korea-like and Japanese-like tendencies than are usually recognized.

The demographic transition is not complete for the low-income countries even though these countries have shown a marked reduction in fertility in recent years. Many of the barriers to fertility reduction in traditional societies remain in place. Reluctance to use family planning techniques, for cost or other reasons, puts families at risk of having unwanted children. The lack of education limits economic opportunity and, especially for women, severely constrains their labor market participation. And, there are many countries where there are formal restrictions or taboos placed on married women's work activities outside the home. Yet, as we will see in Chapters Three and Four, a common characteristic among those countries that have not completed the transition is that they share a high mortality rate relative to the developed world. Why don't the two rates equilibrate at a higher level to produce a low rate of population growth? The problem is that death rate is not only still relatively high, but it is more variable. The gap between fertility and mortality remains high because the target is not the number of children born, but rather the completed family size. As noted, the low-income countries are exactly those that are experiencing the highest rates of HIV/AIDS infection. The fertility rate and mortality rate are causally related.

From a world perspective, the last main phase of the demographic transitions for the lagging countries will continue to contribute to a falling world population growth rate. This rate has been declining since the 1960s. By 2050 it will have fallen to approximately 0.5% per year, the lowest growth rate in modern history – see Figure 2.9.

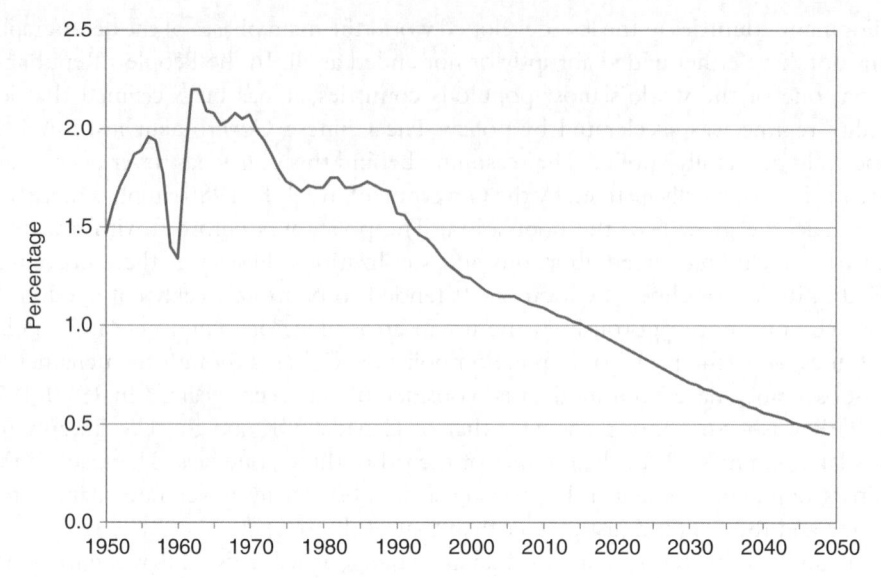

Figure 2.9 World Population Growth Rates, Actual and Projected, 1950–2050.
Source: US Census (current), *International Data Base*.

Although the world's population will enter a regime of below NRR by 2050, according to the UN projections, it is unlikely that the demographic transition will be completed for all countries until about the end of the century. India, which is well into the final phase, will not likely complete the transition until late in the century. By that time it will have replaced China as the world's most populous country. By 2050 only the least developed countries, many of which are in sub-Saharan Africa, will be above net replacement fertility by the conventional measure, that is, NRR = 2.1 – see Table 2.1, above. However, much depends on the incidence and virulence of HIV/AIDS.

2.8 Variation

In pre-modern society the *long-run* growth rate of population was modest as we reported in Chapter One. Although both the birth and death rates were very high by modern standards, the birth rate was generally larger than the death rate. Both varied considerably in the *short-run*, with the death rate being more responsive to the variations in economic circumstances. This, of course, highlights one of the key historical issues of population growth: the strength of an economy consistently to produce the means of subsistence (foodstuffs, clothing, and shelter) at a level substantial enough to avoid highly variable death rates. Similar to most population issues, this has both time and distributional dimensions. The latter might be by sector of the economy, by industry, by geographic area, by employment or by income levels. In an otherwise well-functioning economy, any failure that produces lower incomes (for all or some), in turn weakens the health of the population and makes its members more susceptible to disease and the maladies associated with a low standard of living. This increases both *morbidity* (a decline in healthiness) and mortality. For any individual, a severe

> ## More Terms
>
> *Endemic*: a condition such as a disease that is commonly found in a particular population.
>
> *Epidemic*: pathogens or microbes, such as some viruses, which, when they enter the human body, give rise to disease or death. They normally are external to the country (region, continent) and usually infect many individuals more or less simultaneously. The epidemic may spread in various forms: by body fluids such as blood and saliva or spread from other animal species. They are likely endemic, but become virulent when a change such as an environmental shift occurs, that favors them and they have a greater chance of entering the human system. If the disease is particularly widespread, it is epidemic. The Hantavirus (Pulmonary Syndrome) of 1993–1997 in the southwestern US was an epidemic in the native Indian population.[22]
>
> *Pandemic*: if an epidemic has no boundary or is not restricted to a particular population, it is said to be pandemic. The influenza outbreak in 1918–1919 was spread world-wide and is one of the modern instances of a pandemic disease.

income decline may produce deprivation such that death through disease, malnutrition and starvation results. Indeed, if widespread, this may cause the mortality rate to rise above the birth rate for some time producing negative growth – a decline in population (assuming no substantial out-migration from the economy). This was a common fate of many in history.

From time to time there were eruptions of a disease that had a wide-spread effect. Such eruptions were either *epidemic* or *pandemic*. Some have already been mentioned. Such exogenous population catastrophes produced large increases in mortality. It is the suddenness of these shocks that delivers the impact. Mortality shocks, however, are generally less damaging to a population's ability to recover than a fertility shock of the same magnitude. There is an important qualification to this generalization: provided the population is not on an irreversible declining growth trajectory. Although each mortality catastrophe had its own epidemiological history, they can be classified by some common characteristics:

- The spread of human or animal-human disease was a product of increased contact among populations, particularly with increased international trade and increased migration.
- The failure of the food supply because of plant or animal diseases, short-run climate change (floods and droughts) also contribute.
- The failure of the food delivery or distribution mechanism through interruptions such as war or civil unrest.
- Some of these catastrophes will be examined in detail later (Chapter Ten). There is also a fourth type of population catastrophe which is all the more terrible because of its cause, direct human action: genocides, ethnic cleansings, pogroms, forced migrations and slavery, all have their long sad histories.

Most wars of pre-modern times took relatively small tolls of human life, at least directly. This, however, could be a large *proportional* effect if a country's population was small or if the deaths were narrowly distributed in age (usually 20–45 years of age) and gender (male). It is perhaps no coincidence that early 19th century, post-Napoleonic War French literature is full of unmarried women! Indirectly, wars were often responsible for widespread economic chaos, devastation and starvation far in excess of the direct losses; there were spill-over effects. Calculation of the numerical human loss does not give us the full demographic or economic effects of these catastrophes. Claudia Goldin and Frank Lewis, in their study of the US Civil War, show how important it is to measure the losses in human capital terms both because it is a more accurate economic assessment in terms of lost consumption and it shows how the effects of a war persist long after the event.[23] *Human capital* is simply the value of the investment in the individual over their lifetimes. It includes the rearing and education cost (both the explicit payment of education fees and upkeep and the opportunity cost of being out of the labor market while receiving the education) and the value of further work experience.[24] All of that is lost because of needless death.

2.9 Globalization, Macroeconomics and Population

Globalization is a loosely defined term used to describe the long distance reach of economic, social and political forces and their integration. Some see the global extension of these forces as essentially modern, a product of instant and secure communications. To be sure we have only used the term recently. Historians, however, find compelling evidence that these forces have been operating to integrate economies for some time, the key criterion being that the markets in the various far locations interact with one another. Globalization thus produces a price convergence. On a broad scale this has been happening since the early 19th century – some say even earlier, it largely being a matter of scale and narrowness of definition. For population historians there is the same dilemma. The flow of migrants has always been present but their global span in substantial numbers can, somewhat arbitrarily, said to be also a product of the 19th century. Largely referring to the trans-Atlantic movements of people, the "age of mass migration" is dated to the years after the Napoleonic Wars. This makes the globalization of population flows coincident with the early stages of the demographic transition and the 19th century growth in world trade. Not surprisingly, the flows of information, trade and capital are part of the same phenomenon.

Before the modern age, a state with a larger population generally had a larger army than a state with a smaller population and, consequently, more power. With the power, more resources could be acquired. However, the history of warfare also informs us that smallness of size could be overcome by technology: Greek naval strategy during the Persian Wars; the Mongols' use of cavalry under their brilliant leader Genghis Khan; the English with the long-bow in the 14th and 15th centuries; and so on. The combination of size *and* advanced technology together was the likely guarantor of success. (Recent modern wars with a guerrilla or irregular component occasionally prove an exception.)

So, long before the history of the modern age, a large population was recognized as important. But, if the marginal social cost of acquiring more resources (a greater army) was greater than the marginal social benefit (the income gained through power), a country or empire could become too large. It was then vulnerable to the predation of others. That is, there were offsets as more recent history also testifies.

No historical circumstances determined a country's macroeconomic performance more than its endowment of resources. What constitutes a resource both varies over time and with technology. Historically, the United States was exceptionally well-endowed in land, mineral and other natural resources, fuels, river systems to provide transport, to name but a few. The only resource that was not abundant historically was the human one. Early in its history, American economic growth took on the characteristics of this endowment and developed along lines that were labor-saving and used other resources.[25] Relative factor prices at work again! It dictated conservation of the use of the *relatively* more expensive factor of production. There is, of course, no unique combination of resources that will be better than any other. This includes population as labor. However, if key factors are insufficient or lacking, even in a world of flexible factor proportions, they will impose constraints that limit economic growth.

> Long-run macroeconomic or aggregate economic performance is usually measured by the rate of growth of GDP per annum on a sustained basis. It can also be assessed by the behavior of key macro indicators such as the money supply, labor unemployment and investment. In history, measures of GDP are rare and even the best do not extend further back than the mid-19th century. Consequently, we use those indicators that are more readily available, or can be constructed, when assessing aggregate economic behavior. Short-run macroeconomic growth may exhibit fluctuations or instability. These are departures from the long-run performance trends.

Location and climate are also key endowments. The Dutch and Italians (Venetians) from the late Renaissance until the 18th century used their favorable endowment of coastal locations with maritime expertise to exploit international trade opportunities. In turn, by the late Renaissance period both economies had developed advanced (for the day) financial markets that provided the means of financing its trade. In general, economic growth has appeared more robust in the temperate climate zones; elsewhere climate has imposed severe tests. Limits placed on agriculture by the short growing season of northerly latitudes and the desert areas of Australia and Africa were difficult to overcome. In general, the endowment of an economy was more likely to direct a particular path of development than forestall it completely. For instance, French industrial development was inhibited in the 19th century by its lack of industrial energy supplies, coal in particular. Some countries, such as Canada, had ample coal resources but they were at locations that made exploitation uneconomic, at least until recently. Yet, macroeconomies do adapt, and Canada's modern economic history is one of an industrial development using motive energy in the form of hydro-electric power, as opposed to heat energy, with no obvious detrimental effect on the long-run rate of economic growth. Where you start, what your endowment is, matters. Where you go is path-dependent. Each step in the historical development evolves from the previous one.

But endowments are not fixed in the long run. Both technological changes and price changes determine what is deemed a resource at any particular time. Land and mineral resources in production, for instance, were dependent on prices. As the prices, or rents, of resources rose in response to prices of products using those resources, there was a search for more resources. There is a long history of agricultural land being reclaimed from coastal and river marshes, low lying wetlands and the heath lands throughout the world.[26] Substantial amounts of land were claimed or re-claimed from waste lands in English and Welsh agriculture in the 18th and 19th centuries through enclosures. The draining of the fens was even earlier. The 'new world' city of Boston, Massachusetts, covers roughly twice the land area today it covered when the Puritans arrived in 1630 as a result of leveling hills and filling bays. Better drainage was one key to increasing the usable acreage on US farms in the settled areas of the American Midwest beginning in the 19th century. The ratio of the improved acreage to the total farm acreage increased by a multiple of three between 1860 and 1914 without any change in the land area.[27] Exploitation of the newly found resources was dependent on how much it cost the owner to bring them into production and the price the user was willing to pay for them. It took a rise in the price of oil and a decline in its cost of production to bring the oil resources of the Alberta tar sands into economic use. Offshore oil reserves (North Sea, Nigerian coastal waters, the Gulf of Mexico, for instance) have all been added to national endowments in recent years. In general, minerals share this characteristic; we tend to find more of them when we look for more of them – at a cost. As more non-renewable natural resources are discovered today, it must be true that less will be available in the future, so there is an ultimate problem. The historical evidence also suggests that technological changes have made it possible for us to be successful in finding substitutes for truly scarce non-renewable resources. Of course, we might be critical and note that the environmental costs have not been properly counted.

Demographers theorize that there was/is an optimum population for any economy given its endowment of resources. A population that is either smaller or larger than the optimum would yield a lower real income per capita. But because resource endowments are not fixed and because output and factors prices continually adjust, there is no population stock that is uniquely best in the historian's world of continual change. Notions such as under-population or over-population are misleading, except in extreme circumstances. The modern question to ask is: what would be the effect of slightly more or slightly fewer humans? The answers are not obvious.

Over-population has been from time to time a theme of popular debate and scientific concern. Frequently dire outcomes have been predicted usually, and wrongly, based on long-run population projections that were extrapolations from short-run data trends. A strenuous popular debate took place in the 1960s. Some good arguments came from this debate. In their influential 1964 book titled *Too Many Americans*, the sociologists Lincoln and Alice Day wrote of the US over-population crisis stressing the negative economic externalities.[28] When the book was published the population of the United States was about 189.2 million. The quality of life, they argued, would diminish as more people crowded on to a fixed geographic landscape with a set of natural resources growing slower than population. Total resource use would rise but per capita resource use would inevitably decline, they argued. The current population of the US is 308.7 million, well beyond the Days' worst fears. By many of the conventional measures, such as GNP per capita, Americans are better off today than four decades ago and have a higher measured quality of life. To be sure, there are some characteristics of economic life that have deteriorated over the past four or five decades but the quality of life is a combination of characteristics. While it is harder to find an uncrowded beach or campground site due to both the rise in population *and* the rise in real per capita income, there are more offsets. There are many more choices of products, foodstuffs and public goods whose existence depends on scale. It is a matter of choices and trade-offs, trade-offs that include private and publicly consumed goods and services – and an understanding of the social costs.

From a macroeconomic perspective, is an economy with 1000 people each with a real income of $100 the same as an otherwise identical economy of 100 people each with a real income of $1000? The aggregate income in both cases is the same, but the larger-population economy is disadvantaged in one respect. This is because, at the personal level, its ability to save is related positively to income. The entire flow of income is largely taken up by consumption. The cross-sectional marginal propensity to save is very low, perhaps even negative. In contrast, the smaller-population economy will generate savings *from the same level of aggregate income*. Saving provides the means of acquiring productive capital, so the larger-population economy is far less able to undertake investment on its own. If foreigners are willing to lend to the larger-population country in the form of a capital inflow, the lack of sufficient domestic savings is not an insurmountable barrier to economic growth. To import capital, however, the economy must have sufficient income per capita on a sustained basis to generate a flow of *imports* (which is usually achieved by generating a flow of exports).[29]

The smaller-population country with the high per capita income is also favored by the income elasticity of demand. The growth in the *relative size* of various sectors in the economy is determined by the growth of demand for that sector's goods and services. For instance, agricultural goods may be a large part of the economy, say 75%. If the income elasticity of demand is less than one for agricultural goods, as income per capita grows, the agricultural industry will grow, but it will not grow as rapidly as total income (see Appendix 2.1). The income elasticities of demand for the various sectors tend to be arranged in a hierarchy with necessities like foodstuffs being lower than those faced by manufactured goods and services. Thus, the low per capita income society will generate little change in the sector composition of its economy while the higher income economy will exhibit more.[30] As noted earlier, it is these shifts that are fundamental to historical economic development.

However, some modern economies have a history of being agricultural for long periods of time, but only if they can export their agricultural products. That is, they expanded by finding new consumers (and new agricultural goods) beyond their borders: 19th century Argentina, Australia, Canada and the United States. This required innovation within agriculture or technical change to support the expansion. Many of these economies found their industrial and service sector shares increasing most rapidly during periods of agricultural export booms (e.g., *ante bellum* cotton in the United States or the early 20th century wheat in Canada).

Despite having the potential for economic growth as a result of favorable income elasticities, the high-income, low-population economy may not grow because it is *absolutely* too small. First, there is not enough demand to generate scale effects, which are necessary to drive down per unit costs. This deficiency can be overcome by finding an export market for its goods. The size of the combined domestic and export market determines the extent to which specialization is successful. Second, specialization is also limited by the small size of the labor force and its limited skill set. This, in turn, limits the extent of cost reduction strategies in the production of goods and services. Yet, this too can be overcome by net immigration and tapping the pool of those not working, but capable, such as women (see the discussion of the increasing female participation rate earlier in this chapter). But a strategy of increasing the population depends on attracting people with the needed skills. The economic transition will take place more rapidly if the human capital is matched to the industrial needs than if it is not.

If the small size of the population is a disadvantage without compensating trade, does this mean that the large population economy is advantaged?[31] The answer to this question is: it depends! First, it depends on the endowment of resources (other than population). Anthropology informs us that the great civilizations of pre-conquest Central America disappeared in large measure because the population became too large to be supported by its agriculture. But that can only be part of the explanation. The fact that they had no capacity to adjust or to apply technical change must bear part of the burden of explanation.[32] Second, provided an economy's endowment contains sufficient quantities of other factors, a larger population can adapt by an investment in human capital. With a more highly skilled work force there is more flexibility. Skills are generally acquired through the process of formal education. There are individual exceptions, but not many. Education is highly correlated with social, occupational and geographic mobility, and these, in turn, are population attributes associated with high levels of macroeconomic performance. Last, there may be circumstances where the population may be too large to be consistent with economic development, even in a world of flexible factor proportions. Nico Voigtländer and Hans-Joachim Voth calculate that 18th century China was one of those economies whose population was too large with respect to its resource base, that it had not produced the economic conditions to reduce fertility and permit even a modest gain in per capita income. At the same time, England's [or more properly Britain's] population was changing in a way that promoted economic growth by reducing dependency.[33]

2.10 Institutional Change and Externalities

An economy's aggregate economic performance is directly determined by how well its institutions evolve and how rapidly they adapt to an increasing, or a decreasing, population. Institutions are economic, political and social constructs that are produced by the need to solve problems that: i) are beyond the scope of the individual action; ii) result in a market outcome that is prejudicial to individual welfare and/or economic growth, and iii) produce external effects as by-products of the production (or consumption) of goods and services. Neither the positive effects (social benefits) nor the negative effects (social costs) are gathered or borne respectively by the individuals who produce them, at least not in the first instance. This is a situation commonly known as "market failure."[34]

In some cases the institutions of society are so ingrained that they are thoroughly embodied in custom. Some are deeply human and perhaps a product of our biology, such as monogamous marriage (if not monogamous sex) and the family.[35] But even these institutions solve the economic problem of who takes care of the children (i.e., who bears the cost of fertility). Other types of institutions have evolved as society tried to manage the external effects related to authority and governance. Forms and levels of government have varied throughout history, although they all share the characteristic of providing publicly consumed goods and taxing to pay for them. This they do with greater or lesser efficiency and with greater or lesser public consent. Perhaps the greatest of the publicly consumed goods is the framework called *law*.

The framework of law born out of custom is a social good. But this does not mean that its *contents* are necessarily widely supported, and it indeed may be antithetical to economic progress. For instance, the European feudal system of the Middle Ages locked labor into a type of perpetual contract that inhibited its movement, both geographically and occupationally. That is, it prevented the flexibility that efficient economic adjustment required such as flexible factor prices. Therefore, the prevailing law was, on occasion, only changed by force or by demonstration. Peasant wars and protests were generally unsuccessful in military terms during the Middle Ages and Renaissance, but the peasants' (labor) views often later prevailed in law.[36] For instance, labor shortages after the 14th century plagues contributed to the end of feudal contracts as we will see later – Chapter Ten. Of course, the content of the law could equally support economic development. An example frequently cited is the early development of corporate law in the United States.[37]

Even More Definitions

Social benefits: the benefits that accrue to society at large and cannot, in whole or part, be appropriated by the individual (e.g., a pure water distribution network).

Social cost: the cost that a society must bear that cannot, in whole or in part, be charged to the individual that causes the negative externalities that generate them (e.g., airborne pollution).

Social overhead capital: often referred to as collectively consumed goods that convey social benefits but that are created by an act of capital formation (e.g., economic infrastructure like a transport system).

One area of law that occupies an important historical position is that of property rights. The assignment of property rights gives the power of resource exploitation either to private parties or to the general public. The economic problem with land, water or marine natural resources is that, if held and used by the general public, there are no barriers to limit use and, therefore, no incentive to conserve. Indeed, there is a perverse incentive to exploit rapidly because no one individual can profit from good husbandry. Land in England held "in common" historically was thought to be over-used, hence the phrase "the tragedy of the commons." Much of this common land was privatized from the 15th through 19th centuries. The gains in productivity were once argued to be substantial from privatization, known as enclosures, but recent research by Robert Allen has called this into question.[38] In fisheries, the effects are clear as common access to a fishery drives down the fish stocks and productivity falls along with labor employment. Cannery Row on California's Monterey peninsula was once a thriving fishery, but has become yet another mall. The policy solution has been the government management of these fisheries as if they were sole owned (usually through some form of limited licensing). Through the application of law and custom, the assignment of property rights in a host of applications solves a serious externality problem.

Of course externalities are often negative. The social cost they impart is a real cost. Some of the negative externalities that have been of historical importance to population growth are water-borne and air-borne pollution, and the effects of congestion. One of these is the effective elimination of human and animal waste from the immediate environment and the provision of clean water. As urbanization increased over the past two hundred and fifty years, this problem became more and more acute. The solution to this negative externality was the vast expenditures by the national, regional and municipal government on sanitation facilities (waterworks and sewer systems), which also had large macroeconomic implications.[39] (Even in rural areas, the closeness of human habitation to farm animals became a breeding ground of disease and an effective means of its spread.) One critical element was required to make these public goods successful: an understanding of the germ theory. Naturally, the operation of this type of social overhead capital required new institutions most of which involve government. In the 19th century, this was a force behind the enlargement of city and regional governments. Not only did governments have to provide these public goods (sanitation works), but they had to devise methods of paying for them. The tax base was extended and refined. Compulsory taxation was the only method of funding the projects and avoiding the "free rider problem."[40] Solving the public good issues was one of the key features of improving the human lot; improving health and reducing mortality, the subject of the next chapter.

Appendix 2.1

Income Elasticities of Demand and Sector Shares

In a closed economy, the income elasticity of demand will directly determine the sector shifts, the changes in the industrial structure discussed earlier. Where:

a_i is the ratio of the share of the ith sector in Y relative to its share earlier;
R_t is the rate of growth of total output per capita over the same period;
R_i the rate of growth of the ith sector per capita over the same period;

Y is total output which equals total income in the circular flow; and
ε_{Yi} is the income elasticity of demand and is the percentage change in the quantity of i demanded/percentage change in Y, or (R_i/ Rt).

It can be shown that:

$$a_i = (1 + \varepsilon_{Yi} R_t) / (1 + R_t).$$

If the goods of the ith sector exhibit an $\varepsilon_{Yi} = 1$ then the sector shares will not change over time which is given by $a_i = 1$. On the other hand, if $\varepsilon_{Yi} > 1$ then the ith sector will expand relative to the total economy, $a_i > 1$.[41] The opposite is the case if the income elasticity of demand is less than one.

Endnotes

1. United Nations (current) United Nations Population Division – see General Sources. When presenting estimates based on United Nations Population Division, we cite the medium projections. The UN prepares four projections each based on different assumptions about futures changes: constant refers to the projection assuming current fertility and mortality will not change whereas the low, medium, and high level projections are based on low, medium, and high levels of expected fertility and mortality.
2. They are: Italy, Romania, Poland, Germany, Japan, Republic of Korea, Japan and the Russian Federation.
3. Kuznets (1966). The capital-output ratio for the transport sub-sector (services) is six times that of manufacturing.
4. UN, *The World Bank Group, Millennium Development Goals*. htpp://www.developmentgoals.org/Poverty.htm
5. Lee (2003).
6. Between apprentice and master is the rank of journeyman. A journeyman in a trade usually received higher wages than an apprentice but also suffered from lengthy periods of unemployment.
7. Coleman (2002).
8. Caldwell (2004).
9. The mortality of the entire age group must ultimately equal one.
10. Goldin (1990).
11. Fernandez (2007).

12 van de Kaa (1987).
13 Lesthaeghe (1995).
14 Lesthaeghe and Neidert (2006).
15 McLanahan (2004). The study does not distinguish by region presumably because of the difficulty of securing income inequality by state.
16 Coleman (2006).
17 Currently there is a large Polish immigration to the UK, part of the flow from Eastern Europe. Devine (2006) notes the huge Scottish migration (of mostly ordinary individuals) to Poland in the early 17th century is still evident in the Polish versions of Scottish names.
18 Greenhalgh (2003). A fascinating article by Greenhalgh (2005) links the "one-child" to the scientific/military thought in China and its obsession with control theory. Although published later than the above, it was evidently written before Geenhalgh (2003).
19 n.a. (2003).
20 Annual rates of population growth for 2000–2005 are: US 1.03, Canada 1.01; China 0.67; and UK 0.46.
21 Cheng (1993).
22 American Museum of Natural History, website: http://www.amnh.org
23 Goldin and Lewis (1975).
24 This argument is perfectly general in that it could apply to anyone who died before the end of their working life. The social cost, net of benefits, is larger in the young.
25 Wright (1990).
26 See Wheeler (1965). The use of sea dykes by the Dutch is legendary.
27 *US Historical Statistics*, Agriculture.
28 Day and Day (1965).
29 Capital flows are offset by the entire current account of the balance of payments. Usually exports and imports are the largest part of the current account.
30 Some goods are associated with a negative income elasticity of demand and are referred to as inferior goods. The percentage increase in income per capita actually results in less being demanded.
31 Dasgupta (2000).
32 Mann (2005).
33 Voigtländer and Voth (2006).
34 An undesirable market outcome from, say, the perspective of the distribution of income is not a "failure" even though injurious. A market failure is when the good or service is socially desirable but no market solution exists for its provision by individual agents (firms). The market failure is solved by the provision of the good or service directly by the public sector (in whatever form it takes) or through public subsidy to induce private agents (firms) to produce them.
35 See Adshade and Kaiser (2007).
36 Lichbach (1994).
37 See, for example, Hovenkamp (1991).
38 Allen (1992). Allen has argued that the traditional histories of the enclosures in England have overstated the benefits. The marginal contribution to productivity growth in agriculture from enclosure was very modest; the effects were largely re-distributional.
39 Cain (1978).
40 For a discussion of externalities and institutional economics, see Papandreou (1994). The "free rider" problem arises when no one individual can be excluded from the use of a collectively consumed or public good even if they choose not to pay.
41 Kuznets (1966).

References

Allen, Robert C. (1992) *Enclosure and the Yeoman: The Agricultural Development of the South Midlands, 1450–1850*, Oxford: the Clarendon Press.

Adshade, Marina and Brooks Kaiser (2007) "The Origin of the Institutions of Marriage," working paper presented to the Canadian Learned Societies, Halifax, Nova Scotia, May 2007.

Cain, Louis P. (1978) *Sanitation Strategies for a Lakefront Metropolis, The Case of Chicago*, DeKalb Ill.: Northern Illinois University Press.

Caldwell, John C. (2004) "Demographic Theory: A Long View", *Population and Development Review*, **30**(2) (June), 297–316.

Cheng, C.Z. (1993) "The Fertility Decline in China: The Contribution of Changes in Marital Status and Marital Fertility", *Asia – Pacific Population Journal*, **8**(2), 55–72.

Coleman, D.A. (2002) "Replacement Migration, or Why Everyone is Going to Have to Live in Korea: A Fable for Our Times from the United Nations", *Philosophical Transactions: Biological Sciences*, Vol. 357, No. 1420, Reviews and a Special Collection of Papers on Human Migration, (Apr.), 583–98.

Coleman, David (2006) "Immigration and Ethnic Change in Low-Fertility Countries: A Third Demographic Transition", *Population and Development Review*, **32**(3) (Sept.) 401–46.

Dasgupta, Partha (2000) "Population and Resources: An Exploration of Reproductive and Environmental Externalities", *Population and Development Review*, **26**(4) (Dec.), 643–89.

David, Paul A. (1996) *Technical Choice Innovation and Economic Growth: Essays on American and British Experience in the Nineteenth Century*, Cambridge: Cambridge University Press.

Day, Lincoln and Alice Day (1965) *Too Many Americans*, New York: Dell Publishing Co.

Devine, Thomas Martin (2006) *Scotland's Empire, 1600–1815*, London: Penguin Books, 11–13.

Fernandez, Raquel (2007) "Women, Work, and Culture," NBER Working Paper Series, National Bureau of Economic Research, Working Paper 12888, http://www.nber.org/papers/w12888

Goldin, Claudia D. (1990) *Understanding the Gender Gap: An Economic History of American Women*, New York: Oxford University Press.

Goldin, Claudia D. and Frank D. Lewis (1975) "The Economic Cost of the American Civil War: Estimates and Implications", *The Journal of Economic History*, **35**(2) (June), 299–326.

Greenhalgh, Susan (2003) "Science, Modernity, and the Making of China's One-Child Policy", *Population and Development Review*, **29**(2) (June), 163–96.

Greenhalgh, Susan (2005) "Missile Science, Population Science: The Origins of China's One-Child Policy", *The China Quarterly*, **182**, 253–76.

Hovenkamp, Herbert (1991) *Enterprise and American Law, 1836–1937*, Cambridge, Mass.: Harvard University Press.

Kuznets, Simon Smith (1966) *Modern Economic Growth: Rate, Structure, And Spread*, New Haven: Yale University Press.

Lee, Ronald (2003) "The Demographic Transition: Three Centuries of Fundamental Change", *Journal of Economic Perspectives*, **17**(4) (Fall), 167–90.

Lesthaeghe, R. (1995) "The Second Demographic Transition in Western Countries: An Interpretation", in *Gender and Family Change in Industrialized Countries*, eds. K.O. Mason and A.-M. Jensen, Oxford, England: Clarendon Press, 17–62.

Lesthaeghe, Ron J. and Lisa Neidert (2006) "The Second Demographic Transition in the United States: Exception or Textbook Example?" *Population and Development Review*, **32**(4) (December), 669–98.

Lichbach, Mark I. (1994) "What makes Rational Peasants Revolutionary?: Dilemma, Paradox, and Irony in Peasant Collective Action", *World Politics*, **46**(3) (April), 383–418.

Mann, Charles C. (2005) *1491: New Revelations of the Americas before Columbus*, New York: Vantage Books.

McLanahan, Sara (2004) "Diverging Destinies: How Children Are Faring under the Second Demographic Transition", *Demography*, **41**(4) (Nov.), 607–27.

n.a. (2003) "China Amends One-Child Policy", *Reproductive Health Matters*, **11**(21), Integration of Sexual and Reproductive Health Services: A Health Sector Priority. (May), 194.

OECD (2007) *Factbook 2007: Economic, Environmental and Social Statistics*, Paris, http://www.oecd-ilibrary.org/economics/oecd-factbook_18147364

Papandreou, Andreas A. (1994) *Externality and Institutions*, Oxford: the Clarendon Press.

van de Kaa, D.J. (1987) "Europe's Second Demographic Transition," *Population Bulletin*, **42**, 1.

Voigtländer, Nico and Hans-Joachim Voth (2006) "Why England? Demographic Factors, Structural Change and Physical Capital Accumulation during the Industrial Revolution", *Journal of Economic Growth*, **11**, 319–61.

Wheeler, David L. (1965) "Land Reclamation in the Po River Delta of Italy", *Land Economics*, Vol. 41, No. 4 (Nov.), 376–82.

Wright, Gavin (1990) "The Origins of American Industrial Success, 1879–1940", *American Economic Review*, **80**(4) (Sept.), 651–68.

Part Two
Growth and Dispersal of the Human Population

Chapter Three
Mortality: The Fourth Horseman

3.1 What Do People Die From?

In the developed world today, most people die from degenerative disease, the result of old age, congenital factors or life-style choices. Of the major killers, there are slight differences for men and women, and there is some variation among high-income countries to which differences in diet are a likely contributor. Historically, in contrast, death was largely associated with communicable disease, parasites, malnourishment and starvation. The same is true, to some degree, in certain less-developed countries today. The World Health Organization, for instance, estimates that 11 million infant deaths occur each year from causes that are largely preventable.[1] Absolute levels of deprivation weaken the body's capacity to resist disease, and, although the proximate cause of death might be the communicable or parasitical diseases, the underlying cause is a lack of food and potable water, poor sanitation, lack of access to basic medical care and/or inadequate housing. Modern medicine, improved public health and hygienic practices save many individuals who otherwise would have died before these practices became widespread. The fundamental changes in the causes of death are often called the *epidemiological transition* and are part of the broader demographic transition.[2] This change and its causes and consequences are the subjects of this chapter.

Prior to modern times about one in every two children born failed to reach the age of twenty. In addition, adults tended to die earlier than they would today. There are two issues at hand. First, did the rise in individual real incomes by itself play a role in reducing the death rates, and, if so, how? Second, did the rise of scientific thinking and its promotion depend on a growth in real income (GDP adjusted for prices changes)? The evidence suggests that it did. But once started, the saving of lives could dramatically increase due to scientific breakthroughs that are more or less fortuitous or not immediately related to income. These exogenous scientific discoveries were frequently costly to implement, however. We will examine these issues later in this chapter.

The Children of Eve: Population and Well-being in History, First Edition.
Louis P. Cain and Donald G. Paterson.
© 2012 Blackwell Publishing Ltd. Published 2012 by Blackwell Publishing Ltd.

With surprising frequency, in a historical context, the human population was subject to sudden, widespread disease and other deprivations. Consequently, not only was mortality high, it was highly variable. Such episodes are symbolized by the four horsemen of the apocalypse: plague (pestilence), famine, war and death. Plagues generally refer to *epidemics* and are diseases that rapidly spread in one area (region, nation or continent); they are called a *pandemic* when they occur on a worldwide scale. The virulence of each disease, the method and speed of transmission, and the susceptibility of the population all were factors in determining the death-toll of the disease. Although the spread of many diseases and their reduced effect in recent times has lessened the ravages, many of the infectious agents of diseases, called pathogens, mutate so that the medical fight against them is an on-going battle. The next horseman is famine. It is generally the result of crop or other agricultural failure brought on by unexpected changes in the weather patterns, plant disease, or an infestation of pests. A break-down of the food distribution system often compounds the problem in low income per capita countries, and it most frequently breaks down when there is a calamity such as an outbreak of plague or a war (including civil unrest). The result is malnutrition and starvation and the opportunistic diseases that thrive in the collapsed social infrastructure and the weakened bodies.[3] The horsemen seldom ride alone.[4]

The causes of death today are summarized by the World Health Organization's single cause descriptions – Table 3.1. The table distinguishes three main categories. First, worldwide, the majority of people die from non-communicable conditions, most common are: cardiovascular (heart and stroke); cancers of various types (malignant neoplasms); respiratory failure; and diseases of the digestive system. Since many of these are related to age, as humans live longer there is a greater likelihood of these conditions leading to death. The second category is communicable disease, including perinatal and nutritional conditions. Within this grouping, infectious, parasitic and respiratory disease account for over one quarter (26.0%) of all deaths in all categories.[5] The final category, injuries, accounts for less than 10% of total deaths. While most of the deaths are due to agricultural and industrial accidents, domestic accidents (including transport) and misadventure, almost one-third of the total are intentional, culpable homicides and infanticides.

Table 3.1 reveals that, for any single cause of death, there is: i) a huge variation across geographic areas, and ii) a wide disparity in infant mortality. These two effects are of course linked in that communicable disease is the major killer in sub-Saharan Africa (and a large proportion of that is due to HIV/AIDS) and child mortality is very high. The variation across geographic areas is a relationship between ill health and death on one hand, and national income per capita on the other. Individual susceptibility to communicable diseases is a matter of the absolute poverty levels in the country where they live and one's place in the income distribution. High-income citizens of low-income countries are exposed to less disease than their poorer companions. Low-income countries tend to lack the social and medical infrastructure that reduces the exposure or the spread of diseases or, once endemic, limits their consequences.

Many disease pathogens originate in domesticated animals and thus are associated with the historical rise of settled agriculture. As the numbers of domestic livestock increased, the density of the rat population also increased. Vermin are efficient carriers of pathogens. We believe certain diseases such whooping cough, scarlet fever,

Table 3.1 Estimates of Deaths by Causes, World and Select Areas 2002.

	World	The Americas	Europe	Western Pacific	South-East Asia	Africa
		Percentage				
Mortality Stratum#		VLC VLA	VLC VLA	LC LA	HC HA	HC VHA
Coverage (millions) Sub Area*	6225	334	415	1562	1293	361
Population Estimate (millions)		*853*	*878*	*1718*	*1591*	*672*
Cause						
I. Communicable diseases, maternal and perinatal conditions and nutritional deficiencies	32.1	6.1	6.2	14.6	41.3	73.7
Infectious and parasitic diseases	19.1	2.5	1.3	7.2	20.4	56.8
Respiratory infections	6.9	2.7	4.4	3.7	10.8	9.0
Maternal conditions	0.9	0.0	0.0	0.2	1.3	2.1
Perinatal conditions	4.3	0.6	0.3	3.2	7.5	4.5
Nutritional deficiencies	0.9	0.3	0.2	0.2	1.3	1.3
II. Noncommunicable conditions	58.8	87.5	89.0	74.8	48.8	19.7
Malignant neoplasms	12.5	23.6	26.5	18.2	7.2	3.6
Other neoplasms	0.3	0.6	0.8	0.2	0.1	0.1
Diabetes mellitus	1.7	3.1	2.4	1.6	1.5	0.7
Nutritional/endocrine disorders	0.4	1.2	0.7	0.4	0.2	0.2
Neuropsychiatric disorders	1.9	6.4	4.7	1.3	1.7	0.8
Sense organ disorders	0.0	0.0	0.0	0.0	0.0	0.0
Cardiovascular diseases	29.3	37.9	41.1	31.9	26.6	9.0
Respiratory diseases	6.5	7.3	5.6	14.4	5.8	2.2
Digestive diseases	3.5	3.6	4.6	4.0	3.3	1.4
Diseases of the genitourinary system	1.5	2.4	1.6	1.6	1.2	0.9
Skin diseases	0.1	0.2	0.2	0.0	0.1	0.2
Musculoskeletal diseases	0.2	0.6	0.5	0.2	0.1	0.1
Congenital abnormalities	0.9	0.5	0.3	1.0	1.0	0.6
III. Injuries	9.1	6.3	4.8	10.6	10.0	6.6
Unintentional	6.2	4.4	3.5	7.2	7.5	3.8
Intentional	2.8	1.9	1.3	3.4	2.5	2.8
Total Deaths	100.0	100.0	100.0	100.0	100.0	100.0

Note: WHO estimates and not those reported by specific countries.
#Mortality Stratum refers to the WHO description of death patterns in an area: VLC and VLA means "Very Low Child Mortality" and "Very Low Adult Mortality"; LC and LA means "Low Child Mortality" and "Low Adult Mortality"; HC and HA "High Child Mortality" and "High Adult Mortality"; and VHA means "Very High Adult Mortality". For detailed definitions see the original table and WHO categories.
* refers to the population of the selected sub-area in the mortality stratum, the total population of the area is given below this number. HIV/AIDS dominates in Africa and South East Asia.
Source: WHO (2004), *World Health Report*, Geneva, Annex Table 2.
http://www.who.int/whr/2004/en/09_annexes_en.pdf

Table 3.2 Human Disease, Its Origins and Conditions of Spread.

Human Diseases	Origin	Pathogen
Measles	cattle	virus
Tuberculosis	cattle	bacterium
Smallpox	cattle (cowpox), other livestock	virus
Influenza	pigs, wild birds, domestic poultry	virus
Pertussis (Whooping Cough)	pigs and dogs	bacterium
Falciparum Malaria	chickens and ducks	parasite
West Nile Virus (flu-like with fever)	wild birds/domestic animals	virus
Bubonic plague	rodents/rat fleas	bacterium
Poor Sanitation/Overcrowding		
Diarrhoea	animal fecal matter	virus, bacteria, parasites
Cholera	animal fecal matter	virus

Source: US National Library of Medicine and National Institutes of Medicine (2007), *Medline Plus*, Bethesda, MD: US Government. http://www.medlineplus.gov

measles, influenza and smallpox were far less prevalent in hunter-gather societies. Some populations, such as those in the Americas prior to contact with Europe and Africa, had not acquired immunity to diseases such as smallpox because they lacked the domesticated animals found elsewhere. Table 3.2 lists some of the major communicable diseases and the domestic animals (and their companions) that carry the pathogens. Once the pathogen has made the species-leap, the disease often becomes resident in human populations. Some diseases are non-viral in origin. The parasitic disease of malaria and the bacteria that cause tuberculosis remain major killers despite attempts to eradicate them.[6] And a further problem is the association of tuberculosis with another killer, HIV/AIDS. Since HIV/AIDS is an attack on the immune system, infected persons are less able to fight off the increasingly virulent TB.[7] Other diseases, such as influenza, are viral. Viruses, as is well-known, mutate frequently so, for example, no influenza epidemic is exactly like the previous one.

The third category in Table 3.1 is trauma, a surprisingly large killer at 9.1% of all deaths worldwide. While most of these deaths are accidental or a result of negligence, almost one-third is a result of intentionally delivered trauma – 2.8 of the 9.1%. It is likely that the overall trauma-related deaths were much greater in historical periods. For instance, traumas, such as broken bones or deep cuts, can now be treated more effectively and do not lead to death. Furthermore, many of the associated effects of trauma, particularly infections, have been eliminated or reduced by modern drug therapy and hygienic practice. There is no reasonable way of knowing whether intentional trauma deaths have increased proportionately over our long history. What is known is that deadly conflict has always been with us.

Evidence for pre-Columbian North America, for instance, suggests that there was a relatively high level of violent deaths among the various population groups and that

Table 3.3 Battle Connected Deaths in International Wars and Civil Wars, 1816–1980.

	1816–1848	1849–1881	1882–1914	1915–1947	1948–1980	Totals
Number of International Wars	20	28	24	20	26	118
Battle Connected Deaths, 000s	349.7	1314	9025	16849	3374	30912
National Civil Wars	12	20	18	15	41	106
Battle Connected Deaths, 000s	93	2892	388.0	2622	3022	9017

Notes: Battle connected deaths are assigned to the year in which the war began. These deaths are military and include: 1) deaths; 2) wounded who subsequently died as a result of the war; 3) deaths while in the military; and 4) in the case of civil wars, to account for guerrilla warfare, civilian casualties.
Source: Singer and Small (1982), Tables 7.3 and 16.1 and 70–1.

the frequency of this increased as populations became more densely settled on the land.[8] For more modern times, since the end of the Napoleonic Wars in 1815, the approximate number of military deaths in international and civil wars (to 1980) is estimated to be about 40 million – see Table 3.3. This includes members of the military who died of infections as well as trauma, but it does not include all the private citizens who died as a result of war. Probably the greatest war-related loss of life prior to the 20th century was that during the Taiping Rebellion in China (1850–1865) with a total of military and civilian losses of 20 to 30 million. In more recent history, the Second World War had many *intentional* deaths that were not directly battlefield losses: the approximately 6 million victims of the Holocaust in Europe. The fire-bombing of cities added many more. But there were also deaths that were *unintentional* by-products of war, the results of displacement, scarcity of foodstuffs and hunger, and the spread of diseases among a weakened population, both military and civilian. The USSR suffered staggering losses in the Second World War (The Great Patriotic War from 1941 to 1945 as it was known) of approximately 17.9 million civilian deaths.[9] Total war losses of 26.6 million were no less than 13.5% of the 1941 population.

Direct military deaths in wars are generally made up of younger age males. This concentration of the deaths in one cohort, if substantial in number, has an effect on the way populations grow because of the lack of marriageable males. Thus, a cohort of women found it more difficult to find a partner as the gender ratio declined for that age group. The net consequence was a dramatic fall in the pattern of births. The slow growth of the French population in the aftermath of the Napoleonic Wars is due, in part, to this effect.

> The *gender* or *sex ratio* is the number of males per 100 females – or the other way around, so check definitions carefully. It is often expressed for a cohort as, for example, the ratio of males in the age range 20–39 to the number of females in the same age range.

3.2 Infant and Child Mortality

The crude death rate (CDR) measures the number of deaths per year per 1000 individuals.[10] There are many factors that influence its value so we standardize by characteristic in order to tell where the variation in the overall CDR is found. For example, the CDR is extremely sensitive to the age structure of the population. If a population has more people in the age range of greatest risk to die, the CDR will be higher. Today, for instance, we have an aging population in most countries of the world so we should expect, other things being equal, the CDR to rise since everyone drops off the peg at some point. In order to normalize for this effect demographers often calculate the number of deaths per 1000 individuals in an age range; for example, the death rate of young adults is the number of deaths in the age range 19–24 as a proportion of the population of the same age expressed per 1000. (If 2 300 people out of a population of 1 000 000 dies, the death rate is 2.3 per 1000). We know that gender is important as women are exposed to a risk that men are not: the possibility of death in childbirth. So we may wish to separate the death rate of young adults by gender. Our ability to calculate and use specific death rates is limited only by the information available.

By far, childhood represents the age of greatest historical risk of unexpected death. These death rates are traditionally broken into four parts:

- neonatal mortality: deaths in the first 27 days of life;
- infant mortality: deaths in the first 12 months of life;
- child mortality: deaths in the first five years of life; and
- youth mortality: deaths in the first 19 years of life.[11]

Infant mortality includes neonatal deaths and the other categories are likewise inclusive. Figure 3.1 shows child mortality. But often researchers have a particular research aim for which more precision is needed, and they report the rates *net* of the others. For instance, Ó Gráda in his study of child death in Victorian Dublin and Belfast uses the child mortality rate where child is defined as the range of one to four years of age.[12] Each age category is chosen to highlight a particular susceptibility. To complicate matters, the clinical causes of death in history are often hard to identify because they were not known at the time. Furthermore, the symptoms were not accurately diagnosed and recorded well. So, even with modern knowledge, it is often difficult to identify the causes of death in retrospect. Even the specific age at death is often not available in historical records.

Currently, 90% of all child deaths, those to age five, are accounted for in 43 less-developed countries. Approximately 40% of those are actually neonatal deaths.[13] Throughout the world the child mortality rate has fallen in recent years although the proportionate saving of life occurs least in the high mortality countries. This is often referred to as the "Matthew Effect."[14] The term expresses the tendency for the greatest benefits go to those that have the most. While this is neither wholly true nor, if true, universally true, as an inspection of recent growth

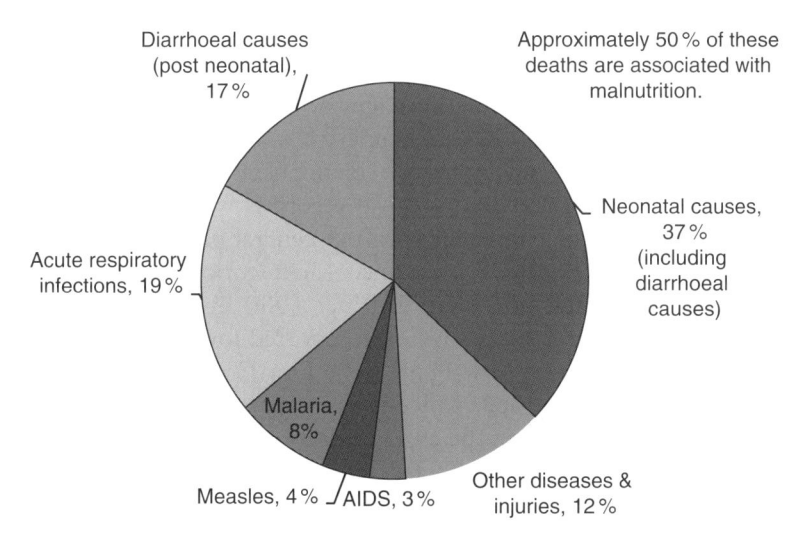

Figure 3.1 Causes of Child (Under Five) Mortality World-Wide, 2000–2003.
Source: United Nations (2004) *Millennium Indicators Database*.

rates of national incomes reveal, there is a strong historical basis for it: where you start matters! For the low-income countries these figures indicate poor living conditions, the poor health of the mothers and the general malnourishment of the population. The question is: were these the conditions of history? The answer is, alas, not straightforward.

Age-specific death rate (deaths by age): number of persons in an age bracket who die in a year, expressed as a number per 1000 in the age bracket (at the beginning of the year)

or

Other specific death rates: by gender; by marital status; by location; by income and ... so on.

Infant mortality rate: number of children (0 to 12 months) who die in a year, expressed as a number per 1000 of children born in the year of the same age range. Also *neonatal* (0–28 days), *child* (0–4 years) and *youth mortality* (6–19 years) *rates*. (We defined these as rates above.)

Where the time span of the group is greater than one year, it is an average. Demographers use both inclusive and exclusive rates. That is, child mortality is sometimes given net of infant mortality.

First, most of the evidence for mortality rates for years before the middle of the 19th century comes from partial evidence of the death records and usually involves backward projections.[15] Few jurisdictions kept or required a universal registration of deaths prior to this time. Researchers have spent much effort, and used considerable ingenuity, to amass indirect evidence that takes us back to the 16th century. Earlier than this date the historical record is written from fragmentary evidence. Nonetheless, it is consistent with the general pattern of high mortality with much geographic variation. For instance, the historical infant mortality rates were probably in the range of 200 to 250 per 1000 live births for late Tudor England and Wales.[16] Similar rates have been reported for other countries including 17th century colonial US, New France, the Low Countries, France and parts of northern and western Europe. Indeed, from the mid-16th to the late 18th century there was little change in the average although there were substantial year to year variations associated the outbreaks of contagious disease, local fluctuations in agricultural productivity (income), and long-term economic swings. The rise in the late 17th century was followed by a decline to trend. The late 17th century records also suggest a difference in infant and child mortality between rural (lower) and urban (higher) mortality – farming and industrial based, respectively. Thus the infant and child mortality rates were very sensitive to the structure of the economy and how it was changing.[17] A downward drift of the infant mortality rate is evident by the about the time that the gains from the industrial revolution in the late 18th century, however slight, began to have an effect on household consumption patterns. But, even in those circumstances the (mean) infant mortality remained above 150 per 1000, and it stayed there until the beginning of the 20th century.[18]

An alternative hypothesis is associated with Gunnar Fridlizus and Alfred Perrenoud. Drawn from their separate investigations of 17th and 18th century European countries, they claim that the declining mortality among the young was not so much a product of growing per capita income as a change in many disease patterns. This *virulence theory* proposes that this particular historical period witnessed a decline in the potency of certain diseases which limited their spread, albeit for unknown epidemiological reasons. Also, for the countries investigated, they claim there was neither evidence of increases in agricultural output nor broad evidence of an improved standard of living.

Even in high-income countries, the neonatal and infant death rates remained high by modern standards until very recently, although not as high as its historic heights. For example, on a world scale, infant mortality in the last 30 years rate fell to one-third of its 1971 level. Again the evidence is widespread and the rapid decline began much earlier for the high-income countries. Here shown in Figure 3.2 is the decade-by-decade decline of infant mortality since the mid-19th century for the US. For the most advanced of western European and North American countries, the infant mortality began a long downward drift some time in the early 1700s. Although varying by country, by the late 19th century infant mortality had declined to a number of approximately 150 deaths per 1000 live births (as noted above). Quantitatively, by far the most significant savings of young lives began in the very late 19th century, similar to what happened in the US.[19] The precipitous fall of infant mortality rates resulted

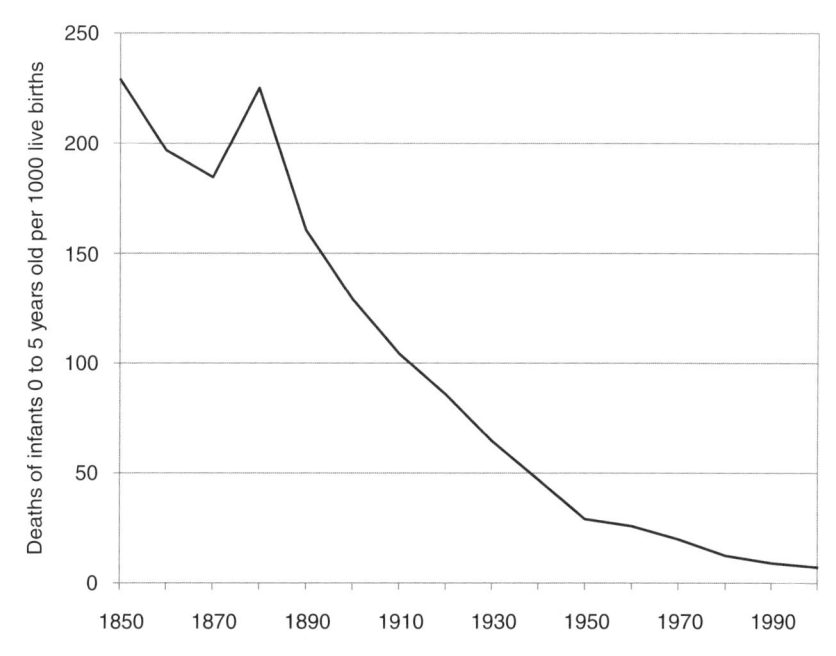

Figure 3.2 Infant Mortality Rate, United States, 1850–2000 – deaths of infants 0 to 5 years old per 1000 of live births.
Note: Interpolated Census data.
Source: Haines (2006) *US Historical Statistics*, Series Ab 920.

from a combination of social spending on water and sewage systems, improvement of the housing stock, and medical and hygiene practices, an important component of which were the new antiseptic procedures. We also cannot rule out the supposed decrease of the virulence of some disease pathogens. The first half of the 20th century witnessed this continued and dramatic decline that was widespread in the high income/industrialized countries and of approximately the same dimensions and timing.

3.3 The Probability of Death and Life Expectancy

If mortality rates are known by age of death, either from populations or samples, then life expectancy can be calculated. However, in order to know the probability of dying at any particular age, we need a large amount of historical information about a population. Only a few countries' populations have death records that are sufficiently complete to permit gazing into the past earlier than the mid-19th century with large data samples: Canada (specifically Quebec), France, Norway, Sweden and Switzerland (Geneva) – and from which life tables are constructed.[20] For others we rely on relatively small samples and backward projections based on these samples. For instance, we rely for much pre-1850 data for the US on the colony/state of Massachusetts.

Gravestone, 1742

Typical gravestone from the 18th Century with its images of death: skull, cross-bones, hour-glass, spades and funeral drapes.
Source: The authors' photograph, Cramond Kirk, 2010.

Robert Bourbeau, Jacques Légaré, and Valérie Émond have calculated the probability of death for male and female members of selected birth cohorts from 1801 to 1941 in Canada. Some of their results are in Figure 3.3.[21] They are remarkably revealing:

- Each successive birth cohort (separated by 30 or 20 years) has a lower probability of death at *every age*.
- The probability of dying while very young (as expected) was very high but then declined rapidly by age so that, for the 1941 cohort, youths of 10 to 13 years of age were the least likely to die of any age group.

Mortality: The Fourth Horseman

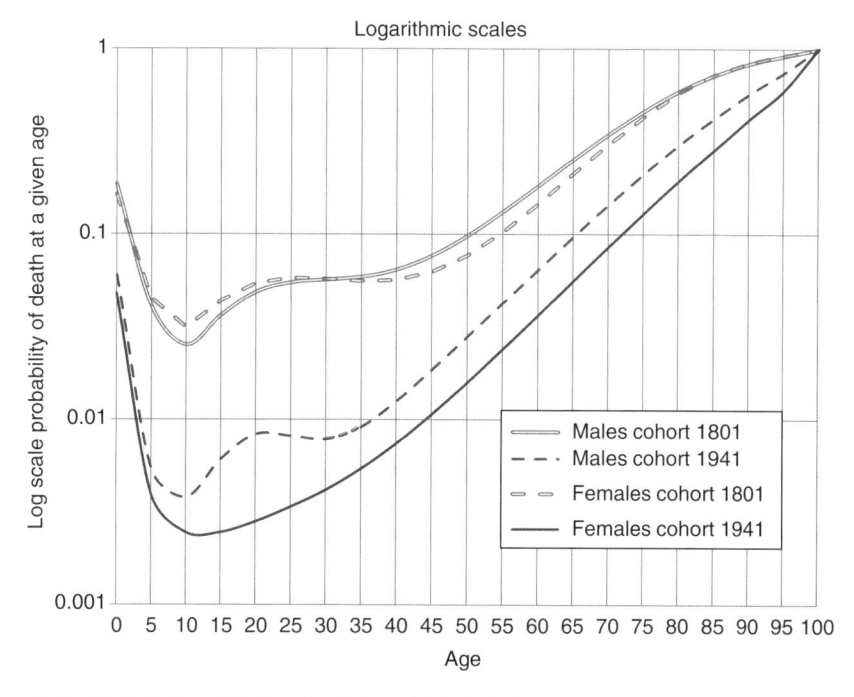

Figure 3.3 Probability of Dying for Selected Birth Cohorts, Canada, 1801–1940.
Notes: Data for the years prior to 1851 are from the Province of Quebec.
Source: from data in Bourbeau, Légaré, and Émond (1997).

- The decline in infant mortality is clearly evident by the inward shift (lower age) and steeper fall of the probability of death curves.
- For both males and females there was a sharply increased risk of dying in the age range of 20 to 30 years of age *except in the female 1941 birth cohort*.
- The pattern and level of the probability of death was roughly the same for males and females with the two exceptions: i) that noted immediately above and ii) at older ages where females generally live longer.

Females were exposed to the probability of death associated with giving birth – usually from an infection contracted and carried by the care-giver assisting the birth. However, as if not to be outdone, males were exposed to a different risk, that of death due to accidents, other trauma and misadventure. So the profile of mortality looked remarkably similar but for different reasons. So why are the probabilities so different for the 1941 birth cohort? Just as neonatal mortality was plummeting in the first five decades of the 20th century so was the risk of maternal death. For the 1941 birth cohort of females the risk of death due to giving birth becomes barely measurable – see later in this chapter. For the males, however, while the risk of death due to work-related accidents falls there is a new risk, death due to motor vehicle accidents, a product of affluence. This is widely supported in the North American data. Suicide rates also increased (and, for certain US inner-city youths, so did death due to gunshots).

How long did people live, on average, in early societies? The evidence is abundant but fragmentary. However, archaeological evidence from gravesites suggests that about

5000 years ago North American Indian hunter-agriculturalists had a life expectancy at birth of only about 18.9 years. In ancient Egypt (and Nubia) around 1050 BC, in an economy dominated by sedentary agriculture, life expectancy at birth was about 19.2 years. Two populations widely separated in time, geography and the economic basis for society share a common expectation of life even although the patterns of disease were different. Perhaps this defines the minimum average life expectancy in any sustainable population?[22] There is considerable scholarly debate about the appropriate calculated life expectancy at birth of ancient Mediterranean peoples. It centers on the sufficiency and reliability of data and the models used for the backward projections. Some of the suggestions are: 23.0 years for Greeks of 670 BC, 26.5 for Egyptians of the Ptolemaic period and about 25.0 to 30.0 years for the Romans of the 1st century.[23] Yet, almost 1500 years later, at the beginning of the modern era, and using better evidence, the life expectancy at birth was in the same range, only 23.6 for the Swiss in Geneva (1625 to 1649).[24]

If we judge by the later Geneva data, there was an increase in life expectancy over the course of the 17th century which is consistent with modest growth in agricultural productivity. For Europe in general, as noted earlier, the rise of life expectancy in the 17th and 18th centuries has been attributed to the deceased virulence of some diseases, the virtual disappearance of bubonic plague, and the first treatment to counteract smallpox (still relatively primitive). All undoubtedly were contributors. But by the 1700s it was Northern Europe which led the mortality decline. But why was Northern Europe so different? In Sweden, for instance, life expectancy at birth was 38.3 for females (lower for males) in the 1750s. This was approximately five full years greater than for similar countries in North Western Europe. France at this time had a life expectancy of 28.7 years.[25] Several explanations account for Sweden's lead in lowering the probability of death. First was the early appearance of public health awareness under enlightened government policies. For instance, Sweden introduced training for midwives about this time, well in advance of other European countries. Second, was the rise in per capita income in the urban areas, which was probably greater than that in comparable areas of England and Wales. Third, there was a lower incidence of infant mortality from exposure to water-borne bacterial disease both because i) there was increased understanding of the association between poor public hygiene and disease, and ii) the promotion of breast-feeding which reduces the hazard of exposing young children to bacteria-infected water.[26] No one explanation of the falling mortality likely dominates in the first phases of the great mortality decline; all had a role. Unfortunately, we lack the detailed side-by-side information for most countries but it does seem that the Nordic countries led the (albeit slow) decline in mortality in the 18th century.[27]

With the fall of mortality rates in North America and Western Europe, life expectancies at birth rose. Of course, one of the arithmetic reasons for the great decline, especially evident in the late 19th and early 20th centuries, was decline in the percentage of the population at greatest risk, the young. As explored in the next chapter, the decline in fertility also played a role so we cannot assume simple cause and effect. As historians, probably the most frequently neglected question and the one most relevant to ask is: was the change in the rate (death, fertility, disease, etc.) brought about by a change in the age-structure of the population?

Cohort Analysis

Cohort: the population (or a sample) born in a certain time period or a group fixed in time by some shared characteristic, e.g.: all females born in Scotland in the years 1871–1876; and all members of the 1963 graduating class of Princeton University.

In Figure 3.4, the life expectancy histories, for males, for several countries whose death rates have today reached very low levels are reported. Following this (in Figure 3.5) are (separate) male and female life expectancies for the United States in the 20th century. That is, the time series of life expectancy at birth (and the corresponding fall in the age specific death rates) broadly follows the rapid rise in the Western European and North American economies (measured in real GDP growth) in the late 19th and 20th centuries. Naturally, the death rates and corresponding life expectancies have stabilized in recent years. We may anticipate that any further changes will be relatively modest. Thus, for the developed western economies and some Asian ones the historical mortality pattern conforms to that predicted by the demographic transition. Of course, there were variations both over time and between

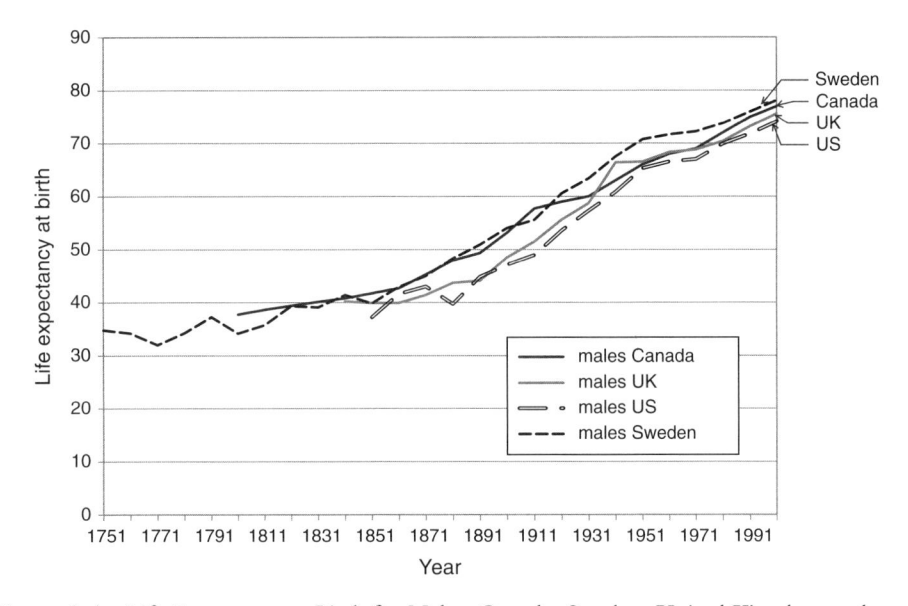

Figure 3.4 Life Expectancy at Birth for Males, Canada, Sweden, United Kingdom and United States, 1750–2000.

Note: The data are for either the year noted or the census one year earlier. Canadian data up to 1921 are based on ten-year cohort data and subsequently on three-year averages. The 20th century US data are the recalculation of Smith and Bradshaw.

Source: Bourbeau, Légaré, and Émond (1997); Haines (2006), *Human Mortality Database* (current): Haines (2006), *US Historical Statistics*, AB 644; Office of Health Economics, UK (current): Smith and Bradshaw (2006); Statistics Canada, Catalogue no. 91F0015MPE, Table 4.1.

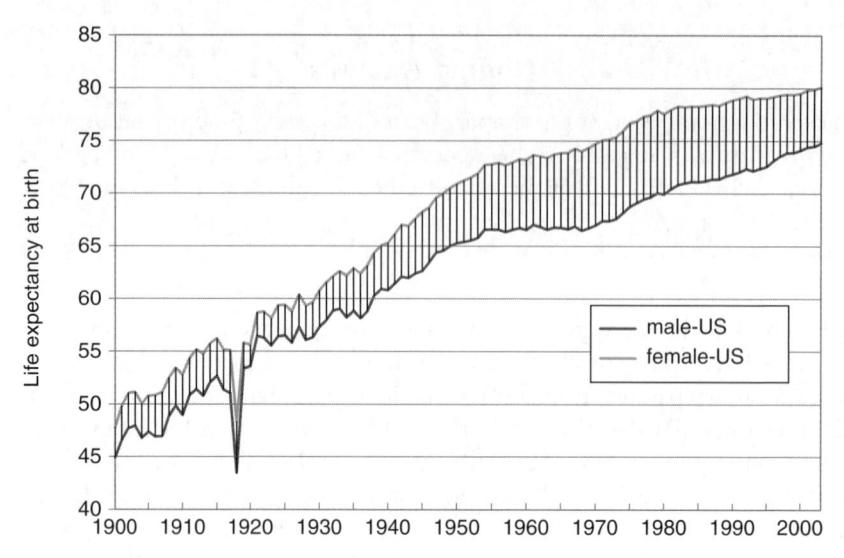

Figure 3.5 Life Expectancy at Birth of US Males and Females in the 20th Century.
Note: The great dip in the life expectancies of both genders is a result of the influenza epidemic of 1919 – see Chapter Ten.
Source: data from Smith and Bradshaw (2006).

countries which will be explored later. The current low income countries have life expectancies at birth that are much higher than those of, for example, Western Europe of the early 17th century. Sub-Saharan life expectancies today are roughly comparable to those of North America and Western Europe of 150 years ago.

A pioneering study of life expectancies in the United States was conducted by the 18th century Harvard professor, Edward Wigglesworth. He estimated the life expectancy at birth (for both sexes combined) at 36.4 years at the end of the American Revolution (1789).[28] Life expectancy at age 20 in 1789 was 34.2 years, which is slightly lower than that of Geneva citizens for the same decade, the 1780s. Thanks to the current research of the scholar Michael Haines, we now have detailed life tables for the US from 1850 onward – some of these data are in Figure 3.5. From 1850 to 1900 there was a gain of about ten years for both men and women.[29] These data along with those of 1789 strongly suggest that the gains in the second half of the 19th century were more rapid than those of earlier periods. But this was not an American exception, the pattern was common to North America and Western Europe.

Since the great gain in life expectancy at birth was the declining death rate of the young (0–19 years of age), the interesting question is how long did adults live? One of the great fallacies of thinking about people in history is to imagine that people were old when they exceeded their life expectancy at birth. How old is old? Old age certainly came earlier than it does today, but not as early as one might think. Before the industrial transformation in Europe, an individual born in the early 1600s had a life expectancy of about 25 years, as noted above. Yet, this does not mean that an individual was old if, for instance, they were 35 years old. The historical life tables indicate that a 20 year-old could expect to live another 33 years. That is, if one survived the devastating mortality of childhood and young adulthood then the

Table 3.4 Life Expectancy and Projections for England and Wales, 1841–2020.

	At Birth		At age 45		At age 65	
	Male	Female	Male	Female	Male	Female
1841*	40.2	42.2	23.3	24.4	10.9	11.5
1850*	39.9	41.9	22.8	24.1	10.8	11.5
1860*	39.9	41.9	22.8	24.1	10.8	11.5
1870*	41.4	44.6	22.1	24.1	10.6	11.4
1880*	43.7	47.2	22.1	24.1	10.3	11.3
1890*	44.1	47.8	22.2	24.2	10.3	11.3
1900*	48.5	52.4	23.3	25.5	10.8	12.0
1910*	51.5	55.4	23.9	26.3	11.0	12.4
1920*	55.6	59.6	25.2	27.7	11.4	12.9
1930*	58.7	62.9	25.5	28.3	11.3	13.1
1940**	66.4	71.2	27.4	31.5	12.8	15.3
1950**	66.5	71.2	26.8	30.7	12.0	14.4
1960**	68.3	74.1	27.3	32.2	12.2	15.4
1970**	68.8	75.1	27.2	32.7	12.0	16.0
1980***	70.4	76.6	28.3	33.7	12.8	16.8
1990***	73.2	78.7	30.3	35.1	14.0	17.8
2000p	75.6	80.3	32.6	36.6	15.7	18.9
2010p	77.6	81.7	34.4	37.8	17.3	19.9
2020p	78.8	83.0	35.4	39.0	18.2	20.9

Notes: p = 2000-based population projections.
* Figures are based on English Life Tables.
** Figures are based on Abridged Life Tables.
*** Figures are based on future lifetime.
Source: United Kingdom (current), *Government Actuary's Department*.

chances were reasonable for both men and women that they would live into their 50s (life expectancy at 20). And, if you lived to be 50 years old then it was likely that you would live another 15.8 years. At the risk of generalizing, old age probably began in a person's 50s. In early 17th century England, Shakespeare died when he was 54 at the onset of "old age". However, by the end of the 18th century an individual 30 years of age would live into their early 60s on average (slightly more for females and slightly less for males). Based on the Geneva data this was a gain of 7.9 years (slightly less for France and Sweden) with the most significant gains coming in the second half of the 1600s.[30] Thus, the historical world was one in which there were old people by our standards, just far fewer of them.[31]

For England and Wales we see the gains in adult life expectancy in Table 3.4. An average man and women aged 45 years can expect to live 50% longer than their mid–Victorian counterparts. While gains are still being registered by each new generation reaching retirement age, they have been small. Planning a pension scheme in the late 19th century was very different from that of today – more on this in Chapter Nine. The longer lives of those over 65 years of age, with current retirement ages, gives us the modern problem of increasing dependency of the elderly. In the US and elsewhere the gap between male and female life expectancy at birth increased through the 20th century only showing a convergence in the last two decades, see Figure 3.5. Failure of any pension scheme whether it is private or of government origin will be borne by the elderly single females of the population.

In the early 19th century, the English actuary/mathematician Benjamin Gompertz devised the *law of mortality*. In modern terms, this is a law of "system failure" that relates age and adult (post-reproductive age) death. The deaths are "all-cause" in that no particular cause is identified. It is an approximation, but one that fits very well for roughly the ages 25–35 to 80–90. The range of its accurate coverage will vary from one population to the next. Although it cannot be measured in history beyond about 100 years ago, it is thought to be generally applicable to older members of the population. The frequency of death rises geometrically with age, which is, of course, linear. To the Gompertz age-related algorithm, another 19th century actuary William Makeham added a non age-related term. Both Gompertz and Makeham were interested in the relationship between the frequency of death and age because of the usefulness of that prediction in the insurance industry. The Gompertz-Makeham approximation is thus the sum of the two separate arguments:

Law of Mortality: $\mu_x = A + B \cdot c^x$,

Where μ_x is the frequency of death at age x;
c is the coefficient of aging, c > 1
B is a constant, B > 0; and
A is background constant, non age-related rate of mortality, A ≥ –B.

Within the age range noted, the Gompertz-Makeham approximation has proven remarkably good at predicting death frequencies for relatively homogeneous populations. (Indeed, it has proven useful to estimate the deaths of various non-human populations from fruit flies to bacteria).

Two particular phenomena, themselves interesting, associated with death and age, limits the usefulness of the Gompertz-Makeham approximation over the entire lifespan. First, death rates at young ages are not well predicted essentially because they are not usually the result of regular system failure. Even although the death rates are high among the young, sometimes very high, they are brought about by non-age related events: poor nutrition, infection (or, perhaps, infectious diseases), disease, and so on. Second, for the very old there is actually a sudden deceleration of the μ_x term brought about by a change in the relationship between death and very old age. The reason, according to Shiro Horiuchi and John Wilmoth, is that healthier individuals appear selected by their physical characteristics to survive into very old age, so we end up with a non-representative group. It is also possible that at very old ages the rate of decay slows down – good news for some of us.[32] For the age range between the limits the so-called *intrinsic mortality* (the system failure component of mortality) has not been fixed over time but has varied with:

- lifestyle (superior nutritional and appropriate exercise choices);
- pharmaceutical advances (insulin, for example); and
- surgical advances and treatment protocols.[33]

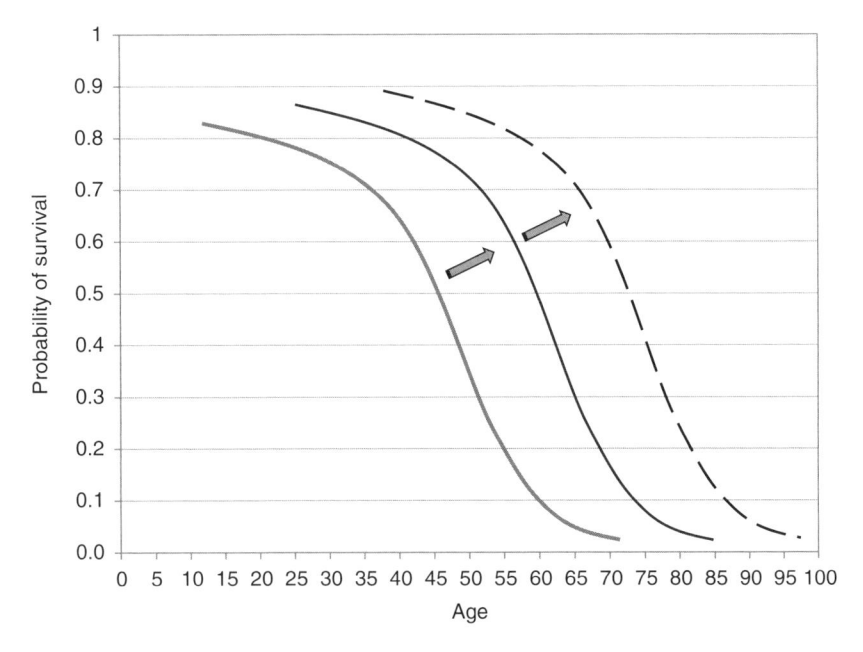

Figure 3.6 The Probability of Survival in History, 'Rectangularization'.

These of course are the results of growing income and of technological advances; income growth and technology are related, although not in a straightforward way, as we shall see later. The net result is that the intrinsic mortality has shifted over time and extended the age range over which the Gompertz-Makeham approximation holds true. (From the frequency of mortality at any given age we can compute the probability of death and its counterpart, the probability of not dying or survival.) The shift in the intrinsic mortality also changed the shape of the survival curve – the probability of not dying at any given age. The ugly but useful term of "rectangularization" describes how the curve shifts outward over time as the effects operate.[34] How these have changed over history is given in Figure 3.6.

The background non-age related mortality pattern has also changed over time and, although this has had a positive effect in recent times, as economic historians we cannot assume that this has always been so. Distinctions may be made in the survival curve: by gender, by time, and by location. For instance, there was (is) a higher rate of death for older males compared to the similar cohort of females. This is expressed in the much longer life expectancy at age 60 for females in western and Asian countries. While the basis of this shorter life for males is not well understood, it is likely that there are both biological and economic reasons. The current age expectancy gap has shown a decline in recent years in most OECD countries. This has led to speculation that as women face less arbitrary discrimination in labor markets (and their working lives become more like those of men) they will tend to have similar mortality patterns. This supposes that a key element in separating the genders is workplace stress. The reduction of the gap is brought about by the rise of the male life expectancy relative to that of the females.[35] However, female life expectancies are still, and have been throughout history, greater than males. There have been direct economic consequences of this: single, elderly women are usually amongst the poorest groups in society – more in Chapter Seven. It has always been so.

3.4 Seasonal Pattern of Death

The anthropological evidence suggests that, when humankind moved into settled communities associated with agriculture, the mortality rate rose. This, as noted before, was brought about by the increased contact with disease pathogens due to the proximity of domesticated fowl and livestock. Furthermore, the density *within* the habitations was increasing thereby creating an environment for the effective spread of disease among the families who lived there. In addition, housing was frequently shared with domestic animals – they were a welcome source of heat. The houses were usually closely arranged in a village or town pattern. Most early farming was conducted with people living in villages venturing out to tend their land holdings. The result was that disease spread rapidly from one family to another. Even when individual farms were created separately from a village, the underlying cause of disease spread did not diminish much. Of course, the economic issue is why did humankind choose to farm with social arrangements that seemed to maximize the mortality rate? First, there was no knowledge of disease and the nature of its spread. To the people involved, the disease pools created by sedentary farm life were an unintended, and not understood, consequence of the arrangements. Second, the new social arrangements certainly created benefits that reduced the variability of supply. Villages provided insurance as defence against incursions and threat to the sedentary farm system. Third, common-field holding, with widely separated plots and fields, spread the ownership or entitlement over the geography and, thus, was a method of risk-sharing: the risk of flooding, of poor soil quality, or other natural calamities.

The time pattern of mortality over the year followed a regular cycle. However, the seasonal pattern was different in the rural areas from that in the towns and cities. In the farming areas, it was coincident with the annual farm cycle. Deaths were low in the late summer and autumn. This is the period of the year when food is most abundant. Food was relatively plentiful even in the early winter because of the end of season slaughter of animals. However, in the late winter and early spring, inventories of food ran down, and in a bad year might be exhausted, and death rates rose to their highest for the year:

- Food became less abundant (and more expensive), and malnutrition increased in severity and occasionally there was starvation.
- Insufficient household heating and inadequate clothing made weakened people vulnerable to infections.
- In colder climates with both people and animals kept indoors longer there was an increase the exposure to disease pools.

Death rates remained high in the spring and early summer (peak mortality was in April/May depending on the location) and then fell dramatically as fresh food

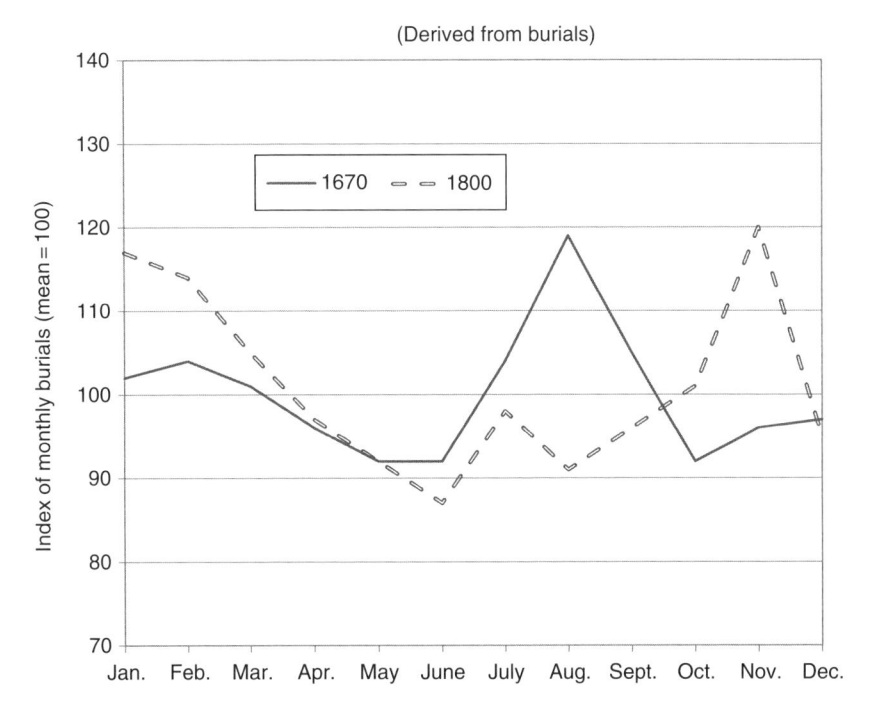

Figure 3.7 Urban Mortality in London by Month, 1670 and 1800.
Source: data from Landers and Mouzas (1998).

appeared as the weather warmed. Thus we find the same seasonality in 17th century England as in farming areas throughout north-western Europe (and probably also in North America).[36] This variability moderated over the course of the "long 18th century."[37] By the middle of the 1800s, nonetheless, rural mortality still showed greater seasonal variation than that of the towns and cities.[38] This *does not* mean that mortality was lower in urban areas and higher in rural areas, it was not. Woods estimates that the life chances were, in general, 1.5 times greater in the rural areas (measured in terms of life expectancy).[39] Throughout the 19th century, as agricultural income variability fell, the extreme variability of the annual mortality cycle moderated (extraordinary events such as the Irish Famine of the 1840s notwithstanding – see Chapter Five).

Well into the 20th century *annual* urban mortality was generally greater than rural mortality and sometimes very much greater. Urban areas also experienced seasonal variation of mortality, but a different one from the rural areas. In the pre-modern period (before c.1800) the peak in the death rates over the year generally occurred in late summer. (Rural mortality in late summer was at a seasonal low). The deaths during the peak were mostly from diseases that were water borne. They disproportionately affected the very young. A new peak emerged in absolute terms – see Figure 3.7 – in the late autumn and early winter to about February.[40] However, by the late 19th century in most areas of Western Europe and North America, this peak had largely disappeared. Since this was well before the large social investment in sewage systems and clean water supplies, researchers have hypothesized that there was either an exogenous change in the virulence of some of the water borne disease pathogens or a change in the environment in which they thrived. Perhaps both conditions held.

The extreme nature of the seasonal peaks fell in both rural and urban mortality began to moderate in the late 19th/early 20th centuries along with the fall in the annual mortality toll in western countries. Yet, there the rural-urban difference had proven remarkably persistent for a long time.

3.5 Seasonality and Longevity

For those born before World War II, the season of their birth was an important predictor of longevity. The theory behind this unexpected finding is the much-debated "fetal origins hypothesis" of David Barker and others.[41] They argue that malnutrition at very young ages, including *in utero*, influenced morbidity and mortality later in life. Low birth weights were associated with maternal malnutrition, and this contributes to greater morbidity at older ages from cardiovascular disease, hypertension, and type 2 diabetes. In addition, maternal infections from diseases such as tuberculosis impaired fetal growth. The nutrition and infection explanations are complementary mechanisms tying morbidity in early and later life.[42] Both have found empirical support.[43]

In the Northern Hemisphere, mortality at age 50 and over was higher for those born in the spring and lower for those born in the autumn. In the Southern Hemisphere, the pattern was reversed, as are the seasons. The difference in life span between peak and trough ranged from 0.6 years in Austria and Australia to 0.3 years in Denmark. The number for the US was 0.4 years, but with considerable regional variation as might be expected. New England (0.31 years) and the Middle Atlantic (0.36 years) were much lower than the East South Central (0.86 years) and the West South Central (0.69 years).[44] One expects the US South to have been less healthy because of the greater proportion of fried foods in that diet and a higher incidence of infectious diseases, parasitic diseases, and gastroenteritis.

Before World War II, the influences of both nutrition and infection were highly seasonal. The typical diet in the early years of the 20th century was different from that at the beginning of the 21st century. The availability and prices of fresh fruits and vegetables varied over the year, and people ate less of them. People ate less meat and more starch. Nutritionists even argued that green vegetables demanded more energy for digestion than they supplied. The nutrition explanation has more to do with the quality and variety of the food available, especially during the winter and spring, than its quantity. Although severe malnutrition was limited in all the countries studied, there was inadequate nutrition in those days during the winter and early spring. Since a fetus has its greatest weight growth during the third trimester, Northern Hemisphere infants born in the spring spent their third trimester *in utero* during a period of relatively poor nutrition, while the opposite was true for infants born in the fall.

The incidence of infectious disease depends on the climate and on the seasons of the year. Gastrointestinal infections were more common in summer; there was (and is) a correlation between the incidence of water- and food-borne infectious diseases and warmer temperatures. In the late 19th century, the movement of non-pasteurized milk without adequate refrigeration contributed to many ailments including gastroenteritis, a major contributor to the infant mortality rate.[45] Respiratory infections (airborne diseases), spread in poorly ventilated conditions, were more common in autumn and winter. Current research cannot distinguish between the period *in utero* and the first year of life. Thus, we cannot determine whether mother's nutrition during pregnancy or infectious disease in the first year of life is of crucial importance. It is the case, however, that before World War II, Northern Hemisphere babies born in the spring experienced a transition from a period of less adequate nutrition to one of more infection. The opposite was true for those born in the fall, and the pattern was reversed for Southern Hemisphere babies.

3.6 Urban Mortality

Before 1900, urban mortality was substantially higher than rural mortality in both Europe and North America, particularly for infants and children. Even the earliest of systematic research, in the late 19th century, reported that life expectancy at birth in Massachusetts cities was almost seven years less than that in the state as a whole.[46] There are numerous reasons proffered for the higher urban mortality rates. Urbanization and industrialization were co-temporal. The need to ship food from farm to city in the age before refrigeration meant that urban food supplies were less healthy. The large numbers of people moving into the cities meant that new diseases arrived daily, and the large numbers of people living in close quarters meant that disease transmission was easy.[47]

In 1900 the US Bureau of the Census created the Death Registration Area (DRA), which included ten states and the District of Columbia. The DRA rates were based on the registration of deaths shortly after they occurred; the Bureau's Census of Mortality rates (which date from 1850) are the result of the enumerator asking how many deaths had occurred the previous year.[48] The Bureau's initial estimates using the DRA were that life expectancy at birth in 1901 was ten years less for white males born in cities than for those born in rural areas; for white females, the difference was about seven years. There are, however, several problems with the original DRA data. In particular, it covered only 26.3% of the US population and, more importantly, the areas were ones in which urban and foreign residents were over-represented, and blacks were under-represented. Consequently, using the DRA information, the overall US mortality was overestimated by failure to recognize the urban distinctiveness.[49]

The US Census Bureau itself also became aware of the rural-urban differences in mortality and conducted a number of regional studies. In 1942 one important study compiled a historical life table for urban and rural areas in 1830.[50] It revealed that life expectancy at age ten was:

- 51 years in 46 small New England towns (mostly in Massachusetts);
- 46 years in Salem, MA (pop. 14 000) and New Haven, CT (11 000); and
- about 36 years in New York City (203 000), Philadelphia (80 000), and Boston (61 000).

Thirty years later these results were criticized for confusing urban-rural differences in longevity with regional disparities in mortality.[51] Deaths in smaller towns, it was claimed, were likely to have been under-registered and subsequent corrections reduced the difference somewhat.[52]

Similar disparities in urban and rural mortality were discovered in Europe. David Glass found life expectancy at birth in England and Wales in 1841 to be 40.2 years for males and 42.2 years for females. However, life expectancy in London was only 35 years for males and 38 years for females, and the numbers were even lower for the industrial cities of Manchester and Liverpool.[53] On the continent, between 1816 and 1820 female life expectancy at birth in the *département* of the Seine, that included Paris, was 30.83 years, more than eight years below that of France as a whole.[54] The gap then widened to ten years in 1851–1855 before falling to eight years in 1876–1880 and to 4.6 years in 1901–1905. This was similar to Germany in 1900–1901 where male life expectancy at birth was about four years lower in urban than in rural areas, but female was only about a year and a half lower.[55]

In the late 19th century, most differences in urban and rural mortality were due to differences in infant and child mortality.[56] This was due primarily to infectious diseases, whose incidence was influenced by living standards and improvements in public health, particularly water and sewer systems.[57] The US Children's Bureau reported that the difference between rural and urban infant mortality rates was nine per 1000 at 1915 but fell to just over one per thousand by 1921. As late as 1939 statisticians for the Metropolitan Life Insurance Company calculated that rural mortality rates remained lower than urban mortality rates, although the disparity between cities of different sizes had essentially disappeared.[58] From a longer perspective, the infant mortality rate in English cities with more than 100 000 inhabitants was 42% higher than in rural areas in the 1850s but the gap had widened to 46% by the early 1900s.[59]

While the difference was *smaller* in certain parts of continental Europe this has been attributed to *higher* infant mortality rates in both German cities and rural areas than elsewhere.[60] In Germany, 1875–1877, the infant mortality rate was only 10% higher in urban areas than in rural areas and the same was roughly true of the Netherlands in the late 19th century.

There have been five explanations offered for the upward trend in the urban-rural difference in the 19th century and the decrease in the 20th century. These five are: improvements in the standard of living, improvements in medical science, advances in sanitation systems, improvements in the fluid milk supply, and changes in migration patterns.

Improvements in the Standard of Living. In a series of articles culminating in his book, Thomas McKeown (1976) holds that improvements in nutrition were primarily responsible for the increase in life expectancy occurring during the 19th century.

Although many have challenged McKeown's emphasis on the role of nutrition over all other factors in the decrease in mortality, none deny that nutrition was a factor.[61] The nutrition hypothesis can explain why urban mortality would exceed rural mortality in two ways. First, rural residents, who tended to be farmers or farm workers, had better access to cheaper and healthy food. Second, although average incomes tended to be higher in cities, personal income inequality tended to be lower in rural areas.[62] This suggests that cities had a higher proportion of residents living in poverty, without adequate access to nutrition and that areas or individuals with lower incomes or socioeconomic status had higher mortality.[63]

Improvements in the Science of Medicine. Advances in medical science contributed substantially to the decline in mortality, particularly in urban areas. The most important development was the acceptance of the *germ theory* of disease by both the medical profession and the public. Before 1880, the dominant theory was the miasmatic theory: foul odors released by decomposing matter caused disease. In some cases (e.g., better ventilation and clean streets) the older theory led cities to do the right thing for the wrong reason, but other actions (e.g., as an undue emphasis on the dangers of sewer gas) were cosmetic at best. As Nancy Tomes pointed out, it was the germ theory, with its emphasis on preventing the spread of harmful bacteria that led to measures such as water filtration and chlorination, the scientific testing of water and food for contaminants, and public health campaigns against such leading causes of death as tuberculosis and infantile diarrhoea.[64] Further, the application of proper sanitary techniques within the home greatly reduced the spread of infectious disease.[65] Since these public and private innovations were generally applied sooner in urban than in rural areas, urban mortality declined faster in the late 19th and early 20th centuries than rural mortality. On the other hand, McKeown is probably correct in arguing that advances in medical practice did little to reduce mortality before World War I as these were limited primarily to the development of sterile surgical techniques, inoculation and vaccination for smallpox, and an antitoxin for diphtheria.

Advances in Sanitation Systems. McKeown, however, underestimates the effect of public health measures. The great reduction in the incidence of waterborne diseases, such as cholera and typhoid fever, which these public health innovations brought about also greatly reduced mortality from airborne diseases by improving the quality of nutrition and reducing other insults to the body.[66] The provision of clean water was responsible for almost half of the total mortality reduction occurring in cities during the early 20th century, including three-quarters of the fall in infant and two-thirds of the decline in child mortality.[67] Expenditures on sewer systems and refuse collection and disposal significantly reduced cities' mortality rates from waterborne disease, but expenditures on water systems were less effective, with the exception of cities drawing their water supplies from rivers.[68] The provision of potable water, however, was one of the first major public health innovations and was largely in place so the incremental expenditures had a smaller mortality payoff in the late 19th/early 20th century. A fall in the mortality rate from typhoid, a waterborne disease, a proxy for water quality, was associated with a significant fall in the mortality rate from pneumonia, which was not a waterborne disease.[69] This supports the Mills-Reincke phenomenon: as cities began to filter their water supplies, death rates from non-waterborne diseases often declined in greater proportion than did death rates from water-borne diseases. Much of the variation in mortality in three French *départements* in the 19th century could be explained by differences in the quality of the water and sewer systems.[70] In Chicago, the provision and improvement of the public water supply lowered the city's mortality rate between 35 and 56% from 1850 to 1925, a result attributable primarily to eradicating typhoid.[71]

Improvements in the Milk Supply. Closely aligned with public health improvements were improvements in the quality (and quantity) of the milk supply. These improvements reduced excessive infant mortality in the cities, particularly during the summer months – see earlier. In the mid-19th century, urban-rural disparities in infant mortality widened as cities began to import milk over longer distances, often under unsanitary conditions. The greater relative anonymity of sellers also led to the adulteration of milk and the sale of "swill milk" that had been collected from cows fed on the by-products of distilleries. Over the course of the late-19th and early-20th centuries numerous changes were made. Milk was tested, first for adulteration and later for bacteria content, and regulations were adopted regarding the handling and sale of raw milk. In particular, laws were passed requiring pasteurization and attempts were made to eradicate bovine tuberculosis. There were public education campaigns encouraging breastfeeding or the use of safe milk. First iceboxes and later refrigerators in the home kept milk from spoiling. Finally, in some cities, safe milk was distributed at subsidized prices to mothers in urban slums, where infant mortality rates were extremely high.[72] In both Europe and North America, the home delivery of milk gained popularity in the early 20th century.

Changes in Migration Patterns. A final explanation for the pattern of urban-rural mortality rates is that large waves of internal and international migrants to urban areas increased the incidence of infectious diseases. Diverse groups of people who previously had not been exposed to one another's diseases came into contact with each other under crowded conditions. Foreign migrants, in particular, were vulnerable because of the stresses associated with the transatlantic passage. An increase in migration in the late 19th century significantly increased the crude death rate in large American cities.[73] Earlier, in 1850, according to an extensive study, any location that had access to regional transportation networks via a water route significantly increased the exposure of its resident population to the higher mortality associated with the volume of internal and international migrants.[74] Yet, this cannot explain the fact *urban mortality declined more rapidly than rural mortality in the late 19th century.* Any negative effects of immigration on mortality had to have been offset by something like the effects of improvements in living standards and public health.

The study of past urban-rural mortality differentials and the burden of disease have particular relevance for the developing world today.[75] Not only are diseases such as malaria and tuberculosis still common in the developing world, but

3.7 The Mortality Transition: Crude Death Rates

The slow pre-1800 decline in the crude death rate gathered momentum and, in Western Europe, by the late 19th century had travelled about half the distance of the transition (Figure 3.8). There were yet gains to be made, as noted earlier, the most significant of which were in the first half of the 20th century. Variations in country performance are largely explained by the different degrees of urbanization, the amount of spending of social infrastructure and local improvements in the standard-of-living. But not only did the CDR decline to its modern level, its variance also declined. Apart from human inspired catastrophes such as wars and their spillover effects, since the great influenza pandemic of 1919 Western Europe and North America have been spared (and taken pre-emptive measures to limit) major afflictions which move the national mortality rate significantly. There are of course many life-saving gains in the future from appropriate medical and drug therapies, social investment and poverty relief that might be expected. The AIDS/HIV epidemic, and others, have smaller aggregate effects than the great scourges of pre-20th century history: smallpox, cholera, influenza, typhus, polio, scarlet fever and many others. The same is not true of the less developed world, as has been noted.[76]

For the US, the aggregate CBR is available only for the years after 1900 due to the way the national census was constructed. With this deficiency over a crucial period, the state records for Massachusetts fill in the broad picture of the 19th century from 1855 onward.[77] In general terms, there is no reason why the state's CDR should vary significantly from the national one. It of course would be higher than the unobserved national CDR because of the higher rate of urbanization in the state relative to the nation. For aggregate statistics we cannot go further into the past with direct evidence. Yet, for Canada we can. The records of mortality are remarkably complete for the Roman Catholic population of Quebec so that a CDR can be calculated.[78] We might argue that there is no major distinction (there are many minor ones) between the demography of New France/Quebec and that of the other British North American colonies during the US Colonial Era and little thereafter that are not accounted for by measurable population differences such as the rural-urban mix.[79] (Quebec is contiguous to the US and shared similar economies with the New England states.) A reasonable inference is that the earlier stages of the US demographic transition can be mirrored by the Canadian data. Certainly by the year that the US (Massachusetts) data begins the CDRs in the US and Canada/Quebec are roughly equal. So, the US in 1800 would be estimated to have had a CDR similar to that of Canada and North Western Europe, somewhat below 30 per 1000.

The next task is to account for the long run decline in the fertility rate. Key to understanding this is the question: what was the relationship between mortality and natality – measured by the crude death and birth rates respectively?

(a) Europe: Norway and Sweden

(b) Europe: England (and Wales) and France

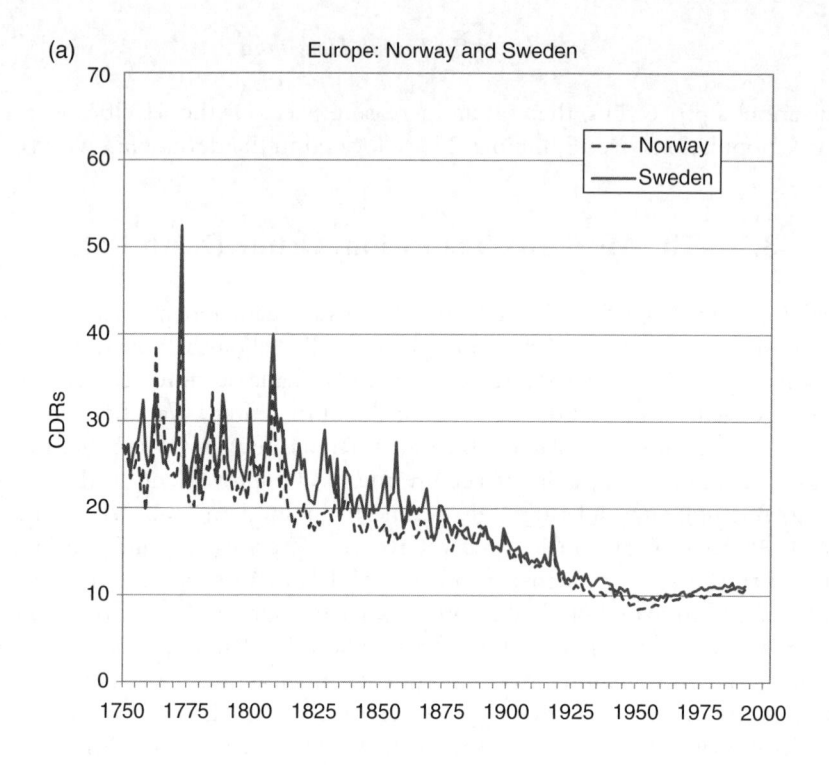

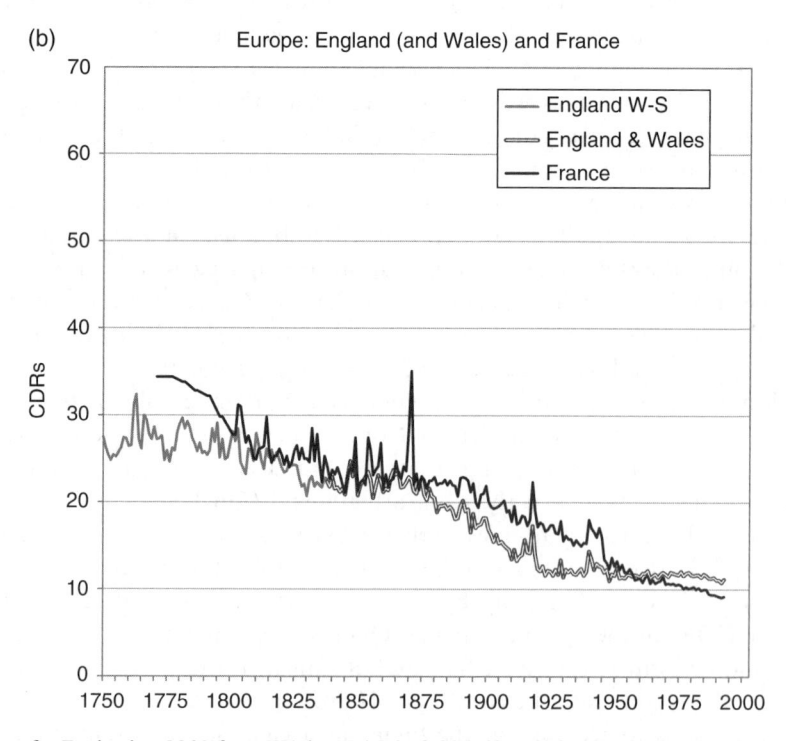

Note: Data for England to 1838 from Wrigley and Schofield (1981) and Official Estimates for England and Wales thereafter. The French data prior to 1801 are from Bourgeois-Pichat (1965); they are interpolated from five year averages. "W-S" refers to the "Wrigley-Schofield estimates".

Figure 3.8 (*Continued*)

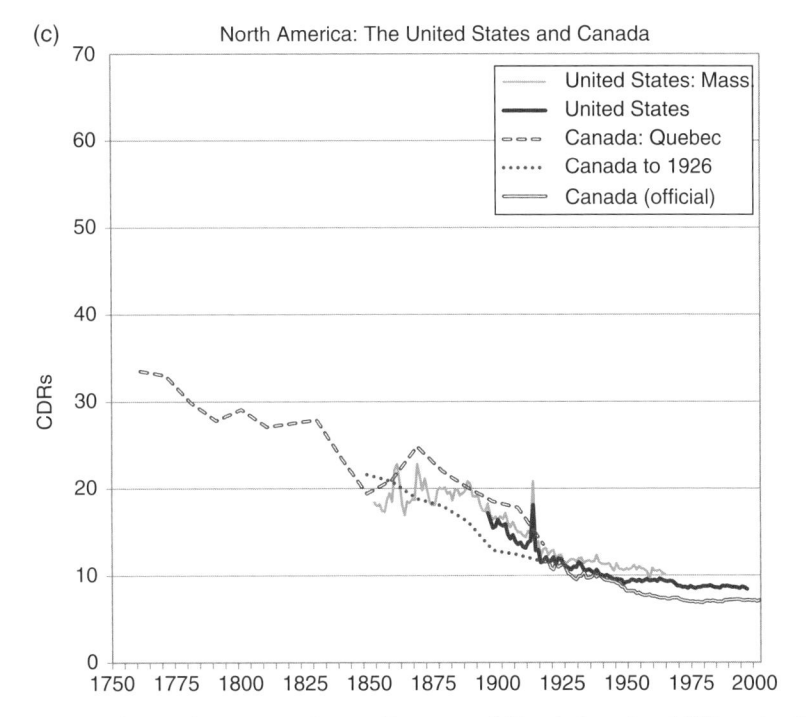

Figure 3.8 Crude Death Rates in Western Europe and North America, 1750 to the Present.
Note: Data prior to 1880 for Quebec are for the Roman Catholic population only. All data prior to 1921 are interpolated for the ten year census intervals. Between 1976 and 1998 the data are interpolations for the five year census intervals. The US data are for all individuals; where no national figures exist, historians use the CDR of the State of Massachusetts.
Sources: Bourgeois-Pichat (1965); Haines (2006), *US Historical Statistics*, Series Ab 988 and Ab1048; Henripin and Peron (1972); *Historical Statistics of Canada*, Series B18; Mitchell, *International Historical Statistics*, Series, 93–117; Statistics Canada (various) including Canadian Census data; US Census data; and Wrigley and Schofield (1981).

Endnotes

1. Children under 12 months of age. World Health Report for 2005, http://www.who.int/whr/2005/en/index.html
2. Omran, (1971) and Salomon and Murray (2002).
3. Bacci (1991).
4. The Horn of Africa (Somalia. parts of Ethiopia, Sudan, Eritrea) provides startling examples of the near total paralysis of the food distribution system. Even the UN and other charitable agencies are frequently frustrated in their efforts to provide relief.
5. Infectious and parasitic diseases: Tuberculosis; STIs excluding HIV (Syphilis, Chlamydia Gonorrhoea); HIV/AIDS; Diarrhoeal diseases; Childhood diseases (Pertussis, Poliomyelitis, Diphtheria, Measles, Tetanus); Meningitis; Hepatitis; Malaria; Tropical diseases (Chagas disease, Schistosomiasis, Leishmaniasis, Lymphatic filariasis, Onchocerciasis) Leprosy; Japanese encephalitis, Trypanosomiasis Trachoma); Intestinal nematode infections (Ascariasis, Trichuriasis, Hookworm disease); Respiratory infections (Lower and Upper respiratory infections incl. Otitis media).
6. Drug resistant strains of Mycobacterium tuberculosis and Mycobacterium bovis give rise to the fear that the incidence of tuberculosis may again rise.

7   Centers for Disease Control and Prevention (Nov., 1999), "The Deadly Intersection Between TB and HIV", Bulletin, Department of Health and Human Services, US Government – http://www.cdc.gov
8   Ubelaker (2000).
9   Ellman and Maksudov (1994), Table 1. The figure was arrived at taking the estimated total deaths minus the recent estimate of military deaths (22.6–8.7 millions). See also: Haynes (2003).
10 For very low rates of mortality, it is sometimes expressed per 10 000.
11 Notice that these rates are inclusive but it is essential to check the exact definition for each study since sometimes they are not. For example, child mortality is often measured as 1–4 years.
12 Ó Gráda (2004).
13 UN, Statistics Division … 1.
14 Dzakpasu, Kramer, and Allen (2000).
15 Tropical diseases were not of course prevalent in northern hemisphere countries.
16 Based on the backward projections; Woods (1997). Schellekens (2001).
17 See Chapter Two.
18 Woods (1997).
19 Haines (1985).
20 For a discussion see: Perrenoud (1984). For the US see: Vinovskis (1972), 184–213 and for England and Wales see: Wrigley and Schofield (1981).
21 Bourbeau, Légaré and Émond (1997).
22 See Chapter Three for a discussion of CBRs and sustainability.
23 Hielte (2004).
24 We cannot reject the possibility that the data are not comparable.
25 Perrenoud (1984), Table 7.
26 Högberg (2004); Sundin (1995); Fridlizius (1984).
27 Vinoviskis (1971). Vinovskis argues that Wigglesworth adjusted his estimates of a lower calculation by methods that cannot now be duplicated and treats this figures as a plausible, well-educated guess.
28 Life expectancy at birth   1850   1900
    white males   37.2   47.1
    white females   39.4   48.4

Haines and Avery (1980), "The American Life Table of 1830–1860…", Haines (2006), "Vital Statistics," *U.S. Historical Statistics,* chapter Ab. Life tables for "All Races" and "Non-Whites" are available from 1900 onward.
29 Data from Perrenoud (1984), Table 7; Fridlizius (1984).
30 "Old" is a subjective notion. Human rights legislation in many world jurisdictions now forbids age discrimination, such as mandatory retirement.
31 Horiuchi and Wilmoth (1998).
32 Olshansky and Carnes (1997); Kesteloot and Huang (2003).
33 Wilmoth and Horiuchi (1999).
34 For instance, see: UK (2008), Health Expectancy, National Statistics. http://www.statistics.gov.uk
35 Wrigley and Schofield (1981).
36 The long 18th century refers to the period between the radical change in government in the United Kingdom in 1689 – the Glorious Revolution – and the fall of Napoleon at Waterloo in 1815.
37 Hayward, Pienta and McLaughlin (1997).
38 Evidence from: Jonsson (1984).
39 Woods (2003).

40 One of the reasons that researchers cannot be more precise is that the most frequently found evidence, the bills of mortality, did not give information that conformed to modern medical diagnoses of disease.
41 See, for example, Barker (2002).
42 Finch and Crimmins (2004).
43 Doblhammer (2003); see also Ferrie, Rolf and Troesken (2007).
44 Doblhammer (2003).
45 See Lee (2007).
46 Weber (1899).
47 New York (2007).
48 Higgs (1979); Condran and Crimmins (1980).
49 Preston and Haines (1991); Haines (1977).
50 Vinovskis (1972) gives a critique of the early life tables.
51 *Ibid*. Life expectancy at ages 10–14 in Massachusetts towns with less than 1000 inhabitants was estimated to be 52.5 years but 46.7 years in towns with 10 000 or more inhabitants.
52 A number of other demographers have calculated large disparities between rural and urban mortality rates. See Condran and Crimmins (1983), Haines (1977), Higgs (1973), Yasuba (1962), and Dublin and Lotka (1945).
53 Glass (1973). See also Szreter and Mooney (1998).
54 Preston and van de Walle (1978).
55 Vogele (1998).
56 Kunitz (1983).
57 Duffy (1990); McKeown and Record (1962); McKeown (1976); Melosi (2000); and Preston and Haines (1984).
58 Woodbury (1926).
59 Williams and Galley (1995); see also Huck (1995) and Woods, Watterson, and Woodward (1988).
60 Williams and Galley (1995) and van Poppel, Jonker, and Mandemakers (2005).
61 Szreter (1988); Riley (1990) and Woods (2003).
62 McLaughlin (2002).
63 Among the studies that provide evidence for this are Steckel (1988); Condran and Cheney (1982); Crimmins and Condran (1983); Haines (1995); Woods, Watterson; and Woodward (1988).
64 Tomes (1998).
65 Both Tomes (1998) and Mokyr (2000) point out this could be overdone.
66 Harris (2004).
67 Cutler and Miller (2005).
68 Cain and Rotella (2001). See also Gaspari and Woolf (1985).
69 Condran and Crimmins (1983). Condran and Cheney (1982) found evidence that water filtration reduced the incidence of mortality from typhoid, but they found no evidence that it reduced infant and child mortality rates from diarrhoeal diseases; both had been declining for at least 20 years before filtration.
70 Preston and van de Walle (1978).
71 Ferrie and Toesken (2008).
72 See Beaver (1973); Meckel (1990a and b); Lee (2007); and Olmstead and Rhode (2004).
73 Higgs (1979) study of 18 US cities.
74 Haines, Craig and Weiss (2003) using data from over 1200 US counties in 1850.
75 Riley (1990, 2005).
76 Ó Gráda (2004).

77 See Haines (2006) and Zopf Jr. (1992).
78 Henripin and Peron (1972). *Quebec* refers to New France (1765–1790), Lower Canada (1791–1840), Canada East (1841–1867) and Quebec thereafter.
79 Infant mortality was notably different between the French and English speaking Quebecers of the late 19th and early 20th century. This too can be largely attributed to the rural and urban differences of the two groups.

References

Bacci, Massimo Livi (1991) *Population and Nutrition: An Essay on European Historical Demography,* Cambridge: Cambridge University Press.

Barker, David J.P. (2002) "Fetal Programming of Coronary Heart Disease," *Trends in Endocrinology & Metabolism,* **13**(9), 364–8.

Beaver, M.W. (1973) "Population, Infant Mortality and Milk", *Population Studies,* **27**(2), 243–54.

Bengtsson, Tommy, Gunnar Fridlizius and Rolf Ohlsson (eds.) (1984) *Pre-Industrial Population Change: The Mortality Decline and Short-Term Population Movements,* Stockholm: Almquist and Wiksell International.

Bourbeau, Robert, Jacques Légaré and Valérie Émond (1997) *New Birth Cohort Life Tables for Canada and Quebec, 1801–1991,* Ottawa: September, Statistics Canada, Catalogue No. 91F0015MPE.

Bourgeois-Pichat, J. (1965) "The General Development of the Population of France Since the Eighteenth Century", in D.V. Glass and D.E.C. Eversley, eds. *Population in History, Essays in Historical Demography,* Old Woking, Surrey: Edward Arnold Publishers.

Cain, Louis P. and Elyce J. Rotella (2001) "Death and Spending: Urban Mortality and Municipal Expenditure on Sanitation", *Annales De Demographie Historique,* **1**, 139–54.

Condran, Gretchen A. and Rose A. Cheney (1982) "Mortality Trends in Philadelphia: Age- and Cause-Specific Death Rates 1870–1930", *Demography,* **19**(1), 97–123.

Condran, Gretchen A. and Eileen M. Crimmins (1983) Mortality Variation in U.S. Cities in 1900: A Two-Level Explanation by Cause of Death and Underlying Factors", *Social Science History,* 7(1), 31–59.

Cutler, David and Grant Miller (2005) "The Role of Public Health Improvements in Health Advances: The Twentieth-Century United States", *Demography,* **42**(1), 1–22.

Doblhammer, Gabriele (2003) "The Late Life Legacy of Very Early Life," *Max Planck Institute for Demographic Research Working Paper WP 2003–030,* September.

Dublin, Louis I. and Alfred J. Lotka (1945) "Trends in Longevity" *Annals of the American Academy of Political and Social Science,* 237, World Population in Transition, 123–33.

Duffy, John (1990) *The Sanitarians.* Urbana, IL: University of Illinois Press.

Dzakpasu, Susie, K.S. Joseph, Michael S. Kramer and Alexander C. Allen (2000) "The Matthew Effect: Infant Mortality in Canada and Internationally", *Pediatrics,* **106**(1), e1–5.

Ellman, Michael and S. Maksudov (1994) "Soviet Deaths in the Great Patriotic War: A Note" *Europe-Asia Studies,* **46**(4), 671–80.

Ferrie, Joseph and Werner Troesken (2008) "Water and Chicago's Mortality Transition, 1850–1925," *Explorations in Economic History,* **45**(1), 1–16.

Ferrie, Joseph, Karen Rolf and Werner Troesken (2007) "The Past as Prologue: The Effect of Early Life Circumstances at the Community and Household Levels on Mid-Life and Late-Life Outcomes," Working Paper, January.

Finch, Caleb E. and Eileen M. Crimmins (2004) "Inflammatory Exposure and Historical Changes in Human Life-Spans," *Science,* **305**(17), 1736–9.

Fridlizius, Gunnar (1984) "The Mortality Decline in the First Phase of the Demographic Transition: Swedish Experiences", in Bengtsson *et al.*, 71–109.
Gaspari, K. Celeste and Arthur G. Woolf (1985) "Income, Public Works, and Mortality in Early Twentieth-Century American Cities Income, Public Works, and Mortality in Early Twentieth-Century American Cities", *Journal of Economic History*, **45**(2), 355–61.
Glass David V. (1973) *Numbering the People: the Eighteenth-Century Population Controversy and the Development of Census and Vital Statistics in Britain*, Farnborough: D.C. Heath.
Haines, Michael (1995) "Socio-economic Differentials in Infant and Child Mortality during Mortality Decline: England and Wales, 1890–1911", *Population Studies*, l. **49**(2), 297–315.
Haines, Michael R. (1977) "Mortality in Nineteenth Century America: Estimates From New York and Pennsylvania Census Data, 1865 and 1900", *Demography*, **14**(3), 311–31.
Haines, Michael R. (1985) "Inequality and Childhood Mortality: A Comparison of England and Wales, 1911, and the United States, 1900", *Journal of Economic History*, **45**(4), 885–912.
Haines, Michael R. (1989) "American Fertility in Transition: New Estimates of Birth Rates in the United States, 1900–1910", *Demography*, **26**(1), 137–48.
Haines, Michael R. (2006) "Vital Statistics, Chapter Ab", *U.S. Historical Statistics*.
Haines, Michael R. and Roger C. Avery (1980) "The American Life Table of 1830–1860: An Evaluation", *Journal of Interdisciplinary History*, **11**(1), 73–95.
Haines, Michael R., Lee A. Craig and Thomas Weiss (2003) "The Short and the Dead: Nutrition, Mortality, and the "Antebellum Puzzle" in the United States", *Journal of Economic History*, **63**(2), 382–413.
Harris, Bernard (2004) "Public Health, Nutrition, and the Decline of Mortality: The McKeown Thesis Revisited", *Social History of Medicine*, **17**(3), 379–407.
Haynes, Michael (2003) "Counting Soviet Deaths in the Great Patriotic War: A Note" *Europe-Asia Studies*, **55**(2), 303–9.
Hayward, Mark D., Amy M. Pienta and Diane K. McLaughlin (1997) "Inequality in Men's Mortality: The Socioeconomic Status Gradient and Geographic Context", *Journal of Health and Social Behavior*, **38**(4), 313–30.
Henripin, J. and Y. Peron (1972) "The Demographic Transition of the Province of Quebec", in D.V. Glass and Roger Revelle (eds.), *Population and Social Change*, London: Edward Arnold, 213–31.
Hielte, Maria (2004) "Sedentary Versus Nomadic Life-Styles: The 'Middle Helladic People' in Southern Balkan (late 3rd & first Half of the 2nd Millennium BC)", *Acta Archaeologica* **75**, 27–94.
Higgs, Robert (1973) "Race, Tenure, and Resource Allocation in Southern Agriculture, 1910", *Journal of Economic History*, **33**(1), 149–69.
Higgs, Robert and David Booth (1979) "Mortality Differentials within Large American Cities in 1890", *Human Ecology*, **7**(4), 353–70.
Högberg, Ulf (2004) "The Decline in Maternal Mortality in Sweden: The Role of Community Midwifery", *American Journal of Public Health*, **94**(8) (Spring), 1312–20.
Horiuchi, Shiro and John R. Wilmoth (1998) "Deceleration in the Age Pattern of Mortality at Older Ages", *Demography*, **35**(4), 391–412.
Huck, Paul (1995) "Infant Mortality and Living Standards of English Workers During the Industrial Revolution", *Journal of Economic History*, **55**(3), 528–50.
Jonsson, Ulf (1984) "Population Growth and Agrarian and Social Structure: Some Swedish Examples", in Bengtsson *et al.*, 223–54.
Kesteloot, H. and X. Huang (2003) "On the Relationship between Human All-Cause Mortality and Age", *European Journal of Epidemiology*, **18**(6), 503–11.
Kunitz, Stephen J. (1983) "Speculations on the European Mortality Decline", *Economic History Review*, New Series, **36**(3), 349–64.

Landers, John and Anastasia Mouzas (1998) "Burial Seasonality and Causes of Death in London 1670–1819", *Population Studies*, **42**(1), (March), 59–83.

Lee, Kwang-sun (2007) "Infant Mortality Decline in the Late 19th and Early 20th Centuries: The Role of Market Milk," *Perspectives in Biology and Medicine*, **50**(4), 585–602.

McKeown, T. (1976) *The Modern Rise of Population*, London: Edward Arnold.

McKeown, T. and R.G. Record (1962) "Reasons for the Decline of Mortality in England and Wales during the Nineteenth Century", *Population Studies*, **16**(2), 94–122.

McLaughlin, Diane K. (2002) "Income Inequality in America: Nonmetro Income Levels Lower Than Metro, But Income Inequality Did Not Increase as Fast", *Rural America*, **17**(2), 14–20.

Meckel, Richard A. (1990a) " Immigration, Mortality, and Population Growth in Boston, 1840–1880", *Journal of Interdisciplinary History*, **15**(3), 393–417.

Meckel, Richard A. (1990b) *Save the Babies. American Public Health Reform and the Prevention of Infant Mortality, 1850–1929*, Baltimore: Johns Hopkins University Press.

Melosi, Martin V. (2000) *The Sanitary City: Urban Infrastructure in America from Colonial Times to the Present*, Baltimore: Johns Hopkins University Press.

Mokyr, Joel (2000) "Why 'More Work for Mother?' Knowledge and Household Behavior, 1870–1945", *Journal of Economic History*, **60**(1), 1–41.

New York City (2007) *Summary of Vital Statistics 2006 for the City of New York*, Bureau Of Vital Statistics, New York: New York City Department Of Health And Mental Hygiene. http://www.nyc.gov/html/doh/html/vs/vs.shtml

Ó Gráda, Cormac (2004) "Infant and Child Mortality in Dublin a Century Ago", Marco Bresci and Lucia Pozzi (eds.), *The Determinants of Infant and Child Mortality in Past European Populations*, (Forum, Italy: Udine), 89–104.

Olmstead, Alan L. and Paul W. Rhode (2004) "An Impossible Undertaking: The Eradication of Bovine Tuberculosis in the United States", *Journal of Economic History*, **64**(3), 734–72.

Olshansky, S. Jay and Bruce A. Carnes (1997) "Ever Since Gompertz", *Demography*, **34**(1), 1–15.

Omran, A. (1971) "The Epidemiological Transition: A Theory of the Epidemiology of Population Change", *Milbank Memorial Fund Quarterly*, **49**, 509–38.

Perrenoud, Alfred (1984) "Mortality Decline in Its Secular Setting", in Bengtsson *et al.*, 41–69.

Preston, Samuel H. and Michael R. Haines (1984) "New Estimates of Child Mortality in the United States at the Turn of the Century", *Journal of the American Statistical Association*, **79**(386), 272–81.

Preston, Samuel H. and Etienne van de Walle (1978) "Urban French Mortality in the Nineteenth Century", *Population Studies*, **32**(2), 275–97.

Riley, James C. (1990) "The Risk of Being Sick: Morbidity Trends in Four Countries", *Population and Development Review*, **16**(3), 403–32.

Riley, James C. (2005) "The Timing and Pace of Health Transitions around the World", *Population and Development Review*, **31**(4), 741–64.

Salomon, J.A. and C.J.L. Murray (2002) "The Epidemiologic Transition Revisited: Compositional Models for Causes of Death by Age and Sex", *Population and Development Review*, **28**, 205–28.

Samuel H. Preston and Michael R. Haines (1991) *Fatal Years: Child Mortality in Late Nineteenth-Century America*, Princeton, N.J.: Princeton University Press.

Schellekens, Jona (2001) "Economic Change and Infant Mortality in England, 1580–1837", *Journal of Interdisciplinary History*, **32**(1), 1–13.

Singer, J. David and Melvin Small, *Correlates of War Project*, Inter-University Consortium for Political and Social Research (ICPSR), Study 9045. webapp.icpsr.umich.edu/cocoon/ICPSR-STUDY/09905.

Sundin, Jan (1995) "Culture, Class, and Infant Mortality during the Swedish Mortality Transition, 1750–1850", *Social Science History*, **19**(1), 117–45.

Smith, David W. and Benjamin S. Bradshaw (2006) "Variation in Life Expectancy During the Twentieth Century in the United States", *Demography*, **43**(4), 647–57.

Steckel, Richard H. (1988) "The Health and Mortality of Women and Children, 1850–1860", *Journal of Economic History*, **48**(2), 333–45.

Szreter, Simon and Graham Mooney (1998) "Urbanization, Mortality, and the Standard of Living Debate: New Estimates of the Expectation of Life at Birth in Nineteenth-Century British Cities" *Economic History Review*, New Series, **51**(1), 84–112.

Tomes, Nancy (1998) *The Gospel of Germs: Men, Women, and the Microbe in American Life*, Cambridge, Mass.: Harvard University Press,

Ubelaker, Douglas H. (2000) "Patterns of Disease in Early North American Populations", in Michael R. Haines and Richard H. Steckel (eds), *A Population History of North America*, Cambridge: Cambridge University Press, 51–97.

van Poppel, Frans, Marianne Jonker and Kees Mandemakers (2005) "Differential Infant and Child Mortality in Three Dutch Regions, 1812–1909 Differential Infant and Child Mortality in Three Dutch Regions, 1812–1909", *Economic History Review*, New Series, **58**(2), 272–309.

Vinovskis, Maris A. (1971) "The 1789 Life Table of Edward Wigglesworth", *The Journal of Economic History*, **31**(3), 570–90.

Vinovskis, Maris A. (1972) "Mortality Rates and Trends in Massachusetts Before 1860", *Journal of Economic History*, **32**(1), 184–213.

Vögele, Jörg (1998) *Urban Mortality Change in England and Germany, 1870–1913*, Liverpool: Liverpool University Press.

Weber, Alfred (1899) *Growth of Cities in the Nineteenth Century: a Study in Statistics*, New York: the Macmillan Company.

Williams, Naomi and Chris Galley (1995) "Urban-Rural Differentials in Infant Mortality in Victorian England", *Population Studies*, **49**(3), 401–20.

Wilmoth, R. John and Horiuchi Shiro (1999) "Rectangularization Revisited: Variability of Age at Death within Human Populations" *Demography*, **36**(4), 475–95.

Woodbury, Robert Morse (1926) *Infant Mortality and Its Causes, With an Appendix on the Trend of Maternal Mortality Rates in the United States*, Baltimore: The Williams & Wilkins Company.

Woods, R.I., P.A. Watterson and J.H. Woodward (1988) "The Causes of Rapid Infant Mortality Decline in England and Wales, 1861–1921, Part I", *Population Studies*, **42**(3), 343–66.

Woods, R.I., P.A. Watterson and J.H. Woodward (1988) "The Causes of Rapid Infant Mortality Decline in England and Wales, 1861–1921, Part II", *Population Studies*, **43**(1), 113–32.

Woods, Robert (2003) "Urban-Rural Mortality Differentials: An Unresolved Debate", *Population and Development Review*, **29**(1), 29–46.

Woods, Robert, (1997) "Infant Mortality in Britain: A Survey of Current Knowledge on Historical Trends and Variations", In Bideau *et al.*, *Infant and Child Mortality in the Past*, 75–80.

Wrigley E. and R Schofield (1981) *The Population History of England, 1541–1871: A Reconstruction*, Cambridge: Harvard University Press.

Yasuba, Yasukichi (1962) *Birth Rates of the White Population in the United States, 1800–1860, an Economic Study*, Baltimore: Johns Hopkins Press.

Zopf Jr., Paul E. (1992) *Mortality Patterns and Trends in the United States*, Westport, Conn.: Greenwood Press.

Chapter Four
The Fertility Transition

4.1 The Fertility Transition

Some economic forces acted largely on fertility, the invention and increased supply of cheap contraceptive techniques being an example. Some were quite sudden in their appearance, while others operated more slowly. Some forces operated to lower both mortality and fertility but not necessarily to the same extent and not necessarily at the same time. And, they varied for different episodes of history and for different societies. As the theory of the demographic transition (Chapter Two) conjectures, there is a link between mortality and fertility. However, the link is a complex one. The fertility decline was, in some periods of history, essentially local such as that in early 19th century North Western Europe. By the second half of the 20th century, however, the fertility decline was global.[1] Even the high birth rate countries of today have substantially lower fertility than they did 50 years earlier. Thus the fertility transition was universal but diverse in cause and time. This chapter explores the fertility transition: the movement from high birth rates to low birth rates and the reasons for it.

For any given geographic area of Western Europe and North America, the fertility transition began slowly and followed an inverted "S" shape. For these continents, the assignment of dates to the fertility transition's beginnings is necessarily imprecise as it began very slowly. (The same is not true of those regions that entered the fertility transition in more recent times.) For Europe the fertility transition started some time in the late 18th century. One researcher, Andrew Hinde, claims that for England it began in about 1750.[2] Hinde's dating can be easily accepted although some argue earlier and some argue later. In North America, however, it began a little later than 1750 although it is a matter of dispute as to when. For all Western Europe and North America the transition was well underway by the early 1800s and progressed through its most rapid phase in the late 19th and first half of the 20th centuries, as we will see later.

The Children of Eve: Population and Well-being in History, First Edition.
Louis P. Cain and Donald G. Paterson.
© 2012 Blackwell Publishing Ltd. Published 2012 by Blackwell Publishing Ltd.

Fecundity is the capacity or potential of a female (or a couple) to reproduce. Female fecundity varies with age with peak fecundity usually in the late 20s and early 30s. Women are typically fertile only between the ages of 15 and 49. There is also a decline in fecundity with length of marriage and change in marital coital patterns. Fecundity is a physiological measure unlike the fertility rate which is an outcome measure.

Lactational amenorrhea is the post-partum infertile period. It tends to increase with the age of the mother. Breast feeding, which increases in the length of the woman's infertile period after a live birth, will also reduce fecundity.

The *crude marriage (or nuptiality) rate* (CMR) is the number of marriages in the population of a given geographical area in a given year, per 1000 of total population (mid-year). If the population is an elderly one, it will have a lower marriage rate than one with a large proportion in the marriageable age range (a young population). Occasionally it refers to nuptiality as a proportion of a female age group, such as the marriage rate of women aged 26 to 30 years of age.

Married refers to a self-reported state of being married. However, historical data often only reflect church or other legalized marriage, such as that drawn from the marriage registers. Individuals living apart but married are classed as married whereas not married includes those living together who have never married, widows and widowers and divorcees. Some modern countries, such as Canada and The Netherlands, recognize same sex marriages.

For some purposes it is helpful to define *first marriage*, the marriage of single individuals (or females) who have never previously been married. For instance, the age at first marriage generally represents the beginning of a female's being "at risk" to bear children.

Age specific marriage (or nuptiality) rate refers to the numbers of marriages of those of a certain age range in the population of a given geographical area in a given year per 1000 of total population (mid-year) in that age range.

Divorce: The crude divorce rate is the frequency of the formal dissolution of marriage. It is defined for the whole population of a given geographical area in the same manner as the crude marriage rate. A percentage calculation is also used, such as the number of divorces of first marriages as a percentage of first marriages, and so on. Often this rate is calculated for the age of a marriage such as the number of divorces of first marriages that occur within ten years of being married as a percentage of first marriages.

Illegitimacy ratio: the number of births of illegitimate children per 1000 live births (usually converted to a percentage). The definition of "illegitimate" makes little sense in the modern era and has largely been abandoned. Historically, it meant a birth outside of wedlock.

4.2 The Queen and the Anabaptists

Queen Anne of the United Kingdom (1665–1714) was pregnant 18 times. Only five children were born live and of these only one survived infancy, although he too died at age 19. If not the greatest possible number of unsuccessful pregnancies for one woman, it was a record for a reigning monarch.[3] She left neither a biological nor a dynastic heir. One group of people, however, has tested the upper bounds of successful human breeding potential. The Hutterites, an Anabaptist sect, live in several farming "colonies" in the prairie region of North America.[4] While they share the same mortality pattern as surrounding communities they are remarkably different in other respects. They are self-contained communities who do not practice any type of artificial birth control, share all income and resources equitably, encourage fertility and, as a group, are subject to neither in-migration nor out-migration. In general, they thrive in a relatively prosperous economic environment. They are believed to represent the highest found fecundity in a normal age-distributed population.

The Hutterite population achieved a remarkable Total Fertility Rate (TFR) of 10.9 in the first half of the 20th century. "Were this population to marry early, have no *lactational amenorrhea*, and no sterilization or parity-connected decline in coitus, then the observed mean birth intervals would be reduced slightly, and the TFR would be about 15.0 per woman."[5] Fifty years on, at the beginning of the 21st century the highest national TFR is 7.8 for the low-income country of East Timor (2005) and that country has a high mortality rate.[6] Today's very high fertility countries are roughly what we would expect of pre-modern Europe.[7] Given that most of the Hutterite children survived, this means that the population grew at a high annual rate of 4.13%, calculated for 1946–1950.[8] With this growth rate the population would double in about 17.25 years – see Figure 4.1.

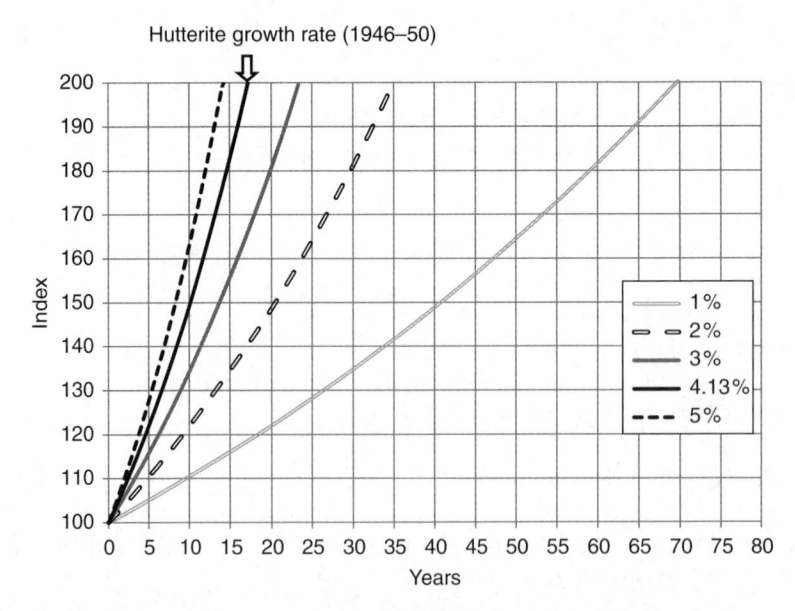

Figure 4.1 Time Taken for Population Doubling With Different Growth Rates.

Rule of 69

This is an *approximation* that is used predict how long it takes for a population, or any amount, to double under different assumptions about the rate of growth (or the interest rate):

$n \approx 0.69/r$ where n is the number of years and r is the rate of growth.

In the above figure n ≈ 35 when the r is 2% (0.02).

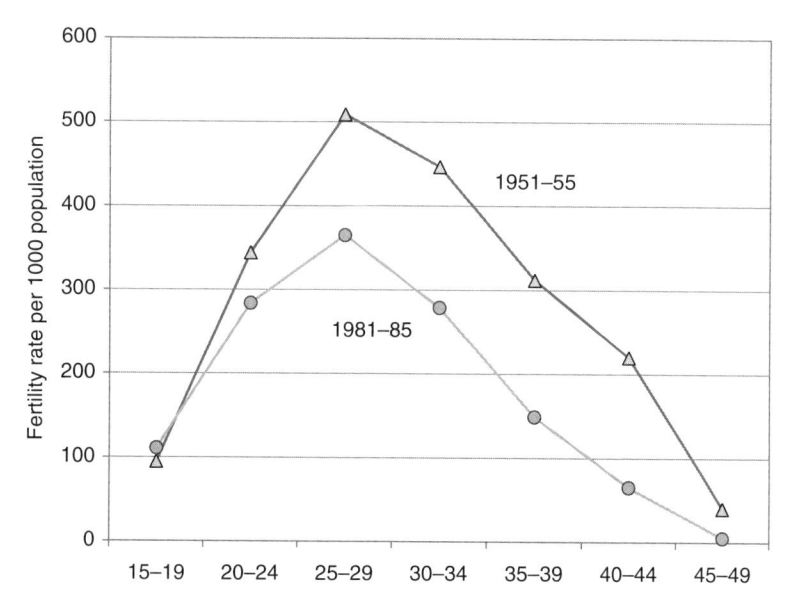

Figure 4.2 Annual Age Specific (Nuptial) Fertility Rates for Dariusleut Hutterites, 1961–5 and 1981–5.
Source: Nonaka and Peter (1994), Table 2.

Yet, there is evidence that the Hutterites did take actions that limited their fertility. Marriage before the age of 20 was/is discouraged. Also, while Hutterite women spend less time breast-feeding, compared to the surrounding population, the *post-partum* infertility gap does, nevertheless, lengthen with the age of the mother. Figure 4.2 presents the married fertility rate of one of the distinct Hutterite groups. In 1951–5, young married Hutterite women between the ages 20 to 24 years (inclusive) each gave birth to approximately 2.5 children – an age specific fertility rate of 509 per 1000. Yet, what is also evident is that the relatively stable fertility pattern has changed in more recent times. Even the Hutterites are moderating their historically high fertility. Exactly what led to the recent fertility decline cannot be identified with great assurance. Increased birth spacing, especially among older women, points to a lengthened period of post-partum infertility (longer time breast feeding), abstinence and even some forms of birth control.[9] We may also conjecture that the lack of cheap land on which to set up new "colonies" has acted as a brake on fertility (new colonies tended to be established after the settled location reaches a population total of about 100). Although these communities live in isolation, although not of one another, perhaps, the wider world is having an influence.

So the Hutterites provide us with an important historical instance of a high-fertility regime, possibly the highest fecundity ever for a relative stable population. We now know the upper bound. Furthermore, their experience indicates the main questions to be asked:

1. If there were resource (income) constraints, how did fertility adjust?
2. How did populations limit births before the availability of cheap and effective artificial contraception?
3. How does the advent of artificial contraception alter fertility patterns?
4. Were changes in the fertility pattern related to changes in mortality (remember that the Hutterite history of recent years has been that of a low mortality regime)?

Hutterite fertility was, nevertheless, outdone by exceptions such as Queen Anne, an outlier even in her own time. Her continuing pregnancies, as noted earlier, left her with only one child who survived infancy. This suggests that the *completed family size* is a key determinant of fertility. In order to see how this works we need a model.

4.3 Strategic Choice

For most of history the provision for the care of the elderly has been the responsibility of the younger, working generation. At the family level an *implicit contract* has been agreed. At the nation-state level the contract might be explicit and guaranteed in law such as old-age benefits, social insurance or tax concessions. However, the working-age generation finances not one but two generations of non-workers; the elderly and the young. Earlier we saw how the balance between the young and the elderly has changed in recent history. Philip Neher has suggested that we view this in a three-generation context.[10] The working generation will progress on to become non-workers, or retirees, just as the young will become workers, as the generations move on.

A peasant farmer, with a fixed plot of land, generates income, a farm crop, when labor is applied. This crop is also income to the farmer. The income can be wholly consumed by the farmer (the marginal propensity to consume = 1) or partly transferred as consumption to the elderly and the young. The redistribution of consumption to the young may be regarded as saving. Even in its simplest expression this gives rise to a fairly complex optimization problem for the working generation farmer. First, there is the constraint of providing for the older generation as seen in Figure 4.3. The desired level of the transfer of income is presumably beyond the bare minimum for existence since the older generation's experience will be the working parents' in the future – that is the nature of the implicit contract. However, if family income falls, as it might do with a fall of agricultural prices, all will be subject to a decline in the transfer. How they share the family cutbacks is itself not a straightforward problem. Second is the problem of selecting the number of children to have. The working parents know that the transfer of income to the young varies directly with the number of children. It too may vary from time to time with the family's income receipts. So

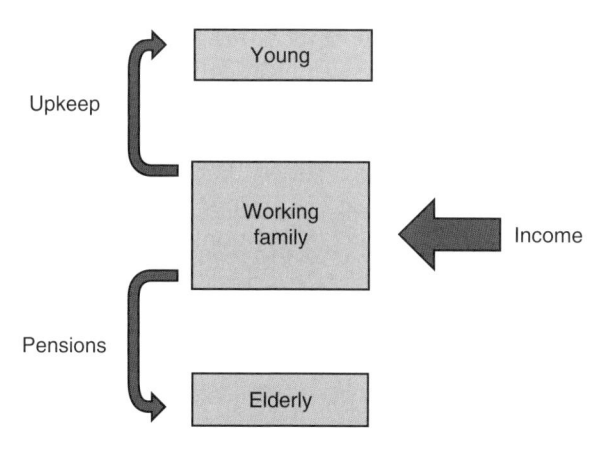

Figure 4.3 Intergenerational Income Transfers and Implicit Pensions.

the parent's consumption goes down by the transfer of consumption to the old and the young. The working parents also wish to avoid having too many mouths to feed because that exposes them, and the others, to the subsistence margin.

But, as the parents think ahead, there is the issue of how many children are required to secure comfort in their old age yet not degrade their current income to poverty levels, that is, what is the optimal number of children. In this sense, fertility is said to be endogenous.[11] But in a traditional society only male children can provide for the next generation; females move on to become part of someone else's household. Approximately one in two children born will be female (in a large sample). In addition, one in two children will die before age 20 (again, in a large sample in a pre-industrial society). Therefore the problem is to have sufficient children to guarantee at least one male surviving to age 20. The combination of gender and survival of the young may induce some insurance taking in the form of more children which ultimately proves to be unnecessary for the goal of funding retirement. This is the difference between expected or *ex ante* and actual or *ex post* outcomes. Any increase in the actual number of children (or their greater longevity) causes the transfer of consumption to the young to rise. This does not mean that the optimal family has four births of children to ensure one male survival. The reason is that children are also workers while they are in the household and as long as their (net) marginal product is positive there will be an income benefit for the family. So even if working with a fixed acreage of land there may be economic reasons for having larger families.

As extended by Mukesh Eswaran, the model gives a framework for explaining a fertility transition. A radical change in the mortality of the young will take several generations to convince peasant farmers to lower family fertility and assure them that the drop in mortality is permanent.[12] That is, the peasant farmer has to be convinced by the evidence of survival that the lowering of the expected number of children will not prejudice his own retirement. To maintain the high fertility in the face of a decline in the mortality of children reduces current consumption of the working adults (with a constant income) by more than is necessary. The (net) marginal product of extra children is now negative. But as emphasized in the last chapter, another reason for maintaining a relatively high fertility regime is the extreme volatility of the death rate in a high mortality regime. So, for the farmer to change his plans, not only does the infant mortality have to fall but there must be evidence of a fall in its variance.

Critics of this approach claim that the model above is too simple. First, it does not take into account that children may be desired for other reasons. Families do not live in social isolation but are part of a larger society. For instance, in a traditional society the number of sons might ensure a gain in prestige just as more daughters provide more opportunities for strategic economic relationships with other families. These political relationships can be a means of acquiring more resources, thereby increasing family income. They can also be a form of economic insurance. Second, and in the same vein, there may be dynastic concerns of a political nature in a society where power is exercised by the number of loyal warriors. This of course can backfire as in the famous case of Henry II of England and his sons. Ordinarily, the number of children is a way of ensuring the power to control and maintain resources. Third, if children are viewed as a retirement compensation scheme, even in traditional societies there may be other assets that are superior. For example, a reduction in the number of dependants might permit saving (the MPC<1).[13] The saving could be put to the purchase of these assets. These then could yield a return for subsequent retirement or be sold-off as the occasion demanded or both. Even in a traditional economy there were surprisingly many assets that could be acquired; the acquisition of land (rights) probably among the most common. Some medieval monasteries in Europe even offered annuities to peasant farmers. For a tithe of a percentage of gross receipts for most of the working life, the religious house would guarantee support in old age. Over time, as commerce developed and spread and industrialization took place, there were more and varied savings vehicles, assets that could be held. That is, while there was a lack of a market to provide the exact savings vehicles for the provision of pensions, there were alternative savings instruments.

Children are valued for many reasons within a family. The decision-making about whether to give birth to a child or not is intensely personal and is governed by many factors: economic, social, psychological and biological. Yet, taken together, there is a remarkable similarity in the human reaction to these forces at any moment in history with similar background conditions. Becker in his many writings on the economics of the family has used these similarities to systematize this aspect of human behavior.[14] With this in mind, we can think of children as yielding certain benefits and incurring costs. Some of the benefits are economic, as in the model of peasant behavior noted in the last section. But some of the benefits may be psychological – the sheer pleasure of having the little darlings around. These non-pecuniary benefits, nonetheless, can be valued in the foregone opportunity sense. What non-child benefit was given up for the psychological benefit of having a child? Similarly, there is a set of costs associated with having and maintaining children. This means that we can think of the demand for child as a response to their prevailing price where the price is measured as the benefits minus costs.

Benefits and costs, however, are not instantaneous but will occur throughout the life of the child and are flows over time. In the equation below:

PV = the present value
B = expected value of benefit; time is indicated by the subscript.

i = the discount rate
C = expected cost which results from a child; and

$$PV = B_0 - C_0 + \frac{B_1 - C_1}{1+i} + \frac{B_2 - C_2}{(1+i)^2} + \frac{B_3 - C_3}{(1+i)^3} + \cdots\cdots + \frac{B_n - C_n}{(1+i)^n}$$

The benefits and costs of the child are summed over the life of the child in a discounted fashion. That is, the marginal rate of time preference (i) means, from today's perspective, benefits in the future are worth less than those of today. So are costs. The discount rate represents the alternative use of resources over time, the opportunity cost. So a Present Value (PV) is calculated. However, the parents considering whether or not to have a child do not know the *actual* future benefits and costs; they are not actual values, because they lie in the future, but *expected* ones.

The benefits can be summarized as:

- the future pension-like benefits that the child will confer;
- children's future repayment of rearing costs – other than pension benefits;
- the current income and imputed earning possibilities of the child; and
- the imputed psychic income derived from the child.

Whereas, the costs are itemized as:

- housing;
- rearing (food and clothing);
- supervisory;
- education; and
- opportunity cost of spouse (women) not working or scaling back of workload.

In modern, western society the PV term may well be negative if we assume the pension benefit is zero (there are superior saving vehicles) and measure the income flows implications and the non-cash imputed psychic income benefits. Xavier Mateos-Planas calls the PV term "the net cost of children parameter" when accounting for modern fertility patterns, neglecting the benefits as minor and giving no weight to the psychological benefits.[15] In history, however, these benefits and costs could be relatively large and subject to change especially when we give weight to Neher's pension argument. Prior to the industrial transition and the major sectoral shifts when most income was derived in agriculture, the configuration of benefits were relatively larger and the costs smaller. For instance, young children could be set to farm tasks at an early age such as gathering eggs from the henhouse. Older girls could act as gooseherds or shepherdesses. Older boys could contribute to the manual labor of the farm. Since these tasks disappear with urbanization as the sectors located in the towns and cities gain importance, the children's income earning possibilities change in character and are likely to be zero until a later age.[16]

Costs also differed with the industrial composition of the economy. As the economy became more urbanized, the cost of housing became more expensive per square meter. This resulted in higher housing costs and more densely populated dwellings, exactly the characteristics that gave rise to the unhealthy nature of cities prior to the late 19th century. Many costs also became explicit once the family was located in an urban center. A vegetable garden (tended by children) in the rural areas could provide an income benefit that in a town or city was replaced by an additional food cost. Supervisory costs were also different in a rural and urban landscape. Older children could look after their younger siblings in the relative freedom of the country whereas in the urban areas supervisory costs were higher and were not relegated so easily. They, like food costs, took on an explicit nature requiring cash (income). Thus, the economies of scale in family size were less obvious in the towns and cities. Indeed, there may have been diseconomies of scale in family formation. Last, with the rise of individual real income there were possible expenditures denied to earlier generations the most important of which was childhood education. In summary, the history of fertility's benefits and costs to the family is the history of i) urbanization, ii) the economics of the family unit, and iii) the rise of real income per capita.

4.4 When to Marry

The Hutterites, as we have seen, abstained from pre-marital sex with the result that almost no children were born to very young mothers. In general, in most societies where children are born within a marriage, delayed sexual contact reduced the "at risk" factor to have children. It also reduced the risk of setting up a new family or household before the economic basis for a new family was secure. Before the advent of artificial birth control and a full understanding of the female fertility cycle, unanticipated pregnancies did occur but, if both parties were unencumbered, a marriage was hastily arranged in normal circumstances. In Shakespeare's time, the average age of (first) marriage was 26.0 for a woman and 28.0 for a male.[17] So much for Juliet, as Peter Laslett has commented.[18] At the end of the 20th century, the age at first marriage for females was 27.1 and for males 29.1 years.[19] Within a narrow range the secular trend is remarkably stable over long periods of time as seen in Figure 4.4. But, as this figure also implies, there were short-run variations from the trend to which, according to Wrigley and Schofield, the gross reproduction rate was sensitive in the late 18th century.[20] The decline in the age at marriage that took place in the early 19th century was a departure from this fairly constant trend, but it appears only in the English data and is temporary. However, the general trend was not significantly different from the pattern of most Western European countries of the 19th century as illustrated in Table 4.1. So the high age at marriage, relative to the start of the female reproductive life, did limit fertility; it had a rationale in the economics of the family. Even though one of the major trends in this period was urbanization Nicholas Crafts found that there is a very weak relationship between the changes in the age at marriage and urbanization, not enough prior to 1850 to influence the rate of growth of the English population.[21]

There were no legal or societal prohibitions on very early marriage in England (or Italy) of the early 1600s and presumably also in earlier periods. However, there were significant practical limitations rooted in the economics of the family. Those who could afford to marry at a very early age, and were so disposed, were those who could escape the income constraint of the ordinary family. This mainly applied to élite, high-income families and to female members of that class of folk. Of course marriage could

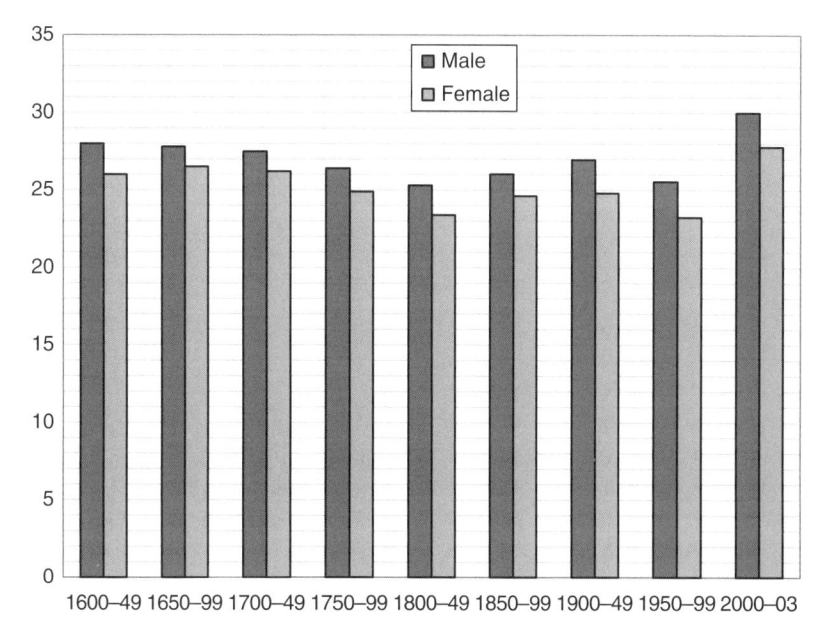

Figure 4.4 Mean Age at First Marriage, England 1600–2003.
Note: The above are 50-year means except for the last period. There is a conflict in the English data based on different measurements and samples. The Wrigley and Schofield data record a much sharper drop in 19th century rates whereas the Census from 1851 shows a consistently higher figure, a figure that accords more with the European continental Census data (see Table 4.1).
Source: Wrigley and Schofield (1981), 255, Table 7.26; UK (current), *National Statistics* on-line: http://www.statistics.gov.uk.

also cement strategic alliances between families and be part of a broader contract to the transfer of property. So, Juliet's mother who urged her daughter to marry (some bloke other than Romeo) was voicing an option not wholly unusual for a rich family. More variation of *planned* marriage at early ages was expected. The age at first marriage is essential information as it determines the "at risk" factor to have children. The longer marriage is postponed the shorter the period in a traditional marriage and the fewer the children.

In early North America, under conditions of relative land abundance which are often described as non-Malthusian, we would predict a lower age at marriage. This did indeed occur but not by as much as might be expected. In France's main colony of New France, in the early 18th century, the mean age of first marriage was 22.9 for females and 26.9 for males.[22] This, as Jacques Henripin has pointed out, was far from the upper bound fecundity. It led to a population doubling in about 30 years whereas with greater fertility, in the range of TFP = 13, the population would have doubled in 22 years – see Figure 4.1. Denied an inflow of immigration, New France's official policy was to encourage early marriage, but it had only a small effect.[23] In British colonial North America, there was a substantial flow of immigration so that the population grew much more rapidly. There were simply more people and more in the age range of peak fecundity.[24] Colonial America (US) too had a lower age at marriage compared to England in the same period, but it was very similar to that of New France. It also was more variable by location and it changed more

Table 4.1 Age at (First) Marriage for Selected Western Countries, 19th Century.

		(mean age)					
	Period	Male	Female		Period	Male	Female
Italy	1861	27.3	23.5	England	1816		25.5
	1871	27.3	23.3		1851	26.9	25.8
	1881	28.2	24.1		1871	26.4	25.1
	1901	27.7	24.1		1891	27.1	26.0
Spain	1797	24.5	23.2	Ireland***	1861	30.1	26.7
	1887	27.0	24.2		1871	30.2	26.4
	1900	27.4	24.5		1881	30.9	27.3
France	1800–9	28.4	26.3		1891	31.6	28.2
	1820–9	27.5	26.0	Germany	1880	28.1	25.5
	1850–9	28.1	24.9	Norway	1851–5	28.7	27.1
	1870–9	28.0	24.3		1861–5	29.2	27.2
	1890–9	27.8	24.1		1871–5	28.7	26.6
USA*	1850	25.3**	21.3*		1886–95	28.2	26.4
	1860	25.0**	21.4**	Canada#	1858–60	24.4	20.6
	1880	26.8	23.1		1871–5	25.0	21.4
	1890	27.6	23.6		1881–5	25.8	22.5
	1900	27.4	23.7		1891–5	25.6	22.9

Note: * USA Singulate age for all races. ** Median age for whites only. *** Post-famine.
\# Data from Ontario for those born in Canada only. If we include the foreign-born the means are higher for both males and female.
Source: US, *Bureau of Census*; Rettaroli (1990), Table 1, 412; Ward (1990), Table A-1.

over time. The mean age of marriage, particularly that of women, started much lower than that in England in the 1600s, but it increased so that there was little to distinguish the colonies and the mother country in this regard by the time of the revolution – see Table 4.2.[25] Location and the passage of time, however, may be the same thing. When any location in the colonies became more densely populated and the frontier of settlement retreated westward, the cost of establishing an independent household rose as the price of land increased. The ability to set up an independent household, or its near prospect, was normally a pre-requisite for a marriage to take place. In addition to the rise in age of marriage there was a decline in completed family size within marriage pointing to some further deliberate family limitation.[26]

The implications from the evidence of the age at marriage are conclusive:

- Fertility at the start of the transition was already regulated (lower than it could have been) by the high mean age at first marriage.
- The great fertility transition came about without any substantial alteration in the age at first marriage.

Changes in fertility resulted from married couples choosing to have fewer children, that is, the TFP of married women fell. The only other demographic explanation would

Table 4.2 Age at Marriage for Several Locations in Colonial US, 17th and 18th Centuries.

	Males	Females	Place
1652–1700	27.2	21.1	Ipswich, Mass.
1700–1749	27.6	23.9	Northampton, Mass.
1750–1799	28.5	25.5	Northampton, Mass.
1756–1785	26.8	23.4	Quakers (Middle Colony)
1781–1800	26.3	24.5	Hingham, Mass.

Note: The numbers include only white individuals (data for blacks is not available for this period) and exclude "immigrants" although new settlers will be included in the various locations. Some low ages of marriage were reported for females only and these tended to be in samples drawn from the élite populations in Virginia and Maryland.
Source: adapted from Wells (1992), Table 1, 88–89.

be that the marriage rate was declining. There were, however, no long-term changes in the proportions of single males and females getting married. Yet, there were, as noted earlier, some important short-run variations in the marriage rate. There are also two such oddities in the recent phases of the fertility transition in North America and Europe. First was the rapid decline in the in the age at first marriage, particularly of women, beginning in the middle of the 20th century – see Figure 4.5. Second is the remarkable reversal of this decline in the last quarter of the century and which continues today. Yet, throughout this gyration in the age of marriage, fertility continued to fall.

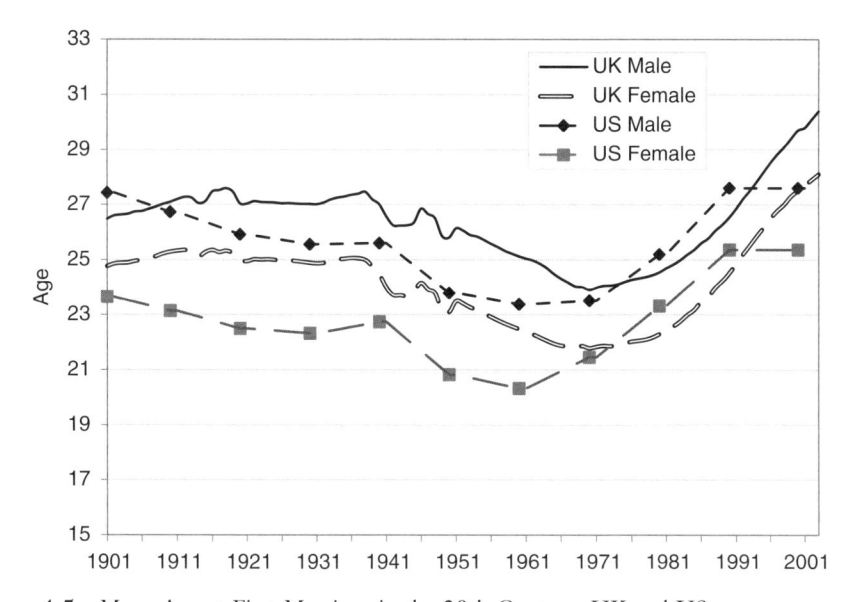

Figure 4.5 Mean Age at First Marriage in the 20th Century, UK and US.
Note: The differences in the age structure because of immigration to the US generate more marriages in the young age group which draws down the US mean.
Sources: UK (current), *National Statistics*, On-line and US (current), *Bureau of the Census*.

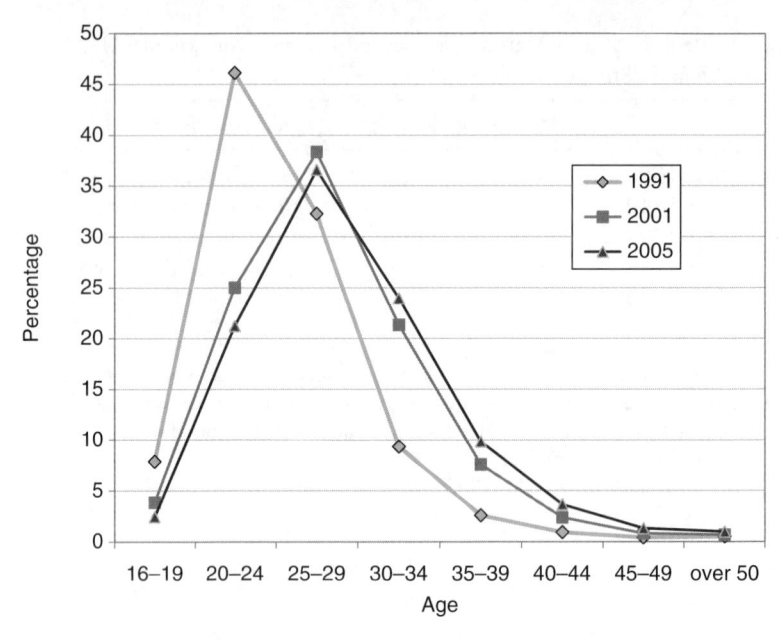

Figure 4.6 Percentage of Marriages of First Married Couples by Age of Bride for England and Wales, 1991, 2001 and 2006.
Source: UK (current), *National Statistics* On-line.

It seems that the decreasing age at marriage was a result of the change in social mores that accompanied the post-World War II years. We may hypothesize that, as marriage became more about companionship and less about children, more people took the non-marriage option. The non-marriage option was chosen at first by those with higher levels of education and higher levels of income. This left lower income individuals, those who tended to get married at a younger age, more prevalent in the marriage market dragging the mean age downward. With the increased spread of cheap contraceptive techniques beginning in the 1960s, these individuals too began to eschew marriage and this caused the age at marriage to rise. Marriage is not considered a necessary social option by many as we have seen (Chapter Two). The evidence is found in the marriage rate by age of first marriage. The recent figures for England and Wales are typical for most Western European and North American countries. In 1991 about 46% of all first marriages were in the age range 20 to 24 years of age (of bride); by 2005 it had fallen to 21%. In marked contrast, the first marriage rate of the 30 to 34 years of age group increased to a staggering 24% from 15% in the same period.[27] As seen Figure 4.6, the first marriage profile by age has become less peaked in recent times reflecting the change in social circumstances. There is some evidence to suggest that in the past marriage caused children – although there were exceptions to this tendency as noted later. Now, it is increasingly the case that children cause marriage.[28]

The late age of marriage of women relative to their reproductive cycles and the proportion of the female population that "never married" were both fertility limiting behaviors. They were evident long before the demographic transition got underway. However, the same fertility limiting results were also achieved, in the case of China, but by other means. First, most evidence from Chinese history before the mid-20th century presents a strong cultural preference for male children.[29] Surviving male children were necessary for their role in ancestor worship, for instance. This also explains the high rate of male adoption. The male preference was reflected in the sex ratio. There is, however, no convincing evidence of wide-spread female infanticide. It did occur but only in times of economic stress. Rather, female children were given a lower level of care than males, especially in the first year of life, and consequently died more frequently – much as seen in parts of the world today where there is an otherwise unexplained gender imbalance, see Chapter Eleven. This, according to James Lee and Feng Wong, led to several effects.[30] First, there was competition among the males for the available women whose fates were largely controlled by a traditional family. As a consequence the age at first marriage of females was much lower than that found in the contemporary western society. The age of males at first marriage was about the same. Recall that the pattern of marriage in the west was generally that of the males and females in the same age range with males usually only a couple of year older than the females. Second, the sex ratio imbalance led to a cohort of unmarried men! And, there were relatively few unmarried females.[31]

Chinese fertility was lower than it otherwise would have been due to the lost fertility of the missing females. Offset against that was the high proportion of females who did marry – a lower "never married" rate than that of the west. Yet, alone the missing females and high proportion of women who did marry would not be enough to account for the lower than expected rate of growth of the Chinese population in the years after 1700 (abnormally high mortality has been rejected by most researchers). While the married females spent more time at risk to bear children than their western sisters the marital fertility of Chinese females was about 30 to 40% lower than that of the Europeans. There being no good evidence of wide-spread abortion practices, the burden of explanation lies either with greater periods of *lactational amenorrhea* or with a reduced rate of marital coital frequency. Maybe the greater age difference between the partners and the fact that most were arranged marriages influenced the latter.[32]

The Chinese path to, and through, the demographic transition offers an appealing variant of a now well-known process. In charting its course researchers now dismiss the long-held notion, attributed to Malthus, that mortality played the positive check role in limiting the growth of the population. The balance of argument is now on the preventative checks of fertility limitation. That being so, the economic history question that goes begging is: was there a growth in agriculture income (productivity) that would explain the demographic behaviour?

4.5 The "Never Married"

While limiting the number of children by postponing marriage (relative to the start of reproductive cycle in both men and women) fertility was also below potential by the fact that some individuals neither married nor cohabited. This historically could arise for several reasons. Some people did not get married because their sexual preferences were same-sex or that they were in a profession or vocation that demanded celibacy such as the church orders (nuns, monks and priests). There were also those who because of mental or physical infirmity were unattractive marriage partners and remained single. And, there were undoubtedly those who simply did not wish to marry and for whom the religious alternative was not attractive. Perhaps the greatest impediment to marriage, however, was a general imbalance in the gender ratio. In any country there may not be enough members of the opposite sex, generally in the same age range, to satisfy the demand for spouses. The very unbalanced sex ratio in early French Canada was noted earlier (Chapter Two). However, most frequently it was the absence of males that was a problem. Males were more likely to be military casualties in wars. France lost approximately 1.4 million men in the Napoleonic Wars and this unbalanced the sex ratio sufficiently that it affected the age structure of the population for decades in echo-like phenomena.[33]

Many other countries suffered the same fate such as Russia after World War II. France recorded about 1.3 million direct military and 0.25 million non-military deaths in 1914–18.[34] Since most deaths were of males, the sex ratio in the age range 20–40 years of age was particularly distorted. Overall the French sex ratio dropped from 0.967 (male to female) to 0.906 over the years from 1911 to 1921.[35] This was almost three times the drop in the UK sex ratio.[36] France lost the "demographic resiliency inherent in a young and fertile population".[37] Interestingly, the secondary sex ratio (the percentage of males born to total births) often is observed to increase temporarily in the aftermath of war. This appears to be the result of increased coital frequency *and* the increased likelihood of males being born when conceived in the earlier stages of the female monthly fertility cycle.[38]

Even if the sex ratio was about one there could be local gender imbalances that do not show up in the aggregate record (although it could be revealed by micro-level inspection). This is most likely when, apart from unattached young men, local populations display little geographic mobility. Marriage is a phenomenon that is essentially local in character. People married those they knew or met and with whom they formed a relationship. Men were historically more mobile than females and tended to enter the migration stream more frequently – to the towns and to other countries. For instance, the migration of males from the farms to the towns tended to leave more women in the rural areas and an excess supply of males in the cities and towns. Local gender imbalance was a barrier to family formation and caused the lowering of the local marriage rate. In such circumstances, men would return home to seek a wife or, perhaps, send for a female of known acquaintance. But sending home for a bride unknown to the potential groom was relatively rare. (Even arranged marriages, where the principals have not first met, tended to be local but also extremely rare in Western Europe and North America.)

The marriage market, as discussed in Chapter Seven, was far from perfect, resulting in a certain group of people who never married. Also the economic circumstances of a male may make marriage prospects slight. The long training period of apprenticeships, for instance, and their onerous, time-consuming duties prevented marriage by denying the pay that could support a new marriage as an independent household. Often it was a violation of an apprentice's contract to marry before completion of service. In the case of women the care of elderly parents or younger siblings often blocked the female's chances of finding a mate.

The British Census of 1861 reveals that over most English counties between 10 to 15% of women aged 45 to 49 were spinsters (never married).[39] A similarly high proportion of men did not marry. This was common throughout Western Europe.[40] Some of these women, but not many, did marry in subsequent years for companionship and income and wealth sharing and not for the reason of having children. Jane Austen's young English women of the late 18th and early 19th centuries were obsessed, as were their mothers, by the prospects of marriage and the financial security it brought. Her heroines were of course non-working women of the minor landed gentry. What her romances illustrate is how narrowly defined class distinctions constrained the choices of both women and men. For different reasons, but related to income prospects, class gradations of the lower income members of society also defined the choice set.[41] As class barriers tended to weaken the never married proportions tended to fall slightly. The changes in class distinctions which we might date to the early 20th century changed this. For instance, during the First World War the mortality rate of young officers was extremely high and substantially reduced the marriage prospects of a similar (upper-middle) class of young women. However, there is no evidence to suggest any significant effect on the marriage rate of this class of women, as one might expect. They revised their expectations ("lowered" their standards) and did get married. Did the weakening of class barriers, as happened during the war, permit this or did the desire to get married weaken the class barriers? Cause and effect are not clear. What is evident is the general tendency for a while for English women to marry older men, presumably a result of the shortage caused by the carnage of the young men in war.[42]

In North America the proportion of the never married was always lower than that in Western Europe.[43] Even when the age at marriage caught up with the English one in the early 19th century there was still a greater overall fertility as the proportion of fecund married couples was greater.[44] At the same time that the English never married rate was in the range of 10% to 15% the United States registered about half that amount.[45] All the indirect evidence is consistent that this was also true of the 17th and 18th centuries. More resources in the form of farm land bettered income prospects and encouraged marriage. The rise of the never married proportions of the white population over the late 19th and early 20th centuries probably is a result of the geographic dislocation associated with the rapid change in the structure of the economy. As Figure 4.7 also illustrates, we get a window into the marriages of the black population of the US. There were demonstrably fewer men and women left unmarried than in the white population. Black women, at least until the mid-20th century, were less likely than their white sisters to become unwed spinsters. For both black and white men and women the proportion of their populations which never married was far from constant although it changed least for black women. On the other hand, the proportion of black men showed the greatest short-term instability. We reconcile these two observations by noting that the black marriage rate (where both partners were black) must too have been more variable than the white marriage rate. This had led the demographers Catherine Fitch and Steven Ruggles to conjecture a relationship between the rise in the *median* age at first marriage and the rise in the never married proportion.

From 1960, as we have seen, everything changed. The black population of the US was beginning to explore a greater range of occupations with longer periods of education. The general reaction of Black Americans was the radical postponement of marriage to a later date. The single best correlate of an increasing age of marriage is the time spent in education.[46] Apart from the never married there were other historical population members

Figure 4.7 Percentage of the Native-Born Population (Aged 45–54) Which Never Married, 1850–2000.
Note: Census data and those for 2000 are actually 1999).
Source: data from Fitch and Ruggles (2000), 85.

who were *not married*. These were the widows and widowers. With the high mortality of adults, the death of a spouse before expected was a more frequent event than today.

4.6 Illegitimacy

Violation of the widespread convention of no pre-marital sex involved major social sanctions if revealed. But the violation could also be overlooked or, at least, made right. Evidence drawn from several London parishes in the late 16th and early 17th centuries suggests about 17% of women were pregnant at the time of marriage. This was probably a little *less* than for the country as a whole.[47] The social stigma of "bastardry" for the child and the social estrangement of the mother were thus avoided. While it also solved the problem of child support, there was a huge economic penalty for the young couple since it required them to set-up a new household (family) before they were financially able – that is, when they otherwise would have chosen not to do so. This high percentage of marriages by pregnant women varied from time to time in history, just as the overall marital fertility did, but it also varied by regions and countries, at least until very recent times.

Of course, illegitimate births did happen. Throughout history many illegitimate births went unrecorded and many of these children were simply absorbed into the large families with, we presume, the appropriate "lies" told to any inquiring official. Social norms and religious attitudes, which were frequently different by class, determined the degree of social odium suffered by the child and its mother. Women bore the main brunt of the often brutal economic and social consequences. Even for married women in colonial Massachusetts, for instance, any births within 32 weeks of marriage often resulted in the public condemnation of illegal "fornication."[48] The overwhelming economic characteristic of those who gave birth to illegitimate children was that they were poor. They were the parents who could not afford to legitimize the child through a marriage. Extra-marital affairs also produced children and poverty. Only a small proportion of illegitimate births were the product of liaisons of the well-to-do with working-class women in which case the child and mother were occasionally provided for. Most were not. The celebrated, but impecunious, poet Robert Burns was the father of seven illegitimate children in his lifetime. In 1785/6 alone, he fathered three illegitimate children (one set of twins) by two different women. He was courting a third who may have been pregnant at the time of her premature death later in the year. At the same time he also published the famous Kilmarnock Edition of his poems. It was a busy year!

Despite the changes in social attitudes to pre-marital sex and the legal changes in the rights of the child and its mother, the white illegitimacy rate in North Carolina, for instance, was roughly comparable in 1970 to that estimated from the Census of 1850.[49] In England the rate of illegitimacy rose through the late 18th century and then declined in the second half of the 19th century and continued that course into the first half of the next, roughly coincident with the great fertility decline. But in the years following 1940 it rose again to about its historical levels. The reasons for this apparent cycle are not well understood. For the first phase of the cycle, attempts to link the illegitimacy rate to the changes in real wages have proven fruitless. But most observers still maintain that there was a link between the rise of working class incomes and the decline of illegitimacy. Peter Laslett, who has written extensively on illegitimacy in history, estimates that that at its historical zenith in the second quarter of the 19th century the birth of illegitimate children accounted for between 5.0 to 6.5% of all births.[50] This is consistent with the illegitimacy ratios for the US and North West Europe. At the same time, in some countries and regions the ratio was much higher, 9.5% in Scotland, for instance.[51] Within each country there was a wide disparity in the regional illegitimacy ratios.[52]

Today in society in Western Europe and North America, the older definitions of illegitimacy hardly apply. However, if one persists in using them, they reveal a remarkable rise in the illegitimacy ratio. The reason for this rise (and the abandonment of the older definitions) is, of course, that many people are choosing to have children outside the traditional scope of marriage. Many of these children are, nonetheless, part of functioning families. So using the data (where it actually exists) and projecting backwards makes little historical sense. Yet, there is still a problem: unanticipated births to single mothers do occur and single mothers with children are among the lowest in the income distribution of families.

4.7 The Seasonal Pattern of Birth

Just as there was a seasonality of death, there was a distinct pattern in the births of children that varied over the year. It took the form of a regular cycle of births, by month. The birth cycle tended to shift over time. In pre-modern times in both Europe

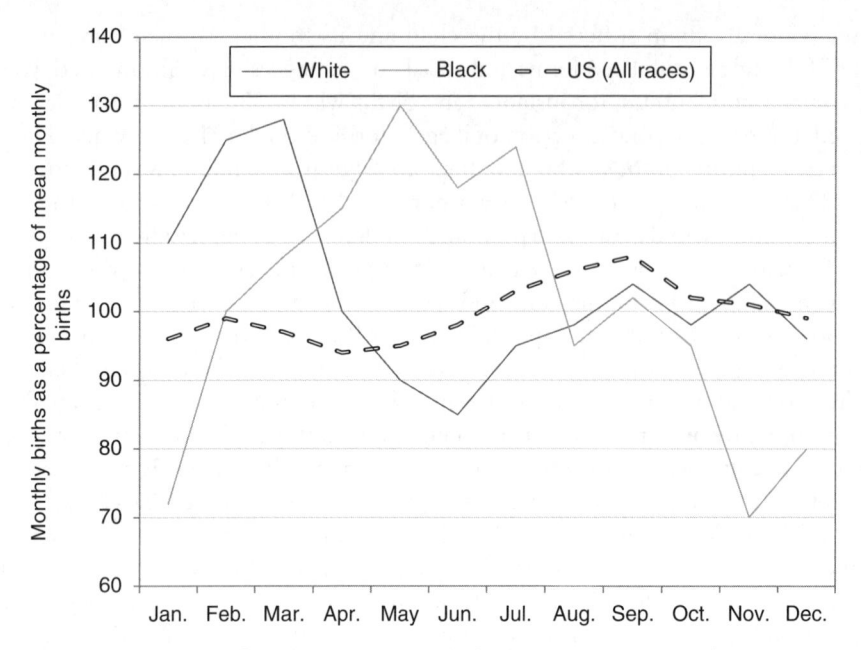

Figure 4.8 The Timing of Births: White and Black Births in Virginia, 1651–1744 and US Births (All Races), 1947–1976.
Source: data are from Middlesex County, Virginia and US. Based on Rutman, Wetherell, and Rutman (2001), 324 and Seiver (1989), 90.

and North America the cycle rose to its highest level in late winter and early spring (March–April). For instance, in North America in the 17th and 18th centuries, evidence from Virginia shows that the births of white children usually peaked in March but that the births of black children in peaked somewhat later May.[53] In recent history (1947–1976 seen in Figure 4.8), however, the average peak births in the US occurred in September/October and this, in turn, implies a changed pattern of coital frequency, nine months earlier. In the early period, the coital frequency was highest in the summer months. The harvest-time tumbles in the hay led to pregnancies that were obvious in a few months and, as a consequence, an increased frequency of early winter unions and late winter births. Coital frequency is now highest in the early to mid-winter period.

The shift in the US seasonality of births rests on the change in coital frequency and calls up several, offsetting considerations. First, modern research has shown that very high ambient temperature and humidity both inhibit the rate of coital frequency and lower sperm counts in the males. Second, the seasonality of births has distinct regional patterns. As the US expanded from the Northern and Mid-Atlantic Coast Colonies to include more southern areas, and in the 19th century the US population expanded into these hotter regions, so the *average* for the country became more influenced by the hot climate areas. But, the regional seasonality in the US Northern states also changed, probably in the 19th century, to reflect the same pattern as the US South. The explanation for this, we conjecture, is the earlier lack of personal privacy in the pre-modern house particularly the "bed." Beds and bedrooms were shared and public places: they were not the private places of today. Human modesty caused young couples, married or not, to seek privacy outside the house, and this was more conveniently done in the summertime. As family income increased, space within the household increased and so did the possibility of private moments. At the margin, conception was turned from an outdoor summer sport to an indoor winter one. So the early birth seasonality was brought about by the overriding concern for privacy *despite* the hot weather adverse effect. In very recent years the proliferation of air-conditioning, itself a sign of growing affluence, is thought to be an influence moderating the seasonality of the CBR.[54] The cycle of seasonality in births is much flatter. In Western Europe, however, and generalizing from the evidence for Sweden, peak births occur in March/April suggesting a mid-summer conception. But there, with the lack of prolonged hot weather regimes, the ambient temperature appears not to play a role.[55]

4.8 Disruptions

Unanticipated economic shocks, if they were profound, had almost instant effects on fertility. Take the exogenous shocks that took place in Finland in the 19th century. Finnish CBRs were trending downward in the 19th century. On three distinct occasions harvest failures led to famine. The most severe of these was a harvest failure in 1867/8 which led to a sudden, violent increase in mortality – especially among the young and elderly. Deaths during famines mostly come in the form of communicable disease as the general health of the population declines and Finland was no exception. Since this was a harvest year that witnessed widespread crop deficiencies in Europe and North America the price of grain rose consequently. Imports of grain from the food abundant countries were limited and high priced. The excess deaths, over those that would otherwise be expected, were large, about 100 000 or about 8% of the population.

Some of the deaths were of married individuals and that meant that fewer people were likely to breed. So part of the lost births was made up of those who would have been born in normal circumstances but who weren't because of the death of possible parents. Lost births were also due to men being separated from women as they roamed the countryside in search of employment or food. The marriage rate was also lower as it tended to be in famine-stressed populations. All combined to lower the fertility rate. A weakened population will have more spontaneous terminations of pregnancies and thus the birth rate will be depressed even further. Last, severe malnutrition lowers the levels of the hormones *testosterone* and *leptin* which not only dampen *libido* but made successful pregnancies less likely.[56] Thus the exogenous shock that took the death rate up simultaneously took the birth rate down. However, recent evidence about those children who survived the severe food deprivation and its aftermath, including those *in utero*, suggests that they did not suffer from reduced life expectancy as a group.[57]

As Figure 4.9 shows, the famine of 1867/8 was one of the most severe of the shocks to hit the Finnish people but by no means the only one. As in other famine shocks, local change of the sex ratio as a by-product of the crisis, was quickly restored to normal once the economic *status quo* was restored. The Finnish famine crisis affected young men and young women similarly. However, there are often sex ratio

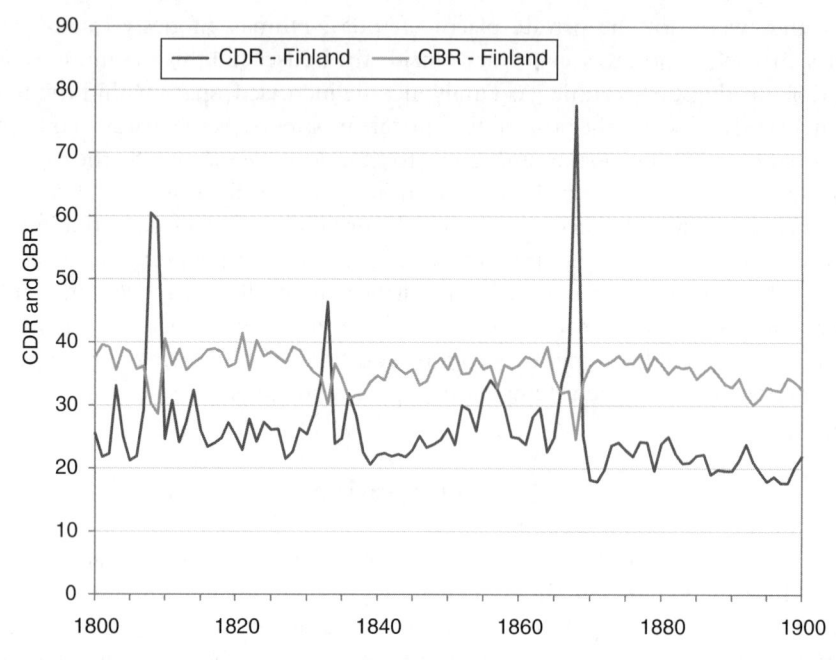

Figure 4.9 Finnish CDRs and CBRs in the 19th Century.
Source: data from Mitchell (2007) *International Historical Statistics*, 93–117 – see General Sources.

changes that take some time to adjust and cause longer periods of disequilibrium. Such was the case in France after World War I, as we have seen. Today in countries such as Somalia and Eritrea, there are people facing food crises who are on the move. Similar to the Finns of a century and a half ago, they are migrating to seek succour, primarily in nearby countries. During a crisis, their marital fertility is much reduced. However, unlike the Finns, these refugees are drawn into a network that may result in their settling in another country. The evidence supports the view that when the refugee group is kept together and material well-being returns to a reasonable level, marital fertility reverts to the norm of the home country. Even when they are dispersed in other countries where there are other co-nationals and co-religionists, there is a tendency for their completed family size to echo normal home conditions. However, as cultural influences become more diffuse, fertility gravitates to the average in the new country.[58]

4.9 The Fertility Transition: Crude Birth Rates

The evidence of the fertility transition in North Western Europe and North America is shown in Figure 4.10. As suggested earlier, the fertility transition was universal but diverse in terms of its timing and extent. Regional and local influences gave each country a slightly different detail but the over-riding causes were the same everywhere and interrelated: changes in per capita income, changes in the structure of output (income) and trade, urbanization, resource availability including land, changes in technology and the knowledge base of society (education), changes in the economic consequences of having children and changes in social attitudes.

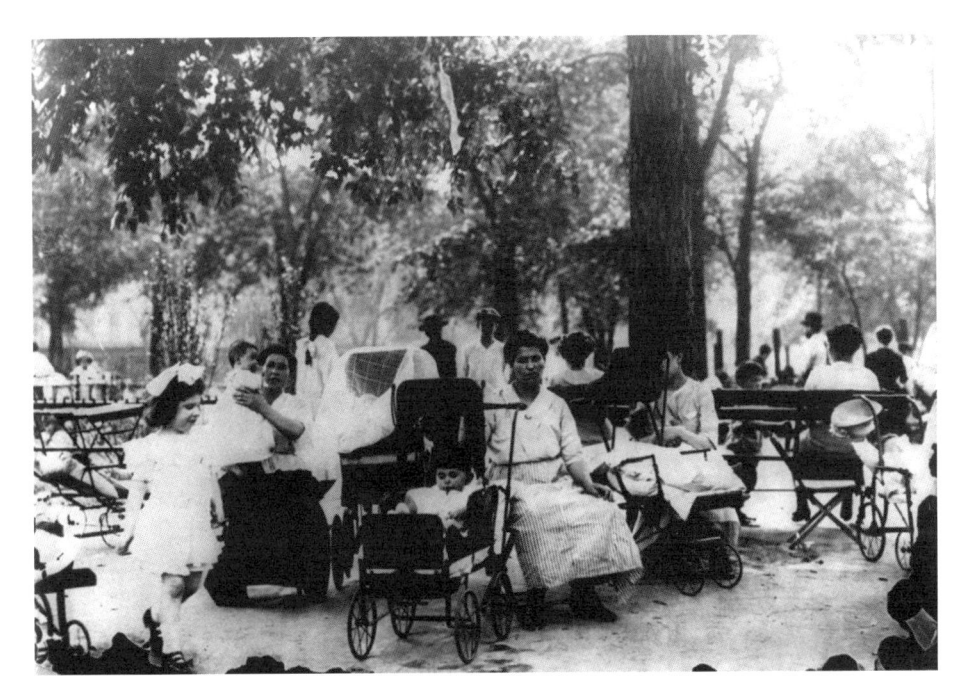

Women and Children, c. 1908

Family sizes were becoming much smaller in the early 20th century. This photo of women (mothers and nannies) and children was taken on a hot day in a New York City park. The clues that indicate that these are fairly affluent families are seen by the state-of-the-art baby carriages and the patent leather shoes worn by the girl in the bottom left.
Source: Library of Congress, Prints and Photographs Division.

The first major distinction is that countries started in 1800 at various levels of birth rates. North America in 1800 had CBRs that were much higher than those found in contemporary Europe. This is not an accident of cutting into the historical series when the countries were at different phases of economic or demographic development. The evidence is scattered, much of it estimated but abundant. All indicates that from the beginning of the white settlement in North America when compared with, for instance, England confirms a CBR gap of roughly 10 to 20 births per thousand. The lowest estimated CBR for the pre-1800 US white population is 47.6 and the highest 55.0.[59] But, as noted earlier and as will be examined later, there were substantial differences in the CBRs between regions. A CBR for the black population is not a relevant comparison prior to the end of slavery in 1865 (although the fertility of the small free black population supports the view that it was not much different from their white neighbors).[60] The highest CBR for pre-1800 England, estimated by Wrigley and Schofield, is 39.8 in 1797 – which is much higher than the retrospective long run average.[61] All countries of Western Europe had similar lower birth rates, or lower, than England.

What gave rise to the greater number of births per 1000 of population in North America? For the early US and its colonial period, the gap between its CBR and that of the old world would have been slightly greater because of the lower female age at first marriage of the North Americans compared to Europe, as discussed earlier. North American women spent more of their lives "at risk" to bear children. This is, however, far

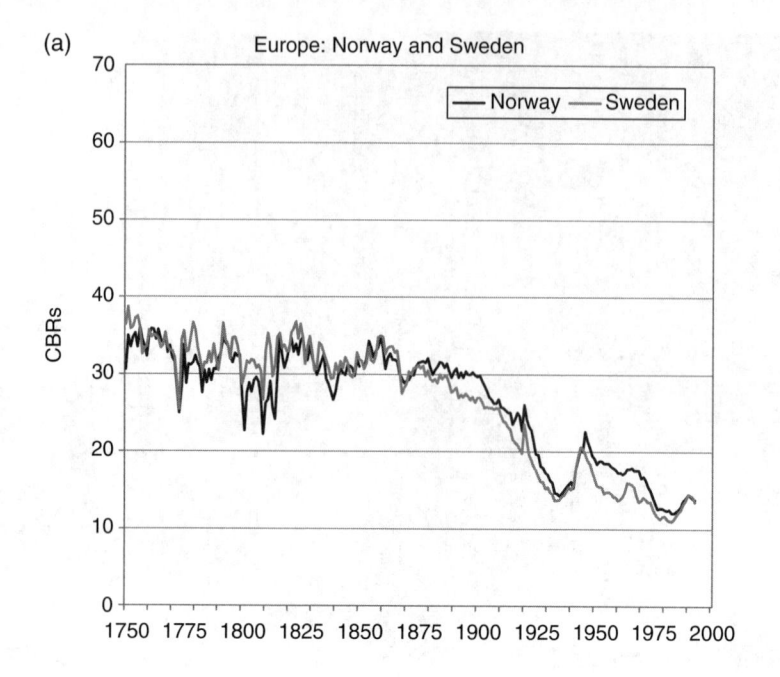

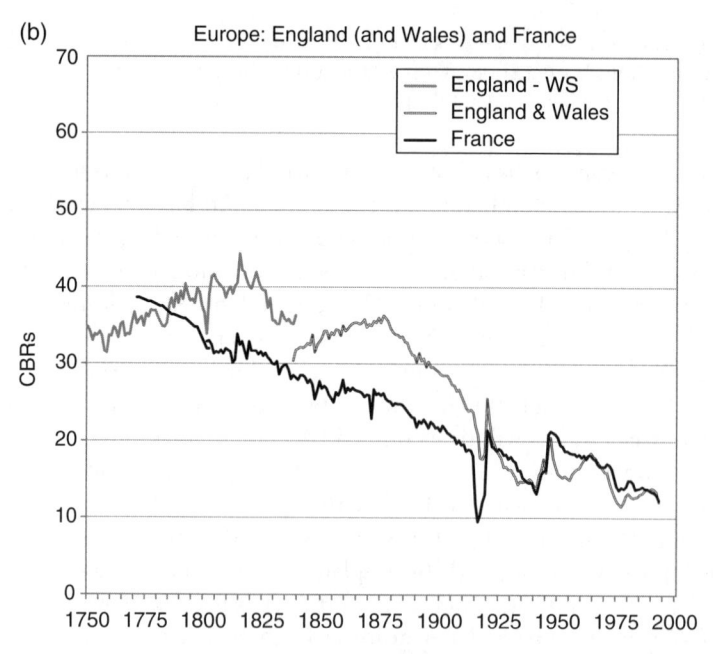

Note: data for England to 1838 from Wrigley and Schofield (1981) and Official Estimates for England and Wales thereafter. The French data prior to 1801 are from Bourgeois-Pichat (1965); they are interpolated from five year averages.

Figure 4.10 (*Continued*)

(c) North America: The United States

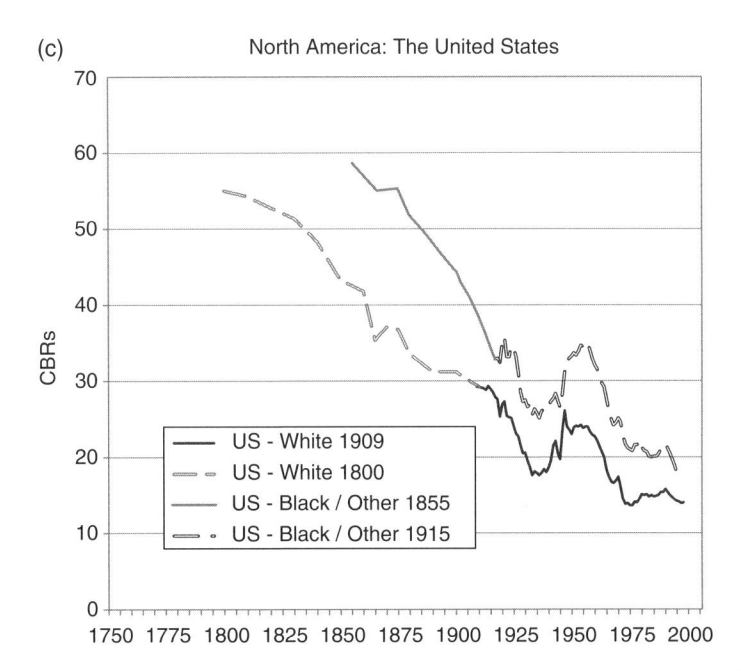

Note: Black/Other. Data for Black Americans for 1855 to 1915 and to 1885 were reported as decade or five-year averages. The post-1916 data are for all non-White races (Black, Asian, Pacific Islanders and American Indians). Unique CBRs for the Black population in the modern era have only been reported by the US Census since 1964. In the 1990s the Black CBR was, on average, 0.6 higher than the CBR for all non-White races.

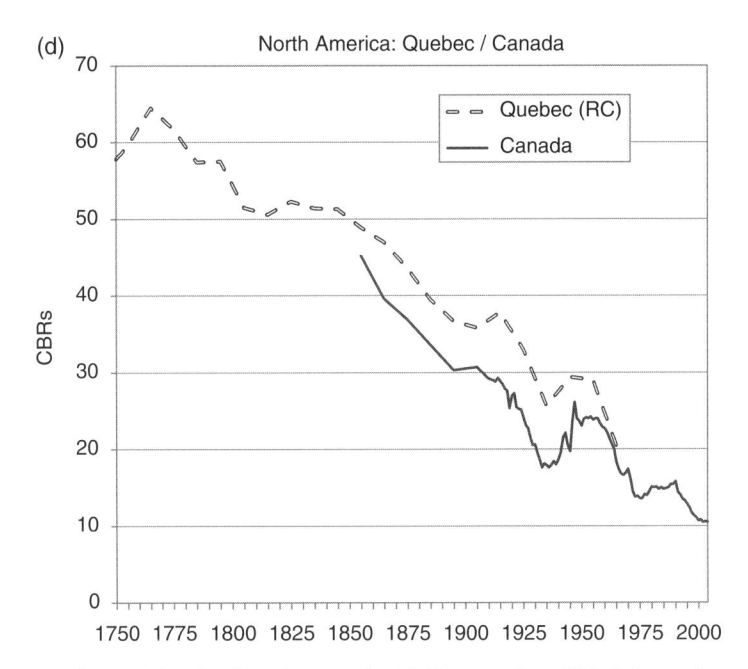

(d) North America: Quebec / Canada

Figure 4.10 The Fertility Decline: Two and a Half Centuries of Birth Rates from 1750.
Note: The data are mid-point averages for the census periods; other values are interpolated ones. The data are annual after 1921. The Quebec figures are for the Roman Catholic population until 1890 and thereafter for all residents of Quebec. The Quebec population was more rural than the Canadian average population.
Sources: Bourgeois-Pichat (1965); Haines (2006), *US Historical Statistics*, Series Ab 988 and Ab1048; Henripin and Peron (1972); *Historical Statistics of Canada*, Series B18; Mitchell, *International Historical Statistics*, Series, 93–117; Statistics Canada (various) including Canadian Census data; US Census data; and Wrigley and Schofield (1981).

from the complete explanation. Compared to Europe, British and French North Americans registered higher first-marriage rates of those below 45 years of age (both women and men) and a lower proportion of never-married males and females. More women were "at risk" and this also helped sustain the initial gap and its continuance, albeit a shrinking one, until the third quarter of the 19th century. But North American women, even allowing for earlier age at marriage, throughout their married life had more children than their European sisters. That is, total fertility rates (TFR) were higher in North America; women had shorter gaps between pregnancies and did not reach the end of their effective (not biological) reproductive lives until later. At the end of the 18th century the number of children born live per married woman in the US was 7.24.[62] English women of the same period had two fewer children. As the lower CBRs for 1800 imply and what we know of mortality rates, Norway, Sweden and France had even lower TFRs – see previous figures. The last thing that could explain the CBR gap between North America and Europe is the age structure of the population. In an orderly growing society we would expect the age structure of the population to be stable, apart from short run variations as mentioned earlier. But the North American population was not stable. It was continually enriched by a flow of immigrants. This flow was not of the numbers that would be experienced later, in the 19th century, during the "age of high immigration" but it was sufficient to give a larger number (proportionally) in the age ranges where family formation normally occurred. Immigrants shared the common characteristic of youth. Thus, the CBR was higher than it would otherwise have been had no immigration occurred.[63]

In retrospect, the decline in the crude birth rate gathered slow momentum in the late 1700s in Northern Europe, and was evident in the United Kingdom in the early 19th century and North America by the second quarter of the century. The first movement of the CBRs in the fertility transition was very modest. Then, beginning about 1875 birth rates began to tumble and in a remarkably short time, 50 years, had achieved the major part of their decline. By 1925 in Western Europe and North America CBRs hovered around twenty per thousand. Since then the decline has been more gradual and, as discussed earlier, has now gone below the net replacement level. It will be recalled that these CBRs are, however, national aggregates. The fertility transition in almost all countries showed considerable variation. The first variation was that between regions in the same country. There were considerable gaps between regions that were persistent for some time (again apart from the short-run variations). Regions with a higher proportion of employment in manufacturing and services tended to have lower than average fertility. In contrast, the more rural regions where agriculture was predominant had higher birth rates. This characteristic has been labeled by demographers as the "urbanization" explanation for the rather obvious reason that industrial and service activities usually take place in urban centers. For instance, rural and urban Ireland had sharply different completed family sizes in the late 19th century with rural areas being larger. Not only were rural families larger but they were larger for any age of (women) at marriage.[64] Regional variations have been found for France, including pre-transition ones, Sweden and many other countries.[65] Regional distinctions in fertility within the US and Canada from the earliest times reflected that this was a continent of new European settlement. Land was relatively abundant for the young but was located at or near the frontier of settlement – we will explore the economics of land settlement later. Another source of variation has been associated with ethnicity or race. As seen in Figure 4.10, Canadians from Quebec, who were largely French-speaking and Roman Catholics, and black Americans had distinct and higher fertility than the general societies of which they were a part.

Religion and ethnicity have often been singled out as separate identifiers of distinct demographic behavior. However, religion and ethnicity are themselves rarely causes of this variation. Quebec, for instance, for most of its history was a distinctly rural society relative to Canada as a whole. It is entirely likely that a large part of the separate fertility pattern was due to the rural-urban distinctiveness and hence per capita incomes. Yet, we know that religious attitudes tend to be reinforced in traditional societies so we cannot rule out religion and cultural distinctiveness altogether. Black Americans historically have always been distinct in their demographic behavior from the white population of the US. There are many reasons for this but most important was the lack of freedom (either under slavery or other restrictions) and which, in turn, limited their geographic, occupational and social mobility. The consequences are well-known and well-documented. Black Americans as a group occupied a uniquely low position on the income distribution. One of the key features in determining the place in the income distribution is their level of education.

In the 1960s and 1970s demographers began to worry about the problem of overpopulation. It is not entirely clear what they meant by this although behind their reasoning was the notion that economic resources would be insufficient to sustain the growth of per capita income. In recent years, from about 1975 to the present as we have seen, the opposite issue has become one of concern: is the rate of population growth adequate to maintain income in the face of declining fertility? CBRs are now at their historical low hovering slightly above ten per 1000 for most OECD countries. This is a number, as we have seen, that is well below net replacement.

The long run downward trends of the CBRs which describe the fertility transition were interrupted from time to time. A certain amount of variation is to be expected in the CBRs; it is the white noise of our historical data. The most common sources of variation are the unanticipated (economic) shocks of history such as brutal famines and devastating wars. Deaths rise because of the shocks and births fall because of the adjustments in the sex ratios, again a result of the shock. Thus during crises the marriage rates fall either because of deaths (males killed in war) or an out-migration of males looking for employment affecting both the marriage rates and marital fertility. Unanticipated economic shocks, if they were profound, had almost instant effects on fertility.

Some of the variation that we see in fertility time series (actually almost any economic time series for that matter) cannot be adequately explained. There is simply a spectrum of white noise. Of course, if we had a complete history of the universe and were clever enough to trace every event, we would find that past events have a lingering but diffuse tendency. They are the statistical echoes of past short-run disturbances that reverberate demographically through the generations. One of those events of fairly recent origin and one that has yet not disappeared into white noise is the demographic bulge, and its echoes, of the post-Second World War baby boom – see Chapter Nine.

4.10 Farms and Towns

The aggregate CBRs hide substantial variations in sub-national or regional fertility which are averaged out in the aggregate. One of these differences, part of the fertility transition, was the urban-rural distinctiveness. But the fertility transition was also marked by great difference in fertility among the rural areas themselves. Since this differential rural fertility was related to economic opportunity on the land it was more prevalent where land was still relatively available (cheap). In the centuries to about 1900 this largely occurred in the Americas, Australasia and Siberian Russia. Thus, while the rural-urban fertility gap was found everywhere, it was only in the "areas of new settlement" that a substantial fertility gap existed within the rural or farm sector.

The rural-urban fertility differential was brought about by the higher cost of raising children in urban areas and the reduced gross contributions of children to family welfare. Fertility in the towns was generally lower than that on farms. Added to this were the growing possibilities in the urban areas for women's wage employment which raised the opportunity cost of having children. (An exact calculation would involve estimating the implicit income of farm wives and subtract it from the urban wage income.) Thus, despite the fact that mortality was higher in the urban areas until the mid-20th century in Western Europe and North America there was a persistent lower fertility in the urban areas. The model in Section 4.3 would otherwise lead to the conclusion that births would rise to compensate for the additional child mortality in the cities. But, as we have seen, the underlying, steady-state conditions (assumptions) do not account for the dynamic changes in the source of income family income and the associated costs. The move from the farms to the towns and cities fundamentally altered the economic relationships within the family. But those relationships also were disturbed by growing farm productivity itself.

The fertility distinction among the rural areas themselves witnessed some areas of high birth rates and some of low ones. This was most noticeable in North America and the other areas where there was an economic frontier of new farm settlement. The key to explaining this difference was the price (or value) of land. Farms nearer the ports (for export of their produce) or towns for domestic sales earned economic rents (surpluses) of location. These rents were capitalized into the land values of the farms. In this fashion land values were higher in some areas and lower in others, the old and the newly settled areas respectively. The rise of the land values meant that the farmer no longer had to rely, or rely totally, on his children for support in their old age. They could sell the farms and provide resources for their own old age. Of course they had to own the property rights to the farm – freehold. This possibility gave rise to three economic problems. First, the land could now be sold by the current generation at the end of their working lives for provision of their incomes in the form of an annuity. That is, there were now superior assets to children, marketable land. (The farm could still be kept within the family and ceded to the eldest male child but there was a clear opportunity cost of following that course of action.) Second, since the next generation often anticipated the sale of the family farm they moved out while their parents were still working the farm. There was a shortage of labor. Third, the net effect of the decline in the death and birth rates was an increase in the number of children surviving into adulthood.

Detailed analysis of the US Census by Richard Easterlin and others reveals that in the 19th century the ratio of children, aged 0 to 9 years, to women aged 16 to 44 years was much higher in the areas of new settlement than in the old settled regions.[66] (Recall from Chapter Two that the census only records who is alive on the day of the count and so a fertility rate is not observed; the child/woman ratio is best measure that can be drawn from the typical census.)[67] In the northern farm states as the rural density increased, the value of land (in constant dollars) increased and the rate of growth of the rural population declined with a decline in the child/woman ratio. Easterlin observed that the same process occurred in all northern states but that there was a difference of timing. In the mid-century, the difference in the child/woman ratio was substantial: in the range of 2000/1000 in the newly settled areas such as Illinois, Iowa and Nebraska and in the range of 800/1000 in the older farm areas such as New York and New Hampshire. Roughly the same numbers have been found for similar rural areas of neighboring Canada.[68] The younger generation was migrating to the areas where setting up a farm was relatively cheaper because of cheaper land prices. Or, in some instances, land could be acquired under the Homestead Act (1862) free of most charges. (Canada also had homestead provisions to encourage western settlement.) Thus, the age distribution of the farm populations was skewed so that the newly settled regions contained a more fecund population. As the farm frontier filled up the difference in the child/woman ratio became smaller and the newer settled areas experienced a child/woman decline. Behind this was a particular system of family bequests.

The bequest model, also attributed to Easterlin, argues that while the capital value of the farm could provide the resources to retire it was more likely that it became the incentive for the designated inheritor (usually the eldest son) to continue to work the farm. He then became the *de facto* farm operator and provided for his parents' retirement. Ultimately, with the death of the parents, he inherited. Under Anglo-American law, he was the sole beneficiary. But what happened to his brothers and sisters? They did not inherit. The issue is that the law may dictate a legal course of action but that is not how families operate. They function on a set of implicit understandings about the desired economic welfare of the family members. Within these norms there would be a wide array of choices. Some families may operate as a quasi-socialist state and be a utility equalizer while others may simply guarantee minimum survival. Family "black sheep," because of their being economic free-riders, were often assigned a low(er) level bequest. The bequests worked in the following manner: the designated heir acquired the farm and had clear legal title; he then mortgaged the farm for some part of its value and received cash; the cash was then distributed to his siblings so they, in a roundabout way, received some part of the estate. The cash received by the brothers *and* sisters was then used to finance the migration to the towns or more remote farm areas where the land was cheaper – lower economic rents of location. Thus, in the newly settled areas the migrants could acquire land equivalent in acreage with only part, and indirect, inheritance. The bequest model has inherent appeal. It explains the mobility of the North American farm population between rural areas. But as the land at the frontier became fully settled and as markets expanded their scope the price of land rose and ultimately choked off the inflow from other rural areas. The age structure of the farm population in the newer areas of settlement no longer was dominated by the fecund young.

We do not know how widespread the pattern of bequests and informal payments was in 19th century North America. Certainly it was restricted to the more affluent farmers. Farmers who had no land-ownership rights and those who had small farms were poor and did not leave wills, the principal source of the evidence. Of course, while the farm-to-farm migration was financed by the bequests there were many who moved to the farm frontier with little or no family resources other than their optimism. The bequests also were a major source financing another important migration: the rural-urban shift. In this respect some investigators have found evidence that the female siblings were also beneficiaries with, in some cases, relative large cash settlements compared to those of their brothers.[69] With much of the young population gone to the far-away farms and the cities fertility in the older farm districts fell.

The bequest model in a farming context provides an explanation of differential regional rural fertility and the decline in rural fertility nationally. It also provides a causal sketch of a singular North American population phenomenon, the very high initial fertility and then its decline in the US ante-bellum period when the economy was still overwhelmingly rural. More than half of all labor prior to the US Civil War was employed in agriculture; the non-agricultural labor force was not dominant, accounting for more than 50% of all employment, until the 1880s.[70] To be sure, in the late 19th century the fertility became dominated by that of the towns but its initial phases of its decline were largely rural.

No such case can be made for Western Europe where all explanations rest on the transition from rural areas to urban ones. The bequest model has, however, limitations when it comes to explaining the quantitatively more important phenomena, the decline in fertility associated with the rural-urban shift. To be sure some farmers' sons and daughters can take their bequest and set up in the towns. An alternative is to imagine the bequests be given during the early part of life as education. (The peasants and procreation model of earlier has no productivity increases or technical change.) Education is an investment in human capital and, because it is embodied in the individual, is mobile. Both geographic and occupational mobility are a function of education. In such a framework, the elder generation is now funded in retirement by the working generation with higher incomes.

Endnotes

1 Caldwell (2001) and Hirschman (2001).
2 Hinde (2003) dates the fertility transition to 1750–1950.
3 A case is reported in the early 20th century of an Austrian woman who had 32 children of which all but four were born live. Eaton and Mayer (1954).
4 The main concentration of Hutterites is in the Canadian provinces of Alberta and Manitoba, and Montana and South Dakota in the United States. Eaton and Mayer (1954).
5 Robinson (1986).
6 WHO (current), *Core Health Indicators*.
7 Hirschman (2001).
8 Eaton and Mayer (1954), 45.
9 Nonaka, Miura and Peter (1994). See also: Sato, Nonaka, Miura and Peter (1994); Larsen and Vaupel (1993) and Heckman and Walker (1990).
10 Neher (1971). This assumes that there are no other "assets" that are either available or provide a higher rate of return.
11 Morand (1999).
12 Eswaran (1998).
13 In the Neher model one can regard the transfers to children as a form of saving.
14 Barro and Becker (1989); Becker and Barro (1988); and Febrero and Schwartz (1995) for Becker's collected essays to 1992.

15 Mateos-Planas (2002).
16 Lindert (1978).
17 Wrigley and Schofield (1981). Estimate based on their reconstruction of parish records and is the average mean values for 1600–49.
18 Laslett (1965) and Laslett (1983).
19 Average mean values for 1996–9. The numbers for 2000–3 are even higher: 27.8 for females and 30.0 for males: UK (2008), *National Statistics*, http://www.statistics.gov.uk
20 Wrigley and Schofield (1981).
21 Crafts (1978); Crafts and Ireland (1976).
22 Desjardins (1995).
23 Henripin (1957).
24 The population of New France went through several cycles resulting from the large inflow of women in the 1660s (see Chapter One) before the age stabilized.
25 Wells (1992).
26 Osterud and Fulton (1976).
27 Certain problems arise when comparing across countries. First, the US Census arranges its evidence by median age not mean age. The median will always be lower than the mean. In Canada, where same sex unions are permitted in some provinces, the marriage forms (Ontario) do not now identify the gender of the partners.
28 Steele, Kallis, Goldstein and Joshi (2005).
29 Lavely, Lee and Feng (1990).
30 Lee and Feng (1999b).
31 Lee and Feng (1999a); Campbell, Feng and Lee (2002); and Wolf (1995).
32 Wolf (2001).
33 n.a. (1946).
34 n.a. (1946).
35 We assume that the Influenza Pandemic of 1919 affected both genders about equally.
36 Mitchell (2007) – see General Sources.
37 n.a. (1946). French losses of children never born (assuming the pre-war fertility levels) were 1.7 million.
38 Graffleman and Hoekstra (2000).
39 Crafts (1978). The entire range was 7.2% to 17.7% with the majority of counties with over 10%. Woods and Hinde (1985).
40 Hajnal (1953).
41 See the classic play by Harold Brighouse, *Hobson's Choice*. *Hobson's choice* is a phrase which indicates a choice of only one option. Brighouse's play emphasizes the small, intra-class distinctions that constrained choices. It is also a terrific film with Charles Laughton and John Mills.
42 Bhrolchain (2001).
43 Haines (1996).
44 Hajnal (1965).
45 The English data measure from the perspective of the 45–49 age group whereas the US data represent the 45–54 age group, the differences caused are likely minor and for our general purposes can be neglected.
46 Fitch and Ruggles (2000).
47 Finlay (1979). Finlay cites the Laslett national evidence (but drawn on a smaller samples) of 21% rate of pregnancy at time of marriage.
48 In her fascinating history, *Daughters of Eve*, Else Hambleton (2004) documents histories from the US colonial era.
49 Newcomer (1990). Newcomer calculated that the 1850 in North Carolina the illegitimacy rate was 0.012

50 Laslett (1977).
51 Leneman and Mitchison (1987). See also: Sklar (1977).
52 Goose (2006).
53 Rutman, Wetherell, and Rutman (2001).
54 Lam, Miron and Riley (1994).
55 Lam and Miron (1994).
56 Ó Gráda (2007).
57 Kannisto, Christensen and Vaupel (1997).
58 n.a. (1946).
59 Gemery (2000).
60 Lindert (1978).
61 Wrigley and Schofield (1981).
62 Osterud and Fulton (1976).
63 Gemery (2000).
64 Anderson (1998). For the years 1881–1888 the completed family size by age at marriage was:

Mean age at Marriage	Completed Family Size Urban Ireland	Completed Family Size Rural Ireland	Mean Age at Marriage	Completed Family Size Urban Ireland	Completed Family Size Rural Ireland
15–19	7.98	8.52	20–24	6.91	7.69
25–29	5.19	6.46	30–34	3.69	4.96
35–39	2.18	3.54	40–44	0.93	2.17

65 Mosk (1980), 77–90 and Mroz and Weir (1990), 61–87.
66 Easterlin (1976a) and Schapiro (1982). See also: Bogue (1976) and Easterlin (1976b).
67 The child/woman ratio is an indirect measure of fertility. It does not account for: births and deaths that happened between the census dates; maternal mortality and children absent on the census date.
68 McInnis (1977).
69 Di Matteo (1997).
70 *Historical Statistics of the US*, Series Aa 185–187.

References

Anderson, Michael (1998) "Fertility Decline in Scotland, England and Wales, and Ireland: Comparisons from the 1911 Census of Fertility", *Population Studies*, (1998) **52**, 1–20.

Barro, Robert J. and Gary S. Becker (1989) "Fertility Choice in a Model of Economic Growth", *Econometrica*, **57**(2) (March), 481–501.

Becker, Gary S. and Robert J. Barro (1988) "A Reformulation of the Theory of Fertility", *Quarterly Journal of Economics*, **57**(1), 1–25.

Bhrolchain, Maire Ni (2001) "Flexibility in the Marriage Market", *Population: An English Selection*, **13**(2) 9–47.

Bourgeois-Pichat, J. (1965) "The General Development of the Population of France Since the Eighteenth Century", in D.V. Glass and D.E.C. Eversley, eds. *Population in History, Essays in Historical Demography*, Old Woking, Surrey: Edward Arnold Publishers.

Bogue, Allan G. (1976), "Comment on Paper by Easterlin", *Journal of Economic History*, **36**(1), 76–81.
Caldwell, John C. (2001) "The Globalization of Fertility Behavior", *Population and Development Review*, **27**, Supplement: Global Fertility Transition, 93–115.
Campbell, Cameron D., Wang Feng and James Z. Lee (2002) "Pretransitional Fertility in China", *Population and Development Review*, **28**(4), 735–50.
Crafts, N.F.R. (1978) "Average Age at First Marriage for Women in Mid-Nineteenth-Century England and Wales: A Cross-Section Study", *Population Studies*, **32**(1), 21–5.
Crafts, N.F.R. and N.J. Ireland (1976) "A Simulation of the Impact of Changes in Age at Marriage before and during the Advent of Industrialization in England", *Population Studies*, **30**(3), 495–510.
Desjardins, Bertrand (1995) "Bias in Age at Marriage in Family Reconstitutions: Evidence from French-Canadian Data", *Population Studies*, **49**(1) (March), 165–9.
Di Matteo, Livio (1997) "The Determinants of Wealth and Asset Holding in Nineteenth-Century Canada: Evidence from Microdata", *The Journal of Economic History*, **57**(4), 907–34.
Easterlin, Richard A. (1976a) "Population Change and Farm Settlement in the Northern United States", *The Journal of Economic History*, **36**(1), 45–75.
Easterlin, Richard A. (1976b) "Reply to Bogue", *The Journal of Economic History*, **36**(1), 81–3.
Eaton, Joseph W. and Albert J. Mayer (1954) *Man's Capacity to Reproduce: The Demography of a Unique Population*, The Free Press: Glencoe, Ill.
Eswaran, Mukesh (1998) "One Explanation for the Demographic Transition in Developing Countries", *Oxford Economic Papers*, April, **50**(2), 237–65.
Febrero, Ramon and Pedro S. Schwartz (1995) *The Essence of Becker*, Stanford: Hoover Institution Press.
Finlay, Roger A. P. (1979) "Population and Fertility in London, 1580–1650", *Journal of Family History*, **4** (Spring), 26–38.
Fitch, C.A., and S. Ruggles (2000) "Historical Trends in Marriage Formation, The United States 1850–1990", L. Waite, C. Bachrach, *et al.*, editors, *Ties That Bind: Perspectives on Marriage and Cohabitation*, New York: Aldine de Gruyter.
Gemery, Henry A. (2000) "The White Population of the Colonial United States, 1607–1790", in Michael R. Haines and Richard H. Steckel (eds.), (2000) *A Population History of North America*, Cambridge: Cambridge University Press, pp. 143–90.
Goose, Nigel (2006) "How Saucy did it Make the Poor? The Straw Plait and Hat Trades, Illegitimate Fertility and the Family in Nineteenth-Century Hertfordshire", *History*, **91**(304), 530–56.
Graffelman, Jan and Rolf F. Hoekstra (2000) "A Statistical Analysis of the Effect of Warfare on the Human Secondary Sex Ratio", *Human Biology*, **72**(3), 433–45.
Haines, Michael R. (1996) "Long Term Marriage Patterns in the United States from the Colonial Times to the Present", *NBER Working Papers*, Historical Papers **80**, 1–38. See also Michael R. Haines (2006) Chapter Ab, Vital Statistics, *Historical Statistics of United States from the Colonial Times to the Present*, New York: Cambridge University Press.
Hajnal, John (1953) "Age at Marriage and Proportions Marrying", *Population Studies*, 7(2), 111–36.
Hajnal, John (1965) "European Marriage Patterns in Perspective", in *Population in History, Essays in Historical Demography*, eds. D.V. Glass and D.E.C. Eversley, London: Edward Arnold, 101–43.
Hambleton, Else L. (2004) *Daughters of Eve: Pregnant Brides and Unwed Mothers in Seventeenth Century Massachusetts*, New York: Routledge.

Heckman, James J. and James R. Walker (1990) "Estimating Fecundability From Data on Waiting Times to First Conception", *Journal of the American Statistical Association*, **85**(410) (June), 283–94.

Henripin, J. (1957) "From Acceptance of Nature to Control: The Demography of the French Canadians", *Canadian Journal of Economics and Political Science*, **23**(1), 9–19.

Hinde, Andrew (2003) *England's Population, A History Since the Domesday Survey*, London: Hodder Arnold.

Hirschman, Charles (2001) "Comment: Globalization and Theories of Fertility Decline", *Population and Development Review*, **27**, Supplement: Global Fertility Transition, 116–25.

Kannisto, Väinö, Kaare Christensen and James W. Vaupel (1997) "No Increased Mortality in Later Life for Cohorts Born during Famine" *American Journal of Epidemiology*, **145**, 987–94.

Lam, David A., Jeffrey A. Miron and Ann Riley (1994) "Modeling Seasonality in Fecundability, Conceptions, and Births", *Demography*, **31**(2), 321–46.

Lam, David and Jeffrey A. Miron (1994) "Global Patterns of Seasonal Variation in Human Fertility", *Annals of the New York Academy of Sciences*, **709**, 9–28. 1994. Reprint 440.

Larsen, Ulla and James W. Vaupel (1993) "Hutterite Fecundability by Age and Parity: Strategies for Frailty Modeling of Event Histories", *Demography*, **30**(1) (Feb.), 81–102.

Laslett, Peter (1965) *The World We Have Lost*, New York: Charles Scribner's Sons.

Laslett, Peter (1977) *Family Life and Illicit Love in Earlier Generations: Essays in Historical Sociology*, Cambridge; New York: Cambridge University Press.

Laslett, Peter (1983) *The World We Have Lost, Further Explored* 3rd edn, London: Methuen.

Lavely, William, James Z. Lee and Wang Feng (1990) "Chinese Demography: The State of the Field", *The Journal of Asian Studies*, **49**(4), 807–34.

Lee, James Z. and Wang Feng (1999a) "Malthusian Models and Chinese Realities: The Chinese Demographic System, 1700–2000", *Population and Development Review*, **25**(1), 33–65.

Lee, James Z. and Wang Feng (1999b) *One Quarter of Humanity: Malthusian Mythology and Chinese Realities, 1700–2000*, Cambridge, Mass.: Harvard University Press.

Lee, James Z., Cameron Campbell and Wang Feng (2002) "Positive Check or Chinese Checks", *The Journal of Asian Studies*, **61**(2), 591–607.

Leneman, Leah and Rosalind Mitchison (1987) "Scottish Illegitimacy Ratios in the Early Modem Period" *Economic History Review*, 2nd ser. XL, **1**, 41–63.

Lindert, Peter H. (1978) *Fertility and Scarcity in America*, Princeton, N.J.: Princeton University Press.

Mateos-Planas, Xavier (2002) "The Demographic Transition in Europe: A Neoclassical Dynastic Approach," *Review of Economic Dynamics*, **5**(3), 646–80.

McInnis, Marvin (1977) "Childbearing and Land Availability: Some Evidence from Individual Household Data", in R.D. Lee, *Population Patterns in the Past*, New York: Academic Press, pp. 201–28.

Morand, Olivier F. (1999) "Endogenous Fertility, Income Distribution, and Growth", *Journal of Economic Growth*, **4**(3), (Sept.), 331–49.

Mosk, Carl (1980) "Rural-Urban Fertility Differences and the Fertility Transition", *Population Studies*, **34**(1) (March), 77–90.

Mroz, Thomas A. and David R. Weir (1990) "Structural Change in Life Cycle Fertility During the Fertility Transition: France Before and After the Revolution of 1789", *Population Studies*, **44**(1) (March), 61–87.

n.a. (1946) "War, Migration, and the Demographic Decline of France" *Population Index*, **12**(2) (April), 73–81.

Neher, Philip A. (1971) "Peasants, Procreation, and Pensions", *American Economic Review*, Part 1, **61**(3), 380–9.
Newcomer, Susan (1990) "Out of Wedlock Childbearing in an Ante-Bellum Southern County", *Journal of Family History*, **15**(3), 357–68.
Nonaka, K., T. Miura and K. Peter (1994) "Recent Fertility Decline in Dariusleut Hutterites: An Extension of the Eaton and Mayer's Hutterite Fertility Study", *Human Biology*, **66**(3), 411–20.
Ó Gráda, Cormac (2007) "Making Famine History", *Journal of Economic Literature*, **45**(1), 5–38.
Osterud, Nancy and John Fulton (1976) "Family Limitation and Age at Marriage: Fertility Decline in Sturbridge, Massachusetts 1730–1850", *Population Studies*, **30**(3), 481–94.
Philip, Verwimp and Jan Van Bavel (2005) "Child Survival and Fertility of Refugees in Rwanda", *European Journal of Population*, **21**(1), 271–90.
Rettaroli, Rosella (1990) "Age at Marriage in Nineteenth Century Italy" *Journal of Family History*, **15**(1), 409–25.
Robinson, W.C. (1986) "Another Look at the Hutterites and Natural Fertility", *Social Biology*, **33**(1) (Spring–Summer), 65–76.
Rutman, Darrett B, Charles Wetherell and Anita Rutman (2001) "Rhythms of Life: Black and White Seasonality in the Early Chesapeake", in Robert I. Rotberg, ed. (2001) *Population History and the Family*, Cambridge, MA: MIT Press, pp. 319–43.
Sato, T., K. Nonaka, T. Miura and K. Peter (1994) "Trends in Cohort Fertility of the Dariusleut Hutterite Population", *Human Biology*, **66**(3), 412–31.
Schapiro, Morton Owen (1982) "Land Availability and Fertility in the United States, 1760–1870", *The Journal of Economic History*, **42**(3), 577–600.
Seiver, Daniel A. (1985) "Trend and Variation in the Seasonality of U.S. Fertility, 1947–1976", *Demography*, **22**(1), 89–100.
Sklar, June (1977) "Marriage and Nonmarital Fertility: A Comparison of Ireland And Sweden", *Population and Development Review*, **3**(4), 359–75.
Steele, Fiona, Constantinos Kallis, Harvey Goldstein, Heather Joshi (2005) "The Relationship between Childbearing and Transitions from Marriage and Cohabitation in Britain", *Demography*, **42**(4), 647–73.
Ward, Peter (1990) *Courtship, Love, and Marriage in Nineteenth-Century English Canada*, Buffalo: McGill-Queen's University Press.
Wells, Robert V. (1992) "The Population of England's Colonies in America Old English or New Americans?", *Population Studies*, **46**(1), 85–102.
Wolf, Arthur P. (1995) *Sexual Attraction and Childhood Association: A Chinese Brief for Edward Westermark*, Stanford: Stanford University Press.
Wolf, Arthur P. (2001) "Is There Evidence of Birth Control in Late Imperial China?" *Population and Development Review*, **27**(1), 133–54.
Woods, R.I. and P.R.A. Hinde (1985) "Nuptiality and Age At Marriage in Nineteenth-Century England", *Journal of Family History*, **10**, (Summer), 119–44.
World Health Organisation (current) *Core Health Indicators*, WHO Statistical Information System (WHOSIS): http://www.who.int/whois/database/core.
Wrigley E. and R. Schofield (1981) *The Population History of England, 1541–1871: A Reconstruction*, Cambridge: Harvard University Press.

Chapter Five
Long Distance Migration

5.1 The Migratory Instinct

Humans have always been restless and mobile. Even the movement of early *homo sapiens* out of Africa was motivated, we presume, by a need to acquire more food, clothing and peaceful surroundings. In modern terms, we call this a larger and more stable source of income. Nomadic peoples from the earliest times wandered in direct response to the need for additional pasture to keep their growing flocks of sheep and goats (resources). Great migrations took place more or less continuously.[1] For instance, the Celts' westward migration within Europe in pre-history was a likely response to economic and political pressure at their eastern border. The citizens of imperial powers such as the Egypt, Greece and Rome spread to the empire's hinterlands; many stayed. In time, these imperial countries were beset by great barbarian invasions. The Visigoths, in the 5th century, moved westward within the Roman Empire, sacked Rome and eventually claimed land in southern Europe. Other barbarian sweeps followed. The Huns were, within several centuries, followed by the Mongols from Central Asia who not only spread westward but eastward into China where they established their own dynasty (the Yuan). Religion presented a motivation, or pretext, for expansion and subsequent settlement, such as the Muslims in the 8th and 9th centuries moving through North Africa into the Iberian Peninsula and East Africa, and the Spanish moving into large portions of South America in the 16th and 17th centuries. On a smaller scale, the emigration from England and Holland to the North American colonies in search of religious toleration had, like all others so motivated, both an economic motivation and consequence. The motives for migration are seldom uni-causal. But, whether part of a voluntary international movement, expelled, or migrating for other reasons, choices had to be made.

For some, the choices were limited or essentially non-existent. There is a rather touching statue just outside Liverpool Street Station in London. It depicts a group of several children, of various ages, all looking slightly lost. Each has a suitcase and a

The Children of Eve: Population and Well-being in History, First Edition.
Louis P. Cain and Donald G. Paterson.
© 2012 Blackwell Publishing Ltd. Published 2012 by Blackwell Publishing Ltd.

personal possession, a toy, doll or book. The statue is a memorial to the "kinder transport," the Czech Jewish children whose anxious parents sent them to Britain by rail in 1939 to avoid repression and the coming holocaust. It also commemorates those people who engineered the transport at some danger to themselves. Wars were not the only cause of flight; as we well know there have been many types of human action, and indeed inaction, that caused widespread human suffering and death for those left behind. Unfortunately, memorials to peoples bravely fleeing to safety are common; for example, there are the recently erected memorials in Helmsdale, Sutherland, to the Scottish Highlanders forced off their crofts in the 18th and early 19th centuries and into the migratory stream and the one in Grosse Île, Quebec, to the starving Irish who landed at Quebec in the famine years of 1847–1849. There are many other flights to safety that are not memorialized – but remembered. The pogroms aimed at displacing European Jewry in the 19th and 20th centuries are celebrated in Yiddish literature for the resilience of those displaced.

In less traumatic circumstances, there were times when the basically rural population of Europe migrated to the towns with increasing frequency: as trade and port cities grew, as administrative centers evolved, and as industries such as the woolen trades became specialized. Yet, it was not until the early modern period (the 17th and 18th centuries) that the structure of the European and North American economies started to change systematically from agriculture to a more diversified industrial/service base. The movement of people became part of that change. It had three main components:

- the rural-urban shift;
- regional (internal) migration; and
- long distance or international migration.

The industrial transition loosened the population, or parts of it, from its traditional rural roots by the changing demand for labor. As reflected in the growing discrepancy between agricultural and non-agricultural wages (incomes), this labor flow proceeded more or less continually until the present day. In OECD countries and some others, however, it has slowed both in absolute numbers and proportional terms as the agricultural sector has become too small a part of developed economies to be the source of many migrants of any sort.

Regional migration within a country, including the rural-urban shift, and international migration are closely related historically. To take one example: farm laborers in Southern Italy decided to move northward to Milan in pursuit of higher wages. Once the question of migrating had been introduced, some would now consider, and could afford, a longer migration from rural Italy to, say, Boston or New York. So the decision to be an international migrant can be a two-stage process. An individual may be a regional migrant first and subsequently an international migrant, presumably based on acquiring information and amassing the funds to finance the international move. Naturally, the timing and intensity of flows varied with both the economic conditions of the migrant-receiving and migrant-donor countries. These are often referred to as the "pull" and "push" forces of migration respectively.

The most potent of these forces is the "better living" that international migrants expect to achieve in the country to which they go. This is typically expressed in terms

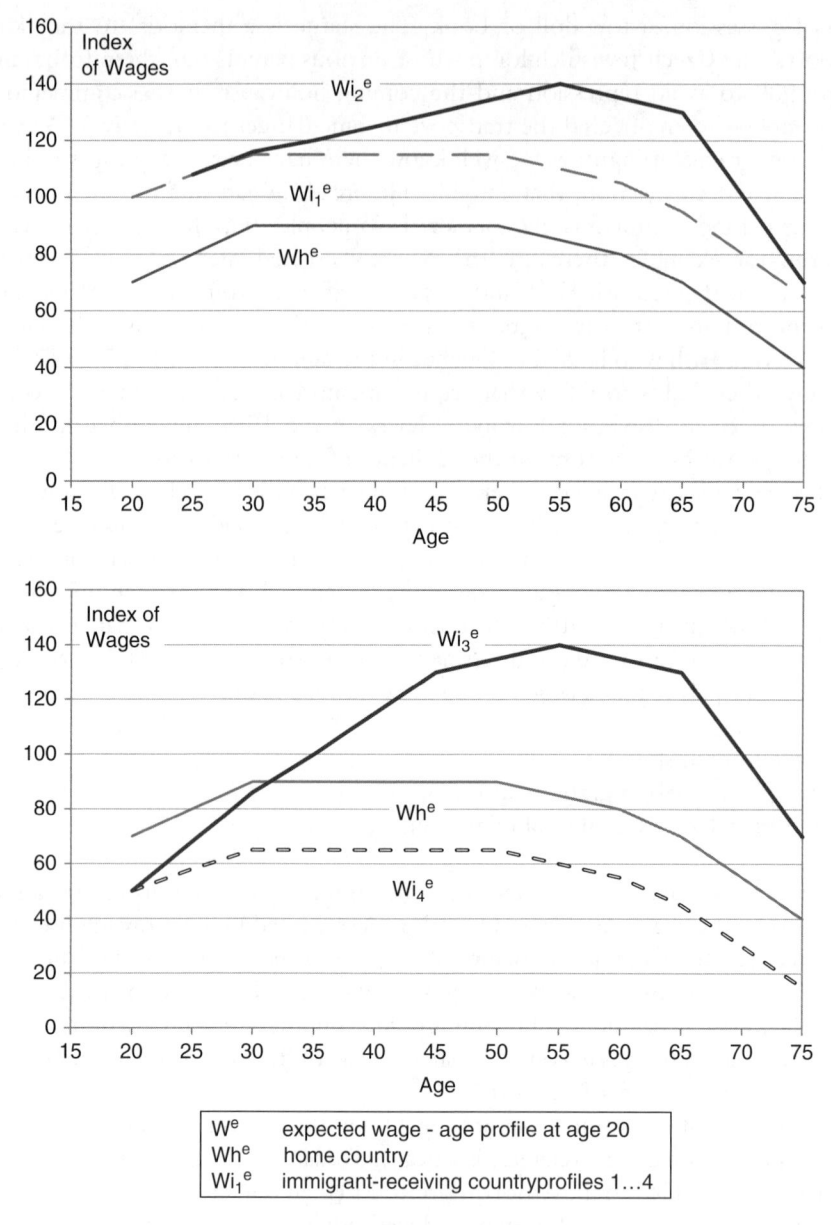

Figure 5.1 Expected Wage Profiles by Location.

of wages or incomes – the assumptions are that all income is earned income and that the immigrant has a fixed level of human capital or education. Figure 5.1 shows several examples of the expected wage profiles for a 20-year-old hypothetical immigrant and their wage profile at home.[2] The home wage-age profile is relatively flat reflecting either a low level of skills or a lack of rewards with experience – in labor markets today such a profile would generally be predicted for an individual with a low level of education and no prospects of job advancement. However, for this potential immigrant the wage profile may not simply be higher but take on a different shape Wi_2^c. That is, the wage continues to rise and peaks much later in life due to job advancement available only in the new country of settlement. If the *expected* (*ex ante*) wage is the *realized* (*ex post*) wage, the migration is clearly successful. But what if the realized wage profile is lower than expected? The migration might still be successful if a wage profile differential between that of home and immigrants-receiving country is positive and compensates for all the costs of migration. The second panel of Figure 5.1 shows alternate expected wage profiles from migration. One is wholly below the home wage-age profile and is unlikely to induce migration. The second, and by far the more interesting and historically more representative case, shows a wage-age profile that is initially below the home wage but rises above it at some later age, here about age 30 (Wi_3^c). The current wage would not induce migration by itself. However, the higher wages beyond age 30 would be a stimulus to movement if their future value is taken into consideration from the outset and offsets the early wage losses. And because these are future values, this requires calculating the familiar discounted present value.

In order to induce migration the present value of the alternatives must be positive and take into consideration the (fixed) costs of migration. To this we might add the value of the immigrant child. Even today when asked the reasons for migration the immigrants will often respond that they migrated for the sake of the children to have a better life. The cost of international migration may be too high to compensate for the present value of the expected wage differential (income) and thus migration will not occur. It is, after all, the *net present value* from migration that is the key to the decision to migrate. Not only are there the costs of transport, plus any costs associated with financing them, but there are the costs (gains) of i) asset disposition; and ii) uncertainty. The disposition of assets (in the home country) and their replacement (in the immigrant-receiving country) is fraught with uncertainty. These assets include personal possessions and housing but may also include the cost of earning assets such as sewing machines or, if the international migration is a rural to rural one, a farm disposition and acquisition. This asset transfer problem is going to make older individuals more cautious about moving as they have more assets, and therefore more to lose, than younger potential international migrants – the less wealthy.

There are also the less adventurous among us and those who hold a special affection for the society and place in which they currently live, the so-called *psychic benefits* derived from remaining in place. Most people ignore or resist the temptation to move or are unaware of the benefits to becoming international migrants. Thus social scientists seeking to explain a flow of immigrants are looking for causes *at the margin*. First, there may be ignorance of the fact that a wage differential exists between countries especially as this differential necessarily is an average. Second, even when the average differential is known with some certainty, there may be uncertainty about where any one individual (the decision-maker) may end up on the wage distribution in the receiving country. Third, the cost of international migration may have simply been too high to compensate for the expected higher wages (income) - all appropriately discounted.[3] Clearly, few did such calculations but rather asked questions that amounted to getting the same information: Will I be better-off? Will I be better-off in the long run? How much better-off will I be? Will I have friends or family there? Is it true, as I've heard, that New York (or Iowa, Manitoba, Christchurch, Woolongong) is really quite nice?

When labor migrates from a lower to a higher wage area, it changes the supply of labor in both places. An increased supply of labor pushes wages down in the one area, and the decline in the labor supply pushes wages up in the other. In the economic theory of trade, this flow of labor with its international equilibrating wage tendency is called *factor price equalization*. Economic historians look for real wage convergence (where the nominal wage of labor is adjusted for the cost of living at the chosen locations).[4] Even if labor were immobile between economies, international trade would itself induce factor price equalization. The reason for this is that countries would specialize in the production of commodities that employed relatively more of the abundant factor within their own economies, thereby conserving on the use of the scarce, and more expensive, factor. This theory, the *Hecksher-Ohlin* model of trade, predicts that a country's exports will embody the country's abundant factor of production.[5] Even without a flow of international labor or other factors of production, there should be a convergence of factor prices between countries. The historical problem is that, when we look at the massive migrations of the 19th and 20th centuries, both of these economic trends occurred. The international flow of goods and services and the increased flow of labor were not substitutes, but complements, in the process of economic growth. Although far from complete, both the convergence of real wages and that of commodity prices were the hallmarks of the increased globalization.[6]

International migration was also accompanied by a flow of capital. The countries of Argentina, Australia, Canada and the United States, for instance, borrowed massively from Europe in the long 19th century (to World War I). Much of the capital originated in Britain and was financed out of the positive balance of payments on current account. In turn, a large share of this capital was used to finance expansion of the transport infrastructure – particularly the large, transcontinental rail projects in these countries – and the growth of cities and towns. In North America, rail expansion onto the Great Plains and Prairies brought huge amounts of land into production. The expansion into Russian Siberia also brought new agriculture and new settlement as a result of an eastward expansion. In other areas such as Europe, China, India and Africa, railways encouraged new and higher productivity uses of land. Throughout the main phases of demographic transition, land, far from being a fixed factor of production, was rapidly expanding at the extensive margin, as were capital and labor. The demand for labor was shifting upward (outward) causing the wage convergence to slow down (if not reverse itself) from time to time.

5.2 Who's In and Who's Out

Historians face a difficult problem, one that persists even in today's world, and that is counting the numbers who entered into the international migration streams. For the period before the modern age of record keeping, which we may date to the mid-19th century, all counts are based on the ingenuity of historians using local historical knowledge, shipping and port records, military records and incomplete censuses.[7] The reason such censuses exist is the same that the Romans used: to determine who is to be taxed and to have a ready roster of (loyal) fighters available for local duty. Even when record keeping became more thorough, the count of immigrant arrivals was still incomplete, missed counts and "illegal" immigration notwithstanding. Also, countries were generally more concerned about the people who entered than those

Table 5.1 Region of Birth of the Foreign-Born Population of the United States: by Percentage, 1850 to 1930 and 1960 to 1990.

	Total	Europe	Asia	Africa	Oceania	Latin America	Northern America
1850	100.0	92.2	0.1	-	-	0.9	6.7
1860	100.0	92.1	0.9	-	0.1	0.9	6.0
1870	100.0	88.8	1.2	-	0.1	1.0	8.9
1880	100.0	86.2	1.6	-	0.1	1.3	10.7
1890	100.0	86.9	1.2	-	0.1	1.2	10.6
1900	100.0	86.0	1.2	-	0.1	1.3	11.4
1910	100.0	87.4	1.4	-	0.1	2.1	9.0
1920	100.0	85.7	1.7	0.1	0.1	4.2	8.2
1930	100.0	83.0	1.9	0.1	0.1	5.6	9.2
1960	100.0	75.0	5.1	0.4	0.4	9.4	9.8
1970	100.0	61.7	8.9	0.9	0.4	19.4	8.7
1980	100.0	39.0	19.3	1.5	0.6	33.1	6.5
1990	100.0	22.9	26.3	1.9	0.5	44.3	4.0

Source: US Bureau of the Census (1999) *The Foreign-Born Population of the United States*, Table 2, Internet Release, 9 March 1999.

who left. Even today most countries do not have a formal process of counting permanent departures – the emigrants. (Modern OECD governments go to great lengths to estimate, not count, the emigrants through tax records, government benefits records and the like.) Unfortunately, for the counters, we only have a census at regular fixed intervals to verify the numbers (see Chapter One). By comparing the censuses over time, we measure the change in the size of the population. New population additions are made up of those born and new immigrants, both of which can be counted by the census. There are only two exits. The first is death, which we can also count from death registration records. The other is emigration which becomes the residual, balancing number. Of course, we have to account for those who are born and new immigrants who have been registered between the censuses in one country and then either die or migrate to another country.

Every emigrant should be an immigrant somewhere. Unfortunately for the historians, there was not a systematic way in which immigrants were recorded. For instance, if we try to account for the substantial emigration from Canada by looking at the immigrant counts in the US (we know that overwhelmingly Canadians migrated to the US prior to 1945), the numbers are not even close. A Canadian may have been born in the UK, carried to Canada by its immigrant parents, spent almost their entire life in Canada, and then as an adult emigrated to the US. When that person entered the US, he or she was recorded as an immigrant from Britain because of their place of birth. Each country had its own standards and thus immigrants were recorded by some as: from their place of birth, last country of residence, last country of permanent residence, or citizenship. So the historical US records of immigrants will only note those who were Canadian-born and not our imagined British-born Canadian emigrant. Modern records are more complete (see Table 5.1).

The flow of immigrants on a year-to-year basis contributed to the stock of immigrants measured in the censuses. Thus countries have a stock of immigrants that reflects the cumulative inflow of past immigration, net of deaths and departures. The stock is defined to include anyone living, no matter what their current citizenship, who once had been an immigrant. Thus, the Canadian and Australian immigrant stocks are dominated by the British and Western Europeans, despite the fact that most of their immigrants in recent years are of Asian and South Asian origin. It takes time for the stock to adjust, but it will do so more rapidly in the near future as the British immigrant stock is an elderly one. Until recently (the 1980s) the same was true of the US where the stock of immigrants was largely of European origin. However, the flow of immigrants to the United States has recently been dominated by Latin Americans and Asians, and is of such numbers, that it has overwhelmed the stock resulting from the immediate post-1945 immigration boom which was largely European.[8]

5.3 Migration of the Unfree

During the US colonial period (1607–1775) there were over three-quarters of a million immigrants. A full 72.2% of these immigrants came in some form of bondage – see Table 5.2. Black slaves from Africa were by far the most numerous, but there were also convicts, prisoners and indentured servants mostly from Britain. The free voluntary immigrants to Colonial America accounted for only slightly more than a quarter of the total in the years leading up to the American Revolution.[9] But North America (including the Caribbean) was far from the only destination of the unfree: South America accounted for the largest number of transported African black slaves leaving an indelible imprint on the population. Prisoners and convicts were also shipped to Australia, but at a different time.

A. Slaves

In pre-modern history slavery was a relative common condition. Most ancient peoples kept slaves. Slavery could be a perpetual condition and inherited by children or it could be limited to the lifetime of the individual. The Persians, Greeks and Romans typically enslaved those whom they conquered. These were not necessarily different people, just enemies. The original purpose of slavery was to remove a population from its home (and source of income) so that it could not take up the conflict again. However, slaves also provided labor that did not require the payment of wages, but it was not costless. Classicists insist that slaves were a consequence of war, not a cause of it. While this may be true, the ratio of slaves to freemen in ancient Athens was at least 2 to 1 and maybe as much as 3 to 1. This suggests that replenishment of the stock of slaves was necessary from time to time to maintain it at existing levels. As the conquests became more distant from the homeland, the enslaved were naturally more distinct in terms of customs, languages and religions and could be regarded as inferior. Therefore, in the eyes of the enslavers, their condition was justified. The Romans shipped large quantities of slaves from the periphery of their empire to Italy to work the stone and salt quarries and row in the galleys (ships). But, the Romans

Table 5.2 Immigration into the US during the Colonial Period by Legal Status and Condition of Servitude.

	Unfree by Condition of Servitude				
	Slaves	Convicts & Prisoners	Indentured Servants	Free	Total
1607–1699	33 200	2 300	96 600	66 300	198 400
1700–1775	278 400	52 200	103 600	151 600	585 800
Total	311 600	54 500	200 200	217 900	784 200
Percentage	39.7%	6.9%	25.5%	27.8%	100.0%

Source: Adapted from Fogelman (1998), Table 1.
NB: rounded to the nearest 100.
Includes political exiles and kidnap victims as prisoners.

also employed slaves as domestic servants and, on occasion, in highly responsible positions. Greek slaves were particularly prized.[10] As empires expanded more and more, slaves were transported long distances and became an important element of the human migratory stream.

From the 9th to the 18th century, for instance, people were rounded up in the Caucuses and Eastern Black Sea regions and sold into slavery. They were then marched to various points of the Islamic empire. Known for their fighting ability, the captives were compulsorily converted to Islam and mustered into the armies of the caliphs. Clearly an incentive was needed and that was a promise of freedom (manumission) at the end of their period of service. The Mamluks, as they were known, became a formidable fighting force sometimes supplementing armies of non-slaves and sometimes being the entire fighting force. Originally mustered by the Assabid Caliphs of Turkey, they frequently assumed local power themselves after the caliphate collapsed in various regions as far flung as western India to Egypt. In Egypt, the Mamluks became the ruling elite in the 13th century and held power for 300 years in Cairo, all the while continuing to purchase more Mamluks (in the tens of thousands) for their armed forces.[11] The Mamluks were renowned for the defeat of the Mongol armies in 1260 – clearly they were slaves of a different sort.

Yet there is nothing in the sad history of the institution of slavery to compare to the massive movement of black slaves from Africa to the Americas. Where it existed in the new world, it was generally profitable and an economically viable institution.[12] Slaves were principally used as manual labor in the tobacco, rice, sugar and cotton plantations of the West Indies, South America and what became the US. As such slavery existed until the middle of the 19th century. However, the trade in slaves, as distinct from their ownership and use, was made illegal in the early part of the century due in great measure to the highly charged campaigns of the English reformer William Wilberforce. These campaigns aroused public indignation on both sides of the Atlantic. As a result, Britain passed the Abolition of the Slave Trade Act in 1807 although slavery itself was not made illegal in Britain and its Empire until 1833. In the year following the British 1807 act the United States legislated:

Be it enacted by the Senate and House of Representatives of the United States of America in Congress assembled, That from and after the first day of January, one thousand eight hundred and eight, it shall not be lawful to import or bring into the United States or the territories thereof from any foreign kingdom, place, or country, any negro, mulatto, or person of colour, with intent to hold, sell, or dispose of such negro, mulatto, or person of colour, as a slave, or to be held to service or labour. [original spelling].

[*Public Statutes … of the United States of America*, Statute II, Chap.XXII, 2 March 1808.]

But, only the end of its Civil War in 1865 brought an end to black slavery in the US.[13] Spain and Portugal finally agreed in 1815 to the abolition of the slave trade within five years. France temporarily outlawed slavery at the time of its Revolution, but slavery was reinstated and lasted there until 1848. Likewise, Holland did not ban the holding of slaves until the 1840s. It has been estimated that altogether approximately 9.5 million individuals were transported as slaves from Africa to the Americas from the 17th to the early 19th centuries.[14] Most slaves were destined for the West Indies and Brazil. A minority went to the other South American countries, and only about 10% of those were landed in the British North American colonies (as distinct from the British West Indies) and later the US (see Figure 5.2). The journey to the Americas from Africa has been the subject of much historical inquiry just as it was a highlight of the Wilberforce abolitionist campaigns: the wretched conditions of transport by sea, the over-crowding and unsanitary conditions. While the abolitionists of the day evoked tearful sympathy describing these conditions, the voyage characteristics were

Figure 5.2 Import of Black Slaves to the British West Indies, British North America and the US, 1630–1800.
Note: British North America includes only the British Colonies that became the US.
Source: data from Carter (2006), *US Historical Statistics*, Table Ad3–15.

actually fairly similar to those experienced by the crews and fare-paying passengers. Of course the slaves suffered indignities that the fare-payers did not: the degrading human bondage and rape of female slaves. But, there were actual incentives for the slavers to keep the slaves alive and healthy as the value of the slave was realized at the end of the voyage. The carrier with fare-paying passengers had no such incentive which, at the margin, might reduce mortality on the voyage. Certainly, the Middle Passage, as the various mid-latitude trans-Atlantic sailing routes from Africa to the Americas were collectively known, never produced the high rates of mortality experienced in the North Atlantic during the Irish Famine years of the late 1840s (see later).

In general, the mortality of slaves on the Middle Passage declined from the high figures in the 17th century at about the same rate as the deaths of immigrants on the North Atlantic – from about 16% in the late 17th and early 18th centuries to rates about 7.7%.[15] A large part of this decline was due to the decreased length of voyages, the increased efficiency of vessels and the scale economies of slave gathering – the latter made voyages shorter as ships no longer undertook coastal cruises to pick up slaves at the various way points. Some routes on the Middle Passage continued to be more dangerous in large measure because of their long voyages. By only measuring the mortality on the voyages we overlook the long period of captivity before the trans-Atlantic shipment.[16] We conjecture, in the absence of quantifiable evidence, the mortality in this period was high. If the deaths before leaving Africa were equal to those on the voyages, the slave migration in total probably killed one able bodied male for every three enslaved. The toll may have been higher among women and children.

B. Convicts and Indentured Servants

Apart from slavery there were other forms of migrant bondage, although not ones that usually resulted in a permanent alienation. From time to time in the 17th century prisoners and convicts were sent from Britain to the British North American Colonies (later to Australia). The object was simple: remove the most troublesome of British society, a classic push force. James Butler, a late-Victorian historian, noted that many of these were political prisoners including those captured in the English Civil War, Cromwell's Wars against the Scots and the Irish, and the various uprisings of the period.[17] However, in 1718, in the aftermath of the Jacobite Rising of 1715, the policy of shipping undesirables to the colonies became systematic in English law; the passing of the *Transportation Act* permitted such a sentence.[18] Most of those transported were serious felons having committed more than one offence. A significant minority was guilty of capital crimes such as counterfeiting, kidnapping, highway robbery, manslaughter and murder. There were about 160 crimes punishable by death, but an individual might be allowed to live on condition they transported themselves out of England. Capital crimes, when leniency was exercised or a pardon from the death sentence was granted, were typically punishable by a seven-year, a 14-year or, on occasion, a life sentence. The labor service of the convicts and prisoners were auctioned off in the colonial markets. Since convict laborers could return to Britain at the conclusion of their sentence, and runaway convicts often made it back as well, it is uncertain how exactly they added to the population. Most who had served their sentences probably stayed in the colonies, albeit in a different area than their penal service. Because of the social odium, they sought out the anonymity of the frontier or the growing towns. Once their sentences were complete, the ex-convicts were no more likely to be guilty of offences than the general population.[19] Although most colonies received shipments of prisoners (and there were objections to them in several colonies), the favored destination was the tobacco-growing areas, particularly Maryland, Virginia and the Carolinas.

With the Revolution the transportation of convicts to the US came to an end. However, the role of recipient was quickly taken up by Australian penal colonies, Botany Bay and Van Dieman's Land. They were different from those of America in that they were established in a land with very few free immigrants in the early settlement period – and many of those were government officials who did not remain. The result was the transported prisoners contributed more to the growth of the Australian population than prisoners had to that of the US. In the 1820s more than half the Australians were prisoners-bondsmen. Even by 1841 over 20% still were in bondage – new shipments and those serving out their terms.[20] This does not include those who completed their sentences and remained in Australia.[21] Nor does it include the children of the original prisoners, and their further progeny. Perhaps the large number (and proportion) of the population that originate from convict labor accounts for the Australian retrospective pride in these tough antecedents.

Unlike the case of the North American colonies where there was a ready demand for labor as household servants and agricultural workers, there was no such exuberant demand in Australia. Wasn't the transportation of prisoners halfway around the world not a rather expensive way of getting rid of the troublesome elements, especially if there was little existing demand for their services? With the loss of the Thirteen Colonies there were few alternative places to send convicts that were relatively secure. Plus, there was another motive. Britain was in the throes of rebuilding its empire, and peopling the continent with British folk, albeit the more desperate ones, was part of the strategy.

Indentured servitude was the device developed to increase the migration of white European workers to the labor-short North American colonies. Almost as many people arrived in the colonies as indentured labor as arrived as free citizens. Researchers have documented how well-organized the markets were for indentured servants.[22] An individual would contract with a ship captain or merchant to work for a specified number of years (usually between four and seven) in return for transportation across the Atlantic plus specified payments (usually food, clothing, housing, or perhaps some education or training in a craft or skill). Also specified was an amount of money or land to be paid when the contract was successfully completed, largely to help assure that the contract would be successfully completed. There was a good deal of bargaining between potential servants and those contracting with them. The holder of the contract in England paid the cost of the trip. When the ship arrived in North America, the contracts (and the people) were sold, usually onboard the ship. The purchase price, which depended upon the servant's age, sex, and skills, was equal to the realized cost plus about a 50% markup.

When the colonies adjoining Chesapeake Bay first discovered that crops were most profitably grown under a plantation system, the demand for indentured servants soared. A sample of over 20 000 indentures taken from surviving ship records suggests the majority chose to go to the Chesapeake. These individuals were predominantly young males in their late teens and early 20s who were farmers, artisans, (unskilled) laborers, and domestic servants.

For example, Walter Gibson, a ship's master and merchant of Glasgow, published a broadsheet in 1683 in which fares for the voyage to Carolina were listed at £5 per adult. Once settlers had reached the colony each was eligible to apply for 70 acres of land from the colonial government for a fee of one penny per acre. There were terms, not onerous, that had to be fulfilled. But there was another pitch in this advertisement:

> To such as are desirous to Transport themselves to the said colony of Carolina, and are not able to pay their Passage; If they be Tradesmen, who have past their Appentiship in any Handy-craft; The said Walter Gibson is content to Transport them on his own Charges, they obliging themselves to Serve him three years, during which time he will furnish them sufficiently with Meat, Cloaths and other necessaries. At the issue of the time of their Service, they are to have settled upon them and their Heirs from the Government, each of them fifty Aikers of Ground, they paying one Penny Sterling per Aiker yearly ... [Original spelling retained.]
>
> Gibson (1683), *Proposals*, 1.

Each person in the family, including servants, was eligible to receive the same land allowance. Folk without a trade had to serve Gibson for four years and settlers under 18 had to fulfill a service period of five years but were able to apply for the same land allocation on the same terms.[23] Indenture contracts had status in courts of law, and servants could appeal to the courts for violations of their rights.[24] Once the indenture was completed, the former servant was a member of the free population; children born of indentured servants during servitude were born free.

A related group was known as *redemptioners*. Most came from Germany and had a slightly different status than the English indentured servants. While English servants usually came over alone, the Germans came in families, bringing their own supplies and movable property with them.[25] The ship captains that brought them generally allowed them time to arrange payment for their passage after arrival.

The rather abrupt shift from reliance on white servants to black slaves at the turn of the 18th century was attributed to the wars of King William III and, especially, those of the reign of Queen Anne. These wars reduced the supply of prime-aged males, which in turn reduced contract lengths, thereby increasing the effective price.[26] With the return of peace, the market for indentured servants revived, but not to its previous numbers. On average, black slaves cost more than white servants because their "contract" to the buyer was for a longer time period. Thus, slaves tended to be more profitable to those involved in their transport and initial sale.

European immigrants wanted land for themselves, and there was unlikely to be a sufficient supply of indentured servants to meet the labor demand in the South. Although Virginia and Maryland were major destinations for indentured servants in the 17th century, by the 18th century, when potential servants had more choice, they chose to avoid the Southern colonies. Why this was true is not entirely clear. Most 18th-century white immigrants went to Pennsylvania where land was readily available and the institutions were liberal. But the same could be said of Virginia. The temperature-humidity mix of the middle colonies was as oppressive as that of the southern ones. Jefferson's comment that, "In a warm climate, no man will labor for himself who can make another labor for him," is just as true for residents of other climates.[27] The fact that the South has warmer winters than the North should have made it attractive to Europeans. Further, if wages were high enough, they could "make" others labor.

Near the end of the 18th century, white servitude was declining in competition with wage labor. In the free market, white skilled workers were able to negotiate wages that were higher than the comparable real income derived from a contract of indenture. The rising demand for labor drove up the price of non-free white labor compared to that of black slaves leading to a decline in servitude. Nonetheless, in 1787, when the US Constitution was being written, white servitude still had to be taken into account, and it lingered on. A study of German redemptioners concludes the end came about 1820.[28] Only 18 indentured servants arrived in 1820 and only 19 in total during the following 10 years. Most of these were children.

Concurrently, US judges began to refuse to imprison people for debt. If the indenture contract was not enforceable, it lost value. Negotiated wage contracts were more efficient, and any break by the employee before the contract expired released the employer from the obligation to pay wages.[29] The other obligations of indenture (e.g., room, board, clothing, medicine, education in a trade, and payment at the end) did not apply to wage labor. However, as indentures disappeared, turnover costs increased, especially for employers who required more labor than their families could supply. When the cost of searching for workers and the cost of going without labor during a critical period was high, employers (i.e., Southern plantation owners) were attracted to slavery to mitigate these costs.[30]

C. Child Migrants

There were other forms of near bondage in immigration history, although few were as touching as the case of the "home children." Beginning in the third quarter of the 19th century, there was a philanthropically inspired and managed movement of children from Britain to the "white" colonies and dominions. The home children were orphans, abandoned children, and other impoverished youngsters from Britain. Under the supervision of guardians, they were collected from the orphanages and shipped to Australia, New Zealand and Canada. The children were often referred to as "Barnado Children" after the principal charity active in securing better lives for the youngsters. It was classic Victorian "do-goodism." The scheme continued in operation into the 1930s (we have abundant details from the shipping records.)[31] For the most part, these children were sent to the farming districts of older settlement, those districts where the fertility rates were low because of the aging population – as seen in Chapter Four. In total, somewhat over 100 000 children were shipped from Britain to Canada under this scheme. Some of these children did indeed enjoy better lives. They were given some education, tutored in farm and domestic skills, and were more or less adopted into the family to which they were sent. Others were sent to farms where they were treated as chattel labor under brutal conditions. It was, at best, a scheme with mixed human results. Surprisingly, a similar scheme between Britain and Australia was instituted after the Second World War and lasted until 1967. It too had very mixed results.

5.4 The Atlantic: Waves of Immigration

The years between the American Revolution in 1776 and the defeat of Napoleon in 1814 were ones of turmoil in the international trading economy and the small, but steady, flow of trans-Atlantic migrants was similarly interrupted. With the restoration of peace in the early 19th century the trans-Atlantic component of international migration grew to such unprecedented heights that economic historians have labeled it the "age of mass international migration." Between 1815 and World War I approximately 55 to 60 million moved from Europe to North and South America.[32] The flow of immigrants into North America in the decade after 1815 was initially much the same in character as in the 18th century: they came mainly from England, Scotland, Wales and Ireland with a sprinkling from Germany. But the volume was different, higher. Depression in British agriculture, demobilization of the armed forces, the re-alignment of British industry to peacetime conditions, and growing urban unemployment caused massive dislocation. While the fall in the cost of passage played a role in making emigration from Britain more attractive than earlier, it was the capacity that

Immigrants Arriving at Ellis Island for Processing

Much of the great flood of pre-1914 Migration to the United States entered through the Ellis Island Immigration Station.
Source: Detroit Publishing Company Collection, *Library of Congress*, Prints and Photographs Division Washington.

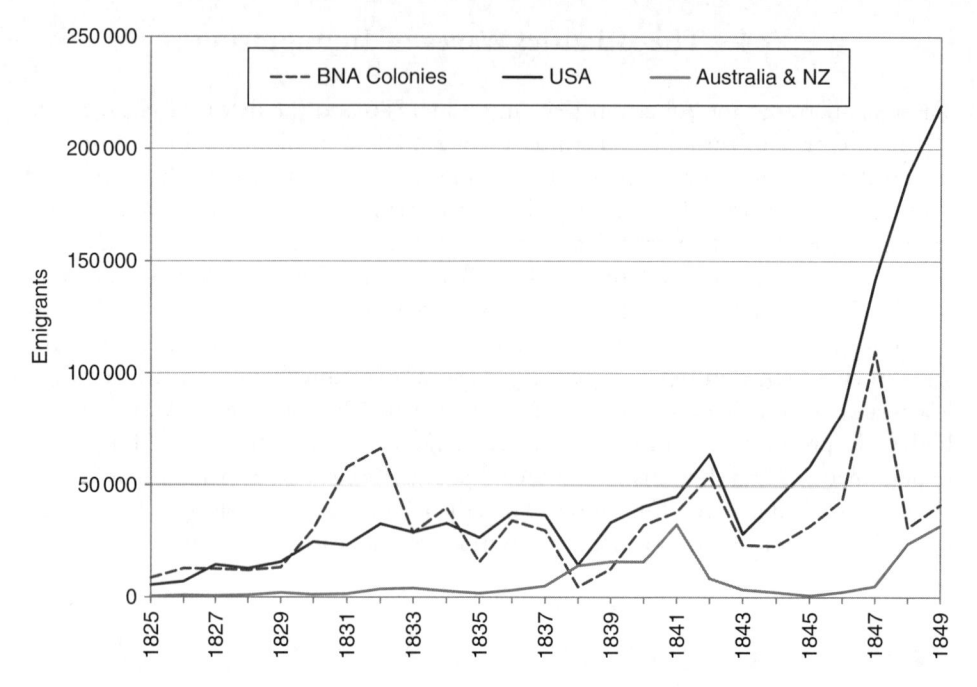

Figure 5.3 Annual Emigration of the British by Destination, 1825–1849.
Source: Colonial Land and Emigration Commissioners data from *The Illustrated London News*, Saturday July 6th 1850.
BNA Colonies: Upper Canada, Lower Canada, Nova Scotia, New Brunswick, Newfoundland, and the British West Indies.

the ships now offered that made mass movement possible. Between 1825 and 1850 more than 2.25 million British emigrants left for the British North American colonies and the US – see Figures 5.3 and 5.4. These included the many Irish who left what was then Great Britain and Ireland (see Diasporas later in this chapter).

The emigration from Europe to the "New World" had its distinct ethnic characteristics. In the years before the US Civil War the sources of immigration expanded to include a large flow of Germans whose instincts to enter the migratory stream were heightened by the unsuccessful Revolution of 1848 and its chaotic aftermath. At about the mid-century mark, the now substantial flow accelerated. The Germans were followed by the Scandinavians. As the century wore on the western Europeans were joined by, first, the southern and then the eastern Europeans. By the beginning of the First World War, the majority of immigrants were non-English speaking. The broad features of this migration were shared with British North America (Canada) but with different timing. The Spanish and Portuguese also entered into the trans-Atlantic migration, but they went principally to South America (Argentina, Chile, Brazil and Uruguay). Spanish emigrants in particular rejected the lure of the US, but, drawn by culture and language, they preferred the Latin south (98% of all emigrants prior to 1914).[33] But many Italians and British also added to this flow, especially that to Argentina and Chile. The Italians had specific geographic preferences that changed quite dramatically about 1900. From 1876 to 1900 for every Italian who went to North America more than two found a home in South America. From the turn of the

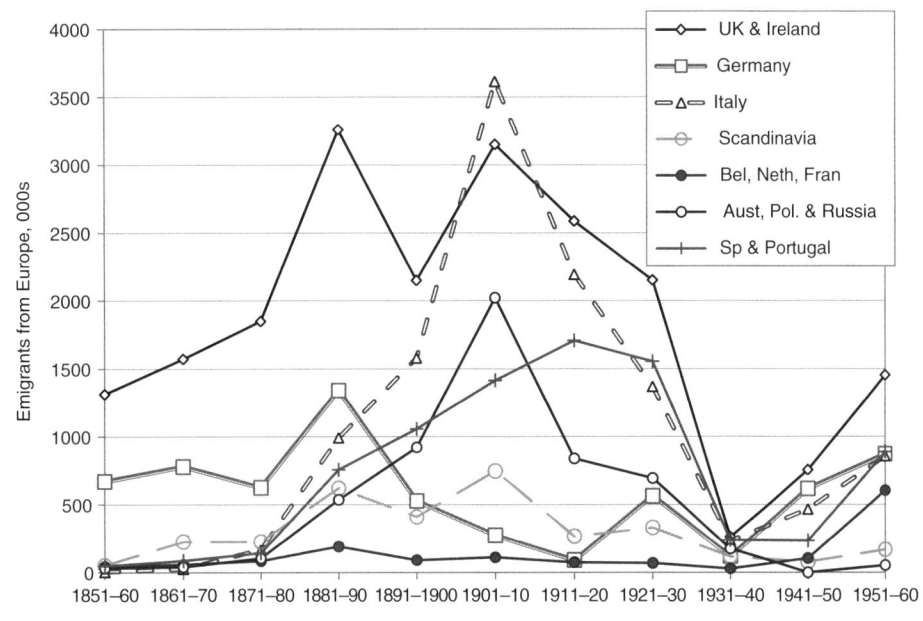

Figure 5.4 Emigration from Europe by Decade, 1851–1960.
Notes: Figure refers to emigration to countries outside of Europe. Scandinavia is: Denmark, Finland, Norway and Sweden. Germany after 1941 includes only West Germany. Netherlands excludes emigration to the Dutch Overseas Colonies. The UK figures date from 1853 and until 1870 excludes the direct emigration from Irish ports. Some of the data that overlap World War II are truncated.
Source: Mitchell (1998) *International Historical Statistics: Europe*, 129 – see General Sources.

century to the First World War, however, the flows changed destinations with 2.4 Italian immigrants now going to North America for every one going to South America.[34] This changing flow mirrors the changing pace of economic growth in the respective hemispheres.

Immigration to "lands of new settlement" before 1914 has often been viewed by historians as happening in distinct waves, most importantly by Brinley Thomas and Arthur Lewis.[35] Since these waves can be characterized by the new groups entering the migratory stream, sometimes as a majority, they raise a critical question: why do they become trans-Atlantic migrants in numbers at a particular period or date? The answer, anticipated earlier in this chapter, is that the historical process is dependent on dislocation in the home country. In some cases, the dislocation was caused by calamity. Most usually, however, it came about because of newfound economic strength in the home country, albeit modest. If the home economy is a traditional one with little change in the structure of employment, by industry, only a few individuals, at the margin, will become migrants. When, however, the home country begins to industrialize, there is an internal reorganization of labor markets in response. Labor moves from the traditional economic activity to the expanding sector. Attracted by higher wages reflecting a higher marginal product of labor, the workers must relocate *within* the country to take advantage of the higher income possibilities, rural-urban and inter-regional migration. There is a long-standing debate among economic historians about whether emigration and internal migration are positively or negatively related. The evidence largely supports the positive relationship.

Information, too, begins to flow more widely and abundantly. Shaken from their traditional roots in agriculture or low-productivity industries, labor becomes more open to the prospects of international migration. International migration was very often a two- or multi-stage process. So, for example, we find the Italians cast themselves into the international migratory flow just as the Italian economy shows signs of economic reorganization and real income per capita growth in the late-19th century. Thus, the background conditions of the waves of trans-Atlantic migration were the emergence of modern economic growth in the home countries. Waves of immigration, however, cannot go on with the same or growing intensity. It is the home economy "wage effect" that puts on the dampers. Real wages at home reacted to the loss of labor through immigration; they also responded to the continuing change of the structure of the economy in the home country.[36] The international migrants expected the real wage differential between the donor and host countries to narrow.[37]

For potential immigrants, the attractive forces of North and South America in the years before 1914 did not send out steady signals. The frontiers were expanding westward. The frontiers drew in-migrants, both domestic and international. Some responded to the free farm land or its low price. After the US Civil War was over the provision of the Homestead Act (passed in 1862) had effect, and there was a flood of migrants to take advantage of its grants of free land. The US and Canadian railroad (railway) companies actively promoted the land they acquired from their governments.[38] The Canadian frontier settlement lagged behind the US expansion by about three decades (and this fact was itself instrumental in the cycles that were generated). However, the gains (economic rents) were not simply in agriculture. They were in mineral industries and in processing the products of agriculture (meat packing, grain milling) and, importantly, shipping. Transport was one of the keys to the westward expansion, a necessity to exploit the frontier gains. The US and Canada built canal systems, the most significant were the Erie Canal and the Welland Canal, in each country respectively. The Erie linked the western regions, of the day, to the main export market in New York. The Welland linked the western Great Lakes to Lake Ontario and the St. Lawrence River and the Oswego Connector of the Erie. Canal building was replaced in the 1840s and 1850s by railroad (railway) building, and after the US Civil War the rail network became a trans-continental one. The relevant feature, for our purposes, was that canals and railroads were massive undertakings that were by their very nature "lumpy." They sucked in labor, and other resources, *for the construction period* and then had little further need of them. On-going labor demand was for the operation of the transport network and farming. But most immigrants did not go to the farm-frontier areas, although many did: they went to the manufacturing and service centers that prospered because of the growth brought about by expansion.

Immigrants tended to be young. This (net) flow of immigrants added to the population of the receiving countries in ages typically associated with family formation and child-bearing. It has, as we have seen, the opposite effect on the immigrant-sending or donor countries. The historical pattern of fertility in those countries receiving immigrants was, in general, higher as a result of the changed age-structure of the population, now biased toward the young. (No country which began to receive the immigrants in the 19th century had yet entered the low birth and low death rate phase of the demographic transition.) Where these immigrants located geographically in the economy also mattered. Naturally, this was determined by the demand for the skills that the laborers supplied. Even within a country, as we have seen, both fertility and mortality were sensitive to location, especially at the level of the most basic distinction of place, rural and urban.[39] Thus, in an historical sense, it is not realistic to view the demographic transition separately from the flows of new (net) immigrants.

During their transitions from an agricultural to manufacturing- and service-based industry many economies achieved an extraordinary high level of investment. The high investment rates propelled the transition at a more rapid rate than otherwise possible. Since these investment rates were well beyond the capacity of domestic savings to finance, capital inflows provided the difference. A capital inflow is nothing more than an international transfer of savings and was often linked to another transfer, the transfer of human resources. When these two flows happen together *in significant amounts* the capital flow is said to be "population-sensitive." The massive flow of immigrants to the expanding "new" world economies, from the "old" world economies of Europe, in the 19th and early 20th centuries also witnessed an unprecedented flow of capital (savings) in the same direction. Each flow was a response to the higher rewards expected in an economy that was expanding more rapidly than another. Yet human and capital flows are not always found together. Much, it appears, depends on size. Small marginal benefits may be sufficient to attract financial arbitrage and result in an import of capital but insufficiently large to cover the transactions costs of human migration or open the wage differential. So we frequently find that capital flows are not directly "population-sensitive." Foreign direct investment, for instance, where capital flows are designed to overcome barriers to trade and labor flows, is another example. (Foreign direct investment is investment by firms and usually takes the form of setting up manufacturing plants and distribution facilities.) The (savings) capital flow is actually a substitute for the inhibited labor flow in this instance. In the years before the First World War, international flows of labor and capital often occur together but we should not be surprised when there are exceptions.

The international migrants carried their savings and any movables with them as property when they migrated. The balance of payments name is cash and settlers' effects. Important as these are to the individuals, however, they contribute only a small percentage to the net capital flow. But from the migrants' point-of-view, this was a vital flow. The success in establishing themselves on a farm, in housing or in business or a profession often depended on this endowment brought to the new land.

Quantitatively more important from a balance of payments perspective was the transfer of demand into the country whose wage rates induced the immigration. To explain this we must remember that non-tradable goods made up the greatest part of consumption. Housing, school services, medical and educational services can normally only be produced and consumed at the point of residence.[40] Young immigrants (remember that youth is their principal demographic characteristic) moved their demand for housing from their home country to their new country.

This further spawned a demand for social infrastructure, much of it urban. For instance, even when the western farm sector was expanding most rapidly in North America of the 19th century, the population of the urban areas in the east was expanding even more rapidly. The needed infrastructure included water and sewage systems, roads, urban lighting (both gas and electricity), railroads and urban transport systems and the like. Immigrant-receiving countries were mostly current-account deficit countries in a balance of payments sense. That is, they typically imported more than they exported. The US, Canada, Australia, New Zealand, South Africa, Argentina, Chile, and Brazil were all countries with this immigration and balance of payments profile.[41] During the Victorian era and up to World War I, they were all exporters of primary produce (grains, cotton, cattle and meat products, other farm produce, timber, minerals, and coffee). These net current account deficits were offset by capital account surpluses – think of this as an export of bits of paper, the paper representing the debt instruments such as bonds – as the overall balance of the international accounts is zero. Thus, when we look at the security placements in the world capital markets, dominated by Britain until 1914, they overwhelmingly represent the social overhead capital projects either directly or indirectly through national, provincial, state and city government debt.[42]

The overall timing of the capital inflows corresponds to the pace of the domestic restructuring. The faster the transition of the share composition of industry, the higher the rate of investment and the higher the reliance on imported capital (savings). Of course, there is circularity in this reasoning as one feeds on the other. What set these forces in motion were the great opportunities for rents in the "new" economies. By the same argument, it is the diminution of the economic rents that slows down the boom – the lumpiness referred to earlier. Over the course of the boom we find large immigrant flows and population-sensitive capital flows. As many historians have observed the pace of economic development (real GDP growth) in these new immigrant-receiving countries, and particularly the capital imports, has a cyclical quality. Not surprisingly, savings transferred to the expanding economies was at the expense of domestic investment in the home country. So too, was the imbedded human capital that we today call the 'brain-drain'.[43] Particularly after about 1850 when world commodity and capital markets were more integrated, the typical cycle was about 15 to 25 years in duration (the Kuznets Cycle). Kuznets Cycles were unique to the years between the early Victorian age and the outbreak of World War I.[44]

5.5 Unbalanced Cargoes

Prior to the 19th century, trade on the North Atlantic was carried out in relatively small ships. While there had been some growth in the size of vessels over the course of two centuries, the average 18th century Atlantic trading vessel out of Philadelphia was still less than 200 "measured" tons.[45] The exports they carried from North America were largely tobacco, rice, wheat and flour, indigo, dried fish, and naval stores (specialized lumber, rope, tar and pitch, and turpentine). Ships clearing Caribbean ports in Jamaica, Grenada and Antigua tended to be a little larger as they carried goods such as raw sugar, molasses and rum. The goods shipped from Europe westward across the Atlantic were manufactured goods and specialized foodstuffs such as spices and, famously, tea. However, relative to the goods carried later, most eastbound cargoes, tended to be of high value relative to their bulk.

Yet, in the early 19th century, there was a revolution in shipping led by the demand for ships to carry low value, high bulk goods on the eastward voyage across the Atlantic. Once the political troubles between the US and Britain were resolved in the aftermath of the Napoleonic Wars, the US became a major shipper of cotton and wheat. Somewhat earlier, British North America (Canada, New Brunswick and Nova Scotia) became Britain's woodyard, to use Arthur Lower's well-worn phrase.[46] Shippers responded by becoming more specialized, expanding vessel size, and increasing the number of ships. The average size of a sailing ship landing at the port of Quebec in 1800 was less than 150 registered tons. By 1851 it had risen to over 400 tons.[47]

The rise of the average capacity of the Atlantic fleet created a problem of unbalanced cargoes. The westbound voyage could not generate a similar volume of high value/low bulk traffic leading to what Harold Innis called the problem of unused capacity.[48] He raised the questions – which he answered correctly – what price to charge on the westbound voyage for the space and what would occupy it? The solution was to carry immigrants and price the space using marginal cost principles. The increase in the supply of passenger travel space forced the price (cost to the immigrant) down. Most historians date the beginning of the age of mass trans-Atlantic migration to the immediate post-1815 years, the time when the price of westbound space declined significantly. The lowest quality passage, steerage class, was about £5 (approximately $24US) for the westward voyage in 1820s from Liverpool to Philadelphia. While this was about the same nominal fare being charged in 1684, in real terms (relative to the rise in average earnings) it was about one-third.[49] Fares on the ships offering the poorest quality of steerage class, the timber ships, charged even less.

But passenger transport also became more practical as ships became larger and more efficient. Voyage times became shorter and more predictable, also contributing to the decline of cost per voyage. By the 1840s the new steam ships appeared. At first, the technology was applied to sailing ships as an auxiliary source of power – see Figure 5.3. Later, with the further enhancement of engine efficiency, exclusively steam-powered ships appeared. They were capable of meeting a relatively rigid time schedule and reaching more ports in Europe. For instance, in 1847 the first regular sailing by direct route to a continental European port, Bremen, was established by the SS *Washington* out of New York (an auxiliary). The demonstration of the latent passenger demand further spurred the development of specialized, fast ships to transport passengers and the mail. Passenger fares on the packet ships from Liverpool to Philadelphia fell to less than £3 10s by the mid-19th century, and declined further by the end of the century.[50] By this time there were regular voyages of steamships devoted to passenger traffic – the precursor of the modern ocean liner. These ships were also capable of filling the hold with other goods such as wheat and cattle on the east-bound voyage.[51] The unused capacity problem did not disappear in the bulk trades however, and many immigrants, but now a minority, in the late-19th century still took the trip in the old-style sailing vessels. By the beginning of the 20th century, however, sailing ships as passenger vessels had largely disappeared. The reduction of the barrier of the high fares on the trans-Atlantic passage was one of the many reasons for increased international migration.

The increase in passenger volume led in the early 19th century to the development of a European network of sea shipping routes, opened as feeders to channel passengers to the ports serving the US and Canadian migrant traffic. By mid-century, the growth of railway networks further linked places remote from the sea to the ports. The catchment area of potential migrants expanded enormously as the price of land transport fell. To a contemporary in mid- to late-19th century Europe, it must have seemed that the whole continent was on the move.

5.6 Information and Advertising

Information about costs and benefits of relocating was the key to the decision to become an immigrant or not. It had two dimensions: quantity and quality. Prior to the 19th century this information was typically modest in quantity and of uncertain provenance. It was only slowly transferred from the individuals in the host country to those in sending countries and within the latter area disseminated in an idiosyncratic manner. Furthermore, there is a ubiquity factor: the more people talked about America or Australia or South Africa the more people were open to the idea of emigration to these places. The Chinese who came to the west coast of North America in the 19th century were told stories at home of the "Land of the Golden Mountain" just as the Irish fed themselves on the myths of New York and Boston. Of course, the myth might just be that, a tall story. But it was a story that was widely spread and so came to be believed in some measure. However, for emigration to take place on a systematic basis the information had to pass a quality test of reasonableness and experience. Folk who signed on with Walter Gibson certainly had good information as far as it went. But they may not have fully comprehended the conditions under which they would serve, probably in the tobacco fields of Virginia. Part of the 19th century revolution in the technology of transport was the more rapid spread of information. Facilitated by a greater speed, variety and ease of communication (newspapers, telegraphs, the trans-Atlantic cable and international postal services) this meant a greater reliability about the information both by virtue of timeliness and source. This was particularly vital in reporting about labor market opportunities and the prospects for settlement. Information from distant locations fell in price and improved in quality and both gradually enlarged the catchment area of possible migrants. Alas it was also true that the new communications gave rise to advertising and persuasion some of which was hugely misleading. Thus, some of key elements promoting the international, and internal, mass movement of people came into being. Now, letters could be sent home regularly at low cost in which the personal fate of the past immigrants could be assessed by the potential emigrants. The high time-cost barrier was systematically reduced.

Indeed, one of the best predictors, in an historical sense, of where the immigration would come from was the stock of immigrants already in place, at least, when the flow was increasing. People informed one another, spoke of the benefits, spoke of their difficulties and even conveyed vital labor market information.[52] Thanks to the exhaustive research of Simone Wegge into the social networks of German migrants in the mid-19th century, we know more about these processes and how they worked. In predicting, retrospectively, who might enter the migratory streams, family ties were very important, as were the close ties associated with the villages from which they came. Further, she found that the links were acted upon fairly soon after the first family member established themselves in the US, although some family networks operated for at least a decade. The village-family networks lasted much longer.[53] The case of immigrants coming from Hesse-Cassel was not unique: "If you come to Boston, I can arrange a job on my worksite." In addition, successful immigrants remitted cash to their homes which helped to finance (through grants or loans) the next generation of immigrants. These are known, in a balance of payments sense, as "immigrants' remittances." This flow of cash was accompanied by an equally vital flow of subtle information, largely immeasurable but much of it of good quality.

Information also came in the form of advertising. Some of this was blatant propaganda of self-seeking opportunists: the land development companies, the railroads with their land grants to sell off and individual employers looking for cheaper labor. But it was not necessarily a zero-sum game; the immigrant gained too. Public policy was also part of this mix as North American, Australian, New Zealand and South African provinces, states and national governments sought out and tried to attract immigrants. So too did South American countries such as Chile, Argentina and Brazil. These governments sponsored speaking tours (often bringing successful immigrants back to their places of origin), held town meetings, and published newspapers and pamphlets devoted to the cause of emigration and why their location was the most-favored.

We also cannot dismiss the effects of dramatic events as advertising. Gold discoveries such as those in California in 1840s, Australia in the 1880s and the Klondike in the 1890s, to name a few, attracted world-wide attention and induced a sudden influx of immigrants: gold rush fever. Ships set out for the west coast of North America, for instance, laden with the hopeful in 1848. But the high expectations were seldom met. The locals got there first. Even then, apart from a fortunate few, the gold rushes never did pay off for the miners/immigrants. Those who benefited were those who provided the services.[54] However, the disappointed hopefuls mostly did not return home; they moved on to take up jobs in the rapidly expanding economies of the countries in which they now found themselves (although likely in an impoverished state).

5.7 Remittances: Then and Now

Immigrants' remittances are money and goods that immigrants send to their countries of origin. For any country, this is a net flow. The payment of such remittances was common throughout the age of mass migration, but their volume increased significantly in the last third of the 19th century when the international transfer of funds became easier and immigrants became wealthier. Gary Magee and Andrew Thompson estimate that, between 1875 and 1913, US immigrants of British origin remitted approximately 16% of their earnings back to the UK.[55] The majority of remitters were motivated by four factors. First, remitters had a sense of obligation to help finance the next round of emigration (usually of other family members). Successive waves of migration were thus self-financing so long as the chain was not broken. Second, there was a desire to provide material support to those who remained at home. Indeed, the "new economics" of labor migration argues that remittances were part of an implicit contract between immigrants and the families they left behind – it was the expected thing to do.[56] The decision to migrate was inseparable from the remittance decision for many. For instance, the many ethnic Chinese laborers who went to 19th century North America (and elsewhere) through revolving labor contracts sent a high proportion of their (low) wages home simply to afford a higher standard-of-living for parents, spouses and children in China.[57] Many, particularly the Southern European immigrants to North America, came with no such guarantee of employment but were similarly motivated.[58] However, there was also a third motivating factor: investing activities, acquiring and maintaining a home in their native country for planned retirement. Last, we must note that as several recent natural disasters reveal, émigrés contribute generously to (welfare) relief efforts in their country of origin.

Today, the World Bank's reports of remittance flows throughout the world indicate that they have been growing rapidly. As measured in US dollars, migrant remittance inflows increased from $2 billion in 1970 to $35 billion in 1985 and to $132 billion in 2000. The estimate for 2008 is $433 billion, and it has been argued that the true amount could be as much as 75% higher.[59] Clearly much of this increase is due to greater diligence in tracking the flow; individual countries are doing a better job of collecting data and more countries are reporting to the World Bank. Because these flows were (and are) much larger than had been recognized previously, the question is raised as to what extent these remittances contribute to economic development in the receiving country? How are the families and friends that receive the monies using this income flow? For one group, the return migrants, the answer is clear: saving in the form of assets – see the next section of this chapter. One answer to this question, however, is clear in the case of Nepal and Malawi: the funds used contribute to the education of the young who receive more schooling than otherwise would be the case.[60] Other questions are the subject of debate by development researchers who typically examine the problems of a particular country. But, at this juncture, there are few general lessons to be drawn.

The ten top countries in the World Bank database for 2007 with respect to absolute amount of migrant remittance inflows measured in millions of US dollars are given in Table 5.3.

There are few surprises here; these are generally large countries with a large number of their native-born living elsewhere, but the right hand column has been included to indicate that, with the exception of the Philippines, these large dollar amounts are in reality a small percentage of the country's GDP. Perhaps a more informative way of looking at the World Bank data is to look at the top ten countries with respect to percentage of the country's GDP. With the exception of Lebanon, these are all classified as either "low-income" or "lower middle-income" countries. Remittances make a significant contribution to the immigrant-sending countries. While we lack the data to examine this as carefully as might be desired, it seems likely that the

Table 5.3 Remittances by Absolute Amount and Rank by Percentage of GDP, 2007.

	Rank by Amount				Rank by % of GDP		
Rank	Country	Remittances $US millions	% of GDP	Rank	Country	% of GDP	Remittances $US millions
1	India	38 666	3.29%	1	Tajikistan	45.54%	1750
2	China	32 833	1.02%	2	Tonga	39.37%	100
3	Mexico	27 136	2.65%	3	Moldova	34.08%	1897
4	Philippines	16 302	11.32%	4	Lesotho	27.70%	443
5	France	13 745	0.53%	5	Guyana	25.78%	278
6	Spain	10 739	0.75%	6	Lebanon	23.69%	6000
7	Poland	10 496	2.49%	7	Samoa	22.83%	135
8	Germany	9839	0.30%				
9	Nigeria	9221	5.57%				
10	Belgium	8557	1.89%				

Source: United Nations (2008) *Migration and Remittances Factbook 2008*, http://www.un.org/esa/population/publications/2009Migration_Chart/ittmig_wallchart09_table.xls.

motivation and uses of these remittances has not changed much over the centuries. What has changed is the ease with which monies can be moved internationally, and the increase in volume has made this an important element for future study.

5.8 There and Back Again – Reverse Migrations

We do not know with any certainty where emigrants go (see earlier – Who's In and Who's Out).[61] Even today it requires a highly focused investigation and plenty of research dollars, and time, to discover the truth of the matter.[62] But there are some vital clues and some historical results. In the late 20th century in the United States approximately 30% of all the foreign-born residents (citizens and legal permanent residents) enter the emigration stream. This has been surprisingly constant for the entire century.[63] According to the last full census about one-quarter of a million permanent US residents left the US each year in the decade of the 1990s to take up permanent residence elsewhere. Over 80% of these emigrants were foreign-born.[64] We do not know that they all are true return migrants (returning to their country of origin) but many, probably a majority, are. Similarly, in the United Kingdom in 2006 and 2007, the emigration flow (about 63% of the immigrant flow) was made up of a slight majority of non-British citizens (51%) and of the remainder who are British citizens many of which would be foreign-born. (The British do not collect the same data as the US). The institutionalized free movement of labor within the European Union gives a range of flexibility to British migrants and a higher ratio of emigrants to immigrants than the US, an option not available to non-Europeans and, of course, not available to US emigrants. Germany too, whose data more resembles that collected in the US, finds that foreign-born residents are approximately 10% of the total population, and about 80% of the outflow, similar to the US.[65]

> *Return migration*: immigrants to a country who have full-time residence status and who return to their country of origin (for a period of at least one year). They may have host country citizenship. Historically, before the 1920s, countries were more relaxed about citizenship and many immigrants never acquired the citizenship of their new country.
>
> *Temporary migrants*: immigrants who have limited rights of residence such as "guest workers," workers on specific term contracts and harvest time agricultural labor. Historically, many individuals did have a right to stay in the host country but chose not to do so either because of their contracts provided passage home or there was active discrimination directed at them. Chinese workers often fell into this group. The Chinese refer to temporary migrants as "swallows."
>
> *Visitors*: Some temporary migrants are technically "visitors." Many such visitors come from northern countries taking up winter residence in warmer climates, such as Spain and Florida; they are often referred to as "snowbirds."

But we know a little bit more of the recent German return emigration than we do of most others. Return migration was closely associated with remittances, as noted earlier. A close association with the family at home and individual life-cycle planning seem to lie behind this link between return and remittances. The latter suggests that individuals planned to return home although not necessarily at the beginning of their immigration experience. The more highly educated are more prone to return migration than those with low levels of human capital *provided* the labor markets in the country of origin are relatively open. Those whose actual income was well below that that was reasonably expected, whatever their level of education, were more likely to go home.[66] Women tended to carry more of their "being a migrant" advantage home to their labor markets of origin than men.[67] The causes of return migration were likely the same in the past as they are today. To be sure, the institutional setting was different, such as the lack of open labor markets in the country of origin, and the costs and penalties higher than they are now. This was a barrier to return.

Nevertheless, immigrants did return home. Even in the 17th century folk were returning to England from the New England colonies. The number can never be known as most left quietly with no records of their movements kept. Of those who left records, the highly educated, puritan zeal to proselytize at home seems to have motivated some to return. Many returned for more prosaic reasons, such as not adapting to the new world and escaping debt.[68] And, as mentioned earlier, an unknown but

Table 5.4 Italian Emigration by Destination, for Periods, 1876–1976.

	Total Emigration	Annual Average	Destinations				
			Europe	South America	North America	Other	Return
	millions	000s	Percentage				
1876–1900	5.3	212.0	48.5	35.0	15.0	1.5	
1901–1915	8.8	587.0	41.0	17.0	40.0	2.0	50.0
1916–1942	4.4	163.0	51.5	19.0	25.0	4.5	52.0
1946–1976	7.4	239.0	68.5	12.5	12.5	6.5	58.0

Source: data from Bailey (1999) 24.

large number of convicts and prisoners returned to Britain. The return of the British immigrants continued and probably reached its height, in both absolute and proportional terms, in the 50 years before the First World War. But the British were not alone.

The years of high Italian immigration to the Americas are highlighted in Table 5.4. In the years 1870–1929, more than 50% of the immigrants returned home. Italy had one of the highest rates of return migration and unlike the British return was much more dominated by acquisition of home country assets and the life-cycle retirement motives. (Southern Europeans, in general, appear more drawn back to their countries of origin than most.) The author Dino Cinel argues that the remittances associated with the return migration, actual and anticipated, were "one of the most important dynamics in the Italian economy and society during the half-century 1875–1925."[69] It touched so many families and reached a volume that inspired a national debate about how the imported savings could be directed in a macroeconomic sense.

No immigrant group had a higher rate of return migration than the Japanese who entered the US before the Second World War – a staggering 85% of the 288 thousand immigrants who had arrived since the inception of Japanese immigration in the third quarter of the 19th century. Japanese immigrants, like their Chinese and other East Asian counterparts, had come under increasing anti-oriental prejudice with its origins in the late-19th century. By the period 1913–1925 this reached fever pitch with many states, especially in the west, restricting the ownership of agricultural land by Japanese immigrants.[70] Not surprisingly, faced with this xenophobic attitude, the Japanese immigrants and many of their American-born children (Nisei) chose to leave. The exodus drew disproportionately from those connected to agriculture (market gardening) including the large number of farm laborers who made up the ethnic Japanese population of the US. The end result was that the Japanese population who were left in the US was comprised of the successful professionals and therefore was (or looked) essentially "middle class" – which itself has engendered a debate about the success of the Japanese in America.[71] There is little question that the majority of Japanese immigrants intended to reside permanently in the US. Circumstances did not permit them to do so.

5.9 Diaspora

The term "diaspora" was first used to describe the removal of the Jews from their biblical homeland during the Babylonian Captivity and their subsequent spread and, often forced, movement throughout the world. In recent years the word has come to be applied to many other distinct ethnic or culturally-defined populations who shared some general characteristics of spread and forced movement. Thus in addition to the Jewish diaspora, we may talk of the African diaspora with its origins in Arab/European/American slavery and include the migrations and settlement of, say Afro-Caribbeans in Britain during the 20th century. Diasporas transcend national boundaries. And, diasporas may be found in the following list (with their initial cause):

- the Acadians, military-political resettlement in the 18th century;
- the Armenians, political repression in the 19th and 20th century;
- the Eritreans, political repression and poverty late-20th and early-21st^t centuries;
- the Chinese, forced labor contracts and poverty in the late-19th and early-20th centuries;
- the European gypsies, ethnic discrimination in the 19th and 20th centuries;
- the Highland Scots, agricultural displacement in the 18th and 19th centuries;
- the Indians, forced labor contracts in the 19th and 20th centuries;
- the Irish, recurring famine conditions and poverty in the 19th and early-20th centuries;
- and many others.

What unites the various elements of the list is that there is an event such as a famine or political repression or religious or cultural intolerance that sets the forces of diaspora in motion.

A. The Chinese

The control of the highly centralized Qing government of China began to break down in the 19th century. As it did, the pace of migration of the Chinese population sped up both within China and, through emigration, to other countries. The background of this change was a growth of family size – the very beginning of the demographic transition. Specific disruptions caused by the Opium Wars (1839–1842), the Taiping Rebellion (1850–1864) and the Boxer Rebellion (1898–1901) helped further to create an unsettled economic climate. So too did the many local outbreaks of violence that troubled China in the waning years of the Qing Dynasty. Yet, the prime mover, on the supply side, was the grinding poverty in the well-settled areas. Some migrants were attracted by the greater income opportunities of the frontier areas of China, and even peasants who were legally tied to the land (about 10% of the population) entered the migratory stream. But, it was not always the poorest who responded. Some better-off peasant families also moved, and in this sense their movement resembled the frontier migration of American farm families in the 19th century.[72] So, too, the Chinese began to explore labor markets and trading opportunities abroad. It was the beginning of the mass spread of the ethnic Chinese to all corners of the world. It has been estimated that in 2000 34 million Chinese-born migrants lived outside China in 140 countries of the world. Today there are more as Chinese emigration has increased in the past decade – although numbers are difficult to measure. These *tangren*, as they call themselves, do not include those of Chinese ethnicity who were born outside China, residents and nationals of other countries.[73] In many cases the second, and subsequent, generations of ethnic Chinese have rejected or just simply lost their ancestral identity, and often lost their Chinese language skills. Thus, the number of ethnic Chinese abroad is very much more, but unknown, than the overseas Chinese-born population.

But it is perhaps not the numbers that are so surprising. China through most of history has had the world's largest population so emigration when it did take place was inevitably large. What is surprising is the rapidity of the Chinese diaspora and its extent. For instance, when the revolutionary patriot Sun Yat Sen raised money to finance his political cause in the late-19th century, he traveled to, and was able to gather funds from, a large and geographically diverse expatriate and ethnic Chinese community. Most of the migrants who went overseas came from Southern China, particularly the southern provinces of Guangdong and Fujian. The 19th century Chinese emigration was, on the demand side, essentially a response to: i) the demand for unskilled labor, and ii) the economic opportunities from trading. The Chinese diaspora, as noted, grew extremely rapidly in the second half of the 19th century and quite naturally it focused, in the first instance, on the countries of South-East Asia particularly the Malay States (now Singapore and Malaysia).[74] Britain and France signed a migration treaty with China in 1860 in order to ensure a steady flow, indeed an increased flow, of labor to their South East Asian colonies. Unlike the western countries of the US, Canada, New Zealand and Australia, the South East Asian countries and European colonies of the region never introduced draconian anti-Chinese legislation. This is not to say that the migration was not troubled by discriminatory practices on the part of governments, it was. There were even legal barriers placed on the Chinese returning from abroad by the Chinese government itself although they were often overcome by specific treaties such as that noted above.[75] However, the fever pitch of Western, and so-called White, countries was generally avoided.

In a relatively short period of time Singapore became an ethnically Chinese enclave, as seen in Table 5.5. The Chinese in Singapore were quick to exploit the trading ventures of the region. In order to explain this success historians point to the adaptability, education and entrepreneurial spirit of the Chinese throughout South East Asia.[76] Chinese traders, some of whom lived outside of China, were very familiar with the commercial possibilities in the Straits of Malacca and the South China Sea areas. Indeed, many of them, according to Wang Gungwu, were familiar with the British and Dutch trading regimes and their practices and were quickly adapted to Singapore.[77] However, Singapore was unusual in that the ethnic Chinese became the majority population – thereby contributing to the break with the rest of the Malay States. In most South East Asian countries into which Chinese migrants flowed in great numbers they remained a minority (Malaya, Indonesia, Thailand, Burma, the Philippines and the countries of Indo-China).[78]

The first recorded Chinese in Latin America were earlier than the 19th century. William Bernstein describes the petition of Mexico City "barbers" in 1635 against the

Table 5.5 The Chinese Population of Singapore, 1824–1947.

Year	Total Chinese	Chinese Male	Chinese Female	Population of Singapore	% Chinese To Total Population
			(000s)		
1824	3.3	3.0	0.4	10.7	31
1834	10.8	9.9	0.8	26.3	41
1849	28.0	25.7	2.2	52.9	53
1860	50.0	46.8	3.2	81.7	61
1871	50.1	46.6	7.5	97.1	56
1881	86.8	72.6	14.2	139.2	62
1891	121.1	100.4	21.5	184.6	66
1901	164.0	130.4	33.7	228.6	72
1911	219.6	161.6	57.9	303.3	72
1921	317.5	215.9	101.6	425.9	75
1931	421.8	263.2	158.6	567.5	74
1947	730.1	387.9	342.3	940.8	78

Note: These data are the ethnic populations, not simply those born in China.
Source: Freedman (1957), p. 25 and Ee (1961), 50.

Chinese barbers who had settled there. There was also an early 17th century migration to Peru associated with the trans-Pacific trade in gold-silver (eastward) and Chinese silk (westward). Since this trade was conducted through the Philippines, it is not surprising to find that it induced a movement of people from China to Manila as well. Migration tended to follow trade. Chinese manual laborers were imported to work the mines.[79] In the latter half of the 19th century when the diaspora gathered force, Chinese settlement was encouraged in Brazil where state-sponsored tea agriculture was introduced in the mid-19th century. The authorities sought cheap but experienced tea workers from China. In other areas the Chinese migrants provided the usual unskilled labor. There was, for instance, a substantial migration to Latin America and the Caribbean, particularly Peru and Cuba, where the "coolies" were employed in the mines and sugar cane fields. The latter was a direct consequence of the abolition of slavery in Cuba in 1845; the first Chinese arrived in Cuba two years later as indentured servants.[80]

In North America, the first Asian immigrants arrived in the US and Canada during the gold rushes of the 1840s and 50s where, amongst other things, they contributed to the local taxes to such an extent that anti-Chinese local sentiment did not get political backing at this time.[81] Economic self-interest overcame stark prejudice. (The coincident gold rushes in Australia signaled the first arrival of the Chinese in that continent.) The mammoth projects of trans-continental railway building were also underway in the aftermath of the US Civil War and the Chinese provided the brute labor particularly in the western states, territories (and provinces). Notably, the anti-Chinese sentiment began as these projects wound down. The Chinese advantage in supplying the labor lay in vast quantities without affecting the price of labor. Even during World War I tens of thousands of Chinese laborers were recruited to dig the trenches and to carry-on the civilian building repair and menial work vacated by the French conscripted into the army. Aided by the Allied governments many traveled across the Pacific and through the US on sealed trains before crossing the Atlantic to France.

Many, if not most, of the Chinese laborers were principally interested in remitting funds back to families. It was often based on a family decision which may have included the choice of which son would be the emigrant. Many who emigrated on limited labor contracts repeated the experience and so became permanent "temporary residents" much like the many guest workers in post-1945 Europe. Others became trapped in a form of "debt-peonage." Gangs of laborers were recruited in China by China-based recruiters acting for foreign contractors and for overseas Chinese merchants who financed the migration. Somewhat similar to the indentured servants of the 17th and 18th centuries' migration from Europe, the merchants would pay for the passage and other expenses, one of which was an immigrant "head tax." Workers were required to reimburse the merchants who paid the passage and head tax, but, because they often had not paid in full by the end of their period of contract service, they were required to extend their stay and agree to new labor contracts. They were caught in a revolving debt trap. While indentured service was illegal in the US by this time (the late 19th century), there is compelling evidence to show that extra-legal means were used to enforce the practice. One of contributing factors was the immigrants' ignorance of alternatives because of the cultural and language barriers.[82]

It was very difficult, especially after the 1880s, for an existing Chinese migrant to North America to sponsor his spouse and family because of either the prohibitions or the very high head tax applied to the Chinese women migrants.[83] A stated objective of the anti-Chinese policy which emerged in the last quarter of the century was to discourage the permanent settlement of the Chinese immigrants by forcing a low sex ratio (females to males) in the community, thus preventing new families and the re-unification of existing families. The consequence was a population of aging men far from the families they supported. There were, however, loopholes as the government's anti-Chinese policies were also generally class-based, and exceptions were made for merchants' families. It is also highly likely that many laborers evaded the prohibitions and "were hidden in plain sight."[84] Perhaps the exclusionary tactic was not as effective as once believed. Apart from manual labor, in the late-19th century, the low (offer) wage Chinese were beginning to move into domestic service industries directly and indirectly, such as laundries, just as women were beginning to exit domestic employment and expand the range of their work choices in increasingly industrializing economies.

Today, the Chinese diaspora consists of many individuals who are not Chinese nationals and are members of the diaspora only through their ethnicity, itself a somewhat imprecise concept. (Where ethnicity is a characteristic actually identified by modern censuses, it is through self-declaration.) For instance, from the last complete census of the United Kingdom (2001), 0.42% of the population describe themselves as ethnic Chinese – a small ethnic group by British standards. Almost 30% of these were British born and an additional 40% were born in countries other than China and Britain. The latter are the ethnic Chinese who were immigrants from Hong Kong (under British rule) and other countries as varied as South Africa and Malaysia.[85] That is, more and more the ethnic Chinese diaspora takes on characteristics separate from the ancestral home. Even these links and associations are weakening, including for the reason of mixed ethnic marriages, "neither *hauqiao* nor *hauren*."[86] The same acculturation trend is found in the United States, Canada, Australia and New Zealand. In the US, for instance, the ethnic Chinese are one of largest minority groups, 3.54 million (2007), after the Hispanics, in the non-white and non-black populations. Almost two million of the ethnic Chinese are US-born and many of them have long family histories in the US. So too, the Canadian population is 3.9% made up of those with Chinese ancestry. Many of those chart their family trees to the first settlements in British Columbia. But, migrants from the People's Republic of China and Taiwan are now among the larger immigrant groups in contemporary North America and Australia. Some within the ethnic Chinese communities are caught between two cultures.[87]

B. The Irish

One part of the British exodus in the early 19th century was the Irish. Ireland suffered a series of bad harvests and local famines and for many years in the early 19th century the Irish made up the largest single component of the British emigration. (About 1.5 million people left Ireland, for all destinations, during the years 1815 to 1845.)[88] Driven by famine conditions and desperate poverty, it may seem surprising that so many favored the British North American colonies compared to the US before the mid-1840s. The most common route to North America was via Liverpool, and a large Canadian fleet of timber ships were available to take passengers. That they landed in Quebec City did not mean that the Irish stayed in British North America however. A large, but unknown, proportion of them subsequently left for the US where canal and later railroad building and the rapidly burgeoning industrial economy provided employment. For Canada, the Irish were the accidental tourists of the day; it was simply a matter of getting on the first available ship in the port of Liverpool. The Irish diaspora reached a climax in the 1840s. Bad as the earlier crop failures had been, none equaled the widespread famine conditions which prevailed in 1846 with the failure of the potato crop.[89] It became known as the Irish Famine (by the world) or the Great Hunger (by the Irish) and resulted from the blight which rotted the potato crop; potatoes were the staple crop of domestic consumption.

Ireland had a pre-famine population of 8.18 million, according to the Census of 1841, but this had declined by 1.62 million by the time the worst of the famine was over, according to the Census of 1851. The difference is deceptive. How many Irish died in the famine interval and how many left Ireland to feed the diaspora? To get to the correct (approximate) number of those who died due to the famine we have to add the children who were born in the census interval (some of whom may have died), subtract the number who would have died in normal circumstances for Ireland, and then count the emigration and the immigration – the latter being presumably very small. These values are, however, not recorded accurately. Joel Mokyr and Cormac Ó Gráda, nonetheless, estimate that, after accounting for the census under-reporting of deaths and other biases, approximately 1 million deaths were directly attributable to the famine conditions in Ireland in the late 1840s.[90] The other part of the population loss which came from emigration was approximately 1.28 million.

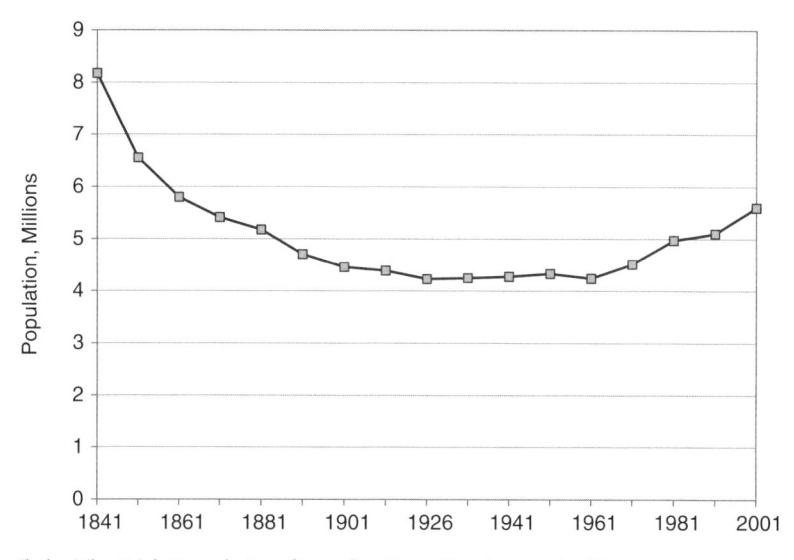

Figure 5.5 The Irish Population from the Great Famine to the Present.
Source: data from Central Statistics Office, Ireland and Northern Ireland Statistics and Research Agency.

Many who left escaped across the Irish Sea to England and Scotland to become absorbed in the industrial population of those countries.[91] (Ireland was no stranger to large scale emigration as about 1.5 million people left in the 30 years before the famine conditions of 1846.) The majority of the emigrants (923 000) took the first available ship to North America or traveled to Liverpool and Glasgow to subsequently embark on the trans-Atlantic journey.[92]

The consequence of this emigration was a decline in fertility because of the loss of young people of child-bearing age. Yet, there is no evidence to suggest a reduction of married woman's age-specific fertility in those who remained. The continual stream of departures and its effects on the age structure and sex ratio, however, did result in an Irish population that declined for one hundred years.[93] Irish agriculture then began a long and slow adaptation to the change in the human resources available, a process that was assisted by the removal of the Corn Laws in 1846 – which had help breed the hot-house conditions of pre-famine agriculture. Not until the second half of the 20th century did the Irish population increase again (see Figure 5.5). The effect on the regions to which the Irish went was also profound. Carrying a relatively low level of human capital they provided the workforces for the mines and the factory systems that were emerging in North America and Britain. Irish immigrants to the US improved their lot, but their income gain was far less than that for many other groups. The Irish tended to congregate in the cities and maintained their social and religious distinctiveness. They also, for the first generation immigrants, retained their demographic distinctiveness with a high marital fertility.[94] There is an on-going debate among historians of the Irish as to why the emigration came to be seen "as exile and banishment rather than a quest for opportunity and self-improvement."[95] The celebration of St. Patrick's Day throughout North America (and now also in Ireland) is a harkening back to the black days of the 19th century – a mixture of pathos and exaggerated romantic attachment. After all, no country has ever surrendered a greater continuing percentage of its population to emigration.

C. The Jews

The second major Jewish dispersion, after that conducted by the 5th century BC Assyrians, began in the 1st century AD as a result of "The Great Revolt" against the Romans. From then on, faced by repression in their native land, Jews began a migration that initially took them to other parts of Africa and Asia, and ultimately all over the globe. But by the 4th century, the Jewish community in Egypt had largely disappeared, the Jewish population of Palestine was in decline, and Babylon had emerged as the centre of Jewish life. Thereafter, Jewish political authority in the original homeland was surrendered unwillingly to the successor imperial powers, religious invaders and occupiers. The list is long: the Byzantine Empire, Arab empires centered in Damascus and Baghdad, European Christian states, the Egyptian Mamluks, the Ottoman Turks and the British mandate (from the League of Nations). It was not until the late-19th century that Jews began returning to Palestine to form a national home, by deliberate policy and weight of numbers. The Jewish state of Israel was created in 1948.[96] Two millennia of a people being separated from a national home raise the age-old question much discussed by Jewish and non-Jewish scholars alike: are the Jews one ethnic group or many, and does the religious identification provide the over-arching cultural identifier?

In the mid-19th century, there were significant Jewish populations in Eastern Europe, particularly Poland and Russia. From then to the eve of World War II, the Jewish population expanded, from a little over 2 to 32 million people. It then fell dramatically with the Holocaust and its subsequent demographic consequences. Maristella Botticini estimates that the 2007 population (13.155 million) was less than half of the 1939 population, with the largest concentrations now in Israel, North America and Western Europe – see Table 5.6. Similar to many groups not covered in a national census and given self-declared characteristics they are extremely difficult to count. Precision is made more difficult in this case by the strict (when applied) matrilineal definition of Jewish.[97]

There are two major features of the Jewish diaspora over the ages.[98] First, Jews have always been a minority in the places where they have lived outside of Israel – often a very small proportion of the population where they lived. In that, they are very different from the Chinese diaspora whose numbers often led them to become a significant part of the host's population as in Taiwan, Singapore and the countries of South East Asia. As a minority with a history of being persecuted, the greater heterogeneity of the society into which they came, the less likely any one group is singled out for discrimination. Jews, in the US for instance, have long played an activist role in shaping a liberal immigration policy to favor the non-Europeans.[99] The second feature of the Jewish diaspora since the Middle Ages in Western Europe, and later North America, is that it has been overwhelmingly urban in character. However, it is not sufficient to observe that the occupations chosen were ones practiced in urban centers (although they were). The occupational choices were strategically made. Jewish migrants entered skilled occupations or became merchants that embody a good deal of human capital such as the professions of medicine and financial intermediation and

Table 5.6 Countries Ranked by Size of Its Jewish Population, 2007.

Country	Jewish Population	Percentage of World Jewish Population
Israel	5 393 400	41.0
United States	5 275 000	40.1
France	490 000	3.7
Canada	374 000	2.8
United Kingdom	295 000	2.2
Russia	221 000	1.7
Argentina	184 000	1.4
Germany	120 000	0.9
Australia	104 000	0.8
Brazil	96 200	0.7

Note: The Jewish population of Israel is 74.9% of the total Israeli population (does not include West Bank and Gaza).
Source: Della Pergola (2007) *American Jewish Year Book*, Tables 5 and 8.

the mercantile ventures of the diamond trade and the fur trade. As such, skills and specialized talent are the most highly portable form of capital investment, in this case human, should relocation be required. The argument that the diaspora led Jews to invest in their human, as opposed to physical, capital because of its portability is compatible with the argument that restrictions and prohibitions against Jews led to those occupational choices.[100] Indeed, restrictions against Jewish land ownership and merchant guild proscriptions against Jewish membership directed these occupational choices. In 1931 in Toronto, a fairly typical small North American city of the period, Jews were under-represented in occupations such as stationary engineer, police, civil engineer, and metal molder and over-represented in the fur and textiles merchant trades, and the professions such as dentist, physician and lawyer.[101]

If the Jewish diaspora was proportionately small in the various host countries, and absolutely small in some cases, was there an advantage to small size? For instance, Avner Greif argues that Jewish merchants who engaged in long-distance trade during the Middle Ages were successful because they were members of a relatively small community. The case of the Maghribi traders of the Mediterranean is illustrative of what Greif calls the "community responsibility system" which enabled merchants to protect property rights, thereby facilitating spot exchange of chattels between buyers and sellers from different localities, different countries.[102] The system required that both legal and political power in each community be the responsibility of those who stood to gain from exchange. Local courts had the incentive to enforce contracts between locals and outsiders and to protect the property rights of those from outside that locality. Even in the absence of formal institutions, members of what today are called commercial or trade networks could use community sanctions to minimize opportunistic behavior. The group could ostracize, even exclude from the network, those who violated or abused basic trade relationships. In fact, there were often personal, even family, connections between traders located at distant points. One often finds in commercial networks that community members retain the ability to read and write in their own language as well as develop linguistic skills in other languages. This enables them to use their native language within the group and to use alien languages for transactions with local customers. Thus, in markets where information could be privately held, the Jewish traders had a cost advantage in operating within such a framework in Europe and North America in the same fashion as the Chinese traders in Asia.[103] It also gave them a global reach not available to local traders.

A major transformation of the Jewish diaspora began in the last quarter of the 19th century with the widespread emigration out of Eastern Europe. The new center of Jewish influence became that of the diaspora in North America/Western Europe, with the former having greater numeric significance. Then after the ravages of the Holocaust and the creation of the modern state of Israel the dual definition of Jewry became that of the diaspora *and* the homeland. The transformation began with the large influx into the US from the Russian and Austro-Hungarian empires driven by the land displacement policies (pogroms) of these regimes.[104] Similar to many migrations, it often involved stops along the way. For instance, we now know that there was a substantial flow through France and England, particularly Paris and London, that ended up in the US after some time.[105] Nonetheless, many did remain in France and England. Both countries, which now count among the largest of the Jewish diaspora nations, had long histories with their Jewish populations. Both had expelled the Jews in the Middle Ages, re-admitted them in the early modern period when well established (although small) communities were established. Members of the diaspora included the 18th century international financiers of the Rothschild family and, we need to mention David Ricardo, the great economic thinker and member-of-parliament. Benjamin Disraeli, the mid-Victorian era Prime Minister of Britain, was the poster-child of successful adaptation (despite private pain). And therein lay the dilemma of those of the diaspora, the trade-off between integration and distinctiveness.

The greatest part of the Jewish diaspora is found in the US and is derived from the Jewish immigration prior to the late 1920s. Most of these immigrants were poor and had levels of literacy lower than that of other European immigrants. They clustered together in low-priced housing of the larger North American cities, primarily New York. They worked in low wage industries and faced quite explicit anti-Semitic discrimination, the most pernicious of which were the barriers to higher education. Opposition to discrimination took two forms; the persistent resistance and the integration of the Jewish-Americans into the American social fabric. This, in turn, gave the Jewish diaspora of North America a liberal political quality. The Jewish immigrants of the late-20th and early 21st centuries (also mainly from Russia) often do not share the earlier attitudes.[106]

5.10 The Barriers Go Up

When the Irish arrived in North America during the Famine Years of the 1840s, their ships often carried a yellow flag at the masthead. This was the signal that the ship was carrying disease; cholera and smallpox were the most frequent and most feared. The ship would be quarantined, and medical inspectors alone determined when and if the immigrants could land – or could only land to be admitted to a quarantined segregation station. In this era the only restriction that immigrants faced was that of the health inspector. However, in the later part of the 19th century governments began to adopt new policies that limited entry to their countries or severely restricted certain immigrants when they landed. In the US it began with the anti-Chinese sentiment of the late-19th century. Erika Lee argues persuasively that in this racial discrimination was the origin of the modern notion of America as its own "gate-keeper."[107] Canada almost step-by-step followed the US lead in various forms of anti-oriental legislation that surfaced in the 1880s although there were some critical differences – Canada did not have a complete ban on workers from China until 1924.[108] Australia, at roughly the same time, followed suit and by the beginning of the 20th century had in effect what came to be known as a "White Australia" policy. Who was responsible for the anti-Chinese bias in legislation? Some blame the trade unions while others suggest that politicians led the movement in response to a general climate of economic pressure. While it was true that Chinese immigrants provided cheap labor, they often worked in non-competing (dual) labor markets. However, by the late-19th century, three of the great immigrant receiving-countries were virtually closed to East Asian immigrants, or, if admitted or already resident, were allowed only limited access to pursue employment and enjoy a settled life.

It was an easy step to extend the discriminatory policies to cover other Asian immigrants. So-called "gentlemen's agreements" limited the flow of Japanese-born migrants from Canada to the US and between Japan (which was interested in limiting emigration) and the North American countries. But bizarre regulations also created a high barrier to entry such as, in the British case, the requirement that South Asian migrants journeying from India to Empire countries must do so without breaking their journeys, which included the ship calling into any other port *en route*!

Before World War I, non-Asian immigrants faced few such barriers to entering the US. That changed in the aftermath of the war. Restrictive immigration policies have been the norm in most developed countries since then, although they loosened to some extent in the last decades of the 20th century. Why did they change when they did? Since the European migration across the Atlantic contributed to American economic growth before the war, why restrict it after the war? A part of the answer is that some factions within the US had been trying to restrict it via a literacy test since the 1890s.[109] An act passed both houses of Congress in 1892, but was vetoed by the president. Congress did not override the veto. Similar bills were introduced periodically thereafter with the support of both capital and labor. Indeed, such an act passed in 1912, but with the same result as the one two decades. In 1917, when a literacy test finally did pass Congress, it did so over a presidential veto.

As Claudia Goldin noted, "The ultimate switch in policy is not hard to explain. The perplexing part of the legislative history of immigration restriction is its timing."[110] The usual explanation given for why the measure finally passed is that a combination of nationalism and chauvinism developed during World War I. Fear of European "radicalism" and the resurgence of protectionist sentiment, together with organized labor's resistance to the influx of any new waves of immigrants on the pre-war scale, produced sufficient political support for restriction.[111]

As a result, immigration rates in the US fell over the first half of the 20th century. They began to increase in the second half, but not back to 19th-century levels.[112] Immigrants were a small proportion of the total population during the 20th century, but they remained a significant contributor to the rate of population growth. In the 1950s, legal immigration was responsible for roughly one-tenth of population growth, and the comparable figure today is roughly one-third.[113]

The Immigration Act of 1965 shifted policy away from geographical quotas toward a set of standards that emphasized labor market skills, the reunification of families, political asylum, and other humanitarian aims. In the aftermath, the proportion of immigrants arriving from developing countries has increased.[114] Yet, immigrants with professional occupations comprise about 25% of legal immigrants today as compared to about 1% in the first decade of the 20th century.[115] Similarly, those reporting their occupation as domestic servant or laborer constitute about 20% of today's flow as compared to 70% in that first decade. Illegal immigrants, estimated at about 30% of the legal flow, are more likely to be unskilled.

Similar trends are present in Canada, Australia, New Zealand and the European Union.[116] Immigration policy in developed nations today has to grapple with attracting productive immigrants but also allow for the re-unification of families, granting asylum to those in peril in their home countries, maintaining the security of their borders, and even the potential for "trafficking in human beings." Given that these goals may conflict, this is not an easy task. The subject of granting citizenship to a large number of immigrants who have been living illegally in the US for decades has become a "hot button" political topic. It is no less so in the European Union. The attempt to develop common immigration policies across the EU has articulated principles, but, like the US, has not been able to pass legislation.[117]

5.11 The Walker Thesis, Displacement and Savings

In the late 19th century, Francis Amasa Walker (professor at Yale, then president of MIT, the American Economic Association, and the American Statistical Association), theorized that, given American conditions, there was some maximum rate of population growth – a distant echo of Malthus. This meant that each European immigrant filled a place that would otherwise have been occupied by a native-born American. This was tantamount to saying that each European immigrant meant one less native-born American in the population:

> Foreign immigration into this country [US] has ... amounted not to a re-enforcement of our population, but to a replacement of native by foreign stock. That if the foreigners had not come, the native element would long have filled the places the foreigners usurped ...
> Dewey (1899) 425[118]

The Walker Thesis, as this view came to be known, was examined by Paul Uselding who observed that: i) there never was a maximum growth rate and ii) each European immigrant represented a capital transfer from Europe to North America. The value of the transfer was equal to the rearing cost of the migrant to the age of migration.[119]

Since most immigrants were young males and females ready to enter the labor force, North America got the benefit of their training without incurring the cost. In this, Uselding elaborated the idea found in the work of an Italian statistician,

Agostino de Vita, who argued that the American capital stock in 1914 was little more than the accumulated cost of rearing, feeding, educating and transporting the millions of European migrants to the United States. The consequence of the Atlantic migration was to "free" American resources to build the capital equipment the immigrants used as part of their labor. This is why North America was able to pull ahead of the Europeans economically. Unfortunately, de Vita overstated the case, but Uselding, nonetheless, pursued the basic idea using known data. He concluded that during the period between 1839 and 1859 the additional capital formation due to immigration was within 5% to 10% of GNP. Later with co-researcher Larry Neal, they expanded the calculations to the period between 1790 and 1912. They concluded that, by the end of the longer period, the additional capital stock created by immigration was 10% to 20% of GNP.[120] Thus, immigration meant that the American economy grew faster than it would have otherwise. This positive impact of immigration was apparent before the US Civil War.

The growth effects of immigration, however, did not benefit everyone. Joseph Ferrie's work demonstrates that the arrival of immigrants, particularly Irish immigrants, during the 1850s had a negative impact on native-born American craft workers. This seems to be a result of the fact that the highest rates of immigration were realized just when the American economy began to industrialize:

> Though their [the Irish] arrival apparently led to some down-grading of native skilled workers, they may have also paved the way for less skilled natives to enter factory work as well, by being available just as employers were preparing to change their production processes.
>
> Ferrie (1997) 208[121]

Robert Gallman further noted that, by 1860, probably 35% of the adult males in the Northern states were foreign-born (half the Union army was foreign-born during the US Civil War of the 1860s).[122] Consequently, he added a caveat to the Walker thesis: since most of the immigrants stayed in the cities, the migration of native-born Americans to urban areas was less rapid than it would have been otherwise. If native Americans were more likely to stay in rural areas where the birth rate was higher, the native-born American birth rate was higher than it would have been had more moved into the growing cities.

5.12 A Final Word on Long Distance Migration

Where there is a push from an emigrant-producing area and a pull to an immigrant-receiving one, long distance migration is likely to provide positive net benefits in the aggregate to both areas. Adjustments will be required, and not everyone will benefit, especially those whose skills put them in direct competition with immigrants. However, not all long distance migration is associated with economic incentives and an open market. Over time, imperial countries have expelled their citizens from the mother country and forced movements of their captives. While this may have positive net benefits in the aggregate, there are equity issues that transcend any consideration of efficiency. Finally, in spite of potential net benefits, countries have taken steps to limit immigration when socio-political concerns trump economic ones. The lost benefits are the opportunity cost of the ignorance, fear, and prejudice that underlie many of those restrictions.

Appendix 5.1

Net Present Value of Migration to the Individual

In order to induce movement the expected net present value of migration to the individual must be equal to or greater than zero. Of course, the values anticipated may not be realized. The expected net present value is calculated as:

$$NPV \geq \{(Wi_0^e - Wh_0^e) - C_0\} + \{(Wi_1^e - Wh_1^e)/(1+r)\}$$
$$+ \{(Wi_2^e - Wh_2^e)/(1+r)^2\} + \{(Wi_3^e - Wh_3^e)/(1+r)^3\} + \cdots\cdots$$
$$+ \{(Wi_n^e - Wh_n^e)/(1+r)^n\}$$

where

C	Transport costs
Wh	Wages at home
Wi	Wages in immigrant-receiving country
0,1 ... n	time
r	discount rate
NPV	Net present value

Hatton and Williamson employed a similar method to estimate the average lifetime gains of income of various US immigrant groups in 1905.[123] With the use of data on wages, imputing a variable skill premium by group, including the costs of immigration, and employing a discount rate of 10% they estimate the following gains by country of origin for the individual on average and in percentage terms:

Germany	63%
Britain	58
Ireland	51
Italy	83
Spain	167
Sweden	50

Endnotes

1. Forster (2004).
2. If migration was delayed, to say age 25, the profile of expected (and actual) wages would be different and so with every possible migration age. It would be more accurate to talk about a family of expected profiles, some perhaps higher but some lower then the ones shown.
3. See Appendix 5.1 for a formalized statement of the net present value calculation.
4. The wage deflator is usually taken as the implicit GDP price deflator or a near historical substitute.
5. The Hecksher-Ohlin model is named after the two Swedish economists who amplified the basic comparative advantage Ricardian model of trade.

6 Freeman (2006); Hatton and Williamson (1998); and Taylor and Williamson (1997).
7 During the colonial periods in both French and British North America, soldiers who were about to be shipped home were often give the option of demobilization in North America. The reasons were the same that the Roman Army gave: to have a ready force of loyal fighters available for local duty.
8 Censuses do count the illegal immigrants (but not separately), but, since "illegals" try to avoid the government agents any reporting, this group is under-represented.
9 This is simply the cumulative flow of immigrants and thus does not include the progeny of those immigrants.
10 Finkelman and Miller (1998) and Wiedemann (1981).
11 Humphreys (1977a and 1977b) and Jackson (1990).
12 Fogel (1989).
13 Lincoln's abolition of slavery in 1863, the Emancipation Proclamation, only applied to the break-away Confederate States of America. Slavery existed in Maryland and the District of Columbia until 1865.
14 Curtin (1969).
15 These figures are from Cohn (1985) Table 1. The last figure is a trans-Atlantic route weighted (by number of voyages) mean calculated by the authors.
16 Haines, McDonald and Shlomowitz (2001); Grubb (1987); and Richardson (1987).
17 Butler (1896) and Smith (1934).
18 Ekirch (1985).
19 Ekirch (1987).
20 Robson (1965).
21 Lewis (1988) argues that the return rate was about 6% in the period 1796–1810.
22 Galenson (1977) and Galenson (1981) both argue that indentures follow from the English legal notion of "service in husbandry."
23 Gibson (1683).
24 Either party could sue if the contract's terms were not fulfilled.
25 See Grubb (1988).
26 Grubb and Stitt (1994).
27 Jefferson (1788).
28 Grubb (1994).
29 Horwitz (1997).
30 Hanes (1996).
31 Parr (1980).
32 Two-thirds of total immigrants from all sources to North America amounted to approximately 40 million from 1850–1913. Hatton and Williamson (2005).
33 Sanchez-Alonso (2000).
34 Bailey (1999).
35 Thomas (1972), Thomas (1973 and 1954) and Lewis (1978).
36 Hatton and Williamson (1998).
37 Friedberg and Hunt (1995).
38 Green, MacKinnon and Minns (2002).
39 Ferrie (1999).
40 These non-tradable goods and services may contain tradable components.
41 The US became a net capital exporter in the first decade of the 20th century. All others remained net capital importers.
42 The US balance of payments changes fundamentally in the first years of the 20th century.
43 Cervantes and Guellec (2002).

44 Because of lags in immigration to the stimuli and because of the lack of precise and accurate historical data it has been difficult to show the relationship between immigration and capital flow econometrically.
45 McCusker (1997), Table 3.2, 53. See also the discussion about "registered" and "measured" tonnage.
46 Britain deliberately switched its imports from the Baltic countries to BNA due to the war by imposing a high tariff on Baltic timber and lumber in 1805. This did away with the transport cost disadvantage. Lower (1974).
47 Registered tonnage probably underestimates the measured tonnage by about 33% according to McCusker (1997).
48 Innis (1956).
49 Gibson (1683): Killick (2008), Table 3c.
50 Killick (2008).
51 Harley (2008).
52 Wegge (2003).
53 Wegge (2008).
54 Clay and Jones (2008).
55 Magee and Thompson (2006).
56 Lucas and Stark (1985).
57 Chen (1939).
58 Baines (1994).
59 Freund and Spatafora (2005); Mansoor and Quillin (2007).
60 Bansak and Chezum (2009); Davies, Easaw and Ghoshray (2009).
61 Borjas and Bratsberg (1996).
62 Ley and Kobayashi (2005). These are known as longtitudinal studies and are based on individual life records. They are, one hopes, a representative sample of the emigrants.
63 Mulder, Guzmán and Brittingham (2002); Jasso and Rosenzweig (1982).
64 'Emigration is defined as the number of US permanent residents departing from the United States to reside abroad. This population accounts for the departure of both native and foreign-born legal residents. The departure of unauthorized migrants, migrants from Puerto Rico, and temporary migrants is excluded.' Mulder *et al.* (2001), *US Census Bureau...*, Table 7.
65 Gundel and Peters (2008). Net immigration is only 22.7 thousand with gross emigration 639.0 thousand in 2006. See also OECD (2008) and Tannenbaum (2007).
66 Arrivals in UK, averaged 584 000 for the years 2006 and 2007, and emigrants averaged 370 000 of which 189 000 were not British citizens. Data are not kept in such a way as to make the UK and US comparable. Emigrants are in this UK definition those who remained outside the UK for at least one year. UK (2009) *National Statistics*, Emigration.
67 Co, Gang and Yun (2000).
68 Delblanco (1986).
69 Cinel (1991).
70 The Supreme Court of the United States held in 1922 that ethnic Japanese were ineligible to become naturalized citizens. Suzuki (1995).
71 Suzuki (1995) and Higgs (1978).
72 Campbell and Lee (2001).
73 Poon (2007) and Ng (1998).
74 Ee (1961).
75 Ee (1961).
76 For a brief history of some of the prominent Chinese businessmen in South East Asia, see Mackie (2004). Also see Charney, Yeoh and Kiong (2003).

77 Wang (1991).
78 Pan (1990).
79 Bernstein (2008).
80 Chang-Rodríguez (1958).
81 Kanazawa (2005).
82 Cloud and Galenson (1987). These views are disputed by McClain (1990), but rebutted in Cloud and Galenson (1991).
83 Walker (1977). North of the border, the Canadian head tax was imposed by authority of the *Chinese Immigration Act* of 1885. It was $50 per individual and was subsequently raised several times being $500 at the end of Chinese immigration in 1923, the *Chinese Exclusion Act*. The latter was loosely based on the US *Chinese Exclusion Act* of 1882.
84 Chew and Liu (2004).
85 United Kingdom (2010), *National Statistics On-Line*, Census 2001 and Table 3.7. Also see Census Release: Ethnicity and Religion, Table 2. The non-white ethnic population of England and Wales is 8.7% of the population. The mixed ethnic group accounts for 1.4%.
86 Wang (1998), 15–33. *Huaqiao* refers to the Chinese nationals overseas whether intending to remain or not whereas *Huaren* refers the overseas Chinese with more distant links to China.
87 Pan (1990). Also see her charming and insightful foreword in her *Sons of the Yellow Emperor*. The same theme is explored in the novel by Terry Woo (2005), *The Banana Boys*, Toronto: COR.
88 Mokyr (1983).
89 Mokyr (1983).
90 Mokyr and Ó Gráda (2002).
91 Boyle and Ó Gráda (1986) Table A1. On a personal note [DGP]: My mother remembers, with great affection, her grandmother who was carried as an infant in arms by the family escaping from Ireland in 1849.
92 Akenson (2009).
93 See also the decline of the native Indian population of North America in Chapter Ten. Guinnane (1997).
94 Guinnane, Moehling and Ó Gráda (2006).
95 Kenny (2003).
96 Metzer (1978).
97 See discussions in the *American Jewish Year Book* (Della Pergola, 2007).
98 Milfull (2007) and Botticini (2003).
99 MacDonald (1998).
100 Botticini and Eckstein (2005). The former argument is associated with Brenner and Kiefer (1981) and earlier with Sombart (1951, 1911); the latter argument, with Roth (1945). Arguments emphasizing the desire to maintain religious identity were offered by Weber (1952) and Kuznets (1960).
101 Hiebert (1993).
102 Grief (2006).
103 Olegario (1999).
104 Gold (1999).
105 Estimating the flow through of Jewish immigrants has always been difficult simply because they might often be classified by the officials as Poles if they were Polish speaking and did not otherwise reveal their identities: Gartner (1960). For a contemporary statistical profile of London's Jewish community see Piggott and Lewis (2006).

106 Gold (1999). Nor do they share the same low level of educational attainment and relative poverty as the earlier group.
107 Lee (2002).
108 Ward (2003).
109 Such tests normally required an immigrant to demonstrate the ability to read an excerpt from the US Constitution in a language of his or her choosing.
110 Goldin, (1994). An excellent discussion of policies restricting immigration can be found in Hatton and Williamson (2005), chapters 8 and 9.
111 Jenks and Lauck (1926); Hutchinson (1949). Brinley Thomas (1954, 1973) argues that US immigration restrictions after 1921 enhanced the rise of totalitarianism in central and eastern Europe. According to Thomas, because the escape route to American had closed, local governments in central, southern, and eastern Europe were forced to find places at home for increasing populations. The results were protectionism, large-scale government intervention in economic life, and, ultimately, totalitarianism.
112 One reason for the fall is suggested by Ferrie (2005) in which he argues that both intergenerational occupational mobility and geographic mobility declined in the US in the first half of the 20th century.
113 Hatton and Williamson (1998).
114 Borjas (1992). Interesting discussions of current immigration policy can be found in both Hatton and Williamson (2005) and in Borjas (1999).
115 The corresponding figure for employed natives is around 16%. See Simon (1999).
116 Green and Green (1999).
117 See, for example, European Union, *Europa, Summaries of EU Legislation* and United States, Congressional Budget Office, *Immigration Policy in the United States*.
118 The quotation above can be found in Walker (1899), vol. II, a compendium of Walker's writing. This is taken from a paper entitled "Immigration and Degradation" that appeared earlier in *The Forum*, vol. 11, 1891. Walker's presidential address to the AEA in December 1890 dealt with immigration issues and he returned to the subject often over the next decade or more.
119 Uselding (1971).
120 Neal and Uselding (1972).
121 Lazonick and Brush (1985) suggest these immigrants were more easily "driven" by foremen to greater effort and individual productivity increases than was true of native-born Americans. The estimate is based on the work of Soltow (1975).
122 Gallman (1977), 27–31.
123 See Hatton and Williamson (2005) Tables 5.2 and 5.4 for details.

References

Akenson, Donald (2009) *The Irish in Ontario: A Study in Rural History*, 2nd ed., Montreal: McGill-Queen's University Press.
Bailey, Samuel L. (1999) *Immigrants in the Land of Promise, Italians in Buenos Aires and New York City, 1870–1914*, Ithaca and London: Cornell University Press.
Baines, Dudley (1994) "European Emigration, 1815–1930: Looking at the Emigration Decision Again", *Economic History Review*, **47**(3), 525–44.
Bansak, Cynthia and Brian Chezum (2009) "How Do Remittances Affect Human Capital Formation of School-Age Boys and Girls?" *American Economic Review*, **99**(2), 145–8.

Bernstein, William J. (2008) *A Splendid Exchange; How Trade Shaped the Modern World*, New York: Grove Press.
Borjas, George (1992) "National Origin and the Skills of Immigrants in the Postwar Period," *Immigration and the Work Force: Economic Consequences for the United States and Source Areas*, eds., George Borjas and Richard B. Freeman, Chicago: University of Chicago Press.
Borjas, George (1999) *Heaven's Door*, Princeton: Princeton University Press.
Borjas, George J. and Bernt Bratsberg (1996) "Who Leaves? The Outmigration of the Foreign-Born", *The Review of Economics and Statistics*, **78**(1), 165–76.
Botticini, Maristella (2003) "Jewish Diaspora," in Joel Mokyr, ed., *The Oxford Encyclopedia of Economic History*, Oxford: Oxford University Press.
Botticini, Maristella and Zvi Eckstein (2005) "Jewish Occupational Selection: Education, Restrictions, or Minorities?" *Journal of Economic History*, **65**(4), 922–48.
Boyle, Phelim P. and Cormac Ó Gráda (1986) "Fertility Trends, Excess Mortality, and the Great Irish Famine", *Demography*, **23**(4), 543–62.
Brenner, Reuven and Nicholas M. Kiefer (1981) "The Economics of the Diaspora: Discrimination and Occupational Structure," *Economic Development and Cultural Change*, **29**(3), 517–34.
Butler, James Davie (1896) "British Convicts Shipped to American Colonies", *American Historical Review*, **2**(1) (Oct.), 12–33.
Campbell, Cameron and James Lee (2001) "Free and Unfree Labor in Qing China Emigration and Escape among the Bannermen of Northeast China, 1789–1909", *History of the Family*, **6**, 455–76.
Carter, Susan B. (2006) " Decennial Net Migration to English America, by Region and Race: 1630–1800", *Historical Statistics of the United States*, Table Ad3–15.
Cervantes, M. and Guellec, D. (2002) *The Brain Drain: Old Myths, New Realities*, Paris: Directorate for Science, Technology and Industry, OECD.
Chang-Rodríguez, Eugenio (1958) "Chinese Labor Migration into Latin America in the Nineteenth Century", *Revista de Historia de América*, **46** (Dec.), 375–97.
Charney, Michael, Brend S.A. Yeoh and Tong Chee Kiong, eds (2003) *Chinese Migrants Abroad*, Singapore: Singapore University Press.
Chen, Ta (1939) *Emigrant Communities in South China: A Study of Overseas Migration and Its Influence on Standards of Living and Social Change*, New York: Institute of Pacific Relations.
Chew Kenneth S.Y. and John M. Liu (2004) "Hidden in Plain Sight: Global Labor Force Exchange in the Chinese American Population, 1880–1940", *Population and Development Review*, **30**(1), 57–78.
Cinel, Dino (1991) *The National Integration of Italian Return Migration, 1870–1929*, Cambridge: Cambridge University Press.
Clay, Karen and Randall Jones (2008) "Migrating to Riches? Evidence from the California Gold Rush", *Journal of Economic History*, **68**(4), 997–1027.
Cloud, Patricia and David W. Galenson (1987) "Chinese Immigration and Contract Labor in The Late Nineteenth Century", *Explorations In Economic History*, **24**, 22–42.
Cloud, Patricia and David W. Galenson (1991) "Chinese Immigration: Reply To Charles McClain", *Explorations In Economic History*, **28**, 239–47.
Co, Catherine Y., Ira N. Gang, Myeong-Su Yun (2000) "Returns to Returning", *Journal of Population Economics*, **13**(1), 57–79.
Cohn, Raymond L. (1985) "Deaths of Slaves in the Middle Passage", *Journal of Economic History*, **45**(3), 685–92.
Curtin, Philip C. (1969) *The Atlantic Slave Trade: A Census*, Madison, Wisc.: University of Wisconsin Press.

Davies, Simon, Joshy Easaw, and Atanu Ghoshray (2009) "Mental Accounting and Remittances: A Study of Rural Malawian Households," *Journal of Economic Psychology*, **30**(3), 321–34.

Delbanco, Andrew (1986) "Looking Homeward, Going Home: The Lure of England for the Founders of New England ", *The New England Quarterly*, **59**(3), 358–86.

Della Pergola, Sergio (2007) "World Jewish Population, 2007", *American Jewish Year Book*, **107**, 551–601.

Ee, Joyce (1961) "Chinese Migration to Singapore, 1896–1941", *Journal of Southeast Asian History*, **2**(1), 33–51.

Ekirch, A. Roger (1985) "Bound for America: A Profile of British Convicts Transported to the Colonies, 1718–1775", *The William and Mary Quarterly*, Third Series, **42**(2) (April) 184–200.

Ekirch, A. Roger (1987) *Bound for America: The Transportation of British Convicts to the Colonies, 1718–1775*, Oxford: Clarendon Press.

European Union (current), *Europa, Summaries of EU Legislation* at http://europa.eu/legislation_summaries/justice_freedom_security/free_movement_of_persons_asylum_immigration/jl0001_en.htm.

Ferrie, Joseph P. (1997) "The Entry into the U.S. Labor Market of Antebellum European Immigrants, 1840–1860", *Explorations in Economic History*, **34**(3), 295–330.

Ferrie, Joseph P. (1999) *Yankeys Now: Immigrants in the Antebellum United States, 1840–1860*, New York and Oxford: Oxford University Press.

Ferrie, Joseph P. (2005) "The End of American Exceptionalism? Mobility in the U.S. Since 1850," *Journal of Economic Perspectives*, **19**(3), 199–215.

Finkelman, A. Paul and Joseph C. Miller, eds., (1998) *Macmillan Encyclopedia of World Slavery*. New York: Macmillan Reference USA.

Fogel, Robert William (1989) *Without Consent or Contract: The Rise and Fall of American Slavery*, New York: W. W. Norton.

Fogleman, Aaron S. (1998) "From Slaves, Convicts, and Servants to Free Passengers: The Transformation of Immigration in the Era of the American Revolution", *Journal of American History*, **85**(1) (June), 43–76.

Forster, Peter (2004) "Ice Ages and the Mitochondrial DNA Chronology of Human Dispersals: A Review," *Philosophical Transactions: Biological Sciences, The Evolutionary Legacy of the Ice Ages*, 359, 1442, 255–64.

Freedman, Maurice (1957) *Chinese Family and Marriage in Singapore*, London: H.M. Stationery Office.

Freeman, Richard B. (2006) "People Flows in Globalization", *The Journal of Economic Perspectives*, **20**(2) (Spring), 145–70.

Freund, Caroline L. and Nikola Spatafora (2005) "Remittances: Transactions Costs, Determinants, and Informal Flows", *World Bank Policy Research Working Paper no. 3704*, Washington, D.C.: World Bank.

Friedberg, Rachel M. and Jennifer Hunt (1995) "The Impact of Immigrants on Host Country Wages, Employment, and Growth." *Journal of Economic Perspectives*, **9**(2), 23–44.

Galenson, David (1977) "Immigration and the Colonial Labor System: An Analysis of Length of Indenture," *Explorations in Economic History*, **14**(4), 360–77.

Galenson, David (1981) *White Servitude in Colonial America: An Economic Analysis*, New York: Cambridge University Press.

Gallman, Robert E. (1977) "Human Capital in the First 80 Years of the Republic: How Much Did America Owe the Rest of the World?", *American Economic Review*, **67**(1), 27–31.

Gartner, Lloyd P. (1960) "Notes on the Statistics of Jewish Immigration to England 1870–1914", *Jewish Social Studies*, **22**(2), 97–102.

Gibson, Walter (1683?) *Proposals. Walter Gibson, Merchant in Glasgow, To Such Persons as are Desirous to Transport Themselves to America*. Glasgow (?).

Gold, Steven J. (1999) "From "The Jazz Singer" to "What a Country!" a Comparison of Jewish Migration to the United States, 1880–1930 and 1965–1998", *Journal of American Ethnic History*, **18**(3), 114–41.

Goldin, Claudia (1994) "The Political Economy of Immigration Restriction in the United States, 1890 to 1921," in Claudia Goldin and Gary Libecap, eds., *The Regulated Economy*, Chicago: University of Chicago Press.

Green, Alan G. and David A. Green (1999) "The Economic Goals of Canada's Immigration Policy: Past and Present", *Canadian Public Policy/Analyse de Politiques*, **25**(4), 425–51.

Green, Alan G., Mary MacKinnon, Chris Minns (2002) "Dominion or Republic? Migrants to North America from the United Kingdom, 1870–1910", *Economic History Review*, **55**(4), 666–96.

Grief, Avner (2006) *Institutions and the Path to the Modern Economy: Lessons from Medieval Trade*, Cambridge: Cambridge University Press.

Grubb, Farley (1987) "Morbidity and Mortality on the North Atlantic Passage: Eighteenth-Century German Immigration ", *Journal of Interdisciplinary History*, **17**(3), 565–85.

Grubb, Farley (1988) "The Auction of Redemptioner Servants, Philadelphia, 1771–1805," *Journal of Economic History*, **48**(3), 583–603.

Grubb, Farley (1994) "The End of European Immigrant Servitude in the United States: An Economic Analysis of Market Collapse, 1772–1835," *Journal of Economic History*, **54**(4), 794–5.

Grubb, Farley and Tony Stitt (1994) "The Liverpool Emigrant Servant Trade and the Transition to Slave Labor in the Chesapeake, 1695–1707: Market Adjustments to War," *Explorations in Economic History*, **31**(3), 376–405.

Guinnane, T.W. (1997) *The Vanishing Irish: Households, Migration, and the Rural Economy in Ireland, 1850–1914*, Princeton: Princeton University Press.

Guinnane, Timothy W., Carolyn M. Moehling and Cormac Ó Gráda (2006) "The Fertility of the Irish in the United States in 1910", *Explorations in Economic History*, **43**, 465–85.

Gundel, Sebastian and Heiko Peters (2008) "What Determines the Duration of Stay of Immigrants in Germany? Evidence from a Longitudinal Duration Analysis", *International Journal of Social Economics*, **35**(11), 769–82.

Haines, Robin, John McDonald and Ralph Shlomowitz (2001) "Mortality and Voyage Length in the Middle Passage Revisited", *Explorations in Economic History*, **38**, 503–33.

Hanes, Christopher (1996) "Turnover Costs and the Distribution of Slave Labor in Anglo-America," *Journal of Economic History*, **56**(2), 307–29.

Harley, C. Knick (2008) "Steers Afloat: The North Atlantic Meat Trade, Liner Predominance, and Freight Rates, 1870–1913", *Journal of Economic History*, **68**(4), 1028–58.

Hatton, Timothy J. and Jeffrey G. Williamson (1998) *The Age of Mass Migration: Causes and Economic Impact*, New York and Oxford: Oxford University Press.

Hatton, Timothy J. and Jeffrey G. Williamson, (2005) *Global Migration and the World Economy*, Cambridge: Cambridge University Press.

Heavner, Robert (1978) "Indentured Servitude: The Philadelphia Market, 1771–1773," *Journal of Economic History*, **38**(3), 701–13.

Hiebert, Daniel (1993) "Jewish Immigrants and the Garment Industry of Toronto, 1901–1931: A Study of Ethnic and Class Relations", *Annals of the Association of American Geographers*, **83**(2), 243–71.

Higgs, Robert (1978) "Landless by Law: The Japanese Immigrants in California Agriculture to 1941", *Journal of Economic History*, **38**(1), 205–51.

Horwitz, Morton (1997) *The Transformation of American Law, 1780–1860*, Cambridge: Harvard University Press.

Humphreys, R. Stephen (1977a) "The Emergence of the Mamluk Army", *Studia Islamica*, **45**, 67–99.
Humphreys, R. Stephen (1977b) "The Emergence of the Mamluk Army (Conclusion)", *Studia Islamica*, **46**, 147–82.
Hutchinson, Edward (1949) "Immigration Policy Since World War I," *Annals of the American Academy of Political and Social Science*, **262**, 15–21.
Innis, Harold A. (1956) "Unused Capacity as a Factor in Canadian Economic History", in M. Q. Innis, *Essays in Canadian Economic History*, Toronto: University of Toronto Press, pp. 141–55.
Ireland, Republic of (current), *Statistics, Population*, Central Statistics Office Ireland, http://www.cso.ie/statistics/Population1901-2006.htm.
Jackson, Peter (1990) "The "Mamlūk" Institution in Early Muslim India", *Journal of the Royal Asiatic Society of Great Britain and Ireland*, **2**, 340–58.
Jasso, Guillermina and Mark R. Rosenzweig (1982) "Estimating the Emigration Rates of Legal Immigrants Using Administrative and Survey Data: The 1971 Cohort of Immigrants to the United States", *Demography*, **19**(3), 279–90.
Jefferson, Thomas (1788) *Notes on the State of Virginia*, London: John Stockdale.
Jenks, Jeremiah and Jeff Lauck (1926) *The Immigration Problem*, New York: Funk & Wagnalls.
Kanazawa, Mark (2005) "Immigration, Exclusion, and Taxation: Anti-Chinese Legislation in Gold Rush California", *Journal of Economic History*, **65**(3), 779–805.
Kenny, Kevin (2003) "Diaspora and Comparison: The Global Irish as a Case Study", *Journal of American History*, **90**(1), 134–62.
Killick, J.R. (2008) "North Atlantic Steerage Fares, Mortality, and Travel Conditions: Evidence From The Cope Line Passenger Service, 1820–1870", Leeds University, Prepared for the Economic History Society (March).
Kuznets, Simon (1960) "Economic Structure and Life of the Jews," in Louis Finkelstein, ed., *The Jews: Their History, Culture, and Religion*, vol. 2, Philadelphia: Jewish Publication Society of America.
Lazonick, William and Thomas Brush (1985) "The 'Horndal Effect' and Early US Manufacturing," *Explorations in Economic History*, **22**(1), 53–96.
Lee, Erika (2002) "The Chinese Exclusion Example: Race, Immigration, and American Gatekeeping, 1882–1924", *Journal of American Ethnic History*, **21**(3), 36–62.
Lewis, Frank (1988) "The Cost of Convict Transportation from Britain to Australia, 1796–1810", *Economic History Review*, **41**(4), 507–24.
Lewis, W. Arthur (1978) *Growth and Fluctuations, 1870–1913*, London & Boston: G. Allen & Unwin.
Ley, D. and Kobayashi, A. (2005) "Back to Hong Kong: Return Migration or Trans-national Sojourn?", *Journal of Transnational Affairs*, **5**(2), 111–27.
Lower, Arthur R.M. (1974) *Great Britain Woodyard: British America and the Timber Trade, 1763–1867*, Montreal: McGill–Queens University Press.
Lucas, Robert E.B. and Oded Stark (1985) "Motivations to Remit: Evidence from Botswana", *Journal of Political Economy*, **93**(5), 901–18.
MacDonald, Kevin (1998) "Jewish Involvement in Shaping American Immigration Policy, 1881–1965: A Historical Review", *Population and Environment*, **19**(4), 295–356.
Mackie, James (2004) "Five Southeast Asian Chinese Empire Builders: Commonalities and Differences", in *Chinese Migrants Abroad*, eds. Michael W. Charney, Brenda S.A. Yeoh and Tong Chee Kiong, Singapore: Singapore University Press, 3–22.
Magee, Gary B. and Andrew S. Thompson (2006) "'Lines of credit, debts of obligation': migrant remittances to Britain, c.1875–1913," *Economic History Review*, **59**(3), 539–77.
Mansoor, A. & Quillin, B., eds. (2007) *Migration and Remittances: Eastern Europe and the former Soviet Union*, New York: The World Bank.

McClain, Jr., Charles J. (1990) "Chinese Immigration: A Comment On Cloud And Galenson", *Explorations In Economic History*, **27**(3), 363–78.

McCusker, John J. (1997) "The Tonnage Of Ships Engaged In British Colonial Trade During The Eighteenth Century", in *Essays in the Economic History of the Atlantic World*, ed. John J. McCusker, New York and London: Routledge, pp. 43–75.

Metzer, Jacob (1978) "Economic Structure and National Goals – The Jewish National Home in Interwar Palestine," *Journal of Economic History*, **38**(1), 101–19.

Milfull, John (2007) "Exile, Diaspora and Jewish Identity", *Diaspora(s): Movements and Cultures*, eds. Nicholas Hewitt and Dick Geary, Nottingham: Critical, Cultural and Communications Press, 7–15.

Mokyr, Joel (1983) *Why Ireland Starved: A Quantitative and Analytical History of the Irish Economy, 1800–1850*, London and Boston: Allen and Unwin.

Mokyr, Joel and Cormac Ó Gráda (2002) "What Do People Die of During Famines: the Great Irish Famine in Comparative Perspective", *European Review of Economic History*, **6**, 339–63.

Mulder, Tammany J., Betsy Guzmán and Angela Brittingham (2002) " Evaluating Components of International Migration: Foreign-Born Emigrants", Population Division, US Census Bureau, Washington, D.C. 20233. http://www.census.govwww.census.gov.

Mulder, Tammany J., Frederick W. Hollmann, Lisa R. Lollock, Rachel C. Cassidy, Joseph M. Costanzo and Josephine D. Baker (2001) *US Census Bureau Measurement of Net International Migration to the United States: 1990 to 2000*, Population Division Working Paper No. 51, Washington: U.S. Census Bureau.

Neal, Larry and Paul Uselding (1972) "Immigration, A Neglected Source of American Economic Growth: 1790–1912," *Oxford Economic Papers*, **24**(1), 68–88.

Ng, Wing Chung (1998) "Becoming 'Chinese Canadian': The Genesis of a Cultural Category", in *The last Half Century of Chinese Overseas*, ed. Elizabeth Sinn, Hong Kong: Hong Kong University Press, 203–15.

OECD (2008) "Economic Effects of Migration on the Home Country: A Simple Life-cycle Model". *OECD Development Centre*, Vol. 2007, 16, 56–69 and "Return", 122–30.

Olegario, Rowena (1999) "'That Mysterious People': Jewish Merchants, Transparency, and Community in Mid-Nineteenth Century America", *The Business History Review*, **73**(2), 161–89.

Pan, Lynn (1990, 1994) *Sons of the Yellow Emperor*, London: Secker and Warburg.

Parr, Joy (1980) *Labouring Children: British Immigrant Apprentices to Canada, 1869–1924*, London: Croom Helm.

Piggott, Gareth and Rob Lewis (2006) *2001 Census Profile: The Jewish Population of London*, London: Greater London Authority.

Poon, Wei Chi (2007) " Displaying History: The Challenges of Creating a Chinese Overseas Exhibition", in *Chinese Overseas: Migration, Research and Documentation*, Tan Chee-Beng, Colin Storey and Julia Zimmerman (eds.), Hong Kong: The Chinese University Press, 387–408.

Richardson, David (1987) "The Costs of Survival: The Transport of Slaves in the Middle Passage and the Profitability of the 18th Century British Slave Trade", *Explorations in Economic History*, **24**, 178–96.

Robson, L.L. (1965) *The Convict Settlers of Australia*, Melbourne: Melbourne University Press.

Roth, Cecil (1945) *The Jewish Contribution to Civilisation*, Oxford: The East and West Library.

Sánchez-Alonso, Blanca (2000) "Those Who Left and Those Who Stayed behind: Explaining Emigration from the Regions of Spain, 1880–1914", *Journal of Economic History*, **60**(3), 730–55.

Simon, Julian L. (1999) *The Economic Consequences of Immigration*, 2nd ed., Ann Arbor: University of Michigan Press.

Smith, Abbot Emerson (1934) "The Transportation of Convicts to the American Colonies in the Seventeenth Century", *American Historical Review*, **39**(2) (January), 232–49.

Soltow, Lee (1975) *Men and Wealth in the United States, 1850–1870*, New Haven: Yale University Press.

Sombart, Werner (1951, 1911) *The Jews and Modern Capitalism*, Glencoe, IL: Free Press.

Suzuki, Masao (1995) "Success Story? Japanese Immigrant Economic Achievement and Return Migration, 1920–1930", *Journal of Economic History*, **55**(4), 889–901.

Tannenbaum, M. (2007) "Back and Forth: Immigrant's Stories of Migration and Return", *International Migration*, **45**(5), 147–75.

Taylor, Alan M. and Jeffrey G. Williamson (1997) "Convergence in the Age of Mass Migration", *European Review of Economic History*, **I**, 27–63.

Thomas, Brinley (1954, 1973) *Migration and Economic Growth; a Study of Great Britain and the Atlantic Economy*, Cambridge: Cambridge University Press.

Thomas, Brinley (1972) *Migration and Urban Development: a Reappraisal of British and American Long Cycles*, London: Methuen.

United Kingdom (current) *Census Reports*, Northern Ireland Statistics and Research Agency: http://www.nisranew.nisra.gov.uk/census/Census2001Output/PopulationReport/populationreport1.html.

United States (2006) *Congressional Budget Office*, Immigration Policy in the United States, (February) at http://www.cbo.gov/ftpdocs/70xx/doc7051/02-28-Immigration.pdf.

United States Bureau of the Census (1999) *The Foreign-Born Population of the United States*, Table 2, Internet Release, 9 March 1999, http://www.census.gov/population/www/documentation/twps0029/tab02.html.

Uselding, Paul (1971) "Conjectural Estimates of Gross Human Capital Inflow to the American Economy," *Explorations in Economic History*, **9**(1), 49–61.

Walker, Francis A. (1899) *Discussions in Economics and Statistics*, edited by Davis R. Dewey, New York: Henry Holt and Company.

Walker, Townsend (1977) "Gold Mountain Guests: Chinese Migration to the United States, 1848–1882", *Journal of Economic History*, **37**(1), 264–67.

Wang, Gungwu (1991) *China and the Chinese Overseas*, Hong Kong: Times Academic Press.

Wang, Gungwu (1998) "Upgrading the Migrant: Neither *Huaqiao* nor *Huaren*", in *The Last Half Century of Chinese Overseas*, ed. Elizabeth Sinn, Hong Kong: Hong Kong University Press, 15–33.

Ward, W. Peter (2003) *White Canada Forever*, 3rd ed., Vancouver: UBC Press.

Weber, Max (1952), *Ancient Judaism*, translated and edited by Hans H. Gerth and Don Martindale, Glencoe, IL: Free Press.

Wegge, Simone (2003) "The Hesse-Cassel Emigrants: A New Sample of Trans-Atlantic Emigrants Linked to Their Origins", *Research in Economic History*, ed. Alexander J. Field, Boston: Elsevier Science, 357–405.

Wegge, Simone (2008) "Network Strategies of Nineteenth Century Hesse-Cassel Emigrants", *History of the Family*, **13**, 296–314.

Wiedemann, Thomas (1981) *Greek and Roman Slavery*, Baltimore: The Johns Hopkins University Press.

World Bank (2008) *Migration and Remittances Factbook 2008*, http://www.econ.worldbank.org/external/.

Chapter Six
Regional Migration

6.1 Introduction

There is nothing in the theory of migration that separates regional from intercontinental migration except the tyranny of distance.[1] Regional migration is the movement of peoples i) within a country irrespective of distance; and ii) over short distances irrespective of borders. Since some movements over short distances are to nearby countries and since national borders do matter, we make a distinction between migration within a country, called *internal migration*, and that migration which crosses borders. These, however, are not straight-forward distinctions. A move from New York to Los Angeles is more like a move between New York and London than one between New York and nearby New London, Connecticut. It may even involve the same amount of culture-shock! So, internal migration may involve long distances. Yet, some migration which crosses borders, say a move between Toronto (Canada) and Buffalo (US), could be construed almost as internal migration since familiar laws, political systems and language exist on both sides of the border. Undoubtedly the familiarity itself is a product of distance; Toronto and Buffalo are only a few miles apart. In an historical context, as we shall see later, the Canadian and US peoples generally ignored the border in their migratory behavior until the 1920s. In recent years, European countries have increasingly harmonized their laws and immigration practices permitting the easy movement of labor with the European Union so the movement between countries is more like internal migration.[2]

Distance, as we have seen, imposes various costs that tend to be greater the longer the move. These costs become barriers to migration. Historically, such barriers were lower the closer the migrant's home was from the intended destination. Not surprisingly, more people moved short distances than moved long distances in response to a higher expected income. From the long run perspective of either an immigrant or emigrant society, regional migration and intercontinental migration are closely

The Children of Eve: Population and Well-being in History, First Edition.
Louis P. Cain and Donald G. Paterson.
© 2012 Blackwell Publishing Ltd. Published 2012 by Blackwell Publishing Ltd.

associated. Those who move within a state, province, or nation will usually outnumber those who move between states, provinces or nearby nations. They, in turn, will usually outnumber those who migrate long distances between far countries and continents. The historical correspondence was never perfect. It simply took time for individuals making decisions to work through all the changes in relative wages.

As the pace of economic activity increased, resource reallocation did too, the demand for factors being a *derived demand*. People moved to higher paying jobs internationally, which reduced the domestic labor supply and thus raised wages (a home wage effect). But the rise in home wages was uneven. Higher productivity industries and other expanding sectors of the economy were more likely to raise their wages first because they were the ones more likely to lose workers to the international migratory stream. Remember, the higher the level of an individual's human capital, the greater the likelihood of their successful migratory movement. (However, we must be very careful about what defines human capital. For example, a peasant from the steppes of Russia may have exactly the appropriate level of farming human capital to cultivate the northern plains of North America.) So an induced movement of labor took place internally. This process created excess labor demand, at current wages in the industries and firms from which the internal migrants left, so the process repeated itself, and continued to do so sequentially. Naturally, history is not always this straightforward. Nevertheless, high-productivity industries lead because their wages, competitively set in the labor market, are generally higher than other wages. Where these industries are located determines the patterns of regional labor migration.

Real wages higher than those in agriculture and traditional industries tended to attract migrants, particularly those with specialized skills and those in a position to acquire new skills. Migrants with high levels of transportable skills tend to be young. So it is not surprising that they, who faced fewer pecuniary and non-pecuniary costs of migration, were (and are) more likely to migrate. The probability of making a job-related move has tended, in normal circumstances, to follow a distinct pattern with age — see Figure 6.1. To the extent that the migration requires the acquisition of new skills, the investment in those skills can be discounted over a greater length of time.[3] Older migrants are unlikely to invest in their own human capital when the present value of future income is small, or even negative. There usually is, however, a tail at the end of the age-probability distribution as the older folk move in retirement to be with their children who migrated earlier. Of course, in recent times this is also accounted for by those who retire to more gentle climates or places with a lower cost-of-living. At young ages the probability of migration is also high; children move with their parents. Young adults leave home and become, by definition, "movers" or, in other words, migrants.

The greater the regional out-migration, the greater is the movement of people *within* the region. For many who reject or do not consider moving to another region, there are vacancies created by the out-migrants into which they might move. And, an economy losing labor to long-distance and regional out-flows may still continue to attract low-skill (low-pay) workers from those locations where the wage rate is even lower. Return migrations, evident for long-distant migrants, also swell the inflows – although in most situations we do not have accurate measures of the numbers returning. As the cost of movement falls, transient labor movements also become more common. As the

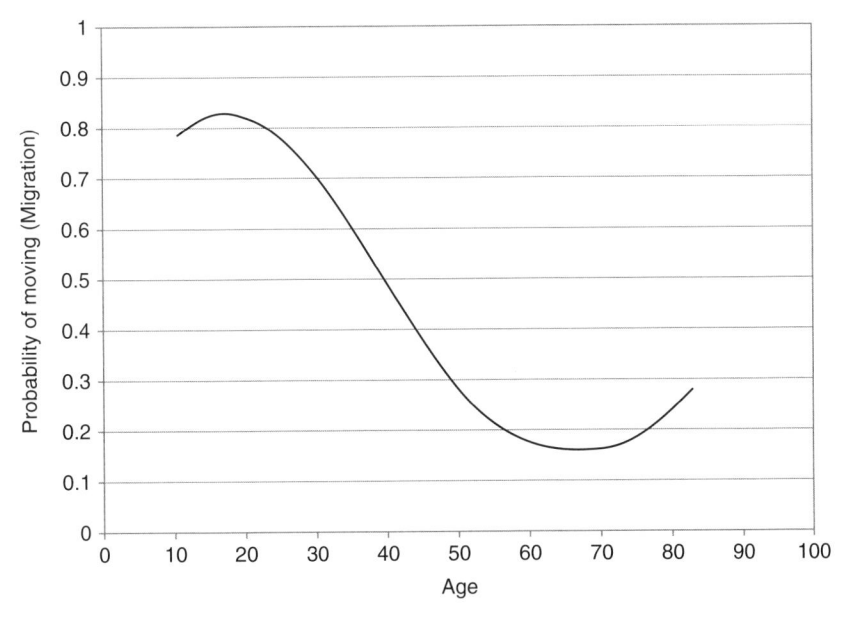

Figure 6.1 Probability of Entering the Migratory Stream by Age.
Note: Although the probabilities vary from case to case, they invariably take the same age related shape. The ones used here are only suggestive and for the modern era. Migration refers here to "movers," those who are not at the same address the following year (or for census purposes, five or ten years). It is high at young ages because young adults leave the family home, they move.
Source: see for example Steckel (1988). As age increases the expected income becomes less likely to exceed the migration costs or sufficient to induce migration.

transport network spread its tentacles in the 19th century, trains of harvest-time workers became common in both Europe and North America – sometimes carrying their labor thousands of miles – for several weeks of remunerative, back-breaking work.

6.2 The US Westward Movement and Other Frontiers

Europeans first settled the Atlantic shore of North America, making their way inland along the many rivers that flowed to the ocean. The original British grant to the Virginia Company of London had been "from sea to sea," but only a few hearty souls made their way over the Appalachian Mountains. As a result of the French and Indian War (the Seven Years War), the British took over French interests in Canada, increased taxes on the colonists and, in the Royal Proclamation Line of 1763, forbade settlers from living west of the rivers that flowed into the Atlantic. In the Quebec Act of 1774, the British gave that colony (province) all the land west of the Ohio River. Since Quebec was largely Roman Catholic, this proved an additional provocation to New England's Protestants. Like the act closing the Port of Boston, this hastened the American Revolution.

Following the Revolution, when the Americans became responsible for the land west of the Appalachians, George Washington worried about losing that land to

Railroad Poster Advertising a Land Sale

Railroads in the North American West sold land to both immigrants and domestic farmers who wished to move west. Uncultivated land at some distance from the railroad was also available at nominal rates through the homestead provisions of both the US and Canadian governments.
Source: Library of Congress, Prints and Photographs Division, Washington.

Table 6.1 Regional Distribution of the US Population, 1790–1860.

	1790	1830	1860
Total Population	3 929 214	12 860 702	31 443 321
	%	%	%
Old Areas			
New England	25.7	15.2	10.0
Middle Atlantic	24.4	27.9	23.7
South Atlantic	47.1	28.3	17.1
New Areas			
East North Central	0.0	11.4	22.0
West North Central	0.0	1.1	6.9
East South Central	2.8	14.1	12.8
West South Central	0.0	1.9	5.6
Mountain	0.0	0.0	0.6
Pacific	0.0	0.0	1.4

Source: Haines (2006) *US Historical Statistics*, Aa 36–45 – See General Sources.

France or Canada unless the mountain barrier could be overcome. To that end, he organized the Patowmack Company to extend the Potomac River as a canal that went up into the mountains. While that canal proved unsuccessful, the more northerly Erie Canal and the National Road helped thousands migrate from east to west.[4] This was the first of three major internal migrations within North America. Indeed, the North American population demonstrated a continuing characteristic: its exceptional mobility. The second saw the white agricultural population migrate to newly growing cities, while the third saw the black population of the United States migrate from rural areas in the South to cities in the North.

The initial westward migration was a simple story of colonizing new land (see Table 6.1). At the time of the first US census in 1790, almost 95% of the population lived in rural areas (places under 2500 residents). As early as the end of the 17th century, more settlers were leaving New England to go west than were entering New England from elsewhere.[5] Over the half century following that first census, the total population of the US more than quadrupled, and the rural share of the population fell to 90%. The largest city in 1790 was just under 50 000 residents; that would increase tenfold over those 50 years. After 1840, the rural share would fall at roughly 5% per decade for more than a century. As might be predicted, the east to west migratory movement of the mid-19th century followed an age profile similar to Figure 6.1 according to Richard Steckel.[6] However, a different age profile (almost the reverse) was observed for the smaller west to east migration – settlers returning home. The westward movement of the population before the US Civil War was higher from the Northern than the Southern states. After the US Civil War this migration took on a scale that had not existed earlier. Contributing to that scale was the new trans-continental rail network.

All conceptions of the frontier have an imperial cast to them as they ignore the presence of indigenous peoples as landowners. Nonetheless, to geographers, the frontier is defined by where people were at any historical moment (i.e., far from the market or

> *Economic rent* is the surplus that can accrue to any scarce resource (or factor of production). It is most frequently applied to the analysis of natural resource use, including the location of land, specialized labor and capital. Since economic rents are pure surpluses, they can be bid away (or taxed away) without causing the factor to leave its current use. That is, the resource is paid more than its opportunity cost.

metropolitan center). It is an area characterized by low population densities. The economic frontier defines the limit of economic activity for a market. At the economic frontier the cost of producing and transporting a good (say, wheat) theoretically equals the price of the output. That is, there is no economic profit or economic rent. This is in keeping with the work of German geographer Johann Heinrich von Thünen who tried to understand how agriculture functioned.

In the first part of his book *Der Isolierte Staat* (1826), von Thünen looked at a market in relation to the agricultural land surrounding it and the rent that had to be paid to use that land. His isolated state had a relatively large town (market) in the middle of a fertile, homogeneous plain on which resources were evenly distributed. For simplicity, he assumed that the plain was circular and ended in wilderness. Transportation on the plain was equally costly in all directions. There was trade between the town and the plain – food was exchanged for manufactured goods. As would be true of all economic location theory that followed von Thünen, the location of the initial town had to be assumed, and for present purposes he assumed it at the center of the circle. The question von Thünen then asked was: how will agriculture be arranged on the plain?

His conclusion was that agriculture would be arranged in concentric zones. Those products that were expensive to transport, that had to be sold fresh (usually in small quantities), would be produced in the zone closest to town. The market price of the product in the town, identical for all purveyors of that product, would have to be sufficient to cover the opportunity costs of the farmers and the transport costs of the most distant producer. One of the farmers' opportunity costs is the rent on land. Since farmers located a greater distance from town would have greater transportation costs, but would receive the same market price for their output, it was logical to expect that land rents would decrease with increased distance. The frontier was reached at a distance where the revenue obtained from producing a crop and transporting it to market was not sufficient to cover the production and transportation costs. Production on the frontier would be for self-sufficient consumption only.

The frontier line is not fixed. It will move outward from the central market if either the price of the product rises or the costs of producing and/or transporting the product fall. Conversely, if the price of the product falls or production and transport costs rise, the frontier line moves inward. So exactly where the frontier is located is highly variable in the short-run because of the fluctuations of prices and costs. Yet, as historians we observe that people moved and settled beyond the economic frontier, why? There were no current economic circumstances that would induce them to do so. Yet, there may be future benefits if prices of the output are predicted to rise and costs are predicted to fall in the long-run. Settlement beyond the economic frontier is a pre-emptive claim on future incomes.

While each of von Thünen's concentric zones contains a single type of production, it is reasonable to assume that more than one product could be produced near the frontier and that the frontier line would be slightly different for each (e.g., cattle or grain). The farm that specialized in cattle production would face very different prices for its output and different production and transport costs. Since cattle could be taken to market (or the closest rail-head) on their own hooves (as it were), the transport costs would be relatively low. In both North and South America, the cattle frontier normally preceded the arable agricultural frontier (wheat and corn). So ranchers and cowboys on the pampas and on the plains made their presence felt before the farmers. Individuals might stake out a land claim and raise cattle until the wheat frontier caught up, then either switch to the more remunerative crop or sell their land to a farmer.

One of the facts that confound historians is that the farm frontiers of North America, Australia, Russia and Argentina were expanding most rapidly in the 19th century when the international prices of many foodstuffs, especially wheat, were falling rapidly. These international prices of most commodities were set in the British market, particularly Liverpool, that port being the nexus of trade. The geographic expansion of the growing networks of maritime transport and rail traffic produced scale effects and, as noted earlier, efficiency gains; the costs of transport fell even more rapidly than the prices. The result was that farm-gate receipts increased throughout the second half of the 19th century and up to World War I. Hence large land rents were created encouraging the continued expansion of the farm frontier. Of course, there were short-run interruptions from time to time caused by price instability. The expansion was not smooth, the lumpiness of rail investment among other reasons, but the trend was continuous until about World War I.[7] If we take widely dispersed locations throughout the world, we can observe the same process happening everywhere; that is, there was global commodity price convergence.[8]

The American frontier had disappeared by the 1890s according to the US government. This meant that there was no longer a continuous line along which land was available for settlement. The announcement that there was no more frontier somehow shocked the collective psyche of Americans and gave rise to an intellectual movement associated with Frederick Jackson Turner known as the Frontier Thesis.[9] The descriptive sketch of the Frontier Thesis attempts to analyze what happens when there is no more land available for settlement. The frontier was unique in a political, sociological and economic sense. It is the story of how the world will be different when no land for settlement is available. For economists, the Frontier Thesis is useful because it directs attention to land rents and the margins of economic activity. Yet the thesis is silent on technical change and any change in the intensity with which factors are used. It is in many ways a lament. Nonetheless, the Frontier Thesis still haunts the historical and cultural landscape. Was the frontier a safety-valve for excess population in the east? No. There was never such a massive movement of people that, by itself, would have made a difference. Or, was it a potential safety-valve, but never an actual one; people just dreamt of getting away to the frontier? Was it the place, as some claimed, where new social institutions were created, new ideas were uninhibitedly created and the fierce independence of the American character was forged? It was a harkening back to something uniquely American. As cultural historians have noted the birth of Hollywood was contemporary to the intellectual concern about the loss of frontier. Cowboys who are often the central characters of early film are, in part, a creation of the Frontier Thesis and the romanticism it inspired.[10]

The frontier is the same as the economic historian's extensive margin. We can think of economic growth as the end result of two processes. First, additional resources (inputs) produce more income (output); this is often referred to extensive economic growth. Second, the growth of income (product) may be a result of using resources (inputs) more efficiently. This is productivity growth or growth at the intensive margin. Both types of economic growth happen simultaneously. Most studies of the importance of the two suggest that extensive growth was the dominant contributor during the 19th but by the early 20th centuries it was productivity, growth at the intensive margin.[11]

Although we normally do not think of British agriculture as having an expanding frontier-like extensive margin, it did. British agriculture was stretched outward (and upward into the hilly and poorer soil quality land) by the persistently high prices during the French Revolutionary and Napoleonic Wars. The Corn Laws, noted earlier, were meant to protect the farmers and their landlords against any fall in price. Passed by parliament, in the interests of landlords, these laws limited, in a variety of complex ways, the import of wheat from outside UK – even from Britain's own colonies at times! The price of grain was kept (much) higher than it would otherwise have been. David Ricardo in his *Principles of Economics and Taxation* (1817) took issue with the Corn Laws because they caused a massive transfer of income to (established) agricultural landlords from urban workers and manufacturing employers. Real wages were kept low by the high price of bread and grains, and manufacturers faced worker pressure for higher money wages to compensate. As noted in Chapter Five, the Corn Laws were repealed in 1847 in the wake of the Irish famine. The consequent fall in the economic rents forced the arable frontier to shift inward and, at the same time, released both labor and capital to other uses, mainly in urban areas. The repeal has come to mark the beginning of the transition of political power from landed to town and industrial interests.

6.3   Urbanization and Industrial Change

By the middle of the 19th century, in Western Europe and North America, at the peak of the first industrial revolution, both international and internal migrants were attracted to places where the demand for labor was high and growing. This generally meant an urban area.

Was there some economic logic for the existence of urban areas? And why was industry attracted to them? One thread of analysis that followed from von Thünen's pioneering work is *central place theory* and its early development by another German, August Lösch. Central place theory is a story of specialization. It is the rationale of why people move to urban areas. To begin with, everyone is living on a self-sufficient farm.[12] Suppose at one of those farms someone decides to specialize in a specific economic activity (bake pies or shoe horses). To do so, it would have to be economically advantageous. In particular, that person would have to expect to be able to earn as much from one hour baking pies as they would have earned had they worked that hour on the land. Further they must earn as much from one dollar invested in capital goods for their specialty, such as anvils, as they would from a dollar spent on farm equipment. And, the other farmers would have to find that it was cheaper to patronize the specialist rather than making the goods themselves.

There are a number of reasons why specialization should reduce cost. Specialization means that:

i. Individuals with different physical attributes, different tastes, different talents, are allowed to concentrate on what they do best;
ii. Tools, often costly tools, unique to a particular task, are kept in use more of the time;
iii. Labor does not lose time moving from task to task (e.g., you don't have to start a fire every time a horse needs to be shod); and
iv. Learning-by-doing, the development of specific knowledge and muscle memory typically enables a specialist to complete tasks in significantly less time than a generalist.

In short, specialization should reduce the costs of all involved through the operation of the *principle of comparative advantage*. What is true of the trade between nations should also be true of trade between individuals; by specializing in what one does best, and trading with others, wealth should increase. In the early years, many North American farmers had been European artisans before they migrated. A few years on the land enabled them to purchase the equipment they needed to return to their craft. But what was their market?

The extent of the market is determined by the inter-play of the various transport costs of producing and selling the good. At the limit, the cost savings of producing the good equals the transportation costs (and the consumer/farmer is indifferent between going to the specialist and doing it himself). Following von Thünen, we can think of a circle with a radius equal to that range as being the market area of a good.[13] Market areas will be larger, and the number of specialists will be fewer, when: i) the savings from specialization are large, which will occur when the capital requirements are significantly large; ii) the transportation costs are low (per ton-mile), which will be true when services are involved; and iii) the commodity is easily stored and purchased infrequently (goods such a tablecloths or furniture). In turn, the size of the market area determines the number of specialists of each type that can profit (on the flat, featureless plain).

But why would a few specialists locate together to form villages? What are the advantages of co-location? Quite simply, if someone opens a general store, a specialty that would be expected to have a small market area given that it frequently sells perishable goods, it is to the advantage of a blacksmith or a cooper, goods with larger market areas, to locate next door. Co-location enables farmers to further reduce transportation costs by combining trips. This ultimately leads to a hierarchy of urban places. Located in the largest places will be the specialists with the widest market areas. In late nineteenth century North America, this would have included food wholesalers and silversmiths, among others. The central city will contain many specialists of common goods given the concentration of population. At the other extreme, a general store, some sort of mill, and the county seat of government generally meant that a small village would have a long life.

Thus, urban places must be considered in the context of surrounding urban places as the economic life of each depends on what is happening there and in neighboring places. One can think of all the towns in a region forming a system, and all the regions forming a national system of urban places and their hinterlands. This system develops concurrently with the transportation network. The number of central places and their spacing is a function of transport technology, which changed over the 19th century from trails, to canals, to railroads and ultimately to automobiles and trucks (lorries). As a result, transportation costs fell, widening market areas. At the beginning of the 19th century, a large proportion of what was offered for sale in a city like Philadelphia came from a radius of 50 miles around the city. At mid-century, a producer of chairs in Chicago was protected from lower-cost chairs produced in Philadelphia by the costs of shipping the chairs between the two cities. By the end of the century, transport costs had fallen to where chairs, wherever they were produced, could be sold in a national market. This means that those transport technology changes altered the hierarchical system of urban places, bringing more specialists to some places and causing specialists to leave others.

The story so far has emphasized commerce, the buying and selling of goods and services, potentially on a large scale, which involve some transportation. Central place theory is largely about commercial cities. The linkage between urbanization and industrialization, the movement of labor from the farm to the factory, requires that industry be attracted to commercial cities. What economic logic underlies that movement?

It is normally assumed that when deciding where to locate economic activity, say a factory, firms want to minimize the cost of the product at the point of purchase. Basic economic theory focuses on the inputs and the output, but there are two other costs that are important to this decision. First, factories themselves are places where inputs are transformed into products, it takes power to effect that transformation. Before the invention of the steam engine, which evolved from the Newcomen engine of 1712 to the Boulton-Watt steam engine of 1763, factories were located adjacent to rivers to make use of water power. Such locations characterized production in Europe and North America into the early 19th century. Second, there are the transportation costs of moving the inputs to the factory and the output from the factory to the market. For any given product, the cost of that product at the market customarily will differ between alternative factory locations because: i) a location is closer to an input source, ii) a location is closer to the market, and/or iii) certain inputs that have to be bought at the factory (e.g., power) are cheaper at one location.

Economic historians have found that a primary determinant for urban locations is the presence of breaks-in-transport. Not surprisingly cities can be found at coastal harbors (Amsterdam, Boston, London, Liverpool and Vancouver), rapids or falls in a river (Buffalo and Montreal), or a connection between a river and lake (Chicago). Concentrations of economic activity often attract governmental activity such as military establishments (forts) or administrative centers (places where law courts meet regularly). At seaports, one expects some sort of immigration and customs control as well as facilities for naval stores. If we look at the historical record of new settlements, a break-in-transport together with a rich hinterland and its developmental capabilities was relatively rare in a world of differentiated topography so that cannot be the whole explanation.

The clustering of economic activity leads to cost savings known as *agglomeration economies*. These particularly affect costs external to the firm. Generally, economists discuss three distinct phenomena under this heading.

i. *Urbanization economies.* These are reflected in the infrastructure, labor pool, and quality of life that results from a clustering of population. If a firm is otherwise indifferent between locating at the relatively unpopulated source of raw materials and the populated market, the existence of good schools, cultural institutions, and the like may swing the balance.
ii. *Industrialization economies.* These are effects resulting from the clustering of industrial activities giving rise to an "industrial climate." When there are a large number of producers in a single industry in one place, any one plant can be quite small, quite specialized, and survive. In a smaller place, that plant will have to do many more things for itself as the goods and services found in larger places are absent. To take a simple example, in a large market with many television stations, a firm that does nothing but repair television cameras might survive. In a small market, there may only be one potential customer. Lacking sufficient business, the specialty firm chooses not to locate there, leaving the one station to send its cameras to the larger market for repairs or to find the ability to do it themselves.
iii. *Localization economies.* These effects result from the clustering of specific activities that favor specialized facilities, labor pools, vocational training, political lobbying, and many others. There are three sources of localization economies: i) the industries that develop as a result of increasing returns to scale in intermediate inputs for products, ii) the benefit to the firm of having access to a wide variety of labor (labor pooling) that provides employment opportunities, and iii) the relative ease of communication, supplies, laborers and innovative ideas due to the proximity among firms.

For any or all of these reasons, industry has been attracted to commercial centers. In turn, internal and international migrants have flowed to the labor pools as urban places have grown.

It is said that Lösch devised his scheme of overlaid market areas while driving across the undifferentiated plain of Indiana in the early years of the 20th century. One can imagine von Thünen's isolated state in the early 19th century when industry was only beginning to have an impact. Neither of these are the world in which we live today. The small and medium sized towns dotting the Indiana countryside in Lösch's day have been transformed by the interstate highway system and shopping malls.

6.4   The Rural-Urban Shift

In the pre-modern world most people lived and worked in rural areas either on farms or the villages that serviced them. In medieval Europe, commerce was viewed as a pleasant interruption of normal life in the form of the weekly market and occasional market fairs. The market towns expanded in number and increased in size with more and more regular trade. They also grew as military, ecclesiastical and administrative

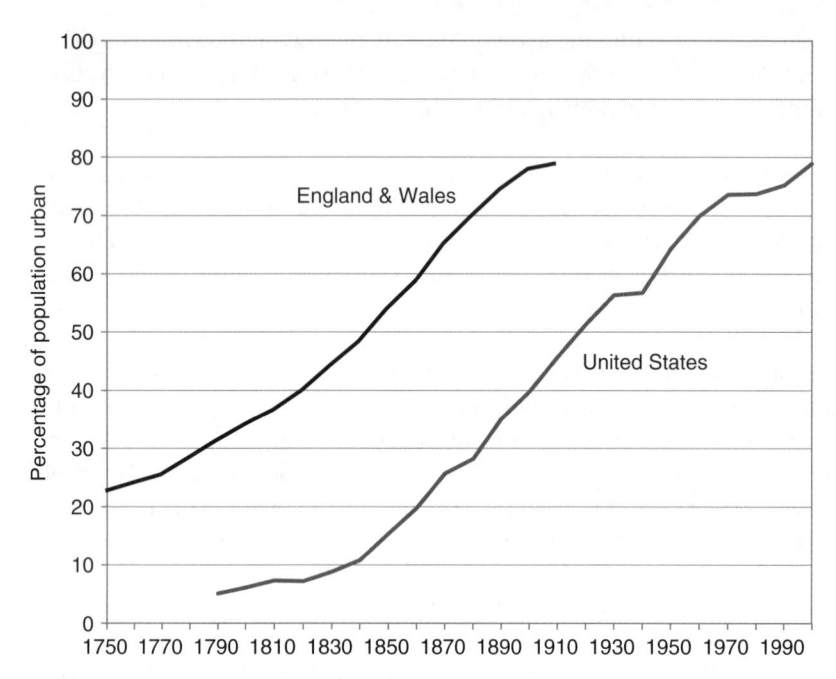

Figure 6.2 Periods of Rapid Urbanization, England and Wales and the United States, 1750–2000.
Note: The data for England and Wales are linear interpolations for 1761, 1781 and 1791. The English and Welsh data are offset by one year (i.e. 1811 not 1810). Urban in England and Wales is defined as towns above 2500 in population and the US data are urban if more than 1000 persons per square mile.
Source: data from the *US Census* and Grigg, 1980.

centers coalesced with the commercial needs. Winchester in Southern England is a prime medieval example of a commercial center (the grain trade), administrative capital and a principal bishopric, all benefiting from the cost saving of agglomeration. Such towns sucked labor out of the rural work force. Periods of vigorous coastal and overseas trade expansion also witnessed the growth of urban ports as trans-shipment points and rudimentary financial centers, as in the woolen trades of the 14th century. Notably the Low Countries and England had the highest rates of early urbanization in Northwestern Europe with their great port cities of Amsterdam and London.

So when we intercept the rural-urban shift in the 18th century, it was already well underway. In 1751, well into the period that generally marks a rise in European agricultural productivity and trade, the urban population of England and Wales was 22.7% of the total (living in towns with populations greater than 2500).[14] This level of urbanization was not evident in the US until over 100 years later – see Figure 6.2. Of course the expansion of the agricultural sector in the US helped dampen the apparent rural-urban shift. With their large agriculture bases, France and Sweden were slow to urbanize; they also lacked the dynamic extensive margin as the US did with the same spreading effects to industry – the production of farm machinery on a large scale for instance.

By the first decade of the 21st century, the rural-urban shift was, if not complete, slowing down in the developed countries of the world as the proportions of the population approached 75% urban – see Figure 6.3. In some large countries the

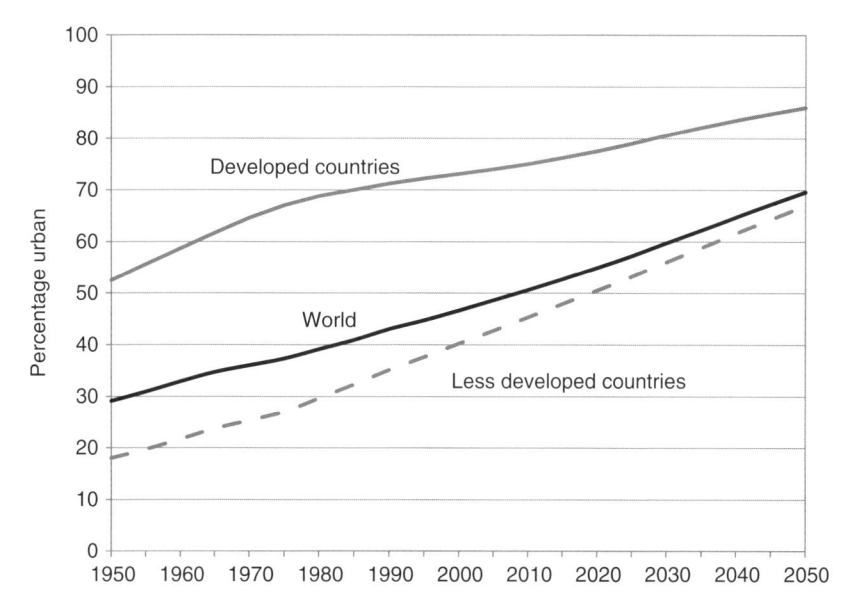

Figure 6.3 Percentage of the World's Population in Urban Areas, Actual and Projected, 1950–2050.
Notes: Developed countries are all regions of Europe plus Northern America, Australia/New Zealand and Japan. Less developed countries are all regions of Africa, Asia (excluding Japan), Latin America and the Caribbean plus Melanesia, Micronesia and Polynesia. Urban refers to populations living in areas classified as urban according to the criteria used by each area or country.
Source: United Nations (2010) *World Population Prospects*.

percentage urbanized was approaching 90% (United Kingdom and Australia) indicating that there the shifts are almost over as the rural economy has few remaining citizens to surrender to the urban areas.[15] Developed countries with vigorous, high-productivity farm sectors, although often highly subsidized ones, still have rural workforces in the 20% range, although even for these countries the urbanization rate is increasing, albeit slowly (Canada, France and the United States). Japan's massive subsidy programs to rice agriculture and rural development helps keep the rural population much higher than it otherwise would have been – approximately 23% of the population in 2007.

It was not until 1850, when the US census first asked about a person's state of birth, that internal migration in the US could be measured with any accuracy.[16] At first, it was only for whites. Table 6.2 reports the percentages of people born in the state where they were counted by the census in any year, those born in contiguous states, and those born in other states. What are omitted are those born in outlying territories (of which there are fewer and fewer as time passes), in foreign countries or in passage, and those who did not report a state of birth. It should be noted that this is an underestimate of migration. A person who was born in the East, migrated to the Midwest as a young adult, and was living in the West at the time of the census would appear in this data to have but one move, not two. If, ten years later, that person were back in the Midwest, the data would reflect only one move, not three. Further, the deaths of migrants are treated the same as the deaths of natives. Consequently, migrants who die prior to being counted in the census in their new location are not captured by the data.

Table 6.2 Percentage of the White US-Born Population, Residence by State of Birth, 1850–1990 (Excluding Territories).

		% Born in		
Year	Total-White	State	Contiguous State	Other State
1850	17 772	76.7	11.9	11.3
1860	23 353	75.1	10.8	13.9
1870	28 096	76.0	9.9	14.1
1880	36 843	76.8	9.7	13.5
1890	45 862	77.5	8.9	12.9
1900	56 595	78.2	9.8	11.6
1910	68 386	77.2	10.3	12.0
1920	81 108	77.1	10.7	11.7
1930	95 498	76.2	11.3	12.0
1940	106 796	77.3	10.6	11.7
1950	124 383	74.0	10.6	14.2
1960	149 544	70.7	10.1	16.1
1970	169 274	68.0	9.8	17.2
1980	183 207	68.1	10.5	20.5
1990	194 458	66.9	10.6	21.6

Source: Haines (2006) *US Historical Statistics*, Ac 1–42 – See General Sources.

The shares in Table 6.2 are relatively constant over time; however, since 1900 the share of those located in the state where they were born has been falling.[17] It is a bit higher in 1940 following the Great Depression, and the increase is much greater than the decadal increases during the years after US Civil War. These increases may be a bit misleading as the average age in the United States was falling throughout the period. If internal migrants are typically people in their late teens and early 20s, then, everything else equal, an increase in the birth rate will lead to a higher share of people living in the state where they were born.

Additional information was added in 1947 when the Current Population Survey was introduced. In most years, respondents were asked whether, within a specified period of time, they had moved to a different house, county, or state. This made it possible to look at those who stayed in one place versus those who moved in terms of the type of move, but by then internal migration, if it was westward, was to an urban place, not to the agricultural frontier.

By the 1850s, the mechanization of agriculture through such devices as the reaper was increasing the average size of a farm and reducing the demand for farm labor. New power sources were freeing factories from locations near water, while other technological changes were increasing the demand for industrial labor. Industrialization and urbanization went hand in hand. In the US in 2008, more the one out of every ten households relocated. This is consistent with the trends of near past. About 2% of the total number of households moved to a new county of residence whereas a similar number moved to a new state of residence.[18] The remainder moved within the county from smaller to larger towns or moved within the towns.

6.5 Town and Farm and the Changing Economic Role of Children

Children in a farm or rural setting have traditionally played an important role in the rural labor force. As noted earlier (Chapter Three), they undertook many farm tasks even from very early ages. In the years of high fertility, older children also played a supervisory role with their younger siblings that released their mother's labor to other tasks. Much of this changed when the family moved to an urban location. The price of housing was greater, and, just as importantly, it became explicitly a cash purchase or rental. In town, it was much more difficult to accommodate more children simply by extending the dwelling to provide more space. On the farm, a family in the same circumstance built an extension on to the farm house. The town house was not only higher priced, but it was built on far less land than the farm house. The same was true of external space, places where children could play and entertain themselves.

The urban location also took away many of the opportunities for children to contribute to family income in an incidental way. The labor of children in the urban areas tended to be "all or nothing." Since the alternative to work for wages was normally schooling, not only did the family forgo income, but there was a cost of maintenance in terms of food and clothing. Child-rearing costs were much higher in the town. (We postpone discussing the macroeconomic effect of this general phenomenon until Chapter Nine.) Naturally, in the face of these increased costs, family size adjusted, as we have already seen. The family issue often became one of affording to send the children to school or otherwise acquire more human capital. While rural schooling was valued for the basic literacy and familiarity with numbers it taught, most human capital for the practice of farming was learned by imitation, and instruction about management was absorbed on the farm. The ambitious farm child could take this formal schooling further, provided the family could afford it (the opportunity cost of the labor and explicit educational outlays). Or, they could find a patron – a wealthier relation or a local worthy, perhaps a minister or priest. Competitive examinations might provide a way, if the reward was sufficient (e.g., the recruitment for the civil service in China or school scholarships in Scotland). But this was rare. Similarly, the urban children's schooling was hostage to the family's ability to absorb the opportunity cost of the child not working, child-rearing costs and the explicit payments for education. There were alternatives; the aspiring urban family might seek apprenticeships for their sons and training, such as milliners, for their daughters. As we will explore later (see Chapter Seven), the urban environment meant a wholly new type of family organization.[19]

6.6 The Great Black Migration in the US

In the years prior to the US Civil War the black population lived in the Southern states as slaves in permanent bondage. There were a few "free blacks" who lived apart from their owners (within a slave state), if they had certificates attesting to their status. Free black citizens had always existed in the North, as did black slaves, albeit in much smaller numbers than the South. Abolitionists encouraged undermining the slave

On the Way to Freedom, 1862

A group of so-called 'contrabands' in Virginia in the early stages of the US Civil War. (Their status is not recorded accurately). They were the beginnings of the northward flow that would gather momentum and become the Great Migration at the end of the 19th century.
Source: James F. Gibson (photographer), Images of African - American Slavery and Freedom, *Library of Congress*, Prints and Photographs Division, Washington.

system by propaganda and by political lobbying. Another way, albeit illegal, was actively to encourage escape, but this proved successful for only a small number of slaves. Early on, it was usually sufficient for a slave to reach a non-slave state or territory to effectively become free – a slave could be returned from a non-slave area if found, but usually only after the case was proven in the local jurisdiction – often unsympathetic to the slave-owner if far enough north. However, in 1850 the US adopted the Fugitive Slave Law to assuage Southern feelings in a vain attempt to avoid the war which many saw coming. The new law gave much greater power to the slave-owner, including the right of hot pursuit and assistance from local federal and local officials in securing a runaway slave.[20] No longer could the escapee rely on the slow and inefficient administration of the old laws. Now they had to flee the country.

The Underground Railroad was a network of dedicated white and black abolitionists in both the North and South who aided slaves on their northward journey. Many of the blacks were themselves escaped or former slaves. One was Harriet Tubman, who became rightly famous (at the time as well as now) for being one of the persistent and successful "conductors" on the railroad. However, with the 1850 law in place, freedom could only be guaranteed by escape across the border into Canada where slavery did not exist. Former slaves crossed the Detroit and St. Lawrence Rivers and became Canadian residents. After the Civil War, in 1865, with the abolition of slavery, many returned to the US, but others remained in their new homes to become a permanent part of the community. Although the Underground Railroad carried only

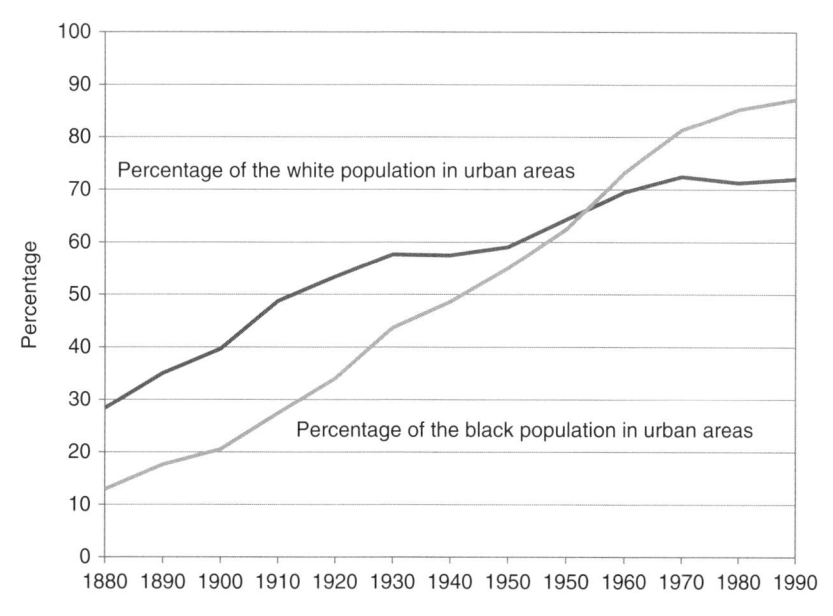

Figure 6.4 The Percentage of the US White and Black Populations, Living in Urban Areas, 1880–1990.
Source: Haines (2006) *US Historical Statistics*, Aa 716–75 – See General Sources.

a tiny fraction of the slaves in the South to freedom, it became important as an idea, a symbol. The North, be it Canada or the Northern States, was well-known as a place of succour, freedom and likely success. Yet, apart from the immediate *post bellum* wanderings of the slave populations in search of families, former slaves did not leave the South in great numbers when the war ended. If this is a puzzle, it has its answer in the functioning of the labor market.

The black population of the US in the late 19th century was mostly rural with relatively low levels of skills compared to the more urbanized white population – after all, they had mostly been deprived of an education. As noted earlier, the white population was increasingly found in cities and towns with a majority becoming urban dwellers for the first time just before World War I. The black population did not see a majority of its numbers in the urban areas until after World War II. Whites included both those who migrated from rural areas within North America and those, largely European, immigrants who overwhelmingly settled in urban areas. The black population was almost exclusively native-born and largely stayed close to their rural roots. Yet, when we view urbanization from today's perspective, the black population is more urbanized than the white – see Figure 6.4. What had changed?

The widespread adoption of the mechanical cotton picker after World War II led to the elimination of sharecropping in cotton, one of the most common relationships between black labor and white landowners. The reduced demand for farm labor contributed to the *Great Migration*, in which large numbers of rural Southern blacks migrated to Northern central cities. This migration had begun in the years before World War I when job availability and expected industrial wages pulled some to the north, but it accelerated in the years after World War II when more were pushed out of agricultural jobs.[21] Given that the US Civil War had ended in 1865, what took free blacks so long to migrate? The answer is that the large wave of unrestricted European immigration before World War I kept wages from rising rapidly, especially in the unskilled labor market which most black migrants entered. Northern employers, by and large, preferred white immigrant labor over domestic black labor. Labor unions were also reluctant to admit black workers. Furthermore, blacks were seen as potential strike-breakers. William Collins' study of black migration showed that blacks moved at times and to places where international immigrants were relatively scarce.[22] This suggests that immigration restrictions such as those adopted after World War I are important in explaining the timing of the Great Migration by allowing an upward drift in wages.

6.7 Declining Regions: Dust Bowls and Yorkshire Coal Mines

The sources of regional migrants in the 19th and early 20th centuries were generally areas with a high proportion of traditional farming – small towns and rural industries. Compared to the areas of (net) in-migration, incomes tended to be lower because the structure of wages was lower in such areas. Maine in the US, New Brunswick in Canada and Northumberland in the UK were all such areas. Year after year these areas fed people into the migratory streams. Yet despite the net migratory loss, their populations still grew; high fertility overwhelmed the net migration effect. At least it did until the recent past with the plunge in modern fertility leaving the two effects in, at best, rough balance. The relative declines in fertility and aggregate income in the low income regions will likely cause such areas to lose population. This has already happened in several states in the US.

In a classic essay with the splendid title of "Other Wests Than Ours," the economic historian Herbert Heaton called attention to the other geographic expansions of the modern period and what propelled them.[23] Not surprisingly there were many common features to all these expansions. One of the largest (and much neglected by historians) expansions was the eastern movement of the Russian population. Russian expansion into Siberia was initially a search for furs (sable, seal and sea otter). In this there was a similarity between the North American fur frontier and the expansion into Eastern Russia/Asia.[24] Siberia rapidly developed into a highly productive agricultural region once the transport infrastructure was in place. However, Siberian agriculture was much more labor intensive. During the Tsarist regime and into the modern Soviet period, Siberia also witnessed forced in-migrations of exiles from central Russia. All that changed with the collapse of the Soviet regime. Birth rates fell, as they were falling elsewhere, but death rates rose as a result of a history of neglect with respect to the necessary social apparatus to deliver effective medical care. Added to this was an increase in out-migration. The migration effect was in part the result of the newly-opened national economy of the 1990s which drew off the better educated to the cities of western Russia, and, in part, it was a result of the poor performance of the agricultural sector. This had an adverse effect on net population fertility. The otherwise fragile balance of net fertility and out-migration was tipped overwhelmingly towards de-population. Siberia has been losing population at an unprecedented rate.[25]

Population readjustment may be brought about by over-expansion of the frontier in the face of unsustainable price rises. For instance, in the vigorous expansion following World War I, based on rising prices and rising productivity, many of the agricultural and mineral frontier areas of North and South America, Australia and New Zealand were forced to contract. But, for the most part, these were *relative* declines. What brings about an absolute decline, such as the de-population of Eastern Russia? One cause is the despoliation of the natural resource base. The Kansas dust-bowls of the 1920s and 30s and the closure of the Yorkshire coal mines of the 1970s have that in common. In Kansas (and surrounding states) inappropriate farming techniques left the topsoil hostage to the wind, and, in the case of the Yorkshire mines, the amount of exploitable coal (at existing market prices) simply ran out. The consequence was a very high rate of unemployment which increased the rate of out-migration. Industries in some declining regions failed to invest and, as such, fell behind as technological productivity advanced, thereby losing their comparative advantage. Why they did so is a hot topic in history with the answers ranging from cultural dispositions, failure of enterprise, market conditions that suddenly changed and the social failure to invest in human capital. Many traditional industries, particularly heavy industries like iron and steel production and shipbuilding but also light industries such as textile manufacturing, found that they were overwhelmed by new producers in Asia that had not been adequately anticipated. The result was to create the conditions that favored out-migration.

6.8 Inter-Urban Migration

People migrate between cities as well as to cities. To this point we have only discussed urbanization in terms of a single city. Inter-urban migration is one factor that equates the supply and demand for labor within cities. If some residents of one city believe a different city is preferred to where they live now, and if they take into consideration land rents, wages, commuting costs, and the like, it is probable they will move. This suggests that, in looking at a system of cities, equilibrium requires that it be impossible to increase utility through inter-urban migration. This means that any differences in wages between urban areas are compensation for differences in rents, commuting costs, or natural amenities (e.g., beaches, mountains).

The price of land tends to be higher in larger cities than in smaller ones. First, assume rents at the periphery of each city are equal to the marginal product of agricultural land and that is independent of the size of the city. One mile closer to city the rents must be higher in order for urban uses to bid the land away from rural uses. Since the larger city is expected to cover a larger area than the smaller one, the periphery is farther from the center. Thus, at a given distance from the city center within the two cities, the rent in the larger city should be higher than in the smaller city. Assuming other things are equal in the two cities (an unlikely assumption), then a potential employee now living in the smaller city would have to be offered a higher wage to compensate for the higher rents if an employer is trying to induce them to move to the larger city. If other things are not equal, if commuting costs are higher in the larger city, if the larger city is in a colder climate, then there are additional reasons for compensating wage differentials.

Looking at the same situation from the perspective of the firm, locating in the larger city involves a trade-off between the positive reasons for locating there (e.g., a break-in transport, agglomeration economies) and the negative impact of higher rents and higher wages. These higher costs are an incentive for smaller cities to make their sites more attractive to firms now located in larger cities. This suggests that, in the future, smaller cities are likely to grow faster than the larger cities, that equilibrium for a system of cities requires the absence of profit-enhancing moves by employers as well as the absence of utility-enhancing moves by potential employees. This impetus spawned the growth of "new towns" in Europe with the state providing the social capital such as parks, open spaces and other public amenities. With the rural-urban shift largely over in European and other OECD countries, future migration will largely be inter-urban.

6.9 Migration: In the Neighborhood

A. Scotland – England

"The noblest prospect which a Scotchman [sic] ever sees is the high road that leads him to England!"[26] This pronouncement by Samuel Johnson, the famous English literary figure and wit, in the 1780s was nothing more than an observation of his time. Ever since, generations of Scots have taken umbrage. Unfortunately for the umbrage-takers, Johnson was correct in many senses. After the Act of Union in 1707 the Scottish and English economies were as thoroughly integrated as any two could be. Trade between the two nations increased as new markets were exploited and Scotland was brought within the scope of the highly-protectionist British mercantile policy.[27] Scots saw the opportunities Union presented and made the most of them. Although many Scots made their homes in England before the Union, the new economic unit of 1707 simply elevated the prospects of successful migration.[28] The Edinburgh-London road, the A-1 in modern times, took many south; it carried those with skills likely to be demanded in the South. It took the products of a high-quality education system and the ideas of the Scottish Enlightenment, which blossomed in the late 18th century.

Among those Scots who migrated was the politically ambitious and talented Dundas family who became a dominant force in the British government in the late 18th and early 19th centuries. They are venerated in the names of towns and streets throughout the world, three in Australia alone. Dundas Street threads through Southern Ontario and, as such, is found in many of its towns and cities. It was the English's turn to take offense, just as they might today with the Scots' hold on elected government: successive prime ministers, Tony Blair and Gordon Brown, plus former Chancellor of the Exchequer Alistair Darling are all Scots. David Cameron, the new prime minister just passes for English; his name and honourable antecedents betray him.

Scotland historically had one of the highest long-term rates of out-migration in Europe.[29] There was persistent international migration to the "new world" countries, especially at times of economic turbulence (e.g., the late 18th and 19th century Highland Clearances and, more recently, the rapid decline in the 1950s and 1960s of many of Scotland's traditional industries).[30] Despite the international out-migration, many of the migrants remained in the United Kingdom and followed Johnson's road. Some of those internal (to Britain) migrants were temporary or "transient." The movement of Scottish harvest-time labor to England from the pastoral farming areas of northwest Scotland was substantial and included many young women. The income they earned was essential to the maintenance of their families' farms at home. Transient workers also moved about within Scotland. For instance, many from the Highlands and Western Isles went to the northeast for the fishing season.[31] But it was the movement of those who permanently stayed outside Scotland that had the greatest demographic effect. In the late 19th century, the out-migration was sufficiently large that the sex-ratio in Scotland became decidedly skewed. The exodus carried away many more men than women. This resulted in a low rate of marriage and a high proportion of females "never-married" compared to England and Wales. Never married females as a group was half again as large in Scotland in the late 19th century, 19.7% compared to 13.0% for England, according to the exhaustive study by Michael Anderson and Donald Morse.[32] For those that remained in Scotland, marital fertility was very high by English standards. But this is an illusion. Scottish families were statistically much like English families in pair-wise comparisons. But the Scottish population was less urbanized than the English one. As a result proportionately more exhibited the higher fertility commonly found in rural areas. Despite this, the net result of these forces was that overall Scottish population growth was very much less than that of England or Wales.[33]

In the 20th century, migration to the rest of the United Kingdom was highly sensitive to the economic climate in England. When that climate was less attractive the flow swung heavily towards emigration overseas. This was the case in the 1950s and 1960s. It was likely so in deeper history, but there is no firm quantitative evidence to prove it. Recent history, however, has witnessed a reversal of the historical trends in internal migration. From 1991 to the second quarter of 2009, Scotland gained more people from internal migration from the rest of the UK than it contributed, 3.73 and 3.41 million respectively. The net inflow varied year-to-year with the business cycle; it was positive in years of the resource booms in oil and gas and negative in years of slower economic growth.[34] Similar to all the regional migration within the UK, at times of high local employment, not only is the outflow less, but some of the Scots in England returned home. Many of these migrants are highly specialized, highly paid workers of the off-shore oil industry and its service sector. In general, there is little that distinguishes the Scottish movement around the UK apart from a few rigidities in the labor market. For example, Scotland has a different law system which makes movement of highly skilled lawyers difficult. There is a greater tendency for workers in Scotland to acquire skills on-the-job relative to England. This tends to give Scottish workers a lower "quit rate." It means there is a greater likelihood that Scottish firms retain workers that otherwise might have been released through redundancy into the general labor market.[35]

B. Canada – USA

While the British and European Union labor markets have become more integrated in recent years, not all have. Those of two near neighbors have become less so: Canada and the United States. Each is the other's largest trading partner and is a signatory to a free trade agreement (the North American Free Trade Agreement – NAFTA). However, they do not share a common labor market.[36] NAFTA, which also includes Mexico, was not intended to cover labor flows even before Mexico joined the agreement. Migration between the US and Canada and *vice versa* were subject to increasingly restrictive immigration regulations, with the US rules becoming more exclusionary since the bombing of the World Trade Center in 1993 and the attack of 2001.

Despite decades of gross immigration over the period, 1850–1931, there was only a small net population gain in Canada due to significantly high emigration. The country, of course, is unique in sharing a landmass with the dynamic economy of the United States and, until the 1920s, a border that was completely open to the movement of people. (The Mexico-US border was never as open). For the entire second half of the 19th century, measured decade by decade from the censuses, Canada lost more people to emigration than it gained from immigration. A variant of the Walker Thesis (see Chapter Five) crops up in the history of Canada's population. It was called the *Displacement Thesis* and was first noticed in the early 1930s. The thesis claimed that European immigrants were displacing the native-born Canadians and pushing them to the US. The history was not so simple. Differentially higher rates of economic growth in the US were so attractive that they induced substantial migration, the migrants were sucked into the US economy. Canadian growth rates were high enough to attract some immigrants from overseas, but not high enough to divert many of them from the US to the northern country. Nor were the growth rates high enough to retain Canada's own population. It was not the recent immigrants to Canada who then left, though some did, but the native-born who elected to move to the higher wage alternative. After all, they probably knew the US more intimately than the foreigners from overseas. Furthermore, for large parts of Eastern Canada, the rural-urban shift was in full force. A US city might both be closer and better known than the home cities of Canada, for example. For many in south-western Ontario, Detroit, Buffalo and Cleveland were closer than Toronto, Montreal or even Hamilton. By 1900 the Canadian-born who lived in the US represented no less than 22.0% of the Canadian population, although they were clearly a much smaller proportion of the US population.[37]

Between 1871 and 1901 Canada also lost population to the US farm frontier by a substantial emigration of Canadian farmers, approximately 225 000. These farmers were responding to the cheap price of very fertile land in the US. This was before large parts of the Canadian prairies were favored by cheap transport and low cost farm infrastructure.[38] It was not until after about 1901 that the Canadian west attracted large-scale immigration – some was from the US and some of that, in turn, was the Canadians (or their children) who had earlier migrated to the Great Plains states. Once the immigration tide turned in the years just before the 20th century, Canada's net immigration increased substantially. However, immigration and emigration, in the Canadian case, were highly correlated. In the twenty years or so before World War I, generally buoyant economies in both Canada and the US induced migration in and out, with large shifts in the industrial structure and hence changes in the demand for labor.[39] Such was the porosity of the Canadian-US border that Canadians migrated to the US cities and states that were growing most rapidly just as those living in the

US did. Canadian migrants to the US tended to have a higher accumulated human capital than the immigrants from overseas. And, in contrast to earlier, a very large proportion of immigrants to Canada were from the US, many of whom were farmers seeking land in the now fertile northern prairie.[40] The inter-play of migratory streams between the US and Canada came to an end in the wake of the restrictive US legislation of the 1920s and its subsequent rigorous enforcement. Two countries that persistently shared population migration, each being to the other a long-term source of immigrants and their embodied savings, thereafter contributed relatively few migrants to each other.

Today, Canadian migrants to the US total between 5000 and 10 000 annually. It is roughly balanced in both directions. These are trivially small in both absolute and proportionate terms compared to the Canada-US migrations of the past. Now these small streams of migrants are made up mostly of highly educated workers (teachers, university faculty, lawyers, nurses, physicians, engineers, economists and computer scientists) going in *both* directions. While the high quality of the human capital in the migratory stream is generally referred to as a "brain drain," the absolute numbers and the human capital balance suggest that it is a tiny problem at best.

6.10 The Undocumented

By the post-1945 years and the upwelling of immigration after the war, the great immigrant-receiving countries (USA, Canada, Australia, New Zealand, UK, Argentina, Brazil and Chile) again found that new arrivals contributed significantly to population growth. In the US in the 1950s, legal immigration was responsible for roughly one-tenth of that growth. Today, with the fall in fertility, the comparable figure is almost one-third.[41] The US Immigration Act of 1965 shifted policy away from geographical quotas toward a set of standards that emphasized labor market skills, the reunification of families, political asylum, and other humanitarian aims. (Australia, Britain and Canada had similar policy shifts.) The low birth rate in the US meant that the native population did not supply as much labor as the market demanded at current wage rates. The limits placed by US policy made it more difficult for immigration to make up the difference. As the source of migrants has shifted toward developing countries, on average, the skill level of the immigrant population has decreased.[42] In the 1930s and 1940s, Europe accounted for over 60% of the immigrants to the US, with the balance coming from other North American countries, predominantly Canada. In the last two decades of the 20th century, only 12% came from Europe, while Asia was responsible for 35% and the Americas for 49%. Mexico alone has contributed 24% of the legal immigrants.

Both the United States and Canada have immigration regulations that permit temporary migrants from Mexico to work in their countries. However, the elephant in the room is the large number of illegal, undocumented immigrants, approximately one-third of the total immigration flow to the US.[43] Information about these migrants is necessarily less reliable, although in a paper released in 2004, the Immigration Studies Program of the Urban Institute estimated that there was a stock of 9.3 million undocumented immigrants living in the United States in 2002. This was approximately a third of the total foreign-born population.[44] By 2008, the estimate had increased to 12 million.[45] Almost 85% of the undocumented immigrants in the US came from Latin and South American countries, the majority from Mexico alone (60%). (Although not counted among the undocumented, an estimated 1.6 million people were apprehended trying to cross the Mexico-US border in the 2000 fiscal year; most of them were Mexican.) The remainder of the undocumented flow came from Asian countries (10%) and from Europe and Canada (5%).[46] Six states (California, Florida, Illinois, New Jersey, New York, and Texas) held two-thirds of the undocumented immigrants, but the numbers of such immigrants have grown more rapidly outside these states since the mid-1990s. This flow of such immigrants is highly sensitive to the business cycle and has slowed significantly during the economic downturn of the years since 2007.

Approximately 6 million undocumented immigrants are in the US labor force (5% of the total). Virtually all the males (59% of the 9.3 million) are in the labor force, and their labor-force participation rate (96%) is greater than that of legal male immigrants and males who became US citizens because the undocumented are more likely to be young and out of school, less likely to be disabled or retired. They earn considerably less than others in the labor force, but they constitute less than 10% of that country's low-wage workers.[47] The labor force participation of undocumented women is lower (62%) because, being young; they are still in the childbearing years and home with their children. With respect to the children under 18 of these immigrants, there are approximately 1.6 million who are themselves undocumented immigrants plus another 3 million who are US citizens because they were born in the country to undocumented parents.

There are two types of illegal immigrants – those discussed above who have crossed the border illegally and those who crossed the border legally but have overstayed their visa. The latter are both quantitatively and qualitatively different. They are generally better educated and more skilled. Consequently, they are often considered to be less of a problem than those who crossed the border illegally.

John Weeks and his colleagues defined a Migration Propensity Index (MPI) based on US Department of Homeland Security data on those apprehended at the border and census data. They then look for what factors might explain the MPI.[48] In particular, they focus on five factors that have a direct effect on the MPI. The most important is the death rate among males from accidents and violence in their home state in Mexico. This is followed by the total fertility rate and the unemployment rate among young male adults. The fourth factor is the number of businesses per adult male in the 20–34 cohort. The larger the number of businesses, the smaller the size of the business, and the lower the wages paid. The final factor is the percentage of the population aged five and older that speaks an indigenous language; the lower this percentage, the higher the MPI. Mexico's indigenous population is concentrated in the south and only recently began to participate in the flow of migration. Consequently, it has one of the higher rates. These are standard push-pull factors in discussions of legal migration, and it is no surprise they are equally relevant to discussions of illegal immigration.

6.11 Convergence

In nearly all countries for which we have quantitative historical evidence, there has been a long-run reduction of the disparity of real income per capita between different regions of that country. This is new. We know from the history of economic growth that this was not always the case. Economic development does not take place evenly over the landscape. Rather it favors those regions with the resources that are in demand: good farm land, abundant natural resources, low cost fuels, skilled-labor pools, and so on. Thus convergence of incomes was not always evident in the short-run because the labor flow was not in sufficient quantities to overcome the divergence tendency. For instance, the sudden discovery of crude oil raises the income of the oil-producing area immediately (divergence) while the converging effects spreading to other regions requires the tax system to kick in, the labor flows to materialize and the inter-regional trade flows to respond to the new demand. The same is true of sub-regional economies.[49]

In the pre-modern period, labor mobility was often restricted by custom, some other institutional constraints (such as those that bound European peasantry in the Middle Ages), or the costs of movement. Thus, if the economic growth that took place in one region did not draw in the (mobile) labor resource rapidly, the gap in the average income between that region and others would widen. Differential net fertility between regions also had an effect. It is generally agreed there were historical disparities in average personal income across regions in every country at the beginning of the modern period that marked the transition from agriculture to industry. How great these regional disparities were is not well documented. But, if the historical regional pattern of income growth follows the Kuznets conjecture of *personal income* distribution and growth (see Chapter Two), the disparities of income must have been growing. For this, however, we can only rely on indirect evidence. For instance, generally the towns became more prosperous than the country areas.

So, regional personal income disparities persisted, or grew, because labor markets were not well integrated; that is, the flow of labor was inhibited. Convergence of regional incomes, on the other hand, began to take place when labor markets start to integrate sufficiently to overcome these negative effects. The integration of labor markets did not take place all at once, nor did it take place for all labor types. Rather, integration extended its reach as old customs fell by the wayside and as the costs of migration fell. George Boyer and Timothy Hatton suggest that, in late 19th century England and Wales, the degree of integration was such that, on balance, convergent began to replace divergent tendencies in local labor markets.[50] Within the UK's major countries (regions) the convergence tendencies of industrial and agricultural wages of Ireland (prior to the separation from the UK), Scotland and combined England and Wales were evident by the mid-19th century. Regional income growth in Ireland, relative to the British average, was due to *more than* the huge emigration that lowered the population base over which income was distributed. The actual gains in Irish productivity growth (output per worker) and capital investment contributed more.[51]

For the 19th century United States, Richard Easterlin has shown the convergence was underway for income per capita in regional groupings of American states by 1880 and

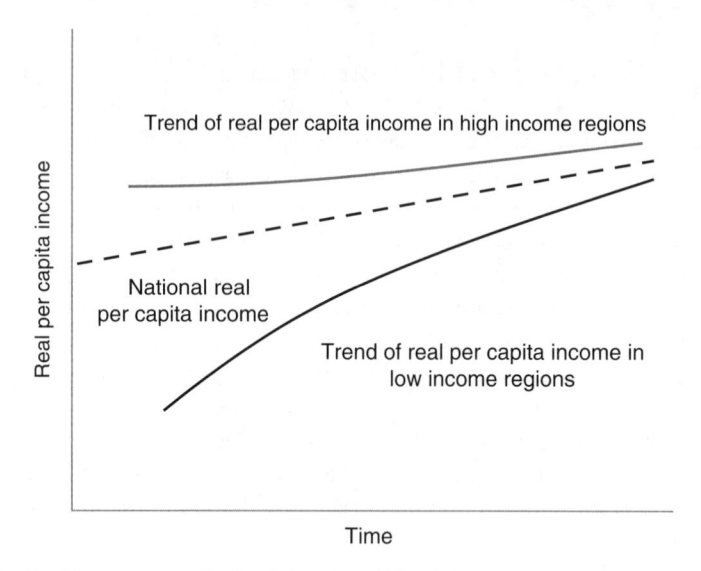

Figure 6.5 Real Income Per Capita Disparities: The Historic Regional Pattern.

may have even been present before the US Civil War.[52] For contiguous states, personal income tended to converge earlier, after 1840.[53] Thus, different measures for different geographical definitions of the US are broadly consistent. While both of these historical income measurements are different and are in nominal terms, subsequent research has shown that the differences in regional per capita real income levels do not seem to be accounted for by differences in regional prices. Nor is regional income convergence explained by the rapid price convergence of this period.[54] What the British and US economies had in common in the second half of the 19th century was the increased integration of *all* markets: commodity, capital, and labor markets. This, in turn, was a product of the new technologies of communication and transport, both of which served to reduce the costs of migration. Today, after decades of convergence, there are still differences in real income per capita between regions of countries. For instance, for the US and Canada, inter-state and inter-provincial per capita income differences are largely explained by differences in the education of the workforces.[55] It is human capital at work again!

The general pattern of the convergence of regional real per capita incomes sees all measures drifting upward. But the movement towards the mean national per capita income is largely from below as the low-income regions more rapidly trend upward than the high-income regions – see Figure 6.5. In part this is due to absolute numbers; the high-income regions become a larger part of the (weighted) national averages, and, consequently, the high-income regional income looks more and more like the national one. (At the somewhat absurd limit, if there were no one left in the low-income region, the national and high-income region would have the same real per capita income.) Yet, there are other reasons to believe that convergence takes place this way, especially in recent years. First, the underlying assumption of wage (income) equality between regions is that all goods are tradable. Clearly they are not. Most consumption is of goods and services that are rooted in geography. Some of these include: the consumption of housing services, primary and secondary school services, medical and hospital services, shopping and many entertainment services, and the like. These cannot be produced elsewhere and imported. Thus there is always a demand for labor, although diminished, in the out-migration region. Second, modern societies engage in a redistribution of income through the tax system, direct transfers to individuals, unemployment insurance schemes, regional transfers, agricultural subsidies and similar fiscal measures that tend to raise incomes that are below the national average. They also slow down the exodus of capital which has a positive productivity effect in the low-income region. When economic growth spreads to the low-income regions, they start to catch up with the high-income regions. In some cases these regions tend to growth faster than the well-established ones, but only if there are favorable endowments of non-labor resources.

The convergence tendencies of real income per capita were found elsewhere in Europe. While convergence likely extended deeper into the historical past, the evidence largely exists for the 20th century. Take, for instance, one of the least developed countries of early 20th century Western Europe, Spain. Per capita income in Spain, as a whole, converged with that of the rest of Europe and also showed rapid internal regional convergence. Also, while it has often been asserted that Spanish regions specializing in mining lagged behind those that did not, this appears to be a myth.[56] Not surprisingly, the more rapid the internal convergence, the more rapid the international convergence of per capita income levels (at least, with related countries). In the European Union today the convergence mechanism is well at work. However, with the admission to the union of countries outside of Western Europe, regional income gaps widened on a once-and-for-all basis as low-income per capita states were admitted. However, the widespread convergence tendency depends on increased spatial contact (trade, human migration and the flow of non-human resources) between the new EU states, their regions, and the enlarged EU. This overall convergence is conditional on adjustment for such things as educational levels.[57]

Sub-Saharan Africa countries, taken together, have not exhibited the convergence tendency of regional per capita incomes found elsewhere. Despite the increased regional integration of markets in recent years, the underlying capital investment has been low and output per worker flagged. In addition, there has been a large destruction of human capital.[58] However, smaller groups of nations within Africa have shown a convergence tendency. Not surprisingly, these are nations that actively promote high degrees of integration through trade and currency agreements. The consequent rate of growth is higher than elsewhere on the sub-Saharan continent, as in West Africa. These countries are often referred to as "convergence clubs."[59] Undoubtedly, the raising of per capita incomes in the least developed countries of Africa depends on the greater harmonization of their markets with neighboring states, greater regional integration on a wider scale, investment in education, investment in the institutional apparatus of law, and a greater stability of government.

6.12 Summary of Part Two – Putting It All Together

The demographic transition was found everywhere in the history of Europe and North America. But it has also been diverse in its detail, as noted in the chapters of Part Two. In this summary we take a long-run view and explore further the evidence of the inter-relatedness of deaths, births, inter-continental and regional migration.

Table 6.3 Average Annual Rates of Natural Increases (CBR – CDR) Per 1000 By 25-Year Periods*.

| | Europe ||||| North America |
	England / England & Wales	Norway	Sweden	France	USA	Quebec / Canada
1750–1774	7.01	6.54	5.64			
1775–1799	10.70	7.88	7.30			
1800–1824	14.80	6.54	6.05	5.33		23.74
1825–1849	12.40	11.68	9.50	4.31		21.73
1850–1874	12.56	13.50	11.46	2.25	19.49	16.42
1875–1899	13.00	13.88	11.61	1.69	13.30	12.88
1900–1924	9.45	12.04	9.07	0.95	13.99	12.89
1925–1949	3.91	7.20	5.07	1.22	9.93	8.29
1950–1974	4.54	8.27	4.66	6.44	10.54	9.34
1975–1999	2.35	4.74	1.06	3.97	6.51	5.60

Source: See Figure 4.10.
NB: France excluding the CBRs and CDRs during the First World War. England to 1838 and England and Wales thereafter. Quebec to 1850 and Canada thereafter.
*Or by part periods.

In general, the greatest rate of natural increase, the difference between the crude birth rate and death rate, occurred once the death rate started to fall sharply and the birth rate was still high (but falling in some circumstances). For the countries at the heart of this study, this occurred in the late 19th and early 20th centuries as summarized in Table 6.3.[60] Within Europe, the trajectory of the rate of natural increase (measured by 25-year averages) differed across countries. England and Wales led. Not surprisingly, Norway and Sweden had similar profiles somewhat later than England and Wales. France was anomalous because of the fertility decline. Although we might expect a strong relationship between *per capita income* growth and the rate of natural increase because fewer people die than formerly in the early stages of the demographic transition, the absence of refined data prior to about 1820/1850 make this difficult to verify.[61] Inferences from the earlier historical (real) wages information, however, accord with this sketch. By the early 20th century, as fertility growth began to slow appreciably, there was a *negative* relationship of per capita income growth and the rates of natural increase.

North America persisted in its difference from Europe. The rates of natural increase remained higher than those of Europe and lasted longer into the first quarter of the 20th century. This difference is attributable to North America's higher initial crude birth rate. This, in turn, was a consequence of two initial conditions. First, North America's farm sector was larger than most European countries in a relative sense, and it was still expanding geographically in an absolute sense. By the second half of the 19th century, many European countries were more urbanized. Second, the high net migration to North America altered the age structure of the population relative to Europe. Indeed, the relative age structure in Europe rose slightly given the large number of international out-migrants from Europe – although evidence of this is hard to identify because of the great number of immigrant-sending countries, thus diluting the measured effect. Immigrants tended to be young, enlarging the population "at risk" to have children and thereby producing an overall higher crude birth rate. This was not a consequence of immigrants having larger families as is sometimes popularly imagined. New immigrants tended to conform to the general fertility pattern of the new countries in which they found themselves. So, even when the average woman in North America was having about the same number of children as her European sister, the presence of more people of child-bearing age meant a higher overall birth rate for the population taken as a whole.

As mortality fell and total fertility declined with a lag, the growth rate of the population rose – see Figure 6.6. Life expectancy at birth rose as the fall in mortality rates was proportionately greater among the young. This meant that the dependency rates rose for the very young and the school age population. As total fertility continued to decline, it no longer added to the overall population growth rate but caused its decline when net replacement fell below 2.1. The overall dependency rates fell sometime shortly after the decline in the growth rates began to register. But, the declining number of children and the increasing life expectancy of the elderly caused a switch in the composition of the dependency rates. As the elderly become an increasing proportion of the population the dependency rate again grew with the non-working elderly becoming dominant.

For both Europe and North America the variability of the crude birth and death rates, hence the rate of natural increase, declined over time. Of course, there were high death toll years and events such as epidemics, pandemics and wars. But, in normal circumstances, the rate of natural increase became more predictable in the short term than it had been earlier. So one of the major consequences, and one too often overlooked, is the stability of the trends in the short-run. While there are many reasons for this new stability, as outlined in earlier chapters, the Western European and North American world has enjoyed more income stability than in the past. The stability of income growth is a product of both size and diversity of modern economies. This lends inertia. The stability of growth is also a result of modern macroeconomic management. These management techniques include:

- the use of built-in stabilizers (fiscal expansion and contraction that is automatically related to income decline and growth, respectively);
- the provision of social welfare schemes which produce an economic safety-net thus narrowing the income distribution by cutting off the lower personal income tail (which is also the most variable part of the income distribution);
- the provision of pensions of various types (state, corporate and personal) that permit more accurate life cycle planning; and
- the trans-national acceptance of responsibility for maintaining economic growth without inflation through such agencies as the World Health Organization, the International Monetary Fund, the World Bank, and the World Trade Organization.

While all of these measures have been applied imperfectly and have many critics, nevertheless it is the case that they have contributed to a reduction of the variability of personal risk and reduced the potential for personal income loss through unemployment. As a result of this greater assurance, personal demographic decision-making takes on a more predictable quality.

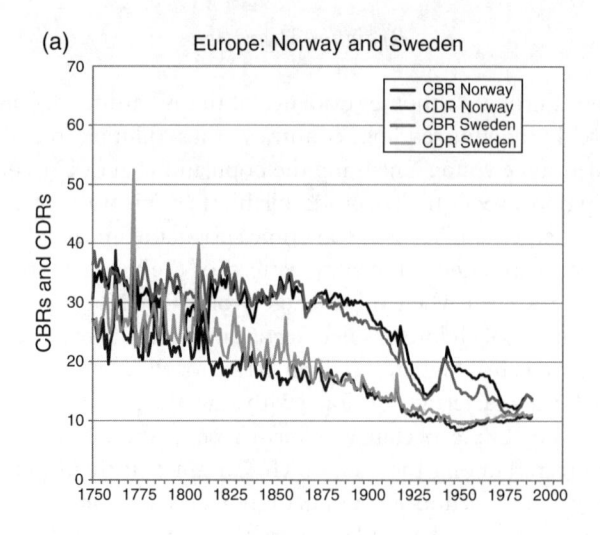

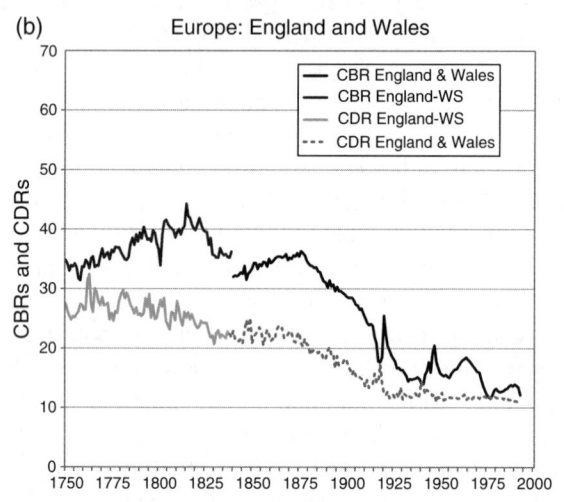

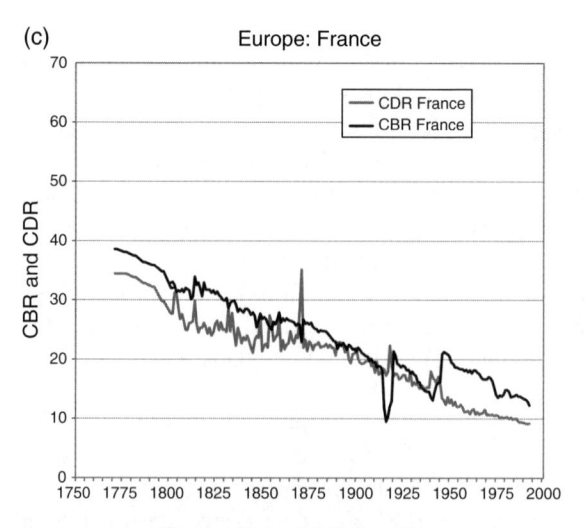

Figure 6.6 (*Continued*)

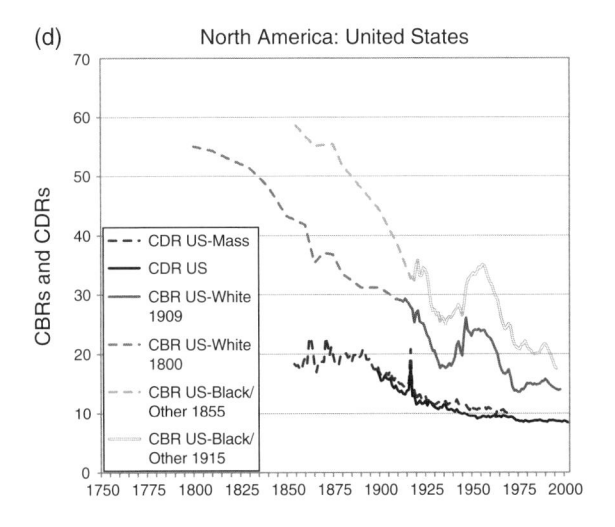

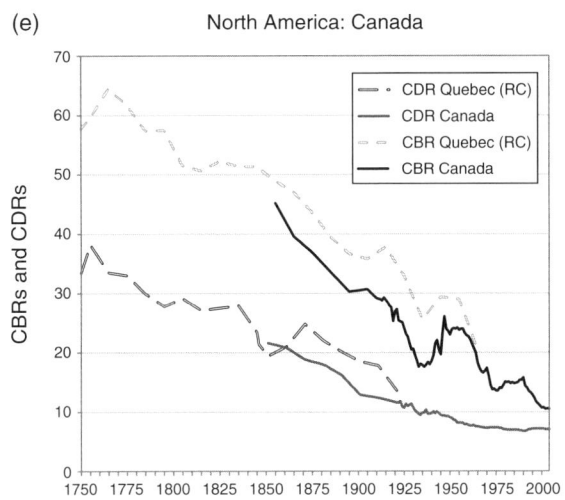

Figure 6.6 The Demographic Transition, 1750 to the Present.

Notes:
England & Wales: Data for England to 1838 from Wrigley and Schofield (1981) and Official Estimates for England and Wales thereafter.

France: The French data prior to 1801 are from Bourgeois-Pichat (1965); they are interpolated from five year averages.

USA: Black/Other. Data for Black Americans for 1855 to 1915 and to 1885 were reported as decade or five-year averages. The post-1916 data are for all non-White races (Black, Asian, Pacific Islanders and American Indians). Unique CBRs for the Black population in the modern era have only been reported by the US Census since 1964. In the 1990s the Black CBR was, on average, 0.6 higher than the CBR for all non-White races.

Canada: The data are mid-point averages for the census periods; other values are interpolated ones. The data are annual after 1921. The Quebec figures are for the Roman Catholic population until 1890 and thereafter for all residents of Quebec. The Quebec population was more rural than the Canadian average population.

Sources: Bourgeois-Pichat (1965); Haines (2006), *US Historical Statistics*, Series Ab 988 and Ab1048; Henripin and Peron (1972); *Historical Statistics of Canada*, Series B18; Mitchell, *International HistoricalStatistics*, Series, 93–117; Statistics Canada (various) including Canadian Census data; US Census data; and Wrigley and Schofield (1981).

Endnotes

1. We borrow this phrase from Blainey (1982).
2. The surge of migration between Poland and the United Kingdom after 2004 is a direct result of the admission of Poland to the EU. See Burrell (2009).
3. Sjaastad (1962).
4. The National (or Cumberland) Road was constructed with federal government money from Cumberland, MD, on the Potomac River to Vandalia, Illinois. It was the gateway to the Ohio River valley.
5. Gemery (2000).
6. Steckel (1989), Fig. 1. He also finds an increase in the probability at ages below 20.
7. Harley (1980).
8. Jacks (2006).
9. See the re-publication of his classic essays: Turner (1961).
10. Danhof (1941); Blake (1995).
11. Wright (1990).
12. Lösch kept the assumption of a perfectly uniform plain and added the assumption that there was a homogeneous distribution of population with like tastes living on the plain. Further, all occupations and production methods were open to all.
13. Lösch recognized that, since a network of circles cannot uniquely exhaust the space in the plain, the edges of the circles would compress into a network of hexagons. This network would develop around the point of the original specialist. So, as in von Thünen, one location has to be given; it cannot be determined from within the system. Suppose that the hexagonal nets for each good are all centered on the original central place. Given each good and service has a different size hexagonal network, there will be clusters of specialists in cities, towns and villages, some large, some small. Lösch (1940, 1954).
14. Grigg (1980).
15. Some countries are essentially city-states and have no rural populations or only miniscule ones, for example: Singapore, Monaco, and Hong Kong, SAR China. UN (2010) Table: Urban and Rural Areas, 2007.
16. See Joseph Ferrie, "Internal Migration," *Historical Statistics of the US*, and Charles Warren Thornthwaite, *Internal Migration in the United States*, Philadelphia: University of Pennsylvania Press, 1934.
17. "Lifetime migration" has been calculated and reported in Table Ac 43–52 of *Historical Statistics of the US*. This table is a large matrix showing both place of birth and place of residence.
18. U.S. Census Bureau, Current Population Survey, 2008 Annual Social and Economic Supplement, "Geographical Mobility: 2007 to 2008," Detailed Tables.
19. Lindert (1978).
20. The *Fugitive Slave Law* of 1850 tightened up the earlier and loosely enforced version of 1783 and extended it.
21. Heinicke (1994).
22. Collins (1997) and Collins (2000).
23. Heaton (1946).
24. Ultimately, the spread of the fur empire was into North America: Gibson (1980).
25. The ratio of the Siberian population of 2002 to that of 1889 is 0.95. Soboleva (2006). Notably, the states in the US that are losing population most rapidly are largely agricultural: Louisiana and North Dakota.
26. Boswell (1991).

27 Paterson (2006).
28 The first king of the two countries (James I and VI) notoriously brought in many Scots to court in London.
29 The emigration rates cited by Anderson and Morse (1993), Table 4 marks Scotland as one of the highest countries of out-migration in non-Mediterranean Europe in the late 19th century.
30 Jones (1970).
31 Devine (1979).
32 Anderson and Morse (1993), Table 2. The never married group is calculated for women aged 45 to 54.
33 Anderson and Morse (1993), 8.
34 Figures from the General Register Office for Scotland (2009), Tables on Migration.
35 Heitmueller (2004).
36 By value, Canada is the single largest market for US exports. The rank order of markets for US exports in 2009 is: Canada, Mexico, China and Japan. Canada has usually been the largest source of imports although China ranked first in 2007 and 2009. United States (2010) Trade Data.
37 Vedder and Gallaway (1970).
38 Studness (1964).
39 Percy and Woroby (1987).
40 Coats and MacLean (1943); Truesdell (1943).
41 Hatton and Williamson (1998), p. 6.
42 Borjas (1992). Hatton and Williamson (2005) discuss "five seismic changes" in their chapter 10. Interesting discussions of current immigration policy can be found in both Hatton and Williamson (2005) and in Borjas (1999). Hatton and Williamson begin a discussion of illegal immigration in chapter 10 and follow it with a discussion of the asylum claim for immigration status.
43 Illegal immigrants are more likely to be unskilled.
44 Passel, Capps and Fix (2004); Passel and Woodrow (1984).
45 Weeks, Stoler and Jankowski (2009).
46 Orrenius and Zavodny (2005).
47 About two-thirds of undocumented workers earn less than twice the minimum wage, compared with only one-third of all workers. Orrenius and Zavodny (2005) argue that "changes in economic conditions and in migration costs affect the skill composition of the migrant flow as well as the number of migrants" (216). They find that "that illegal immigrants from Mexico come from the middle of the sample's education distribution" and that "less-skilled migrants are more responsive than skilled migrants to changes in US wages while the opposite holds for changes in Mexican economic conditions" (237).
48 Weeks, Stoler and Jankowski (2009). The MPI is the ratio of the percentage of all detained Mexicans aged 20–34 who are from a given state in Mexico to the percentage of all Mexicans aged 20–34 that reside in that state.
49 For comparative historical national income figure see Maddison (2005).
50 Boyer and Hatton (1997).
51 Geary and Stark (2002). The study concludes in 1911.
52 Easterlin (1960). Easterlin groups the US states into New England, Middle Atlantic, South Atlantic, East South Central, East North Central, West South Central, West North Central, Mountain and Pacific. Easterlin's data for 1840 is synthetic and is consistent with convergence by construction.
53 Barro and Sala-i-Martin (1992).
54 Roberts (1979).

55 Basher and Lagerlo (2008). This study is a cross-sectional, not a time series, one.
56 Galvão Jr. and Gomes (2007).
57 Tselios (2009), 343–370; Hoffmeister (2009).
58 Ben Hammouda, Karingi, Njuguna and Jallab (2009).
59 Jones (2002).
60 Mateos-Planas (2002).
61 Olney (1983).

References

Anderson, Michael and Donald J. Morse (1993) "High Fertility, High Emigration, Low Nuptiality: Adjustment Processes in Scotland's Demographic Experience, 1861–1914, Part 1", *Population Studies*, **47**(1), 5–25.

Barro, Robert J. and Xavier Sala-i-Martin (1992) "Convergence", *The Journal of Political Economy*, **100**(2), 223–51.

Basher, Syed A. and Nils-Petter Lagerlo (2008) "Per-capita Income Gaps Across US States and Canadian Provinces", *Journal of Macroeconomics*, **30**, 1173–87.

Ben Hammouda, Hakim, Stephen N. Karingi, Angelica E. Njuguna and Mustapha Sadni Jallab (2009) "Why Doesn't Regional Integration Improve Income Convergence in Africa?" *African Development Bank*, 2009, 291–330.

Blainey, Geoffrey (1982) *The Tyranny of Distance: How Distance Shaped Australia's History*, South Melbourne: Macmillan.

Blake, Kevin S. (1995) "Zane Grey and Images of the American West", *Geographical Review*, **85**(2), 202–16.

Borjas, George (1992) "National Origin and the Skills of Immigrants in the Postwar Period," in *Immigration and the Work Force: Economic Consequences for the United States and Source Areas*, Chicago: University of Chicago Press.

Borjas, George (1999) *Heaven's Door*, Princeton: Princeton University Press.

Boswell, James (1990) *Life of Samuel John, Ll. D*, 2nd Edition, Chicago: Encylopaedia Britannica.

Boyer, George R. and Timothy J. Hatton (1997) "Migration and Labor Market Integration in Late Nineteenth-Century England and Wales", *Economic History Review*, New Series, **50**(4), 697–734.

Burrell, Kathy, ed. (2009) *Polish Migration to Britain in the 'New European Union', After 2004*, Farnham, Surrey: Ashgate Publishing.

Coats, R.H. and M.C. MacLean (1943) *The American-Born in Canada*, Toronto: Ryerson Press.

Collins, William (1997) "When the Tide Turned: Immigration and the Delay of the Great Black Migration," *Journal of Economic History*, **57**(3), 607–32.

Collins, William (2000) "African-American Economic Mobility in the 1940s: A Portrait from the Palmer Survey", *Journal of Economic History*, **60**(3), 756–81.

Danhof, Clarence H. (1941) "Economic Validity of the Safety-Valve Doctrine", *Journal of Economic History*, **1**, Supplement: The Tasks of Economic History, 96–106.

Devine, T.M. (1979) "Temporary Migration and the Scottish Highlands in the Nineteenth Century", *Economic History Review*, **32**(3), 344–59.

Easterlin, Richard A. (1960) "Interregional Differences in Per Capita Income, Population, and Total Income, 1840–1950," *Trends in the American Economy in the Nineteenth Century*, Conference on Research in Income and Wealth, Vol. 24, 73–140, Princeton: Princeton University Press.

Galvão Jr., F. and F.A. Reis Gomes (2007) "Convergence or Divergence in Latin America? A Time Series Analysis, *Applied Economics*, **39**, 1353–60.

Geary, Frank and Tom Stark (2002) "Examining Ireland's Post-Famine Economic Growth Performance", *The Economic Journal*, **112**, 482, 919–35.

Gemery, Henry A. (2000) "The White Population of the Colonial United States, 1607–1790", in Michael R. Haines and Richard H. Steckel (eds) (2000) *A Population History of North America*, Cambridge: Cambridge University Press, 143–90.

General Register Office for Scotland (2010) "In and Out Migration between Scotland and Rest of UK, 1991 to March 2009", http://www.gro-scotland.gov.uk/statistics/migration/.

Gibson, James R. (1980) "Russian Expansion in Siberia and America", *Geographical Review*, **70**(2), 127–36.

Grigg, David B. (1980) *Population Growth and Agrarian Change: An Historical Perspective*, Cambridge: Cambridge University Press.

Harley, C. Knick (1980) "Transportation, the World Wheat Trade, and the Kuznets Cycle, 1850–1913", *Explorations in Economic History*, **17**(3), 218–50.

Hatton, Timothy J. and Jeffrey G. Williamson (1998) *The Age of Mass Migration: Causes and Economic Impact*, Oxford: Oxford University Press.

Hatton, Timothy J. and Jeffrey G. Williamson (2005) *Global Migration and the World Economy: Two Centuries of Policy and Performance*, Cambridge: MIT Press.

Heaton, Herbert (1946) "Other Wests Than Ours", *Journal of Economic History*, **6**, Supplement, 50–62.

Heinicke, Craig (1994) "African-American Migration and Mechanized Cotton Harvesting, 1950–1960," *Explorations in Economic History,*, **1**(4), 501–20.

Heitmueller, Axel (2004) "Job Mobility in Britain: Are the Scots Different? Evidence from THE BHPS", *Scottish Journal of Political Economy*, **51**(3), 329–58.

Hoffmeister, Onno (2009) "The Spatial Structure of Income Inequality in The Enlarged EU", *Review of Income and Wealth*, **55**(1), 101–27.

Jacks, David S. (2006) "What Drove 19th Century Commodity Market Integration?", *Explorations in Economic History*, **43**(2), 383–412.

Jones, Basil (2002) "Economic Integration and Convergence of Per Capita Income in West Africa", *African Development Bank*, 2002, 18–47.

Jones, Huw R. (1970) "Migration to and from Scotland Since 1961", *Transactions of the Institute of British Geographers*, **49** (March), 145–59.

Lindert, Peter H. (1978) *Fertility and Scarcity in America*, Princeton, N.J.: Princeton University Press.

Lösch, August (1940, 1954) *Die ra umliche Ordnung der Wirtschaft*. Jena: G. Fischer, Translated as *The Economics of Location* from the 2d. rev. ed. by William H. Woglom with the assistance of Wolfgang F. Stolper, New Haven: Yale University Press.

Maddison, Angus (2005) *World Economy: Historical Statistics*, Paris: Development Centre of the Organisation for Economic Co-operation and Development.

Mateos-Planas, Xavier (2002) "The Demographic Transition in Europe: A Neoclassical Dynastic Approach", *Review of Economic Dynamics*, **5**, 646–80.

Olney, Martha L. (1983) "Fertility and the Standard of Living in Early Modern England: In Consideration of Wrigley and Schofield", *Journal of Economic History*, **43**(1), 71–7.

Orrenius, Pia M. and Madeline Zavodny (2005) "Self-selection among Undocumented Immigrants from Mexico," *Journal of Development Economics*, **78**(1), 215–40.

Passel, Jeffrey S., Randy Capps and Michael Fix (2004) "Undocumented Immigrants: Facts and Figures," Urban Institute, Immigration Studies Program, January 12.

Passel, Jeffrey S. and Karen A. Woodrow (1984) "Geographic Distribution of Undocumented Immigrants: Estimates of Undocumented Aliens Counted in the 1980 Census by State," *International Migration Review*, **18**(3), 642–71.

Paterson, Donald G. (2006) "United Kingdom", *History of World Trade since 1450*, 2 vols, ed. John J. McCusker, New York: Thomson-Gale, 777–83.

Percy, Michael B. and Tamara Woroby (1987) "American Homesteaders and the Canadian Prairies, 1899 and 1909", *Explorations in Economic History*, **24**(1), 77–100.

Roberts, Charles A. (1979) "Interregional Per Capita Income Differentials and Convergence: 1880–1950", *Journal of Economic History*, **39**(1), 101–12.

Sjaastad, Larry A. (1962) "The Costs and Returns of Human Migration", *The Journal of Political Economy*, **70**(5), Part 2, 80–93.

Soboleva, S.V. [trans. Stephen D. Shenfield] (2006) "To Save Siberia from Depopulation", *Problems of Economic Transition*, **48**(11), 77–91.

Steckel, Richard H. (1988) "The Health and Mortality of Women and Children, 1850–1860", *Journal of Economic History*, **48**(2), 333–45.

Steckel, Richard H. (1989) "Household Migration and Rural Settlement in the United States, 1850–1860", *Explorations in Economic History*, **26**(2), 190–218.

Studness, C.M. (1964) "Economic Opportunity and the Westward Migration of Canadians during the Late Nineteenth Century", *Canadian Journal of Economics and Political Science*, **30**(4), 570–84.

Tselios, Vassilis (2009) "Growth and Convergence in Income Per Capita and Income Inequality in the Regions of the EU", *Spatial Economic Analysis*, **4**(3), 343–70.

Truesdell, L. (1943) *The Canadian – Born in the United States*, New Haven: Yale University Press.

Turner, Frederick Jackson (1961) *Frontier and Section: Selected Essays of Frederick Jackson Turner*, Englewood Cliffs, N.J.: Prentice-Hall.

United Nations (2010) *World Population Prospects: The 2006 Revision and World Urbanization Prospects: The 2007 Revision*, Population Division of the Department of Economic and Social Affairs of the United Nations Secretariat, http://www.esa.un.org/unup.

United States (2010) *International Trade Administration*, Department of Commerce, Top Trade Partners, on-line. http://www.trade.gov/td.

Vedder, R.K. and L.E. Gallaway (1970) "Settlement Patterns of Canadian Emigrants to the United States, 1850–1960", *Canadian Journal of Economics*, **3**(3), 476–86.

von Thünen, Johann Heinrich (1826, 1850, 1867) *Der isolierte Staat*, Volumes I, II and III. Translated as *The Isolated State* by Carla M. Wartenberg. Edited with an introd. by Peter Hall. Pergamon Press, Oxford, New York, 1966.

Weeks, John R., Justin Stoler and Piotr Jankowski (2009) "Who's Crossing the Border: New Data on Undocumented Immigrants to the United States," *Population, Space and Place*, (www.interscience.wiley.com) DOI: 10.1002/psp.563.

Wright, Gavin (1990) "The Origins of American Industrial Success, 1879–1940", *American Economic Review*, Vol. 80, No. 4. (Sept.), 651–68.

Part Three
Choices and Their Consequences

Chapter Seven
The Changing Family

7.1 Introduction

The great demographic shift ushered in fundamental changes that were both causes and consequences of changes in the well-being of individuals and families. In Part Two we considered the quantitative dimensions of population change: the increasing numbers, the extension of life and the like. In this part attention turns to the quality of life: the families to which individuals belonged, their health, the economic environment in which they lived and the catastrophes that occasionally overcame them (they too have their quantitative features). It is to the family that our attention now turns. The family is society's most basic social institution, arguably its most important. This chapter is about the family and how it has changed as its economic role has evolved.[1]

One of the many ways our well-being has improved is that the range of options available is now greater. For instance, we have a much greater selection in consumption than earlier generations. The shelves of the typical supermarket have coffee that originates in Africa or South America, but it is roasted in Verona or Seattle and a hundred places in between. For travel we can go by bus, car, train, air and ship – each at different prices. Even for individual goods or services a range of price options is also available to us that were not earlier in history. The range of options is greater for many other choices. One of the most fundamental is the choice we must make concerning our living arrangements. Do we choose to live alone or as part of a family? Or, where choice is limited as in the case of children who are born into a social condition of class, race, sex, and indeed time, what form do these social arrangements take?

The greater the number and variety of people we meet, the broader is our range of human interaction. This diversity is valued for its own sake and for the options it affords. Undoubtedly some of these contacts will result in a negative experience – we've all met unpleasant people, and they've met us. Others may be interactions that neither we nor the other individual choose to pursue. There are also those contacts

The Children of Eve: Population and Well-being in History, First Edition.
Louis P. Cain and Donald G. Paterson.
© 2012 Blackwell Publishing Ltd. Published 2012 by Blackwell Publishing Ltd.

where neither party to the exchange expects anything more than a civil and fleeting interaction. The majority of people fall into this category: the salesperson, the policeman directing traffic, the person that we stand next to in the bus queue and so on. There are yet others with whom we have a more substantial relationship which is developed with greater or lesser intensity: friends, teammates, colleagues, college classmates, fellow supporters of the Chicago Cubs or Newcastle United, and others. But of all the groups with which we are associated, it is our family that occupies a special place.

No simple historical definition can be supplied that encompasses the functional, legal, and emotional dimensions that constitute a family. The family has existed in a huge variety of forms from the multi-generation extended family still found in many less-developed countries to the small nuclear family common in most OECD countries. Usually marriage is the first step in family formation, but it is neither a necessary nor a sufficient step. Today, marriage involves a civil procedure, and in many cases involves a religious ceremony as well. But civil unions are a relatively recent innovation given the long history of the institution of marriage. Civil ceremonies in England date from a specific change in law in 1837.[2] They arose in continental Europe and North America about the same time. This did not mean that it necessarily supplanted the religious ceremony – it was part of them in some cases. The coming of civil unions was a response to populations that were becoming more heterogeneous with the increased migrations of the industrial era.

Historically, the marriage itself took many forms, although in essence it is a promise by two individuals to form a pair-bond. The marriage might have been a formal contract (oaths, witnesses and seals) if dynastic rights or substantial property were involved. Usually, the solemnization of marriage took place in a church, but it was not until after a ruling by the Council of Trent (1545–1563) that the rite of marriage entered the Roman Catholic Church as a sacrament. Not until the mid-18th century did it become a rite of the Church of England (Anglican). Even then, its legal and religious features have varied throughout history. Thus, until the past few hundred years, a traditional marriage only required the promise of mutual permanent affection.[3] Various jurisdictions had different rules on whether the promise had to be witnessed or not. In some the act of living as a couple implied mutual agreement and thus was legal – and after some time the partner often acquired or shared in the joint property – in the form of the common-law union. Society too had a stake in marriage to ensure the welfare of subsequent children and to guarantee the orderly transfer of property that might be required as the family progressed through the life-cycle. In recent years the legal definition of a family has expanded in order to protect earlier forms, such as common-law cohabitation. The family has evolved to include same-sex unions and various other domestic arrangements. However, only a few countries and states recognize the legality of same-sex marriage – although associated "rights" such as legal dependency for tax purposes are recognized more widely.

As we have already seen (Chapter Four), the typical family is a co-operating economic unit whose function is to make decisions about how the income of the group is to be earned and distributed, both in the present and in the future.[4] The economic self-definition of family as a redistributive institution for its members varies by family type. Redistribution raises a compelling distinction: who are family members and who are not? There is a technical definition for census purposes: more than two people who live together and who are related by birth, marriage, or adoption. The household in the census is all those who live in the same dwelling excluding renters. In practice, the family borders are fuzzy and may even change as the need alters. Even in a small, narrowly-defined family, we are more likely to respond with an income transfer to distant family members in an emergency than in unexceptional circumstances. The family also changes as its members age. Parents, once fully responsible for their children's well-being, provide them less and less as they become young adults and earn some income of their own (although they still may be an investment for pension-like purposes as noted in Chapter Four). The obligations of children have also changed over time. As late as the 19th and early-20th centuries, for instance, it was common practice for working, adult children remaining at home to surrender their weekly pay packet to their parents, usually the mother, who would rebate an allowance. This custom is a rarity today although explicit payments for rent and food may result in a money transaction.

The family, as we all know, is a complex unit where social, economic and personal relationships exist in complicated harmony, and occasionally disharmony. It all starts with two individuals who court one another.

7.2 Courtship and Marriage

Young people in pre-modern times, especially if they lived in a village or rural area as most did, would never meet many others of their age group. Of course, they could extend the number of contacts by embarking on an adventure – easier for men than women – such as joining (or being conscripted into) the army, going to sea, emigrating to another country or running away to town. But, most people lived a settled existence prior to the availability of cheap transport and the advent of industrialization. Historically, with life centered in rural and smaller communities, and with less geographic and social mobility, people necessarily had fewer contacts with others. So the dilemma for a young person was: how to choose or find a partner from a limited set of people. Not that the choice was always that of the young people. In many cultures the choice was that of the parents, and even grandparents. Freedom of choice of a marriage partner was a rarity, although limited evidence suggests that parents began to take into account their children's preferences once the income-earning potential of women became evident.[5] Even then, most marriages were the subject of social engineering by the parents or near kin. However, whether it was their choice or their parents, the same paucity of marital options applied. Today, where notions of romantic love are pervasive and the number of people we meet is large, it is difficult to appreciate fully how the choice of a marriage partner was limited both numerically and socially. For instance, in 18th and early-19th century England, a sample of several major rural county parish records reveals that most marriages were of individuals from within the parish. England was predominantly rural in this era. What is surprising, at least at first glance, is the fact that the proportion of marriages with both partners from the same parish actually *increased* with time, at least until 1837. One of the main reasons for this unexpected result was that the parishes themselves were of increasing density; more people, more choice.[6] As society urbanized, the fact that individuals were from the same parish, especially in the towns, does not imply that they were born and lived their lives in that parish; it only implies that there was geographic proximity for the few years prior to marriage. Choices broadened as the young migrated to urban places.

A Receipt for Courtship, 1805

A young man handing a note to a young woman. The note (we learn from its text) is a caricature of romantic courtship.
Source: Originally published: London: Laurie and Whittle, 1805. *Library of Congress*, Prints and Photographs Division, Washington.

Most places of acceptable social contact for young people were, until the 20th century, rather formal, often less so in North America than Europe. The young might meet at church services where a sly look over the pew was all that was permitted. Schools in the Victorian period, where they existed and catered to both sexes, might afford a slightly less informal setting, although, as students rose in the social order, their schools tended to become single sex ones. In rural societies of the 18th and early 19th century, occasional dances provided another meeting place. These were generally arranged and supervised by the more sober-minded seniors to ensure that there was no undue familiarity among the young. Where the geography allowed, people might be invited from the neighboring parishes. With a view to pre-inspection of possible marriage partners, these social affairs were places to assess the compatibility of the youngsters themselves and, for the older adults in charge, to sort out the likely prospects. Such soirées were class restricted. Dances were held in the grand houses or the 'assembly rooms' of towns and villages, but these were affairs of the gentry. The rural working class and farmers had their own dances which were more boisterous affairs than those in the grand houses – think Thomas Hardy. Occasionally they got out of hand and caused anxiety among the supervising seniors; the church denounced them from time to time but did not often stop them. These survive into modern times with the 'barn dance.'[7]

The workplace was also a place to meet others of the opposite sex, but it also was a place of possible sexual misadventure. In the pre-modern and early modern periods in Western Europe and North America, most female employment was physically located in the household or on the farm. Domestic and farm chores or home-based production, such as contract weaving (the putting-out system), provided the opportunity for close personal control. The presence of parents and siblings guarded against too much unwanted attention or too much intimacy amongst those of marriageable age. As Jane Humphries has observed, young women who worked outside the home as live-in domestic servants simply transferred parental authority to a third party.[8] As noted earlier, the vigilance was not thorough and many young women were impregnated by their employers and other males of the employer household. Close parental control still describes the practices in many less-developed countries today. As the economy became more industrialized, more and more women, both unmarried and married, found employment outside of the home. The young necessarily enlarged the contact group but such contact was still in the presence of older women. Industrial and commercial employers tended to separate the male and female workers through distinctly different female and male work tasks. This also had, from the employer's point of view, the benefit of discouraging undue familiarity between young men and women because of the supposed disruptions it might cause. Indeed, they may have been required to do so in order to encourage the supply of female labor often controlled by the fathers and husbands.

In the late 19th century, female participation in the workforce increased, and the physical workplace became less distinct by gender. This was associated with the rise of light manufacturing and the service industry in particular. But the pace of urbanization recruited more women to the workforce from urban areas. Social interaction increased, and parental control lessened. In early 20th century France, three quarters of the marriages resulted from young people meeting each other i) at work, ii) in the neighborhood, or iii) by private introduction. However, the greatest first meeting place of marriage partners was iv) at a public dance. These four meeting places and activities, according to a French survey of the 1980s, are only half as important now as they were in the 1920s – although a public dance still rates highly. Neighborhood meetings, once important, are now not a significant contributor to the finding of a marriage partner.[9] There are now many more 'open' social occasions: college classes, football games, parties, rock-concerts, cruising and others. We suspect that these changes are broadly the same for most Western European, North American, Australian and New Zealand societies notwithstanding the small cultural differences in the courtship ritual. Yet:

> cupid's arrows do not strike the social chess-board at random, but form a diagonal line, perfectly visible in the cross-tabulation of social origins of spouses. How can the multitude of individual love choices converge to give such a result?
>
> Bozon and Heran (1989).

This raises the question: is the choice of a partner in the marriage market strategic? The marriage market is a phrase, recently coined, to analyze the act of finding a partner. Be warned, there is no romance here. It is one of those 'as if' approaches to marriage. Individuals are imagined to choose partners that maximize their joint income streams. The relationship is strategic on both sides of the bargain.[10] It makes little sense for a lower income earner, especially male, to search for a possible partner among the higher income earners as the female would find them a financially unattractive proposition – see Chapter Four on Strategic Choice. Of course, there would be exceptions.

In a male hierarchical system, women often had little choice of partner – although usually a minimum amount of affection between the principals was a prerequisite to any imposed union. The woman's family would offer a *dowry*, a payment to the groom's family which was often passed on to the couple, at least in part. The function of the dowry (the size of which was often determined in the market) was a persuasion that the bride would not be a financial encumbrance on the groom or his family.[11] As such the dowry might consist of property or savings. These may be documented in a formal (legal) agreement as we find in the case of the well-to-do of the pre-modern period. A dowry also might be sufficiently large that it permitted the woman to rise in the class structure. It also worked the other way, as occasionally an implicit dowry was all important since it included a dynastic claim transferred to the new husband – think of this as reducing the necessary cash payment. Medieval history is littered with lesser (but wealthy) nobility marrying women with claims to superior political or social inheritances. But for most folk, the dowry was small and simply confirmed by an oral contract specifying that the bride would be provided with certain goods by her family: cattle, clothes, articles of furniture, bedding and the like. The seeking out of dowries *and* the level of what was to be expected suggests that the parties were of roughly the same income level. Farm laborers tended to marry the daughters of farm laborers; farmers' daughters tended to marry farmers.

Dowries, historically, tended to be more common in highly stratified societies. In contrast to a dowry, a *bride price* is the payment made to the bride's family for her income claims and reproductive potential. These payments by the groom's family were (are) particularly common in pre-industrial societies with less well-established social structures.

The bride price was replaced by the dowry as traditional societies became more commercial and industrial. Dowries are found today in South and Southeast Asia and Sub-Saharan Africa. As Siwan Anderson has pointed out, enforcing the payment of dowries, often paid in installments (some of which come after the marriage), constitute a particular threat to women's safety in areas such as India where dowry-related murder is all too common.[12] Dowries are at odds with freedom of choice and have largely died out as an institution in western societies. An exception is that dowries and bride prices still may be found in some recent immigrant communities.

The lessening of parental or patriarchal control of marriage partners was, as noted earlier, a result of greater contact due to urbanization. Today in Western Europe, North America, Australia and elsewhere, the arranged marriage has given way to greater freedom of choice, to romantic marriage. Pre-selection contact was (is) still stratified, however, with urban location, education, and work force characteristics being the most prevalent and, within these striations, dances continue to attract. All of these are related to income levels. The fact that people of similar social and economic backgrounds and income levels tend to marry each other is not a surprise. The freedom of choice has produced one more result that is very modern – small in number today, but which will increase in the future. Peoples are now marrying across racial and religious divides. Social barriers of race and religion in marriage are being broken down in European and North American society just as earlier legal prohibitions, in some cases, were removed. To be sure, this is a small crack in racial and religious exclusivity. The upswing in the inter-marriage rate was post-World War II. Those at the lower end of the educational scale are least likely to marry outside their ethnicity, while those with higher levels of education are more likely to do so.[13]

The growth of commercial and industrial economies has tended to promote freedom of choice in recent years, and populations are adjusting to it. China is one country going through a romantic revolution. Half a century ago, according to a study of a rural community in Northern China, only about 4% of all marriages fell into the freedom of choice category. The majority were either arranged by families or match-makers. Now, as the Chinese rural economies are becoming more commercialized, about one third of all marriages are between individuals who select their own partner.[14] It is pleasant to speculate that the forces of economic globalization and the spread of love-based marriage are causally linked.

7.3 Household and Family Size

In pre-modern times the typical family was large with several generations living as part of the same household. Sometimes they included nearly-related kin. With the beginning of the industrial and demographic transitions, the geographic mobility of individuals meant that the family, while still large by today's standard, was more spread out. But, at about the same time, child mortality declined so the dependency rate of the young rose and households remained large. In the 20th century, the nuclear

---

US Census definitions

Family Size: Number of individuals in a family. A family is a group of two or more people who live together and who are related by birth, marriage, or adoption.

Household Size: The total number of people living in a housing unit (excludes those in institutional settings – such as group homes, shared units and others). Note that a household can be a few as one person. It takes at least two people to be a family.

Family Household (Family): A family includes a householder and one or more people living in the same household who are related to the householder by birth, marriage, or adoption. All people in a household who are related to the householder are regarded as members of his or her family. A family household may contain people not related to the householder, but those people are not included as part of the householder's family in census tabulations. Thus, the number of family households is equal to the number of families, but family households may include more members than do families. A household can contain only one family for purposes of the modern census. Not all households contain families since a household may comprise a group of unrelated people or one person living alone.

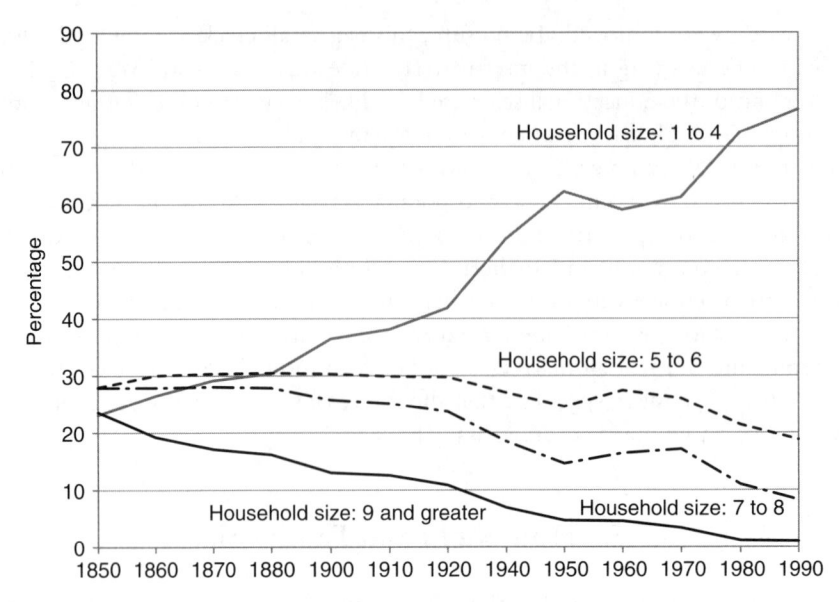

Figure 7.1 Household Size by Decade in the United States from 1850 to 1990.
Source: calculated from data in Haines (2006) *US Historical Statistics*, Ae85–96.

family (parents and a small number of children) evolved out of the fall in fertility and the increase in women's employment outside the home (other things equal). Today the so-called nuclear family is slowly disappearing in the OECD countries and is being replaced by DINKs (double incomes, no kids) and the various other forms of post-second demographic transition families. Nuclear and extended families, however, do still exist. Yet the cross-sectional evidence shows that they are rapidly disappearing. We can square these observations by noting that the modern, and now traditional, nuclear family in which an individual may find themselves is a form that varies with age over an individual's life-cycle. Many families in the developed world today may be part of several types of family in the course of their lifetimes: a non-nuclear family at some stage such as a childless cohabitation, enter a nuclear (perhaps an extended) family with wide contacts when they have children, then withdraw to another type of family such as a retired couple or into a single person household. The fact that families now have fewer children means that there will also be fewer siblings, aunts, uncles and cousins. What *will* we do in a world with so few aunties?

In 1790, at the time of the first US Census, the majority of households had seven or more people in them. An astonishing 29 % of households had nine or more people. Although there is no quantitative evidence for the following 60 years, the pattern of household size appears to have changed only little – see Figure 7.1. But, beginning in 1850, there was a remarkable shift from large to small household size that was continuous on a decade-by-decade basis. By 1990 most people lived in small households (four persons or fewer), and only about one % lived in households of nine or greater. Today, the mean household size is 2.6 persons and the completed family size is 3.2 persons – some children or one of the parents may have left the household making household size smaller. An historical difficulty is that family size (parents and children) and household size is not the same thing. The household may include other relations living with the family and exclude children not living at home. Nonetheless, future household size in the US is predicted to stabilize as we move through the 21st century according to researchers Leiwin Jiang and Brian O'Neill, even with widely varying assumptions about the marriage rate, divorce rate, fertility and life expectancy. The extreme range of their projections to the year 2100 is 2.0 to 3.1 persons per household; their best estimate is about the level we have today, even though they project change in household composition such as more single-persons, more co-habitations and a slight increase in marital fertility.[15]

At the end on the 20th century household size in most developed countries was remarkably similar. Even in the least developed world, the average household size was less than that of the Americans just after the Revolution.[16] As the sociologist David Kertzer notes, there is much debate about the role household size has played in history. Some claim the small nuclear family was an outcome of the industrial transition from agriculture to urban industries. The counter-claim has been that nuclear or small extended households existed before the transition got underway and, indeed, was partly responsible for the faster economic growth of the leading countries. Was it effect or cause?[17] The answer is that it was both; there was feedback. The European marriage pattern with its late age of marriage restricted the marital fertility of households by reducing the 'at risk' period. This created savings (see Chapter Nine). It also meant that the family was more mobile and could relocate to urban centers and establish themselves at a lower cost than larger families. Also, the evidence in Figure 7.1 illustrates that there was a greater variation in US household sizes in 1850 than today. Of the four size groups shown, all were roughly equal in importance in the early US, where the European marriage pattern was also prevalent. The rewards for having fewer children would tend to alter the behavior of those with larger families. After decades of convergence to the small family size, there is now less household variation. Nearly eight out of ten households accommodates four or fewer people.

Within the household, the family is involved in three economic relationships. The first is the set of principles governing co-operation among the members. Who washes the dishes? Second is the issue of who owns the physical edifice where the household lives. Of course, home ownership was a relatively rare event until modern times. (American, Canadian and Australian home ownership was always greater than that in Europe and Asia.) So we must also consider who has the rights of rental, the claim on the tied-cottage or other forms of possible tenure. Third are the obligations of those in the household to the individual(s) who have the established rights of tenure or ownership. As Robert Ellickson argues in his exceptional history of household structure and law, these relationships are mostly informal (or implicit) in order to keep the transaction costs down.[18] However, the terms of co-operation among household members are not always determined in an equitable manner. Patriarchal households are fairly common even today in many parts of the least developed world and are not unknown elsewhere. There, the free negotiation of terms of co-operation among members of the household is not an option. Until the individual (adult) household member has *freedom of exit*, the institution of the household is less flexible. The emergence of a more liberal household arrangement was one of the key foundations of European and North American economic growth. It permitted the supply of labor to expand through its mobility.

7.4 Child Labor

It has only been since the middle of the 19th century that a substantial number of families could afford to give their children a "privileged" upbringing, to forego the additional family income that the children's labor would produce. In most agrarian

Oyster Shuckers in a Canning Factory in South Carolina, 1909

This photograph was part of the evidence collected in 1909 by the *National Child Labor Committee* set up by the US government to investigate the extent of child labor and to make recommendations about uniform laws regulating child labor across the states. It shows, with their reported ages, Josie (5), Bertha (6) and Sophia (10) who worked as full-time oyster shuckers in the Maggioni Canning Company of Port Royal, South Carolina.
Source: Photograph from the records of the US National Child Labor Committee, *Library of Congress*, Prints and Photographs Division, Washington.

societies, children worked (and still work) alongside their parents from the time they were old enough to retrieve eggs from the hen-house. Outside farming, an apprenticeship has been part of an artisan education since the Middle Ages.[19] With industrialization, many children went to work inside the factories with their parents. Even more went to work apart from their parents, a situation that gave rise to much criticism of the basic concept of child labor. As education came to play a greater role in determining one's position in the adult labor force, the children of the bourgeoisie remained in school rather than joining the labor force.[20] However, the practice of child labor is still very much with us, especially in the less developed parts of the world.[21]

It is logical to ask the question, why do children work? It should not be surprising that there is no good answer to the question. There are many motivations, including a desire to work on the part of the children themselves. In addition to the fact that children had traditionally worked, there seems little question that the ample supply of children available at the dawn of the Industrial Revolution coupled with a family's need for income were among the principal reasons for the existence of child labor. It was also the case that there was a demand for the labor of children, especially since their wages were low and they were unlikely to form labor unions. Further, as several scholars have noted, their small stature and nimble fingers were ideally suited to the type of work situations created by the Industrial Revolution in textile mills and mines. As economic development contributed to increasing family incomes and technological change moved away from the small scale, simple machinery that had given children a comparative advantage, child labor disappeared. By World War II, it was largely a thing of the past in developed nations, but it remains in the less developed world.

Historians have largely focused on the large number of children who entered the often-bleak factories of the late 18th–early 19th centuries. They have decried the deplorable conditions of those factories for children, but the adults breathed the polluted air as well – and the whole family had to breathe it at home. Other historians have argued that the decision to work was economically rational, given the alternatives.[22] Clearly, the decision to work is one that was made in the context of the society of which the children were a part. Today, there are laws in many countries that specify the age to which a child must stay in school, but that age is almost always younger than what the law considers to be the age of consent. A child's decision to work may be viewed as unacceptable if the child is 15 and acceptable if the child is 17. For many, especially those children who lived (or live) on farms, there was no decision to make; work was (and is) a natural part of life. And, if we go back into the dim mists of history, everyone worked to survive. The debate over whether children should work first required a great deal of economic development.

Children should be productive members of the family, but in developed countries today those chores are largely unpaid (weekly allowances notwithstanding). Parents had worked when they were children, and they expected their children to work. As suggested above, some boys worked apart from their families as apprentices; girls would leave home around 12 to become domestic servants. By the 16th century, a significant number of young people were employed as servants in husbandry.[23] Living away from home, the girls performed chores such as milking, weeding, and cooking, while the boys looked after the work animals, ploughed, and drove the carts. There is ample evidence that, when the Industrial Revolution arrived, children were not entering the labor force for the first time; their conditions of work changed.[24]

Those conditions were often troubling, even before widespread employment in factories. The most cited example is that of the "climbing boys" of British chimney sweeps. It is alleged that boys as young as four would climb narrow chimneys to scrape soot. Britain's 1788 Act for the Better Regulation of Chimney Sweepers and their Apprentices, was to protect such children. It required that apprentices be at least eight years old, but the Act was generally ignored because there was no means to enforce it.[25] With the first rural textile mills (c.1769), and the expansion of coal mines, the perception of child labor changed for the worst. "The dark satanic mills" of William Blake's poem became, in E.P. Thompson's prose, "places of sexual license, foul language, cruelty, violent accidents, and alien manners."[26] In brief, no place for children, but many of them were assigned to such places by orphanages and workhouses. They received food, clothing, shelter, and (most likely) no wages. Estimates of the number of children employed in rural mills average around a third of that labor force, but the fraction was much higher in certain mills. Children also worked in the mills and mines of Belgium, France, Germany and the US as they industrialized. When the steam engine freed mills from having to locate adjacent to water (so a waterwheel could provide power), the mills became less rural, more urban. The demand for coal increased. Children from poor, working-class families replaced orphaned apprentices. This seems to have intensified the debate over the effect on children, a debate that remains as vigorous today as it was then.

Among those who argued that industrialists were exploiting children and subjecting them to unhealthy working conditions were Friedrich Engels, Karl Marx, and Beatrice and Sidney Webb. Their position was that children as young as five worked indoors, sunrise to sundown, every day but Sunday, in poorly lit, overcrowded factories and mines. They called upon Parliament to pass laws to help correct the situation. On the other side of the debate, Andrew Ure and John Clapham argued that, to make a contribution to their family's income, children were performing light work under conditions little different than those under which they worked before industrialization. Both sides presented an impressive array of information to bolster their position. After a good deal of Parliamentary debate, a Royal Commission was created to investigate the situation. As a result, Parliament passed several laws setting the minimum age of employment at nine and the maximum daily hours at 12 (c.1819) before lowering them to 10 (c.1847). Given the experience with the 1788 law, a cadre of factory inspectors was created to enforce the laws.

The situation in the US was very similar to Britain. Everyone worked on a family farm. Fieldwork was generally the responsibility of men, while women and children performed tasks closer to the house and garden. Children appear to have had a relatively low productivity on northern US farms.[27] Indeed, it has been argued that the first areas to industrialize were those where the productivity of women and children was low relative to adult males.[28] Northeastern women, who were described as "redundant" with respect to agriculture, became actively involved in the putting-out system. By 1832, with the shift away from artisan shops toward small factories, the percentage of young Northeastern women (ages 10 to 29) involved in wage work was 40% of the industrial work force in the Northeast. Typically, they pooled their incomes with other family members.

The first American textile mill, that of Almy and Brown, opened in 1790 in Pawtucket, Rhode Island. The first large-scale New England industrial town was

Lowell, Massachusetts, owned by the Lowells of Boston. In the search for a labor force, Samuel Slater, partner to Almy and Brown, is often credited with launching the family system of labor in which children tended machines for their fathers. The Lowells generally hired single New England farm girls for whom they constructed clean, well-supervised dormitories. The labor of the "Lowell girls" was compensated at a relatively low wage, but the wages the Lowells paid were higher than the girls could have earned by staying on the farm. Although the share of children in the industrial labor force began to decline as early as 1840, it remained an important part of the textile industry into the early 20th century.

The first statistics on child labor in the US are from 1880. For children 10–19, the labor force participation rate was higher for rural children than urban ones, higher for boys than for girls, higher for foreign-born children than for native born, and higher for blacks than for whites.[29] Statistics from the *Cost of Living Survey of 1889–90* indicate that for urban households, the income produced by the children was important to the family's income. The income of the principal breadwinner peaked when he was in his 30s, but his family's income didn't peak until he was in his 50s.[30]

As was true in Britain, the fact that children still held industrial jobs at the end of the 19th century was viewed with alarm. As the high-school movement took hold, it became clear that children who quit school to work were reducing their lifetime income potential, a story that is told today about high-school dropouts.[31] Parents were seen as sacrificing their children's future, but the normal trade-off was an increase in the family's income. Employers were accused of assigning children to dangerous jobs, then bullying them if they showed any hesitancy. As in Britain, the US response to the situation was labor legislation. The first state law was passed in Massachusetts in 1837; in order to be considered for employment in a manufacturing firm, children under the age of 15 had to have attended school for at least three months in the previous 12 months. By 1900, 44 states (and territories) had passed similar laws. On the other hand, federal legislation was ruled largely unconstitutional by the Supreme Court. The most celebrated attempt, the Keating-Owen Act of 1916, was set aside two years later in the *Hammer v. Dagenhart* decision. It was not until the Fair Labor Standards Act of 1938 that a federal statute was found constitutional.[32] By then, child labor had almost disappeared in the US and other developed countries, but not so in the developing world.

The US Department of Labor publishes an annual study on child labor to assure that the country is not unwittingly abetting the problem through international trade. The most recent is entitled *The Department of Labor's 2008 Findings on the Worst Forms of Child Labor*.[33] This is a country-by-country report, and in Table 7.1 the top line reports the average percentage of all countries reporting the percentages of boys and girls aged 7–14 that are working. There are 122 countries cited in the monitoring with details about 75 of them. From these 75 countries averages are computed; only the countries with more than 10% of their children working are shown in the table presented here. It should be noted that the reports are for different years. The percentages of children working in agriculture and the service sector are also reported in Table 7.1. As can be seen, roughly speaking, a quarter of the children in these countries work, a slightly higher percentage of boys than girls. Over two-thirds of them worked in agriculture, and just under a quarter of them

Table 7.1 Children in the Labor Force, Selected High Percentage Countries, Various Years (working children as a percentage of children in the age range).

	Year	Children	Boys	Girls	Agriculture	Services
			7–14 years			
Average of 75 countries		23.7	25.2	22.2	68.7	23.5
Countries with over 10%						
East Timor	2001	85.2	84.5	85.9	91.8	8.2
Ethiopia	2005	50.1	58.1	41.6	95.2	3.4
Cambodia	2000–04	48.9	49.6	48.1	82.3	12.9
Burkina Faso	2003	47.0	46.4	47.7	97.4	2.0
Somalia	2006	39.8	41.2	38.4		
Nepal	1999	39.6	35.4	44.0	87.1	11.0
Tanzania	2001	35.4	36.2	34.5	77.4	22.4
Kenya	2000	32.5	34.7	30.4		
Uganda	2005–06	31.1	32.4	29.8	95.5	3.0
Haiti	2005	29.0	32.2	26.0		
Guyana	2000	26.3	28.7	23.9		
Madagascar	2001	24.3	24.8	23.7		
Ghana	2000	24.2	24.5	24.0	71.0	22.6
Bolivia	2002	23.2	23.9	22.5	76.3	18.8
Peru	2000	22.3	24.0	20.5	73.2	22.9
Guatemala	2003	21.1	26.2	16.0	62.3	24.2
Bhutan	2003	19.6	16.1	22.7	92.2	1.9
Pakistan	1999–2000	16.4	15.8	17.2	78.1	13.4
Paraguay	2005	15.3	22.6	7.7	60.8	32.1
Sri Lanka	1998	15.0	17.9	11.9	71.5	14.8
Bangladesh	2006	13.6	21.3	5.6		
Morocco	1998–99	13.2	13.5	12.8	60.6	10.1
Thailand	2005–06	13.0	13.5	12.6		
Iraq	2006	12.4	15.1	9.6		
Yemen	1999	11.1	11.2	11.0	92.0	6.2
Philippines	2001	11.0	13.4	8.4	65.4	29.4
Columbia	2001	10.4	14.1	6.6	35.6	49.9
Ecuador	2004	10.2	12.6	7.8	71.0	22.9
El Salvador	2003	10.2	13.7	6.5	51.2	35.3

Source: US Department of Labor (2009) *2008 Findings on the Worst Forms of Child Labor.*

worked in the service sector.[34] A country that reported these average percentages is Ghana, and we will take a closer look at what the report had to say about child labor in Ghana.

The countries reported in Table 7.1 were chosen to reflect the diversity of experiences found in the report among all countries with more than 10% of their children working. Far and away, East Timor is the country with the largest percentage of children reported working, and the vast majority of them were in agriculture. Only eight of the 75 reported more than half of their children were in the labor force, and most reported little difference between boys and girls. Other than East Timor, the other seven countries are in Africa. Even in the middle of the distribution, most of the countries are in Africa. Countries from Central and South America, the Middle East, and Asia all reported much lower percentages.

Of the 40 countries reporting a sectoral division of child labor, all but six report that a majority of the children worked in agriculture. The lowest (18.5) was reported in the Dominican Republic where under 6% of the children work and the majority are reported in the service sector. Indeed, the only two countries reporting a greater share of children in the service sector than in agriculture are Chile and Venezuela, where an even smaller percentage of children are in the labor force. The purpose of the Department of Labor report, however, is not to provide such statistics, but to look inside them and see what the children are actually doing. For that, we turn to Ghana.

The agricultural work that occupies 71% of the children involves the production, harvesting, and loading of a variety of food crops and livestock. Under Ghanaian law, the minimum age for employment is 15 for heavy and 13 for light work (that which neither interferes with education nor is harmful to health). The Department of Labor report singled out for special consideration the estimated 1.6 million Ghanaian children involved in the cocoa sector, some as young as five.[35] This work was reported to involve several hazardous tasks, including carrying heavy loads, spraying pesticides, using machetes to clear undergrowth, and burning vegetation. Ghana's service sector employs 22.6% of the children in activities such as street vending and fare collecting. As early as age six, girls in urban areas carry heavy loads on their heads. These girls are often street children and vulnerable to being exploited in prostitution. In the major urban centers, the capital city of Accra and the coastal tourist cites of Elmina and Cape Coast, children are engaged in commercial sexual exploitation and, at least in the coastal cities, the sale of drugs. Ghana's Ministry of Women's and Children's Affairs (MOWAC) estimates that thousands of children are involved in the sex industry in Ghana.[36] Much of this involves the "trafficking" of children and forced labor, both of which are illegal. Ghanaian children are trafficked both internally and to and from neighboring countries in West Africa.

Ghana's manufacturing sector employs 5.8% of the child labor force. Both boys and girls are found in quarrying and small-scale mining activities such as the diamond and small-scale (illegal) gold mining. Both are involved in the fishing industry on Lake Volta; many of them have been transported there.[37] The work is hazardous for the boys who perform tasks such as deep diving and the casting and drawing of nets. Girls are domestic servants and cooks in the lake's fishing villages; they are also involved in the preparation and sale of fish for market. It is traditional in Ghana, as elsewhere, to send children to Koranic teachers, and this may involve a vocational or apprenticeship component. In addition to the education, many of the students are forced by their teachers to obtain money and food, and this usually involves begging.

The Department of Labor report goes on to discuss the efforts Ghana's government is making to reduce abuses. And it should be emphasized, the reason Ghana is discussed here is that, statistically, the numbers it reported are almost exactly equal to the averages for all 75 countries that reported data.

The detail contained in the country-by-country reports of the Department of Labor study hearkens back to the anecdotal evidence one finds in relation to western European and North American children at the beginning of the Industrial Revolution. Absent words like "trafficking," children today work in areas where children have worked for centuries. In many parts of the globe, they continue to contribute to family incomes still too small to enable them to invest in their human capital that would have the potential to increase their family's income in the future. And, in specific parts of the world, investments in human capital are still being denied to women. What Ghana's experience suggests is that child labor is still very much a part of family decision-making. Indeed, note was taken of the fact that some parents still engage in what has been a traditional practice of sending their children to live with more affluent relatives (or family friends). Family connections were, and remain, an important part of the institutional setting in which child labor occurs.[38]

7.5 Family Connections: Networks

Families exist within networks of similar families. Sometimes these families are related genetically as an extended family group (cousins, second cousins, great-aunts and so on) and sometimes they are part of a network linked together by other shared characteristics such as social origins and religious affiliations. We have already seen this at work in the 19th and early 20th centuries in the German and Italian immigrants to the United States. In the less-developed world, they are often part of the mechanism that supplies child labor as we saw in the previous section. Irish policemen came to dominate certain metropolitan police departments in the US in the late 19th century. In Portugal, Basque fishermen banded together, shared information, controlled their output (by capturing the organization of the markets) and through that activity, manipulated prices.[39] Family networks provide benefits for their members, but they often do so by retaining an exclusivity of information which necessarily lessens the opportunities of outsiders (a social cost). At the limit, family networks may act in a collusive fashion or function as a discriminatory mechanism. However, the history is not so clear cut. This section deals with networks in two cases: self-help and business management.

Family networks act as social support for their members. In this sense they are like an insurance scheme (or, as noted in Chapter Four, a pension-like arrangement for close family members). The implicit premium is the reciprocal nature of the obligation to help. In this fashion, "families" may be extended well beyond the immediate family to include close friends who fulfill the same social support on a wider basis. A 1980s study of a low-income population in rural Georgia revealed that women had support networks that were approximately double the number of family relatives. The networks were not large, however, ranging from 6.06 for black Americans to 7.82 for white Americans (means). Professional help was generally absent from the networks of these poor mothers.[40] We do not know whether the experience of these rural folk can be generalized to look backward in history, but it seems likely that we can. Although these rural-poor networks are small, the networks often are quite large. Members of certain religious communities tithe. Historically, they give a portion of their personal incomes (a tenth for example) to provide assistance for beneficial social projects. The insurance premium is now explicit. There is a long history of such tithing in communities such as the Ishmaeli Muslims and the Society of Friends (Quakers). Apart from the social care of their members at a local level, they also engage in support well outside the networks – educational support is an example. Another historical instance of tithing comes from the European monasteries and nunneries during the Middle Ages. They received tithes from the more prosperous with a promise that they never would be left destitute. While acting as a social support network with unwritten (but implicit) terms of reference, yet networks often provided a well-defined benefit for their members at an explicit price.

Such is the case of the mutual self-help societies which arose in Britain in the 18th century and subsequently spread to North America. These organizations were essentially working-class and fraternal. That they had, to our ears, exotic names (Oddfellows, Knights of Pythias and the like) should not lead us to underestimate the seriousness of their purpose. They provided a service which neither families nor the state could provide, an insurance against the risk of unemployment due to illness. Sickness insurance benefits were received by those who were accepted into a fraternal order, enrolled in an insurance scheme, and paid a weekly fee. It also covered accidents and longer-term disability. David Beito and Herb and George Emery have carried out a series of economic studies on these fraternal orders in North America whose provision of health insurance for members was a principal reason for joining. What they have shown is that the fraternal orders were remarkably efficient in providing coverage for their members. Despite being organized at the local level into so-called lodges, they operated on sound accounting principles and got their prices right, neither too high nor too low. They avoided the insurer's free-rider problem (false claims) by two of their provisions. One was the waiting periods before receipt of benefits. Second, a high degree of moral suasion was applied. The elders, the executive of the lodge, would come and visit to ensure the illness benefits were warranted and, because the lodges were essentially local, they brought community social pressure to bear to prevent "malingerers" from applying for benefits. So successful were these fraternal networks that together they covered a large proportion of the white, working class males – a majority in some areas. In parallel, there was a similar set of black-based fraternal orders. It was as if the societies limited their networks to well-perceived risks, within which the moral responsibility of members could be guaranteed. Ultimately the fraternal societies died out in the second quarter of the 20th century. Their demise is a subject of much discussion among economic historians. It is most likely that they succumbed to the employer-based schemes which provided superior benefits and which emerged in order to attract labor to particular employers. Also, and particularly in Britain, the advent of national insurance and universal health arrangements crowded them out.[41] Yet, the importance of the self-help fraternal orders should not be underestimated: for more than a century they provided sickness insurance to a substantial part of the working-class population that was ignored by the market.

Networks were also important in the world of finance. In the Middle Ages, Venetian bankers and Jewish financiers operated their arbitrage over long distances because i) they had developed specific instruments to effect a transfer of savings; and ii) they had a network comprised of individuals who would honor the instruments – bills of exchange, for instance. The individuals regarded their networks as completely trustworthy. The personal relations of the network members reduced the risk of the transactions, thereby making them possible. The networks also allowed individuals to work co-operatively. Ann M. Carlos, Karen Maguire and Larry Neal point to the case of the London Jewish community acting in concert to buy the stock of the Bank of England as it declined in value during the South Sea Bubble in 1720. They voluntarily accepted losses on the bank stock. It is conjectured that this was to prove their reliability and gain a permanent place in the growing London capital market. It is also likely that this action also gained them more social acceptability in the long run.[42] Only a tight network where the participants fully understood the reasoning behind the action and the shared long-run goals could have achieved this outcome.

A key rationale for the existence of networks is that they allay risk. Risk in finance and investment has many dimensions, the principal of which is the flow of knowledge. But it did not always spread with equal ease over distance because of communication inefficiencies and over the technical distance between industries. Networks help leap the barriers to capital formation. During the period between the US Civil War and World War I, several things happened simultaneously: the investment rate rose, industrial restructuring of the economy was rapid, mortality fell substantially, fertility was on a downward path and net immigration flows increased. One key economic feature of this period was the rapid evolution of capital markets. New demands for investment led to the creation of new financial instruments and new markets for their sale. This period has become known as the "age of finance capitalism." In the United States the movement of savings across these barriers to capital formation owes a great deal to the entrepreneurs of the day. Their names are familiar even today.[43] In all these countries the managers of capital were part of networks, albeit very loose ones. They were knit together by social class, education, religious background and, occasionally, by family ties through intermarriage. That is, they went to same schools (or type of school), worshipped in the same churches, were members of the same clubs, married off their children to each other and went to the same places for holidays (Cape Cod or the Isle of Wight).[44] They shared the same values, passed on information to one another and co-operated, sometimes competed, in the same markets. Why would individuals who competed with each other be part of the same network? It is the same as having a hateful cousin. You may not like them but, because you share so many social characteristics, you can read them like a book. That is, and more so for co-operators, information that has not been observed by the market for financial capital is acted upon. The act of moving capital over barriers created rents to scarcity (or super-normal profits). The rents stir others into action and many actors create an institution called the market in the instruments of ownership (bonds, mortgages, insurance and shares, to name a few). The actions of the networks then are beneficial to the emergence of more efficient capital formation, while, at the same time, any attempt by members of the network to act collusively will be to its detriment. It's a trade-off.

7.6 Marital Dissolution

In the days of the Roman Empire divorce (a legal end of marriage) was relatively common, but only for the members of the patrician class (and there were clan grievances to be reconciled). Muslim society also had lax divorce laws, although the untangling of marriage contracts and various families' allegiances meant that it was complex, expensive and, consequently, relatively rare. Pre-modern European marriage dissolution practices are not well-documented except in the case of dynastic separations where an annulment could be sought from the bishop or pope – presumably with the appropriate payments to ease its passage. Perhaps the most celebrated divorces were those of Henry VIII whose domestic affairs were one of the reasons behind the split of the Church of England (Anglican) from that of Rome.

Divorced, beheaded, died;
Divorced, beheaded, survived[45]

memorializes these divorces, and the fates of Henry's other wives – useful in order to keep the order of the queens in mind, a British schoolboy trick! Henry's divorces notwithstanding, neither the Church of Rome nor the Church of England permitted divorce, although they did recognize a legal separation – which naturally ruled out remarriage – except in Henry's case. In the 18th and early 19th centuries in England, divorce was an option only for the very rich since it required the passage of a specific act of parliament naming the individuals. Civil divorce did not become an option in English law until the mid-1850s, and even then it was limited as to cause and unequally applied in the case of men and women.[46] The Matrimonial Causes Act of 1857 and The Divorce Act of 1857 introduced civil procedures for divorce on the grounds of adultery in the suits brought by men. For women the requirement was to find evidence of both adultery *and* other grievous offenses in their suits – adultery was a necessary but not sufficient condition.

In those countries of Western Europe that retained the established Roman Catholic religion, divorce was only introduced as part of a regime change. France, for instance, introduced liberal divorce measures early in the Revolutionary period; it subsequently revoked these laws and made divorce illegal until another sudden change in 1884.[47] Somewhat similar sea changes took place in the divorce laws of the east. Both Japan and China had traditional, but different, marital dissolution practices until recent history. Japan in the pre-modern period had an exceptionally male-oriented divorce law; women had very few rights – if any at all. A Japanese male could simply write a three-line letter to his wife indicating that he divorced her. Interestingly, most marriages so dissolved were early in the union *before* children were born. Today, under its post-1945 law that roughly resembles divorce law in the west, the mean age of divorce is much later in life and normally takes place *after* the birth of children.[48] Although there is some historical questioning of the arbitrariness of pre-modern Japanese practice, there is little doubt about the one-sided benefits. Chinese law also changed radically only in the 20th century with the coming of the Communist Revolution which introduced compulsory mediation as part of divorce. This may reflect an older Confucian Chinese custom. Since the end of the Maoist Era, the country has adopted more explicit and balanced divorce proceedings, but it has not entirely given up on mediation.[49]

As they emerged in the late 16th and 17th centuries, the Protestant states of Europe (except England) permitted divorce from their inception as they did not include

> **Divorce Rates** may be defined in a variety of ways. Below are some of the common variants and where found:
>
> a. the number of *persons* divorced in a year as a percentage of married people (stock) in the same year (mid-year population). *England and Wales.*
> b. the number of divorces in a year per 1000 adults (mid-year population). *USA*
> c. the number of divorces in a year per 1000 married adults (mid-year population). *USA*
> d. the number of divorces in a year per 1000 total population (mid-year population). *OECD*
> e. the number of divorces in a year per 100 marriages in the same year.

marriage as a religious sacrament. Scotland, for instance, gave men and women equal access to divorce either on the grounds of adultery or abandonment. The parties could then re-marry. But, the Scottish divorce rates, for the most part, seem well below the rate of Scottish marriage dissolution despite their liberality. The cost of finding the evidence, witnesses, paying lawyers and, one suspects, the social embarrassment was simply too high. Ordinary families that suffered a broken marriage seem to have simply reconstituted themselves in new, but separate, common-law arrangements (probably as bigamists, but with community acquiescence).[50]

In the second half of the 18th century, roughly coincident with the first phase of the Industrial Revolution in Western Europe, a social change of attitude toward marital dissolution took place. The history of divorce records a fairly sharp increase in divorce proceedings in most non-Roman Catholic jurisdictions in North America and Western Europe. Naturally, there is considerable speculation as to why this occurred and why it was so widespread. Perhaps there were some minor changes in the laws in the late 1700s that seemed very attractive to those at the time, but we do not perceive them as such in the 21st century. But more likely, it was the shifting economic environment of the late 1700s. The period marks the beginning of the shift of the workplace to urban areas, the growth of individual incomes and the growing range of people met – giving rise to new expectations of romantic attachments and new opportunities to commit the act for which divorce was suited to deal. Indeed, adultery may have become a more common occurrence.[51] However, this sudden up-take in divorce proceedings did not lead to further increases. For that we had to wait until the mid-20th century.

Social improvers throughout the Victorian and Edwardian eras brought divorce problems to the public gaze: the fate of abandoned females and children, the non-payment of court awards for maintenance (still a continuing problem) and the drive for equitable access to divorce proceedings by both sexes prior to World War I.[52] The rapidly growing sympathy (admiration) for women's suffrage due to female contributions to the war effort was an important fillip to gender equity concerns. In England The Matrimonial Causes Act of 1923 finally evened the playing field in law: equal access and equal causes.[53] English men and women born in the first five years of the 20th century had a divorce rate of 4% (of their marriages), most of which occurred in the 1920s and 1930s. Then the revolution came. In the aftermath of World War II, many marriages broke down. The pressures of wartime and disrupted lives all contributed. The increased marriage rate led to more divorces with a lag of about a decade. But married people demanded more; it was as if they developed a taste for a new good. Easier access to divorce and expansion of the terms were among the reforms demanded along with a lower price (cost). Those born in the years 1945–1949 and who were married had a 27% likelihood of their marriages ending in divorce (and it is not over yet). Most divorces among this group were not the end of two-parent families, however. Eight out of ten women whose first marriages ended with a divorce remarried, usually within a short period of time. The remarriage rate was even higher for men, over 90%.[54]

The widespread, but much exaggerated, "sexual revolution" of the 1960s was one of many forces that lay behind the movement for a "no fault" divorce system. No fault divorces were first introduced in Sweden in 1915 and, although they became the model for subsequent reforms, did not pass into the law of other countries for about 50 years. Fault of course implies the finding of its proof. This applied in most European and North American legal jurisdictions. There was a loophole. The parties wishing a divorce could collude to find a solution. The typical grounds for divorce by the post-1945 years were: adultery, desertion, physical and mental cruelty, long imprisonment for a felony, and persistent drunkenness. It was by far easiest to collude on the grounds of "adultery" – all that it required was a good story and an actor willing to accept the (small) likelihood of being found out. The institution of the "law of divorce" became untenable under these practices. Divorces increasingly did not involve children. The cultural shift that is the second demographic transition (Chapter Four) was background to the decline in the total fertility rate. Within marriages, children tended to be born later in the life of the mother. So in more and more marriages, the existence of children and their welfare was not an issue. "No-fault" divorces found a general legal and popular acceptance where one individual could initiate the proceedings and freely declare that the marriage had irretrievably broken down.[55] The granting of a divorce generally involved a short period during which the divorced person could not re-marry – a puritan holdover. The divorce patterns of the recent past, since the reforms of the 1960s and 1970s, have been very similar across countries. Divorce rates rose after the reforms of the late 1960s and 1970s for about ten years or so then stabilized and very recently have begun to decline – see those for the United States and England and Wales in Figure 7.2.

How much the divorce law reforms contributed to the divorce boom is a matter of controversy. Some observers claim that the reforms were responsible for a permanent rise of the divorce rate by about one-sixth. Others claim that much of the divorce boom was due to the rush for earlier dissolution of unhappy unions and that moved the divorces forward by about a decade.[56] This was a once-and-for-all shift, and, thereafter, the greater reluctance of young people to enter a marriage and the increased non-marital cohabitations meant that the stock of marriages in the years 2000–10 did not face the same high risk for divorce as earlier marriages. However, the probability of divorce from a first marriage tends to be close to 50%, and the probability of a

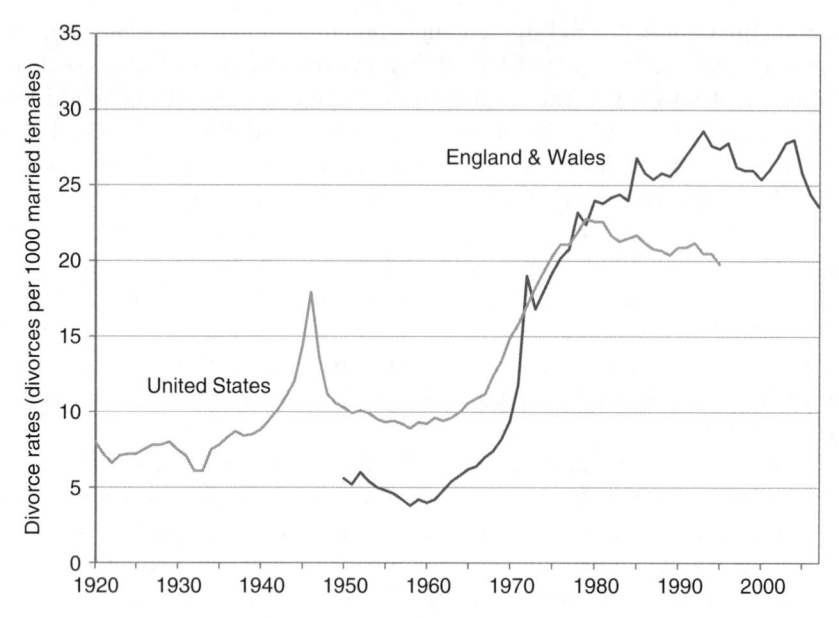

Figure 7.2 Divorce in the United States and England and Wales, 1920–2007.
Note: The broad features of Canadian divorce rates followed that of England and Wales. About 40% of Canadian marriages end in divorce. This includes all marriages whether first, second, third or other. The data also show that the divorce rate is generally higher for each subsequent marriage after the first.
Sources: UK (current), National Statistics On-Line, *Historic Divorce Tables: United States* (current), National Vital Statistics, CDC On-Line.

second divorce is even higher. As observed across the US social spectrum, divorces become more frequent the lower the income of the male partner. There does not appear to be any relation to female income.[57] From the point of view of the individuals, the issues of divorce now become: the division of assets of the marriage and the compensation to spouses, if indeed there are mandated payments. From a social perspective we have to ask if and how the divorce puts families at risk to become poor.[58]

7.7 Married Women's Property

Modern feminist historians argue that marriage and how it was (is) arranged has much to do with individual male-female power relationships. In a historical context, for instance, marriage usually meant an actual transfer of the female's property to the male spouse or, at minimum, a transfer of a claim to her property. Prior to the reforms of the 19th century in Western Europe and North America, this meant that married women had few rights to property, although they did have some. For instance, the settlement of a sum of money on a woman in her right was a common practice of the wealthy. These were called dower arrangements and, amongst other reasons, were designed for her provision should she be widowed, which was likely given life expectancies. They were kept separate for the male spouse's property by a legal trust. Although a woman's legal rights to own and dispose of property ceased to exist once married, they could return in widowhood. On the other hand, a "never-married" woman had more or less complete authority over her property on the death of her father. This might have been a reason for choosing that state and may explain the high rates of the "never-married" which we find occasionally over time. Changes in the legal property rights of married women were effected over the course of history by two other major developments: the changing legal status of primogeniture and married women's participation in the workplace.[59]

Primogeniture is the legal imperative of passing on an entire estate to the eldest son. It is often held that the law of primogeniture was partly responsible for the late age at marriage of European males. The eldest son would have to wait until his father's demise before being able to set up an independent household. There are several problems with this argument. First, younger sons, those who were not scheduled to inherit, also displayed a late age at marriage. Their economic independence was hardly fashioned by the death of a father. Second, most males in countries under primogeniture did not inherit anything. The heritable right of farm tenure as a renter/tenant might be an exception to this for ordinary folk, but tradition suggests that this right was essentially conveyed long before a parent's death, and the legal transfer was made later. Third, where we have side-by-side examples of the two legal systems – primogeniture and multi-geniture – as in pre-Revolutionary US and colonial New France, both had very similar ages at marriage for men *and* women. To be sure, it was slightly lower than that of their European brothers and sisters, but it was not that much lower. Further, one would expect a North American to have a lower age at marriage because of the relative abundance of land and the ease of establishing an independent household. Finally, as noted in Chapter Four, primogeniture was a legal practice that was widely violated by a family's internal redistribution of the father's estate.

The law regarding women's property holdings within the family began to change in the 19th century on both sides of the Atlantic. The pace of change was slow because, it is claimed, the modification of the law was in male hands. The economic pressures, however, were evident to all. Male-held property could be sought in the courts by a creditor seeking relief, but what of the assets that a female held in her own right and what of the assets legally held by the male spouse but brought into the marriage by his wife? The laws were for the most part ambiguous. This was complicated by two other contemporary practices. First, if male-held assets were hidden in the wife's portion, did this disguise make them free from claims? It did not. Second, what happened to the assets or the debts of the male spouse when he absconded? It appears that in North America the assets of the male spouses usually escaped effective detection when pursued for reasons of debt or marriage breakdown; the geography was too large. To resolve these issues, in the quarter century before the US Civil War, many US states enacted protection for the family by making the wife's assets unassailable in the face of the husband's debts.[60] In the case of marriage breakdown, where the male had absented himself, the courts generally found for the female spouse, and the assets that the woman bought into the marriage were held to be hers. The courts were motivated by welfare concerns for the abandoned family.[61] Still, women did not have the right to dispose of their property, or mortgage it in the case of real property.

By the late 19th century, the greater female participation in the labor force precipitated another significant change in the law concerning women's property rights. There was pressure to permit married women to enter into contracts, the pre-requisite to business activity. A female's earnings prior to the changes were held to be those of the male spouse. The freeing of women from this obligation encouraged, at the margin, many married women into employment and business activity. Where these laws were enacted, there was an appreciable increase in female-headed businesses.[62] In England the major shift in family affairs took place with the passage of The Married Woman's Property Act in 1871. This law was the outcome of same social and economic pressure that had been building in North America. It was bolstered by the famous, and much-discussed, 1861 essay of John Stuart Mill, *The Subjection of Women*.[63] Prior to the 1871 act, English women appeared to have more, albeit limited, rights of property than their North American sisters, but they had fewer rights over earnings and contracts. Recently, May Beth Combs has analyzed the investment behavior of married women and found that there was a considerable change in attitude once married women were given security over their own property; they increasingly held their assets in personal (movable) as opposed to real estate.[64] Many other jurisdictions passed similar laws that established married women in the same legal category as men and single women. However, they typically did not give women claim to assets in the husband's name which the family accumulated over its lifetime, thus denying the woman the right to her value added. For recognition of that claim, women had to wait another century – long after there was a substantial rise in married women's labor force participation. As the legal historian Lori Chambers notes when commenting on a Canadian law similar to the 1871 British act, "[it] had done nothing to address the imbalance of economic power within most marriages or to deconstruct the social belief in marital unity, male authority and wifely obedience."[65] In the 20th century, as women's labor force participation continued to increase and as the divorce rate soared, the number of families headed by a working single mother increased. One consequence of the intersection of social change and the law was that families headed by a single mother were more likely to be poor than other types of families.

7.8 Poverty: One-Parent Families and Elderly Females

Poverty lowers individual self-worth, shortens the time spent in education, inhibits geographic mobility, leads to poor nutritional standards, causes poor life-style health choices, subjects the individual to more periods of unemployment and is often associated with sub-standard housing. It has many characteristics of a disease and is too easily passed on within families. Many would argue, correctly, that the history of the past 50 years or so has seen the long-run fall of poverty rates in most countries. Most developed countries have at least halved the percentage of their population in poverty. But, even the developed world did not collect evidence on poverty until relatively

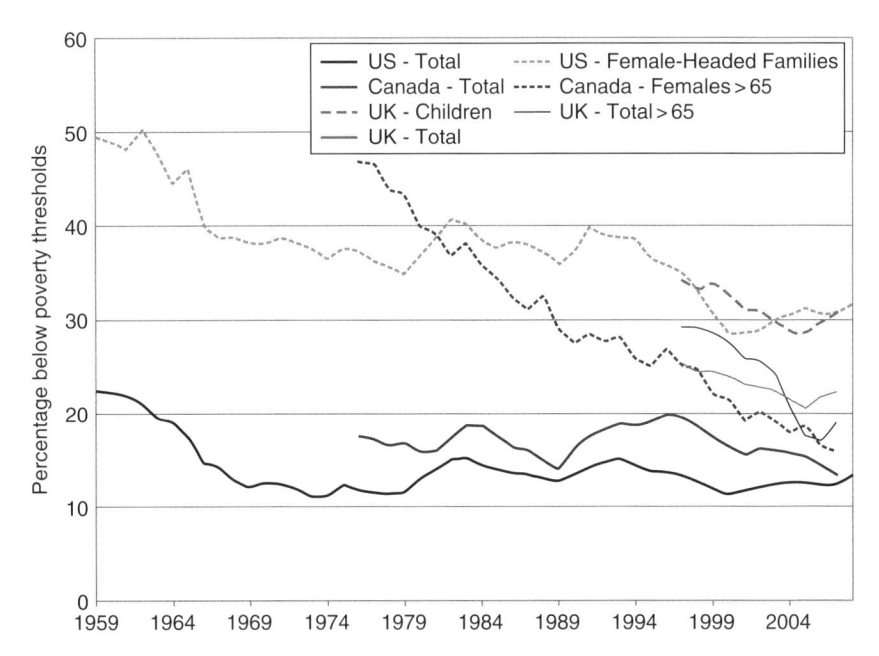

Figure 7.3 Poverty Rates in United States, Canada and the United Kingdom, 1959–2007/8.
Notes: The UK data prior to 2002 exclude Northern Ireland. UK data are based on the 60% threshold of median income.
Source: US Census data in DeNavas-Walt, Proctor and Smith (2009), Table B-1. Statistics Canada (current) 202082/7; *US Historical Statistics*, Be 260–411.

recently. Definitions of poverty vary widely by country. Any comparison of poverty rates over time across countries is fraught with problems. Nonetheless, Figure 7.3 represents the course of poverty rates for three OECD countries: Canada, the United Kingdom and the United States. Some other countries did better; some other countries did worse. Within countries, some groups fared better than other groups in experiencing poverty declines. But, in all countries, two groups are particularly at a high risk: children and the elderly.

Poor children are much more likely to come from female-headed single parent families. In all OECD countries today, female-headed single parent families as a percentage of all families with children have more than doubled in the past half century. The second major high-risk group is the elderly. Their increased life expectancy and their growing numbers mean that another high-risk group is increasing proportionately. A focus on these groups gives us a window into the past levels of deprivation. It also informs us of the major social policy initiatives that are on the agenda for action.[66]

Today in the developed world of OECD countries, no less than 12% of children live in poverty. However, there is considerable variation. The Scandinavian countries (Denmark, Norway, Sweden and Finland) register less than 5% child poverty whereas in four countries of the OECD group (the US, Poland, Mexico and Turkey) about one in every five children lives in poverty.[67] For international comparisons, the OECD defines child poverty as those children living in a family whose income is less than one-half of the median family income. (The median income is the income that is found at the mid-point of the population.) It is a relative standard. Some individual countries define poverty by different standards or thresholds based on calculated standards-of-living. European countries use the OECD-like definition but occasionally set different levels. For instance, the United Kingdom uses a 60% rule; any family with income below 60% of the median family income is judged as 'in poverty'. The United States uses a threshold approach where the poverty level is calculated annually by the US Bureau of the Census to set the upper bound on the poverty scale and sets the threshold. This calculation is based on the minimum cost-of-living for individuals and families. It includes such items as: food, clothing, accommodation, the cost of health insurance premiums and transport. Furthermore, it allows for adjustments for the ages of those included and their family relationship – a child in a family does not require the exact same expenditures as an adult. Different thresholds define poverty for families of different compositions and sizes. There is no best solution to the definitional issues, although the threshold definition does provide the flexibility for calculating regional variations in both income and the cost-of-living.[68] The same is true of Canada which uses similarly calculated thresholds to define those living with a low income (a euphemism for poverty).[69]

Since poverty thresholds were first developed in the 1960s, the US poverty levels have declined during periods of economic growth and have increased when growth slowed. For instance, the US poverty rate in 1999 was back to what it had been 20 years earlier paralleling the rates of economic growth in the 1980s and 1990s. Since the beginning of the 21st century, poverty rates have shown a persistent rise. Here the rising income inequality bears the blame. Elderly people living alone, single-parent households, ineffective public education are among the reasons the number of poor has increased even as average income has risen.[70] The distribution of US family incomes in 1980 was similar to that in 1947, but then the share of income going to the top fifth, particularly the top 5%, began to increase. In 2007, the top fifth of all families enjoyed more than 49.7% of total family incomes, compared with a mere 3.4% for the lowest fifth. This increase was due to an enormous increase in the ratio of professional and executive compensation to that of the average worker.[71] The data also show black and Hispanic families had disastrously high poverty levels. The median income of black families was 54.3% that of white families in 1950. By 1975, the percentage had risen to 61.5%, but it fell back to 56.4% by 1981. But then it rose again, reaching 65.8% in 1999, before falling back to 63.1% in 2006. Overall, Hispanic households have fared better than black households, but both constitute a larger percentage of the lower parts of the income distribution than white households. Indeed, racial discrimination and educational disadvantages act against minority groups, even though the payoffs to economic success tend to be the same as those for whites (e.g., rock stars and athletes are likely to receive equal remuneration regardless of race).

Details from the US and Canada reveal that poverty is not necessarily a permanent condition. People drift in and out of poverty as their personal circumstances change, principally whether they are employed or not. The part of the population that is always in poverty, the chronically poor, is actually much smaller than the poverty rate.

Only 1.8% of the US population was chronically poor over 48 months in 2006–2007 for instance. In Canada over the same period the incidence of permanently low income was remarkably similar to the US. Certain groups, apart from those defined by family status, are at greater risk to enter the poverty rolls. These are for the most part the groups with the lowest levels of educational attainment and are, hence, at higher unemployment risk. In the US these include the Hispanic and Black Americans. In Canada they are comprised of Native Indians, visible minorities and recent immigrants and persons with disabilities.[72] In the United Kingdom they include immigrant groups, particularly those from Africa, Pakistan and Bangladesh and those of low levels of education. Levels of education and immigrant status in the case of the three countries noted above are highly correlated.[73] The worrying tendency is the persistence of poverty among groups. From the US, and likely elsewhere, family structure is not only an important characteristic determining poverty, but it is the best predictor of the next generation's risk of poverty. Children in poor families receive less education, are exposed to greater unemployment risks and have less geographic mobility. Daughters of a white, poor and unmarried mother themselves have a 1 in 12 chance of ending up in the same condition. For Black American mothers and daughters, however, the probability of ending up in the same condition is much higher: one in three![74]

Although the rates are declining in recent years, the principal family characteristics that give rise to child poverty are still the same: female single-parent households and sole elderly females. Of the former, the single-parent family headed by a female is up to five times more likely to be in poverty than the male headed counterpart. Joblessness adds to the risk. To reduce the child poverty rate, individual countries make direct transfer payments to poor families. For instance, if we take an area where the child poverty rate is extremely high, such as the former East Germany, the payment of direct transfers and tax reductions by the federal government of Germany reduced the rate from over 35.2 to 16.2% in 2004.[75] Still large but the policy direction is clear: the larger are the income transfers as cash and near-cash (food stamps or housing allowances, for instance), the more families are raised from poverty and the scandalous proportion of their children living in poverty reduced.[76] The transfers, however, have to be targeted and delivered efficiently. For elderly females the picture is also bleak. Their simple longevity condemns them, along with the inadequacy of pensions, and their situation only ameliorated by targeted transfer payments. Also, many OECD countries have been going through a period of increasing income inequality in the past two decades. In the US and the UK, as noted earlier, wages at the low end of the income distribution are not keeping up with those at the higher end of the income distribution. In the short run this offsets the long-run fall in the poverty rate, but not always completely.

It is only since governments aggressively took on the function of income redistribution in the 20th century that substantial reductions in poverty rates took place. To be sure, governments often accepted this explicit role reluctantly. We do not know the proportion of people who were poor historically. When historians discuss poverty in the past, they normally mean the abjectly poor; they are limited by available evidence, and their numbers are only conjecture. Even then there is ample evidence of an anecdotal nature that suggests that poverty was endemic in industrial societies prior to the modern era. Like the poor of today, most were not in perpetual poverty but suffered in episodes. The majority of the poor, again like today, were the working poor. The poor suffered when the economy was performing badly or employment prospects diminished, and the incidence of poverty increased as the newly poor were drawn into the group. Also, like today, specific parts of the life-cycle and particular family types left individuals vulnerable. In the industries which were facing reduced demand the nominal wages of the workers were bid down. Workers' incomes may also be reduced by decreased hours of work available to them. Or, as occasionally happened, the real cost of living increased due to a rise in the price of basic commodities causing severe economic distress for families. When these events happened, it produced social unrest. "Food riots" or "bread riots" were a common feature of the industrial past and, earlier still, in the rural economy. These happened as reactions to a sudden emergency, but they also occurred when long-grinding poverty reached a tipping point.

The death of a spouse was often the devastating event signaling poverty, especially if it was the death of the male partner. The surviving female partner and children had very few options. If relatively young and not too encumbered with children, the woman could seek a new partner and remarry. Otherwise, children were often abandoned to their fate or added to the child laborers similar to those we see in the less developed countries of today. In pre-modern times, the relief of paupers, as the destitute were known, was left to the religious authorities and to the occasional beneficence of the crown. The giving of coins or alms-giving on designated saints' days and the establishment of alms-houses for the elderly poor were among measures commonly used for what must have been generally ineffectual poverty relief. Systematic attempts to alleviate poverty on a nation-wide basis were first introduced in late Elizabethan England and Wales with the Poor Law in 1597 and 1601. It established the parish as the main administrative and decision-making unit. Relief was targeted at the "deserving poor" who were defined as the aged, the sick and the very young. Parish rates-payers were taxed to provide the funds which were paid out to the individuals where they lived. It was termed "outdoor relief." The level of the relief and to whom it was distributed was determined locally. It was, in this sense, a local system that was mandated nationally.[77] But the Elizabethan Poor Law was not a flexible institution as industrial and demographic change overtook it. Parishes ceased to be small places where the deserving poor were easily identified. Those parishes which offered higher levels of benefits attracted the mobile poor of those parishes which provided lower benefits. Work relief payments made to the working poor were abused by employers to lower the wages they paid. Since these employers were often the local landlords who controlled the boards which administered the system, they were widely suspected of being corrupt. The growth of towns and cities meant that many parishes were urban and incapable of disbursing funds in a way that was designed for a stable rural economy. The Poor Law with all its inequities, idiosyncrasies and defects spread to the English, later British, colonies to become the basis of their support of the deserving poor.[78]

Based on the English Poor Law the colonies in North America adopted the same type of legislation on a colony-wide, later state-wide, basis. The administrative unit was the municipality or, as in the case of the rural area, county level government although the province (colony) also had some financial responsibility. Unlike England, the majority of the chronically poor was urban or those who had drifted to the urban centers. Various schemes were tried to take care of the increasing number of urban poor. These included paying for the board and lodging of employable poor. Some of the chronically poor, especially the young, were sold into indentured contracts. Pauper apprenticeships were financed in some areas. Boston experimented with a linen factory designed specifically to employ the poor.[79] Because the North American poverty problem was essentially an urban one, the colonies came to rely on a new 18th century development, the workhouse. Boston, New York and Philadelphia all had workhouses by the mid-18th century, and, by the Revolution, they had become the central institution for public-sector poverty relief. Private sector charities, mostly churches, were also motivated to act by the need so evident of the unattended poor. As a system, poverty relief was never more than a patchwork. By the 19th century many workhouses had devolved to specialize in the delivery of their various services: orphanages for the very young; insane asylums for those with mental health problems including senility and training centers in domestic serves for young females. One area where the workhouses had a lasting legacy was in the treatment of the sick poor and elderly; the workhouses (or almshouses) became hospitals. Some of the famous and more progressive hospitals of the modern era had workhouse antecedents such as the Philadelphia General Hospital and New York's Bellevue Hospital.[80]

In England, the system of outdoor poor relief failed because it did not have a systematic way of providing for the growing urban poor. The New Poor Law of 1834 was the remedy of the reform. It superseded the act which had existed since the early 1600s – and which now became known as the Old Poor Law. Workhouses, some of which predated the reform, became the agency of urban relief.[81] These austere places did improve somewhat as the 19th century wore on as humanitarian public campaigns were mounted against their conditions. Nor was Britain alone as workhouses became the main social welfare institution in many countries. Russia had a well-organized set of workhouses in its main cities in the late 19th century as did Germany and France.[82] Orphanages were built to take care of the abandoned, destitute children. In the 1870s the child-migration schemes (Chapter Five) were introduced in an often misguided attempt to look after the welfare of the older young. The internal placement of young girls as domestic servants was also a common practice. Anne Shirley of *Green Gables* fame was sent as an orphan to a farm of elderly adults (who were ultimately quite nice).

The late Victorian period also saw the growth of many private-sector charities each with its targeted group of clients such as the homeless, the elderly and the children. They were often financed by corporate donors or led by them and financed by public subscription. In most countries, the conditions of the chronically poor did improve in the late 19th century, although often not enough to raise them out of poverty. Beatrice and Sidney Webb were the poster children of the new social movement sweeping Europe and North America motivated in large measure by the plight of the poor. Thanks to the public pressure on the state, treatment of the poor did become more humane. Social legislation was continually improved to cope with the growing numbers and changing patterns of the poor. Some countries, however, resisted this growing social concern or met it only minimally. Japan's social policy, for instance, continued to regard poverty as a moral failing and its legislation of the 1920s was directed more to changing the behavior of the poor rather than to ameliorate their condition and understand its causes.[83] It was well into the 20th century that a thoroughly new way of caring for the poor came about: in Britain, national insurance for the working poor came into being in 1911 but it was not until the post-1945 "welfare state" that the non-working poor were directly assisted. In the US, the New Deal legislation of the 1930s was targeted initially at out-of-work portion of the labor force but was later expanded to cover social security for the aged (over 65 years of age), survivors such as widows and the disabled. One of its current key features is the Medicaid program for the indigent and the Medicare program for the elderly – federal health insurance programs.

If we are to judge by the levels of poverty among the single-headed households and the elderly, there must have been a large unseen and un-remedied problem throughout the period of industrial transformation in Europe and North America. From the mid-20th century the trend of the proportion of the poor in the overall population has declined. Earlier in history it was unlikely less. That the incidence of poverty has declined and shifted in composition means of course that we have only tackled the general problem, and that not enough, and not the specific problems.

Endnotes

1. Tilly and Cohen (1982).
2. Anderson (1975).
3. Coontz (2004); see also Coontz (2005), a book which examines the history of marriage.
4. Becker (1991).
5. De Moor and Van Zanden (2010).
6. Ginther and Zavodny (2001); Snell (2002).
7. For a study of courtship rituals see Ward (1990).
8. Humphries (1987); Horrell and Humphries (1995).
9. Bozon and Heran (1989); Rosenblatt and Cozby (1972).
10. Becker (1973); Becker (1974).
11. See Botticini (1999); Botticini and Siow (2003).
12. Anderson (2007).
13. Fryer Jr. (2007) and especially see Tables A2 and A4.
14. Yan (2002).
15. Jiang and O'Neill (2007); Brower and Ruggles, *US Historical Statistics* – see General Sources.
16. Only the Republic of Ireland, Poland and Romania of all European countries were above three persons per household (3.6, 3.2 and 3.1 respectively). The highest number of persons per household was in sub-Saharan Africa although there was a great range and many countries where the counting is known to be inaccurate or non-existent. Angola and Burkino Faso registered about 6.0. United Nations (current) Table 6.
17. Kertzer (1991).
18. Ellickson (2006).
19. See, for example Hamilton (1996).
20. See, for example, Moehling (2005).
21. There are two encyclopedic studies of child labor: Hindman (2009); Hobbs, McKechnie, and Lavalette (1999).
22. See Nardinelli (1990).
23. Kussmaul (1981).
24. Pinchbeck (1930).

25 See Tuttle (1999).
26 Thompson (1966).
27 Craig (1993).
28 Goldin and Sokoloff (1982), and by the same authors (1984).
29 There is no clear age range for child labor. The young end of the range is the age at which society finds work an acceptable alternative; the older end is the age at which childhood gives way to adulthood.
30 These statistics are cited in Whaples (2005).
31 Goldin and Katz (2008).
32 The employment of those 16 and under was prohibited, but the law also established a national minimum wage that effectively increased children's wages, thereby decreasing demand.
33 US Department of Labor (2009). This is a report required by *The US Trade and Development Act* of 2000.
34 *Ibid.*, pp. xxi–xxxiv. These pages are summaries of the specific categories discussed in each of the country reports.
35 *Ibid.*, which cites Tulane University (2008).
36 *Ibid.* Ghana was one of 24 countries that adopted the Multilateral Cooperation Agreement to Combat Trafficking in Persons and the Joint Plan of Action against Trafficking in Persons, especially Women and Children in West and Central African Regions. Enforcement has been described as modest.
37 *Ibid.*
38 The context of this remark was that this arrangement is one that has been exploited by those trafficking in children.
39 Hess (2010).
40 Gaudin and Davis (1985), Tables 1 and 2. The authors' sample was chosen from those on the food stamp program.
41 Beito (2000); Emery (2010); Emery and Emery (1999); Emery (1996).
42 Carlos, Maguire and Neal (2008), 728–48.
43 In the US: Cooke, Gould, Vanderbilt, Carnegie, Lodge and Cabot. In Canada: Hamilton-Merritt, Massey and Aitkin (Beaverbrook). In the UK: Mond, Brunel, Lever and Guiness.
44 There is a large literature on the historical sociology of class links and markets. Inkster (1988); Levine (1980); Lisle-Williams (1882); and Porter (1957).
45 Katherine of Aragon, Ann Boleyn, Jane Seymour, Ann of Cleves, Catherine Howard and Katherine Parr.
46 Gibson (1994); Stone (1981, 1990).
47 Phillips (1979); Fine and Fine (1994).
48 Cornell (1990).
49 Huang (2005).
50 Leneman (1996); Leneman (1998).
51 See *The Matrimonial Causes Act of 1923*; Gibson (1994).
52 Stone (1990).
53 Gibson (1994).
54 Schoen and Baj (1984).
55 Allen (1998); Vlosky and Monroe (2002).
56 Wolfers (2006).
57 Burgess, Propper and Aassve (2003).
58 OECD (current) "Family Database".
59 Mill (1869, 1909).
60 Chused (1985).

61 Backhouse (1988); Di Matteo (1997); Inwood and Van Sligtenhorst (2004).
62 Kahn (1996) is a study of patents filed by women in the 19th century.
63 Mill (1869).
64 Combs (2005).
65 Referring to the married *The Married Woman's Property Act of 1884* of Ontario. Chambers (1997).
66 Brewer, Muriel, Phillips and Sibieta (2008); Smock, Manning and Gupta (1999).
67 OECD (current) Chart C08.1 – the figures used are for the mid-decade 2000–2009.
68 DeNavas-Walt, Proctor and Smith (2009).
69 Collin and Jensen (2009).
70 Basic poverty data for the period 1959–2006 can be found in *Statistical Abstract*, 2009, Table 693.
71 There is always more inequality in the distribution of wealth than in the distribution of income.
72 DeNavas-Walt, Proctor and Smith (2009) and Collin and Jensen (2009).
73 Kenway and Palmer (2009).
74 Musick and Mare (2004), Table 2.
75 Corak, Fertig and Tamm (2008).
76 Renwick, Trudi and Bergmann (1993).
77 Slack (1990).
78 Nash (1976); Taylor (1969); and Schneider (1938).
79 Huang (2006); Murray and Herndon (2002).
80 Rosenberg (1982).
81 MacKinnon (1987).
82 Bradley (1982).
83 Tipton (2008).

References

Allen, Douglas W. (1998) "No-fault Divorce in Canada: Its Cause and Effect", *Journal of Economic Behavior and Organization*, **37**, 129–49.

Anderson, Olive (1975) "The Incidence of Civil Marriage in Victorian England and Wales", *Past and Present*, **69**, 50–87.

Anderson, Siwan (2007) "The Economics of Dowry and Brideprice", *Journal of Economic Perspectives*, **21**(4), 151–74.

Backhouse, Constance B. (1988) "Married Women's Property Law in Nineteenth-Century Canada", *Law and History Review*, **6**(2), 211–57.

Becker, Gary S. (1973) "A Theory of Marriage: Part I", *Journal of Political Economy*, **81**(4), 813–46.

Becker, Gary S. (1974) "A Theory of Marriage: Part II", *Journal of Political Economy*, **82**(2), S11–S26.

Becker, Gary S. (1991) *A Treatise on the Family*, Enlarged edition, Cambridge, MA: Harvard University Press.

Beito, David (2000) *From Mutual Aid to the Welfare State: Fraternal Societies and Social Services, 1890–1967*, Chapel Hill: University of North Carolina Press.

Botticini, Maristella (1999) "A Loveless Economy? Intergenerational Altruism and the Marriage Market in a Tuscan Town, 1415–1436." *Journal of Economic History*, **59**(1), 104–21.

Botticini, Maristella and Aloysius Siow (2003) "Why Dowries?", *American Economic Review*, **93**(4), 1385–98.

Bozon, Michel and François Heran (1989) "Finding a Spouse: A Survey of How French Couples Meet", *Population: An English Selection*, **44**(1), 91–121.

Bradley, Joseph (1982) "The Moscow Workhouse and Urban Welfare Reform in Russia" *Russian Review*, **41**(4), 427–44.

Brewer, Mike, Alastair Muriel, David Phillips and Luke Sibieta (2008) *Poverty and Inequality in the UK: 2008*, London: Institute for Fiscal Studies.

Brower, Susan and Steven Ruggles, "Population in Households, by Household Size: 1790–1990", Table Ae85–96 in *Historical Statistics of the United States* – see General Sources.

Burgess, Simon, Carol Propper and Arnstein Aassve (2003) "The Role of Income in Marriage and Divorce Transitions among Young Americans" *Journal of Population Economics*, **16**(3), 455–75.

Carlos, Ann M., Karen Maguire and Larry Neal (2008) "'A Knavish People…': London Jewry and the Stock Market during the South Sea Bubble", *Business History*, **50**(6), 728–48.

Chambers, Lori (1997) *Married Women and Property Law in Victorian Ontario*, Toronto: University of Toronto Press.

Chused, Richard H. (1985) "Late Nineteenth Century Married Women's Property Law: Reception of the Early Married Women's Property Acts by Courts and Legislatures", *American Journal of Legal History*, **29**(1), 3–35.

Collin, Chantal and Hilary Jensen (2009) *A Statistical Profile of Poverty in Canada*, Social Affairs Division, Ottawa: Library of Parliament.

Combs, Mary Beth (2005) "'A Measure of Legal Independence': The 1870 Married Women's Property Act and the Portfolio Allocations of British Wives", *Journal of Economic History*, **65**(4), 1027–57.

Coontz, Stephanie (2004) "The World Historical Transformation of Marriage", *Journal of Marriage and Family*, **66**(4), 974–9.

Coontz, Stephanie (2005) *Marriage, A History : From Obedience To Intimacy, Or How Love Conquered Marriage*, New York: Viking Press.

Corak, Miles, Michael Fertig and Marcus Tamm (2008) "A Portrait of Child Poverty In Germany", *Review of Income and Wealth*, **54**(4), 547–71.

Cornell, Laurel L. (1990) "Peasant Women and Divorce in Pre-industrial Japan", *Signs*, **15**(4), 710–32.

Craig, Lee A. (1993) *To Sow One Acre More: Childbearing and Farm Productivity in the Antebellum North*, Baltimore: The Johns Hopkins University Press.

De Moor, Tine and Jan Luiten Van Zanden (2010) "Girl Power: The European Marriage Pattern and Labor Markets in The North Sea Region in the Late Medieval and Early Modern Period", *Economic History Review*, **63**(1), 1–33.

DeNavas-Walt, Carmen, Bernadette D. Proctor and Jessica C. Smith (2009) *Income, Poverty, and Health Insurance Coverage in the United States: 2008*, U.S. Census Bureau, Current Population Reports, P60-236, Washington, D.C.: U.S. Government Printing Office.

Di Matteo, Livio (1997) "The Determinants of Wealth and Asset Holding in Nineteenth-Century Canada: Evidence from Microdata", *Journal of Economic History*, **57**(4), 907–34.

Ellickson, Robert C. (2006) "Unpacking the Household: Informal Property Rights around the Hearth", *The Yale Law Journal*, **116**(2), 226–328.

Emery, Herbert (2010), "Fraternal Sickness Insurance", *EH.net*. Encyclopedia, http://eh.net/encyclopedia/article/emery.insurance.fraternal

Emery, Herbert and George Emery (1999) *A Young Man's Benefit: The Independent Order of Odd Fellows And Sickness Insurance in the United States and Canada, 1860–1929*, Montreal: McGill-Queen's University Press.

Emery, J.C. Herbert (1996) "Risky Business? Nonactuarial Pricing Practices and the Financial Viability of Fraternal Sickness Insurers", *Explorations in Economic History*, **33**, 195–226.

Fine, Mark A. and David R Fine (1994), "An Examination and Evaluation of Recent Changes in Divorce Laws in Five Western Countries: The Critical Role of Values", *Journal of Marriage and Family*, **56**(2), 249–63.

Fryer Jr., Roland G. (2007) "Guess Who's Been Coming to Dinner? Trends in Interracial Marriage over the 20th Century", *Journal of Economic Perspectives*, **21**(2), 71–90.

Gaudin, Jr., James M. and Katheryn B. Davis (1985) "Social Networks of Black and White Rural Families: A Research Report", *Journal of Marriage and Family*, **47**(4), 1015–21.

Gibson, Colin S. (1994) *Dissolving Wedlock*, London: Routledge.

Ginther, Donna K. and Madeline Zavodny (2001) "Is the Male Marriage Premium Due to Selection? The Effect of Shotgun Weddings on the Return to Marriage", *Journal of Population Economics*, **14**(2), 313–28.

Goldin, Claudia and Lawrence Katz (2008) *The Race between Education and Technology*, Cambridge: Harvard University Press.

Goldin, Claudia and Kenneth Sokoloff (1982) "Women, Children, and Industrialization in the Early Republic: Evidence from the Manufacturing Censuses," *Journal of Economic History*, **42**(4), 74–74.

Goldin, Claudia and Kenneth Sokoloff (1984) "The Relative Productivity Hypothesis of Industrialization: The American Case, 1820 to 1850," *Quarterly Journal of Economics*, **99**(3), 461–87.

Hamilton, Gillian (1996) "The Market for Montreal Apprentices: Contract Length and Information," *Explorations in Economic History*, **33**(4), 486–523.

Hamilton, Gillian and Aloysius Siow (2007) "Class, Gender and Marriage", *Review of Economic Dynamics*, **10**, 549–75.

Hess, Andreas (2010) "Working the Waves": The Plebeian Culture and Moral Economy of Traditional Basque Fishing Brotherhoods", *Journal of Interdisciplinary History*, **40**(4), 551–78.

Hindman, Hugh D., ed., (2009) *The World of Child Labor: an Historical and Regional Survey*, Armonk, N.Y.: M.E. Sharpe.

Hobbs, Sandy, Jim McKechnie and Michael Lavalette, eds (1999) *Child Labor: a World History Companion*, Santa Barbara, Calif.: ABC-CLIO, 1999.

Horrell, Sara and Jane Humphries (1995) "Women's Labor Force Participation and the Transition to the Male-Breadwinner Family, 1790–1865", *Economic History Review*, **48**(1), 89–117.

Huang, C.C. (2005), "Divorce Law Practices and the Origins, Myths, and Realities of Judicial 'Mediation' in China", *Modern China*, **31**(2), 151–203.

Huang, Nian-Sheng (2006) "Financing Poor Relief: In Colonial Boston", *The Massachusetts Historical Review*, **8**, 72–103.

Humphries, Jane (1987), "'… The Most Free From Objection…' The Sexual Division of Labor and Women's Work in Nineteenth-Century England", *Journal of Economic History*, **47**(4), 929–49.

Inkster, Ian (1988) "Cultural Enterprise: Science, Steam Intellect and Social Class in Rochdale circa 1833–1900", *Social Studies of Science*, **18**(2), 291–330.

Inwood, Kris and Sarah Van Sligtenhorst (2004) "The Social Consequences of Legal Reform: Women and Property in a Canadian Community", *Continuity and Change*, **19**(1), 165–97.

Jiang, Leiwen and Brian C. O'Neill (2007) "Impacts of Demographic Trends on US Household Size and Structure", *Population and Development Review*, **33**(3), 567–91.

Kenway, Peter and Guy Palmer (2007) *Poverty Among Ethnic Groups: How and Why Does It Differ?*, New Policy Institute, York, UK: The Joseph Rowntree Foundation.

Kertzer, David I. (1991) "Household History and Sociological Theory", *Annual Review of Sociology*, **17**, 155–79.

Khan, B. Zorina (1996) "Married Women's Property Laws and Female Commercial Activity: Evidence from United States Patent Records, 1790–1895", *Journal of Economic History*, **56**(2), 356–88.

Kussmaul, Ann (1981) *Servants in Husbandry in Early Modern England*, Cambridge: Cambridge University Press.

Leneman, Leah (1996) "'Disregarding the Matrimonial Vows': Divorce in Eighteenth and Early Nineteenth-Century Scotland", *Journal of Social History*, **30**(2), 465–82.

Leneman, Leah (1998) *Alienated Affections; The Scottish Experience of Divorce and Separation, 1684–1830*, Edinburgh: Edinburgh University Press.

Levine, Steven B. (1980) "The Rise of American Boarding Schools and the Development of a National Upper Class", *Social Problems*, **28**(1), 63–94.

Lisle-Williams, Michael (1882) "Merchant Banking Dynasties in the English Class Structure: Ownership, Solidarity and Kinship in the City of London, 1850–1960", *British Journal of Sociology*, **35**(3), 333–62.

MacKinnon, Mary (1987) "English Poor Law Policy and the Crusade Against Outrelief", *Journal of Economic History*, **47**(3), 603–25.

Mill, John Stuart (1869, 1909) *The Subjection of Women*, London, New York: Longmans, Green.

Moehling, Carolyn (2005) "'She Has Suddenly Become Powerful': Youth Employment and Household Decision-Making in the Early Twentieth Century," *Journal of Economic History*, **65**(2), 414–38.

Murray, John E. and Ruth Wallis Herndon (2002) "Markets for Children in Early America: A Political Economy of Pauper Apprenticeship", *Journal of Economic History*, **62**(2), 356–82.

Musick, Kelly and Robert D. Mare (2004) "Family Structure, Intergenerational Mobility, and the Reproduction of Poverty: Evidence for Increasing Polarization?" *Demography*, **41**(4), 629–48.

Nardinelli, Clark (1990) *Child Labor and the Industrial Revolution*, Bloomington: Indiana University Press.

Nash, Gary B. (1976) "Poverty and Poor Relief in Pre-Revolutionary Philadelphia", *The William and Mary Quarterly*, Third Series, **33**(1), 3–30.

OECD (current), "Family Database", OECD – Social Policy Division, Directorate of Employment, Labor and Social Affairs, http://www.oecd.org/els/social/family/database

Peter Kenway and Guy Palmer (2009) *Poverty Among Ethnic Groups How and Why Does It Differ?*, New Policy Institute, London: Joseph Rowntree Foundation.

Phillips, Roderick G (1979) "Le Divorce en France a la Fin du XVIIIe siècle", *Annales, Histoire, Sciences Sociales*, **2**, 385–98.

Pinchbeck, Ivy (1930) *Women Workers and the Industrial Revolution*, London: George Routledge and Sons.

Porter, John (1957) "The Economic Elite and the Social Structure in Canada", *Canadian Journal of Economics and Political Science*, **23**(3), 376–94.

Renwick, Trudi J. and Barbara R. Bergmann (1993) "A Budget-Based Definition of Poverty With an Application to Single-Parent Families", *Journal of Human Resources*, **28**(1), 1–24.

Rosenberg, Charles E. (1982) "From Almshouse to Hospital: The Shaping of Philadelphia General Hospital", *The Milbank Memorial Fund Quarterly. Health and Society*, **60**(1), 108–54.

Rosenblatt, Paul C. and Paul C. Cozby (1972) "Courtship Patterns Associated with Freedom of Choice of Spouse", *Journal of Marriage and Family*, **34**(4), 689–95.

Schneider, David M. (1938) "The Patchwork of Relief in Provincial New York, 1664–1775", *The Social Service Review*, **12**(3), 464–94.

Schoen, R. and J. Baj (1984) "Twentieth-Century Cohort Marriage and Divorce in England and Wales", *Population Studies*, **38**(3), 439–49.

Slack, Paul (1990) *The English Poor Law, 1531–1782*, Economic History Society, Basingstoke, Hampshire: Macmillan.

Smock, Pamela J., Wendy D. Manning and Sanjiv Gupta (1999) "The Effect of Marriage and Divorce on Women's Economic Well-Being", *American Sociological Review*, **64**(6), 794–812.

Snell, K.D.M. (2002) "English Rural Societies and Geographical Marital Endogamy, 1700–1837", *Economic History Review*, **55**(2), 262–98.

Stone, L. (1981) "Family History in the 1980's." *Journal of Interdisciplinary History*, **12**, (Summer), 51–87.

Stone, Lawrence (1990) *Road to Divorce: England 1530–1987*, Oxford : Clarendon Press; New York : Oxford University Press.

Tanner, Andrea (1999) "The Casual Poor and The City Of London Poor Law Union, 1837–1869", *The Historical Journal*, **4**(2), 183–206.

Taylor, James Stephen (1969) "The Mythology of the Old Poor Law", *Journal of Economic History*, **29**(2), 292–7.

Thompson, E.P. (1966) *The Making of the English Working Class*, New York: Vintage Books.

Tilly, Louise A. and Miriam Cohen (1982) "Does the Family Have a History? A Review of Theory and Practice in Family History", *Social Science History*, **6**(2), 131–79.

Tipton, Elise K. (2008) "Defining the Poor in Early Twentieth-Century Japan", *Japan Forum*, **20**(3), 361–82.

Tulane University (2008) *Annual Report: Oversight of Public and Private Initiatives to Eliminate the Worst Forms of Child Labor in the Cocoa Sector in Cote d'Ivoire and in Ghana*, Payson Center for International Development and Technology Transfer, New Orleans, September 30.

Tuttle, Carolyn (1999) *Hard at Work in Factories and Mines: The Economics of Child Labor During the British Industrial Revolution*, Boulder, CO: Westview Press.

United States Department of Labor (2008) *Forced Labor, and Human Trafficking*, Bureau of International Labor Affairs, Office of Child Labor, Washington, D.C.: Government Printing Office.

United States Department of Labor (2009) *Findings on the Worst Forms of Child Labor*, Washington: U.S. Government Printing Office.

Vlosky, Denese Ashbaugh and Pamela A. Monroe (2002) "The Effective Dates of No-Fault Divorce Laws in the 50 States", *Family Relations*, **51**(4), 317–24.

Ward, Peter (1990) *Courtship, Love, and Marriage in Nineteenth-Century English Canada*, Buffalo: McGill-Queen's University Press.

Whaples, Robert (current) "Child Labor in the United States". *EH.Net Encyclopedia*, edited by Robert Whaples. October 7, 2005. URL: http://eh.net/encyclopedia/article/whaples.childlabor

Wolfers, Justin (2006) "Did Unilateral Divorce Laws Raise Divorce Rates? A Reconciliation and New Results", *American Economic Review*, **96**(5), 1802–1820.

Yan, Yunxiang (2002) "Courtship, Love and Premarital Sex in a North China Village", *The China Journal*, **48**, (July), 29–53.

Chapter Eight
Health and Well-Being

8.1 Introduction

An individual's well-being is intimately connected to their family's health. Health issues, however, often create a lock-in feature: the link between poor health and poverty. For instance, continuing poor health, episodes of ill health, mental and psychological distress or general anxiety all contribute to the lowering of personal income potential. Not surprisingly, the primary determinant of the social/economic standing of individuals is the standing of their parents. If ill health occurs in early life, and especially if it persists, education and training are interrupted and curtailed. Thus poor health deprives the individual of developing the human capital with which they might escape the family's social/economic status if that status is low. Without the requisite human capital, individuals are destined for low-paying jobs. The family's burden of care for a child in poor health, especially if persistent, robs them of the time to engage in activities other than that care, reduces the child's contributions to family income and imposes extra costs of maintenance associated with ill-health. In extreme cases, ill-health can lower the family's well-being such that they fall in the social order or establish the social and economic conditions for continuing poverty as we saw in Chapter Seven. It is no coincidence that the cycle of poor health and the cycle of poverty are part and parcel of the same phenomenon.[1]

Poor health can result from many root causes. First, there are specific maladies that are a product of the environment in which the family lives and works. Workers in coalmines have a greater tendency to develop lung diseases such as *pneumoconiosis* (black lung disease) or *silicosis*. Sometimes the general environment creates distinctions in patterns of illness (morbidity) such as those we find historically between rural and urban environments. There are yet others that are a result of the family's nutritional standard. These vary both across the income distribution and across history. As personal incomes rose, nutritional choices increased and scientific advances provided evidence of

The Children of Eve: Population and Well-being in History, First Edition. Louis P. Cain and Donald G. Paterson.
© 2012 Blackwell Publishing Ltd. Published 2012 by Blackwell Publishing Ltd.

which were the healthier nutritional selections. The available and affordable choices at any time are often reflected in birth weights, adult weights and the heights of individuals; each of these anthropometric measures, as they are called, shows considerable variation throughout modern history. The modern health problem of obesity amply demonstrates that health changes are not always positive. If the family income is low, it will tend to be poorly housed, and housing quality is one of the key historical features explaining the prevalence of communicable disease, part of the poor health cycle in history. Advances in health care have raised hopes that a solution to many health problems can be found. These are the subjects of historical interest in this chapter.

8.2 Glasgow: Then and Now

One of the key centers of the British industrial revolution was the Scottish city of Glasgow. By the mid-19th century it was a thriving manufacturing center (tobacco processing, shipbuilding, and textiles) and one of the largest ports in Britain after Liverpool and London. Because of its proximity to Dublin and Belfast, it was also one of the main cities to absorb the Irish diaspora of the 1840s – which provided ample cheap labor for its factories and shipyards. About this time it was noted that many in Glasgow (especially children) were short in stature and had malformed skeletal structures of which the most visible feature was "bow" or "bandy" legs. The explanation is that they had a disease symbolic of the industrial revolution in Northern Europe and northern parts of the United States: rickets. Rickets is a disease that impedes the normal growth of the skeleton and is most noticeable in the long bones and spine. It was evident in the early 19th century, but it was not clinically described (in Glasgow) until 1884. Rickets results from an inability of the body to process sodium and phosphate because of a lack of vitamin D. Vitamin D, in turn, is produced in the body by two means: through an adequate and well-balanced diet and by exposure to sunlight. Although rickets had been described even in ancient history, its source/cause was not known. It was not until 1922 that the direct relationship between the lack of exposure to sunlight and rickets was identified.[2]

With the beginning of widespread industrialization the disease became more common as the two effects of insufficient diet and lack of sunlight reinforced one another. By no means was rickets confined to Glasgow, as indicated by the term given to it by the Dutch in the 17th century, "the English disease."[3] A recent study shows that it was also prevalent in late medieval Britain, but it was related to socio-economic status rather than urbanization.[4] It was also endemic in the northern states of the US, particularly in New England. Rickets was the quintessential modern industrial disease. It was associated with youngsters spending long hours in indoor workplaces. Second, it was made more likely due to aerial pollution. Good air quality was impaired by the burning of coal for both factory and domestic heat. As a result, early industrial cities were shrouded in smog that effectively blocked out the sunshine. This was exacerbated by the reduced hours of sunlight in the northern climes. A cloudy location simply added to the effect. Third, even in the cities with higher wages than the surrounding countryside, there were huge pockets of urban poor with inadequate diets. Glasgow had it all.

Many of those with adequate income to provide minimum healthy diets, with sufficient vitamin D, often did not do so.[5] The early 19th century New Lanark experiment of building a model industrial (small) town in the countryside with a healthy environment and safe and healthy workplaces was a direct response to urban blight and poor living conditions, including the malady of infantile rickets. The project was the brain-child of the social reformer Wilfred Owen. Unfortunately, there were no general lessons learned from this social experiment, although everyone agreed that the countryside was a healthier environment even for those engaged in industrial pursuits. As a consequence, there were no changes to the urban environment that can be directly attributed to the project. As late as 1920, the poorer children of the "laboring class" still showed the symptoms of inadequate diet, below average height.[6] The disease persisted for a long time because, apart from diet, the remedy required the elimination of the pollution created by extensive coal burning. Those contracting rickets did not die of the disease and, consequently, the fight to eradicate rickets did not take on the same urgency as, say, eliminating cholera. Nevertheless, by the mid-20th century, infantile rickets had largely disappeared.

To everyone's surprise, in the late 20th century, rickets made its reappearance in Glasgow. But Glasgow was different than it had been even 50 years earlier. Gone was the severe aerial pollution of the past as coal burning was banned. Workers spent fewer hours in the workplace (usually indoors) and had higher real incomes. Children under 16 had been removed from the workplace by education and social policy. Furthermore, the social safety net removed people from abject levels of poverty. Why then did rickets make a comeback? The answer is not straightforward. Similar to most British cities in the post-1950 years, Glasgow experienced a substantial immigration from South Asia, mostly Pakistan, India and Bangladesh. These new arrivals had adequate and well-balanced diets in the countries where they originated, countries that were also sunny. South Asians normally have a high level of melatonin in the skin, and the dark pigmentation filters the sunshine's deleterious effects. Once in northern cities, with their much reduced hours of sunlight, these individuals were acquiring sodium and phosphate deficiencies because of their lower capacity to absorb vitamin D from the environment.[7] Diets, of course, tended to be culturally acquired and passed on from one generation to another. The balance within the diet that was optimal in South Asia was seriously lacking in vitamin D in Northern Europe. The disease had, in some sense, gone full cycle.

8.3 Morbidity

Morbidity is the incidence of ill-health or disease in a population. Its effect on the size of a population and the growth of that population depends on how morbidity affects both birth and death rates. Here we are concerned with morbidity's effects on the quality of life. The higher morbidity is in a country, the greater is the depreciation of the quality of life. Jane Austen died when she was quite young, aged 41. She died of a condition that today would be quite treatable, Addison's Disease. (Think how many more wonderful novels she would have written had she lived.) The last years of her life were probably lived in discomfort. However, not all morbidity is a product of disease, environment and inadequate nutrition. It was also the result of unrelenting and back-breaking toil producing physical and mental stress.

With the greater understanding of medical science including the role of hygiene, immunization, refined clinical diagnoses, and the general growth of health systems, there was a general improvement in the quality of life. Also the removal of the conditions in which disease flourished allowed developed countries to eradicate many of the great historical killers and debilitating infectious diseases. Smallpox, cholera, diphtheria and malaria were all substantially reduced in the 40 years prior to World War I and contained or eradicated soon after (and by the 1950s in the cases of the last two). Added to the eradicated list in the third quarter of the 20th century were whooping cough, polio and typhoid fever with measles and scarlet fever gone by the 1990s.[8]

One pernicious condition continued well into the 20th century, to be sure with decreased frequency of occurrence. "Childbirth or childbed fever," as it was called historically, is a condition that occurs in women after giving birth. It is an infection of the uterus which causes extreme pain and was the leading cause of death of women in childbirth until the second half of the 20th century. (It was also called *puerperal fever* and more recently *endometritis*.) As seen in Chapter Four, this was the special mortality risk that women ran historically during their reproductive lives. In the 18th and 19th centuries it killed about 25% to 30% of the women who contracted the disease. This meant that about 15 to 20 live births per 1000 were accompanied by the death of the mother. Since the disease also occurred in epidemics, the mortality rate could be three times that level on occasion. The disease's organism belongs to the *streptococcus* family of bacteria and is spread only through contact, which thrives in crowded conditions both in the home and in the hospital. Carriers of the disease likely included those assisting at the birth including the physicians (who were male) in the lying-in hospitals. Hospitals of the early 18th century probably had an incidence of this disease that was higher than home births, but by the later years of the 1700s the infection rate was about the same. Little was known of the disease or its transmission until the change of thinking brought about by the epidemiological transition of the 19th century. Indeed, Ignaz Semmelweis' classic experiment in the 1840s into the origin and spread of puerperal fever was a key moment in the development of germ theory.[9] Women in continental Europe seem to have had a higher mortality rate due to this condition than their counterparts in Britain and North America until the attack on the disease in the 20th century. There is some disagreement among historians as to the origins of this difference (which probably can never be resolved and therefore provides good historical tilting grounds). The most likely explanation lies in the pathology of the disease, its frequency and virulence and the physical conditions of its spread such as hospital over-crowding and poor clinical practises.[10]

Similar to the inadequate reporting of rickets, most historical information does not give sufficient clinical detail about a particular disease or malady for accurate identification before about 1900. Prior to the age of modern medicine, clinical signs of ailments were too often overlooked or not understood; in retrospect, misdiagnosis was common. Furthermore, most countries lacked a central reporting mechanism with specific standards to reckon the prevalence of any malady. Even with up-to-date knowledge it is difficult for medical historians to confirm an ailment from the historically reported evidence. This does not mean that some reasonable inferences cannot be made from data that were imperfectly understood at the time. Today, in contrast, morbidity data sheds light on the incidence of a well-defined affliction, a disease or an injury, or an aggregation of those elements.

> **Disability Adjusted Life Years (DALYs)** are the sum of years of potential life lost due to premature mortality and the years of productive life lost due to disability.[11]

Table 8.1 presents a more complicated construct, the World Health Organization's (WHO) estimates of Disability Adjusted Life Years (DALYs). In the table, the total DALYs are reported by condition for the world, then the percentage accounted by each geographic region is indicated. The ratio of the DALY percentage to the population percentage affords a good idea of the incidence of each condition in each region. Unfortunately, such data is only available for the past few years. What exists from earlier times is generally for one condition in one place at one time. What is immediately apparent is that Africa, with just over a tenth of the world's population, accounts for just under a quarter of the DALYs for a variety of conditions. By these measures Africa accounts for over a half of infectious and parasitic diseases which includes killers such as malaria and diarrhoea. Almost four-fifths of HIV/AIDS losses occur in Africa. Sadly, if that was not enough, over three-fifths of the world's DALYs as a result of war were suffered in Africa. For the Americas, the figure that stands out is that for "violence," and that together with the figure for Africa accounts for well over half of the world's total. Heart disease and cancer, the two major diseases with respect to mortality, are more or less evenly distributed with respect to DALYs per capita by region. Europe is the exception for "Cardiovascular diseases" and "Malignant neoplasms" – cancers. In both cases, Europe's percentage of world DALYs is about 60% above its share of the population. The Eastern Mediterranean is the exception for "other neoplasms." This category includes skin and brain cancers. While it has a much smaller claim of DALYs, it is highly concentrated. The ratio in the Eastern Mediterranean of the percentage of world DALYs for that category to its share of world population is roughly 2.6!

In Table 8.2, we take a look at two conditions by country in the WHO data. The two are HIV and tuberculosis. As noted HIV/AIDS is a particular problem for Africa; tuberculosis is most prevalent in the Southeast Pacific. Their incidence is relatively low. (Consequently, the morbidity rates are reported per 100 000 of the relevant population.)[12] Both of these conditions appear to become more common as the Human Development Index (HDI) rank falls (see Obesity and the BMI later). Given the concentration of HIV in African countries, this is not surprising. A simple arithmetic mean (unadjusted for population size) over all the WHO reporting countries suggests that the rate in the "High Human Development" countries is less than a tenth of what it is in "Medium Human Development" countries. The "Low Human Development" countries, which are exclusively African in our abbreviated table, have an average only slightly larger than the "Medium" group. Tuberculosis demonstrates a similar pattern.

Table 8.1 Disability Adjusted Life Years (DALYs) by Cause for the Year 2000.

	Total DALYs in millions	Africa	Americas	Eastern Mediterranean	Europe	Western Pacific	South East Pacific
Percent of World Population		10.6	13.7	7.9	14.4	25.4	27.8
All Causes	1468.1	23.6%	9.8%	9.2%	10.2%	29.1%	17.9%
I. Communicable, maternal, perinatal and nutritional conditions	601.9	41.9	4.5	10.4	2.3	31.5	9.1
A. Infectious & parasitic diseases	341.4	52.5	3.4	9.2	1.6	26.4	6.7
HIV/AIDS	71.8	78.5	4.1	1.3	1.5	12.6	2.0
B. Respiratory infections	91.7	34.8	3.8	11.8	3.3	36.5	9.7
C. Maternal conditions	33.2	34.0	5.7	13.2	2.5	34.6	9.9
D. Perinatal conditions	101.9	20.5	7.8	11.8	2.9	41.7	15.2
E. Nutritional deficiencies	33.7	26.9	6.3	12.7	5.2	35.7	13.0
II. Noncommunicable diseases	681.4	9.1	14.2	8.1	16.8	26.6	24.9
A. Malignant neoplasms	74.4	6.2	14.8	5.0	23.4	18.0	32.5
B. Other neoplasms	1.7	8.9	15.5	20.9	16.4	19.0	19.0
C. Diabetes mellitus	15.5	6.9	21.3	7.7	14.0	29.6	20.2
D. Endocrine disorders	8.1	15.5	27.6	10.4	12.5	14.4	19.1
E. Neuropsychiatric conditions	188.4	9.1	18.5	7.6	15.4	24.9	24.3
F. Sense organ diseases	66.0	12.9	8.8	10.2	9.3	32.1	26.6
G. Cardiovascular diseases	144.2	7.3	10.5	8.1	23.5	28.8	21.7
H. Respiratory diseases	53.8	9.8	14.3	6.7	12.9	28.3	27.9
I. Digestive diseases	45.8	10.8	11.9	8.6	15.4	31.0	22.1
J. Genitourinary diseases	14.9	13.5	12.7	10.0	11.9	26.9	24.6
K. Skin diseases	3.6	22.2	12.5	8.8	9.0	28.9	18.3
L. Musculoskeletal diseases	29.1	7.3	14.2	5.9	19.1	22.8	30.5
M. Congenital anomalies	28.6	11.8	12.2	15.4	7.2	32.7	20.4
N. Oral conditions	7.2	7.8	17.6	11.9	13.9	28.3	20.3
III. Injuries	184.8	17.5	10.8	9.4	11.4	30.3	20.4
A. Unintentional injuries	133.7	15.6	8.6	10.5	10.8	32.9	21.2
B. Intentional injuries	51.1	22.5	16.4	6.4	12.8	23.5	18.2
Violence	21.7	25.4	30.0	5.5	10.7	16.6	11.8
War	8.1	63.0	1.8	12.6	6.0	13.2	16.6

Source: World Health Organization (current). http://www.who.int/healthinfo/global_burden_disease/DALY6_00_2004.xls

Table 8.2 Morbidity Rates by Development Status, Current (ranked by incidence of TB; highest 5 and lowest 5 by development category).

		HIV	TB			HIV	TB
		per 100 000 population				per 100 000 population	
No.		2005	2006	No.		2005	2006
	High Human Development				Lowest		
	Highest			90	Fiji	<500.0	30
1	Romania	n.d.	140	91	Tunisia	115	28
2	Malaysia	391	125	92	Lebanon	114	12
3	Russian Federation	775	125	93	Jamaica	1371	8
4	Korea, Republic of	<100.0	123	94	Jordan	n.d.	6
5	Croatia	n.d.	64		**Low Human Development**		
	Lowest				Highest		
42	Norway	67	4	95	Sierra Leone	1361	977
43	Canada	222	4	96	Côte d'Ivoire	6442	747
44	Finland	<100.0	4	97	Burundi	3132	714
45	USA	508	3	98	Dem. Rep. of Congo	2933	645
46	Iceland	<500.0	3				
	Medium Human Development			99	Mozambique	14 429	624
	Highest				Lowest		
47	Swaziland	34 457	1084	103	Senegal	837	504
48	South Africa	16 579	998	104	Burkina Faso	2004	476
49	Togo	2879	787	105	Guinea	1475	466
50	Cambodia	1468	665	106	Tanzania	5909	459
51	Namibia	17 676	658	107	Niger	998	314

Notes: HIV cases in 15 year olds and older. TB all confirmed cases.
Source: World Health Organization (current).
http://www.who.int/whosis/indicators/compendium/2008/3pmr
http://www.who.int/whosis/indicators/compendium/2008/2ptt

A third disease worth mentioning in the WHO data is poliomyelitis, which, as noted above, has been eradicated, at least in countries where children are routinely vaccinated against it. Indeed, many countries simply do not report a figure to WHO because it is so rare an occurrence. However, it is clear that the disease survives in pockets in and around India as well as central Africa. In 2007 there were 1102 confirmed cases of poliomyelitis in seven countries.[13]

The prevalence of poor health and disease (morbidity) reduces economic well-being. While it is dangerous to draw conclusions from data that are limited to a single year, there seems little doubt that, in general, the economic (welfare) loss attributable to morbidity decreases as the level of human development increases. This raises many issues (and this is not the place to address questions about them) concerning the cost of health care, access to health care, and the like. However, health care cannot be the entire story. The incidence of HIV/AIDS across regions and countries is a function of many more things than income per capita. Social customs seem a particularly promising place to look for an answer.

8.4 Early Populations and Nutrition

Basal metabolism is the amount of energy required for the basic functioning of the body systems in a resting state. It is life at its most basic. By the early 20th century, the number of calories required for basal metabolism had been calculated. The caloric requirements for specific activities were not estimated until the mid-20th century. Before World War II, there were studies that attempted to link specific nutritional deficiencies and specific ailments. In the decades after the war nutritional scientists and physiologists began what has proved to be a continuing research theme on the synergy between nutrition and disease and infection.[14] Two sources of vital information were identified in the 1970s: food-supply estimates and anthropometric data.

The first historical food-supply estimates were produced by Jean Claude Toutain as part of a project to examine the course of French economic growth following the Industrial Revolution.[15] This was done by converting the agricultural accounts into the output of nutrition (calories and other nutrients) available for human consumption using what are called "National Food Balance Sheets". Estimates are available by decade from 1785. Similar estimates have been made for Great Britain. They are available for the half-centuries between 1700 and 1900 and by decade for the 20th century.[16]

Surprisingly, the Industrial Revolution and its aftermath brought only a modest improvement in nutritional status. Figure 8.1 measures the calories per capita that were available to French and British workers. For the first 150 years or so, food would have been at least 50% of the average working family's expenses; any improvement in the living standards should be apparent in their food consumption. The value for France in 1705 is on a par with that of Rwanda in 1965, the year when that country was the lowest in the World Bank's report. Great Britain began at a slightly higher level, but, in 1850, it was still only about 75% of current levels. These figures only measure quantity; the quality of foodstuffs was also poor and often monotonous. Even after allowing for the lower food consumption of women, children, and the elderly, it seems clear that prime-age males had far less energy for work than their modern counterparts.

> **Baseline nutritional maintenance** consists of two components. The basal metabolic rate accounts for about four-fifths of the total. It is the amount of energy required to keep the body functioning when it is at rest. The other fifth is the energy needed to eat and digest food and for essential hygiene.

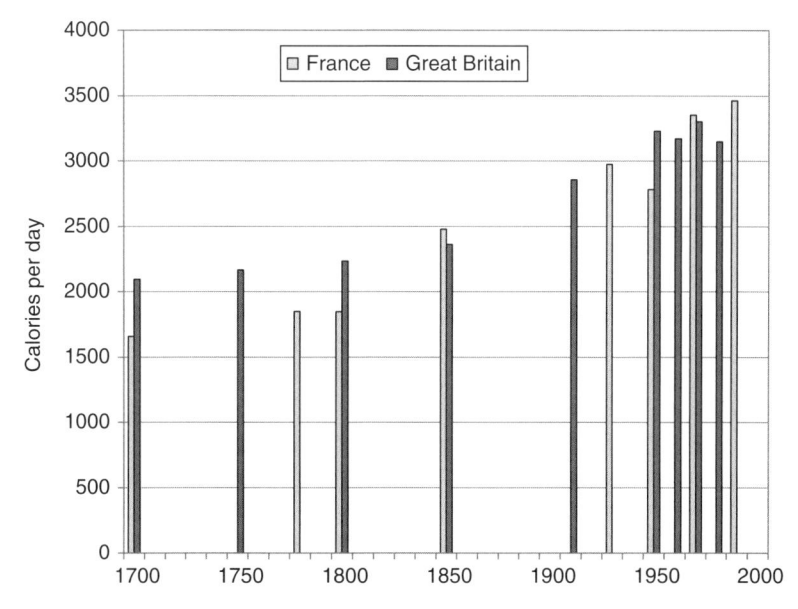

Figure 8.1 Secular Trend in the Daily Calorific Supply Per Person in France and Great Britain, 1700–1989.
Source: data from Fogel (2004).

Evidence of the effects of food supply on human well-being is in the historical anthropometric data (on weight, height, BMI, etc.) which has been collected for some time. Beginning in the early 1700s, the Swedish and Norwegian armies systematically recorded the height of recruits. As we have seen, by the middle of the 18th century, similar data was available for Britain and its colonies. Weight data are not readily available for another century, not until the platform scale appears. Once it was recognized that body build predicted health and mortality, economic historians such as Robert Fogel and his students Dora Costa, John Komlos and Richard Steckel began systematically recovering this information.[17] The data were put to many uses, one of the first was to explain the secular decline in mortality we first visited in Chapter Three.[18] Here we will focus on the height of individuals.

Height is the anthropometric variable about which we have the most data. It can be inferred from the length of the femur, and there are human skeletal remains that go back many millennia.[19] By the 17th century, height was being used as a way of identifying and recognizing individuals. Consequently, the militaries of many countries have records of heights over many years. Heights were also used to identify individuals shipped from one place to another such as convicts, indentured servants, and slaves. As Richard Steckel notes:

> Stature [height] measures performance by health history rather than inputs to health, which has the advantage of incorporating the supply of inputs to health as well as demands on those inputs ….
>
> Steckel (1995).

The height of individuals is the output measure of nutritional inputs (and the nutritional inputs may have competing demands). Steckel reminds us that using stature as an indicator of well-being is consistent with Amartya Sen's approach to the standard of living.[20] Sen argues that measuring the standard of living requires a balancing of "functionings," defined as the living conditions that can/cannot be achieved, and "capabilities," defined as the ability to achieve a particular living condition. He does not believe that a statistic such as real GNP (or GDP) per capita alone can capture the standard of living, although he agrees that the standard of living is influenced by such a statistic. As the quote above avers, height measures the supply of inputs an individual consumes net of the demand placed on those inputs.

Most measures of a population's health status are positively correlated with measures of their income or wealth, as noted earlier. Similarly, a population's height is positively correlated with its per capita income. Using height as an approximate measure of welfare circumvents the well-known conceptual problems that arise when a measure related to GNP and GDP is used. Indeed, a population's average height is a measure of consumption (as opposed to output) that reflects an individual's needs. As with rickets, extreme poverty results in malnutrition, a retardation of an individual's growth, and, thus, shorter people (stunting). Thus, if income inequality causes some individuals in a population to consume too little food and health care, that should be reflected in differences in height between poor and rich.[21] As noted, height information is available when other data either are missing or are of questionable value. It is available for times and places, for subgroups within a population, where income measures are not.

Given the calories consumed by the average European in the 17th century, it seems reasonable to conclude that they must have been much shorter than current-day Europeans. This is certainly true of Americans. Today, the average US adult male is about 177 cm tall and weighs about 78 kg. Baseline nutritional maintenance for such an individual requires almost 2300 calories per day, which is more than the average daily total for British males in 1800. The data in Table 8.3 confirm this supposition. Europeans in the mid-18th century were much shorter than they are today.

Was the same true of Americans? The stature evidence is consistent with the notion that the colonial economy experienced slow, steady growth. The average adult height of those born between 1720 and 1740 was relatively constant at about 171.5 centimeters, but those born in the mid-1750s were about a centimeter taller. The average for those born between 1780 and 1830 was relatively constant at about 173 centimeters.[22] As is immediately obvious, these are very similar to the contemporary heights reported in Table 8.3. What John Komlos has termed the "antebellum puzzle" is that stature then decreased (see Figure 8.2). This is a puzzle because "the nutritional status of a population was hardly expected to decrease when per-capita income increased by some 50% between 1830 and 1860."[23] Life expectancy also fell on average for those born over those years.[24] Robert Fogel argues that, while average food consumption (gross nutrition) remained high, the average quantity of nutrients (net nutrition) most likely fell. Although, as Robert Gallman and John Wallis note, this is the only evidence suggesting there was a decline in personal income and wealth, Komlos is convinced there is a link to growing inequality: "The 'antebellum puzzle' implies … that during the early stages

Table 8.3 Average Final Heights of Men Who Reached Maturity Between 1750 and 1975.

(in cms. per quarter century)

Century-Quarter	Great Britain	Norway	Sweden	France	Denmark	Hungary
18th – 3	165.9	163.9	168.1			169.1
18th – 4	167.9		166.7	163.0	165.7	167.2
19th – 1	168.0	166.7	164.3	165.4	166.7	
19th – 2	171.6	168.0	165.2	166.8	166.8	
19th – 3	169.3	168.6	169.5	165.6	165.3	
20th – 3	175.0	178.3	177.6	174.3	175.0	170.9

Source: data from Fogel (2004).

of modern economic growth, progress was not uniform in all dimensions of human existence".[25] The principal nutrient, the consumption of which declined in per capita terms, was meat.[26]

There is also some evidence suggesting that, Fogel's long average estimates in Table 8.3 notwithstanding, the height of British males also declined in the first half of the 19th century, approximately 1820–1850/60.[27] This coincides with the American ante-bellum height puzzle (and it may be related through the increased price of meat as protein). Earlier, both Britain and France in the 18th century saw improvements in nutritional standards that were so slight that any change in the distribution of nutrients could have a fairly serious and negative effect on heights.

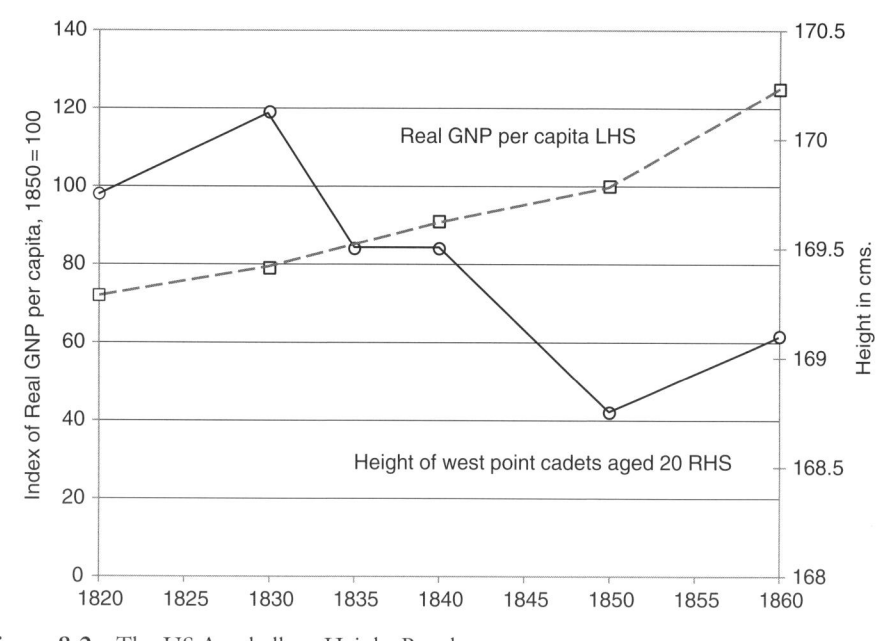

Figure 8.2 The US Antebellum Height Puzzle.
Source: data from Weiss (1994) Table 1.6 and Komlos (1987).

The evidence is not conclusive. However, the "biological standard of living" did not improve markedly in the early period of the Industrial Revolution.[28]

Anthropometric measures reflect income inequality through nutritional deprivation. For example, average heights are sensitive to the distribution of income as well as its level. They reveal something about the consumption of nutrition by the poor. Stature, a person's natural height, is a *net* measure of consumption that reveals both the supply of health inputs at a point in time and the demand placed on those inputs. Thus, differences in stature attributable to nutritional deprivation are a reflection of income inequality. If all classes of the population have equal access to nutrition, and equal information about its effects, it seems reasonable to conclude that those who are malnourished lack the income to purchase equal amounts of nutrition. Per capita income, however, is not the only factor that affects stature. Personal hygiene, public health measures, and the disease environment affect illness, and work intensity is a function of technology, culture and methods of labor organization. In addition, the relative price of food, cultural values such as the pattern of food distribution within the family, methods of preparation, and tastes and preferences for foods may also be relevant for net nutrition.[29]

8.5 Birth Weights

Prior to the 20th century, infant mortality tended to be lower the higher the occupational status (or social status) of the family; the children of higher income families had superior health outcomes to those of poorer ones. One survey of 1883 revealed that the children of urban professionals at the end of their growth spurt were much taller than those born to town artisans and country laborers. At the end of their respective growth spurts, the difference was 19.4 centimeters (7.6 inches) for boys and 14.9 centimeters (5.9 inches) for girls. For the desperately poor or orphaned boys of 18th century London, the gap between their stature and that of the upper/professional class boys was even larger. The stature of the poor, as Roderick Floud and Kenneth Wachter point out, suggests that they were malnourished throughout their growth period.[30] What was their condition at birth?

No single measure is as good a predictor of subsequent infant survival and adult health as the birth weight of infants. Low birth weight is linked to the slow growth of adolescents by the common lack of nutritional sufficiency in both circumstances. Thanks to pioneering work by the historian Peter Ward, who assembled a vast array of hospital records, we now have historical observations dating back to the mid-19th century.[31] Since the optimal birth weight range is bounded by 3500 to 3900 grams, those with a birth weight lower than normal were likely to suffer higher mortality and greater morbidity. For instance, cardio-vascular deaths are much higher in those with low birth weights than those with birth weights in the normal range (allowing for full gestation of the fetus). Compared with contemporary (late 20th century) information from the same locations, the European city maternity hospitals of Vienna, Edinburgh and Dublin had roughly twice the percentage of low-weight births in the late 19th and early 20th centuries. Since we know that nutrition was improving during this period, even for the low-income families, it is most likely that low birth weight babies were even more common earlier in the industrial age. This stands in marked contrast to the North American cities of Montreal and Boston where, in the main maternity hospitals, the percentage of low birth weight babies has approximately remained the same from the late 19th century to the present. Just as importantly, their mean birth weight was high, even within the normal range of today. While well-off females in North American cities tended to deliver their babies at home, even the less well-off females had superior access to nutritionally balanced diets (calories and protein) compared to their European peers. Yet things were not universally better. Babies born to black mothers in the Boston Lying-In Hospital from 1872 to 1900 were more than twice as likely to be of low birth weight (12.3%) than white mothers (5.9%).[32] Although North American birth weights today do not differ significantly by socio-economic class, they did historically.[33]

Fetal weight gain largely occurs in the last trimester of pregnancy so those that had access to sufficient food at this time tended to have higher birth weight children. Apart from higher family income, there were other economic characteristics that might have ensured a higher birth weight in the mid-19th century. Proximity to food sources (e.g., urban allotments or farms) meant that the price of foodstuffs was lower, or produced by one's own labor, and, consequently, the mother-to-be had access to marginally more calories. Domestic servants also had access to food that was different from other members of the working-class. Often with the tacit agreement of the household in which they served, servants were permitted to take discarded but perfectly acceptable food. Of course, many of these domestic positions offered food as part of the compensation. On the other hand, a variety of social conventions could result in an inordinately low level of nutrition for future mothers. As the female head of the household, she was usually the person who allocated the food within the family and often did without in order to make sure that the others of the family did not suffer nutritional deprivation. Thus, we have an historical problem of looking for the income distribution (rarely available) and the distribution of nutrition within the family (also, rarely available). In addition, the nutritional state of the mother was dependent on the variation in income over time. Since the year-to-year variation was greater than in modern economies, any decline in income adversely affected the poorer mothers.

8.6 The Human Development Index

In 1979, Morris Morris proposed a "physical quality of life" index, a weighted sum of life expectancy at birth, the infant survival rate, and the adult literacy rate in an attempt to measure improvement in longevity.[34] The United Nations Development Program adopted the Human Development Index (HDI) based upon Morris's work.[35] In the HDI, per capita national income is used rather than the infant survival rate. All three variables are indexed to the same base, and the HDI is simply the sum of the three normalized indices. Applying this index in a historical context is often problematical given the likely absence of data on any or all of the component series.

In the case of the United States, a consistent series on life expectancy is available only from the middle of the 19th century. Dora Costa and Richard Steckel used

Table 8.4 The Costa-Steckel Human Development Index (HDI) and its Components for the United States, 1800–1970.

Year	HDI	Income per capita	Literacy	Height in cm
1800	0.580	302	0.724	172.9
1810	0.588	318	0.725	173.0
1820	0.603	326	0.737	172.9
1830	0.624	349	0.745	173.5
1840	0.617	391	0.761	172.2
1850	0.632	430	0.780	171.1
1860	0.661	523	0.803	170.6
1870	0.702	659	0.800	171.2
1880	0.735	909	0.830	169.5
1890	0.750	1113	0.867	169.1
1900	0.802	1395	0.893	170.0
1910	0.865	1747	0.923	172.1
1920	0.884	1743	0.940	173.1
1930	0.894	2025	0.957	173.4
1940	0.936	2370	0.971	176.1
1950	0.951	3133	0.974	177.1
1960	0.955	3623	0.978	177.3
1970	0.962	4774	0.990	177.5

Source: data from Costa and Steckel (1997).

height to substitute for life expectancy as a measure of health.[36] They normalize literacy rates between 0 and 1 with the lowest rate assigned a value of 0, the highest a value of 1, and the ones in the middle scaled accordingly. The minimum height is that of the Bundi of New Guinea (132 cm), while the maximum was the tallest national population found in 1990 (approximately mean value of 180 cm). The minimum per capita income was the estimated price of a subsistence diet ($140 in 1970 dollars), while the maximum was the United Nations' estimate of the upper bound ($1660 in 1970 dollars).[37] Their calculation of HDI for the US from 1800 to 1970 is in Table 8.4. The calculated HDI is relatively high, even before the US began to industrialize. The numbers for the early 1800s are higher than for many less developed countries in the world today. Where one starts matters!

During the years characterized by the *ante-bellum puzzle* (discussed earlier), the index essentially stagnates. Although both per capita income and literacy were increasing, height was decreasing. Despite average height decreases through 1890, increases in per capita income cause the index to increase after the US Civil War. These data are depicted in Figure 8.3 and are presented with similar calculations made for the United Kingdom, Sweden, and Germany. As can be seen, there is a marked upward trend between the late 19th and mid 20th centuries in all four series during the period that corresponds with industrialization. Given the assumptions that have to be made to calculate HDI, particularly the choosing of maximum and minimum values for each component series, the relative position of the series is not

Figure 8.3 Historical Human Developments Indexes, Select Countries, 1755–1980.
Note: Interpolated data between data points.
Source: data from Steckel and Floud (1997).

as important as the fact that all four move in the same manner. The United States and Western Europe experienced similar gains in welfare as measured by the Costa-Steckel HDI – see Figure 8.3.

8.7 Obesity and the BMI

The conventional definition of obesity makes use of the Body Mass Index (BMI), weight divided by squared height. An obese person is one whose BMI exceeds 30. A BMI between 20 and 25 is conventionally thought to be optimal as in Figure 8.4 (although relative morbidity and relative mortality for middle-aged Norwegian males appears to be roughly equal for BMIs from 22 to 28). A BMI below 20 is considered thin; a BMI between 25 and 30 is overweight. As Cutler, Glaeser, and Shapiro note, between 1894 and 1961, the average BMI for men in their 40s rose from 23.6 to 26.0.[38] Thus, by 1961, American males were at the margin between being of optimal weight and being overweight. Over the last four decades of the 20th century, average BMI for that group increased by an additional 0.7. This put many more individuals into the less healthy portion of Figure 8.4. The magnitude of the danger can be seen by examining OECD statistics for the percentage of the total population considered to be obese.

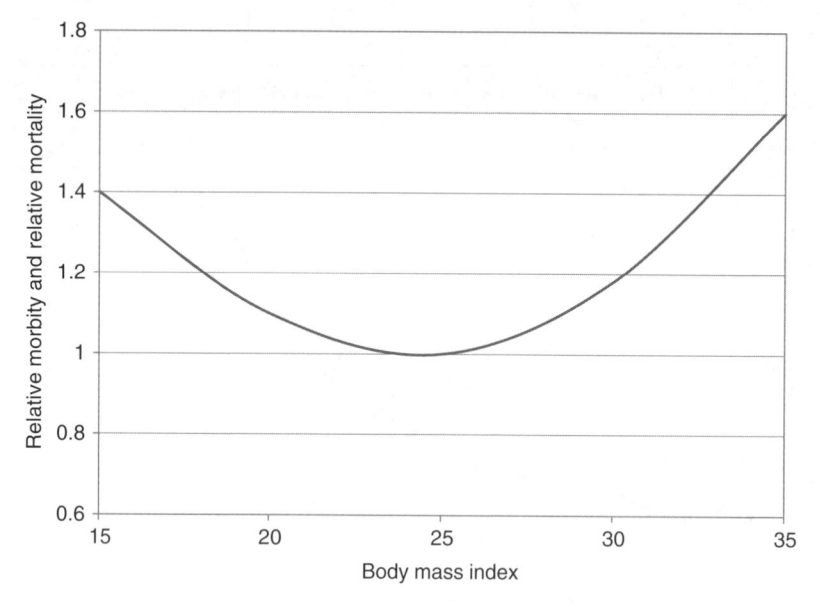

Figure 8.4 BMI and Relative Morbidity and Mortality.
Note: standardized for height.

> **The Body Mass Index (BMI)** makes use of the most commonly available measures of physical adult stature: height and weight. It is calculated as:
>
> $$\text{BMI} = \text{weight in kg} / [\text{height in m}]^2$$
>
> It is an indirect measure of body fat.[39]

One of every three Americans is now considered obese as is apparent from Figure 8.5. While the problem is less severe elsewhere, every country has shown an increase in the percentage obese over the period 1991 (or thereabout) and 2006. The eight countries leading the weight gain over this interval were: Austria, Finland, France, Japan, Netherlands, Sweden, the United Kingdom and the United States.[40] Even countries with small proportions of their populations classed as obese such as Japan have participated in the average weight gain. As of 2006, Mexico was just behind the US at about 30%, but this was not a North American phenomenon; Canada was 12 percentage points lower. At the other end of the distribution, both Korea and Japan were below 5%.

If a person maintains a stable weight, then on average the caloric intake equals caloric expenditure. The cause of the weight gain has to be caloric imbalance. There are three ways in which people burn calories. The first is basal metabolism, the energy expended to keep the body going. The heavier the individual, the more energy that is required. The second is the processing of food. Recall that these two together

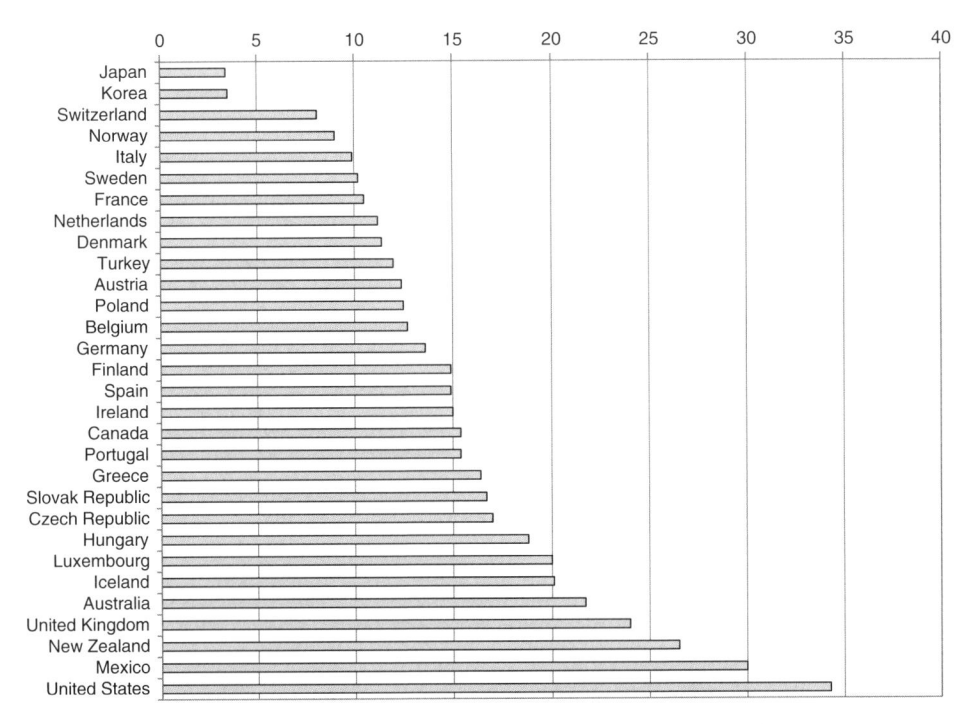

Figure 8.5 Percentage of Population Obese, Selected Advanced Industrial Countries, 2007.
Notes: Obese is a BMI>30 kg/m^2.
Source: OECD Factbook (2010) *Obesity*, 232–3.
http://www.oecd-ilibrary.org/economics/oecd-factbook_18147364

comprise baseline nutritional maintenance. Together they account for roughly 70% of the daily energy used by most people. The third way, the remaining 30%, is physical activity. The American weight gain of recent years, 1991 to 2006, translates to less than 150 calories per day. This is quite small, equal to roughly one additional can of a non-diet soft drink or one mile less walked per day.

Table 8.5 puts the American situation into a historical context. Using data from a sample of Union Army veterans for the late 19th and early 20th century contrasted against the National Health and Nutrition Examination Survey (NHANES) for the final quarter of the 20th century, Lorens Helmchen and Max Henderson paint a stark picture of change.[41] Over the century, there was a large, relatively continuous move out of occupations that required large inputs of energy (e.g., agriculture, heavy manufacturing) toward those that required much less (e.g., services). As a result, BMIs increased as did the percentage (and the standard error) of people regarded as obese. It seems clear changes in the labor market help explain the long-run trend in Table 8.5, but they cannot explain the recent short-run acceleration in the prevalence of obesity. Those who argue that the recent epidemic has been caused by such a shift are really talking about the increase between 1895–1900 and 1976–1980 more than that of recent years.

Studies such as the US Department of Agriculture's *Continuing Surveys of Food Intake by Individuals* from the late 1970s and early 1990s, studies based on

Table 8.5 BMI and Distributions Statistics for US White Males, 1890–2000.

		(Non-Hispanic by Age Group)				Obesity Prevalent
		BMI				
Age	Period	Mean	Q1	Q3	90%	%
Years						
40–49	1890–1894	23.2	21.0	24.7	27.3	3.7
	1976–1980	26.5	23.9	28.9	31.0	15.8
	1999–2000	27.8	23.9	29.5	34.5	24.4
50–59	1890–1894	23.0	20.8	24.4	27.0	3.4
	1976–1980	26.2	23.9	28.0	31.4	13.8
	1999–2000	29.1	25.1	32.4	36.1	35.0
60–69	1890–1894	22.9	20.7	24.4	26.9	2.9
	1976–1980	25.9	23.4	28.2	30.6	13.4
	1999–2000	29.2	25.6	32.9	35.9	41.3

Notes: drawn from Union Army veterans sample and the NHANES Q1–25th percentile; Q3–75th percentile; 90%–90th percentile; Obesity Prevalence-proportion BMI> = 30 which is the threshold for obesity in this table.
Source: data from Helmchen and Henderson (2004).

personal recall, report more than enough additional calories consumed to account for the increase in average weight.[42] The biggest share of these additional calories is derived from snacks, an increase in the frequency of caloric consumption. Calories consumed at dinner actually decreased. These data contradict two conventional explanations for the increase in obesity; large portion restaurant meals and fattening fast food meals.

That people have chosen to "eat out" or consume "take-aways" more often is a logical result of an increase in the opportunity cost of time attributable to decreases in tax rates and the narrowing of the gender wage gap which have lowered the relative cost of food prepared outside the home. This does not necessarily mean that people choose to eat out, but it does mean that they spend less time in preparing meals at home. David Cutler, Edward Glaeser, and Jesse Shapiro argue that the explanation for the increase in obesity has to do with a technological change, the decline in the time cost of food preparation.[43] This is clearly represented by the microwave oven. In 1978, only 8% of American homes had microwave ovens, a percentage that increased to 83% by 1999.

There is a high correlation between the percentage of microwave ownership and obesity across countries. In the United Kingdom, which had a percentage increase in obesity similar to the US, roughly two-thirds of homes have microwave ovens. At the other extreme, Italy, where obesity has been much less of a problem, reports that only 14% of homes possess microwaves. Americans spend an average of 34 minutes per day on meal preparation; Italians, over 86.[44] An implication of the decline in the time spent at home to prepare meals is that there is a good deal more professional food preparation involved in what individuals eat. This is reflected in the fact that the share of the cost of food going to farmers fell from 44% in 1972 to 23% in 1997. Given that the time cost of food reflects the opportunity cost, this reduction means that one should expect an increase in food consumption.

While technological change in agriculture has reduced the price of (and hence increased the demand for) calories, the burning of calories through exercise has become more expensive. The movement from manual labor to more sedentary automation increased incomes, but it meant simultaneously that fewer calories were burned as a result of the work that generated those incomes. Exercise shifted from labor to leisure, and it became necessary to join a gym, jog, play squash or the like in order to accomplish what once was a by-product of work. This increased the price, hence reduced the demand, for exercise. Thus, the effect of the increase in food consumption was reinforced.

There are social as well as private costs connected to obesity, and this raises the question of the extent to which governments should become involved. This, in turn, leads to the question of the benefits and costs of alternative public policies.[45] When, within a society, few people are obese, there is generally a stigma attached to it. However, as obesity becomes more common, as has been happening, the stigma wanes. As the cost of being obese falls, as more people become obese, the health cost rises. Government programs such as Medicare and Medicaid (US), the National Health (UK) and the public health systems of countries such as Canada and France among others are affected. On the one hand, the increase of morbidity increases costs, but, on the other, the increase in mortality decreases costs. This suggests the net effect is not likely to be very large. There is also an externality associated with health insurance in the US created by the fact that weight is not a variable used in setting premiums, but this effect is also likely to be small, especially when one considers other "risky" behaviors in which individuals indulge. Nor is there rate discrimination in the public health systems of countries with 'nationalized medical and hospitalization' systems.

The most frequently discussed public policy to counteract obesity is education. There is a suspicion that the negative health effects caused by obesity are not as well understood as they should be, and neither are the foods that contribute to obesity. Nutritional labeling is required on most, but not all, food products.[46] In addition, over the period covered by Figure 8.4, in the United States and elsewhere, a diet industry has emerged. Discussions of the effects of obesity are commonplace in popular media. There are good reasons to believe obese people understand how they got that way and they perceive obesity as part of a broadly-defined problem of behaviors, lifestyles and circumstances. They further understand that obesity is not as a narrowly-defined medical problem that can be dealt with in isolation.[47] And, as Tomas Philipson and Richard Posner argue, "uneducated persons have less of an incentive to invest in their health because their longevity and their utility from living are below average."[48]

Obesity, however, is not simply a result of the choices individuals make or their lack of self-control. There are physiological factors that are part of the equation as well as ample evidence that socio-economic status matters. Giorgio Brunello, Pierre-Carl Michaud, and Anna Sanz-de-Galdeano found that the BMIs of individuals from high- and low-status homes converge over the life cycle in the European countries they examined. On the other hand, they diverge in the US, a difference they attribute to European welfare policies.[49]

Other policy options that have been discussed include taxes, regulating fast food sales, and an adaptation of the anti-tobacco program. A variety of tax options have been proposed, but there is a strong suspicion that, for any type of tax, the social costs of collecting the tax would be greater than the social benefits from reducing obesity.[50] Several communities have required fast food restaurants to make nutritional information for their products readily accessible to consumers at their stores; several schools have begun to limit what is available to their students in campus vending machines. Potentially more effective than these steps are regulations on the advertisements of fast food restaurants. The US food industry is that nation's second largest advertiser (automobiles are first). Such regulations would be consistent with one of the policy options directed at reducing tobacco consumption. Other components of the anti-tobacco program do not have clear analogs for obesity reduction. One does not need to smoke to survive, so limitations on where one can consume food are more annoying than helpful. And because food is a necessity, a high tax on food would be regressive.[51] All things considered, given the data presented above, none of these options is likely to have a large effect if the basic cause of obesity lies in snacks. This presents a problem for policy as one person's snack is another's meal.

8.8 Household Space

It is in the home that most of us generally feel most safe, especially if surrounded by the comfort of family. Unfortunately, household or domestic space has always been one of the most dangerous of places. Events and conditions within the home can contribute to high levels of transmission of non-fatal and fatal diseases as noted in Chapter Three. Both the quality and quantity of housing directly affect the general health of individuals. Water-borne and air-borne pathogens are more easily transmitted where individuals share a common water source and live in close proximity. Take the case of the disease diarrhoea. Historically, this was one of the main killers of young children and still is today in developing countries. It is highly correlated with child morbidity as the conditions that cause diarrhoea are repeated. There are many methods of transmission of the pathogens responsible but most of the infection takes place because of a lack of basic hygienic practices: contaminated water (tied to the washing of hands or absence thereof) and the presence of flies. Much of the disease transmission is by the mother who unwittingly does not wash her hands, or cannot because of the absence of clean water, and thus the disease enters the prepared food supply – it may even makes the breast-fed infant vulnerable.[52] As noted in Chapter Four, the provision of the public amenities of potable water and sewage systems can reduce the incidence of water-borne diseases. Air-borne diseases are spread by similar intimate processes.

The quality of domestic space was critical in determining the rate of morbidity. For instance, modern studies have found that allergies and childhood asthma are positively related to cockroach infestations. They are also associated with dust mites, mice and mold, which are more common in poor quality housing.[53] By the mid-19th century, low quality urban housing, particularly tenements, attracted civic government attention throughout Europe and North America. Subscriptions were solicited from those better-off to fund the building of sanitary housing for the poor, many of whom were working poor. Model tenements with affordable rents were established in British

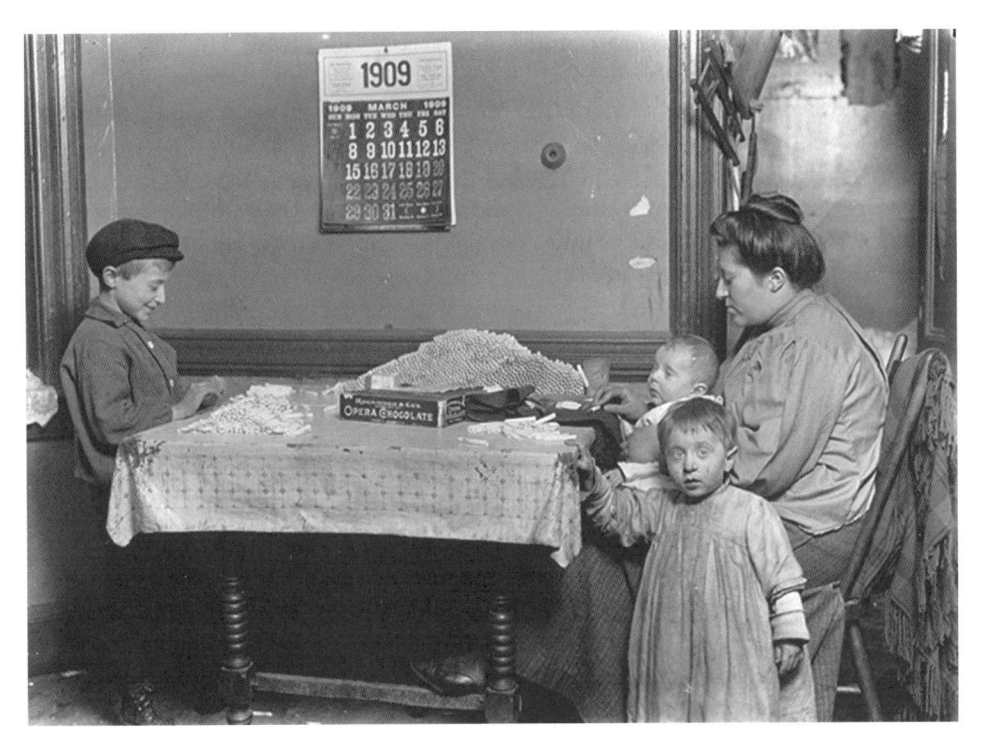

Poverty, Single Parenthood and a New York City Tenement, 1909

A young widow and boy rolling papers for cigarettes in a dirty New York City tenement in 1909. Piece-work compensation for such tasks was typically very low.
Source: Photographer Lewis Wickes Hines, 1909. Photograph from the records of the US National Child Labor Committee, *Library of Congress*, Prints and Photographs Division Washington.

cities and, consequently, the disease rates were much lower than elsewhere in similar urban landscapes, much to the satisfaction of the Victorian improvers.[54] They took self-congratulatory delight in the reduction of alcoholism, prostitution, gambling, unwanted pregnancies and other "moral vices." However, such well-intentioned schemes could be nothing more than a model and had, in aggregate, little effect on the morbidity patterns. Victorian paternalism and Dickensian literary outrage did, however, bring life to a much more practical and effective result. This was the creation of boards of sanitary inspectors as part of the public health civic initiatives in many countries in last half of the 19th century. The boards brought pressure to bear on the landlords to improve ventilation, water and sewage facilities. Yohanna von Wagner was one such inspector in Yonkers, New York.

> ... I begin to inspect the plumbing [cellar], and unless the house is new the pipes or construction are generally defective. ... When I go to the upper floors the living-rooms over the cellars are damp and also very unhealthy. The tenants have malaria, rheumatism, and tuberculosis, and the children have bronchitis and do not thrive, and even on the upper floor all complain of ill-health.
>
> Yohanna von Wagner (1902).

While not the first woman to occupy such a role, she made a compelling (and reasonably successful) public case for the appointment of more women as inspectors because they were effective in educating women householders in the need for hygienic practices.[55] Her results were similar to those made by the trained midwives (female) in Sweden a century earlier. The public health concerns voiced by the new sanitary inspectors, and publicity surrounding the findings, made the interplay among the causes harder to ignore: i) lack of education; ii) poverty, poor housing; and iii) disease and other ill-health.

Low birth weight is such a good predictor of subsequent morbidity because it is the first in a sequence of deleterious personal medical events. Evidence from the very early part of the 20th century in the US shows that those who suffered from tuberculosis in childhood had a much higher risk of strokes and cancer in later life. Typhoid is associated with later elevated risks of heart disease and kidney disease.[56] What linked the two sets of medical conditions were the poor housing and the inability to escape from it, since there is no known scientific link between these health outcomes. Geographic mobility usually derived from occupational mobility, and a route to higher incomes, was also a product of education and literacy.

Of course, not all accommodation in urban areas was sub-standard in its day. In the late 19th century new designs for specific urban dwellings emerged that were a sharp departure from the past. Urban tenements with ample ventilation, and air shafts, were a response to the interior poor air quality, for instance. Design innovations included increasingly the water closet and running water. For the better-off families row (terrace) housing gave them private household space in densely populated neighborhoods. New transport technology such as the urban tramways (inter-urbans as they were called in the US and Canada) permitted the escape from the immediate vicinity of the workplace as workers now could use these new public amenities to travel over the cityscape. They permitted the city to spread, and low cost suburban areas grew. The free-standing, single-family resident house became more common. Outside the urban core the well-off families could aspire to a 'villa', a house with its own garden, much promoted by the real estate developers of the day.[57] Hampstead Garden suburb in London and Kenilworth outside Chicago were only two of the tonier (up-market) residential areas created in the early 20th century. Each city had its counterpart.

Where there is more disease, there are usually more deaths. Until about the mid-20th century, the rate of mortality was higher in the urban areas than it was in the rural areas. However, most evidence suggests that the morbidity rate was exactly the opposite; it was higher in the rural areas and villages.

8.9 Health and Hospital Care Systems

Embryonic national health care systems first emerged in the late 19th century. They were an outgrowth of the co-operatively-run employment insurance schemes which had proven successful in providing limited health benefits. The breath of their coverage and their provision of cheap medical care on a wide scale in North America has often been cited as one the reasons for the late emergence of national health schemes in the US and Canada (see the previous chapter). In Europe the friendly societies were similarly successful, but their limited coverage simply drew attention to those left out;

they became a model for subsequent health care provision. The national schemes were always social insurance based with medical care as a secondary benefit. It is no coincidence that national pension benefits emerged at the same time as these early national health schemes. For the national provision of health care three institutional innovations were required: i) the extension of their coverage beyond the workers who made direct contributions to the elderly, the disabled and children; ii) the high degree of compulsion required of the schemes; and iii) the method of funding them by the national government. Most were a variant of the plan first introduced in Germany in 1885 which was compulsory and funded by general taxation to the extent that individual premiums did not cover all of the enlarged coverage. Direct subsidy of the friendly societies to extend coverage to those who did not pay premiums was also tried. Before 1900 the countries of Belgium, Sweden, Denmark and France had all introduced national health schemes. The effect of these, according to the research of Calman Winegarden and John Murray, was to accelerate the reduction of mortality and raise the life expectancy further – death rates were declining rapidly in the 40 years before World War I as mentioned earlier. The saving of lives came in the general form of better care for the sick and not in finding a cure for a particular medical condition. Fewer people died in all categories of ill-health as opposed to the saving occurring from the eradication of one medical condition.[58]

Over relatively short histories, the nations of the OECD group of countries have each created a national health system. They are remarkably similar in that the systems are designed around the broad issues of public health care, individual medical and hospital services. They are also remarkably different from each other in their fiscal construction and how the services are delivered. All seem to work, although all seem to have weaknesses. On the demand side there are issues: access to services, waiting lists for procedures, affordability and many others. On the supply side there are: human capital issues, payment to services providers, physical facilities, appropriate technologies and many others. These health systems also struggle with the issue of effectiveness and, indeed, even measuring effectiveness. Not surprisingly, any system-wide comparability is only evident in gross terms given the variety of national organizations, the mix of public and private funding, and coverage. Or, specific conditions and remedies can be evaluated for a narrowly defined health outcome or clinical procedure. Some of the non-OECD countries also have national health systems but they are, for the most part, of a more fragile construction. Many non-OECD countries have none; public health, medical and hospital services are managed and funded by private payments and, where there is a public input, it is on an *ad hoc* basis. Early research by Victor Fuchs in the 1960s and 1970s documented the long-suspected, positive relationship between expenditures on health care and income, on the one hand, and between expenditures on health care and health status, on the other. This includes both private and public sector spending.[59]

Life expectancy at age zero is one of the basic measures of a population's health and, as we have seen earlier, one of the key components of the Human Development Index. Figure 8.6 shows that high per capita spending on health care is accompanied by high (unisex) life expectancy at birth. Of course, higher spending in aggregate does not guarantee a higher level of health outcomes, although it is a very good start. The outcome of high life expectancy is achieved not through spending in any one year but by the cumulative spending (investment) over many years, and the countries with the

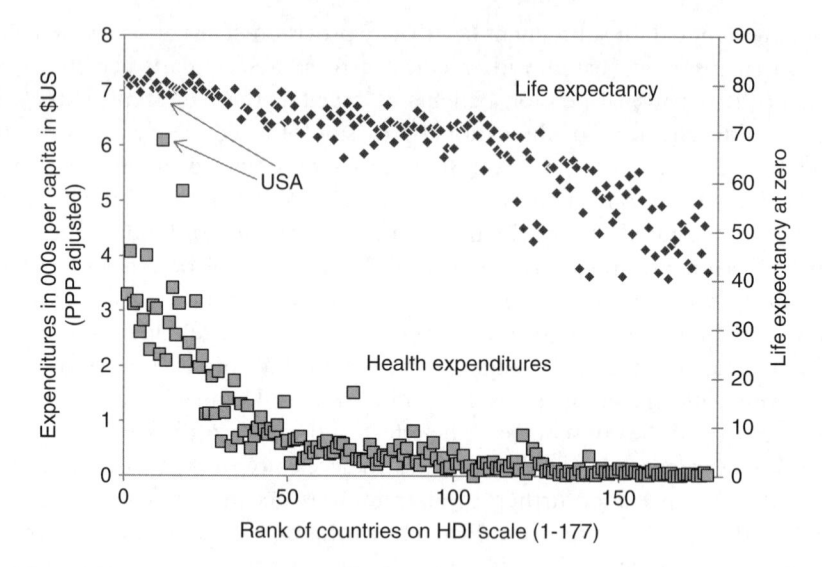

Figure 8.6 Life Expectancy and Health Expenditure Per Capita, By Country, 2004.
Note: this figure includes data for 177 countries. It omits data from Saudi Arabia, various Gulf States and Singapore. All are high HDI countries with abnormally low *apparent* expenditures on health as a proportion of GDP. The other omissions are those countries with small populations and/or faulty data. The $US are converted using purchasing power (rather than exchange rates).
Source: WHO, World Health Statistics (2010), http://www.who.int/whosis/whostat/EN_WHS10_Full.pdf

highest life expectancy (>75 years) all have a long history of such spending. Yet, of the 177 countries measured by the HDI, about 136 are currently spending less than $1000 US per person on health and medical care; 41 countries spend less than $100 US – see Figure 8.6. The latter are mostly sub-Saharan African and South Asian nations with little economic history of coordinated health expenditures and a more recent history of AIDS – see Chapter Ten.

As more countries provide high quality medical care we would expect a convergence of the life expectancy at birth (adjusted for expenditure). Yet one troublesome trend has emerged in recent years. Among the highly developed nations life expectancy is increasing least rapidly in the United States. This has created a *differential* life expectancy that is increasing. Compared to Canada, Japan and several European countries the gap is significant. In the 1970s the differential was non-existent between the US and this "peer" group.

Where $[L^c us_0 / L^c p_0]$ = the ratio of the life expectancy at age zero in the US to the life expectancy at age zero in the countries of Canada, Germany, France, Japan, Switzerland and the United Kingdom:

$$[L^c us_0 / L^c p_0]_{1975} = 1.00 \qquad [L^c us_0 / L^c p_0]_{2004} = 0.97.$$

This despite an increasing ratio of expenditures, US to "peer" group, over the same period from 1.30 to 2.00.[60] That is, now with an estimated per capita expenditure of $6096 compared to $3041 in the peer group, the US has a health outcome less desirable than those particular countries who spend very much less. There are several issues that flow from this observation. First, life expectancy is only one health measure, a very important one, but nonetheless only one. We must take into account other health trade-offs such as campaigns to lower the adult smoking rate. This policy has been more successful in the US than in Europe. It is counted as a health expenditure in Europe whereas in the US and Canada it falls to the remit of other agencies and is not usually counted. Second, the underlying data are not comparable through the period of the comparison. For instance, a country with a higher *differential* proportion of its population from countries such as Mexico and those of Africa, to name a few, will find that they have more people with health histories that lower *average* health status. Many of the conditions that surface in later life are the product of childhood health and nutrition. Third, also contributing to a lower health status and anticipated earlier in this chapter, the modern disease of obesity may play a role in biasing the US results relative to countries with lower incidence of the disease. The US currently has twice the level of this condition than the "peer" countries – see Figure 8.6 for country comparisons. The same is true of adult diabetes.

A recent review of the US health care system with that of other countries with high levels of per capita spending and high success outcomes, shows that there was no systematic superiority in health outcomes for individual procedures. However, there are signs that the US health system as a whole suffers from barriers to access. These barriers, for example, result in the avoidance of early treatments due to their price (cost). This avoidance may simply raise the cost to the health system because of late diagnoses or delayed treatment making later and more expensive treatment likely.[61] Although this problem largely occurs among those who are self-insured, it also comes from an unawareness of what is available in the public sector (e.g., Medicaid). The poor suffer both from a lack of income and a lack of information. The percentage of the chronically ill skipping care because of costs in 2007 was substantially higher in the US than other OECD countries: US (42%), Canada (14%), UK (9%) and Holland (5%).[62] As various countries in the world come to grips with the growing proportion of GDP that is devoted to health care, they also have to plan for ease of access. Better health care is something we increasingly consume as our income increases. An uneven distribution of health access produces an uneven distribution of health benefits, and that becomes a cost to all. There is also the need for more rational (market) planning across countries. For instance, many suppose pharmaceuticals are available internationally at marginal cost, but the fixed costs of developing them are recovered in the domestic market. Is the resulting system of subsidies equitable?

Improvements in the health and well-being of the population are massive in their scope and they, in turn, have aggregate or macro-economic consequences. These are the next concern of this history.

Endnotes

1 Palloni (2006); Palloni, Milesi, White and Turner (2009).
2 Harris (2002); Rajakumar, Greenspan, Thomas and Holick (2007).
3 Arneil (1975).

4   Pinhasi, Shaw, White and Ogden (2006).
5   Hardy (2003).
6   Tully (1924).
7   Rajakumar and Thomas (2005) detail the re-emergence of rickets in the US.
8   The timing is taken from the Dutch records. The Netherlands is one country that led in the standardizing the diagnosis of disease. Dutch history gives us a clear picture of the disappearance sequence in Western Europe. Wolleswinkel-Van Den Bosch, Van Poppel, Tabeau and Mackenbach (1998).
9   Disinfectant use and hand-washing (chlorinated lime solution) were found to reduce the incidence of puerperal fever. Although the reasons for this outcome were not understood the results were one of the key observations of which Pasteur made use. We are indebted to Professor Peter Ward on this point.
10 DeLacy (1989); Hallett (2005).
11 A more complete explanation of DALYs can be found at http://www.who.int/health info/boddaly/
12 Because any one disease or injury usually affects only a small percentage of the population at any one time, morbidity rates are often expressed on a base of one thousand, or any round number of thousands up to a million. For some diseases and health impairment, where the incidence is rare, the absolute value is reported.
13 India (756); Myanmar (14), Nepal (2); Sudan (1); Nigeria (278); Democratic Republic of Congo (41) and Niger (10).
14 For example, Scrimshaw, Taylor and Gordon (1968).
15 Toutain (1971).
16 Oddy (1990).
17 In addition to height and weight, variables such as the body mass index (the ratio of weight in kg. to height in m^2) and the length of bones measured from skeletal remains have been used. See Fogel (2004); Steckel and Rose (2002).
18 As Fogel (2004) notes, by the early 1970s, the consensus view of what caused the mortality decline was summarized in two United Nations reports: United Nations (1953) and United Nations (1973). The UN explanation focused on five factors:

  • public health reforms;
  • improvements in medical knowledge and practices;
  • changes in personal hygiene;
  • growth in income and living standards; and
  • natural factors such as the decline in the virulence of pathogens.

  This consensus was challenged by McKeown (see Chapter Three) who emphasized the role of improved nutrition. See Harris (2002).
19 See Steckel (2005a); Steckel (2005b); and Steckel and Rose (2002).
20 Sen (1987).
21 Eveleth and Tanner (1990) document that height is correlated with socio-economic status.
22 Costa and Fogel (1997).
23 Komlos (1996).
24 Fogel (1986).
25 Gallman and Wallis (1992); Komlos (1996).
26 Komlos (1987), 201.
27 Floud, Wachter and Gregory (1990); Komlos (1996).
28 Steckel (1995).
29 Steckel (1995).

30 Floud and Wachter (1982); Nicholas and Oxley (1993, 1996).
31 Ward (1993). His main findings are drawn from five major hospitals in Canada, the USA, Ireland, Scotland and Austria.
32 Ward (1993).
33 Costa (1998).
34 Morris (1979).
35 United National Development Programme, *Human Development Report: 1990* (New York: Oxford University Press, 1990).
36 Costa and Steckel (1997). This substitution subtlety changes the definition of HDI as height emphasizes childhood conditions relative to the entire life span; it further introduces a cohort measure into what is otherwise a cross-sectional measure.
37 Costa and Steckel (1997).
38 Cutler, Glaeser and Shapiro (2003). Similar, albeit smaller, changes occurred for men in their 30s.
39 Burkhauser and Cawley (2008) have recently argued that BMI is a noisy measure because it does not distinguish body composition; fat is treated exactly the same as bone and muscle. Those with muscular bodies are likely to be considered obese. They prefer a measure such as total body fat or percentage body fat, but those are much less likely to be available. They argue the BMI measure discriminates against African-derived populations and sub-groups such as West Indians and African-Americans.
40 OECD Health Data (2008).
41 The table from which this has been excerpted contains many more statistics. See Helmchen and Henderson (2004).
42 Enns, Goldman and Cook (1997).
43 Cutler, Glaeser and Shapiro (2003).
44 Brunello, Michaud and Sanz-de-Galdeano (2008), See also Michaud, van Soest and Andreyeva (2007).
45 A particularly interesting discussion of the alternatives can be found in Philipson and Posner (2008).
46 Variyam and Cawley (2006) argue the effects of labelling policies have been limited.
47 Douglas, Greener and van Teijlingen (2008).
48 *Ibid*.
49 Brunello, Michaud and Sanz-de-Galdeano (2008).
50 A direct tax on excess body weight is suggested in Schmidhuber (2004).
51 See Burns (2008).
52 Borooah (2004).
53 Rauh, Chew and Garfinkel (2002).
54 Gatliff (1875).
55 Von Wagner (1902).
56 Clay and Troesken (2006) estimate that if tuberculosis could have been eliminated in 1900 in American cities the cancer and stroke mortality in 1915 would have been 32% lower. By the same reasoning typhoid raised deaths from heart disease by 21% and kidney disease by 23% over the same dates.
57 Ward (1999).
58 Winegarden and Murray (1998).
59 Fuchs (1972).
60 Garber and Skinner (2008), Figures 4a and 4b and OECD (2009), *Health Statistics*, Table 6.
61 Carey, Herring and Lenain (2009); Ahking, Giaccotto and Santerre (2009).
62 Garber and Skinner (2008).

References

Ahking, Francis W., Carmelo Giaccotto and Rexford E. Santerre (2009) "The Aggregate Demand for Private Health Insurance Coverage in The United States", *The Journal Of Risk And Insurance*, **76**(1), 133–57.

Arneil, G.C. (1975) "Nutritional Rickets in Children in Glasgow", *Proceedings of The Nutrition Society*, **34**, 101–8.

Borooah, Vani K. (2004) "On the Incidence of Diarrhoea Among Young Indian Children", *Economics and Human Biology*, **2**, 119–38.

Brunello, Giorgio, Pierre-Carl Michaud and Anna Sanz-de-Galdeano (2008) "The Rise in Obesity across the Atlantic: An Economic Perspective," IZA Discussion Paper No. 3529.

Burkhauser, Richard and Cawley, John (2008) "Beyond BMI: the Value of More Accurate Measures of Fatness and Obesity in Social Science Research." *Journal of Health Economics*, **27**(2), 519–29.

Burns, Cate (2008) "The Vulnerable and the Disadvantaged," *The Australian Economic Review*, **41**(1), 90–6.

Carey, David, Bradley Herring and Patrick Lenain (2009) *Health Care Reform in The United States*, Economics Department Working Paper No. 665, Paris: Organisation for Economic Co-operation and Development.

Clay, Karen and Werner Troesken (2006) "Deprivation And Disease In Early Twentieth-Century America", Working Paper No. 12111, Boston: National Bureau of Economic Research.

Costa, Dora L. (1998) "Unequal at Birth: A Long-Term Comparison of Income and Birth Weight", *Journal of Economic History*, **58**(4), 987–1009.

Costa, Dora L. and Robert W. Fogel (1997) "A Theory of Technophysio Evolution, with Some Implications for Forecasting Population, Health Care Costs, and Pension Costs", *Demography*, **34**(1), 49–66.

Costa, Dora and Richard H. Steckel, (1997) "Long-Term Trends in Health, Welfare, and Economic Growth in the United States," in Richard H. Steckel and Roderick Floud, eds., *Health and Welfare during Industrialization*, Chicago: University of Chicago Press.

Cutler, David M., Edward L. Glaeser and Jesse M. Shapiro (2003) "Why Have Americans Become More Obese?" *Journal of Economic Perspectives*, **17**(3), 93–118.

DeLacy, Margaret (1989) "Puerperal Fever in Eighteenth-century Britain', *Bulletin of the History of Medicine*, **63**(4), 521–56.

Douglas, Flora, Joe Greener and Edwin van Teijlingen (2008) "'Ask Me Why I'm Fat!' The Need to Engage with Potential Recipients of Health Promotion Policy to Prevent Obesity," *The Australian Economic Review*, **41**(1), 72–77.

Enns, Cecilia Wilkinson, Joseph D. Goldman and Annetta Cook (1997) "Trends in Food and Nutrient Intakes by Adults: NFCS 1977–78, CSFI 1989–91, and CSFII 1994–95," *Family Economics and Nutrition Review*, **10**(4), 2–15.

Eveleth, Phyllis B. and James M. Tanner (1990) *Worldwide Variation in Human Growth*, 2nd edition, Cambridge: Cambridge University Press.

Floud, R. and K.W. Wachter (1982) "Poverty and Physical Stature: Evidence on the Standard of Living of London Boys, 1770–1870", *Social Science History*, **6**(4) (Autumn), 422–52.

Floud, R., K.W. Wachter and A. Gregory (1990) *Height, Health and History; Nutritional Status in the United Kingdom, 1750–1980*, Cambridge: Cambridge University Press.

Fogel, Robert W. (1986) "Nutrition and the Decline in Mortality Since 1700: Some Preliminary Findings," in Stanley L. Engerman and Robert E. Gallman, eds., *Long-Term Factors in*

American Economic Growth, NBER Studies in Income and Wealth, vol. 51, Chicago: University of Chicago Press.

Fogel, Robert W. (2004) *Escape from Hunger and Premature Death, 1700–2100, America, Europe and the Third World*, Cambridge: Cambridge University Press.

Federico, Giovanni (2003) "Heights, Calories and Welfare: A New Perspective on Italian Industrialization, 1854–1913", *Economics and Human Biology*, **1**, 289–308.

Fuchs, Victor R. (1972) "The Contribution of Health Services to the American Economy," in Victor R. Fuchs, ed., *Essays in the Economics of Health and Medical Care*, New York: National Bureau of Economic Research.

Gallman, Robert and John Wallis (1992) "Introduction," in Robert E. Gallman and John Joseph Wallis, eds., *American Economic Growth and Standards of Living before the Civil War*, Chicago: University of Chicago Press.

Garber, Alan M. and Jonathan Skinner (2008) "Is American Health Care Uniquely Inefficient?", *Journal of Economic Perspectives*, **22**(4), 27–50.

Gatliff, Charles (1875) "On Improved Dwellings and Their Beneficial Effect on Health and Morals, with Suggestions for Their Extension", *Journal of the Statistical Society of London*, **38**(1) (March), 33–63.

Hallett, Christine (2005) "The Attempt to Understand Puerperal Fever in the Eighteenth and Early Nineteenth Centuries: The Influence of Inflammation Theory", *Medical History*, **49**, 1–28.

Hardy, Anne (2003) "Commentary: Bread and Alum, Syphilis and Sunlight: Rickets in the Nineteenth Century", *International Journal of Epidemiology*, **32**, 337–40.

Harris, Bernard (2002) "Public Health, Nutrition, and the Decline of Mortality: The McKeown Thesis Revisited", *Social History of Medicine*, **17**(3), 379–407.

Helmchen, Lorens A. and R. Max Henderson (2004) "Changes in the Distribution of Body Mass Index of White US Men, 1890–2000," *Annals of Human Biology*, **31**(2), 174–81.

Komlos, John (1987) "The Height and Weight of West Point Cadets: Dietary Change in Antebellum America", *Journal of Economic History*, **47**(4), 897–927.

Komlos, John (1996) "Anomalies in Economic History: Toward a Resolution of the 'Antebellum Puzzle'", *Journal of Economic History*, **56**(1), 202–14.

Michaud, Pierre-Carl, Arthur van Soest and Tatiana Andreyeva (2007) "Cross-Country Variation in Obesity Patterns among Older Americans and Europeans," RAND Labor and Population Working Paper No. 405.

Morris, Morris D. (1979) *Measuring the Condition of the World's Poor: The Physical Quality of Life Index*, New York: Pergamon.

Nicholas, Stephen and Deborah Oxley (1993) "The Living Standards of Women during the Industrial Revolution, 1795–1820", *Economic History Review*, New Series, **46**(4), 723–49.

Nicholas, Stephen and Deborah Oxley (1996) "Living Standards of Women in England and Wales, 1785–1815: New Evidence from Newgate Prison Records", *Economic History Review*, New Series, **49**(3), 591–9.

Oddy, Derek J. (1990) "Food, Drink and Nutrition," in F.M.L. Thompson, ed., *The Cambridge Social History of Britain 1750–1950*, vol. 2, New York: Cambridge University Press.

Organisation for Economic Co-operation and Development (current) [OECD] *Statistics*, Paris: OECD Publishing. http://www.oecd.org/statsportal/

Palloni, Alberto (2006) "Reproducing Inequalities: Luck, Wallets, and the Enduring Effects of Childhood Health, *Demography*, **43**(4), 587–615.

Palloni, Alberto, Carolina Milesi, Robert G. White and Alyn Turner (2009) "Early Childhood Health, Reproduction of Economic Inequalities and the Persistence of Health and Mortality Differentials", *Social Science and Medicine*, **68**, 1574–82.

Philipson, Tomas and Richard Posner (2008) "Is the Obesity Epidemic a Public Health Problem? A Decade of Research on the Economics of Obesity," Working Paper No. 14010, Boston: National Bureau of Economic Research.

Pinhasi, R., P. Shaw, B. White and A.R. Ogden (2006) "Morbidity, Rickets and Long-Bone Growth in Post-Medieval Britain – A Cross-Population Analysis", *Annals of Human Biology*, **33**(3) (May–June), 372–89.

Rajakumar, Kumaravel and Stephen B. Thomas (2005) "Reemerging Nutritional Rickets: A Historical Perspective", *Archives of Pediatrics and Adolescent Medicine*, **159**, (April), 335–41.

Rajakumar, Kumaravel, Susan L. Greenspan, Stephen B. Thomas and Michael F. Holick (2007) "Solar Ultraviolet Radiation and Vitamin D: a Historical Perspective", *American Journal of Public Health*, **97**(10) (October), 1746–54.

Rauh, Virginia A., Ginger L. Chew and Robin S. Garfinkel (2002) "Deteriorated Housing Contributes to High Cockroach Allergen Levels in Inner-City Households", *Environmental Health Perspectives*, **110**(2), 323–7.

Riley, J.C. and G. Alter (1996) "The Sick and the Well: Adult Health in Britain During the Health Transition", *Health Transition Review*, **6**, 19–44.

Schmidhuber, Josef (2004) "The Growing Global Obesity Problem: Some Policy Options to Address It," *eJADE:-Electronic-Journal of Agricultural and Development Economics*, **1**(2), 272–90.

Scrimshaw, N.S., C.E. Taylor and J.E. Gordon (1968) *Interactions of Nutrition and Infection*, Geneva: World Health Organization.

Sen, Amartya (1987) *The Standard of Living*, Cambridge: Cambridge University Press.

Steckel, Richard (1995) "Stature and the Standard of Living," *Journal of Economic Literature*, **33**(4), 11903–40.

Steckel, Richard H. (2005a) "Health and Nutrition in Pre-Columbian America: The Skeletal Evidence." *Journal of Interdisciplinary History*, **36**(1), 1–32.

Steckel, Richard H. (2005b) "Health and Nutrition in the Pre-Industrial Era: Insights from a Millennium of Average Heights in Northern Europe," Allen, Robert C., Tommy Bengtssson and Martin Dribe, eds., *Living Standards in the Past: New Perspectives on Well-Being in Asia and Europe*, Oxford: Oxford University Press.

Steckel, Richard H. and Roderick Floud, eds. (1997) *Health and Welfare during Industrialization*, NBER Project Report series, Chicago: University of Chicago Press.

Steckel, Richard and Jerome C. Rose, editors (2002) *The Backbone of History: Health and Nutrition in the Western Hemisphere*, New York: Cambridge University Press.

Toutain, Jean Claude (1971) *La Consommation alimentaire en France de 1789 a 1964*, Geneva: Economies et Societes, vol. V, no. 11, Librarie Droz, Cahiers de l'I,S.E.A.

Tully, Annabel M.T. (1924) "The Physique of Glasgow School Children (1921-22)", *The Journal of Hygiene*, **23**(2), 186–97.

United Nations (1953) *The Determinants and Consequences of Population Trends*, New York: United Nations.

United Nations (1973) *Determinants and Consequences of Population Trends: New Summary of Findings on Interaction of Demographic, Economic and Social Factors*, New York: United Nations.

United Nations Development Programme (1990) *Human Development Report: 1990*, New York: Oxford University Press.

Variyam, Jayachandran N. and John Cawley (2006) "Nutrition Labels and Obesity," NBER Working Paper 11956.

Von Wagner, Yohanna (1902) "Tenement-House Inspection", *The American Journal of Nursing*, **2**(7) (April), 508–13.

Ward, W. Peter (1999) *A History of Domestic Space: Privacy and the Canadian Home*, Vancouver: UBC Press.

Ward, W. Peter (1993) *Birth Weight and Economic Growth; Women's Living Standards in the Industrializing West*, Chicago; University of Chicago Press.

Weiss, Thomas (1994) "Economic Growth Before 1860: Revised Conjectures," in D. Schaefer and T. Weiss, eds., *Economic Development in Historical Perspective*, Palo Alto: Stanford University Press.

Winegarden, C.R. and John E. Murray (1998) "The Contributions of Early Health-Insurance Programs to Mortality Declines in Pre-World War I Europe: Evidence from Fixed-Effects Models", *Explorations in Economic History*, **35**, 431–46.

Wolleswinkel–Van Den Bosch, Judith H., Frans W.A. Van Poppel, Ewa Tabeau and Johan P. Mackenbach (1998) "Mortality Decline in The Netherlands in the Period 1850–1992: A Turning Point Analysis", *Social Science and Medicine*, **47**(4), 429–43.

Chapter Nine

Macroeconomic Effects of the Industrial Transition

9.1 Introduction

The consequences of demographic change often bring about major shifts in the structure of an economy and thus aggregate economic behavior. In this chapter we focus on the key features of these shifts. Historical economic development, as noted in Chapter Two, is distinguished from simple economic growth by including fundamental changes in the way the economy functions. Economic growth normally accounts for, and perhaps models, the changes in income and income per capita. Historically, economic development means more than economic growth; it is a wider concept. Structural shifts such as the transition from primary production to manufacturing and then to service production are among the concerns of economic development.[1] In this chapter the focus is on the shifts in economic history which had macroeconomic effects that significantly affected the population and its well-being.

First is the major macroeconomic issue of our time: the demographic shock of the baby-boom of the post-World War II years and the stresses it places on the economy. There is no historical precedent for this. Next, but related, is the shift in the aggregate saving of developed economies. This is a topic much beloved of economists and, unfortunately, pretty much ignored by historians and the rest of the world despite its vital importance. This raises the further issue of how society funds an increasingly aging population. The increased dependency of the aged in the face of falling fertility and the reduced dependency of the young create a unique historical problem. The resolution of that problem is made even more critical because of the baby-boom shock. In the long run, greater saving is a sign of greater disposable income. Yet it appears that in most societies individuals use their increased income for greater control of their own time. Time allocation is the way people spend their personal time and how they make trade-offs between work (income-earning time) and personal (non-work time). This has varied both in the workplace and the home. Finally, we examine the

The Children of Eve: Population and Well-being in History, First Edition.
Louis P. Cain and Donald G. Paterson.
© 2012 Blackwell Publishing Ltd. Published 2012 by Blackwell Publishing Ltd.

9.2 Shocks and Echoes – the Baby Boom

Whenever there is a shock or a bulge in a vital statistic, a sudden departure from the trend in birth, death, marriage, or immigration rates, there is a demographic consequence. For instance, a decrease in the marriage rate leads to a fall in the fertility rate. Subsequently, there is an echo of the original shock some time in the future. But such a shock will return with diminished amplitude. And there will be further echoes, again with further diminished amplitude, until all the effects of the original are dissipated as illustrated in Figure 9.1. The reason for the dampening effect is simply that the subsequent events are more spread out or diffuse. Take, for instance, a shock in the form of a sudden decline in the birth rate due to some exogenous factor such as war (as was discussed in Chapter Three). There should be a one-year decline in the marriage rate about 26 years on, then a one-year decline in the birth rate some time later. This accounts for the echo, but not its dissipation through time. For that we must appeal to the distribution of individual fertility; events are not exactly synchronized. In addition, there may be a declining trend as depicted in Figure 9.1.

The greatest shock of recent times is the post-war baby-boom.[2] As discussed earlier, a combination of forces led to an extraordinary burst of births in the post-1945 years, especially in the immigrant-receiving countries. The postponement of children due to the depression of the 1930s, then the war with its rise in female employment and

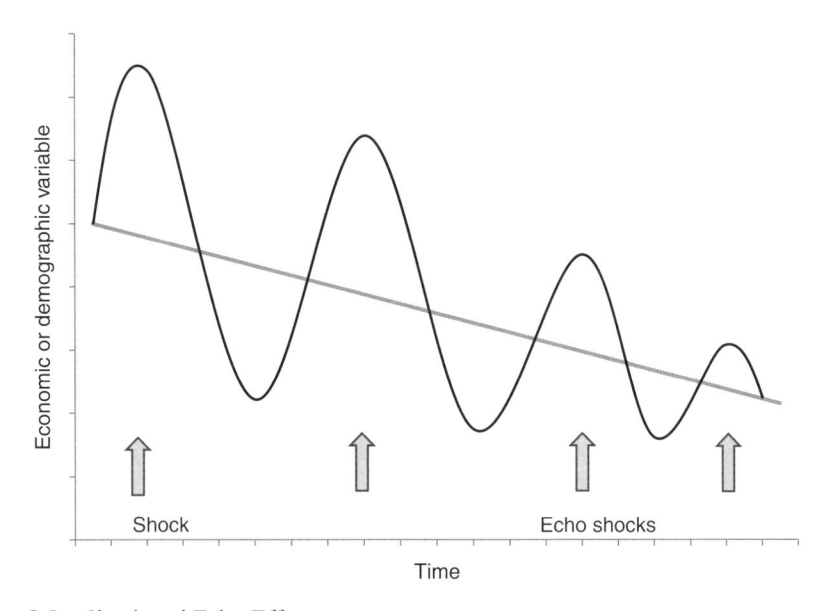

Figure 9.1 Shock and Echo Effects.
Note: Each peak and each trough is closer to the trend (mean) than the previous peak and trough as the shock spreads but dissipates.

income, led to a catch-up effect. To this was added a major flow of immigrants that began once peace had been restored (to the US, Canada, Argentina, Australia, New Zealand and others). This meant that the age-structure of the immigrant-receiving countries shifted towards the young, since the migrants themselves were overwhelmingly young. The rise in the proportion of the population aged 20–40 years of age caused the rise in the CBR which persisted at a high level for about two decades. The consequence was a rise in the number of births and a consequent rise in the dependency ratio. Notice there was no rise in the net fertility rate; it continued its long-run downward trend. Because of the immigrant effect, the baby-boom lasted much longer in North America than in Western Europe. The post-war baby-boom did not peak in Canada and the United States until 1958 and 1961 respectively.

Figure 9.2 shows the population pyramid that mimics the baby-boom. A population pyramid maps the age and sex structures of the population for any moment in time. In normal circumstances, the same number of births is repeated and the age-specific mortality does not change hence the pyramid shape. If age related mortality is low the pyramid will have steep sides; if it is high the sides will be sharply angled. By the first decade of the 21st century, that original shock of the baby-boom has worked its way through the age range, and the leading edge of that group of babies, now referred to as the boomers, is approaching retirement, ages 45 to 65. The echo phenomenon is indeed present, but weak or not so pronounced. The population pyramid also captures the low fertility of the modern era with its sharply contracted number of young children (0 to 5 in the figure).

The baby boom of the post-war period has led to several major macroeconomic stresses. New public and private investment had to be undertaken i) in the form of building the social infrastructure such as schools and universities and ii) privately to provide the housing to accommodate the boom as it grew. Maternity hospitals have to be converted to palliative care. Decommissioning the social infrastructure as the boomer demand, or its echo, passes is another problem. By far the greatest of these problems is paying for the eventual retirement of the "babies" and filling the gaps in the labor force that will be created. It is to this issue that we now turn.

9.3 Children and the Saving Shift

The dramatic rise in the economy-wide savings rates beginning in the middle of the 19th century was made possible by increasing incomes. An increase in saving relative to aggregate income meant that more investment could be financed. This freed up resources for more machinery and equipment, more social infrastructure, more manufacturing plants (and houses) along with greater inventories. These all contribute to the growth of the economy's capital stock, that is, its productive capability.[3] Historically, as aggregate income grew, saving continued to increase and contribute to yet further economic income growth *and* development. The rise in the saving rate tended to be slower in those countries which had experienced their industrial transition earlier in history and more rapid in those economies which followed. The follower economies were also able to access the saving of the countries that had transformed earlier in the form of capital imports which supplemented domestic saving. In the late

Age in five year intervals

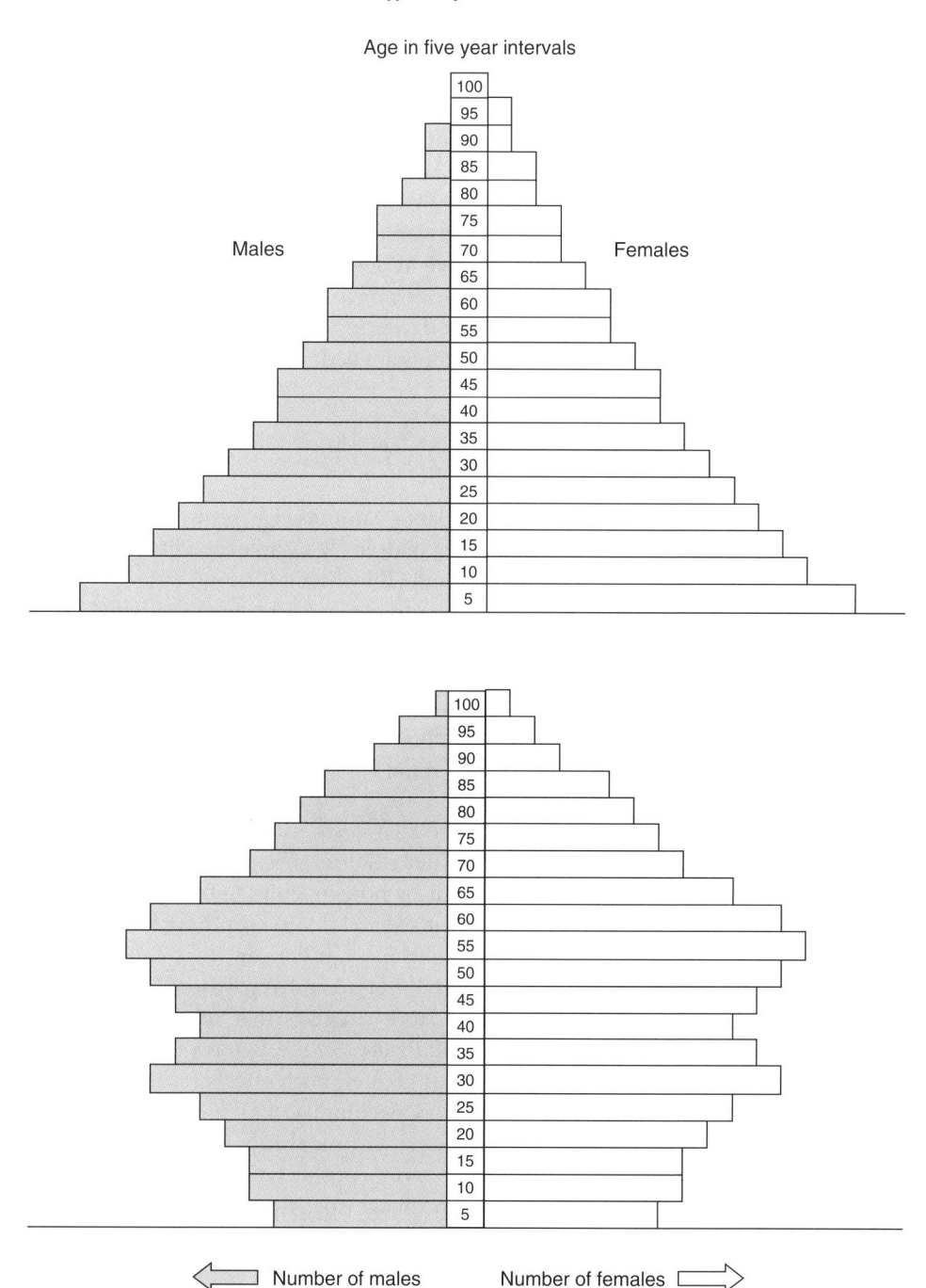

Males | Females

← Number of males   Number of females →

Figure 9.2 Population Pyramids, Representations.
Note: The above are representative population pyramids for the early modern era with its high mortality and for the modern era in OECD and many less developed countries. The latter captures the "baby boom" of the post-1945 era.

19th century countries such as the United States, Canada, Argentina and Australia, among others, all benefited from capital imports originating in Europe, mostly Great Britain.[4] The lower saving rate in these countries in the 19th century was itself a result of higher dependency rates than those of Europe.[5] (Earlier, when discussing immigration, it was seen that the countries of large net immigration had a younger age structure.) However, in the opinion of Jeffrey Williamson, the rapidity of the shift in the US saving rate at mid-19th century was accelerated due to the method of financing, and then retiring, the war-debt from its Civil War.[6] Saving is made up of personal saving and the (net) saving of business and government. The financing of the war by debt issues can be thought of as a government device to force the private sector to save.

Saving is what is left over after all expenditures are deducted from all income and is given by the following:

$$S_t = (E_t + rK_t + R_t) - (C_t + P_t)$$

where S_t is saving, and income is made up of labor earnings (E_t), returns at (r) rate on capital (K_t) and repayments and income from children (R_t), and expenditures are consumption (C_t) and the rearing costs of children (P_t) where t is time.

For each individual family, child-rearing costs rise as child mortality rates drop. However, this is not a straightforward relationship. As the number of children in a family rises, they may not all attract the same rearing costs. Hand-me-down clothes, older children supervising the younger ones and other such family economies make the extra cost of the next child less than the previous one. Some claim that historians have underestimated the economies of scale of the family.[7] But, it is also evident that, with the drop in child mortality, children live longer, and they incur more in rearing-costs as teenagers than they did as infants, so that costs are dependent on the age-structure of the children in the family. The net result is that, when there are fewer children, a family's rearing costs go down but by how much is an open question. As the children age, there will be an offset in that older children cost more.[8]

The fall in fertility and the lowering of child mortality meant that children now survived with greater frequency. This resulted in a greater repayment contribution to family income. The prevalence of child labor suggests that some recapture of rearing costs was made quite early in the child's life. So the P_t term falls and the R_t term rises. Although the fall in rearing costs is greater, both effects result in a rise of saving. This means the family now owns more accumulated savings, which we call capital resources K_t. This, in turn, further adds to income through the return on past savings. And, because income has now risen, more current saving is induced. This is the familiar loop that all starts with the decline in age-specific mortality – particularly among the young.[9]

All historical economies that passed through the demographic transition experienced a rise in the saving rate that in some part was due solely to the adaptability of the family. There was no historical norm since the elements that created the saving (rearing costs, number of children, repayments by children and accumulated savings and their rate of return) varied. Frank Lewis has estimated that about one quarter of the saving shift in the 19th century US was directly attributable to these fundamental changes in demographic behavior. For the United States, the domestic saving rate

Macroeconomic Effects of the Industrial Transition 291

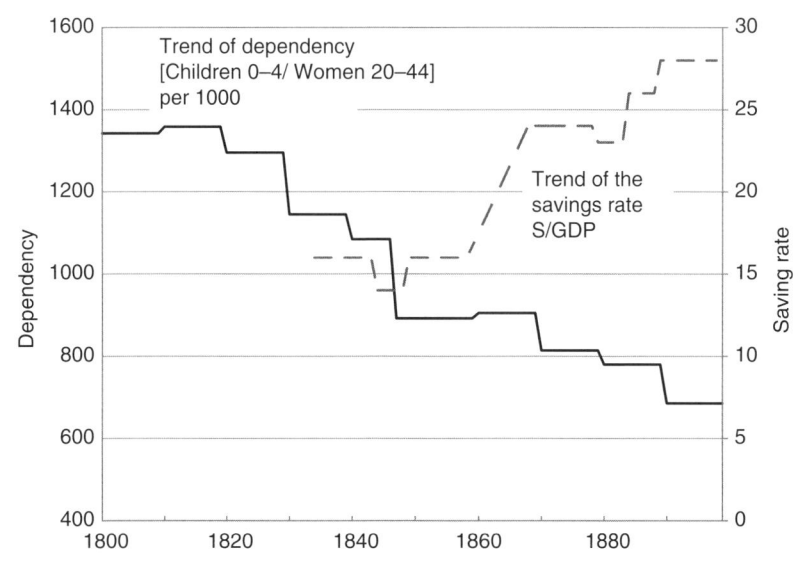

Figure 9.3 Shift in the Saving Rate and Dependency in the 19th Century United States.
Sources: Gallman, 1966; Haines, 2006, *US Historical Statistics*, Table Ab315–346.

(S/GDP) rose by approximately six percentage points in the mid- to late-19th century. In the predominantly agricultural economy, thirty years prior to the US Civil War, it was about 16% of national income. By the late 19th century the savings rate stood at about 22% of national income and, given the relationship between savings and investment, so did the investment rate.[10]

The greatest single economic action of individuals causing the aggregate saving rate to increase was, not surprisingly, the movement from rural to urban places. Opportunities in urban areas in the form of higher wages offered the possibility of a higher income than could be earned by remaining in a rural area. At the start, specialization in the farm-service sector (e.g., meatpacking) and the demand for urban goods and services (e.g., transport) accelerated the trend. Incentives to have fewer children, as has been noted, came to predominate. Figure 9.3 shows the decline in child dependency and the rise in the saving rate in the US in the 19th century.

9.4 Intergenerational Contracts or Life Cycles: Pensions

The industrial transition, the growth in income and the increase in life expectancy gave rise to a large, older, non-working population. This led to a problem: how does society fund the growing aged dependency ratio? It is a modern problem not only because of the unprecedented extension of life expectancy in recent years, but also the rapid decline in the net reproduction rate and the baby-boom generation that is fast approaching retirement. A perfect storm of old-age!

In a simple steady-state world, without demographic change, the model of peasants and pensions in Chapter Four suggests a method of funding pensions through the

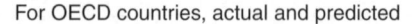

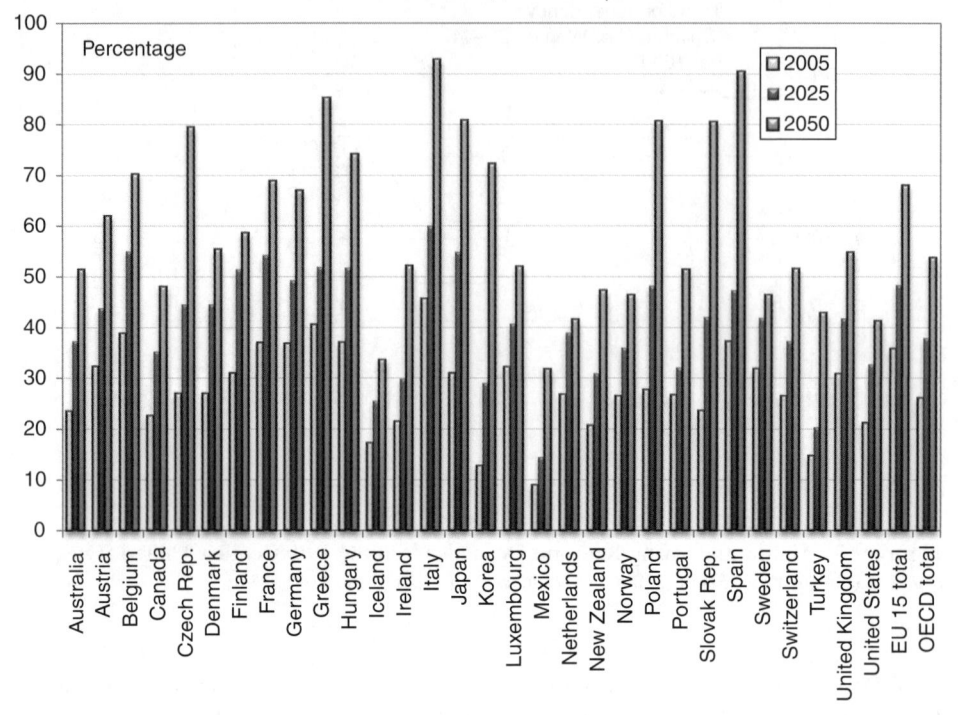

Figure 9.4 Percentage of Inactive Population Aged 65 and Over to the Total Labor Force. *Source*: data from OECD (2008) *Factbook 2007*.

extended family. At the family level, the current generation has less consumption in order that the older generation has some. At the same time provision must be made for the children; they are the pension givers to the next generation of the elderly – their parents. We can think of this as a tax on the current working generation to finance the dependent young and old.

In theory, a state can act much as the simple family economy. In reality, many states do not. For those who do, at the aggregate level, the state acts as the re-distributor of income among generations. It taxes people during their working lives and pays out during their old age. In a steady state, it does both simultaneously knowing that the revenues will always occur in about the same amount as the payouts required. In so acting, the state is both an *inter-generational transfer* device and an *insurer* – offering insurance against the risk of ungrateful offspring or grateful but impecunious children, no children, or no surviving male children. This can only be sustained, however, if the proportion of the dependent aged is not increasing. But the proportions are changing and are projected to do so for some time as illustrated for the OECD countries in Figure 9.4.

But most governments are more than a simple transfer device. They are also mandated to achieve income redistribution goals, some more and some less. Theoretically, nobody is left to starve and die on the streets, although some still do even in the most prosperous of countries. These two roles, however, are in conflict and lead to several basic problems with the inter-generational transfer of retirement funding. They are:

i) What should the state do with the elderly who have never worked and therefore never been taxed? The list is surprisingly long: many married women, the injured, the mentally and physically disabled and the feckless who have never worked.[11]
ii) Should the state provide everyone with the same retirement benefit regardless of their contribution to taxes or should the benefits be proportional to their tax contributions?

There is a trade-off between equity considerations and the willingness of the current working generation to be taxed.

In practice, the state has encouraged part of this function of funding retirement to be assumed by private pension plans through the use of tax incentives – what economists call a *tax expenditure*. But the principle is the same; tax the current workers to fund the retirement of the former workers. This introduces discrimination based on pay that leads to higher pensions for the higher income earners since such pensions usually promise a percentage of salary on retirement. But this strategy leads to yet further problems. If no funds are set aside for future pensions, the corporation, firm or even government agency (including legislators) has assumed a potentially huge unfunded liability. Of course, if a firm carries such unfunded pension liabilities, it can go out of business, and those contributing to its private pension scheme are left empty-handed. For this reason, the courts in most jurisdictions have accorded the pension plan the first right to the firm's surviving assets. So, most firms actually amass a fund of the excess of payments into and out of the plan. When this is done in conjunction with the employees (who also pay in) or their representatives (such as a union) and a neutral agent manages the fund, the plan is outside of the company control. The result is that it reduces the unfunded liabilities and gives some security of funding for future pensioners. If, however, the company simply amasses the fund on its own account, it accomplishes the former but leaves the employees exposed to the risks of corporate use of the fund (and possible loss) and corporate failure.

The only other method of providing for retirement is the *life cycle* approach. Each working generation finances its own retirement through savings set aside for that purpose. Contributions are made to private plans, typically by both the employer and the employee, and these savings are then invested and secured against default. They are not available until a fixed age or retirement date. If a plan experiences excess gains, earnings greater than accountants estimate are necessary for future pensions, those gains are accumulated by the firm and either kept by it or passed on to the members as reduced premiums. Such pensions are *defined benefit* schemes. Typically a defined benefit scheme promises a percentage of salary per year or percentage of some average salary. Often such schemes are portable so there is no, or little, pension benefit loss when moving employment. An alternative scheme which is increasingly popular is the *defined contribution* one. In this case, the employer and employee make regular contributions, say 5% of salary each, and the funds are vested, solely for the use of the employee upon retirement. Defined benefit and defined contribution are different in one important regard: any gains in the defined contribution pension fund from the investment by the fund manager accrue only to the worker. Upon retirement the employee is entitled to a lump-sum payment which typically must be used to purchase an annuity or committed to some other approved financial plan. Most jurisdictions

> ## Pension Terms and Issues
>
> **Life Annuity:** a financial instrument which makes regular (e.g. monthly) payments to individuals for the rest of their lives. It is purchased from an insurance company (usually) and the payments are determined by the purchase price, average life expectancy of the group and the rate of return on the funds not yet disbursed. Various types of life annuities can be purchased: fixed for a certain number of years, joint and last survivor (for spouses), inflation indexed, and so on.
>
> **Defined Benefit Plan:** a plan which defines a retirement benefit such as, the average salary over the best five years' employment (usually the last five years) × some fraction (0.65 is common). Typically both the employer and employee contribute. There may be other benefits such as continued health insurance or life insurance.
>
> **Defined Contribution Plan:** a plan that defines the contributions of the employer and the employee to the pension plan. Such a plan is usually administered by a third party trust. On retirement the individual is given a lump-sum which is the accumulated total contributions and the compound earnings on these contributions over time. Typically, this lump-sum is used to purchase a life annuity although other investment options are available in some jurisdictions.
>
> **Tax Subsidized Retirement Plans:** a plan where the state permits payments into the scheme to be non-taxable benefits. There are limits to how much one can contribute in any year – usually some percentage of income such as 7.5%. Accumulated earnings of the plan are also free of tax. However, when withdrawals are made (through an annuity, for instance) they are taxed as income. In order to avoid using such schemes as a method of estate building and avoiding tax altogether a minimum amount of withdrawal is usually required each year. Some of the schemes below are on this general type.
>
> For an international comparison of various state pensions see: Wakeham (2003). A thorough review of social security schemes is: United States (2009).

offer some tax-sheltering to the pension fund (tax is paid not when the funds are first received, but when they are received as pension) thus increasing its value. Not unreasonably, the fund, at retirement, must be used for the intended purpose.

Pensions are not equal in amount if they provide a payment stream that is based on (or are proportional to) salary or income contributions. As such they discriminate on the basis of the acquired labor market characteristics (education, initiative, aptitude, periods of employment and so on) that determine wages and salaries. However, let's consider a case of what the labor market might consider non-discrimination. A male and female of exactly the same age had identical educations and employment histories.

Each received the same salary at similar points in their careers and has made similar contributions to a pension fund which earned an identical rate of return on investments. Both decided to retire at age 65 and had identical sums for the purchase of an annuity. So far these individuals are identical in all vital respects, and each has ended their working lives with the same pension endowment. They have been treated equitably. But life expectancy at age 65 is greater for women than for men. The lump-sum pension endowment, and its subsequent earnings, has to be spread over more years for the woman and, hence, her monthly pension income in retirement would be lower than that of the man. So a non-discriminating society ends up treating the woman differently by the standard of monthly, or annual, pension payments. How did we end up here?

On the presumption that society does not wish to discriminate among individuals based on *arbitrary* personal characteristics which are those assigned simply by being born (ethnicity, race, gender and so on), but does wish to discriminate among *acquired* labor market characteristics, there is only one possible solution to this ethical dilemma. Even if it were possible, we cannot pay women more simply because they are women in order to give them a large enough pension endowment at age 65 to provide the same monthly income as a man. (A corollary is that woman should not be paid less than men based only on gender.) So the ethical solution is to average the male and female life expectancy tables to reflect unisex life expectancy values. The identical woman and man receive the same compensation throughout their lives and end up with similar pension payments.[12] Many national, state and provincial governments and public institutions have adopted unisex life tables for calculating pension payouts. Few jurisdictions, however, have mandated the use of the unisex life table for pension payments.

Public pensions for the elderly do not follow a common pattern country to country. Yet, most are based on contributions deducted from income or wages as a tax, usually at the source of employment – and remitted from tax revenue. However, individual eligibility varies as does the adequacy of funding with respect to the actuarial goals. Social Security in the US, the State Pension in the UK and the Canada Pension Plan, for instance, are all funded in a different manner. Only the last of these three is actuarially sound. However, all of these countries and most of Western Europe and Canada offer additional plans that are based on funding out of current tax revenues – old age security schemes and income supplements. Herein lie important demographic issues. The population changes that have taken place in the past fifty years or so, increasing dependency and falling fertility, guarantee an increasing need for tax revenue. Indeed, the future tax burden well could be unsupportable. In recognizing this, some measures already have been taken. For instance, the UK Government has announced an increased eligibility age for the State Pension which will be raised to age 68 for both men and women over the course of the next few years. Current eligibility is 65 years of age for men and 60 for women. France, Germany and the US have done the same. While these changes violate the implicit contract with workers, they may be tolerated by them so long as the changes are small. This is politically dangerous territory: anger the taxpayer or anger those receiving or expecting a certain level of retirement funding. Most governments have also begun the transition from an inter-generational mode of funding to that based on a life cycle approach.

In the late 19th century the "age of retirement" was declared to be 70 years of age by the autocratic Prussian Chancellor Otto von Bismarck. Paternalistic in nature, his social policy had the laudable aim of providing a comfortable end to the few final years of life otherwise spent in drudgery. A modest state pension financed the individual's retirement from the workplace. In a rush of similar late Victorian sentiment, many nations copied this policy. Retirement was later reduced to 65 years of age. The cost was not great as the pensions were small and the pensioners did not live much beyond age 65. Private pension plans followed suit, and the mandatory retirement age soon became the norm for members of these plans. These pension plans ran into the actuarial problem of increasing life expectancies of the elderly. This placed additional financial pressure on them. In recent years, the economic and financial burden bumped into another concern, the civil or human rights one. The heart of the issue was a particular view of contesting "rights."

Discrimination on the basis of age was explicit in most of the public and private pension arrangements. Yet, many nations have a prohibition against age-related discrimination in their constitutions, bills, charters and declarations of rights, and by legislation supporting and clarifying human rights.[13] Australia, Canada and the United States, for instance, have more or less abandoned mandatory retirement as required by their courts interpreting domestic law (they still have a minimum age eligibility for age-related benefits). Other nations have prohibitions on age related discrimination, but they do not extend that beyond "retirement age." The United Kingdom, to note one country, has laws against age discrimination in the workplace but also has a national default retirement age of 65 (soon to be raised as noted above). Although a worker can request continued employment beyond their normal retirement date, this is only a right "to be considered."[14] Both the UN and European human rights charters are hopelessly vague on age discrimination, although they are quite forthright on other forms of discrimination.[15] The Court of Justice of the European Communities has recently upheld compulsory retirement policies if they produce a national social benefit. Individual rights and social rights are put in conflict. For instance, age discrimination is permitted in the UK and justified because a national employment strategy exists – although one is hard pressed to find out what it is.[16] In general, there is no certainty that such policies as employment strategies make economic sense despite government claims. As in the British case, to claim that workers must exit the labor market in order to create room for new entrants is a short-run (static) argument, at best short-sighted and wrong in any other time-frame with flexible factors of production and an open immigration policy.

The European so-called solution to the graying of the labor force is to rely on a steady inflow of immigrants, with the appropriate levels of human capital, to forestall market shortages. Of course, many non-European countries also have adopted this policy. The immigrants lower the average age of those being taxed. But, such policy alternatives are, by themselves, doomed to fail eventually. Only if impossibly large immigration flows took place (and they were continued in the future) could such a policy succeed. The only reasonable solution is the extension of the working life and the introduction of greater flexibility about the age of retirement. This makes sense given the greater life expectancy and heightened awareness of the equity issues.[17] The underlying and immediate issue is the demographic bulge that has been working its way through most economies since the end of World War II by raising the dependency ratio.

9.5 The Work-Leisure Choice

The choice between work and non-work, called leisure time, if made voluntarily is another choice with macroeconomic consequences. The choice is one of the affluent and resulted from the long-term rise in workers' per capita income. By revealed preference, workers historically have altered their desired time-pattern of daily work, especially in the manufacturing and service sectors. Workers chose to work less. That is, they chose to take more leisure. (In this context leisure is defined as any time not at work.) In the US, before the Civil War, the workday was from sunup to sundown. Between the Civil War and the World War I, the average hours per day spent in manufacturing occupations dropped steadily, slowly at first and then more rapidly – see Table 9.1. The gain of leisure came from both the reduction of hours spent working each day and the reduction of the number of days worked. The practice of only working a half day on Saturdays became more common. This change in the amount of social time or leisure came about because workers could afford it. The rise in real wages and the fact that proportionately more workers were in the high-wage sector (a result of the industrial shift) meant workers earned more discretionary income. In addition, in some decades, the relative decline in immigration meant that greater attention had to be paid to the demands of domestic workers – for instance, the decades of the 1860s, 70s, and 90s.[18] The increasing pressure to reduce the hours of work was evident through labor unions, government legislation at the state and federal level, and the popular sentiment for social reform. This gain in leisure time was not restricted to manufacturing. Indeed the US federal government's first major intervention to control the hours of work was in the government (service) and later transportation services. Twenty years before the US Civil War a ten-hour day was mandated in the federal civil service.[19] However, it was not until the 20th century that similar legislation was passed which regulated the hours of work of non-federal employees.

Table 9.1 Estimates of the Average Hours Worked Per Day in US Manufacturing, 1850–1919.

Year	Average Hours Worked Per Day
1850	11.0
1860	11.0
1880	10.5
1890	10.3
1900	9.8
1909	9.5
1919	8.7

Source: adapted from Cain and Paterson (1981).

In all European countries that record statistics on the hours of work, an increase in leisure time similar to that in the US and Canada occurred during the first half of the 20th century. The British gain of leisure time was slightly earlier than that in most other European countries. Reduction of the hours of work often took the form of defining a Saturday as a half day of work. The British Factory Act of 1874 became the model by dictating early Saturday closing in the textile industry. By 1920 the tendency was to demand the elimination of some or all Saturday employment. While in countries such as the US, Canada, and the UK, some gains were made in the late 19th century, the major reduction in the hours of work came in the first half of the 20th century. Unfortunately international comparisons are inconsistent in data coverage and definition so ranking the gains is not possible. Nevertheless, the gains in France may have been as high as 28% (1900–1952).[20] At mid-20th century Europeans tended to work slightly longer (44 hours per week) than Americans and Canadians (approximately 40 hours a week). But Europeans tended to have more holidays (which are not part of the computation). Today they are essentially the same, below 40 hours – apart from the longer holidays.[21] Of course, there were variations in the short-run. In the inter-war period some of the reduction in the hours of work was a social response to unemployment as a method of work-sharing (unions), and, as in the British coal mining industry, some additions to hours worked were a demand from employers. However, despite the variation, the long-run trend was for a reduction in the hours worked.

The demand for leisure can be thought of in the continuum of time. Time, say an hour, may be used for either work or leisure but clearly not both at the same time. (This is not to argue that some jobs do have a pleasurable component.) If we value the opportunity cost of time, as the wage rate increases the price of non-working – leisure time becomes more expensive. That is, a worker has to forgo an hour of work, an hour's income, to purchase an hour of leisure time. Normally we would expect an increase in the price to reduce consumption of the good in question. But, as we have seen, there was an absolute decline in the working week. Leisure is a normal good, one which is consumed in greater quantities the more income rises. As the price of leisure rose, the effect of increased income (more consumption of leisure) overcame the effect of the increased relative price of leisure (less consumption of leisure).[22] A recent study in the UK found that, at the existing wage rate, British workers would prefer about 4.3 hours per week more leisure than they are currently consuming.[23] The actual hours of work are greater than the desired hours of work. We suspect that the results of this large-scale British survey are perfectly general in the high income per capita countries.

Modern studies of leisure time use show that we increasingly absorb our free time with socializing with friends, arts and culture, watching television (more for men and less for women), sports (watching), and active leisure activities including sports participation. Even those engaged in active sports and similar activities spend more time watching television and for the population as a whole it is more than twice as much than active pursuits.[24] Clearly our passivity is a cause of the obesity crisis of recent years (see Chapter Eight). But how did the demand for more leisure time manifest itself in the mid-19th century when it first became evident in the decline of time at work?

Popular entertainment, including sport, flourished as the working week shrank in the mid-19th century. Additional leisure time created opportunities for both players and spectators. For example, in England, informal games resembling football (soccer) trace back millennia, but interscholastic competition between English schools were common by 1848.[25] After graduation, former students formed clubs in their home cities. Eventually all-star elevens began to compete. The Football Association was formed in 1863. Eight years later, the year that baseball's National Association was formed in the United States, the association established the FA Cup, an open-entry tournament still in existence.

THE FIRST GYMNACYCLIDIUM FOR LADIES AND GENTLEMEN.

COPYRIGHT SECURED BY PEARSALL BROS.   STARRY & REILLY ENG.

OPENING EXHIBITION AND HOP AT THE GRAND VELOCIPEDE ACADEMY

Or Gymnacyclidium, containing over 8,000 square feet for Riding, with Gallery and Seats for about 1,500 people, by the

PEARSALL BROTHERS!

Originators of Velocipede Schools in this Country, at the

APOLLO BUILDING, CORNER BROADWAY & 28th STREET,

Main entrance on 28th Street.

On **MONDAY EVENING, APRIL 5th, 1869,**

Commencing at 8 o'clock.

MUSIC BY DODWORTH'S BAND.

The Gymnacyclidium: All the Rage in 1869

With growing disposable income, individuals regaled themselves of many new entertainments during the second half of the 19th century: the music halls, vaudeville, spectator and participation sports amongst others. The gymnacyclidium was clearly not for the faint-hearted and catered to a younger set.

Source: *Library of Congress*, Prints and Photographs Division, Washington.

During the last quarter of the century, working-class English men increasingly played football and imitated the club structure. Oxbridge graduates, over-represented both in the Football Association administration and the football-playing population in and around London, refused to play against anyone who was paid to play. Industrial worker-players from the Midlands and the north of England, however, could ill afford trips to distant games as the majority continued to be held outside employment.[26] Given England's compactness, football teams and their fans could leave for most away games Saturday at noon (the end of the British working week until the 1950s), play a game against a closely-matched opponent in the late afternoon, and return home Saturday evening.[27]

In a similar fashion, a few years later in the Northeastern United States, baseball evolved from rounders, a popular children's game. Young men formed social clubs that made arrangements for fields where members could play. The game spread rapidly among the troops during the US Civil War and among the population at large when the troops returned home.[28] In 1862 William Cammeyer made his Brooklyn property available free to local clubs that agreed to let him charge spectators admission.[29] His innovation spread quickly, but soon the teams began to collect the revenues. When receipts surpassed operational expenses, the surplus was used to entice "crack" players away from other teams, though players of more modest talent expected no compensation.[30] Eventually club all-star "first nines" began to travel to play other clubs' all-stars, but there was no consolidated schedule or championship until the formation of the National Association. The greater distances in the United States meant that quality baseball teams had to travel so far that no player could maintain outside employment during the season. Similarly, few supporters could travel to away games, so attendance was almost exclusively local fans. The entire roster of a top American baseball team became fully professional of necessity. Sport had become entertainment, the opportunity to witness the spectacle of professional sport.

Workers also had more leisure time to take an active part in sport. Many factories sponsored work teams both in Europe and North America. Many of these date to the later part of the 19th century. For families, more time was available for entertainment which was supported by the rising incomes. Pianos became a popular purchase for the more affluent families. Sing-songs around the piano became a feature of family life.[31] For the less affluent, and outside the home, minstrel shows were popular events in North America prior the Civil War to be replaced by vaudeville later in the 19th century. In Britain music halls thrived.[32] Usually for men alone, bars and public houses absorbed some of the growing income and expanding leisure hours in alcohol consumption. Since it led to the inevitable social problems and over-spending, thus taking away some of the families' core income, it spawned an active temperance movement that was especially virulent in the US.

To summarize, as incomes rose, as economic growth and development took place working hours began to decrease as a result of a general demand for more leisure. The increase in leisure time led to increased participation in activities that spawned entirely new industries.

A Football (Soccer) Team

Immigrant communities often centered their social activities in clubs. Here the Vancouver Chinese Student Football team in 1926 provided both a sports outlet for these strapping young men and a source of pride for their fellow citizens, especially as they were cup winners.
Source: The Wallace B. Chung and Madeline H. Chung Collection, University of British Columbia.

9.6 Time Spent in Household Work

The drop in aggregate work hours, the increase in leisure time, is often assumed to have led to a dramatic decrease in the time devoted to household work over the first two-thirds of the 20th century. The usual support proffered for this assumption focuses on the diffusion of household appliances that contributed to a reduction in the time required for household production and a reduced cost of having children. The former increased the labor force participation of women; the latter contributed to the baby boom.[33] However, there is no consensus on whether the facts confirm the assumption.

Economists who argue that the facts are in agreement with the assumption generally follow the work of Stanley Lebergott who made rough estimates of the time housewives spent on home production.[34] Valerie Ramey has argued that Lebergott based his estimates, inadvertently, on "the wrong table in a key dissertation and on the assumptions of a social activist (Charlotte Gilman) who conducted no study."[35] Other economists, following on the work of Ruth Schwartz Cowan (1983), maintain that, while technology has reduced the drudgery of home production, it did not reduce the time. Cowan notes:

> modern technology enabled the American housewife of 1950 to produce single-handedly what her counterpart of 1850 needed a staff of three or four to produce: a middle-class standard of health and cleanliness …
>
> Cowan (1983).

By the 1950s the new household technologies and their spread had broken down the older social indicators that marked different levels of personal cleanliness and domestic hygiene.

During the first half of the 20th century, while electricity, gas, and water were being diffused, knowledge was being diffused to housewives that maintaining a clean house and preparing nutritious meals could improve the health of their families. Joel Mokyr (2000), attempting to explain what he termed "the Cowan Paradox," argued that standards of cleanliness and nutrition were increasing at the same time, so that the output of household production rose substantially.

Ramey, focusing exclusively on US data, calculated that, rather than a reduction of the approximately 42 hours per week that Lebergott reported for the period 1900 to 1966, it fell by only six hours for prime age women, and "all of that change could be accounted for by the number and age of children and the increased education levels of housewives."[36] Further, the time spent in home production by prime age men increased by seven hours over the same period. Over the next ten years, women continued to devote less time to home production, a reduction of nine additional hours, while the time spent by men only increased by an hour. The time spent by prime age individuals on average rose a little between 1900 and 1965, then fell by four hours from 1965 to 1975. Over the last quarter of the 20th century, Ramey estimates that hours for prime age individuals fell slightly and then recovered. If the contributions of children and older adults are included in the calculation, time spent in home production per capita, increased by about two hours over the century.

Data from a large number of countries assembled by the Multinational Time Use Study (MTUS) tell a similar story for a more recent period. In the MTUS coding, household work comprises seven major activities: Cooking/Washing Up, Housework, Odd Jobs, Gardening, Shopping, Child Care, and Domestic Travel.[37] Most of these involve several individual activities that may have been reported individually in a national study. For example, Domestic Travel is defined to include such activities as accompanying an adult or child (e.g., taking them to a doctor or to school), travel to and from shopping, and travel to take care of someone else. The MTUS currently has 39 such studies that are coded in a consistent format. Table 9.2 reports the average hours per week women and men each report they expend on household work. Average hours are calculated here only for individuals 18–64 years of age who report that they are not a student. The studies are identified by the country and the year they began. Four did not report numbers for all seven activities, and those are duly noted by an asterisk in the table. The first study was done in 1961; the last, in 2003. The statistical relationship of hours of household work by sex versus year, with controls for the countries with multiple studies (Canada, Netherlands, Norway, UK, and US) suggests women annually reduced the amount of time they spent on household work by 9.5 minutes over those years. Men annually increased the amount of household work they did by 13.0 minutes over the same period. This means that over this 42-year period, the total time men and women spent doing household work annually increased by 3.5 minutes per year, or just under 2.5 hours in total.

Table 9.3 looks at the seven categories for the US individually to better understand what underlies these changes. A simple comparison of the results for 1965 with those for 2003 suggests that the reduction in women's time is largely attributable to Cooking/Washing up and Housework; the other five categories all involved an *increase* in time. The amount of time men spent in household work increased in every category. While men cook and wash up 0.8 hours more than they once did,

Table 9.2 Average Weekly Hours of Household Work, Various Countries, 1960s to Present.

Year	Country	Women	Men	Year	Country	Women	Men
1960s				**1990s**			
1961	UK	34.9	9.6	1990	Netherlands	35.9	16.8
1964	Denmark*	34.6	6.8	1990	Norway	31.5	17.8
1965	USA	40.4	12.0	1991	Germany	40.1	18.8
1970s				1992	Austria	40.1	12.8
1971	Canada	38.0	14.5	1992	Canada	34.4	17.7
1971	Norway	42.5	13.9	1992	USA	27.7	16.9
1974	Australia	40.5	12.1	1995	Netherlands	33.4	17.3
1974	UK	32.6	10.0	1995	UK*	32.5	16.6
1975	Netherlands	40.8	13.3	1998	Canada	31.8	18.6
1975	USA	35.7	16.9	1998	France	36.2	19.8
1980s				1998	USA*	31.6	20.9
1980	Netherlands	40.1	15.1	**2000s**			
1981	Canada	32.0	17.3	2000	Netherlands	35.0	22.0
1981	Norway	34.9	15.8	2000	Norway	31.9	20.6
1983	UK	35.2	15.7	2000	Slovenia	38.0	20.5
1985	Netherlands	37.9	16.6	2000	South Africa	34.7	13.1
1985	USA	32.7	17.6	2000	UK	32.7	19.0
1986	Canada	33.4	16.0	2001	Germany	32.3	18.3
1987	Denmark	27.1	15.6	2002	Italy	39.8	13.7
1987	UK	34.7	18.4	2002	Spain	37.6	12.9
1989	Italy*	41.3	9.7	2003	USA	35.1	23.1

Note: * Did not include information on all categories as earlier surveys.
Source: Multinational Time Use Study data base.

the reduction of 6.7 hours for women is the biggest single change observed. Once again this suggests the microwave oven played an important role, as did dishwashing machines and the sale of prepared foods. Indeed, a significant portion of the price of food now is attributable to the labor of others. Men have increased the amount of housework they do, but women's time has gone down. This calls attention to the increase in the number and efficiency of household appliances and products.

This simple impression seems statistically true.[38] The time women spent on Cooking/Washing up declined an annual average of 11.6 minutes per hour. This is same reduction as the total, meaning that the annual 5.8 minutes per hour reduction in Housework was cancelled by small increases in the other five activities. Men, on the other hand, increased the time they spent on every activity with the largest increase coming in Housework (an annual average increase of 4.5 minutes per hour). The overall annual increase in total time spent by men on household work, 14.7 minutes per hour, was greater than the decrease calculated for women.

If one adds women's and men's times together, even though there are many different living arrangements in the data from married couples to single individuals, the total time spent in household work increased annually by 3.1 minutes per hour between 1965 and 2003, or a total of just less than 2.0 hours in the US. This is

Table 9.3 Average Weekly Hours Spent in Household Tasks, the US, 1965–2003.

Year	Cooking & washing	Housework	Odd jobs	Gardening	Shopping	Childcare	Domestic travel	Total
1965								
women	12.5	11.9	3.0	0.3	2.7	5.7	4.3	40.4
men	1.4	1.2	2.7	0.2	1.6	1.3	3.6	12.0
total	13.9	13.1	5.7	0.5	4.3	7.1	7.9	52.5
1975								
women	10.1	9.0	3.0	0.7	3.6	4.3	4.9	35.7
men	1.5	2.5	4.6	0.7	2.0	1.3	4.3	16.9
total	11.6	11.6	7.7	1.4	5.6	5.6	9.2	52.6
1985								
women	8.8	9.3	1.1	0.8	4.1	4.2	4.5	32.7
men	2.4	4.5	2.4	0.8	2.5	1.2	3.9	17.6
total	11.1	13.8	3.5	1.6	6.6	5.4	8.4	50.3
1992								
women	5.4	7.4	3.2	0.3	3.8	2.7	5	27.7
men	1.8	3.4	4.1	0.3	2.1	0.8	4.3	16.9
total	7.3	10.7	7.3	0.6	5.9	3.5	9.3	44.6
1998								
women	5.6	8.5	1.3	nr	4.6	5.8	5.9	31.6
men	2.5	5.7	2.1	nr	2.5	3.3	4.8	20.9
total	8.1	14.2	3.4	nr	7.1	9	10.7	52.6
2003								
women	5.8	7.7	4.5	1.1	4.2	6.1	5.7	35.1
men	2.2	3.1	5.0	2.2	2.8	2.9	4.9	23.1
total	8.0	10.9	9.5	3.3	7	9	10.6	58.2

nr – not reported.
Source: US Multinational Time Use Study data base.

roughly one half hour less than the average of 2.5 hours for all the countries in Table 9.2. In sum, the weight of the evidence agrees with Ruth Cowan. The two categories on which much of the literature has focused, Cooking/Washing up and Housework, are the only two to show a decrease in the US data. These two, and only these two, agree with Stanley Lebergott. Both Shopping and Domestic Travel show increases of roughly 2.5 hours each, and one suspects this is largely attributable to the amount of time spent driving. The move from neighborhood stores to shopping malls and supermarkets and the involvement of children in more activities to which they are chauffeured for safety reasons involves greater distances, therefore more time.

Given the wide variety of activities that comprise household work, it should not be surprising that, as leisure hours increased, the amount of time committed to household work increased. While that work has come to involve less cooking and cleaning, we've used the hours that have been freed to garden, shop, and give our children a better quality of life – coaching their softball, soccer and hockey teams, for instance.

9.7 Education and Human Capital

In addition to the remarkable increase in physical capital that economic development made possible, the improvement in human capital was vital to the improvement in productivity and consequently individual well-being as we have seen throughout. From society's point-of-view, the increase of human capital formation was vital to both continued growth and development. Modern economists typically measure human capital in terms of years of formal education, but this may obscure other important contributions. For instance, apprenticeship schemes and on-the-job training are not typically counted when the years of schooling are assessed. The result is that we may under-estimate the amount of human capital embodied in the work force. Also not counted are the skills which are passed from parent to child such as those skills involved in farming. Nonetheless, the substantial differences in schooling are one of the distinguishing features of economic development. The least developed countries of today have educational levels lower than those of most of the OECD countries during the mid-19th century. This has been a substantial brake on their ability to improve the well-being of their populations.

In production, increases in the quality of labor make us capable of more and more complex tasks. A unit of labor today is not, on average, the same as a unit of labor historically. So the quality improvement of labor yields a direct gain in output. In addition, changes in aggregate productivity seem largely related to changes in human capital in an indirect way. For instance, the quicker the response of labor to incentives, such as higher wages, the quicker factors will be shifted from the lower to higher output activities (at the margin). So a high degree of industrial, occupational and geographic mobility helps move both labor and capital to their more efficient end-use more rapidly.

In history a major improvement in aggregate human capital came about as adult mortality began to decline, albeit slowly, in Europe and North America in the 17th century. To be sure, there was much variation, but the trend of decline in adult mortality is evident in most available data from Western Europe and North America (Chapter Three). When someone's life is extended, obviously society has access to their human capital longer (even if it depreciates, which itself is an open question). Society saves the resources which otherwise would have to be spent more frequently to train replacements for that person. This is similar to the savings that lead to economic growth when human capital simply arrives embodied in immigrants. Consider carpenters of a certain life expectancy which suddenly rises. Society now has to spend less per year on training carpenters to maintain the same level of services – the same amount has to be spent to train one carpenter in total, but it is spent less frequently. In addition, and in aggregate, a decline in the adult mortality rate means that the economy now has more people in the working-age group, and this gives rise to an increased (derived) demand for human capital formation – more carpenters. This change in the composition of the population with its reduced dependency ratio often has been called the *compositional effect*.

The second aggregate consequence of the increased adult longevity is that it increased the pay-offs to investment in human capital – particularly education – due to the increased growth in aggregate income and the increased length of the pay off period (even when the future is discounted). Even though these effects were small, they did contribute a large proportion of the income gain in the immediate pre-modern and early modern periods, approximately 1675–1800. Thus, a rise in the life expectancy was a long-run source of economic growth.[39]

It is likely that some degree of literacy was necessary to build upon these gains noted above. Perhaps not surprisingly, by the 15th and 16th centuries it was the city states of Italy which likely had the highest proportions of their populations literate. In the 1560s, in Venice, about 26% of the males of school age (up to 15 years of age) attended school, although very few girls did. Most of these schools were communal and secular in nature. Many of them taught mathematics and, what we would call, "business studies" with double entry book-keeping a key subject. The net result was that one-third of the male population and one-eight of the female population was literate – the girls having been home-coached, sent to private tutors or learned to read and write in Sunday school.[40] The story is similar throughout Renaissance Italy. Other countries with high degrees of literacy for the times were Switzerland, Scotland, Germany (Prussia), the Netherlands and the Scandinavian countries – although we cannot be exact because of the absence of historical data. What researchers have proven, rather than simply surmised, is that literacy and quantitative reasoning (numeracy) are highly correlated and that both were more highly developed in Western Europe than Eastern Europe. This cognitive trait gave Western Europe a decided advantage by the early 1600s, and possibly earlier, to seed commercial development that was a prelude to agricultural and then industrial revolutions.[41]

As early as the mid 19th century there was concern in England that it was being outstripped by German and North American education. Table 9.4 shows a German–English gap of about 1.12 years in the average educational attainment. Notably, as Jason Long reports, Prussia had introduced mandatory school attendance in 1763; England did not do the same until 1870. A 19th century attempt to raise school attendance by direct subsidies to privately-run schools produced only a small

Table 9.4 Average Number of Years of Schooling of the Adult Population (15 to 64 Years of Age) of Selected Countries, 1870–2010.

	1870	1900	1930	1960	1990	2010
Select OECD Countries						
Australia	2.12	6.59	8.69	9.24	12.76	13.25
Canada	5.82	7.26	8.07	8.53	12.36	13.30
Denmark	4.74	5.74	6.76	8.50	11.54	12.32
France	4.04	6.63	8.01	8.61	11.61	12.74
Germany	5.25	6.36	7.68	8.94	13.21	12.74
Japan	1.67	2.98	5.90	8.90	11.93	13.11
United Kingdom	4.13	5.84	7.15	8.53	12.28	13.34
United States	5.57	7.09	8.46	10.29	12.76	13.62
Select Less Developed Countries						
Angola	0.06	0.06	0.07	0.10	1.90	2.92
Argentina	1.28	1.74	3.75	6.13	7.69	8.80
Ethiopia	0.07	0.09	0.10	0.12	1.25	2.60
India	0.04	0.04	0.38	1.17	3.15	5.32
Indonesia	0.58	0.58	0.78	1.60	5.98	7.99
Mali	0.09	0.13	0.17	0.21	0.95	1.60

Source: adapted from Morrison and Murtin (2009), Table 3.

aggregate gain.[42] At mid 19th century most Prussian children attended school while only about one-half of the English children did. The individual return to primary education in Britain was low compared to other countries. This is a sign that either the labor markets were not inducing the occupational mobility that other countries were or that the education itself was of low quality.[43] With educational accomplishment of only four to five years of school, a gap of over a year is significant because it is near the literate retention threshold – many adults with low levels of schooling forget their juvenile writing and reading abilities. If the comparison with Germany was galling to the British, the comparison between North American and the British children was even more so – see Table 9.4. In fact, the rise of schooling in Britain during the late 19th century was largely due to more girls entering the school system and not existing groups staying longer. And, for some decades, notably the 1880s, there was actually a decline in the hours spent in school by teenagers.[44] The Elementary Education Act of 1870 (England and Wales) had little observed effect beyond the targeted group of very young children. Historians have often pointed to this educational gap as *one of the sources* of the poor productivity record of Britain in the half century before World War I relative to those countries with higher proportions of their labor force with higher levels of schooling.

No country with a wide educational gap between itself and the leading countries closed it more effectively than Japan. With the Meiji Government which took power in 1868 educational reform began, slowly at first. The educational goals were i) to become accessible – previously it had been class based – and ii) to contribute to the modernization of the economy by building up the human capital stock. By the 1880s the Japanese government had a national system of compulsory elementary school education, but it explicitly rejected Western models at the elementary and high school levels. One of the by-products of this choice was that the system tended to become nationalistic which indirectly supported the cult of militarism in the years after World War I. This necessitated further reforms in the post 1945 period.[45] For university education the model was German. The broad political support of education and a vigorously growing economy meant that by 1930 much of the gap between Japan and the West had been closed. By the 1960s Japanese workers had achieved the country's long-term goals of educational parity with the West. But, they achieved more. The Japanese educational system has a substantially lower drop-out rate through to high school than other OECD countries.[46] This means that Japan not only has a high average level of educational accomplishment but a lower variance in achievement. Although Japanese economic growth has stalled in recent years, the long-term improvement in Japanese well-being was a direct product of the national education strategy.

A national strategy for educational improvement is often held only to be possible in a culturally homogeneous society such as Japan. But, in fact, it was the culturally diverse United States with its large immigrant population that achieved the highest (average) levels of education both in the 19th and 20th centuries. It came in two phases. First was the drive for compulsory primary education funded from local taxation. Second was what Claudia Goldin and Lawrence Katz have called 'the Great Transformation in American education'. Between 1910 and 1940 secondary school education became available to far more teenagers than in most other countries. The high school movement was the result of a no great political, national strategy, but it came from a general sense (indicated by economic factor such as higher wages) that this would improve the lives of individual citizens. It was financed as local supply responses to a demand for education that produced high *differential* rates of return. The egalitarian nature of the school system for the most part, the greater ability to absorb taxes than elsewhere – given the higher per capita income and wealth – and local consensuses were factors in the success of the high school movement.[47] Homogeneity of the population was important but only at the local school level and even then it was more about shared educational goals – how to use schooling to get ahead – rather than being culturally similar.

After World War II the great mushrooming of university enrollment was felt throughout the OECD countries. It happened more quickly in the US than elsewhere. The same trend, albeit somewhat slower, was evident in France and Germany; Britain lagged. Despite the high *differential* pay-off to increased schooling in the US, the rate of return to schooling in fact fell through most of the 20th century – until about 1980. At this point the skill premium, as this differential rate of return is often called, began to increase. Its rise was coincident with the technical revolution wrought by micro-chips and computers. The 20th century trend of declining personal income inequality was reversed in the last two decades of the century. The 20th century also saw the long decline in fertility; the opportunity cost of having children increased. This was itself a product of the reduced barriers facing women in formal education as well as a result of the skills premium. However, as seen elsewhere, those with lower levels of schooling or training and income tend to have a greater number of children than those with higher individual levels of human capital.

Even within the countries of the developed world, some groups did not share equally in their countries' education gains during the 20th century. This was more acute in the US than elsewhere. Without direct national funding, for the most part, its educational system was hostage both to the local willingness and local ability to provide the instruction for its school-aged population. For instance, it took about two generations for blacks who were the grandchildren of slaves to achieve the same level of literacy, occupational status and income as free black citizens' descendants. But the human capital gap between black and white Americans tended to converge even more slowly.[48] The educational gap was a product of several historical forces. First, blacks mostly lived in the South which after the US Civil War was a low income per capita region. It had less to spend on education. This affected all students, black and white. Second, restrictive legislation (called Jim Crow laws in the US although the name has no particular meaning) and racial segregation in the schools existed until the 1960s with its inevitable consequences of discrimination against black youngsters. Fewer resources were devoted to their schooling. Third, for black students the marginal gains to be made from remaining in school were lower than those of whites given the racial discrimination in the workplace. The Great Migration out of the South changed the background conditions as did a radical change in social attitudes, but it took a long time for black and white parity. Today, for the US as a whole, the high school completion rate for black students is the same as the US average – slightly higher for white students and lower for those of Hispanic ethnicity.[49] This is a remarkable change from as recently as 40 years ago when black student high school completion rates were significantly lower.

At the aggregate level the labor productivity gains accounted for by schooling can be thought of as in part *transitional* and in part *sustainable* or on-going. Transitional gains accrue because of changes in the educational system, an increasing proportion of investment devoted to education. Sustainable gains are those that occur due to the high quality of the labor force to work with (exogenous) technical change. Since per capita investment in schooling grew in the 20th century until at least the third quarter, part of the 20th century growth of income in OECD countries was transitional. In the future these countries will have to rely on labor productivity growth that is sustainable which is estimated to be about 1% annually for the US – compared to the combined effects of 1.6% in the 100 years since 1870.[50] Such evidence should be encouraging for the planners in the less developed countries of today. Countries such as those of sub-Saharan Africa with their low levels of schooling in the work force (Angola, Ethiopia and Mali for instance) can gather substantial productivity gains both from the transitional effects by increasing the share of investment in education *and* from sustainable productivity growth. Unfortunately, alone this will not do, as the human capital must have co-operating factors of production and institutions that are sympathetic to economic development.[51]

Historical shifts in the pattern of education, saving, inter-generational transfers and time allocation are all aggregate effects. They took (take) place relatively slowly. However, there were other shifts in the historical economies and their populations that were deleterious and, either rapid or slow, but inexorable. These we call catastrophes, the subject of the next chapter.

Endnotes

1. David and Wright (1997).
2. One of the most popular treatments of this subject is Foot (1996).
3. This is the process known as "capital deepening." See Cain and Paterson (1981); (1986) and Wright (1990).
4. Edelstein (1982).
5. Taylor and Williamson (1994).
6. Williamson (1974).
7. Kelley (1976).
8. David and Sanderson (1987); Turchi (1975).
9. Lewis (1983).
10. Lewis (1983); Williamson (1974).
11. There is a separate argument that the married women with children should be recognized as having contributed to GDP by providing child-rearing services and home care. This, it is argued, should entitle them to a pension that is proportional to their services valued at market prices for the services.
12. Some would argue that this means that in retirement men cross-subsidize women. Such an argument entirely misses the point, however. A Rawlsian definition of equity says that gender should never distinguish parts of the human family.
13. For instance: The Age Discrimination in Employment Act of 1967 and The Older Workers Benefit Protection Act of 1990, United States (1967 and 1990).
14. United Kingdom (2009).
15. United Nations (1948).
16. The Court of Justice of the European Communities (2007), Case C–388/07.
17. Maestas and Zissimopoulos (2010).
18. Whaples (1990).
19. Johnson and Libecap (1994).
20. McCormick (1959).
21. *Ibid*.
22. This results in the familiar backward bending supply of labor.
23. Stewart and Swaffield (1997).
24. Canada (current), Table 113-0001; for the UK see Lader, Short Gershuny (2006); The American Time Use Study can be accessed at http://www.bls.gov/news.release/pdf/atus.pdf
25. Young (1975) and Harris (1975). See Cain and Haddock (2005).
26. London's well-heeled amateur Old Etonians traveled to Lancashire to take on working-class Darwen. "The result was a draw, but Darwen were unable to travel to London for the replay. The Etonians offered to pay their fares, but the Darwen players simply could not afford the loss of wages…." Harris (1975).
27. In 1885, the Football Association reluctantly voted to allow payment for "broken time," or wages lost while playing and traveling. Harris (1975).
28. Harris (1975); Eckard (2005).
29. Kirsch (1989).
30. Within a year of Cammeyer's innovation the *Brooklyn Eagle* reported, "ballplaying has become quite a moneymaking business, many finding it to pay well to play well" (Rader, 2002).
31. Pianos were among the first goods to be sold on credit, an arrangement that requires consumers to earmark future saving to pay for past consumption.

32 For a history of British music hall see Bailey (1986). For North American vaudeville see Bordman (2004).
33 See Greenwood, Seshadri and Yorukoglu (2005); Albanesi and Olivetti (2009). All have argued that improvements in reproductive medicine and the invention of infant foodstuff, often called formula, were important to the increase in women's labor force participation.
34 Lebergott (1976, 1993). See also Fogel (2000); Folbre and Nelson (2000).
35 Ramey (2009).
36 Ramey (2009). Lebergott (1976) excludes the care of the family; Ramey includes it.
37 This is a slightly different definition than that used by Ramey, so the numbers are not strictly comparable.
38 Confirmed by regressions run for each activity and the sum.
39 Using data from Geneva and Venice, Boucekkine, de la Croix and Licandro (2003) estimate that the contribution of increased human capital may have been responsible for 70% of the differential growth rate, 28% from a 'composition effect' and 42% from increased levels of education.
40 Grendler (1989).
41 A' Hearn, Baten and Crayen (2009) argue that there was a closer correspondence between the east and west earlier in history and that the two areas diverged in proportionate literacy and numeracy for about 1000 years before the modern era. They have since converged.
42 Mitch (1986).
43 Long (2006).
44 Lord and Rangazas (2006).
45 Schoppa (1991).
46 Blinco (1993).
47 Goldin and Katz (2001 and 2008); Morrisson, Christian and Fabrice Murtin (2009).
48 For a cohort of blacks and whites that was born between 1950 and 1954 the white-black educational gap was 0.78 years, Sacerdote (2005). Collins and Margo (2003) also provide evidence of black school attendance based on Census data.
49 This is based on those 18 to 24 years of age who are not currently enrolled in secondary schools, United States (2009), Table 10.
50 Rangazas (2002).
51 Jones (2005).

References

A'Hearn, Brian, Dorothee Baten and Joerg Crayen (2009) "Quantifying Quantitative Literacy: Age Heaping and the History of Human Capital", *Journal of Economic History*, **69**(3), 783–808.

Albanesi, Stefania and Claudia Olivetti (2009) "Gender Roles and Medical Progress," National Bureau of Economic Research, Working Paper No. 14873, April.

Bailey, Peter, ed. (1986) *Music Hall: The Business of Pleasure*, Milton Keynes, England: Open University Press.

Blinco, Anne (1993) "Persistence and Education: A Formula for Japan's Economic Success", *Comparative Education*, **29**(2), 1–183.

Bordman, Gerald Martin, ed. (2004) *The Oxford Companion to American Theater*, New York: Oxford University Press.

Boucekkine, Raouf, David de la Croix and Omar Licandro (2003) "Early Mortality Declines at the Dawn of Modern Growth", *The Scandinavian Journal of Economics, Population Dynamics and Macroeconomic Performance*, **105**(3), 401–18.

Cain, Louis P. and David D. Haddock (2005) "Similar Economic Histories: Different Industrial Structures: Transatlantic Contrasts in the Evolution of Professional Sports Leagues," *Journal of Economic History*, **65**(4), 1116–47.

Cain, Louis P. and Donald G. Paterson (1981) "Factor Biases and Technical Change in Manufacturing: The American System, 1850–1919", *Journal of Economic History*, **41**(2), 341–60.

Canada (current) *Indicators of Well-being in Canada*, Human Resources and Skills Development Canada, Ottawa: www4.hrsdc.gc.ca.

Collins, William J. and Robert A. Margo (2003) "Historical Perspectives on Racial Differences in Schooling in the United States", National Bureau of Economic Research, NBER Working Paper 0714352.

Cowan, Ruth Schwartz (1983) *More Work for Mother: The Ironies of Household Technology from the Open Hearth to the Microwave*, New York: Basic Books.

David, Paul and Gavin Wright (1997) "Increasing Returns and the Genesis of American Resource Abundance", *Industrial and Corporate Change*, **6**, 203–45.

David, Paul and Warren Sanderson (1987) "The Emergence of a Two-Child Norm among American Birth Controllers", *Population and Development Review*, **13**(1), 1–41.

Eckard, E. Woodrow (2005) "Team Promotion in Early Major League Baseball and the Origin of the Closed Sports League," *Explorations in Economic History*, **42**(1), 122–52.

Edelstein, Michael (1982) *Overseas Investment in the Age of High Imperialism: The United Kingdom, 1850–1914*, New York, Columbia University Press.

Fogel, Robert William (2000) *The Fourth Great Awakening and the Future of Egalitarianism*, Chicago: University of Chicago Press.

Folbre, Nancy and Julie Nelson (2000) "For Love or Money – Or Both?" *Journal of Economic Perspectives*, **14**(4), (Autumn), 123–40.

Foot, David with Daniel Stoffman (1996) *Boom, Bust and Echo: How to Profit from the Coming Demographic Shift*, Toronto: Macfarlane Walter & Ross.

Gallman, Robert (1966) "Gross National Product in the United States, 1834–1909", in Dorothy S. Brady, ed., *Output, Employment and Productivity in the United States after 1800*, Studies in Income and Wealth, New York: National Bureau of Economic Research by Columbia University Press.

Goldin, Claudia and Katz, Lawrence (2001) "The Legacy of the US Educational Leadership: Notes on Distribution and Economic Growth in the 20th Century," *American Economic Review*, **91**(1), 18–23.

Goldin, Claudia and Katz, Lawrence (2008) *The Race between Education and Technology*, Cambridge, Mass.: Belknap Press of Harvard University Press.

Greenwood, Jeremy, Ananth Seshadri and Guillaume Vandenbroucke (2005) "The Baby Boom and Baby Bust," *American Economic Review*, **95**(2), 183–207.

Greenwood, Jeremy, Ananth Seshadri and Mehmet Yorukoglu (2005) "Engines of Liberation," *Review of Economic Studies*, **72**(1), 109–33.

Grendler, Paul F. (1989) *Schooling in Renaissance Italy: Literacy and Learning, 1300–1600*, Baltimore: The Johns Hopkins University Press.

Haines, Michael R. (2006) *Historical Statistics of the United States*, Ab315–346.

Harris, Harold Arthur (1975) *Sport in Britain: Its Origins and Development*, London: Stanley Paul.

Johnson, Ronald N. and Gary D. Libecap (1994) *The Federal Civil Service System and the Problem of Bureaucracy: The Economics and Politics of Institutional Change*, Chicago: University of Chicago Press.

Jones, Gavin W. (2005) "Human Capital Aspects of Economic Development: A Comparative Perspective in Asia", in eds. Shripad Tuljapurkar, Ian Pool and Vipan Prachuabmoh,

Wiphan Prachūapmo Rūpfōlō, *Population, Resources and Development, Riding the Ages Waves*, Vol. 1, The Netherlands: Springer.

Kelley, Allen C. (1976) "Savings, Demographic Change, and Economic Development", *Economic Development and Cultural Change*, **24**(4), 683–93.

Kirsch, George B. (1989) *The Creation of American Team Sports: Baseball and Cricket, 1838–7*, Urbana: University of Illinois Press.

Lader, Deborah Sandra Short and Jonathan Gershuny (2006) *The Time Use Survey, 2005; How We Spend Our Time*, London: Office for National Statistics.

Lebergott, Stanley (1976) *The American Economy*, Princeton: Princeton University Press.

Lebergott, Stanley (1993) *Pursuing Happiness*, Princeton: Princeton University Press.

Lewis, Frank D. (1983) "Fertility and Savings in the United States: 1830–1900", *Journal of Political Economy*, **91**(5), 825–40.

Long, Jason (2006) "The Socioeconomic Return to Primary Schooling in Victorian England", *Journal of Economic History*, **66**(4), 1026–53.

Lord, W. and P. Rangazas (2006) "Fertility and Development: The Roles of Schooling and Family Production", *Journal of Economic Growth*, **11**, 229–61.

Maestas, Nicole and Julie Zissimopoulos (2010) "How Longer Work Lives Ease the Crunch of Population Aging", *Journal of Economic Perspectives*, **24**(1), 139–60.

McCormick, Brian (1959) "Hours of Work in British Industry", *Industrial and Labor Relations Review*, **12**(3), 423–33.

Mitch, David F. (1986) "The Impact of Subsidies to Elementary Schooling on Enrolment Rates in Nineteenth-century England", *Economic History Review*, **39**(3), 371–91.

Mokyr, Joel (2000) "Why Was There More Work for Mother? Technological Change and the Household, 1880–1930," *Journal of Economic History*, **60**(1) (March), 1–40.

Morrisson, Christian and Fabrice Murtin (2009) "The Century of Education", *Journal of Human Capital*, **3**(1), 2–42.

Rader, Benjamin G. (2002) *Baseball: A History of America's Game*, 2nd edn, Urbana: University of Illinois Press.

Ramey, Valerie A. (2009) "Time Spent in Home Production in the 20th Century United States," *Journal of Economic History*, **69**(1), 1–48.

Rangazas, Peter (2002) "The Quantity and Quality of Schooling and US Labor Productivity Growth (1870–2000)", *Review of Economic Dynamics*, **5**, 932–64.

Sacerdote, Bruce (2005) "Slavery and the Intergenerational Transmission of Human Capital", *The Review of Economics and Statistics*, **87**(2), 217–34.

Schoppa, Leonard James (1991) *Education Reform in Japan: A Case of Immobilist Politics*, London: Routledge.

Stewart, Mark B. and Joanna K. Swaffield (1997) "Constraints on the Desired Hours of Work of British Men", *Economic Journal*, **107**, 441, 520–35.

Taylor, Alan M. and Jeffrey G. Williamson (1994) "Capital Flows to the New World as an Intergenerational Transfer", *Journal of Political Economy*, **102**(2), 348–70.

The Court of Justice of the European Communities (2007) *Case C-388/07*, curia.europa.eu/en/actu/communiques/cp09/aff/cp090019en.pdf

Turchi, Boone A. (1975) *The Demand for Children: The Economics of Fertility in the United States*, Cambridge, Mass.: Ballinger.

United Kingdom (2009) *Age Discrimination*, Direct Government. http://www.direct.gov.uk/en/Employment/DiscriminationAtWork/DG_10026429

United Nations (1948) *Universal Declaration of Human Rights, Adopted and proclaimed by General Assembly resolution 217 A (III) of 10 December 1948*. http://www.un.org/events/humanrights/2007/udhr.shtml

United States (1967, 1990) *The Age Discrimination in Employment Act of 1967 and The Older Workers Benefit Protection Act of 1990*, United States Equal Employment Opportunity Commission, http://www.eeoc.gov/index.html

United States (2009) *Dropout and Completion Rates in the United States, 2007*, Department of Education, National Center for Education Statistics, Washington: http://www.nces.ed.gov/pubs2009/

United States (2009) *Social Security Programs Throughout the World*, Social Security Administration, Office of Policy, Washington: http://www.ssa.gov/policy/docs/progdesc/ssptw/

Voth, Hans-Joachim (2001) *Time and Work in England 1750–1830*, Oxford: Oxford University Press.

Wakeham, Lawrence (2003) *State Pension Models*, Occasional Paper, London: Pensions Policy Institute. http://www.pensionspolicyinstitute.org.uk

Whaples, Robert (1990) "Winning the Eight-Hour Day, 1909–1919", *Journal of Economic History*, **50**(2), 393–406.

Williamson, Jeffrey (1974) "Watersheds and Turning Points: Conjectures on the Long-Term Impact of Civil War Financing", *Journal of Economic History*, **34**(3), 636–61.

Wright, Gavin (1990) "The Origins of American Industrial Success, 1879–1940", *American Economic Review*, Vol. 80, No. 4. (Sept.), 651–68.

Young, Percy M. (1975) *A History of British Football*, London: Stanley Paul.

Chapter Ten
Population Catastrophes

10.1 The Nature of Catastrophes

Long-run economic and population change has taken on a more predictable quality in recent history than it exhibited during the demographic transition. The world economy moves in a smoother way; it has less unexpected variance. Even the economic setbacks and turbulence of the early 21st century bear no comparison to those of earlier history. Unemployment levels, for instance, are neither as persistent nor as high as those of the 1930s and earlier. Undoubtedly there will be future economic and financial crises from time to time, but they will most likely be of short duration. Lest we get too complacent, it is well to remember that "it's a mad world, my masters." The response to these otherwise solvable events could go entirely wrong – high tariffs in a world of declining trade as in the Great Depression, for example. Yet, even in a world of less short-run variability, there is still the potential for the unexpected. Events such as the famines in Somalia, North Korea and elsewhere are all too frequent and devastating. They are made more appalling because the resources are usually at hand to ameliorate the condition and deliver food-aid. Enter the malevolent warlords of various sorts, and the situation is compounded and made tragic. We call events such as these *catastrophes*. In this chapter we examine the consequences of six major external shocks of the population order: the collapse of the environmental basis of two small societies (climate change and natural resources failure); the sad plight of the North American native Indians; famine; the Black Death of the 14th century; the HIV/AIDS crisis and the influenza pandemic.

Population catastrophes take a variety of forms. First, there are those which are sudden and unexpected population events. Propelled by outside forces that are largely unpredictable, the catastrophes often involve death on a large and geographically broad scale. The appearance of famine conditions and the occurrence of new contagious diseases are such cases. Catastrophes may also take a second form, that of

The Children of Eve: Population and Well-being in History, First Edition.
Louis P. Cain and Donald G. Paterson.
© 2012 Blackwell Publishing Ltd. Published 2012 by Blackwell Publishing Ltd.

a *catastrophe path*. This describes a pattern of population growth, or decline, which leads to an undesirable population and economic outcome. If, for instance, the underlying economic base of the economy is deteriorating and there are no viable alternatives, the population is on a catastrophe path to collapse, the case of the Greenland Norse that we will visit later in this chapter is one example. Yet, catastrophe paths in human history that lead to the disappearance of a population are relatively rare and mostly occur in small or isolated populations. The main reason for the rarity of catastrophe paths leading to actual catastrophic outcomes is a self-correcting tendency. In the short term this operates through changes in net migration, but in the longer-run involves fertility adjustment.

Every population crisis is not, however, a catastrophe and are thus frequently misidentified. For instance, population crises at the country level are not necessarily crises for the wider world. The recent emergence of substantial negative population growth rates in some Eastern European countries due to the substantial emigration of the young is often described as a catastrophic decline (see Chapter Two). Since this is a voluntary migration and the emigrants assist in buoying up the declining growth of population elsewhere – where there is an excess demand for labor at current wage levels – world welfare is actually improved. Even the population deficit countries of Eastern Europe will likely experience adverse consequences only in the short-run.[1] Last, and related to the above, a population catastrophe is not necessarily an economic catastrophe. Or, at the least, the population and economic catastrophes are unlikely to be of the same magnitude. This is because of the capacity of the aggregate economy to adjust in the medium- to long-run. Even in the short-run, a 10% fall of the population does not mean that national income (GDP) will fall 10%. Indeed, there is no reason why the end result of the adjustment to the population shock is not an improvement in individual welfare, real GDP per capita. Both wages and prices adjust.

Where population catastrophes involve large numbers of deaths, we naturally respond to the human suffering or cost. Individuals are the victims and die due to no fault of their own. These are sad events. Yet, no matter how intense the tragedy, it should not blind us to the economic consequences of the event. Ultimately the stories of population catastrophes are the stories of economic and human adaptation, including institutional change.

10.2 The Greenland Norse and the Easter Islanders

The great movement of the Norsemen, or Vikings, that began in the 9th century was a response to growing pressure on the farm resources of Denmark and Scandinavia. Initially it took the form of raiding adjacent countries for their loot. Treasure-seeking, however, turned into permanent settlement. There is now considerable question about how violent many of these take-overs were, although there certainly were violent episodes. The Viking expansions spread over much of Europe and beyond. One group settled in Normandy (and a century later became the Norman invaders of Anglo-Saxon England in 1066 AD), another in Sicily and yet others went eastward to Southern Russia and the Black Sea area. Dublin was a Viking trading city as was York in the heart of eastern England. In their longboats (a technological marvel) they sailed to settle Iceland; a breakaway group from the Iceland colony then established themselves in Greenland under the leadership of Erik the Red in 913 AD.

In Greenland the Vikings farmed cattle and sheep which they brought with them. (Some time later they also colonized L'Anse-aux-Meadows on the continent of North America in what is now Newfoundland; this colony had a relatively brief existence.)[2] The Greenland colonies were located in the south (actually called the Eastern Settlement) and west of the country. There they flourished for several hundred years and, at their zenith, probably numbered about 5000 to 7000 individuals. They had a small cathedral as well as churches (they were Christianized early in the settlement period), conducted trade with Iceland and Norway and seemed otherwise a stable settlement. Trade in ivory (walrus) and skins, once important sources of income, did not continue because of new and cheaper sources for both in Africa. Contact with the wider world was reduced and then lost, and the colony died out some time in the early 15th century (some individuals likely remained for some further time). When there was an attempt by the Icelanders to re-establish contact, all they found was the ruined settlements.[3] What happened to the Norse Greenlanders?

Various conjectures were made at the time, and many more have been made since about the fate of the Greenland settlements. The Skaërings (Inuit) were said to have wiped them out. This is unlikely as the Inuit were not residents of Greenland until after the Norse settlement, and the Ellesmere Island and Baffin Island Inuit conducted a small, but presumably, profitable trade with them. From time to time the Norse did run into conflicts with the Inuit on the hunting grounds, but only on occasion. The same charges have been leveled at Basque and Portuguese fishermen, but they too are unlikely culprits. Plague visited Iceland in the late 1300s, but there is no archaeological record of its having reached Greenland. Soil despoliation has been ruled out by modern scientists as an explanation for the demise of the colony.[4] The explanation that has most credence is that the Greenland settlements were indirect victims of climate change.

The settlements had been undertaken in what climatologists call the Medieval Climatic Optimum. This was a warm period in the history of the earth's climate. However, the onset of the Little Ice Age coincided with the population decline in the early 1300s. Earlier, it had been possible for the Greenlanders to gather two hay crops a year, but cooling meant the settlers were reduced to only one crop as the length of the growing period shortened. The climate change brought more frequent and stronger western winds and caused substantial soil erosion.[5] The Arctic winds began to take an ever greater toll on the viability of the crops, and, consequently, the animals that depended on them. Migration by land to a less compromising climate was not a possibility, although some Greenlanders may have escaped on passing ships to Norse Iceland, but, without the wood for ship-building, the sea-route was not an escape. The original ships that brought them to Greenland were long gone. The archaeological evidence suggests that the population failed to reproduce and, in reduced circumstances, descended into poverty, squabbling, starvation and eventual extinction. Bound in by the physical constraints of nature and with little scope for change, technical or otherwise, the Norse Greenlanders were also victims of their inability to adapt. Did they willfully ignore successful adaptation possibilities, as Jared Diamond suggests pointing to the failure to reorient their economy from pastoral farming to fishing and hunting (marine mammals) which they could have learned from the Inuit? Certainly social conventions may depress economic growth and restrict economic development (there are of course many that support it). There is, however, no known case of large societies blindly adhering to social norms in the face of prolonged deprivation let alone starvation and death. More likely, the Greenlanders were simply unaware of the options and how to exploit them, or, if they were aware of them, they could not affect the changes rapidly enough to avoid the catastrophic outcome.

The medieval Greenlanders were not the only population to follow a catastrophic population path. The Easter Islanders in the Pacific left only their great stone monuments. The difference between the Easter Island and Greenland economies was that, while the population declined in both cases, the Greenland population failure was initiated by exogenous or outside forces of climate change. For the Easter Islanders the cause was endogenous. As James Brander and Scott Taylor have argued persuasively, using a predator-prey model from natural resource economics, the Easter Island population went through cycles of boom and decline. These were directly related to the degradation of the island's natural resources, slow-growing palms in this case. The Easter Islanders *might* have been spared the boom-bust population growth path had the renewable natural resources been faster to replicate themselves. Or, given the slow rate of growth of the palms, this fact had been recognized and institutions put in place to manage their harvesting, such as a property exploitation right.[6] The Easter Islanders were using up their capital stock in the form of consumption. Of course, a rationally planned population would have been much smaller, but the economy would have been sustainable. It helps to get the social discount rate right![7]

10.3 North American Native Indians

Another population which was on a catastrophic (declining) path for over 500 years, but which ultimately did survive, is the North American Native Indians/Inuit/Aleuts. This was part of a larger decline of the native population of the entire American continent.[8] Arrayed against these peoples were the many forces of the European newcomers: their cultures and customs, their legal systems and languages, and their germs. The aboriginals of North America, themselves, were made up of various language groups and were genetically distinct populations. They encompassed a wide variety of different cultures and economies that were based on agriculture, fishing as well as hunting. The entire North American population at the dawn of European permanent settlement in 1492 is a matter of conjecture and widely varying estimates.[9] Russell Thornton's recent calculation is that, *at contact*, there were approximately seven million native North Americans. These Indians, Inuit and Aleuts represented about 10% of the entire population of the Americas; a larger share lived in Central and South America. Of those in North America, the Indians were by far the most numerous. Four centuries after the initial contact, in 1901, only 375 000 individuals made up the entire native population.[10] By any reckoning, this was a population on a catastrophe path, doomed by forces largely out of their control. Yet, unlike the Norse Greenlanders, the North American Indian population survived. Today it numbers just over two million. How did this catastrophe path come about and what reversed it?

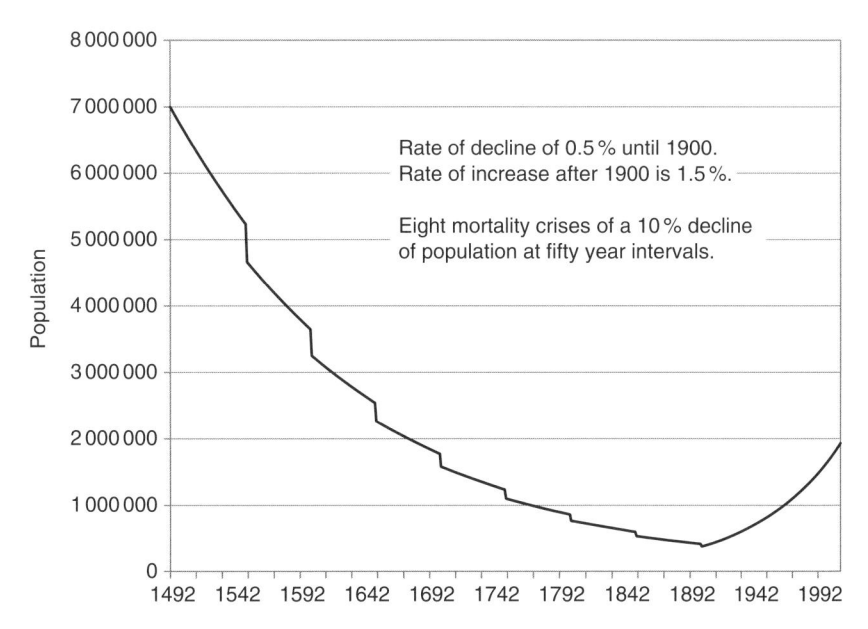

Figure 10.1 A Catastrophe Path: Numeric Illustration of North American Indian Decline and Growth.

If one starts from a contact population of 7 million, a small decline of about 0.5% per year and adds eight (relatively) small population crises of 10% mortality, one produces a population that accords with that of 1901 – see Figure 10.1. If we then suppose that the secular decline became a reasonable secular increase of 1.5% for the remainder of the 20th century, then the model estimates the current population satisfactorily. Notice that the supposed population crises occur about 50 years apart and are quite modest when compared with the historical pandemics of Asia and Europe or the world of more recent times.

The pre-contact population was far from static; it was increasing, like any pre-industrial population, but only very slowly. Warfare was common, and trauma was a frequent cause of death as tribes and "nations" vied for control of local resources. Disease could spread as the Native North American tribes did have limited contact with one another for trading purposes. Yet, as Russell Thornton points out, the conditions for epidemic disease were absent: no high population density and a lack of domestic livestock. This did not mean that the continent was free of disease. Indeed, tuberculosis (there is some argument about this), sexually transmitted disease and parasitical infection were common.[11] The European and African newcomers brought the old world diseases such as smallpox, influenza, cholera, scarlet fever and measles, their domestic livestock and an apparently insatiable desire for land.[12] But they also brought their new institutions, particularly explicit property rights. And they brought the pressures of a new market economy. All spread rapidly, and often did so well in advance of the actual European/African contact.

Take the case of the breakdown of a "Good Samaritan principle" among native tribes. Each native group had well defined hunting territories. To violate the barriers of these territories was a serious matter that invoked a response, usually in the form of a punitive raid. However, if one group came into the hunting territory of the other simply because they were starving, they were permitted to take what they needed for sustenance under the Good Samaritan principle so long as they did not imperil the animal resource. The principle acted, in a modest way, as insurance. However, once the animal hides could be sold (directly or indirectly) to fur traders, the resources took on a new value beyond clothing and food. Furthermore, these pelts could be traded for weapons, such as axes or guns, thus destroying the technical equilibrium in which the tribes existed. Since the neighbor with more and effective weapons was a threat at any time, no further violation of the tribal boundaries was then permitted. The Good Samaritan principle practiced by the groups gave way to an explicit market.[13] There is no consensus about whether intra-native conflict rose or not due to the coming of the newcomers. Certainly there were some major intra-Indian conflicts such as that between the Huron and Iroquois who battled each other for control of the trade routes to the fur trading posts in the 17th and early 18th centuries. But there were likely equally vicious conflicts prior to the Old World contact.[14]

More likely conflict was between the newcomers and the native Indians as the pressure for more land for European settlement built. The history of one-sided promises and radical change in government policy displaced many native Indians from their traditional areas such as the abrogation of the Indian Territory treaty in the years immediately after the American Revolution. This brought migratory population pressure to bear on the neighbors. Then, in some instances, there were the wars between the Indians and the whites; the Shawnee Prophet War (American mid-west in the early 19th century) and the Sioux Uprising (American Plains in the second half of the same century) are only two examples on the regrettably long list. Perhaps no one instance gathers such popular historical attention as the forced migration of the Cherokee. Escorted by the US Army, they were compelled to move from Georgia to Oklahoma (a vastly different environment from their historic habitat).[15] The one thousand miles, the so-called "Trail of Tears," took a toll of about 25% of the Cherokee involved.

Yet, it was neither inter-tribal conflicts nor native/non-native wars and brutality that contributed most to the decline in the North American native population. It was disease spread and its consequences. First, there were the continual epidemics that were local or regional. Some tribes suffered enormous proportional casualties, and their subsequent histories were of decline. Others, such as the Tolowa of California, suffered several times from severe outbreaks of cholera and influenza and yet survived as a nation. The practice of admitting women from other tribes to full status assured that when the local sex ratio was out of balance, more males than females, a socially acceptable in-migration did occur.[16] Even the Abenaki, which was one of the groups of first contact in the 1600s, did not die out. Others were not so fortunate. The Beothuks of Newfoundland/Labrador had completely disappeared by the mid-19th century.[17] A combination of settler brutality and disease were the causes – in proportions unknown.

Thus, the stylized "facts" of the numeric model of Figure 10.1 accord with averages and non-catastrophic crises and predict well the decline in the native population. There was yet one other source of decline in the native Indian numbers: inter-marriage.

Inter-marriage led to a loss of cultural distinctiveness and integration into non-native society. Native peoples then get lost from the "census" count. So common was this in prairie Canada that they formed a distinct, new group with a distinct identity, the Metis – an ethnic mixture of Scots-Indians and French-Indians. But the native population decline was reversed in about 1900. This is the product of: i) a growing resistance to disease among the surviving native populations; ii) a decrease in the virulence of diseases by the late 19th century; and iii) a change in government attitudes, some would say a paternalistic one, to native affairs. This last brought them into the scope of modern medicine with vaccinations, improved housing (and sanitation) on reserves and improved education. In the US the improvement in health outcomes was led in the last half of the 20th century by such far-seeing agencies as the Indian Health Service.[18] However, the process is far from complete. The native Indian population still has a lower life expectancy at birth than the non-native population and has high rates of obesity and alcohol abuse. Notwithstanding these issues, the native North American population recovered from its low in 1901 at a rate of 1.5% per year. It is, at least, no longer imperiled by a declining population and small numbers.

10.4 Famine

Famine is generally the result of crop or other agricultural failure brought on by unexpected changes in the weather patterns, plant disease, or infestations of pests. A breakdown of the food distribution system often compounds the problem in low income per capita countries, and it most frequently breaks down when there is a calamity such as an outbreak of plague or a war (including civil unrest). The result is malnutrition and starvation. Opportunistic diseases thrive in these conditions. An increased mortality is accompanied by "lost" births and stillbirths. Yet historically, famine and hunger are somewhat localized catastrophes. Not all of Ireland suffered equally from the famine caused by the failure of the potato crop – see Chapter Five. Even within an area not all suffered equally. For instance, famine's victims are traditionally the younger and older generations in a population.

The simple arithmetic of population change suggests that famines did not have major long-run effects on the size of a population. A famine that caused, say, a 5% decline in the population over the course of a year would be considered major. If such a famine hit an agricultural country once a decade, a small annual rate of population growth over the other nine years of the decade is all that is required to maintain a stable population over the long run. Although we don't have good data on the quantitative impact of famines before modern times, given what we know about the severity and spacing of famines, it seems doubtful that famine was ever a powerful, general long-run population check – except when it stimulated large and permanent emigration.

When economists think about famine, inevitably their thoughts turn to Parson Thomas Malthus, whom we met in Chapter One. Malthus conjectured that unchecked human breeding would expand at a geometric rate, while the means to sustain the population would expand at only an arithmetic rate. At the limit, there would be an increase in mortality attributable to famine and disease, which he called a *positive check* on population growth. As we saw in Chapter One, the solution lay in *preventive checks* such as a reduction in family fertility; Malthusian pressures generally led to responses such as fertility decline, consumption of foodstuffs normally avoided, small loans, and migration. Malthus expected famine to be a result of such pressures when all other checks failed, "gigantic inevitable famine stalks in the rear and, with one mighty blow, levels the population with the food of the world."[19] Yet there is little evidence that populations have ever reached a Malthusian crisis; famine was more likely to be a cause of Malthusian pressures than a consequence.

Famine generally has been linked to economic backwardness, which generally meant both a lack of infrastructure for dealing with famine itself and the presence of an adverse disease environment. At the turn of the 21st century, famine mortality is largely traceable to poverty-stricken and/or war-torn parts of the world, largely sub-Saharan Africa. For example, 20th-century famines are generally linked to either civil strife and warfare (e.g., the Soviet Union in 1918–22 or Biafra/Nigeria in 1970) or to despotic autarky (e.g., China in 1959–61 or North Korea after 1996). The damage done by famine today is considerably smaller than it was historically. Indeed, we now have the means to eradicate famine.[20] The world grows sufficient food for the existing population, information transmission is essentially instantaneous, and transportation costs minimal, but, in some places the traditional measures for coping with famine (e.g., crop insurance and storage, trade and other means of distribution, and committed public policy and philanthropy) are missing.[21] Only in sub-Saharan Africa has food production fallen behind population growth. Further, totalitarian governments can overwhelm global relief efforts made possible by improvements in communications and the growth of non-governmental organizations; relief may be increasing, but its distribution can be skewed toward those favored by the government. The result is the common symptoms of famine today as well as historically: "rising prices, food riots, an increase in crimes against property, a significant number of actual or imminent deaths from starvation, a rise in temporary migration, and frequently the fear and emergence of famine-induced infectious diseases."[22] Public health measures have probably reduced total famine deaths and reduced the proportion caused by disease, but the majority of the deaths, even today, are likely to be the result of infectious disease. Some diseases are caused directly by the lack of nutrition; others are caused indirectly through the impact of famine on a society. As people wander in their search for food, disease transmission is facilitated through such means as the use of only the most rudimentary sanitary arrangements. Historically, we have little evidence of how many people died of famine before, say, the 17th century in Europe.

The normal cause of famine is crop failure in an agrarian economy. The crops normally failed because of extreme weather conditions: hot and dry or cold and wet. Yet, as Cormac Ó Gráda, the leading modern student of famines, has shown, extreme weather is neither a necessary nor a sufficient condition for famine. In particular, famine was much less likely if the harvest was bad for only one year.[23] The most serious famines were the result of multi-year failures of a staple crop. Unanticipated economic famine shocks could, however, have instant effects on short-run fertility as we have seen in the example of 19th century Finland – see Chapter Four. The famine crisis affected young men and young women similarly. Fertility in general was reduced by the depressed economic conditions. But it was the sudden change in the sex ratio that had the most telling effect. Men migrated to where there was still employment or food available. Local change of the sex ratio as a by-product of the crisis of the 1870s was then restored once the economic conditions returned to normal and the men came home.

Perhaps the most prominent famine is the one attributed to an outbreak of *Phytophthora infestans*, a fungus that destroyed the potato crop, particularly in Ireland. We met this famine in Chapter Five, (section 5.9 on diasporas), and it is a good example of a classic famine. Here, we focus on the famine in Bengal during World War II. It provides a good example of the difference between modern famines in an industrial world and classic famines in an agricultural world. Like many 20th-century famines, it is one where human actions made acts of nature worse.

The Bengali famine is the subject of Amartya Sen's path-breaking *Poverty and Famine*, one of many books and articles on the subject.[24] During the famine, which covered the years 1943 and 1944, two million out of a population of approximately 60 million died. There was also a large decrease in the number of pregnancies. Both the fertility and mortality series reached their extremes in the fall of 1943.

Following the fall of Burma in March 1942 to the Japanese, it was generally thought they would soon invade neighboring Bengal. The small amount of rice Bengal usually received from Burma was no longer available. Bengali rice production along the coast was limited to that needed for local consumption. Sen, whose view is based on the official *Report on Bengal*, argued that what precipitated the famine was an increase in demand financed by public expenditures related to the war. Bureaucratic incompetence and political infighting, speculation and hoarding, made the situation worse. The rice crop of late 1942 was of a bit below normal, but expectations of war led producers and grain merchants to limit the amount released to the market, hoping to earn speculative profits. The inability of the government to deal with this speculation meant consumers tried to purchase rice before prices rose and/or war came to Bengal. This view has been criticized, but it remains the most widely accepted.

Ó Gráda's view is that food was in short supply in 1943 as a result of a poor harvest; it was not a result of hoarding. He notes that Bengal in 1943 "was even more dependent on rice than Ireland had been on the potato" a century earlier.[25] His view differs from Sen and the official view in part because of Sen's failure to use once-confidential correspondence, some of which has long been in the public domain, that tells a story of food shortage. Two of the individuals responsible for drafting the official report commented that by the time their report was written the famine was long over, no one knew what actually happened, and the commission relied on "quite unreliable" data. One piece of evidence cited by Ó Gráda notes that the authorities "would not hear of there being a shortage in Bengal."[26]

One reason for this, and for blaming the problem on hoarding (a centuries-old practice), was the fact that the authorities, following the advice of the military, had purchased the Bengali boats that were large enough to be used by (the possibly) invading Japanese soldiers and destroyed them. The boats were owned by fishermen and boatmen whose livelihood depended on them. Some were used to move the rice crop. Ó Gráda presents two pieces of evidence that the hoarding hypothesis is incorrect. First, he notes that rice prices rose as might be expected in a shortage situation, then fell as the crop was harvested in late 1943, but, contrary to expectations, these price movements were not precipitous. Further, although one official warned that, once the hoards were released to the market, and rice could once again be imported into Bengal, rice prices would plummet, there is no evidence of such an abrupt fall at the appointed time.[27] Second, a high-profile campaign was undertaken to discover hidden hoards of rice, but very little was discovered. Still the authorities continued to claim the food was there somehow even as government-sponsored food pantries were being forced to close for a lack of rice.[28] Work done by the Indian Statistical Institute, cited by both Sen and Ó Gráda, documents that in Bengal

> ... average holding size was too small to provide the rice necessary for subsistence, and that those groups most affected by the famine were already under pressure beforehand. It also found that the famine's impact was regionally very uneven, and that subdivisions with proportionately more families on below-subsistence holdings were more vulnerable to the famine.
>
> Ó Gráda (2008).

The evidence suggests farmers left the land, often for Calcutta, in their search for food. Relief was not forthcoming as it was wartime, and the British authorities were hopeful some of the Bengali crop could be diverted to Ceylon and elsewhere. Ó Gráda quotes the *Economist* as reporting "food ships must come second to victory ships."[29]

It seems clear that, regardless of the posturing of bureaucrats, the Bengali famine was the result of a harvest failure, the effects of which were exacerbated by war and human decisions, whether one adopts the Sen or Ó Gráda view. It was what now gets described as a "twentieth-century" famine to distinguish it from those in earlier times. Harvest failures prior to the war had not resulted in famine. In 1942 when the harvest failed, the outcome of the war was very much in doubt, and it was not clear where the transport capacity could be found to move needed supplies from elsewhere. Had it been found, the famine could have been avoided. Sen blames the "chaos and uncertainty" of the war for the hoarding; Ó Gráda blames "wartime priorities" for the lack of a humanitarian response. In ancient times, a siege leading to famine was a military tactic. In Bengal, millions became unwitting victims of a war that involved issues little related to them, but which nonetheless claimed their lives.

10.5 We All Fall Down! Plague

Even today, children in Britain, and elsewhere, are taught the rhyme:

> Ring around the rosie, A pocketful of posies
> Hush-a, hush-a. We all fall down![30]

Many believe the verse refers to the plague, its symptoms (red circular swellings), the supposed remedy (dried flowers to sweeten the air) and the end result, death. No wonder the folk memory survives into modern times for, as one group of researchers estimates, about 200 million people died worldwide as a result of plague over time. It ranks as the most deadly disease in all of human history. Most of the deaths occurred during three major pandemics:

- The Plague of Justinian, 542 to 750 AD. An outbreak of bubonic plague or possibly of the pneumonia virus (the evidence is not definitive) that killed about

20% of Europe's population. It was also present in Asia and the Middle East and reoccurred in a roughly five-year cycle for about 200 years.[31]
- The Black Death, 1347/8 (lasting in various outbreaks to the mid-17th century). An initial outbreak of bubonic plague (possibly with accompanied pneumonic plague) spread initially along the trade routes from the Caspian Sea and Black Sea areas. The death toll of the 1347/8 outbreak ranged from 25% to 35% of the world's population (in England it has been estimated at 33%.) The Black Death reoccurred in Europe periodically, but with decreasing virulence.[32]
- The Bombay Plague (actually originating in Yunnan, China in 1855), late 19th and early 20th centuries. The bubonic plague pandemic occurred mainly in India and China. Estimated death rates in the affected areas of India and China are about 25%.

The lack of consistent historical evidence about the plagues, their spread and timing, and the economic consequences makes the great killer a bit of a puzzle and a subject of great controversy among historians.[33]

First, there is the problem of reconciling the medical and epidemiological evidence. At the heart of the debate is *Yersinia pestis* which was isolated as the bacterium responsible for the last pandemic. It is also endemic in certain locations of the world today: the Western United States, India, Mongolia, Central Asia and Southern Africa. It can be found on every continent, except Antarctica and Australia. *Yersinia pestis* is the bacterium agent of the Black Death and is further thought to be the likely pathogen of the Plague of Justinian.[34] One group of medical researchers has found DNA traces of *Yersinia pestis* in the preserved tooth marrow of a Black Death victim of the 14th century, although at least one well-respected historian of the plague, Samuel K. Cohn Jr., explicitly rejects the evidence as insufficient (possibly tainted).[35] Cohn also argues that

World Distribution of Plague, 1998

Dark Shaded Areas: Plague occurs in animals.
Light Shaded Areas: Countries reporting plague, 1970–1998
There are typically about 10 to 15 deaths each year in the US.
Source: Courtesy of the Centers for Disease Control.

the symptoms of the Black Death and the Bombay pandemics were different as were their patterns of spread. Notwithstanding Cohn's view, the medical evidence favors the one that it was the same bacterium, although, as Robert Perry and Jacqueline Fetherson in *Clinical Microbiology Reviews* point out, there can be slight variations in the bacterium that can trigger differences in disease and virulence characteristics.[36]

Yersinia pestis is not resident in humans but in rodents such as rats, squirrels and prairie dogs. Its long-term survival depends on a natural resistance in some small mammals. It is transmitted to humans by fleas, especially the rat flea (*Xenopsylla cheopis*). Although about 30 types of flea are capable transmitters (vectors) of the bacterium, the human flea is not one of them. When the disease breaks out among the rodent population, the rat flea becomes infected. As the rats (*rattus rattus*) are not resistant, they die, and the rat flea migrates to another (any) nearby host. Since rats and humans are common companions, the flea bites the new human host. The infected flea then dies.[37] *Yersinia pestis* transmitted in this fashion gives rise to the bubonic plague in humans, named for the red "bubos" that form in the lymph glands of the armpits, groin and neck. Persons contracting the disease generally died with five to seven days, although there was a survival rate of about 25% of the victims. Bubonic plague was not spread from one human to another except in very rare cases of blood contact where the disease became the *septicaemic* plague which was relatively rare but nearly always fatal (even today in one to three days). If the plague infection spread to the lungs of the victims as a secondary infection it could, however, be transmitted from one human to another as an air-borne disease through the water droplets of the human breath. *Pneumonic* plague, as this variant was known, killed very rapidly and nearly 95% did not survive an attack. Today antibiotic drugs can arrest the bubonic plague, and it is seldom lethal. *Septicaemic* and *pneumonic* plagues are still usually fatal because they cannot be identified early enough (see Appendix 10.1 for the plague transmission cycle).

The most recent bubonic plague pandemic, the Bombay Plague, was slow moving over the landscape. In contrast, the Black Death was very fast moving. The outbreak of the 14th century originated in Central Asia in the 1330s and was spread effectively by the overland trade routes, notably the Silk Road.[38] It entered the maritime trade of the Black Sea and was first reported in Mediterranean Europe in December of 1347. It evidently had spread on the Black Sea trade routes in months. The same rapid spread took the plague to Egypt and other parts of the Middle East. Within 12 months it had spread throughout Central and Western Europe and most of Britain. By June of 1348 Northern Europe and all of Britain were reporting deaths. The spread was also influenced by seasonal climate; its geographic spread was more rapid in the summer. The registration of deaths for several Italian cities in 1348 shows that plague deaths peaked in the summer months of May to September with the largest toll in July. There then was a rapid falling off in the autumn and winter when few deaths were registered; the plague reappeared in the early spring.[39] In terms of its spread, some areas of southern Germany and Poland were partially or totally spared; there is no particularly good explanation for this, although the low density of the rat population is often conjectured to be a reason.

The speed of the plague's spread presents a bit of a problem for explanation since *rattus rattus* does not travel very far in its life. The traditional answer is that the rats accompanied international, inter-regional and local trade on ships, in wagons and in carts. The rat flea can live in the hair of camels and horses for short periods – an explanation of its moving down the Silk Road from Central Asia. (Recall the rat flea does not live on the human body.) Yet, even allowing for the trade-based explanation, critics claim that this cannot explain plague's uniform spread and its speed. This has led, in turn, to speculation that the rat-flea-bacterium transmission mechanism is too weak, based on the well-documented Bombay pandemic, and that an air-borne disease is more likely. Air-borne pneumonic plague, however, is a much weaker mechanism of transmission as the bacterium does not typically survive long outside a host.[40] Some historians now suggest that the Black Death was an entirely different disease, a particularly aggressive pneumonia for instance. Or, it may even have been a disease now extinct. The weight of science, however, supports a *Yersinia pestis* based plague. Several explanations for the pace of its spread have been offered, they are:

- that *Yersinia pestis* of the Black Death took a slightly different form from that of the Plague of Justinian and the Bombay pandemic (Biovars *Antiqua*, *Medievalis* and *Orientalis* in historical order);
- that other small mammals which also acted as hosts (squirrels, for instance) played a more significant role than previously thought, and their fleas carried the bacterium;
- that the rat flea (which usually dies in the process of transmitting the disease) developed some sort of immunity, thereby making it a more congenial host. The flea was resident on the rat longer and less likely to pass on the bacterium as suspected in the case of the Bombay plague;
- that *Yersinia pestis* may take mutant forms or have changed characteristics due to changes in their foodstuffs. These protein changes are thought to change the virulence characteristics of the plague.[41]
- that *Yersinia pestis* is very sensitive to external temperature variation and only thrives between 26° and 37° Celsius; and
- that the spread of the disease depends on the density of the rat population and that, in turn, depends on the availability of the rats food supply. If food is more plentiful the rat population grows at a given locality and the greater likelihood of an outbreak of plague.

In summary, while there is historical difficulty in reconciling the various plagues' characteristics (in some but not all cases) and the speed of travel of the Black Death compared with modern plagues, it is still more than likely that these are accounted for by variation of the bacterium and a change in its vectors.

The plagues yet have more puzzles to offer. First, the reoccurrence of the bubonic plague seems to exhibit a cyclical quality. In all, there were 33 outbreaks of the plague between 1347/8 and 1665 – although there were some small local outbreaks afterward. Generally it returned with decreasing death tolls in the infected areas but not always, and occasionally it returned with heightened virulence as it did in "the Great Plague" of 1665 when the death rate in London reached 16%. The crowding in London is reckoned to have increased the plague's mortality toll after the national outbreak of 1347/8. The spread tended to be slower in the rural areas.[42] The affluent citizens of the city took themselves to the country if they could and often to a self-imposed quarantine. Some quarantine measures were also adopted by civic authorities. Many cities closed their ports to shipping during plague outbreaks. Meeting places in the cities were often shut down as in the case of the theatres in Shakespeare's time.

The second on-going puzzle is why did the plague generally disappear from Western Europe in the third quarter of the 17th century? The long-term cooling trend of the environment is suspected of playing a role. Better nutrition and higher living standards probably did not play a role as, during all plague incidents, the well-off usually died with the same frequency as the poor, if they were infected in the same environment. Some individuals in Western Europe, however, seemed to be immune from the plague or survive it while most around them succumbed. Since there can be no acquired immunity from a bacterial infection, there was likely a genetic predisposition to reject the *Yersinia pestis* or at least limit its damage to the body's immune system. As noted earlier, the HIV/AIDS genetic blocker known as CCR5-delta 32 may be linked to this plague resistance quality. The cumulative effects of the plague mortality as it reoccurred would leave the plague-resistant population as a greater proportion of the total population, thereby lowering average mortality. However, while quantifying such an effect is impossible, it may explain the *apparent* declining virulence of the plague.[43] It is now evident that the English population showed more genetic diversity before the Black Death than afterwards. The last part of the explanation for the end-of-plague issue is based on the prevalence of *rattus rattus* (black rat), the reluctant host carrier. The brown rat (*rattus norvegicus*) began to replace the black rat in Britain in the early 18th century and somewhat later in the Americas. It quickly became the dominant rat species in the UK and the USA. Arguments that the plague disappeared with the change in the dominant rat species fail, however, on the issue of timing. Furthermore, the brown rat is an equally congenial host for the rat flea as the black rat. The puzzles remain.

The population of Europe was, according to one estimate, approximately 75 million in 1347. Five years later it numbered only 50 million. For England, there is also a somewhat fragile consensus about the size of the population and the number of fatalities due to the initial outbreak of the Black Death.[44] Andrew Hinde has estimated the pre-Black Death population of England in 1347 to be at a minimum 4.0 million and at most 5.6 million.[45] Most historians favor the upper range of Hinde's figures, and 5.2 million is often used. Although some estimates of the deaths in 1347/8 are upwards of 40% of the population, most seem to favor the more modest 33%! Where there is fragmentary evidence in the form of death records, such as religious communities and town internments, and legal ones in the form of testaments, they suggest a lot of variation between locations both within Europe and, more narrowly, within England. Death in the towns and cities varied by urban densities, much as modern diseases in less developed countries today and Western Europe and North America historically. If the plague reached a village, however, because of the crowded nature of village living, the effect could be equally devastating as that of crowded city. In short, the death toll in Europe (and in the rest of the world where the plague was known to have spread) during the Black Death of 1347/50 was the greatest mortality catastrophe (proportional) the world has ever known. And, as noted, the bubonic plague continued to revisit for 300 years.

The population of England did not regain its pre-1347 level until some time in the late 17th century. The other European countries' populations recovered their pre-plague

Table 10.1 Population of Selected European Countries, 1300–1700.

	(in 000s)				
	1300	1400	1500	1600	1700
England and Wales*	5750	3000	3500	4450	5450
England**	5000	2500	2500	4400	5200
Netherlands	800	600	950	1500	1950
Belgium	1250	1000	1400	1600	2000
Italy	12500	8000	9000	13300	13500
Spain	5500	4500	5000	6800	7400
Total Europe	94200	67950	82950	107350	114950

*These figures are for England and Wales whereas the numbers cited in the text are for England only, hence the difference.
**Allen's figures for England.
Source: Adapted from Table 1 in Pamuk (2007) and Allen (2003), Data Appendix, 435–43.

levels at least a century earlier – see Table 10.1. In England, apart from the initial mortality effect of the Black Death, the re-occurrence of plague at fairly regular intervals caused the general course of English population growth to be negative for at least 75 to 100 years. In about the mid-1400s population started to grow again, but only very slowly on trend with major setbacks in the plague years. So the question becomes: why did the population of England take so long to recover from the effects of the plague and why was the recovery slower than in the continental countries of Europe? The explanation lies in the population consequences of i) real wage changes; and ii) the changes of institutions and property rights.

A sudden increase in mortality meant a decline in the demand for foodstuffs; food in the immediate aftermath was met out of stocks on hand. The first phase of the post-plague period was thus deflationary. This was followed within months by inflationary pressure. The decline in the supply of labor with, a lower but stable demand, likely drove up the wage rate of labor. If the economy operated with *fixed factor proportions*, this would lead to a reduction in the employment of the *non-human* resources, land and capital. Such an outcome also leads to a decline in aggregate income, at least in the short-run, so the demand for all factors, being a derived demand for the output, also declines. Wages would then decline. But since there is no reduction in the supply of the non-human factors such as land, we should expect to see a large quantity of idle resources as these resources, at the margin, lose their economic value. However, and thirdly, economies adjust, and the most common form of adjustment is by re-aligning the way in which factors are combined. This is otherwise known as "technological adaptation or change." That is, the *relative factor prices* dictate the optimal combination of human and non-human resources. As the post-catastrophe world adjusts, it is not subject to fixed factor proportions, but to a world where all factor inputs are variable, that is, an economy with *variable factor proportions*. It is also likely that the output mix of near substitutes will alter as the prices of outputs favor the use of the new relative factor prices. David Haddock and Lynne Kiesling argue that, contrary to the historical claim, land did not go out of production after the Black Death of 1347.

Table 10.2 Land Use in Southern England Before and After the Black Death.

		(percentage of farm acreage)			
Area	Dates	Arable	Meadow	Pasture	Wood
Gloucestershire	1349–54	83.1	8.4	2.2	3.2
King's Norton, Worcestershire	1386–96	81.3	15.1	2.4	1.2
Arden, Warwickshire	1345–55	70.4	8.2	7.2	12.9
Avon Valley and Feldon, Warwickshire	1345–55	95.1	4.4	0.5	0.0
Essex	1272–1307	90.2	3.2	4.2	2.5
Gloucestershire	1485–1500	46.0	13.6	34.5	6.0
King's Norton, Worcestershire	1494–1504	53.3	17.5	22.1	7.2
Arden, Warwickshire	1496–1500	34.5	8.6	38.1	18.7
Avon Valley and Feldon, Warwickshire	1496–1500	56.7	9.4	32.9	1.0
Essex	1461–1485	68.4	7.6	14.6	9.5

Source: from Haddock and Kiesling (2002), Tables 1–5.

Rather it was simply used for different purposes. Labor-intensive agriculture, such as gardening and cropping, gave way to pasture-based cattle and sheep agriculture which conserved on the use of the relatively more expensive factor, human labor.[46] Land in agriculture was not, in any large measure, abandoned back to nature despite the historical claim that it was. The farm land was simply put to the new use, a use that looked less tidy to observers in the aftermath of the plague, and called for rotation of pastures leaving some fields vacant for all or part of the year, again contributing to the general untidiness – see Table 10.2.

In terms of human resources, the great mortality shock to the population caused the real wages of those who remained to rise. Throughout the countries for which we have records, money wage rates rose, and the prices of commodities, particularly agricultural goods, fell, a clear improvement in the standard-of-living for about 75 to 100 years after 1347. But the rise in real wages was neither achieved smoothly nor without turbulence in labor markets. There were vast changes to society. The most important of these was the weakening of the prevailing economic system of feudalism. At the outset it should be noted that feudalism was never a monolithic system, was not the same everywhere, and varied substantially in practice from any later imagined theory. However, feudal arrangements required a high labor/land ratio *and* a lack of alternatives for labor in order for them to work. The Black Death and, subsequently, the decline in population shattered the *status quo ante*.

The institutions that propped up feudalism were largely controlled by the owners of land and other non-human resources – the lords of the manor, *seigneurs* and the crown. Their reactions to the labor shortages of the plague years had contradictory effects. First, if their manors were devastated by the plague, they had to attract new labor, and the only labor available in the short- and medium-run was that from other manors, themselves suffering plague losses. The encouragements were in the form of higher money wages, a relaxation of feudal obligations and promises of a higher standard-of-living in the form of lower food and housing prices. Thus they encouraged breaking the feudal ties that bound a laborer to a particular piece of land and many (implicit) contracts were converted to wage ones. Second, the landlords whose laborers were leaving reacted by raising their wages in order to keep them. They also engaged in non-wage competition for labor services, and a new form of landholding, the leasehold, became more common.[47] Third, to economize, most landlords switched some or all of their land from arable to pasture. Fourth, the landlords experiencing a loss of labor to other estates tried to arrest that flow of labor by trying to enforce the old feudal rights that tied the peasant to a particular piece of land.[48] This, of course, created conflict among the landowners: those who needed the labor and were willing to forgo some of their feudal rights versus those who wanted to keep their peasant laborers from leaving. Since landlords held the power of the state, and the state favored the *status quo*, the landlords had some political success. But the division was not always clear (just as the plague effects were not clear to them) and some argued both positions. Attempts to regulate the labor market by reinforcing old laws and enforcing new ones (e.g., maximum wage rates to be paid) were a patchwork rather than a coherent set of laws.[49]

The reactionary political attempt on the part of the landowners to roll back the new measures of economic freedom evoked a response throughout Europe, including England. Peasant revolts broke out in many countries. Two of the largest were the *Jacquerie* in France and Wat Tyler's (the Peasants') Revolt in England, in 1356 and 1381 respectively. Both were national in scope, although in each instance not coordinated. In both cases also, the attempt to impose new taxes heightened the anxiety that the state (crown) could simply tax away the new-found gains in living standards, the *causa bella*.[50] The timing of the peasant revolts was largely determined by the timing of the political attempts to stop the labor flows in a slightly more relaxed labor market than formerly and impose new taxes. Initially, some concessions were made to the rebels, but the end result was that both revolts were put down ruthlessly. Despite these setbacks, the labor scarcity continued to bring pressure to liberalize labor's working conditions, and real wages continued to rise (see Figure 10.2). The labor markets had rather dramatically changed. Not only did the real wages of farm workers increase, but so did those of urban workers and rural/non-farm workers. As the labor market loosened the constraints of feudalism, labor could migrate to the towns. The buoyant woolen trades provided the demand for labor both directly and indirectly and, from that, the growth of manufacturing. Women's employment as domestic servants also brought women's wage labor into the market on a wholly new basis as they, for instance, took positions in the manor and town houses – formerly occupied by the extended family. The old relationships were being broken down, which is hardly surprising given that the population declined for about 125 years after the Black Death of 1347–50.[51] In his recent biography of Edward III, Ian Mortimer makes the case for projectile warfare (the long bow) robbing the knight of his special status on the battlefield, and this diminution of authority carried over to economic life.[52]

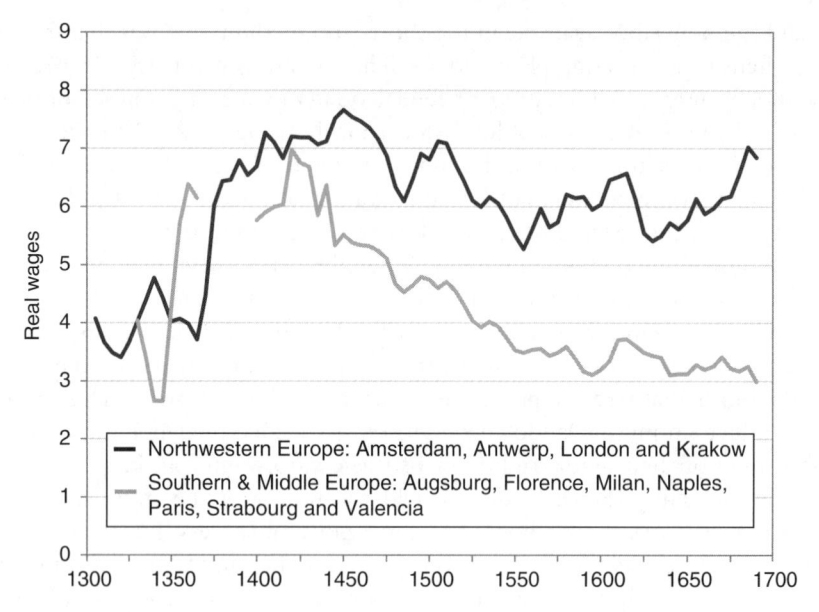

Figure 10.2 Real Wages of Laborers in the Plague Centuries, Various Locations, 1300–1700.
Note: The data presented above are linked ten year averages computed from the Allen series. Real wages are in grams of silver adjusted for the consumer price index. For details on the Allen time series and methods of their calculation see Allen (2001; 2003).
Source: Data courtesy of Prof. Robert C. Allen.

The declining population contributed to a rise in real wages in most European countries following the Black Death, as can be seen in Figure 10.2. This was the result of:

i) the continuing severe labor shortages that the plague caused both during the initial years and during the subsequent outbreaks of the disease at regular intervals, about eight years on average;
ii) the structural change within agriculture; and
iii) the growth of the commercial sector, its urbanizing influence and the resulting changes and increases in the demand for labor.

In England, however, the rise in real wages actually pre-dated the onset of the Black Death in 1347. This upwards movement has been credited to another mortality crisis brought about by the persistent crop failures and famines in the 1320s (the English population was falling from 1320). Yet, the wage increase of the early 14th century was not sustained, and the 20 years or so prior to the pandemic were marked by declining real wages.

For the period after the Black Death, John Munro has shown that the premium for skills such as those enjoyed by masters declined as the real wages of laborers rose more rapidly, at least into the early 15th century. But this is not obvious in the detailed computations and analyses of craftsmen and laborers' real wages by Robert Allen.[53] Nor would the deaths associated with the 1347–50 plague outbreaks *alone* explain the continuous long-term rise of real wages afterward. Real wages in most European centers rose through until the mid-15th century. Rather what we observe is the cumulative outcome of the commercialization of (pastoral) agriculture which began in the late 13th century and which gave rise to the growth of income of, at least, the English population – although it was still subject to short-term crises.[54] An important element of this was the increasing international exports of wool and the gains from this trade were transformed into increasing income – the supply of wool increased because of the switch to pastoral agriculture. Land rents were bid down. The new towns that thrived as the economy diversified gave rise to further urban employment. After about 100 years of rising real wages they turned down. This was mostly a result of a rise in the price of food in the mid-15th century. But, England and the Low Countries fared better than the countries of Southern Europe as a group at this time, and, by the 1600s, there was a clear real wage divide between the northern and southern countries of the continent.[55] In summary, the forces active in the labor market after the Black Death catastrophe were part of late mediaeval structural change leading into the progress of the early modern period.[56]

It took, as mentioned earlier, more than 300 years for the population of England to reach the level it had been on the eve of the Black Death! Even allowing for the continuing toll of plague reoccurrences, the recovery of the population was noticeably slower than that of most European countries whose real wages from the late 15th century onward had declined more sharply than those of England. Of course, we might have underestimated the continuing plague deaths of the 16th and 17th centuries. If not, the burden of the demographic explanation must rest on the failure of fertility. The European Marriage Pattern which, as we have seen in earlier chapters, was one of a relatively high age at (first) marriage of both men and women. Whether or not this marriage pattern, common to Middle and Western Europe, was a product of the forces unleashed in 1347 is a matter of current conjecture. The absence of evidence about pre-1347 marriage patterns is such that this is always likely to be a matter of historical speculation. Some evidence of a greater freedom of choice can be found in the 14th century as family structure was disturbed by the greater mobility found; this would support the delay of marriage hypothesis. The rise of wages raised the opportunity cost of marriage and this too would also suggest delay. However, acting in the opposite direction, the price of land was falling and the lump-sum needed to establish a family easier to amass. So we find contradictory evidence. Most likely the European Marriage Pattern had been well established before 1347 and the plague effect was only marginal.[57] Northern Europe in the 16th and 17th centuries was overwhelmingly rural but unlike Mediterranean Europe in England and the Low Countries the seeds the commercial, agricultural and industrial revolutions were already having a demographic effect.

10.6 The HIV/AIDS Pandemic

One of the most important demographic trends of the late 1900s was the world-wide convergence of life expectancies (at birth). Development policies and increasing income per capita in the less developed part of the world resulted in a dramatic rise in life expectancies. To be sure, the life expectancies in the high-income countries also rose, but at a less rapid rate, and, although the gap between the high- and low-income countries was still large, there was, nevertheless, convergence. Then quite abruptly in

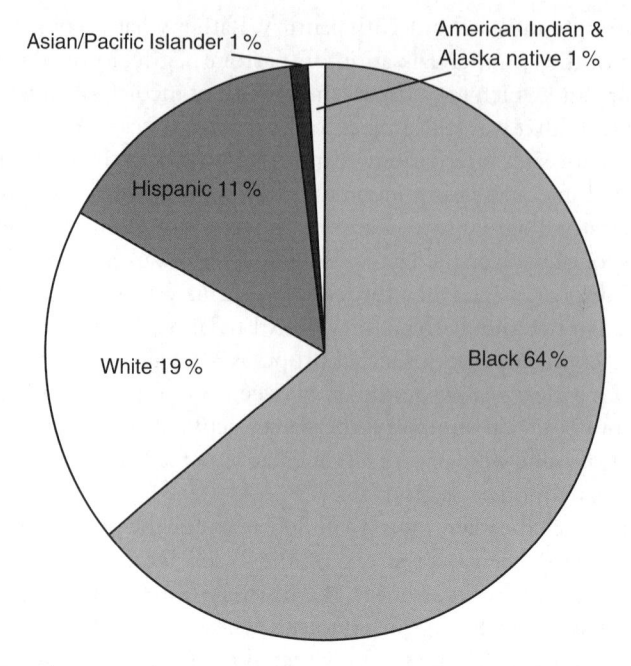

Figure 10.3 Female HIV Infection in the United States Rate by Race-Ethnicity, 2007.
Note: Based of statistics for 33 states. Females account for approximately 26% of total infections in the US. The transmission is primarily (80%) due to high-risk sexual activity with an infected partner. About 16% is due to infection because of intravenous drug use.
Source: data from Centers for Disease Control (2007) *HIV/AIDS and African Americans*, http://www.cdc.gov/hiv

the late 20th and early 21st centuries, the trend reversed itself. In sub-Saharan Africa life expectancy at birth fell by 7% in the decade of the 1990s. Transitional economies as a group saw life expectancy fall by 1.9% in the same decade.[58] In sub-Saharan Africa HIV/AIDS is now the leading cause of death. For example, Botswana's infection rate (2005) is 24.4% of the population aged 15 to 49 years of age.[59] Nor is the disease limited in its continental spread. Brazil, the Bahamas and Haiti in the Americas and Thailand, India and Myanmar in Asia are among the most severely infected countries. Because of the pandemic nature of the disease and its devastating human effects (an estimated 4.9% of all deaths in 2002), it is tempting to draw parallels between the HIV/AIDS pandemic and the Black Death of the late medieval period.[60] Certainly, both catastrophes require us to make a distinction between population outcomes, in welfare terms, and growth effects, in aggregate income (GDP) terms.[61] But unlike the medieval plague whose sources, spread and contagion were little understood by contemporaries, we know a great deal about HIV/AIDS and its epidemiology – although alas still not enough. This means that measures to limit its spread could be effective *if* adequate policies, and funding for them, were generated. Also unlike the plague which struck everyone, the modern pandemic is primarily a disease of the poorest among us. It is therefore very unevenly distributed over the planet. Yet, the scourge of HIV/AIDS which had surfaced earlier (the virus was first identified in 1984) now has a quantitative significance sufficient to affect a world aggregate.

HIV/AIDS is a recently acquired human virus that made the species leap within the past 50 to 100 years from a near relative, the chimpanzee. The conjecture is that infected chimpanzee blood made its way into the human diet via those who hunted the animal for its meat – a relatively rare event in itself. The *human immunodeficiency virus* (HIV) is spread through contact of bodily fluids such as blood, semen, and breast milk and causes a failure of the human immune system. Its victims initially were those who practiced unprotected sex with an infected individual and *haemophiliacs* who acquired it through infected blood products before adequate testing for the disease's presence. Infected needles, especially among drug users, are efficient vectors of the virus. Today, HIV is broadly resident in many populations because it can be passed on to children in the womb and through an infected mother breast-feeding her children. The early stage of the disease (HIV) weakens the immune system and makes the infected person susceptible to conditions such as colds, diarrhoea, and fevers, but it may otherwise be asymptomatic. In the UK, a country with a high level of education and HIV/AIDS awareness, it is nonetheless true that about 25% of infected persons do not know that they are HIV positive.[62] With such a high level of ignorance the potential for spread is very high. The effects of HIV are cumulative, and, after some period, the virus enters the mature stage and becomes AIDS (acquired immunodeficiency syndrome) as the human immune system is overwhelmed. The period of HIV pre-AIDS infection varies from individual to individual and may be as long as ten years. During the AIDS phase, the infected person is subject to opportunistic diseases: skin cancer, lung infections, fungal infections, brain tumors, eye infections, weight loss among others.[63] Since the pattern of these opportunistic diseases varies from person to person, AIDS is a wide spectrum disease or syndrome.

In the high-income countries of Western Europe, North America and Australia, the disease is particularly concentrated in some high-risk groups. Gay men are the group with the greatest likelihood to become HIV-positive. In the initial phases of the disease in the 1980s gay men also accounted for the most new cases reported. However, heterosexuals now account for the most new cases each year, but male-to-male sexual contact is still the single largest category among white men in the US. In both the UK and the US members of the black communities are especially vulnerable. However, of those heterosexuals who become HIV-positive in the UK, slightly over 75% actually acquired the virus overseas. In the US, the African-American population acquired the disease locally and mainly from unprotected sex with an infected partner. For females in the US, as evident in Figure 10.4, blacks bore a heavy burden. Black women account for about 12.5% of the female population, but they are about 64% of those living with HIV/AIDS. That is, a black woman is about nine times more likely to be living with the disease than her white counterpart. Among those with the disease, the black population tends to live shorter lives than other Americans. All of this points to the distribution of income and education being key determinants of a policy to slow its spread. Apart from gay men, most of the HIV high-risk groups are also low-income groups and have a sad familiarity with that we find in the other developed countries. Of course there are exceptions: aboriginals in Canada are a high-risk group whereas in Australia they are not.[64]

The actual amounts of HIV infected people and AIDS victims in countries outside sub-Saharan Africa is about one third of the world's total. Given that they are spread

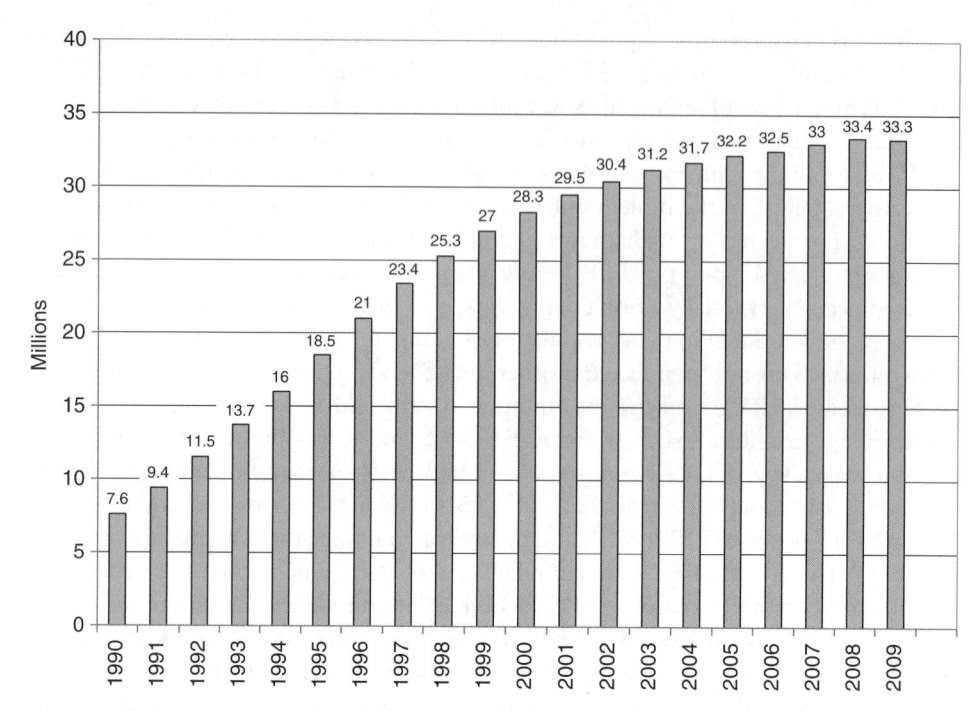

Figure 10.4 Estimated Number of People Living with HIV Globally, 1990–2009.
Source: WHO (2007) *Global Health Observatory*, apps.who.int/ghodata/

over many countries, the aggregate labor market effect of their reduced labor services in any particular economy is very small. In the US 14 561 deaths were attributed to AIDS in 2007. The number of people living with the disease in the same year in the US was 732 514 (263 936 HIV positive and 468 578 AIDS).[65] In the UK and Canada the numbers living with both HIV and AIDS were estimated to be 77 000 and 73 000 respectively in 2007. The UK, with one of the highest incidence of HIV/AIDS in Western Europe, has, nonetheless, about one half of the North American infection rates. In sub-Saharan Africa there are approximately 22 million people who are currently living with HIV/AIDS. The sheer numbers and the poverty of the nations involved require a policy response that is on quite a different scale than that of confronting the pandemic in the affluent countries of Western Europe, North America and Australia-New Zealand.

There is no cure for AIDS. First, if contracted, there are recently developed anti-retroviral drug therapies that modify the damages to HIV positive patients and extend the time before AIDS takes a firm hold. These drugs are complex, varying with the stage of the disease, expensive and costly to administer. Second, there has been an appalling ignorance of the epidemiology of the disease in some highly placed political circles in sub-Saharan African countries. This not only has limited government funds to HIV/AIDS education and treatment, but it has limited public health policy effectiveness by restricting publicity about safe sexual practices and HIV screening. Then there is the dogma of certain religious groups and churches about pre-marital sex, family planning and condom use to name a few, which makes its way into the public policy debate in the affluent countries. Effective assistance offered by donor countries and international organizations is thereby often inhibited. Third, since the only treatment available to HIV positive victims is a drug therapy, the pricing of drugs and the market structure in which the major drug companies operate is a matter of public concern. Drug producing companies (particularly in the US, the UK, France, Switzerland and Germany) have historically enjoyed patent protection (property rights) over their research outcomes which raises the issues of i) how much protection should they have (the answer appears to range between zero and complete), and ii) whether there is a socially more efficient way of drug development. That these are classical and long-standing industrial organization issues does not mean that we are closer to policy solutions. Perhaps not surprisingly, there is evidence of price discrimination *among* low-income countries with higher prices charged in higher-income regimes.[66]

Has the HIV/AIDS pandemic peaked? With the current level of effort (medical best practice, medical technology and public policy) the rate of new infections of HIV positive individuals has moderated in all major regions of the world. However, the number of new HIV infections on an annual basis is still greater than the numbers who die of AIDS-related causes according to WHO sources.[67] The number of people living with the combination of HIV and AIDS is still rising on trend, and will continue to do so for some time – see Figure 10.4. The increasing availability, the lower cost and increasing effectiveness of anti-retroviral drug strategies keeps an increasing number of HIV positive patients alive and functioning and free of AIDS. The total number with the combined disease is larger as a consequence. Stocks and flows again! Unfortunately, there has been a "brain drain" of physicians from high HIV infected countries in sub-Saharan Africa to OECD countries in recent years. This outflow of health care professionals is highly sensitive to the HIV/AIDS spread.[68] As the HIV/AIDS population stabilizes in the near future (projected stabilization is 2025), and as per capita income goes up in the infection-ravaged country (and physicians' salaries), the brain drain of physicians will also moderate or, perhaps, cease.[69] This, in turn, will lessen the severity of the current crisis as more health professional resources are applied to public health policy which should reduce the infection rate and reduce the rate of collapse into the disease's last stages.

The sub-Saharan countries have experienced a higher death rate than would otherwise have prevailed due to the AIDS pandemic. It is these early deaths that lower life expectancy. The decline in the labor supplies of both men and women might cause wage rates to rise, were it not for two offsetting effects. First, there is a decrease in the demand for output, hence a decrease in the demand for labor to produce output. Second, upward pressure on wages simply reduces the high and often disguised unemployment endemic to the region. The net result is somewhat similar to that in England six centuries earlier: there is a reduction of fertility brought about by inducing women to remain in the labor market (or enter it); the price of children has risen. Taking the projections about the most likely course of the disease over time at face value suggests that the population of countries such as South Africa will remain below the hypothesized non-HIV/AIDS alternative for some time. Or, as Alwyn Young estimates, the income (GDP) per capita remains above the non-HIV/AIDS alternative until at least the year 2045.[70] We would expect the gains to be greater in the very low-income countries and smaller in the higher-income countries of sub-Saharan Africa. But the macroeconomic effects do not end here. As Young also computes, the extra gains from reduced fertility and lower aggregate human capital formation (but not individual levels) are sufficient to fund caring for the AIDS victims without prejudicing future generations' economic welfare.[71]

The key to decision-making about adopting HIV-limiting health and safe sexual practices is education. While this may be so in general, there are holes in the argument. For instance, increased years of schooling (in sub-Saharan Africa) are actually *positively* related to the infection rate. This is probably a spurious correlation as it is the rising personal income (which is brought about by higher levels of education) which commercializes sex, and sex-workers have a high rate of infection and tend to pass it on to others. For this reason, sex-workers are a major target group of public policy because of the high payoff (in terms of lives saved) to reducing infections spread by their activities. The second influence of education is on the accumulation of human capital. Many of the victims of AIDS are innocent children whose parents have died of the disease, some of whom have passed on the virus to their children. Such children usually live in depressed circumstances in charity or state-supported orphanages, and the result is that they will receive less in formal education than they would have received with living parents. The per capita human capital reduction is clearly a gross cost at the aggregate level. To this loss, there is an offset that depends on the amount of additional expenditure on health care. Since much comes in the form of capital imports into sub-Saharan Africa, the potential to raise the investment rate is there. We can think of health care as a "leading industry" playing much same type of infrastructure role as railway and like expenditure a century and a half earlier.

10.7 When, Not If? But Not Now! Flu Pandemics

As catastrophes go, near the head of the league table is the great influenza pandemic of 1918–1919. Upwards of 40 million deaths world-wide were directly caused by it during the 18 months of the outbreak – more deaths, as is often pointed out, than attributed to World War One itself. Some epidemiologists argue that even this estimate is far too low, and the actual number of deaths due to the pandemic of 1918–1919 was tens of millions more. We will never know. To place it in some perspective, this particular influenza pandemic brought about many more deaths than AIDS has taken cumulatively since 1981. Its death toll rivals the 1347 episode of bubonic plague (but not all three episodes). Yet, unlike these other catastrophic diseases, most people who contracted the disease survived it. Approximately, one-third of the entire population of the world may have had the virus of this particular influenza strain at some point in the disease cycle of 1918–1919. So it is the common flu, or not-so-common flu as it turns out, that has the greatest potential for human harm. Small changes in the pattern of spread and in individual susceptibility could make flu the greatest catastrophic event of human history. The nature of the virus, ever altering and adapting, makes it still our greatest threat.

> ### Influenza Type A Virus H1N1
>
> [WHO announced today the H1N1 pandemic is over 10/08/2010]
>
> "Influenza is a respiratory infection caused by an RNA virus. There are three main types of influenza virus (A, B, and C); A is the main cause of influenza in humans. Influenza A is further divided into subtypes on the basis of the two classes of surface proteins comprising the outer coat of the virus – hemagglutinin (H) and neuraminidase (N). Virus subtypes are identified by the order in which the protein was discovered; for example, the subtypes now established in the human population are H1N1, H1N2, and H3N2. Although these proteins are attacked by the human immune system, new protein types allow the virus to escape the human body's defenses. Virus subtypes can, in turn, be subdivided into various strains.
>
> Influenza is a seasonal disease concentrated in the cold months of the year in temperate zones and, less strongly, in wet and rainy seasons in tropical zones, although pandemics can emerge at any time during the year. The reasons for its seasonality remain unknown." MacKellar (2007), 427–8.

The particularly deadly influenza virus which spread in the last months of World War I had its *apparent* epicenter in France at staging areas for the allied troops. The ultimate source of the virus is not known. The possibilities are several and not mutually exclusive. The first documented appearance of the virus was in the US at a military base in Kansas. From there, the relatively mild form of the virus was carried to Europe by the troops.[72] The other suspicion is that the influenza virus originated in China since most known sources of outbreaks of flu, before and since, come from Asia. So, some time in the late stages of the war, the influenza virus reached France carried possibly by Chinese workers brought to France for construction work.[73] The flu spread rapidly among the troops, leapt across the war-torn no-man's land with ease and spread geographically outward. During its first phase, knowledge of the epidemic and, where known, its extent were kept from the public due to strategic military concerns and war-time censorship. The inability of the German army to maintain sufficient healthy soldiers at the front in an attack posture seriously weakened that country's resolve, so the influenza outbreak may have hastened the peace. It might be noted that the flu epidemic became known as *the Spanish Flu* simply because the Spanish, who were not actual belligerents in the war, were one of the few countries with a free press which reported the epidemic in its early stages.[74] Undoubtedly, the secrecy which prevailed in the initial months of the flu epidemic allowed it to spread more effectively than otherwise would have been the case with quarantine and isolation measures and greater public health awareness. The epidemic soon reached pandemic proportions.

The influenza virus was subsequently spread by the soldiers returning from duty in the war. It morphed into a pandemic by October of 1918. Indeed, one can hardly

The Great Flu Pandemics of 1918/9

In many countries, police and other public officials wore masks in an attempt to prevent the spread of the flu. The masks proved ineffective.
Source: US Department of Health and Human Services, www.PandemicFlu.gov

imagine an environment more conducive to the spread of flu than the crowded troop-trains and troopships of 1918–1919 headed to Indo-China, Africa, India, Australia/ New Zealand, Canada and the US to name just a few destinations. In the US, it spread outward from the ports and military bases where US soldiers were sent for demobilization. It took similar paths in other countries.

Over the 18-month period of the outbreak the influenza exhibited three distinct mortality phases or patterns of virulence. For England and Wales these were:

Wave I	June/August 1918	Duration:	7 weeks
Wave II	October 1918/December 1919		14 weeks
Wave III	February 1919/April 1919		10 weeks

Apart from minor timing differences, the pattern was about the same in all countries for which we have measurement. Wave II was by far the most deadly taking at its peak four times the number of victims as the peak of Wave I. It was also more deadly because the outbreak lasted longer. Wave III was shorter and, at its peak, took about half the victims as the peak of November 1918.[75]

In the world population not all ran the same risk of dying, however. As evident in Table 10.3, the national death rates due to influenza varied considerably by country. An Italian was about twice as likely to die as an English person, for instance. Within Europe, the disease seemed to be more deadly in the Mediterranean or southern

Table 10.3 Selected National Death Rates Due to the Pandemic Influenza, 1918–1919.

(influenza and pneumonia deaths combined)

Country/Population	Deaths/1000	Country/Population	Deaths/1000
Western Samoa	220.0	Italy	10.6
Alaska (Eskimo)	80.0	Spain	8.3
India*	53.2	Switzerland	6.0
South Africa	43.0	Sweden	5.9
New Zealand (Maori)	42.0	England & Wales	5.8
Gold Coast	40.0	New Zealand (European)	5.8
Nigeria	30.0	USA	5.2
Mexico	23.0	Canada	4.5
USA (Indian)	20.6	Ireland	4.0
Indonesia	17.7	Australia (European)	2.3
Chile	11.0		

*India is the simple average of the rate of Punjab, the Bombay Region and the Central Provinces (our calculation).
Note: For detailed sources of the estimates see Rice and Palmer (1993).
Source: Rice and Palmer (1993), Table 3.

countries.[76] In the densely populated states of India, the pandemic took a particularly large toll – about 13 million.[77] Yet, smaller and isolated communities in Polynesia were at severe risk. The relative isolation of populations, even within countries, meant that they did not have the long historical exposure to flu outbreaks of the past that seemed to confer some form of resistance. And that brings us to one of the most interesting observations about the influenza pandemic: the 1918–19 deaths were concentrated in the age groups of the very young (less than 12 months) and young adults (20 to 40 years of age). While high flu deaths among the newborn might be expected, the fact that otherwise healthy young adults were falling victim was not. As Jeffrey Taubenberger and David Morens have calculated, young adults were more susceptible and died with a greater frequency when compared to their morbidity and mortality in "normal" flu years such as 1928–1929.[78] Furthermore, the older parts of the population, usually among the most susceptible to disease, registered deaths that were consistent with those in non-pandemic/non-epidemic years. The lower than expected death rate among those over 40 years of age suggests that the virus was a mutation of an earlier one imparting some immunity.[79] A particularly bad outbreak of the disease in 1889–1890 is thought to be the source of the partial immunity because i) it is a very similar flu virus; ii) it had a high morbidity rate but low mortality rate so many survivors carried its antibodies; and iii) the age and timing are consistent. The final part of the puzzle is that there is no firm scientific view among virologists about what made this variant of the H1N1 virus of 1918–1919 so deadly.

Unlike bubonic plague and HIV/AIDS the relative burden of economic cost of an influenza catastrophe comes not from the deaths but from illness. Similar to the deaths due to AIDS, the excess deaths due to influenza simply raise the amount of capital per surviving worker in the medium- and longer-term. Productivity both increases and offsets the lost production due to death. There is little effect on economic growth. However, there is a large loss of current income (production) in the short-run. Similar to the bubonic plague real wage effect of 14th century England, in the United States at the time of the influenza pandemic (and subsequently), wage increases were roughly proportional to the mortality loss.[80] Both non-lethal influenza and deaths contribute to the direct costs. In the case of the former the lost income due to absence from the workplace is calculated. Flu usually takes the workers out of the workplace from five to ten days. The current direct cost is equal to the loss of national income. Due to the pandemic of 1918–1919, as has been recently calculated, was a fall in US GDP in 1918 of −0.45%.[81] Not much given the human carnage wrought by the disease.

> Even with modern anti-viral and anti-bacterial drugs, vaccines, and prevention knowledge, the return of a pandemic virus equivalent in pathogenicity to the virus of 1918 would likely kill greater than 100 million people worldwide. A pandemic virus with the (alleged) pathogenic potential of some recent H5N1 outbreaks could cause substantially more deaths.
> Taubenberger and Morens (2006).

Today, societies are faced with a difficult choice. They can devote massive amounts of resources to the on-going stock-piling of anti-viral and antibacterial drugs and vaccines knowing that the probability of their use is extremely small. The influenza Type A virus is more or less continually mutating so that last year's virus from which the anti-viral drugs will be made is not an exact match for this year's virus. Vaccines therefore will be a close match and confer protection, though not complete protection, on susceptible groups. Yet, epidemiologists are of the opinion that the virus can mutate in both small and large ways that make it a continual threat. The institutions which are charged with the responsibility of monitoring the possibility of a flu pandemic, such as the World Health Organization, are often accused of "crying wolf too often." In turn, this weakens the public will.[82] This is especially so when also asked to compute the cost to society. More than one political career has been ruined by the commitment of resources to a pandemic which never materialized in a deadly form. Landis MacKellar has called this "policy-fatigue." Yet, if we scale up the pattern of morbidity and excess deaths from 1918–1919 and apply it to the population of today it suggests a death toll of greater than 100 million (possibly as high as 300 million) depending on the particular fatality rate assumed.[83] To be unprepared would be unthinkable.

10.8 Summary

The threat to individual and family health and well-being posed by infectious disease epidemics and other catastrophic events was, and remains, a concern to people everywhere in the world. As we learn more about the causes of these diseases, climate patterns, and other calamities, there naturally is a hope we can avoid the anticipated catastrophe. And the more things we learn about, the more things there are to go wrong. The news today is filled with stories concerning the growing number of antibiotic resistant micro-organisms, the potential severity of each new hurricane season, or the likelihood of a major earthquake. Environmental threats are dynamic and omnipresent. The realization they can reach you and your family often leads to an outpouring of support independent of a rudimentary benefit-cost calculation. When people do make such a calculation, it logically is limited to private costs, to the effect on the immediate family. The social costs of new threats are seldom discussed. We worry about our employment, but the impact on fellow employees or even the employer is a secondary concern. The macroeconomic effects on, say, the unemployment rate are another step removed. We often don't have a good idea of the probability that any one person will contract the disease. Thus, our focus usually is on the potential benefits of avoiding the catastrophe (e.g., "for a few dollars from each of you, we can cure cancer;" "a few pennies a day can feed a child in a less developed nation;" or "every little donation helps earthquake victims"). With so many competing claims, we need to have a better understanding of the aggregate benefits and costs, of the macroeconomic effects as well as the microeconomic ones. Although well-being has increased over time, it is constantly threatened. New, often now man-made, catastrophes always seem to be lurking in the shadows. None dare call it paranoia.

Appendix 10.1

The Plague Transmission Cycle

1) *Yersinia pestis* is a bacterium that is resident in fleas that infect the wild population of rodents (ground squirrels, prairie dogs) in parts of North America and Central Asia. It is the source of the plague.
2) An outbreak occurs when the conditions favor the virus. The flea population expands as the animal host population expands (because of increased food availability) and the climate conditions are favorable.
3) There is increased contact between the sylvan rodents and other mammals (although all mammals can be temporary hosts) such as horses, camels and, most importantly, domestic rodents. Humans occasionally are infected directly by contact with a flea infected (non-rodent) animal.
4) The close contact between humans and domestic rodents is the most frequent transmission route. The flea leaves the dead host (domestic rodent) and migrates to the human host. The human is infected by the flea bite.
5) Humans do not spread the disease to one another, except in cases noted below, but they may pass on the flea although the contagion is likely the result of living in the same environment with infected rodents.
6) Human may catch the pneumonic version of the plague from infected individuals as this is spread by water droplets in the air. The virus is not robust in the air so transmission by this route is relatively rare.
7) Blood to blood contact between an infected and a non-infected individual is a very efficient transmission mechanism but the *septicemia* version of the plague is even rarer than the pneumonic version.

Endnotes

1. Ignoring political and strategic arguments that relate the size of the army to population size and, for the moment, agglomeration and other scale effects.
2. McGovern (1980).
3. Mikkelsen *et al.* (2001); Pringle (1997).
4. Mikkelsen *et al.* (2001).
5. Jacobsen (1987); Brown (2000).
6. Brander and Taylor (1998).
7. As the American cartoonist Walt Kelly has his main cartoon character Pogo say: "Man does not see the writing on the wall until he has his back to it."
8. See Mann (2006); Crosby (2003b).
9. Denevan (1996).
10. This number is from the combined censuses of the three countries, the US, Canada and Greenland. There is of course great uncertainty about the estimate of the contact population. We have selected the Thornton (2000) estimate which is on the high side. We use it as a basis for later calculations on grounds the upward bias is, for our purpose, more desirable than a downward bias.
11. Thornton (2000).

12 Meister (1976).
13 McManus (1972).
14 See Mann (2005); Crosby (2003b).
15 Perdue (2007).
16 Thornton (1984).
17 Gatschet (1885) offers a near contemporary account.
18 Bergman *et al.* (1999).
19 As Ó Gráda (2009) notes, "the view that Famine was the product of ... overpopulation can be traced back nearly five millennia to the Babylonian legend of Gilgamesh" (8).
20 Kannisto, Christensen and Vaupel (1997). In the final chapter of Ó Gráda (2009) he discusses what can be realistically expected over the next decade or two.
21 Chapter 3 of Ó Gráda (2009) covers historical methods of preventing and coping with famine.
22 Ó Gráda (2009).
23 Ó Gráda (2007).
24 Sen (1981). Our account is based on Ó Gráda (2008). Another version of the story appears as Chapter 6 in Ó Gráda (2009); in particular see the conclusion of that chapter (184–94) where Ó Gráda details concisely the bureaucratic failings of the British.
25 Ó Gráda (2008). The other famine discussed in detail in this paper is the mainland Chinese Great Leap Forward famine of 1959–61.
26 *Ibid.*, p. 24.
27 *Ibid.*, pp. 25–26.
28 *Ibid.*, pp. 26–28.
29 *Ibid.*, 30, from *Economist*, 30 Jan. 1943, 141. News of the famine was viewed in Britain as propaganda from those arguing against the hoarding hypothesis.
30 There is some debate about which plague incident the rhyme refers to (1347/8 or 1665) and exactly what the symbolism means.
31 See Rosen (2007) for a popular and well-argued account of the Plague of Justinian. Dols (1974).
32 Dols (1979).
33 Although somewhat dated, Hatcher (1977) still provides one of the best guides to the controversies of the Black Death. See also: Benedictow (2004).
34 Perry and Fetherson (1997). There are the "three human pathogenic species of *Yersinia* — *Yersinia pestis*, *Yersinia pseudotuberculosis*, and *Yersinia enterocolitica*". Only *Y. pestis* is associated with bubonic plague. Prior to 1967, when it was renamed, the bacterium was known as *Pasteurella pestis*.
35 Raoult *et al.* (2000); Cohn (2002).
36 Perry and Fetherson (1997).
37 *Ibid.*
38 For a good description of the spread of the disease along the trade routes, see Bernstein (2008).
39 Cohn (2002).
40 Several experiments have recently shown that under ideal conditions the *Yersinia pestis* bacterium will live in the soil for several weeks in a laboratory. There has recently been verification of this in nature. Eisen *et al.* (2008).
41 Perry and Fetherson (1997).
42 Shrewsbury (1970).
43 The genetic variation of the British population was much less than that before the Black Death. Topf *et al.* (2007).
44 Bailey (1996).

45 Hinde (2003). Hinde's calculations depend on the assumed base population of 1300 and the assumed growth rate of the post-plague population (his calculations are retrospective).
46 Haddock and Kiesling (2002).
47 Schofield (1996).
48 Hatcher (1994).
49 Cohn (2007). England, under Edward III, passed a law but there is little evidence of enforcement.
50 Both France and England were in the throes of the Hundred Years War hence the need for additional state revenues.
51 Benedictow (2004).
52 Mortimer (2006).
53 Allen (2001); Allen (2003); and Munro (2004).
54 Bailey (1998), 223–51.
55 Allen (2003). Clark (2007) downplays the role of real wages differences between England and Southern Europe. See also Pamuk (2007).
56 For a thorough discussion of wages and the reasons for their performance: see Penn and Dyer (1990).
57 De Moor and Van Zanden (2010).
58 Goesling, Brian and Glenn Firebaugh (2004).
59 UN (2007), *World Population Prospects: The 2006 Revision*, Table A.20. Some smaller sub-Saharan African countries have even higher rates of infection – see General Sources.
60 WHO (2003), *World Health Report*, Statistical Annex, Table 2. HIV/AIDS is the third largest cause of death world-wide but the single largest cause of death in Africa.
61 Young (2005).
62 Power (2004).
63 CDC (2007), *HIV/AIDS Surveillance Report*.
64 The Canadian Government lists the high-risk categories for HIV infection as: gay men, injection drug users, aboriginal people, prison inmates, youth, women, and people from countries where HIV is endemic. Canada (2009), *Health Canada*, http://www.hc-sc.gc.ca/ahc-asc/activit/strateg/int_AIDS-sida-eng.php
65 United States (2008), Tables 8, 13 and 14. WHO (2008), *2008 Report on the Global AIDS Epidemic*, Annex 1.
66 Borrell (2007).
67 WHO (2008), *2008 Report on the Global AIDS Epidemic*, Annex 1.
68 Bhargava and Docquier (2008).
69 Bongaarts *et al.* (2007).
70 Young (2005).
71 Young (2007).
72 The definitive US account is Crosby (1989, 2003a). According to Iezzoni's (1999) popular account, by the spring of 1918 the flu outbreak was documented. There were even discussion among US Government authorities on the subject of slowing down the movement of US troops to the battle front (Europe) and avoiding troop concentrations.
73 Langford (2005). The Chinese workers travelled to France by the route that took them across the Pacific, across Canada and the US to eastern ports and then on to Europe.
74 Hollenbeck (2002).
75 Smallman-Raynor, Johnson and Cliff (2002), Figure 1.
76 Ansart *et al* (2006).
77 The Indian Censuses were remarkably good after 1890.
78 Taubenberger and Morens (2006). These authors then ask the rhetorical question, to which there is no epidemiological answer: where was the virus in the intervening 30 years?

79 Tumpey *et al* (2004).
80 Garrett (2009).
81 James and Sargent (2007). The Canadian Department of Finance estimates. The authors of this study actually argue that their method of calculation, using industrial production, may overstate the loss because of the inability to separate lost industrial production due to the flu deaths from the decline in industrial production as the war ended.
82 Albala-Bertrand (1993).
83 MacKellar (2007).

References

Albala-Bertrand, J.M. (1993) *Political Economy of Large Natural Disasters: With Special Reference to Developing Countries*, Oxford: Oxford University Press.
Allen, R.C. (2001) "The Great Divergence in European Wages and Prices from the Middle Ages to the First World War", *Explorations in Economic History*, **38**(4) (October), 411–47.
Allen, Robert C. (2003) "Progress and Poverty in Early Modern Europe", *Economic History Review*, **56**(3), 403–43.
Ansart, Séverine, Camille Pelat, Pierre-Yves Boelle, Fabrice Carrat, Antoine Flahault, Alain-Jacques Valleron (2006) "Mortality Burden of the 1918–1919 Influenza Pandemic in Europe", *Influenza and Other Respiratory Viruses*, **3**(3), 99–106.
Bailey, Mark (1996) "Demographic Decline in Late Medieval England: Some Thoughts on Recent Research", *Economic History Review*, **49**(1), 1–19.
Bailey, Mark (1998) "Peasant Welfare in England, 1290–1348", *Economic History Review*, **51**(2), 223–51.
Benedictow, Ole J. (2004) *The Black Death, 1346–1353; The Complete History*, Woodbridge, Suffolk: The Boydell Press.
Bergman, Abraham B., David C. Grossman, Angela M. Erdrich, John G. Todd and Ralph Forquera (1999) "A Political History of the Indian Health Service", *The Milbank Quarterly*, **77**(4), 571–604.
Bernstein, William J. (2008) *A Splendid Exchange; How Trade Shaped the Modern World*, New York: Grove Press.
Bhargava, Alok and Frederic Docquier (2008) "HIV Pandemic, Medical Brain Drain, and Economic Development in Sub-Saharan Africa", *The World Bank Economic Review*, **22**(2), 345–66.
Bongaarts, John, Thomas Buettner, Gerhard Heilig and François Pelletier (2008) "Has the HIV Epidemic Peaked?", *Population and Development Review*, **34**(2), 199–224.
Borrell, Joan-Ramon (2007) "Pricing and Patents of HIV/AIDS Drugs in Developing Countries", *Applied Economics*, **39**, 505–18.
Brander, James A. and M. Scott Taylor (1998) "The Simple Economics of Easter Island: A Ricardo-Malthus Model of Renewable Resource Use", *American Economic Review*, **88**(1), 119–38.
Brown, Dale MacKenzie (2000) "The Fate of Greenland's Vikings", *Archaeology*, February, online: http://www.archaeology.org/online/features/greenland/index.html
Centers for Disease Control [CDC] (current) *HIV/AIDS Surveillance Report*, Department of Health and Human Services, U.S. Government. http://www.cdc.gov/hiv
Clark, G. (2007), "The Long March of History: Farm Wages, Population and Economic Growth, England, 1209–1869" *Economic History Review*, **60**(1), 97–136.
Cohn, Samuel (2007) "After the Black Death: Labour Legislation and Attitudes Towards Labour in Late-Medieval Western Europe", *Economic History Review*, **60**(3), 457–85.

Cohn, Samuel K. Jr. (2002) "The Black Death: End of a Paradigm", *The American Historical Review*, **107**(3), 703–38.

Crosby, Alfred W. (2003a) *America's Forgotten Pandemic: the Influenza of 1918*, 2nd edn, New York and Cambridge: Cambridge University Press.

Crosby, Alfred W. (2003b) *The Columbian Exchange Biological and Cultural Consequences of 1492*, revised edition, Westport, CT: Praeger Press.

De Moor, Tine and Jan Luiten Van Zanden (2010) "Girl Power: the European Marriage Pattern and Labour Markets in the North Sea Region in the Late Medieval and Early Modern Period" *Economic History Review*, **63**(1), 1–33.

Denevan, William M. (1996) "Carl Sauer and Native American Population", *Geographical Review*, **86**(3), 385–97.

Dols, Michael W. (1974) "Plague in Early Islamic History", *Journal of the American Oriental Society*, Vol. **94**(3) (July), 371–83.

Dols, Michael W. (1979) "The Second Plague Pandemic and Its Recurrences in the Middle East: 1347–1894", *Journal of the Economic and Social History of the Orient*, Vol. 22, No. 2. (May), 162–89.

Eisen, R.J., J.M. Petersen, M.S. Higgins, D. Wong, C.E. Levy, P.S. Mead (2008) Persistence of *Yersinia pestis* in Soil under Natural Conditions, *Emergency Infectious Diseases*, 14, 6 (June), 941–3. http://www.cdc.gov/EID/content/14/6/941.htm

Garrett, Thomas (2009), "War and Pestilence as Labor Market Shocks: U.S. Manufacturing Wage Growth 1914–1919", *Economic Inquiry*, **47**(4), 711–25.

Gatschet, Albert S. (1885) "The Beothuk Indians", *Proceedings of the American Philosophical Society*, **22**, 120, Part IV, 408–24.

Goesling, Brian and Glenn Firebaugh (2004) "The Trend in International Health Inequality", *Population and Development Review*, **30**(1), 131–46.

Haddock, David D. and Lynne Kiesling (2002) "The Black Death and Property Rights", *The Journal of Legal Studies*, **31**(2), Part 2: The Evolution of Property Rights, S545–S587.

Hatcher, John (1977) *Plague, Population and the English Economy, 1348–1530*, London: The Macmillan Press Ltd.

Hatcher, John (1994) "England in the Aftermath of the Black Death", *Past and Present*, **144**, (August), 3–35.

Hinde, Andrew (2003) *England's Population; A History Since the Domesday Survey*, London: Holder Arnold.

Hollenbeck, James E. (2002) "The 1918–1919 Influenza Pandemic: A Pale Horse Rides Home from War," *Bios*, **73**(1), 19–27.

Iezzoni, Lynette (1999) *Influenza 1918, the Worst Epidemic in American History*, New York, TV Books.

Jacobsen, N. Kingo (1987) "Studies on Soils and Potential for Soil Erosion in the Sheep Farming Area of South Greenland", *Arctic and Alpine Research*, **19**(4), 498–507.

James, Steven and Tim Sargent (2007) "The Economic Impact of an Influenza Pandemic", Working Paper 2007–04, Department of Finance, Government of Canada.

Kannisto, Väinö, Kaare Christensen and James W. Vaupel (1997) "No Increased Mortality in Later Life for Cohorts Born during Famine" *American Journal of Epidemiology*, **145**, 987–94.

Langford, Christopher (2005) "Did the 1918–19 Influenza Pandemic Originate in China?", *Population and Development Review*, **31**(3), 473–505.

MacKellar, Landis (2007) "Pandemic Influenza: A Review", *Population and Development Review*, **33**(3), 429–51.

Mann, Charles C. (2005) *1491, New Revelations of the Americas Before Columbus*, New York: Vintage Books.

McGovern, Thomas H. (1980) "Cows, Harp Seals, and Churchbells: Adaptation and Extinction in Norse Greenland", *Human Ecology*, **8**(3), 245–75.

McManus, J. (1972) "An Economic Analysis of Indian Behaviour in the North American Fur Trade", *Journal of Economic History*, **32**(1), 36–53.

Meister, Cary W. (1976) "Demographic Consequences of Euro-American Contact on Selected American Indian Populations and Their Relationship to the Demographic Transition", *Ethnohistory*, **23**(2), 161–72.

Mikkelsen, Naja, Antoon Kuijpers, Susanne Lassen and Jesper Vedel (2001) "Marine and Terrestrial Investigations in the Norse Eastern Settlement, South Greenland", *Geology of Greenland Survey Bulletin*, **189**, 65–9.

Mortimer, Ian (2006) The Perfect King, London: Jonathan Cape.

Munro, John (2004) "Before and After the Black Death: Money, Prices, and Wages in Fourteenth-Century England", Working Paper No. 24, Department of Economics and Institute for Policy Analysis, University of Toronto, Toronto, Canada.

Ó Gráda, Cormac (2007) "Making Famine History", *Journal of Economic Literature* **45**(1), 5–38.

Ó Gráda, Cormac (2008) "The Ripple that Drowns? Twentieth-century Famines in China and India as Economic History", *Economic History Review*, **61**(1), 5–37.

Ó Gráda, Cormac (2009) *Famine: A Short History*, Princeton: Princeton University Press.

Pamuk, Sevket (2007) "The Black Death and the Origins of the 'Great Divergence' Across Europe, 1300–1600", *European Review of Economic History*, **11**, 289–317.

Penn, Simon A.C. and Christopher Dyer (1990) "Wages and Earnings in Late Medieval England: Evidence from the Enforcement of the Labour Laws", *Economic History Review*, **43**(3), 356–76.

Perdue, Theda (2007) *Cherokee Nation and the Trail of Tears*, New York: Viking Press.

Perry, Robert D. and Jacqueline D. Fetherston (1997) "Yersinia pestis – Etiologic Agent of Plague", *Clinical Microbiology Reviews*, **10**(1), 35–66.

Power, Lisa (2004) "HIV and Sexual Health in the UK: Politics and Public Health", *The Lancet*, **364**, 9428 (July), 108–9.

Pringle, Heather (1997) " Death in Norse Greenland", *Science*, New Series, 275(5302), 924–26.

Raoult, Didier, Gerard Aboudharam, Eric Crubezy, Georges Larrouy, Bertrand Ludes, Michel Drancourt (2000) "Molecular Identification by "Suicide PCR" of Yersinia pestis as the Agent of Medieval Black Death", *Proceedings of the National Academy of Sciences of the United States of America*, **97**(23), 12800–3.

Rice, Geoffrey W. and Edwina Palmer (1993) "Pandemic Influenza in Japan, 1918–19: Mortality Patterns and Official Responses", *Journal of Japanese Studies*, **19**(2) (Summer), 389–420.

Rosen, William (2007) *Justinian's Flea: The First Great Plague and the End of the Roman Empire*, London: Penguin Books.

Schofield, Phillipp R. (1996) "Tenurial Developments and the Availability of Customary Land in a Later Medieval Community", *Economic History Review*, **49**(2), 250–67.

Sen, Amartya K. (1981) *Poverty and Famine: An Essay on Entitlement and Depravation*, Oxford, England: Clarendon Press.

Shrewsbury, John Findlay Drew (1970) *A History of Bubonic Plague in the British Isles*, Cambridge: Cambridge University Press.

Smallman-Raynor, Matthew, Niall Johnson and Andrew D Cliff (2002) " The Spatial Anatomy of an Epidemic: Influenza in London and the County Boroughs of England and Wales, 1918–1919, *Transactions of the Institute of British Geographers*, New Series, **27**(4), 452–70.

Taubenberger, Jeffrey K. and David M. Morens (2006) "1918 Influenza: the Mother of All Pandemics", *Emerging Infectious Diseases*, **12**(1), 15–22.

Thornton, Russell (1984) "Social Organization and the Demographic Survival of the Tolowa", *Ethnohistory*, **31**(3), 187–96.

Thornton, Russell (2000) "Population History of the Native North Americans", in Haines and Steckel (2000), *A Population History of North America*, 9–50.

Topf, A.L., M.T.P. Gilbert, R.C. Fleischer and A.R. Hoelzel (2007) "Ancient Human mtDNA Genotypes from England Reveal Lost Variation over the Last Millennium", *Biology Letters*, **3**, 550–553.

Tumpey, Terrence M., Adolfo García-Sastre, Jeffery K. Taubenberger, Peter Palese, David E. Swayne and Christopher F. Basler (2004) "Pathogenicity and Immunogenicity of Influenza Viruses with Genes from the 1918 Pandemic Virus", *Proceedings of the National Academy of Sciences of the United States of America*, **101**(9) (March), 3166–71.

United Nations (2010) [UN] *World Population Prospects: The 2008 Revision*, United Nations: New York United Nations, and subsequent, annual revisions. http://www.esa.un.org/unpp/

World Health Organization (2008) *2008 Report on the Global AIDS Epidemic*, Geneva: World Health Organisation.

World Health Organization (year), [WHO] *World Health Reports for (year)*, Geneva: World Health Organization. http://www.who.int/whr

Young, Alwyn (2005) "The Gift of the Dying: The Tragedy of AIDS and the Welfare of Future African Generations", *The Quarterly Journal of Economics*, **70**(2), 423–66.

Young, Alwyn (2007) "In Sorrow to Bring Forth Children: Fertility Amidst the Plague of HIV", *Journal of Economic Growth*, **12**, 283–327.

Part Four
Conclusions

Chapter Eleven
Concluding Remarks

The human species once consisted of so few individuals that we were a fragile presence on the earth. But the children of Eve prospered. Within the limits imposed by the environment, the larger the population of any species (animal, vegetable, microbes, viruses or bacteria), the greater were its chances of survival. As the human population grew, genetic diversity followed giving greater protection to the species. Humans also spread geographically, so they were less likely to be hostage to locally disastrous events such as visited on the Greenland Norse. The human population had to live within the constraints of its physical and technical environments; however humankind was lucky in this. We are generalists, not specialists, and this meant that the human population was adaptable. Humans thrived in cool, temperate and warm climates and could do so because of flexibility in their clothing and dietary requirements. Foods as varied as grubs, grasses, fish and Aberdeen-Angus steak were all on the human menu.[1] In short, humans had no narrowly-defined ecological niche and, therefore, lacked specific dependencies. As such, the human family lived outside a species-specific predator-prey framework. This characteristic of adaptability required decision-making and the need to choose between alternatives is the basis of economic behavior.

In the telling of this story many compelling issues have been glossed over. First, for the past several hundred years or so, industrial accidents have paralleled the growth of industry. Mortality and morbidity as a result of industrial trauma have always been with us, but we generally have ignored this cost of the rise of the modern economy. It is hard not to empathize with those who often unwittingly bore the risk and suffered the consequence.

Many of the historical population issues raised here continue to be problems and none more so than the great divides created by the income distribution both between economies and within them. There are other historical issues that are only emerging as present-day concerns crystallize. One of these is the so-called female deficit issue or 'missing women'. Young adult women are not as numerous as they ought to be in

The Children of Eve: Population and Well-being in History, First Edition.
Louis P. Cain and Donald G. Paterson.
© 2012 Blackwell Publishing Ltd. Published 2012 by Blackwell Publishing Ltd.

countries such as India and China given the birth ratios of males and females in general and the standards of nutrition and medical care available. It is often fairly claimed that the preference for male children is so strong some women abort fetuses that are known (by amniocentesis procedures) to be female. In earlier times, infanticide may have been practiced to achieve the same end. In either case, the result was (is) gender imbalance. While abortion and infanticide may be present, there is debate as to whether such practices, by themselves, were (are) so widespread as to have a measurable effect. However, the missing women are more likely the result of other selective practices. Recent research by Siwan Anderson and Deraj Ray has shown that in sub-Saharan Africa, where there is also a strong preference for males, the gender imbalance is not due to selective abortions, but rather comes about because of the lack of medical attention given to female children relative to males. This results in more young female deaths.[2] The 'missing females' debate is far from over.

In most developed countries today, another new issue is emerging that arises from the income distribution of the past few decades. There is a distinct group of people who are increasingly disenfranchised from the mainstream economy. They drift in and out of employment; their low, and sometimes falling, earnings represent a growing social problem. They are generally young, low-attainment workers who have less than a secondary school education. The widening wage, and income, gap between them and their more highly-educated contemporaries has created an expectations gap in a world of transparent opulence. It is this group in which we find a disproportionate occurrence of failed early marriages, single-parent families, above average fertility, consignment to poverty and the like. Apart from the provision of social services, the only solution seems to be adult education and job training – policy options that are often delivered inadequately and clumsily. This group is a growing problem that requires immediate attention because it is over-represented in the prison populations, the welfare rolls and many other indices of social distress such as homelessness, hooliganism, bullying and addiction to alcohol and drugs. They are the developed world's 'have nots'.

Today, we are in the last phases of the greatest population boom in human history. It began in the 17th century and progressed over the 18th and 19th century with increasing momentum. At the beginning of the 20th century the population of the world stood at about 1.55 billion. Over the course of the century it increased four fold to 6.04 billion and has since grown to 7.00 billion. Concurrently, most individuals became substantially better-off. Even the economically disenfranchised generally achieved a higher standard of living than their counterparts did a century ago. We have survived the boom, but we have survived with substantial stress on the capacity of the physical environment. So far technical change has accommodated us.

In the past, population growth projections have often proven wildly inaccurate because they relied too much on short-term estimates during times of unstable mortality and fertility patterns. The current United Nations population projections are based on long-term trends that are much more stable than those of earlier years. For the developed countries, the projections are based on post-demographic transition trends. For the less-developed countries, they take the ongoing transition into account as well as the likely effects on the population of events such as the HIV/AIDS pandemic. Yet even so, the population projections are extraordinarily sensitive to slight changes in the fertility rates (or assumptions about their future behavior). The best estimates of the future size of the human population suggest that by 2050 it will number about 9.3 billion, 2.4 billion more than today (2010).[3] This works out to an average annual rate of increase of a little over 0.7%. By the beginning of the next century the population will be slightly over 10.1 billion. Thereafter, it will stabilize and possibly decrease. If fertility is 0.5 children below the (medium) projection of the UN, the world's population will stabilize in only 40 years (at 8.1 billion). If this comes about many readers of these words will be alive to see world population clocks tick repeatedly on the same number. And, these individuals will also witness the beginning of a long, slow decline in the world's population, one that will continue for the rest of the century and beyond (6.2 billion in 2100).[4] Yet, there is no guarantee that this will be the outcome. If fertility rates prove to be 0.5 children greater than the UN's medium projections, population will grow at a rapid rate into the next century.

From any of these calculations, it is clear that global population growth will take place largely in the less-developed world due to:

i) its greater, although falling, net fertility;
ii) the further saving of infant lives; and
iii) the extension of individual life expectancy.

The latter two causes are the most difficult with which to come to grips because their outcomes depend on how economic resources are committed to those ends. If we are pessimistic about the commitment of such resources, both domestic and foreign, especially in sub-Saharan Africa, then the actual population in 2050 could well be lower than predicted (see Table 11.1). On the other hand, if we are optimistic about our ability to save even more lives and add years to life, then the actual population could be higher than anticipated. Even then, it is unlikely to be very much higher

Table 11.1 Actual and Predicted Population Growth Rates, 1950–2050.

	(average annual percentage)		
	1950–1975	*1975–2009*	*2009–2050*
World	1.89	1.53	0.71
More Developed Regions	1.02	0.48	0.08
Less Developed Regions	2.25	1.82	0.83
Least Developed Regions	2.31	2.5	1.69
Other Less Developed Countries	2.24	1.72	0.65
Africa	2.44	2.59	1.66
Asia	2.11	1.62	0.58
Europe	0.84	0.23	−0.14
Latin America & Caribbean	2.64	1.73	0.55
North America	1.38	1.07	0.62
South America	2.59		
Oceania	2.03	1.49	0.91

Source: Data from United Nations (2009) *World Population Prospects, The 2008 Revision*, esa.un.org/unpp/p2k0data.asp.

because even the less developed world is made up of countries whose demographic behavior is changing in an historically predictable way. We conjecture that these countries will react to the improvement in child mortality and increased life expectancies by further reducing fertility.

Throughout the later phases of the great population boom of the past several hundred years, the forces of globalization have tended to bring about improved well-being by spreading the techniques of fertility control, reducing mortality and opening up migration. In the process they have changed attitudes to marriage, the desired size of the completed family, the role of women in the labor force and the reduction of barriers of discrimination across race, ethnicity, gender and age. In terms of income growth, globalization has spread the gains widely and lent stability to economic performance throughout the world. Yet, there are many criticisms of these forces. In particular, the gains have been gathered disproportionately by the already high-income countries. This inequity may be the result of interference with the tendencies of globalization through policies such as both tariff and non-tariff barriers that prevent the less-developed countries from exploiting their own comparative advantages in international trade. They may also result from globalization forces occasionally being too blunt when dealing with fragile economies with little economic and social capacity to absorb such blows.[5] There are many questions yet to be resolved about how to distribute income gains so as to reinforce the tendency towards convergence. Nonetheless, the fastest growing economies in recent years, notably China and India, have been those that were not long ago consigned to the less developed part of the world.

It is inevitable that the developed countries will contain more individuals who have recent origins in countries other than where they are currently located. The (net) immigration process will ensure this result. As the source of immigrants broadens, the world population is going to become more cosmopolitan. We will live in societies with a wider range of cultural options than in the past. Further, once raised, social and economic concerns such as equality of opportunity cannot easily be suppressed; the genie is out of the bottle. Along with greater ethnic diversity comes the need for increased social accommodation. The last 50 years also witnessed an increase in the rate of inter-marriage between couples with different national, religious, ethnic and racial backgrounds. This is likely to accelerate as the young experience greater diversity in their classrooms and workplaces. Many youngsters with diverse backgrounds will achieve the same level of higher education and professional advancement. Simply put, they will find themselves more frequently in each other's company – perhaps meeting at the 21st century's equivalent of a 19th century barn dance.

Endnotes

1 Richards, Pettitt, Stiner, and Trinkaus (2001).
2 Anderson and Ray (2009).
3 United Nations (2010) *World Population Prospects*.
4 United Nations (2011), *World Population Prospects: The 2010 Revision*. These estimates are adjusted from time to time to account for changes to the currently projected rates. See:

United Nations (2011), News Release, Department of Economics and Social Affairs, Population Division, 3 May 2011.
5 See Sen (1999) and Stiglitz (2006).

References

Anderson, Siwan and Debraj Ray (2010) "Missing Women: Age and Disease", *The Review of Economic Studies*, 77(4), 1262–1300.

Richards, Michael P., Paul B. Pettitt, Mary C. Stiner and Erik Trinkaus (2001) "Stable Isotope Evidence for Increasing Dietary Breadth in the European Mid-Upper Paleolithic", *Proceedings of the National Academy of the United States of America*, **98**(11), 6528–32.

Sen, Amartya (1999) *Development as Freedom*, Oxford: Oxford University Press.

Stiglitz, Joseph E. (2006) *Making Globalization Work*, New York: W.W. Norton and Co.

United Nations vars. [UN] *World Population Prospects:* United Nations: New York United Nations, annual with revisions, http://www.esa.un.org/unpp/

United Nations (2011), News Release, Department of Economics and Social Affairs, Population Division, 3rd May 2011.

General and Frequently Referenced Sources

Canada (current), *Statistics Canada/Statistique Canada*, Ottawa: Statistics Canada. http://www.statcan.gc.ca, http://www.statcan.

Carter, Susan B., Scott Sigmund Gartner, Michael R. Haines, Alan L. Olmstead, Richard Sutch, and Gavin Wright, eds. (2006) *Historical Statistics of the United States, Earliest Times to the Present: Millennial Edition*, New York: Cambridge University Press.

Centers for Disease Control and Prevention [CDC] (current) Department of Health and Human Services, United States Government. http://www.cdc.gov.

Cipolla, C. (1962) *The Economic History of World Population*, Baltimore: Penguin Books.

Human Mortality Database (current) University of California, Berkeley (USA), and Max Planck Institute for Demographic Research (Germany). http://www.mortality.org or http://www.humanmortality.de.

Mitchell, Brian R. (2007) *International Historical Statistics: Europe, 1750–2005*, Basingstoke, Hampshire; New York, N.Y.: Palgrave Macmillan.

Organisation for Economic Co-operation and Development (current) [OECD] *Statistics*, Paris: OECD Publishing. http://www.oecd.org/statsportal/.

Organisation for Economic Co-operation and Development (year) [OECD *Factbook*] *OECD Factbook (year): Economic, Environmental and Social Statistics*, OECD Publishing.

United Kingdom (current) *Government Actuary's Department*, London: HM Government. http://www.gad.gov.uk.

United Kingdom (current) *Office for National Statistics*, London: HM Government. http://www.statistics.gov.uk.

United Nations (2010) [UN] *World Population Prospects: The 2008 Revision*, United Nations: New York United Nations, and subsequent, annual revisions. esa.un.org/unpp/.

United Nations (current) [UN] *Demographic and Social Statistics*, Department of Economic and Social Affairs, New York: United Nations. http://www.unstats.un.org/unsd/demographic/.

United Nations Development Programme (current) [UNDP] *Human Development Reports*, New York: United Nations. hdr.undp.org.

The Children of Eve: Population and Well-being in History, First Edition.
Louis P. Cain and Donald G. Paterson.
© 2012 Blackwell Publishing Ltd. Published 2012 by Blackwell Publishing Ltd.

United States (current) *National Center for Health Statistics*, Department of Health and Human Services, Center for Disease Control and Prevention, http://www.cdc.gov/nchs/.

United States Bureau of Labor Statistics (current) *Data*, Washington: United States Government. http://www.bls.gov.

United States National Library of Medicine and National Institutes of Medicine (2007) *Medline Plus*, Bethesda, MD: United States Government. http://www.medlineplus.gov

Urquhart, M.C. (1965) *Historical Statistics of Canada*, Toronto: Macmillan Co. of Canada; Cambridge: Cambridge University Press. Subsequent edition in 1983 and on-line at *Statistics Canada/Statistique Canada* [see above].

Willcox, Walter F., ed. (1931) *International Migrations*, Vol. I ed. Imre Ferenczi, *Statistics*; Vol. II ed. Walter F. Willcox, *Interpretations*, New York: National Bureau of Economic Research.

World Bank, The (current) *World Development Indicators*, New York. http://www.worldbank.org/data.

World Health Organization (year), [WHO] *World Health Reports for (year)*, Geneva: World Health Organization. http://www.who.int/whr.

Wrigley, E.A. and R.S. Schofield (1981) *The Population History of England, A Reconstruction*, London: Edward Arnold.

Index

Note: Page numbers in *italics* refer to images. Page numbers followed by *f* refer to figures, and those by *t* to tables.

abolition of slave trade, 139–40
abolition of slavery, 160, 171n13, 195–7
Abolition of the Slave Trade Act (Great Britain, 1807), 139
aboriginals *see* indigenous peoples
abortion: forced, 49; gender selection, 111, 354
abstinence, sexual, 106
accidental deaths, 6, 66, 67*t*, 68; disability adjusted life years, 259, 260*t*; males vs. females, 75; Migration Propensity Index, 204; occupational, 66, 75, 230, 353
"Adam," 8
adaptation potential: environmental change, 4, 317, 353; failures, 317–18; social, political, and economic change, 5; technological change, 329
Addison's Disease, 257
adoption, 111, 220, 225
adultery, 115, 237–9
Africa: child labor, 232*t*, 233, 234; disability adjusted life years, 259, 260*t*; famine, 91n4, 322; HIV/AIDS, 5, 49, 66, 259, 334, 336–8, 346n59–n60; polio, 261, 280n13; population growth rates, 355*t*; tuberculosis, 261*t*

African Americans: birth weight data, 267; child labor, 231; crude birth rates, 119, 121*f*, 211*f*; demographic differences, 123; education, 197, 309, 311n48; fertility rates, 123; "free blacks," 195–8; HIV infection, 334*f*, 335; marriage rates and never-married, 113, 114*f*; migration via slavery, 138, 139–41, 196–7; poverty levels, 244, 245; seasonal birth patterns, 116, 116*f*; south-north migration, 195–8, *196*, 309; urban populations, 197, 197*f*; women, labor force participation, 46
African diaspora, 158
Africans, in slave trade, 138–41, 143
age discrimination: modern awareness, 356; work and retirement, 44, 92n30, 296
age-specific birth rate, 40, 41
age-specific death rate, 71
age-specific fertility rates, 101, 101*f*, 163
age-specific marriage rate, 99
agglomeration economies, 191, 192
aggregate data: censuses, 24–5; quality/quantity of life, 15–16
aggregate income *see* gross national product (GNP)

The Children of Eve: Population and Well-being in History, First Edition.
Louis P. Cain and Donald G. Paterson.
© 2012 Blackwell Publishing Ltd. Published 2012 by Blackwell Publishing Ltd.

aging: crude death rate and, 70, 80; disease deaths and, 66; experience, and income effects, 22, 40, 134, 134*f*, 135, 170n2, 231; occupational mobility and, 182, 183*f*; old age classification, 78–9, 92n30; population illustrations, 43–5, 43*f*, 49, 208–9, 295; retirement ages, 44, 79, 295, 296; *see also* pension entries; retirement

agriculture: animal diseases, 12, 58, 66, 68, 82; climate cycles and adaptation, 4, 317–18; commercialization, 333; economic theories, 58, 60n38, 124–5, 186–9, 329–30; export economies, 55–6, 150–151; failures, 6, 66, 117, 162, 199, 321, 322–4, 332; family farm/child labor, 102, 105, 124–6, 195, 228–33, 232*t*,; farmer profit declines, 272–3; food cycles, 82; immigrants in "new world," 148; Ireland, 162, 163, 321; land reclamation/repurposing, 54, 329–30, 330*t*; mechanization, 192, 194, 197; migrant labor, 182–3, 201, 203; population growth rates, 14, 17, 321; prehistoric populations, 11–12, 76; primary economy stage, 33, 35, 35*f*, 36, 133; regional migration, 201–3; slave labor, 139; subsidy effects, 193, 207; Vikings, 317

AIDS *see* HIV/AIDS

air quality: homes, 229, 276; pollution, 58, 229, 256, 257

air-borne plague, 324–7, 344

alcoholism, 275, 300, 321, 354

Aleut population, 318

alimony, 238, 240

Allen, Robert, 58, 60n38, 329*t*, 332, 332*f*, 346n55

alms-houses, 246, 247

Almy and Brown (mill), 230–231

amateur sports, 298–300, 310n26–n27

amenorrhea, 99, 100, 101, 111

American Revolution, 183

amniocentesis, 354

Anabaptists *see* Hutterites

ancient civilizations, 9, 11–12; empires and migration, 132; life expectancy, 76; records, 19–21; slavery, 138–9

Anderson, Michael, 201, 213n32

Anderson, Siwan, 224, 354

Anglican Church, 220, 237

animal domestication, 11, 12

animal-human diseases, 12, 51, 58, 66, 68, 68*t*, 82, 326–8, 339, 344

Anne, Queen of Great Britain, 143

annuity products, 293–5

annulment, 237

"antebellum height puzzle," 264–5, 265*f*, 268

anthropometric data, 262, 263, 266; *see also* birth weights; body mass index (BMI); height; weight

anti-discrimination legislation, 296, 310n13

anti-retroviral drugs, 336, 337

anti-Semitism, 165, 166; *see also* Holocaust, WWII

anti-tobacco programs, 274, 279

anti-viral drugs, 342

apprenticeships, 40, 59n6, 112, 143, 195, 229, 230, 247

Arab empires, 164

Argentina, 165*t*, 187

Armenia, 158

arranged marriage, 221; China, 111, 225; political pairings, 104, 106–7, 224, 236; pregnancies, 106; as rarity, 112, 224

Asia: child labor, 232*t*, 233; emigration, 138, 157–62, 167, 203, 257; influenza, 339, 346n73; plagues, 5, 325–7; population growth rates, 355*t*; *see also* Southeast Asia

Asian Americans: female HIV infection, 334*f*; immigration history, 160–62, 167

Assyrians, 164

asylum seekers, 168, 203, 213n42

Austen, Jane, 113, 257

Australia: census, 24; forced migration, 138, 141, 142, 144; gold rush, 153, 160; immigration and policy, 138, 146*f*, 162, 167, 168; Jewish populations, 165*t*; population decreases, 15; third demographic transition, 48; urbanization, 193, 193*f*

Austria: emigration, 147*f*; weight gain, 270, 271*f*

baby boom (post-1945), 43, 45, 123, 239, 287–8; as demographic shock, 286; generation retirement, 288, 291; population pyramids, 288, 289*f*
Babylon, 164, 345n19
bacterial diseases: animal-human/plagues, 68*t*, 325–8, 344, 345n34, 345n40; history and research, 68, 258, 325–6; water, 76
balance of payments profiles, 60n29, 150, 171n42
banking industry, 235–6
barbarians, 132
Barker, David, 84
"Barnado Children," 144
barriers to education: class, 307; race, 197, 244, 309; religion, 166
barriers to migration/immigration: costs, 15, 135, 149–52, 161, 169, 170, 173n83, 181–2, 205, 206; policies and laws, 167, 168, 173n83, 202–4
barriers to trade, 149, 172n46, 315, 356
basal metabolism, 262, 270
baseball, 299, 300, 310n30
baseline nutritional maintenance, 262, 264, 270–271
basic necessities, 4, 6
battle-connected deaths, 69*t*; *see also* warfare
Becker, Gary S., 104
Beito, David, 235
Bengal, India, famine, 323–4
bequest model, 125–6
Bernstein, William, 159–60
Biafra, 322
birth control and contraception: avoidance, 49, 100; device introduction, and effects, 98, 311n33; fertility pattern changes, 102, 110; HIV/AIDS policy and, 337; influence on culture, 47, 106, 110, 311n33, 356; influences from culture, 100, 101
birth rates: age-specific, 40, 41; developed world, 32, 33, 40, 41, 47; exogenous shocks, 117, 322; fertility transition, 31–3, 98, 118–19, 120*f*–121*f*, 122–3, 209; population shocks, 288; *see also* crude birth rates; fertility rates
birth seasonality: longevity ties, 84–5; patterns, 115–17, 116*f*

birth spacing, and fertility rates, 101
birth weights: health measurement, 84, 256, 266; low birth weight morbidity links, 84, 266–7, 276; records, 20, 266–7
Bismarck, Otto von, 296
black Americans *see* African Americans
Black Death (14th C.), 315, 325–7, 345n33; land use pre-, post-, 329–30, 330*t*, 333; population effects, 12, 329, 329*t*, 331, 333, 346n45; wage effects, 36–7, 329–33, 332*f*
black lung disease, 255
Blair, Tony, 200
body fat, 270, 281n39; *see also* obesity
body mass index (BMI), 269, 270; anthropometric data collection, 263, 271, 280n17; averages, 269; body composition vs., 281n39; morbidity and mortality, 270*f*; obesity definition, 269; white American males, 271, 272*t*
Bombay Plague (19th–20th C.), 5, 325–7
bones, study, 263, 280n17
Boston, Massachusetts, 54
Botswana, 334
Botticini, Maristella, 164
Bourbeau, Robert, 74–5, 75*f*, 77*f*
Boxer Rebellion (1898–1901), 158
Boyer, George, 205
Bozon, Michel, 223
"brain drain," 150, 203, 337
Brander, James, 318
Brazil: immigration, 160; Jewish populations, 165*t*
breastfeeding: HIV, 335; infant health, 76, 88, 274; post-partum infertility, 99, 101
bride price, 224
Brighouse, Harold, 127n41
British Factory Act (1874), 298
Brown, Gordon, 200
Brunello, Giorgio, 273
bubbles, economic, 236
bubonic plague, 5, 324–5, 338; cycles, 324–5, 327–9; disappearance, 76; origin, 68*t*, 325–7, 345n34, 345n40; symptoms, 326
burials, seasonal patterns, 83*f*
Burkhauser, Richard, 281n39
Burns, Robert, 115

Butler, James, 141
Byzantine Empire, 164

California gold rush, 153, 160
calories: distribution, families, 26; metabolism/activity use, 262, 263*f*, 264, 270–71; weight gain, 270–272
Cameron, David, 200
Cammeyer, William, 300, 310n30
Canada: agriculture, 187, 198; censuses, 24, 25, 29n25, 137, 202; crude birth rates/ fertility transition, 98, 118–19, 121*f*, 122–3, 208, 208*t*, 209, 211*f*; crude death rates, 89, 91*f*, 208, 208*t*, 209, 211*f*; divorce, 240*f*, 242; economic history, 53–4; emigration, 137, 201–4; energy policy, 53–4; HIV/AIDS, 335, 336, 346n64; immigration, 138, 144–6, 146*f*, 148, 152, 160–162, 167, 168, 202, 301; immigration policy, 167, 168, 173n83, 202; Jewish populations, 164, 165, 165*t*; labor reforms, 298; life expectancy/death information, 73–5, 75*f*, 77*f*, 94n79, 278; marriage age history, 108*t*, 127n27; native populations, 317, 318, 321; natural resources/trade, 151, 172n46; nutrition and health records, 267; pensions, 295; population aging, 43*f*; population growth/decrease, 15, 60n20; poverty, 243, 243*f*, 244, 245; regional income differences, 206; third demographic transition, 48; total fertility rate, 49, 122; underground railroad, 196–7; urbanization, 193; US border areas, 181, 202; weight gain, 270, 271*f*; westward expansion, 125, 148, 183, 202; *see also* New France
canal building, 148, 162, 185, 190
cancer: cause of death, 66, 67*t*; distribution and disability adjusted life years, 259, 260*t*; other disease links, 276, 281n56
capital crimes, 141
capital flows: macroeconomic views, 55, 60n29, 236, 288, 290; population-sensitive, 149–50, 172n44; remittances, 153–5, 161; transatlantic migration, 136, 149–50, 168–9
capital markets, 150, 236

cardiovascular disease: cause of death, 66, 67*t*; distribution and disability adjusted life years, 259, 260*t*; fetal origins hypothesis, 84; other disease links, 276, 281n56
Carlos, Ann M., 236
catastrophe path, 315–16, 318, 319*f*
catastrophes, 28, 315–16, 342–3; epidemics and pandemics, 51, 66, 319, 338–42; famine, 66, 91n4, 315, 321–4, 332; human-caused, 51, 343; natural disasters, 51, 342–3; plague, 5, 12, 66, 324–33, 325*f*, 329*t*; population crises, 315–21, 319*f*, 353
Catholic marriage and divorce, 220, 237, 238
Catholic populations, Quebec: crude birth rate/fertility transition, 121*f*, 122–3, 211*f*; crude death rates, 89, 91*f*, 211*f*; Protestant relations, 183
Caucasian Americans *see* white Americans
causes of death *see* death, causes
Cawley, John, 281n39
CCR5-delta 32 genetic mutation, 9, 328
celibacy, 111
Celts, 132
census-taking, 19, 22–6, *24*, 37, 137; challenges of ethnicity, 164, 173n105; challenges of migration, 136–8, 155, 156, 162, 183*f*; child/woman ratio, 124–5, 128n71; crude death rate, 89; enslaved peoples, 29n27; family/household definitions, *24*, 220–221, 225; internal migration tracking, 193–4; marriage information, 112–13, 114*f*; native populations, 321, 344n10; treatment of gender, 19, 23, *24*, 26; *see also* US Census/Bureau of the Census
Central America: child labor, 232*t*, 233; civilizations, 56, 318
central place theory, 188–91, 212n12, 212n13
Chambers, Lori, 242
charity records, 20; *see also* relief programs and funding
checks on population growth *see* positive checks, population growth; preventive checks, population growth

Cherokee tribe, 320
Chicago, Illinois, 88, 276
child care: affluent families, *119*; institutional availability, 46; leisure time mix, 305; sibling care, 106, 290; women's careers vs., 46; women's roles/informal labor, 26, 45, 301, 302, 310n11, 311n36
child health, 256, 257, 274–6, 279, 338; *see also* child labor
child labor, 228–34, 246; agriculture, non-family farming, 231, 232, 232*t*, 233; family farming, 102, 105–6, 124, 195, 228–9, 230; laws, *228*, 229–31, 233, 249n32; modern world, 229, 231–4, 232*t*, 257; photographs, 228, *275*; physical size relevance, 229, 230; reports, 231–4, 232*t*; urban settings, 105–6, 118, 122, 195, 230, 231, 256; working family rent contributions, 221
child migrants, 144, 247
child mortality, 70–71, 71*f*, 72, 73*f*, 78, 92n11, 321; heath and sanitation, 86, 87, 93n69, 274; rate declines, 209, 225, 290, 355–6; urban vs. rural, 85, 86, 124; *see also* infant mortality
child poverty, 243–4, 243*f*, 245–7
childbirth, 70, 75, 258, 267
childless couples, 226
children, benefits and costs: costs and saving, 290; family economics, 104–5, 124, 221, 227, 290; household efficiency effects, 301; migration benefits, 135; *see also* child labor
children and divorce, 237, 238, 239
children of undocumented immigrants, 204
child/woman ratio, 124–5, 128n71
China: divorce law, 237; dynasties, 132, 158; economy and population size, 56, 158, 356; emigration/diaspora, 152, 154, 156, 158–62, 160*t*, 164, 167, 173n83, 173n86; famine, 322, 345n25; fertility, 49, 110–111; gender selection, 353–4; genealogy, 21, 162; influenza, 339, 346n73; marriage, 111, 225, 237; plagues, 5, 325; population aging, 44, 49; population growth rate, 60n20; population policy, 49, 60n18, 111; remittances, 155*t*, 161; wars, 28n5, 69, 158

Chinese Exclusion Act (U.S; 1882), 167, 173n83
Chinese Immigration Act (Canada; 1885), 167, 173n83
choice: marriage partners, 221, 223–5; as quality of life improvement, 17, 219
cholera, 68*t*, 87, 89, 166, 257, 319, 321
chronic disease *see* specific diseases
Church of England, 220, 237
church records, 20–21, 29n22, 106, 114, 127n17; marriage, 20, 99, 106, 114, 221
Cinel, Daniel, 157
Cipolla, Carlo, xv
citizenship, 137; illegal immigrants, 168; return migration and, 156
city government: size influences, 58; village/town creation, 190–192
civil marriage ceremonies, 220
civil service jobs, 297
civilian casualties of wars, 69, 69*t*, 322–4
Clapham, John, 230
Clark, G., 346n55
class barriers: education, 307; marriage options, 113, 127n41, 224
climate: economic success and, 53; history, 4, 11, 12, 28n2, 317, 328, 353; migration choices, 143–4, 156, 199, 317; retirement destinations, 182; temperature and birth rates, 116–17
climate change, 315, 317, 318, 328
Clovis people, 4
co-location, 189; *see also* location theory
coal resources: burning and health, 256, 257; industrial demand, 230; mine depletion/closures, 199; mining and health, 255; nations' economic status and, 53–4
cohabitation, non-marital, 47, 220, 226, 227, 239
Cohn, Samuel K., Jr., 325–6, 346n49
cohort data, 22, 77; Human Development Index, 267–8, 281n36; life expectancy, 74–5, 75*f*
coital frequency, 99, 100, 111, 112, 116, 118
Collins, William, 198
colonial areas and societies: British areas, 22, 89, 107–8, 109*t*, 115, 140–143,

140*f*, 159, 183, 185, 246–7, 324, 345n24; disease introductions, 68, 318–21; French areas, 22–3, 89, 107, 108, 112, 127n24, 159, 183; Greenland, 317; immigrants, and forced migration, 138, 139*t*, 141–3; immigrants, voluntary migration, 143–4, 146, 146*f*; militaries, 23, 171n7; poverty relief, 246–7; slaves, 138, 139*t*, 140*f*
Combs, May Beth, 242
commercial networks, 165–6, 235–6
commodity markets, 187, 206
common land, 58, 60n38, 82
common-law marriage, 220, 238
communicable disease: animal-human disease histories, 51, 58, 66, 68, 68*t*; as class, 65, 66, 91n5; death rates, 66, 67*t*, 322; disability adjusted life years and, 259, 260*t*; housing quality, 82, 256, 274; immigration and travel, 166–7; as opportunistic, famines/catastrophes, 66, 69, 117, 315, 321, 322, 342; urban settings, 86, 88; *see also* specific diseases
communication paths: emigrants to home country contacts, 152–3; epidemic information, 339, 342; industries, 236
comparative advantage, 170n5, 189, 199, 356
completed family size, 356; declines, 108; fertility determinant, 102
compositional effect (population), 306, 311n39
compound population growth rates, 13*f*, 29n13, 100, 100*f*, 101, 107
compulsory education, 306, 308
computer technology, 308
conception, males vs. females, 112, 118
consumer safety regulations, 88
consumption: vs. familial redistribution, 102, 292; incomes and well-being, 6, 16, 55, 264, 266; leisure time, 298; long-term comparisons, 16; natural resources, and depletion, 6–7, 11, 186, 199, 315, 318, 320
consumption (disease) *see* tuberculosis
contraception *see* birth control and contraception

contract labor: indentured/forced, 158, 161, 247; piece-work/putting-out system, 223, *275*
convergence, incomes, 136, 205–7, 356
convicts *see* prisoners, convicts, and exiles
cooking, home, 272–3, 302–3, 305
Corn Laws (England), 163, 188
corporate law, 57
cost of living: poverty level considerations, 244, 246; "real cost of living," 246; surveys, 231
Costa, Dora, 263, 267–9, 268*t*
cotton industry, 56, 139, 151, 197
Council of Trent (1545–63), 220
courtship, 221–5, 222
Cowan, Ruth Schwartz, 301, 302, 305
craft production, 169, 223
Crafts, Nicholas, 106
Cromwell, Oliver, 141
cross-border migration, 181, 202–4; *see also* emigration; immigration; regional migration (including internal)
cross-section analysis: data, 21; quality and quantity of life, 16, 267–8, 281n36
crude birth rates, 32; area data and illustrations, 118*f*, 119, 120*f*–121*f*, 122, 210*f*–211*f*; baby boom, 288; demographic transition, 32, 32*f*, 207–9; fertility transition, 118–19, 120*f*–121*f*, 122–3; rural vs. urban, 122–6
crude death rates, 32; area data and illustrations, 89, 90*f*–91*f*, 118*f*, 210*f*–211*f*; demographic transition, 32, 32*f*, 70, 207–8
crude divorce rate, 99
crude marriage rate, 99
Cuba, 160
Cumberland Road (US), 185, 212n4
currency agreements, 207
Cutler, David, 269, 272
cycles, poverty, 242, 244–6, 255, 354

Dagenhart, Hammer v. (1918), 231
DALYs *see* disability adjusted life years (DALYs)
dances, 222–4
Darling, Alistair, 200
Day, Lincoln and Alice, 54–5

de Vita, Agostino, 168–9
death, causes: accidents, 66, 67*t*, 68, 75; global view, 2002, 67*t*; historical, 6, 65–6, 321–2, 324–5, 338; modern, 66, 67*t*, 75, 322, 334, 338, 340–42, 341*t*; wars, 69, 69*t*, 338
death patterns: birth seasons, and longevity, 84–5; seasons of death, 82–4
death probability, 73–82, 81*f*
death rates, 32*f*, 70, 71; age-specific, 71; demographic transition, 31–3, 32*f*, 49, 65, 77, 149, 207–8; developed world, 32, 33, 40, 72–3; developing world, 49, 70–71, 337, 355; exogenous shocks, 117, 322; Irish Famine, 162; law of mortality and, 80; migration propensity factor, 204; *see also* crude death rates; mortality rates
death records, 72, 85, 92n40, 137, 193
Death Registration Area (DRA) rates, 85
debt-peonage, 144, 161
debts: national, state and local, 150, 290; personal, 241
demographic transition, 31–3, 32*f*, 47–9, 77, 149, 207–9; epidemiological transition, 65; fertility rates and, 32, 98, 111, 148–9, 208, 209, 356; illustrations, 210*f*–211*f*; saving rate effects, 290; "second," 46–8, 239; "third," 48; years following/end, 43, 45–50, 226, 315; years preceding, 43; *see also* crude birth rates; crude death rates
Denmark: census, 24; emigration, 146, 147*f*
dependency rate, 44, 45; children, 43, 102, 104, 209, 225, 288, 291, 291*f*; decrease in ratio, 306; retirees/elderly, 43, 44, 102, 209, 295; saving rates and, 288, 290, 291*f*
"deserving poor," 246
developed nations *see* Organization for Economic Co-operation and Development (OECD) nations; specific nations
Dewey, Davis R., 168, 174n118
diabetes, 67*t*, 84, 260*t*, 279
Diamond, Jared, 317–18
diarrheal diseases, 68*t*, 71*f*, 87, 93n69, 259, 274
diasporas: African, 158; defined, 158; Irish, 133, 146, 162–4; Jewish, 158, 164–6

diets: American South, 84; cultural transmission, 84, 257; human history, 353; lower classes, 255, 257; nutrition, health, and longevity, 82–7, 256–7; and obesity, 271–4; standard of living measurement, 19, 86–7; *see also* nutrition, family/personal
digestive system disease: cause of death, 66, 67*t*; disability adjusted life years, 260*t*
"DINKs" (double incomes, no kids), 226
diphtheria, and prevention, 87, 258
direct transfer payments, anti-poverty, 207, 245
disabilities and poverty, 245
disability adjusted life years (DALYs), 259, 280n11; data, year 2000, 260*t*
disability insurance, 235, 277
disaster relief, 154
discount rate, 27, 29n28, 105, 170
disease: communicable class, 65, 66, 91n5, 256, 259; degenerative/modern day, 65, 66, 67*t*; eradication, 68, 88, 258, 261, 280n8; historic views, 5, 12, 50–51, 65, 66, 321; introductions, Americas, 68, 318–21; occupational, 255; productivity and quality of life, 16, 257–8; *see also* animal-human diseases; communicable disease; disease transmission; epidemics; influenza; morbidity; nutrition, family/personal; pandemics; plagues; public health; water sanitation, and disease; specific diseases
disease transmission: HIV, 335, 346n64; influenza, 339–42, 340, 346n73; plague, 325–8, 344, 345n38
Displacement Thesis, 202
disposable/discretionary income, 286, 297, 299
Disraeli, Benjamin, 166
distance, in migration, 181–2
diversity: ethnic, 356; genetic, 328, 345n43, 353
divorce, 236–40; and children, 237–9; as class privilege, 237; defined, 99; laws, 236–9; mean age, 237; rates, 227, 238–40
Divorce Act (England; 1857), 237
Domesday Book, 22

domestic livestock, 66, 68, 82, 319
domestic partnerships, 220
domestic saving rate, 55, 286, 290–291, 291*f*
domestic service, 168; Chinese labor, 161; nutrition benefits, 267; women's labor, 223, 229, 247, 331
domestic space, 82, 274–6, *275*
domestication of animals, 11, 12
"double incomes, no kids (DINKs)", 226
doubling rate, population, 100, 100*f*, 101, 107
dower arrangements, 240–241
dowries, 224
dropouts, 231, 308, 309
drug addiction, 354; *see* also alcoholism
drug therapy, HIV/AIDS, 336, 337
drug-resistant diseases, 91n6, 342
Dundas family, 200
dust bowl (US; 20th C.), 199

East Timor: child labor, 232, 232*t*, 233; fertility and mortality rates, 100
Easter Island, 316–18
Easterlin, Richard, 124–5, 205–6, 213n52
Eastern Europe: emigration, 146, 147*f*, 166; Jewish populations, 164, 165*t*, 166, 173n105; migration to Western Europe, 41–2, 60n17; population decline, 41–2, 42*t*, 316
echo shock effects, 286–8, 287*f*
economic bubbles, 236
economic frontier concept, 185–7, 189, 212n13
economic growth, 53–6, 57, 188, 205, 207; vs. economic development, 33, 56, 286; family size and, 227; poverty and, 244, 246; stability, 209
The Economic History of World Population (Cipolla), xv
economic rent, 186, 188
economic shocks: catastrophes, 315, 316; fertility effects, 117, 123
economic transformation: described, 33–6, 286; income inequality trends, 39*f*, 40; migration, 133, 147–50; mortality rates and, 72
economic well-being: health links, 245, 255, 261–, 266; macro views, 36–40, 55, 219

economies of scale: agriculture, 36; families, 106, 290; national economies, 56
education: adult, 354; average years of schooling by country, 306–7, 307*t*; children, 106, 154, 195, 229, 231, 233, 234, 356; costs and financing, 106, 154, 195; discrimination barriers, 166, 197, 244, 307, 309; fertility rate correlations, 48, 49, 110, 308–9; gaps, 354; health, 273, 335; high school, 231, 307–9; human capital investment, 28, 52, 56, 182, 195, 206, 207, 234, 305–9, 338; infrastructure, 288; inter-marriage effects, 225; males and females, 306–9; marriage age effects, 48, 110, 113; mobility effects, 56, 126, 305, 307; native Americans, 245, 321; parents', effects, 48; post-secondary, 308; poverty and, 243–5, 354; return migration, 156; *see also* apprenticeships; labor skills; literacy
education reform, 307–9
educational attainment, and gaps, 306–7, 307*t*, 309, 311n48–n49, 338
efficiency, labor *see* productivity, labor
Egypt: ancient, 19, 76, 132; Jewish populations, 164; middle ages, 139
elderly care: family economics, 102–3, 103*f*, 291–2; institutional structures, 102, 104, 292–3, 296
elderly women and men, poverty, 80, 82, 243*f*, 244–6, 248
Elementary Education Act (England and Wales; 1870), 307
Ellickson, Robert, 227
Ellis Island, New York, *145*
Emery, Herb and George, 235
emigration: census data, 25, 136–7; information sharing, 152–3; internal migration and, 147–8; population formulas, 14–15, 25, 33, 315, 321; recession effects, 204; reverse migration, 155–6, 172n64; *see also* immigration; specific nations
Émond, Valérie, 74–5, 75*f*, 77*f*
empire size, 53, 56, 132, 142
endometritis, 258, 280n9
energy resources, and economic success, 53–4, 201; *see also* coal resources; oil resources
Engels, Friedrich, 230

England: class barriers, 113, 127n41; coal mining, 199; common land, 58, 60n38, 82; crude birth rates, 119, 120*f*, 208, 208*t*, 210*f*; crude death rates, 90*f*, 208, 208*t*, 210*f*; death seasonality, 82; divorce, 237–9, 240*f*; earnings history, 36–7, 37*f*, 76; economic growth, and population, 56; education, 306–7; emigration, 138, 139*t*, 141–6, 146*f*, 147*f*, 156; fertility transition, 98, 118, 119, 120*f*, 126n2; illegitimacy rates, 115; infant mortality, 72; influenza, 340, 341*t*; labor markets, 205, 330–333; land use, 54, 58, 60n38, 329–30, 330*t*, 333; life expectancy/death information, 76, 77*f*, 79, 79*t*, 86; London mortality, 1670 and 1800, 83*f*; marriage age history, 106, 107*f*, 108, 108*t*, 109*f*, 110, 110*f*, 112–13; marriage history, 220, 221; migration from Scotland, 200–201, 213n28; monarchy, 100, 102, 104, 143, 237, 249n45; never-married, 112–13, 201; poor laws/support, 246–8; population statistics, 328–9, 329*t*, 333, 346n45; real wages, 332–3, 342, 346n55; sports, 298–300; urbanization, 192, 192*f*; wars, 141, 143, 183, 346n50; women's labor force participation, 47; *see also* United Kingdom
entertainment: leisure time choices, 298, 300; sports as social event, 298–300, *299, 301*
entrepreneurs, 236, 249n43
environmental carrying capacity, 10, 10*f*, 11, 353, 354
environmental changes: climate, 315, 317, 318, 328; human migration and history, 4, 10, 11, 317
epidemics: conditions conducive to, 319; defined, 51, 66; effects, 50, 51; native American populations, 319, 320; *see also* plagues
epidemiological transition, 65
eradicated diseases, 88, 258, 261, 280n8
Erie Canal, 148, 185
Erik the Red, 317
Eritrea, 118, 158
erosion, 199, 317
Essay on the Principle of Population (Malthus), 17

Eswaran, Mukesh, 103
ethnic diversity, 356
EU (European Union): membership, 212n2; per capita income convergence, 207; *see also* Europe
Europe: crude birth rates, 119, 120*f*, 122, 208, 208*t*, 209, 210*f*; crude death rates, 89, 90*f*, 208, 208*t*, 209, 210*f*; death seasonality, 82–3; divorce and laws, 237–8; emigration: convicts and indentured servants, 141–3; emigration: indentured servitude, 138; emigration: voluntary, 143–7, 147*f*, 148, 152, 162–4, 167–9, 198, 200–204, 208–9; exports, 150–151, 333; health care, 248, 273, 276–7; illegitimacy rates, 115; immigration policy, 168, 181, 296; infant mortality, 72, 76, 85; influenza, 338–42, 341*t*; internal migration, 181, 212n2; labor reforms, 298; life expectancy/death information, 73, 76, 77*f*, 78–9, 79*t*, 86, 278; marriage age history, 106, 107*t*, 108*t*, 109*f*, 110, 110*f*, 112–13, 122, 227, 333; Mediterranean countries, marriage/family changes, 44, 48; migration history, 132–3; nationalism, 167; never-married, 112–13, 201; nutrition and health records, 256–7, 259, 260*t*, 261*t*, 262–6, 263*f*, 265*t*; plagues and effects, 12, 36–7, 324–33, 329*t*, 332*f*, 346n45; population aging, 43*f*; population growth rates, 328, 355*t*; poverty, 243, 243*f*, 244, 245, 247; slavery, 140; total fertility rate, 41; urbanization, 192–3, 192*f*, 193*f*; world DALY comparisons, 259, 260*t*
"Eve," 7–8, 8*f*
exercise: occupational, 271, 273; recreational, 273, 298–300, *299, 301*
exiles, forced migration *see* prisoners, convicts, and exiles
expected wages, 134–5, 134*f*, 170, 170n2, 181–2
exploration, global: Americas: North, Central, South, 318; Northern Europe, Iceland, Greenland, 4, 316–17
exports: Caribbean goods, 150; European goods, 150–151, 333; North American

goods, 150, 151, 213n36; shifts to net importing, 55–6, 150, 171n41
extended family, 226, 234; *see also* multigenerational family structure
extensive economic growth, 188
externalities, economic, 56–8
extreme weather conditions, 322; *see also* climate

factor price equalization, 136
factories, 34, *47*; air quality, 229, 256, 257; child labor, 228–31; employment for poor, 247; location, 189, 190, 194, 230; skilled/unskilled work, 169; sports teams, 300
Factory Act (UK; 1874), 298
Fair Labor Standards Act (US; 1938), 231, 249n32
families, political relations, 104, 106–7, 113, 224
family economics: costs of children, 104–5, 124, 221, 227, 290; income distribution, 102–6, 103*f*, 126, 220–221; marriage arrangements, 106–7, 221, 223–4, 236, 237; remittances, 153–4, 155*t*, 156, 157, 161; retirement/pension support, 102, 103, 104, 105, 125, 126, 154, 221, 234, 291–2; *see also* child labor
family farms: inheritances, 19, 124–6, 241; labor, 102, 105, 124–6, 195, 228–33 232*t*
family histories, 20–21, 29n22
family immigration and emigration, 143, 153, 161, 168, 203
family limitation: Malthusian theory, 18; national policies, 49, 60n18, 111; pre-history, 10–11; *see also* birth control and contraception
family networks, 234–6
family nurturing: as decision influencer, 26; elder support, 102–3, 103*f*, 154, 234; females' roles, and nutrition, 267, 302; females' roles, and spinsterhood, 112; prehistoric evidence, 9; *see also* child care; family networks
family planning: birth spacing, 101; fertility gap, 47, 124; marriage age, 106–11; postponement of children, 287; primogeniture, 241; reasons for children, 102, 103, 104–5, 110; *see also* abstinence, sexual; birth control and contraception; illegitimacy
family size: child labor issues, 102–4, 105–6; completed, and fertility, 102, 108, 356; decreases, *119*, 291; defined, 225; economies of scale, 106, 290; family incomes and, 102–4, *119*, 227; gaps, desire/reality, 47, 124; history, 225–7, 226*f*; immigrant assumptions, 209; urban vs. rural, 105–6, 122–6, 195, 227; *see also* family limitation
family structure/organization: importance, 219–20; legal definitions, 220, 225; poverty predictor, 245; urban influences, 195, 227; *see also* family size; household size
famines, 66, 91n4, 315, 322–5, 332; fertility effects, 117–18, 118*f*, 123, 321–2; Finland, 117, 118*f*, 322; prevention, 322, 345n21; records and reporting, 322, 323–4; *see also* Irish Famine, 1840s
farming *see* agriculture
fast food, 272, 274
fat, 270, 281n39; *see also* obesity
fecundity, 29n26, 99; colonial North America, 107; Hutterite population, 100–102
female fecundity, 99
female genetics, 8
female HIV infection by race, US, 334*f*
female-headed single parent families *see* single-parent families
Fernandez, Raquel, 45–6, 46*f*
Ferrie, Joseph, 169, 174n112
fertility gap, 47, 124
fertility rates: age-specific, 101, 101*f*, 163; China, 110–111; decline, 45, 76, 98, 122, 123, 126, 163, 198, 208, 209, 226, 288, 355; demographic transition, 32, 98, 111, 149, 208, 209, 356; education correlations, 48, 49, 110, 308–9; Hutterite population, 100–102, 100*f*, 101*f*; immigrant absorption, 41, 44, 48, 107, 148–9, 209; never-married and, 111–13, 122, 201; New France, 17th C., 23; population projection challenges,

354–5; post-demographic transition, 43–5, 354; pre-demographic transition, 43, 149; regional differences, 205; rural vs. urban, 105–6, 122–3, 123–6, 201; second demographic transition, 46–7; societal disruptions and crises, 117–18, 118*f*, 163, 322–3, 333, 337–8; third demographic transition, 48; total (TFR), 40–41, 42*t*, 47, 100, 108, 122, 209; women's labor force participation and, 45, 226; *see also* birth rates; fertility transition

fertility transition, 98, 108–11; crude birth rates, 118–19, 120*f*–121*f*, 122–3; timeframes, 98; youth mortality influence, 103

fetal origins hypothesis, 84–5

Fetherson, Jacqueline, 326, 345n34

feudal system, 57, 104, 159, 330–31, 346n49

filles du roi (New France immigrants), 23, 23, 127n24

finance industry, 164, 166, 235–6

financial instruments, 150, 236, 293–5

Finland: crude birth/death rates, 118*f*; emigration, 146, 147*f*; famine and fertility, 117, 118, 322; weight gain, 270, 271*f*

first marriage, 99; average ages, 106–110, 107*f*, 108*t*, 109*t*, 110*f*, 113, 119, 122; China, 111; cultural influences, 101, 106, 110, 111; divorce probability, 239–40, 240*f*; median ages, 108*t*, 113, 127n27

fishing industries, 58, 201, 233, 234, 317, 323

Fitch, Catherine, 113

fleas, disease transmission, 68*t*, 326–8, 344

Floud, Roderick, 266

flu *see* influenza

Fogel, Robert W., 29n21, 263–5, 263*f*, 265*t*, 280n18

food preparation time, 272–3, 302–3, 305

food preservation and storage, 4, 28n3, 322

food prices: affordability and nutrition, 262, 265–7, 273, 303; farmer profit declines, 272–3; grain, 16, 117, 186–8, 323–4; meat, 265; purchased meals, 272

food riots, 246, 322

food stamps/assistance, 245, 249n40

Football Association (FA), 299, 300, 310n27

football (soccer), 298–9, *301*

forced abortion, 49

forced labor contracts, 158, 161, 247

forced migration *see* child migrants; indentured servants; Native American forced migration; prisoners, convicts, and exiles; slavery and enslaved peoples

foreign-born populations: Germany, 156; United Kingdom, 155–6; United States, 1850–1990, 137*t*, 155–6, 167–9; United States, 21st century, 203–4

formula, infant, 311n33

France: Asian migrant labor, 159–61; crude birth rates/fertility transition, 120*f*, 122, 208, 208*t*, 210*f*; crude death rates, 90*f*, 208, 208*t*, 210*f*; divorce law, 237; emigration, 147*f*; energy resources, 53; food supply/caloric consumption, 262, 263*f*, 264, 265; Jewish populations, 165*t*, 166; life expectancy/death information, 73, 76, 79, 86, 88, 278; marriage age history, 108*t*, 122; marriage history, 223; population data, 69, 72; sex ratio, 112; urbanization, 192, 193; wars, 183, 339, 346n50; weight gain, 270, 271*f*

free blacks, 195–8

"free rider problem," 58, 60n40, 235

freeholders, 16, 124

Fridlizus, Gunnar, 72

Frontier Thesis, 187–8

Fuchs, Victor, 277

Fugitive Slave Law (US; 1850), 196, 212n20

fur trade, 165, 198, 317, 320

Gallman, Robert, 169, 264, 291*f*

gaps in wages/incomes *see* income distribution; income inequality; wage gaps

gastrointestinal infections, 84–5

gay and lesbian populations *see* homosexual populations

gay marriage *see* same-sex marriage

GDP *see* gross domestic product (GDP)

gender differences: census-taking, 19, 23, 24, 26; child labor, 231, 232t, 233; death probability, 75; diseases, 65; divorce rights, 237–9; education, 49, 306, 307; family structures, 103, 104; geographic mobility, 112, 322–3; HIV/AIDS infection, 334f, 335; housework, 302–3, 303t, 304t; legal rights, 19; life expectancy, 16, 75, 77, 78f, 79t, 80, 81–2, 92n28, 295; medical care, 354; nutrition, 262, 267; sex selection, 111, 353–4; wages, 272; war deaths, 69, 112; workplace separation, 223

gender preferences, offspring, 111, 353–4

gender ratios *see* sex ratio imbalances, and migration

genealogy tools, 20–21, 29n22

generations: care for future, 27; ethnic Chinese, 159; family economics, 102–6, 103f, 124, 125, 126, 154, 292; human history, 3; mtDNA transmission, 8; social expectations/patterns, 5

genetic diversity, 328, 345n43, 353

geographic expansion *see* westward expansion, North America

geographic mobility: education links, 56, 126, 305; family effects, 225, 227; gender differences, 112; inequalities/consequences of lacking, 123, 174n112, 221, 243, 245, 276

germ theory, 58, 87, 258

Germany: census, 24; education, 306–7, 308; emigration, 143, 144, 145, 146, 147f, 153, 156, 172n65, 234; Human Development Indexes, 268, 269f; immigration, 172n65; Jewish populations, 165t; life expectancy/death information, 86, 278; marriage age history, 108t; poverty, 245; WWI, 339

Ghana, child labor, 232, 232t, 233, 234, 249n36

Gibson, Walter, 143, 152

Gilman, Charlotte, 301

Glaeser, Edward, 269, 272

Glasgow, Scotland, population health, 256–7

Glass, David, 86

global economic downturn, 2007-, 204

global population estimates: 10,000 BC to 2050, 14t; 40,000 to 8,000 BC, 11; current, 11, 354, 355t; future projections, 31, 41, 49–50, 50f, 59n1, 354–5; total, all history, 14

global trade: child labor awareness, 231; Chinese trading, 159, 160, 166; commodity markets, 187; comparative advantage, 170n5, 189; factor price equalization, 136; globalization inequalities, 356; historical views, 136, 165–6, 315, 317; import/export shipping, 150–151, 172n46; location and success, 53; mass migration and, 52, 136, 149; networks, 165–156; North America, 201–2, 213n36; plague and, 325–8, 345n38

globalization, 356; history, 52, 136; marriage trends and, 225

GNP *see* gross national product (GNP)

gold rushes, 153, 160

Goldin, Claudia, 52, 167, 308

Gompertz, Benjamin, 80

Gompertz-Makeham approximation, 80, 81

Good Samaritan principle, 319–20

grains: agriculture, 9, 187; famine, 323; prices, 16, 117, 186–8, 323–4; trade, 150, 151, 187, 188, 192

grave records and sites, 21, 74, 75–6

Great Britain: Asian colony labor, 159; earnings history, 37f; education, 306–7; emigration, 138, 139t, 141–6, 146f, 147f, 162–4, 200–201; food supply/caloric consumption, 262, 263f, 264, 265; labor markets, 205, 206; regional migration, 200–201, 213n28–n29, 256; urbanization, 192f; *see also* England; Ireland; United Kingdom

Great Depression, 287, 315

Great Hunger *see* Irish Famine, 1840s

Great Migration (African American south-north migration), 185, 195–8, *196*, 309

Greece, ancient: empire and migration, 132; life expectancy, 76; slavery, 138

Greenland Norse, 4, 316–18, 353

Greif, Avner, 165

gross domestic product (GDP), 34, 36; census information, 37, 38f; growth rate

as measurement, 53; Human Development Index, 267, 268t; inadequate measurement for standard of living, 264; industrial transition, 35, 35f; population shocks and catastrophes, 316, 329, 334, 337–8, 342; real GDP, 38f, 77, 150, 205–6, 206f, 264; shares, 33
gross national product (GNP), 34; economic well-being measure, 55, 264; European-American migration and, 169; real GNP per capita, 264–5, 265f
gross reproduction rate, 41
guest workers *see* temporary migrants
guilds, 165
gun violence, 75, 320
gypsies, 158

H1N1 virus, 339, 341
H5N1 virus, 342
Haddock, David, 329–30, 330t
Haines, Michael, 78, 291f
Hammer v. Dagenhart (1918), 231
Hantavirus, 51
Hatton, Timothy J., 170, 205
Haub, Carl, 14
health care *see* medical care
health education, 273, 335
health inspection, 166–7, 275–6
health insurance: employer-based, 235, 276, 294; national, 235, 248, 273, 276–7, 279; obesity and risky behaviors, 273; self-help societies, 235, 276–7; self-insurance, 279
heart disease *see* cardiovascular disease
Heaton, Herbert, 198
Hecksher-Ohlin model of trade, 136, 170n5
height: averages, 264–6, 265t; health measure, 12, 256, 257, 263–8; Human Development Index, 267–8, 268t, 281n36; socioeconomic status and, 264–6, 268, 280n21
Helmchen, Lorens, 271, 272t
hemophiliacs, 335
Henderson, Max, 271, 272t
Henripin, Jacques, 107
Henry II, King of England, 104
Henry VIII, King of England, 237, 249n45
Heran, François, 223

high school education, 231, 307–9
Hinde, Andrew, 98, 126n2, 328, 346n45
Hispanic Americans: education, 309; female HIV infection, 334f; poverty levels, 244, 245
historical records: crude death rates, 89, 90f–91f; death records, 72, 85, 93n40; genealogy tools, 20–21, 29n22; life expectancy, 73–80, 85; marriage, 20, 99; population information, 19–22, 37, 354; *see also* census-taking
HIV/AIDS, 334; blocker genetic mutation, 9, 328; child death, 71t; disability adjusted life years and, 259, 260t; disease history, 334–5; drug therapy, 336, 337; females, by race, US, 334f; global rates, 334–8, 336f; labor effects, 336–8; as modern epidemic/pandemic, 5, 89, 262, 315, 333–8, 354; most-affected areas, 5, 49, 66, 259, 334, 338, 346n59–n60; screening and status, 335, 336; symptoms, 335; tuberculosis, 68
hoarding, 323, 345n29
Hobson's Choice (play; Brighouse), 127n41
Holocaust, WWII, 69, 133, 164, 166
home births, 258, 267
"home children," 144
home cooking, 272–3, 302–3, 305
home heating, 82, 256
home ownership, 227
home safety, 82, 274
homelessness, 354
home-schooling, 306
Homestead Act (1860), 125, 148, 184
homicide, 66, 67t, 224
homo sapiens, 7, 8, 9, 29n11, 132
homosexual populations: HIV infection, 335, 346n64; as "never-married," 111; same-sex marriage, 99, 127n27, 220
Hong Kong, 161
Horiuchi, Shiro, 80
Horn of Africa, 91n4
hospitals: founding/history, 247, 288; health history, 258; records, 20, 266, 267, 281n31
hours worked: housework, 302; manufacturing/offices, 230, 297–8, 297t

household size: defined, 225, 227; history, 225–7, 226f; US, 1850–1990, 226f, 227; US predictions, 227
household space and hygiene, 82, 274–6
housework, 272–3, 301–3, 304t, 305
housing and housing costs: population booms, 288; rural, 195; suburbanization, 276; urbanization, 105–6, 195
human behavior: adaptation, 4, 5, 317–18, 329, 353; demographic change, 26–7; economic perspectives, 27, 28; procreation decisions, 104, 219; and survival, 3–4, 353
human capital, 52, 150; destruction, 207, 338; education as development, 28, 52, 182, 195, 206, 207, 234, 305–9, 307t, 338; estimating, 305; formation shift, 286–7; health and, 255, 338; immigration as transfer, 168–9, 182, 203; investment failure, 199; labor needs/matches, 56, 156, 164–5; wars and, 52
human-caused catastrophes, 51, 343; *see also* warfare
human-caused deaths, 10, 66, 67t, 319; disability adjusted life years, 259, 260t
human consumption *see* consumption
Human Development Index (HDI), 15, 259, 261t, 267–9, 268t, 281n36; country histories, 269f; health care spending and life expectancy, 277–8, 278f
human interactions, 219–21, 223, 236, 356
human origins, 3, 7–9, 353
human rights statutes, 296
human trafficking, 168, 233, 234, 249n36; *see also* slavery and enslaved peoples
Humphries, Jane, 223
Hundred Years War, 346n50
hunger *see* famines; malnutrition; starvation
Huns, 132
hunting, native American, 318–20
hunting and gathering societies: disease history, 66, 68; life expectancy, 76; migration patterns, 3, 11, 12; population patterns, 9–11; transition to agriculture, 11–12
Huron tribe, 320
Hutterites, 100–102, 100f, 101f, 106, 126n2

hygiene and health: baseline nutritional maintenance, 262; domestic, 274–6, 301–3, 305; preventable deaths, 65, 274; technological and societal improvements, 68, 73, 76, 258, 275–6

ice ages, 4, 317
Iceland, 316–17
Iezzoni, Lynette, 346n72
illegal immigration: census issues, 136, 171n8; education, 204; North America, 203–4; unskilled workers, 168, 203; worker wages, 204, 213n47
illegitimacy, 99, 114–15, 127n47
illegitimacy ratios, 99, 115
immigration: "age of high immigration," North America, 122, 145, 171n32, 236; barriers, 15, 135, 151, 161, 166–9, 173n83, 202–4; census-taking and records, 136–8, *145*, 155; education considerations, 308; health effects, 88; non-traditional sources, 48, 60n17; population effects, 41, 42t, 44, 48, 107, 148–9, 209, 288, 290, 356; population formulas, 14–15, 33, 40; wage profiles, 133–5, 134f, 147–8, 170; wages effects, 29n19, 40, 136, 148, 149, 170, 182, 198, 204, 213n47, 316; *see also* migration; specific nations
Immigration Act (US; 1965), 168, 203
immunization, 87, 258, 321; influenza, 342; polio, 261
implicit contracts, 102, 154, 234, 235
importing countries, 150, 171n41, 213n36
income: census data/statistics, 25, 26, 37, 38–9, 39t; choices in family support, 102–5, 221, 290, 292; economic structure transformations, 35; GDP and HIV/AIDS rates, 334, 337–8; globalization and growth, 356; infant mortality and, 266; levels by gender, and divorce, 240; and life expectancy, 65; macroeconomic views, 55, 205; Malthusian theory, 17, 18; marriage and, 110, 221, 223–4, 226; mean levels, 36, 38, 206; nutrition links, 255–7, 264–7, 265f; population growth and, 13, 14, 17, 18, 123; poverty definitions, 243–4;

quality of life and, 16, 37, 133–4; saving possibilities, 288; *see also* gross domestic product (GDP); wages
income convergence, 136, 205–7, 356
income distribution: black Americans, 123; economic structure change, trends, 39*f*, 40; education influence, 123; equalizing factors, 207, 245; health/disease and, 66, 86–7; inter-family, 102–6, 103*f*, 126, 220–221; modern divides and trends, 38–9, 353, 354; population growth, 13; population shrinkage, 205; productivity and investment increases, 205; tax structures, 26–7, 207; UK, 245; US history, 38, 244, 245, 309; *see also* income inequality
income elasticities of demand, 6, 55, 56, 59, 60n30
income inequality, 38–40, 39*f*, 205; "antebellum puzzle" considerations, 264–5; globalization and, 356; and health, 264, 266; and poverty, 244, 245, 264, 266; region assumptions, 206–7; US society, predictions, 48; US/history, 244, 245, 264–5, 308
income variation, 244, 246, 267
indentured servants, 138, 139*t*, 142–4, 160, 161, 171n22, 247
India: census, 24, 346n77; demographic transition, 50; diaspora/emigration, 158, 257; diseases, 261, 280n13; dowry-related murder, 224; economic growth, 356; famine, 323–4; gender selection, 353–4; influenza, 341, 341*t*; plagues, 5, 325–7; remittances, 155*t*
Indian Territory (US), 320
indigenous peoples: HIV/AIDS risks, 335, 346n64; land rights, 185; life expectancy, 76; migration, 204; population catastrophes, 318–21; *see also* Native Americans
indoor sanitation facilities, 24, 82, 84–5, 274, 276
Industrial Revolution, 4, 188; city centers, 256; education preceding, 306; employment and child labor, 229, 230, 234; environmental effects, 6; mortality rates and, 72; population effects, 14, 18, 188, 262

industrial transition, 33, *34*, 35, 35*f*, 133, 286–309; *see also* economic transformation
industry (secondary economy stage), 33, 35, 35*f*, 286
infant mortality, 65, 321; historical records, 72, 73*f*, 75, 86, 266; improvements, less-developed regions, 355, 356; incomes and, 266; influenza, 341; life expectancy and, 16, 76; pre-demographic transition, 43; rate, defined, 70, 71; rate disparities, 66, 70–71, 94n79; sanitation challenges and improvements, 65, 86–8, 93n69; sex preferences/ratio, 111; 2002 rates, 67*t*; urban, 86, 88, 94n79; *see also* child mortality
infanticide, 10, 66, 111, 354
infections: battle trauma, 69; care and treatment, 68; childbirth-related, 75, 258, 280n9; home conditions and, 82, 84–6, 274
infectious disease *see* communicable disease
infertility, 99, 100, 101, 111
infidelity, marital, 237–9
influenza, 68, 89, 315, 321, 338–42; economic/labor effects, 341–2; harm potential, 68, 338, 341, 342; history, 68, 68*t*, 319, 341; pandemic, 1918–19, 5, 51, 78*f*, 89, 110, 338–43, *340*, 341*t*
informal labor market: women, child care, 26, 45, 301, 302, 310n11; women, housework, 26, 301, 302
information flows: finance and investment, 236; international migration, 148, 152–3; trade, 166
inheritances: daughters vs. sons, 19, 126, 241; dower arrangements, 240–241; land and farms, 19, 124–6, 241; wills, 19, 20
Innis, Harold, 151
innovations *see* technology introductions and innovations
inspection, health and sanitation, 166–7, 275–6
institutional change/institutional economics, 56–8, 60n40
insurance, health *see* health insurance
insurance, social, 102, 209, 234–5, 248, 276–7

insurance industry, information gathering, 80, 86
intentional deaths *see* homicide; infanticide; suicide rates; warfare
inter-marriage, racial/religious, 162, 224–5, 320–321, 356
internal migration *see* regional migration (including internal); rural-urban migration
International Monetary Fund, 209
international organizations, 209; *see also* specific organizations
inter-urban migration, 199–200
intravenous drug use, 334*f*, 335, 346n64
intrinsic mortality, 80–81
Inuit populations, 317, 318
investment: economic transformation, 149, 150, 288; education, 306–9; rates, 149, 291
investment instruments *see* financial instruments
Ireland: emigration/diaspora, 133, 145, 146, 147*f*, 152, 162–4, 166–7, 169, 234, 256, 323; family sizes, 122, 248n16; labor markets, 205; marriage age history, 108*t*; population history, 162–4, 163*f*, 205
Irish Famine, 1840s, 83, 158, 321, 323; agriculture following, 188; migration memorials, 133; mortality rates, 141; population effects, 162, 163*f*
Iroquois tribe, 320
Ishmaeli Muslims, 235
Islamic conversions, 139
isolated communities: Hutterites, fertility, 100–102, 100*f*, 101*f*, 106, 126n2; Polynesia, influenza, 341
Der Isolierte Staat (von Thünen), 186–7
Israel: creation, 164, 166; Jewish populations, 164, 165*t*
Italy: cooking/eating habits, 272; emigration, 133, 146–8, 147*f*, 157, 157*t*, 234; literacy history, 306; location and trade, 53; marriage age history, 106, 108*t*; population aging, 43*f*, 44; regional migration, 133, 157*t*

Jacquerie (France; 1356), 331
Japan: agriculture subsidies, 193; divorce law, 237; education, 307–8; emigration, 167; population aging, 43–4, 43*f*, 49; return migration, 157; social policy, 247–8; weight gain, 270, 271*f*
Japanese Americans, 157, 167, 172n70
Jefferson, Thomas, 144
Jewish diaspora, 158, 164–6
Jewish populations: history, 164, 166; occupations, 164, 166, 235, 236; WWII era, 132–3
Jiang, Leiwin, 227
Jim Crow laws (US), 309
job training, 305, 306, 354; *see also* apprenticeships
Johnson, Samuel, 200
Joint Plan of Action against Trafficking in Persons, 249n36
journeymen, 40, 59n6; *see also* apprenticeships
Justinian, Plague of (542–750 AD), 12, 324–5, 327, 345n31

Katz, Lawrence, 308
Keating-Owen Act (US; 1916), 231
Kertzer, David, 227
kidney disease, 276, 281n56
Kiesling, Lynne, 329–30, 330*t*
"kinder transport," WWII, 132–3
Klondike gold rush, 153
Komlos, John, 263–5, 265*f*
Korea: population aging, 43–4, 43*f*, 49; weight gain, 270, 271*f*
Kuznets, Simon, 33
Kuznets curve, 39*f*, 40, 205
Kuznets cycles, 150

labeling, nutritional, 273, 274, 281n46
labor contracts, indentured/forced, 158, 161, 247
labor force: agricultural/non-agricultural balance, 126; children, labor force participation, 229, 231–3, 232*t*; competition for, 331, 332; economic structure transformations, 35, 148; gap effects, 56, 288; immigrants, 48, 56, 203; immigrants, illegal, 204; indentured servitude, 142–4, 160; Malthusian theory, 17, 18, 29n19, 168; migration, 136,

147–8, 168–9, 205, 315; "never-worked," 293; participation (LFP), 45–6, 45f, 204; population as natural resource, 53; retired population ratio comparisons, 292, 292f; shares, 33; women, 45–7, 46f, 47, 49, 56, 81, 124, 204, 223, 226, 242, 287–8, 301, 311n33, 331, 356; *see also* child labor; informal labor market; temporary migrants

labor law: child labor, 228, 229, 230, 231, 233, 249n32; peasant labor, Middle Ages, 57, 205, 331, 346n49

labor pooling, 191

labor skills: human capital development, 56, 305, 306; indentured labor agreements, 142, 143, 144; Irish immigrants, 163, 169; Jewish immigrants, 164–5; job training, 305, 306, 354; master vs. laborer wages, 332–3; specialized/specific/targeted, 56, 149, 168, 182, 188–9, 201; *see also* apprenticeships; unskilled jobs

labor unions: children, 229; pension plans, 293; racial discrimination, 198; work hours issues, 297, 298

lactational amenorrhea, 99, 100, 101, 111

land resources: depletion, and effects, 187–8, 199, 320; economics, agriculture, 53, 54, 58, 60n38, 124–5, 186–7, 202; post-plague effects, 329–30, 330t; property rights/use, 58, 125, 157, 165, 241, 319, 320; sales/allowances to settlers, 125, 143–4, 148, 184; settlements, marriage, and fertility, 101–2, 108, 113, 122, 124–5, 241; traditional economies, 102, 104, 318; urban prices, 199–200

language learning, 166; *see also* literacy

Laslett, Peter, 106, 115

Latin America: emigration, 138, 203–4; immigration, 159–60; population growth rates, 355t

law: framework of, 57; specialized systems, 201

law of mortality, 80

League of Nations, 164

leaseholding, 331

Lebergott, Stanley, 301, 302, 305, 311n36

Lee, Erika, 167

Lee, James, 111

Légaré, Jacques, 74–5, 75f, 77f

leisure time: exercise, 273, 298–300; housework, 301, 305; work-leisure choice, 286, 297–300

Lesthaeghe, Ron, 46

Lewis, Arthur, 147

Lewis, Frank, 52, 290

life annuities, 294, 295

life cycle retirement method, 293

life expectancy, 16, 73–82, 81f, 209, 277; convergence, global, 333–4; decrease factors, 12, 264, 333–4; disease cuts, 5, 333–4, 337; elderly, increases, 243, 245, 291, 296; gaps between nations, 81, 277–9, 278f, 333–4; gender differences, 16, 75, 77, 78f, 79t, 80, 81–2, 92n28, 295; historical records, 73–4, 75–6, 77–80, 77f, 78f, 79t, 85–6; increase factors, 6, 75, 76, 79, 86–8, 277–8, 278f, 333, 355; increases and human capital, 306; nutrition, seasonality, and longevity, 84–5, 117; pre-modern times, 12, 65, 75–6; projections, 79t, 227, 243, 355; racial differences, 321, 335; rural vs. urban areas, 66, 83, 85–6

Lincoln, Abraham, 171n13

literacy: census data collection, 25; history, 12, 306, 307, 309, 311n41; Human Development Index, 268, 268t; immigrant testing, 167, 174n109; trade and learning links, 166

literature, population studies, 17, xv, xvii

Little Ice Age, 4, 28n2, 317

livestock, domestic, 66, 68, 82, 319

livestock production, 187

localization economies, 191

location theory, 186–91

logistic growth patterns, 10, 10f, 11

London, England: capital market, history, 236; football, 300, 310n26; mortality, 1670 and 1800, 83f; plague, 327; port, 192

Long, Jason, 306

long-run growth rates: economy, 53; population, 12–13, 13f, 50, 207–9, 315,

354; population declines/catastrophes, 315, 316; population projections, 54–5, 354–5
longevity: birth seasons and nutrition, 84–5, 117; human capital and, 306
longitudinal analysis: census data, 25; emigrants, 155, 172n62; quality and quantity of life, 15–16; time series data, 21
Lösch, August, 188–9, 191, 212n12, 212n13
low birth weight *see* birth weights
Lowell, Massachusetts, 231
lumber, 150, 151, 172n46
lung disease *see* respiratory infections and disease

MacKellar, Landis, 339, 342
macroeconomics, 28, 53–7, 149, 150, 188, 205; effects of catastrophes, 36–7, 325, 329–33, 334, 337–8, 341–2, 347n81; effects of industrial transition, 55–6, 286–309; management techniques, 209
Magee, Gary, 153
Maghribi traders, 165–6
Maguire, Karen, 236
Makeham, William, 80
malaria, 68, 68t, 88, 258, 259, 275
Malaysia, 159
malnutrition: birth weights, 84, 266; economic causes, 264, 266, 267; famine, 321, 322; hormone effects, 117; in utero, and effects, 84–5, 117; *see also* nutrition, family/personal
malnutrition deaths, 51, 65, 66, 67t; agricultural households, 82; children, 71f; war byproduct, 69
Malthus, Thomas, 17–18, 26, 29n18, 111, 168, 321, 322
Malthusian theory, 17–19, 29n19, 168, 321–2
Mamluks, 139, 164
mandatory education, 306, 308
mandatory retirement, 44, 92n30, 296
manufacturing: hours worked, 230, 297t; as secondary economy stage, 33, 35, 35f, 286
markers, genetic, 8

market failures, 57, 60n34
market integration, 52, 200, 201, 205–7
marriage: civil ceremonies, 220; courtship and, 221–5; defined, 99; dissolution, 236–40, 240f; fecundity, 99; group barriers, 113, 127n27, 224–5; as institution, 57, 99, 110, 220; local nature, 112, 221; property in, 220, 224, 240–242; as sacrament, 220, 237–8
marriage age: education levels and, 48, 110, 113; history, 106–9, 107f, 108t, 109f, 109t, 119, 122, 333; later marriage and fertility, 48, 49, 99, 106–8, 110, 122, 227, 333; Malthusian theory, 18, 107; primo- and multi-geniture, 241; 20th century, 106, 109–11, 109f, 110f, 127n19; young marriage and fertility, 99, 101, 106, 107, 119, 122; *see also* first marriage
marriage attitudes, 356; class barrier breakdowns, 113; companionship desires, 110, 113; decreases in marriage, 110; divorce, 238; fertility rate effects, 44, 48
marriage rate: fertility and, 47–8, 99, 109, 117, 122, 123, 227, 287; gender imbalances and, 69, 112, 113, 117, 123, 201; inter-marriage, 224–5, 356; short-run variations, 109, 287
marriage records, 20, 99, 106, 114, 127n17, 221
Married Woman's Property Act (England; 1871), 242
Married Woman's Property Act (Ontario, Canada; 1884), 242, 250n65
married women's labor force participation, 46f
Marx, Karl, 230
Massachusetts: crude death rates, 89, 91f, 211f; illegitimacy, 115; life expectancy/death information, 73, 85–6, 93n51; Lowell, 231; marriage age history, 109t
Mateos-Planas, Xavier, 105
maternal malnutrition: birth weights, 267; offspring morbidity links, 84, 85
maternal mortality, 70, 75, 258; 2002 rates, 67t; decreases, 75
matrilineal ethnicity, 164
Matrimonial Causes Act (England; 1857), 237

Matrimonial Causes Act (England; 1923), 238–9
"Matthew Effect," 70–71
McKeown, T., 86–7, 280n18
McLanahan, Sara, 48, 60n15
mean income levels, 36, 38, 206
measles, 68t, 71f, 258, 319
meat: hunting, 317–18, 320; nutritional component, 265
Medicaid and Medicare, 248, 273, 279
medical advances: drugs, 68, 326, 336; and life expectancy, 80–81, 87, 277; public health and hygiene, 65, 73, 87, 258; reproductive, 47, 311n33
medical care: access and affordability, 66, 261, 277, 279, 337, 354; costs factors, 273, 279; gender privilege, 354; lacking, death rates effects, 198; lacking, preventable deaths, 65; misdiagnosis in, 258; national expenditures, and life expectancy, 277–9, 278f; native Americans, 321; systems, history, 276–7; trauma, 68; *see also* health insurance; medical advances
Medieval Climatic Optimum, 317
Meiji Government (Japan), 307–8
melatonin, 257
mental health problems, and poverty, 255
mental institutions, 247
metabolism, 262, 270
Metis people, 321
Mexico: child poverty, 243; immigration, 159–60; migration to US, 203, 204, 213n47; NAFTA, 202; remittances, 155t; weight gain, 270, 271f
miasmatic theory (medicine), 87
Michaud, Pierre-Carl, 273
microbes, 5
microeconomics, 28
microwave ovens, 272, 303
Middle East: child labor, 232t, 233; plague, 325, 326; population histories, 11–12; tax records, 20
Middle Passage, 140–141
midwives, 76, 276
migration, 28, 169, 181; climate-related, 143–4, 199, 317; costs influence, 15, 135, 149–52, 161, 169, 170, 181, 182, 199, 205, 206; health effects, 88; human history and scope, 3–4, 7, 9–14, 52, 118, 132–6, 138–52, 164, 166, 316; net present value to individual, 135, 170; plague effects, 331, 332; psychic and social benefits, 27, 135; recession effects, 204; treaties, 159; WWII, 287, 288; *see also* emigration; immigration; inter-urban migration; regional migration (including internal); rural-urban migration

Migration Propensity Index, 204, 213n48
militaries: anthropometric data, 263; employees, 44; population size and, 344n1; pre-modern era, 52–3, 104, 136, 139, 171n7; rosters, 136, 139, 171n7; technologies, 52; *see also* warfare
milk, 85, 86, 88
Mill, John Stuart, 242
Mills-Reincke phenomenon, 88
mineral resources and mines, 53–4, 153, 160, 199, 207; child labor, 229, 230, 233; hours worked, 298; respiratory diseases, 255
minimum wage, youth labor, 249n32
minorities, US *see* African Americans; Hispanic Americans; inter-marriage, racial/religious; Japanese Americans; Native Americans
miscarriage rates, 117
"missing" females, 19, 111, 353–4
mitochondrial DNA (mtDNA), 8, 8f
mixed marriage *see* inter-marriage, racial/religious
modern phase, demographic transition, 32
Mokyr, Joel, 162, 302
Mongols, 132, 139
"moral vices," 275
morbidity: body mass index and obesity, 270f, 273; data use, 258–9, 280n12; defined, 50, 255, 257; industrial trauma, 353; influenza, 341, 342; low birth weight links, 84, 266–7, 276; malnutrition influence, 84, 255, 257, 266–7; ranks by national development, 259, 261t; rural-urban comparisons, 255, 276; stress influence, 257

Morens, David, 341, 342, 346n78
Mormon genealogy, 29n22
Morris, Morris, 267
Morse, Donald, 201, 213n32
mortality, intrinsic, 80–81
mortality, law of, 80
mortality rates: body mass index and obesity, 270*f*, 273; demographic transition, 32, 49, 65, 77, 111, 149, 209; developed world, 72–3; developing nations, 49, 70–71, 356; famine and disease, 17, 321–3, 329; mortality declines, 263, 280n18, 305–6, 355, 356; net replacement rate consideration, 41; population pyramid illustration, 288, 289*f*; pre-modern society, 50, 65, 72, 82; records, 72, 76, 85, 93n40; rural vs. urban, 82–4, 83*f*, 85–9, 93n52, 94n79, 124, 276; slaves, 141; *see also* child mortality; death rates; infant mortality
mortality shocks, 12–13, 13*f*, 19, 29n14, 51
Mortimer, Ian, 331
motherhood, as labor/career, 26, 45, 310n11
motor vehicle accident deaths, 75
multigenerational family structure, 220, 225, 227
Multinational Time Use Study (MTUS), 302–5, 303*t*, 304*t*
Munro, John, 332
murder, 66, 67*t*, 224
Murray, John, 277
musical entertainment, 300, 310n31, 311n32
Muslim populations: African-European migration, 132; divorce laws, 236–7; tithing, 235
mutations: genetics, 8; viruses, 68, 338, 341, 342
mutual self-help societies, 235, 276–7

NAFTA (North American Free Trade Agreement), 201–2
Napoleonic Wars, and era economics, 69, 112, 151, 188
national and regional trade: income convergence and, 207; Native Americans, 319, 320; plague and, 325–8, 345n38; UK, 200
National Association of Base Ball Players, 299, 300
National Child Labor Committee (US), 228
national debt, 150
national food balance sheets, 262
National Health and Nutrition Examination Survey (NHANES), 271, 272*t*
national health care/insurance, 235, 248, 273, 276–7
national income *see* gross domestic product (GDP); gross national product (GNP)
national revolts, 331
National Road (US), 185, 212n4
national security: attacks on, 202; immigration policy, 168, 202, 204
nationalism: Europe, 167; Japan, 308
Native American forced migration, 320
Native Americans: disease introductions, 68, 318–21; education and poverty, 245, 321; HIV infection, 334*f*, 335, 346n64; inter-marriage, 320–321; life expectancy, 76; modern populations, 318–19, 319*f*, 321, 344n10; population crisis, 315, 318–21, 319*f*; westward expansion and, 185, 319, 320
natural disasters: mortality catastrophes, 51, 342–3; relief effort funds, 154, 343
natural resources: consumption and depletion, 6–7, 11, 186, 199, 315, 318, 320; export products, 150, 151, 160, 172n46; national economic performance, 53–4, 205; social benefits of conservation, 27, 58
naturalized citizens, 172n70
Neal, Larry, 169, 236
Neanderthals, 7, 9
Neher, Philip, 102, 105
neonatal mortality, 70–72, 71*f*, 75
net increases, population, 14–15, 33
net present value, migration, 135, 170
net replacement gap, 41, 48, 122, 123
net replacement rate, 40, 41, 47, 209
Netherlands: emigration, 147*f*; infant mortality, 86; location and trade, 53; weight gain, 270, 271*f*
networking, 152–3

networks: commercial, 165–6, 235–6; family, 234–6; support, 234–5; village/emigrants, 152–3, 190, 234, 301
never-married individuals, 99, 111–12; fertility limiters, 110–114, 122, 201; property rights, 241
New Deal legislation, US, 248
New France, 22–3, 29n25, 72, 89, 107, 108, 112, 127n24, 241
New Lanark experiment (Scotland; 19th C.), 257
New Poor Law (England; 1834), 247
"new towns," 200, 333
New Zealand: census, 24; forced migration, 144; immigration/policy, 146f, 168; third demographic transition, 48
Nigeria, 322
"no-fault" divorce, 239
nomadic peoples, 3–4, 9, 11, 132; *see also* migration
non-discrimination, pensions, 294–5, 310n11
non-married cohabitation, 47, 220, 226, 227, 239
non-renewable resources, 53, 54; *see also* mineral resources and mines; oil resources
non-tradable goods, 149–50, 171n40
Norse, Greenland, 4, 316–18, 353
North America *see* Canada; United States; westward expansion, North America
North American native Indians *see* Native Americans
North American trade, 201–2, 213n36
North Carolina, illegitimacy rates, 115, 127n49
North Korea, 315, 322
north-south migration (UK), 200–201
Norway: crude birth rates/fertility transition, 120f, 122, 208, 208t, 210f; crude death rates, 90f, 208, 208t, 210f; emigration, 146, 147f; history, 317; life expectancy/death information, 73; marriage age history, 108t
nuclear family: history, 225–7; structure, 220
numeracy, history, 12, 306, 311n41
nuptiality rate, 99
nutrition, family/personal: baseline maintenance, 262, 264; and birth weight, 84, 266–7; disability adjusted life years, 260t; domestic households, 267, 302; health/longevity and, 12, 82–6, 117, 256–7, 262–6, 279; hormone effects, 117; improvements, 255–6, 266–7
nutritional labeling, 273, 274, 281n46
nutritional science, 262, 302

Ó Gráda, Cormac, 70, 162, 322–4, 345n19–n21, 345n24–n25
obesity, 256, 269–74, 271f, 279, 298, 321
occupational mobility: barriers, 17, 123; education links, 56, 126, 305, 307; families and, 227; housing, 276; Jews, 164–5; probability by age, 182, 183f; quality of life, 17
occupational safety: accidents and deaths, 66, 75, 230, 353; child labor, 229, 230, 231, 233; factory conditions, 229, 230; farming conditions, 233; *see also* hours worked
oil resources: area income effects, 205; booms, and in-migration, 201; cost effectiveness, 54; offshore, 54, 201
"old age": classification, 78–9, 92n30; legal aspects of labeling, 92n30
one child policy, China, 49, 60n18
O'Neill, Brian, 227
Opium Wars (1839–42), 158
opportunistic diseases, 66, 69, 117, 321, 335
opportunity costs: children, 104, 105, 117, 128n61, 195, 308; education, 52, 195; food preparation time, 272–3; human behavior, 26–7; immigration limitations, 169; marriage, 333; property holdings, 124, 186; resources, 186, 187; wars, 6, 52
Organization for Economic Co-operation and Development (OECD) nations: census-taking, 137; crude birth rates, 123; divorce, 238; education, 305, 307t, 308, 309; family size trends, 226; life expectancy gaps, 81, 278–9; migration trends, 200, 337; national health care, 277, 279; national population rates, 41, 43, 43f; obesity, 269–70, 271f; poverty rates, 243–5, 243f; records, 21; retired

population vs. labor force, 292, 292*f*; service economies, 35; social support policies, 48
orphans, 144, 230, 247, 266, 338
Ottoman Turks, 164
out-of-wedlock births, 99, 114–15, 127n47
overpopulation, study and debate, 17–18, 54–5, 123, 322, 345n19
Owen, Wilfred, 257

Palestine, 164
Pamuk, Sevket, 329*t*
pandemics: defined, 51, 66; population tolls, 5, 12, 50, 319, 324–5, 338, 342; *see also* HIV/AIDS; influenza; plagues
panel data, 21
parasitic diseases, 65, 66, 67*t*, 68*t*, 91n5, 259, 260*t*, 319
parental control: child labor, 229; daughters, employment, and safety, 223, 224
parish records *see* church records
passenger travel, ships, 151–2, 162, 166–7; *see also* transportation costs
Pasteur, Louis, 280n9
Pasteurella pestis see Yersinia pestis
pasteurization, 84–5, 88
patents, 250n62, 337
pathogens, 66, 68*t*, 73, 82, 83, 274, 325
patriarchal households, 224, 227
paupers, 246, 247
peasant labor: China, 158; income consumption/redistribution, 102, 104, 126, 291–2; Middle Ages, and law, 57, 205, 331; plague effects, 330–333
peasant revolts, 331
penal colonies, 138, 141–2
pension eligibility, 44, 79, 293, 295, 296, 310n11
pension liabilities, 293
pension planning/schemes, 79–80, 209, 277, 292–6
pensions, implicit, and family support, 103*f*, 105, 221, 234, 235, 291–2; *see also* retirement
per-capita health expenditures, 277–9, 278*f*
Perrenoud, Alfred, 72
Perry, Robert, 326, 345n34

pertussis, 66, 68*t*, 258
Peru, immigration, 160
pharmaceutical drugs, 279, 326, 336, 337, 342
pharmaceutical industry, 279, 337
Philippines: immigration, 159, 160; remittances, 155*t*
Philipson, Tomas, 273
physical space, households, 82, 274–6, 275
pianos, 300, 310n31
piece-work, 26, 223, 275
Plague of Justinian (542–750 AD), 12, 324–5, 327, 345n31
plagues, 5, 12, 66, 325–39; economic effects, 36–7, 325, 329–33, 342; feudalism and, 330–331; global distribution, 325*f*; population effects, 324–5, 328–9, 329*t*, 346n45; research/study, 325–7, 334, 345n30–n31, 345n33–n34, 345n40; resistance, 326, 328; travel and transmission, 325–8, 344, 345n38; *see also* epidemics; pandemics
planned communities, 230–231, 257
pneumoconiosis, 255
pneumonia, 87–8, 327
pneumonic plague, 324–7, 344
pogroms, 51, 133, 166
Poland: child poverty, 243; family sizes, 248n16; immigration and emigration, 60n17, 147*f*; Jewish populations, 164, 173n105
polio, 89, 258, 261
political prisoners, 141
political relations, inter-family, 104, 106–7, 113, 224
pollution, 6, 58, 229
poor health: causes, 66, 255–6, 274–5; poverty links, 66, 242, 255, 264, 266, 276
Poor Law (England/Wales, 1597 and 1601), 246, 247
population aging *see* aging
population crises, 315–21, 319*f*
population growth: catastrophe path, 315–16, 318, 319*f*; doubling rate, 100, 100*f*, 101, 107; economic history and, 17–18, 27–8, 315, 316; environmental carrying capacity, 10, 10*f*, 11, 353, 354; factors and formulas, 14–15, 18, 25,

29n13, 33, 40, 100f, 101, 321; future projections, 31, 41, 42t, 49–50, 50f, 59n1, 354–5, 355t; gender imbalances, 22–3, 69; hunting and gathering societies, 9–12; less developed regions, 32, 33, 41, 42t, 48–50, 354–6, 355t; Malthusian theory, 17–19, 29n19, 168, 321–2; maximum rate (Walker Thesis), 168, 169, 174n118; models, 10f, 13f; modern-day, 31, 40–41, 42t, 354–5, 355t; more developed regions, 31, 32, 33, 42t, 168, 209, 354, 355t; rates considerations, 12–13, 15, 17, 18, 354–5; statistics, 11–14, 14t, 31, 41, 42t, 60n20, 100f, 354–5, 355t; United States, 54–5, 60n20, 167–8; *see also* birth rates; census-taking; demographic transition; fertility rates; global population estimates; immigration; overpopulation, study and debate

population history: death probability/life expectancy data, 73–82; human scope, 3, 7–9, 353–5, 355t

"population pyramid," 288, 289f

population shocks and echoes, 286, 287–8, 287f

population totals *see* global population estimates

Portugal: emigration, 146, 147f; fishing industry, 234, 317

positive checks, population growth, 17, 18, 321–2

Posner, Richard, 273

post-partum infertility, 99–101, 111

potatoes, 162, 321, 322

Potomac River, 185

poverty: cycles, 242, 244–5, 246, 255, 354; data/statistics, 242–3, 243f, 248; definitions, 243–4; elderly, 80, 82, 243f, 244, 245, 248; health issues, 66, 242, 255, 264, 266, 276, 279; history, 245–6; modern famine, 322; reduction and relief, 48, 243, 245–8, 354; single-parent families, 243, 243f, 244–6

Poverty and Famine (Sen), 323

prehistoric migration, 3, 4, 7, 9–14

pre-marital sex: abstinence, 106; HIV/AIDS policy and, 336–7; illegitimate children, 99, 114–15

prenatal nutrition, 84–5, 267

Preston, Samuel H., 29n28

preventive checks, population growth, 18, 111, 321–2

preventive medicine, 279

primogeniture, 241

prison populations (modern day), 346n64, 354

prisoners, convicts, and exiles: anthropometric data, 263; debtors, 144; forced migration, 138, 139t, 141–4, 198; return migration, 157

prisoners of war, 139, 141

probability of dying, 73–82, 81f

probate records, 20

production costs, US economic history, 53

productivity, labor: agriculture income, 58, 72, 76, 111, 124, 193, 230; economic structure changes and, 35–6, 148; education/human capital development, 305, 307, 309; growth, 188; illness and death, 16, 342, 347n81; industry differences, 148, 182, 199; national, 16

professional occupations: Jewish populations, 164–5; modern-day reach, 356; and offspring health, 266

professional sports, 300

propaganda, 153, 195–6, 323, 345n29

property rights: Black Death and, 329; divorce, 240; home ownership, 227; land, 58, 125, 157, 165, 241, 319, 320; in marriage, 220, 224, 240–242; natural resource management, 318; patent protection, 337

prostitution, 233, 249n36, 275, 338

protectionism, 167, 200

psychic benefits, migration, 27, 135

public goods, 16, 29n17

public health: famine fighting, 322; health care systems, 277; HIV/AIDS education/work, 335, 336–8; influenza policies, 339, 342; lives saved, 65, 322; obesity policy, 273, 274; sanitation improvements, 76, 86–8, 274–6; tobacco policy, 274

public services and investment: housing and health, 58, 274–6, 288; negative externalities, 58; transportation, 276, 291

puerperal fever, 258, 280n9
purchasing power parity, 39*t*
"push" and "pull" migration forces, 133, 169, 204

Qing Dynasty, 158
Quakers, 235
quality of life: analysis, 15–16, 54–5, 354; global rankings, 15, 259, 267–9; improvements across history, 16–17, 37, 219, 257, 354; migration factor, 133–4; morbidity effects, 257–9, 261–2; US, 54–5; *see also* standards of living
quantity of life *see* life expectancy
quarantines: effects of lacking, 339; plagues, 327–8; ships' passengers, 166–7
Quebec, Canada: crude birth rates/fertility transition, 121*f*, 122–3, 208, 208*t*, 211*f*; crude death rates, 89, 91*f*, 208, 208*t*, 211*f*; life expectancy/death information, 73, 74–5, 75*f*, 94n79; migration memorials, 133
Quebec Act (British statute, 1774), 183
Queen Anne of the United Kingdom, 100, 102

racial and ethnic prejudice: anti-African American, 197, 198, 309; anti-Asian, 157, 160, 161, 167; anti-Semitism, 165, 166; globalization and, 356; non-whites, 167, 244
racial differences: birth weights, 267; births, timing (US), 116, 116*f*; crude birth rates (US), 119, 121*f*; data gathering, 109*t*, 193, 194*t*, 321; demographic behavior, 123; distinctiveness, 9; education (US), 113, 197, 244, 309, 321; HIV/AIDS infection (females), US, 334*f*; interracial marriage, 224, 320–321, 356; life expectancy, 321, 335; never married (US), 113, 114*f*; women, labor force, 45–6
railways, 34; construction, 136, 148, 152, 160, 190; land sales, 153, *184*; trade effects, 187; westward expansion, 148, *184*, 185
Ramey, Valerie, 301, 302, 311n36–n37
rat- and rat-flea borne disease, 68*t*, 326–8, 344

rates of return, private and social, 27
raw milk, 88
Ray, Deraj, 354
real cost of living, 246
real GDP: demographic transition and, 208; health and standard of living, 264; historic regional patterns, 205–6, 206*f*; as measurement, 77, 150; US, 38*f*; 205–6
real GNP per capita, 264–5, 265*f*
real income: consumption and, 16, 36, 106; convergence, 205–7, 206*f*; growth rates, 38, 38*f*; life expectancy and, 65; Malthusian theory, 18; national income growth and, 38; regional differences/per capita disparities, 38–9, 205–7, 206*f*, 309
real wages, 36; convergence, 136; demographic transition and, 208; emigration and, 148; growth rates, 37*f*; historical trends, 36–7, 297; illegitimacy rates links, 115; increases, and leisure time, 297; Malthusian theory, 18, 29n19; plague effects/changes, 36–7, 329, 330–333, 332*f*, 342, 346n55; traditional industries, 182, 188–9; *see also* wages
recessions: historic perspective, 315; migration declines, 204
"rectangularization," 81, 81*f*
redemptioners, 143, 144
refrigeration, 84–5, 88
regional government, 58
regional income convergence, 205–7, 206*f*
regional migration (including internal), 181–3; demographic transition and, 207–9; examples, 133, 157*t*, 198–9, 200–203; industrialization and urbanization, 147–8, 188; international migration and, 133, 147–8, 181–2; North America, 201–3, 320; state-to-state, US, 185, 193–8, 194*t*, 309; UK, 200–201; *see also* inter-urban migration; location theory; rural-urban migration; westward expansion, North America
regional population distribution, US, 1790–1860, 185*t*
regional trade *see* national and regional trade
relief programs and funding: disease (general), 343; famine, 322, 324; HIV/

AIDS, 337, 338; natural disasters, 154, 343; poverty, 48, 243, 245–8, 354
religious communities, 235, 336–7
religious conversions, 139, 317
religious participation: declines, 47; marriage and divorce, 220, 236–7; migration influence, 132; poverty relief, 246; tithing and social support, 234–5; US, regional differences, 48
remarriage: divorce following, 239–40, 240f; rates by gender, 239; separation and, 237; widows, 246
remittances, 153–5, 155t, 156, 157, 161
rents: economic, 186, 188; family, 221, 227; housing, 195, 227, 274–5; land, 186, 187, 188, 199, 200, 333
Republic of Korea *see* Korea
respiratory infections and disease: cause of death, 66, 67t, 71f; child death, 71f; disability adjusted life years, 260t; H1N1, 339; home conditions, 274, 275; occupational, 255; seasonality, 85
retirement: ages, 44, 79, 295, 296; familial support, 102–5, 125, 126, 154, 221, 234, 291–2; legal aspects, 92n30; mandatory, 44, 92n30, 296; migration, 182; national funding/maintenance, 292–6; OECD populations comparisons, 292, 292f; US trends, 45, 288, 291; worker replacement, 44
return/reverse migration, 154, 155–7, 157t, 159, 182; England-Scotland, 201; west-east, United States, 185
reunification via immigration, 168
rheumatism, 275
Ricardo, David, 166, 188
rice, 323–4
rickets, 256–8
right to vote, 24, 238
riots, 246, 322
Romania, household size, 248n16
romantic love, 221–5
Rome, ancient: divorce, 236; empire and migration, 132; life expectancy, 76; military clashes, 164; slavery, 138–9; tax and census records, 20, 136
Royal Proclamation Line (British statute, 1763), 183

Ruggles, Steven, 113
rule of 69, 101
rural vs. urban fertility and family size, 105–6, 122–6, 195, 201
rural vs. urban health (non-mortality related), 256–7, 266
rural vs. urban morbidity, 255, 276
rural vs. urban mortality, 82–9, 83f, 93n52, 94n79, 124, 276
rural-urban migration, 125–6, 133, 147, 169, 191–4, 200; central place theory, 188–90; declining rural regions, 198–9; economics and taxation, 188; household effects, 227; marriage effects, 221, 223; saving increase effects, 291; US history, 185; *see also* Great Migration (African American south-north migration); urbanization
Russia: agriculture, 187, 198; emigration, 147f; internal migration, 198; Jewish populations, 164, 165t, 166; population declines, 42, 198, 199; Siberia, 124, 136, 198, 212n25; workhouses, 247; WWII deaths and population effects, 69, 112
Rwanda, 262

sacraments, 220, 237–8
same-sex marriage, 99, 127n27, 220
sample data, 21–2
sanitation challenges: agriculture, 58, 66, 82; diseases, 65, 68t, 84–5, 87–8, 322; housing, 82, 274–6; waste from consumption, 7
sanitation infrastructure: private, 24, 82, 84–5, 274, 276; public, 58, 73, 76, 83, 86–8, 321
Sanz-de-Galdeano, Anna, 273
saving and savings: capital flows, 149, 150, 236, 288, 290; dependency rates and, 288, 290, 291f; dowries, 224; family income redistribution, 102, 104, 105, 154, 157, 290, 292; formula, 290; household, 227; interest rates, 27; national aggregate incomes and, 55, 286, 288, 290–291, 291f; personal incomes and, 36, 55, 286, 288, 290
Scandinavian nations: child poverty, 243; emigration, 146, 147f; history, 316–17; *see also* specific nations
scarcity of labor, 331, 332

scarlet fever, 66, 89, 258, 319
Schofield, Ronald, 21, 90*f*, 91*f*, 106, 107*f*, 119, 120*f*, 121*f*, 210*f*, 211
schooling *see* education
schools: food options, 274; privately-run, 306–7; social infrastructure, 288; social opportunities, 222, 236; sports, 299; universities, 308
Scotland, 200; divorce, 238; Glasgow population health, 256–7; Highlands, 133, 158, 200, 201; immigration and emigration, 60n17, 133, 145, 200–201, 213n29, 256, 257; labor market traits, 201; labor markets, 205; migration from UK, 201; migration to England, 200–201, 213n28
Scottish Enlightenment, 200
seasonal migrants *see* temporary migrants
seasonal patterns: birth, 84–5, 115–17, 116*f*; death, 82–4; influenza, 339, 340; longevity, 84–5; plagues, 326
"second demographic transition," 46–8, 239
secondary economy sector, 33, 35, 35*f*, 286
secondary education, 231, 307–9
secondary sex ratio, 112
segregation: gender, 223; race, 197, 309
self-help societies, 235, 276–7
self-identity, ethnicity, 161–2
Semmelweis, Ignaz, 258
Sen, Amartya, 264, 323, 324
separation, marital, 237
septicaemic plague, 326, 344
service economies: body mass index/health effects, 271, 273; child labor, 232, 232*t*, 233; progression/tertiary economy stage, 33, 35, 35*f*, 36, 133, 286
Seven Years War, 183
sewer systems, 86, 87, 88, 274
sex ratio imbalances, and migration, 111, 112, 201; famine, 117–18, 163, 322–3; military deaths, 69, 112, 123; native American in-migration, 320; New France, population imports, 23, 127n24
sex selection, 111, 353–4
sex work, 233, 249n36, 275, 338
sexual abuse and violence: child workers, 230, 233; rape, in slave trade, 141; women workers, 223

"sexual revolution," 239
sexually transmitted disease, 319; *see also* HIV/AIDS
Shakespeare, William, 79, 106, 328
Shapiro, Jesse, 269, 272
Shawnee Prophet War (US; 19th C.), 320
ships and shipping: passenger travel, 151–2, 162, 166–7; records, 20; routes, 152; sail and steam technology, 151; sizes, 150, 151, 172n47; slave experiences, 138, 140–141; trade, 150–151, 187, 326, 327–8; Vikings, 316–17
shock and echo effects, 286, 287–8, 287*f*
shopping, time spent, 302, 305
short-run growth rates: economy, 53; population, 50, 209, 354; population declines/catastrophes, 316, 322; population projections, 54–5
Siberia, 124, 136, 198, 212n25
silicosis, 255
simian diseases, 335
Singapore, 159, 160*t*, 164
single-parent families: anti-poverty supports, 48; illegitimacy and income, 115; nutrition challenges, 267; poverty, 243–6, 243*f*, 275; rate increases, 242
single-person households, 225–7244, 248
Sioux Uprising (US; 1862), 320
Skaërings *see* Inuit populations
skeletal remains, study, 263, 280n17
skills, labor *see* labor skills; unskilled jobs
skin tone, 257
Slater, Samuel, 231
slave armies, 139, 263
slavery and enslaved peoples: abolition, 160, 171n13, 195–7; abolition, trade, 139–40; census/enumeration, 29n27; history and migration, 138–41, 143, 196–7; modern-day trafficking, 233; quality of life improvements, 17; US colonies/states, 138, 139*t*, 144, 195–7
smallpox, 68, 68*t*, 76, 87, 89, 166, 258, 319
smoking, 274, 279
snacking, 272, 274
soccer, 298–9, *301*
social benefits, 57, 274
social class barriers: education, 307; marriage options, 113, 127n41, 224

social class links, 236, 249n44
social costs, 57, 234, 274, 343
social discount rate, 27, 29n28, 318
social events, and courtship, 222–4
social insurance, 102, 209, 234–5, 248, 276–7, 292, 295; *see also* relief programs and funding
social mobility, 17, 56, 123, 221
social networks: class links, 236; emigrants, 152–3, 234, *301*
social overhead capital, 57
social rates of return/discount, 27, 29n27
social reforms, 297
social security programs, 292, 295
social unrest, 246, 322, 331
Somalia, 118, 315
South Africa, 5, 337
South America: child labor, 232*t*, 233; emigration, 204; immigration, 145–8, 157*t*, 160; Jewish populations, 165*t*; native populations, 318; population growth rates, 355*t*; slave trade destination, 138–40
South Asian emigration, 138, 257
South Korea *see* Korea
South Sea Bubble, 236
Southeast Asia: Chinese immigration, 159, 160*t*, 164; marriage economics, 224; trade, 159
south-north migration, US, 185, 195–8, 309
Soviet Union, 198, 322
space, household, and hygiene, 82, 274–6, *275*
Spain: emigration, 146, 147*f*; exploration and settlement, Americas, 318; marriage age history, 108*t*; per capita income, 207
Spanish Flu *see* influenza
specialization, 189; labor skills, 56, 149, 164–5, 168, 182, 188–9, 201; national production, 136, 190, 291; theory, 188–9, 212n12, 212n13
speculation, commodities, 323
sports participation: health benefits, 273; leisure activities, 273, 298–300, *299*, *301*
St. Patrick's Day, 163–4
standards of living: food supply, 19, 262–3; history/study, 19, 86, 262, 330, 331,
354; improvements, 86–7, 89, 354; measurement theory, 264; poverty benchmarks, 244; *see also* quality of life
starvation, 51, 65, 66, 69, 321, 322; agricultural households, 82; population extinctions, 317; *see also* malnutrition
state-to-state migration *see* regional migration (including internal)
steam power, 190, 230
Steckel, Richard, 185, 212n6, 263–4, 267–8, 268*t*, 269
sterilizations, 48
streptococcus bacteria and disease, 258
stress, 81, 257
strikes, labor, 198
stroke *see* cardiovascular disease
structure of economy, 33–6, 133
stunting of growth, 264
sub-Saharan Africa: disease and mortality, 66, 278; education and productivity, 309; famine, 322; fertility rates, 49; HIV/AIDS, 5, 49, 66, 334, 336–8, 346n59–60; household size, 248n16; human origins, 3, 7; life expectancy, 78, 334, 335; marriage economics, 224; medical care and gender, 354; per capita incomes, 207
suburban expansion, 276
suicide rates, 75
Sun Yat Sen, 159
sunlight, 256
supply of labor *see* labor force
support networks, 234–5
survival decisions, 3–4, 353
Sweden: birth rate seasonality, 117; crude birth rates/fertility transition, 120*f*, 122, 208, 208*t*, 210*f*; crude death rates, 90*f*, 208, 208*t*, 210*f*; divorce law, 239; emigration, 146, 147*f*; Human Development Indexes, 268, 269*f*; life expectancy/death information, 73, 76, 77*f*, 79; urbanization, 192; weight gain, 270, 271*f*
swine flu (H1N1), 339, 341
Switzerland life expectancy/death information, 73, 76, 78, 79, 278

taboos, 10–11, 15, 49
Taiping Rebellion (1850–65), 28n5, 69, 158

Taiwan, 162, 164
Talon, Jean, 22–3
tar sands, 54
Taubenberger, Jeffrey, 341, 342, 346n78
tax policy: domestic partnerships, 220; incomes, 40, 207; national health care, 277; peasant concerns and revolts, 331; retirement contributions, 292–5; unhealthy foods, 274
tax records, 19, 20, 22
Taylor, Scott, 318
technological adaptation, 329
technology introductions and innovations: agriculture, 55–6, 192, 194, 197, 273; architecture, 276; birth/death rates and, 33, 47, 98; child labor effects, 229; computers, 308; economic structural transformation, 35–6; environmental carrying capacity and, 10, 10f, 11, 354; household tools, 272, 301–3, 311n33; human capital and, 28, 199, 308; market integration, 206; medicine, 47, 65, 68, 73, 80–81, 87, 258, 277, 311n33, 326, 336; military power, 52; resource substitutions, 54
teenage pregnancy, 48
television watching, 298
temperance movement, 300
temperature and climate *see* climate; climate change
temporary migrants, 156, 161, 172n64, 182–3, 201, 203, 322
terrorist attacks, 202
tertiary economy sector, 33, 35, 35f, 36, 133, 286
testosterone, 117
textile mills: child labor, 229, 230–231; hours worked, 298
theatre, 299, 300, 311n32
"third demographic transition," 48
Thomas, Brinley, 147
Thompson, Andrew, 153
Thornton, Russell, 318, 319, 344n10
Thünen, Johann Heinrich von *see* von Thünen, Johann Heinrich
time allocation: household work, 272–3, 301–5, 303t, 304t; work-leisure choice, 286, 297–300

time series analysis, 15–16, 21; Human Development Index, 267–9, 268t, 269f; real wages: labor in plague centuries, 332f
tithing: peasant farming, 104; religious communities, 235
tobacco consumption, 274, 279
Tolowa tribe, 320
Tomes, Nancy, 87
tools: making, 9, 29n11; use in specialization, 189
total fertility rate, 40–41, 42t, 46, 108, 209; Hutterite population, 100; national rates, 100, 122
totalitarianism: cause factors, 174n110; famine relief prevention, 322
Toutain, Jean Claude, 262
towns *see* "new towns"; village building
trade *see* fur trade; global trade; national and regional trade
trade barriers, 149, 172n46, 315, 356
trade networks, 165–6
trades, Europe, 133, 165, 331, 332–3
traditional phase, demographic transition, 32
"Trail of Tears," 320
training, job, 305, 306, 354; *see also* apprenticeships
transatlantic passage: fares, 143, 145–6, 151–2; immigrant experiences, 88, 140–41, 151, 163; indentured labor, 142–3; slave trade, 140–41; *see also* immigration
transient migrants *see* gypsies; temporary migrants
transition phase, demographic transition, 32
transportation costs: migration, fares, 143, 145–6, 151–2; migration, general, 130, 170, 199, 200, 206; options and choice, 219; production, 189, 190; trade, 172n46, 189, 190
transportation infrastructure construction, 136, 148, 185; urban services, 276, 291; urbanization, 190
transportation sector, economies, 35, 59n3
trauma deaths: accidents, 6, 66, 75, 230, 353; gender differences, 75; Migration Propensity Index, 204; native American societies, 319; rates, 6, 66, 67t, 68;

warfare casualties, 6, 28n5, 69*t*, 112, 118, 322, 324, 338
treaties, migration, 159
tribal conflict, 319, 320
trusts, personal legal, 240–241
tuberculosis, 68, 68*t*, 88, 91n6, 319; maternal infections effects, 84; morbidity rates, 259, 261*t*; other disease links, 276, 281n56; prevention, 87; victims, 275
Tubman, Harriet, 196
Turkey, child poverty, 243
Turner, Frederick Jackson, 187
typhoid, 87, 88, 93n69, 258, 276, 281n56
typhus, 89

"unbalanced cargoes" (ships), 150–151
uncertainty, in migration, 135
underemployment, 246, 354
Underground Railroad, 196–7
undocumented immigrants: census issues, 136, 171n8; education, 204; North America, 203–4; unskilled workers, 168, 203; worker wages, 204, 213n47
unemployment: emigration factor, 145; out-migration factor, 199, 204; poverty and, 242, 245, 246, 248; risk reduction, 209, 235; 20th and 21st centuries, 145, 298; unemployed seeking work, 44, 248; work hours changes, 298
Union Army, records, 20, 29n21, 271, 272*t*
unions *see* labor unions
United Kingdom: agriculture, 188, 198; census, 24, 161, 162, 173n85; class barriers, 113; crude birth rates, 119; earnings history, 36–7, 37*f*, 76; emigration, 137, 138, 139*t*, 141–6, 146*f*, 147*f*, 153, 155, 162–4, 172n66, 200–201; fertility transition, 118, 119, 120*f*; health care, 273; HIV/AIDS, 335, 336; Human Development Indexes, 268, 269*f*; illegitimacy rates, 115; Jewish populations, 165*t*, 166; labor markets, 205, 206; labor reforms, 298; life expectancy, 77*f*, 79*t*, 278; marriage age history, 109*f*, 110*f*, 112–13; monarchy, 100, 102; never-married, 112–13, 201; pensions and retirement, 295, 296; population aging, 43*f*, 295; population growth rate, 60n20; poverty and relief, 243–8, 243*f*; regional migration, 200–201, 213n28–n29; sex ratio, 112; total fertility rate, 49; urbanization, 192–3, 192*f*; weight gain, 270, 271*f*, 272; *see also* England; Wales
United Nations: discrimination policies, 296; Human Development Index, 15, 267, 268; organizations and statistics, 29n24; Population Division and data, 41, 59n1, 354–5, 355*t*, 356–7n4
United States: agriculture, 187, 198, 230; borders, 181, 202, 204; census data, 185, 185*t*, 192*f*, 193, 194, 226–7, 226*f*; crude birth rates, 119, 121*f*, 122, 208, 208*t*, 209, 211*f*, 288; crude death rates, 89, 91*f*, 208, 208*t*, 209, 211*f*; divorce, 238–40, 240*f*; economic growth factors, 169; education, 308–9; emigration, 155, 172n64, 203; exports, 213n36; fertility transition, 98, 118–19, 121*f*; foreign-born populations, 137*t*, 155–6, 167–9, 172n64, 203–4; health care, 248, 273, 278–9, 278*f*; HIV/AIDS, 334–6, 334*f*; household size, 226*f*; housework, 302–3, 304*t*; Human Development Index, 267–8, 268*t*, 269*f*; immigration, 141–8, 145, 146*f*, 150, 152, 153, 160–163, 166–170, 174n106, 198, 201–3; immigration policy, 164, 168, 202–4; immigration records, 137, 145, 203–4; income records, 37, 38, 38*f*, 205–6, 244; infant mortality, 72, 73*f*; influenza, 338–40, 341*t*, 342, 347n81; internal migration, 185, 193–4, 194*t*, 195–8, *196*, 309; Jewish populations, 164, 165*t*, 166; labor force participation, 44, 45, 45*f*, 46*f*, 203, 204; labor reforms, 297, 298; life expectancy/death information, 73, 77–80, 77*f*, 78*f*, 85–6, 88, 93n51, 278–9, 278*f*; marriage age history (including colonial era), 107–8, 108*t*, 109*f*, 109*t*, 119, 122; minority mix, 162; native American history, 320; natural resources, 53, 187–8, 202; never-married, 113; nutrition and health records, 267; obesity, 269–72, 271*f*, 279; population aging, 43*f*, 44;

population rate/growth rate, 54–5, 60n20, 167–8; poverty, 243, 243*f*, 244–5; real GDP per capita, 38*f*; regional population distribution, 1790–1860, 185*t*; regions, seasonality, and births, 84–5, 116–17; regions, seasonality, and longevity, 84–6; saving rates, 290–91, 291*f*; second demographic transition/modernity, 48; slave trade, 138–41, 140*f*; slavery, 139, 144, 195–6; sports, 300; third demographic transition, 48; total fertility rate, 49, 122; urbanization, 192*f*, 193; *see also* westward expansion, North America

universal health care *see* national health care/insurance

university education, 308

unskilled jobs: African Americans and, 197; immigrant labor, 143, 159–61, 168, 182, 203; wage profiles, 134–5, 134*f*

unwanted pregnancy, 275; female employees, 223; marriage and, 106; teenage, US, 48

urban growth: economic structure transformations, 35; immigrant populations, 150, 164, 169, 191; pollution, 58; projections, 193*f*; white and black US populations, 197*f*

urban migration, 199–200

urban mortality: gun violence, 75; historical views, vs. rural, 82–9, 93n52, 94n79, 124; infant, 86–8, 94n79; London, 1670 and 1800, 83*f*

urban poor, 247

urban vs. rural comparisons *see* rural vs. urban fertility and family size; rural vs. urban health (non-mortality related); rural vs. urban morbidity; rural vs. urban mortality; rural-urban migration

urbanization: children and labor, 105–6, 118, 122, 195; health aspects, 85, 88–9, 105–6, 256, 331, 332; industrial change and, 188–91, 194; marriage age and birth rates, 106, 122; rates, 88–9, 150, 192–3, 192*f*, 193*f*; women in workplace, 223, 224

urbanization economies, 191

Ure, Andrew, 230

US Bureau of Labor Statistics, 21

US Census/Bureau of the Census: Death Registration Area creation/information, 85; GDP data, 37; history, 24–5, 226; poverty levels, 244; term definitions, 225; urban/rural life expectancies, 85–6; world population estimates, 14*t*; *see also* census-taking

US Civil War, 28n5; debts, 290; foreign-born soldiers, 169; issues preceding, 196; personnel health records, 20, 29n21, 271, 272*t*; population migration and expansion, 185; postwar expansion, 148; slavery, 140, 196, 197; studies, 52

US Constitution, 24, 144, 251

US Department of Agriculture, surveys, 271–2

US Department of Labor, child labor reports, 231–4, 232*t*, 249n33

Uselding, Paul, 168–9

USSR, in WWII, 69, 112

vaccinations, 87, 258, 321; influenza, 342; polio, 261

van de Kaa, David, 46

vaudeville, 300, 311n32

vending machines, 274

Venice, Italy, 306, 311n39

vermin, 274, 325–7, 344

veterans, records, 20, 271, 272*t*

Vikings, 4, 316–17

village building, 189, 191–2, 200, 257

village networks, 153, 190

Virginia, births by race and season, 116, 116*f*

virulence theory, 72, 76

viruses, 68; animal-human diseases, 51, 68, 68*t*; influenza, 68, 338, 339, 341, 342; *see also* HIV/AIDS; plagues; specific diseases

Visigoths, 132

visitor status, 156

vitamin D, 256, 257

Voigtländer, Nico, 56

von Thünen, Johann Heinrich, 186–9, 191

von Wagner, Yohanna, 275–6

Voth, Hans-Joachim, 56

voting records, 24

voting rights, 24, 238

Wachter, Kenneth, 266
wage gaps: disenfranchised populations, 354; European regions, 333, 346n55; gender, 272
wages: agriculture and traditional industries, 124, 182, 188–9, 205, 331, 333; children, 229, 230, 231, 249n32; expected and realized, migration, 134–5, 134*f*, 170, 170n2, 181–2; gender equity, 295; home wage effect, 182; immigration effects, 29n19, 40, 136, 148, 149, 170, 182, 198, 213n47, 316; Malthusian theory, 17, 18, 29n19; older vs. younger workers, 22, 40, 134, 134*f*, 135, 170n2, 231; pensions and retirement, 293–5; undocumented workers, 204, 213n47; urban rates, 199, 200; *see also* income; real wages
Wales: crude birth rates, 208, 208*t*, 210*f*; crude death rates, 90*f*, 208, 208*t*, 210*f*; divorce, 238, 239, 240*f*; education, 307; emigration, 145; fertility transition, 118, 120*f*; infant mortality, 72; influenza, 340, 341*t*; labor markets, 205; life expectancy, 76, 79, 79*t*, 86; marriage age history, 110, 110*f*; poor laws/support, 246, 247; population statistics, 329*t*; urbanization, 192, 192*f*
Walker, Francis Amasa, and Walker Thesis, 168, 169, 174n118, 202
Wallis, John, 264
Wang Feng, 111
Ward, Peter, 20, 266, 281n31
warfare: casualties, 6, 28n5, 69*t*, 112, 118, 322, 324, 338; distribution and disability adjusted life years, 259, 260*t*; famine and, 321–4; funding, 346n50; historic views, 5–6, 51–3, 68–9; marriage and fertility effects, 69, 112, 113, 118, 123, 287; migration and, 132–3, 183; native North Americans, 319, 320; opportunity costs, 6, 52; weaponry, 331
warm late medieval period, 4
Wars of the Roses, 6
Washington, George, 183, 185
waste and waste management *see* sanitation challenges; sanitation infrastructure
Wat Tyler's Revolt (England; 1381), 331

water pollution, 58
water power, 190, 230
water sanitation, and disease, 76, 83, 84, 87–8, 93n69, 274; *see also* sanitation challenges; sanitation infrastructure
wealth inequality *see* income inequality
Webb, Beatrice and Sidney, 230, 247
weekends, 297, 298, 300
Weeks, John, 204
Wegge, Simone, 153
weight: as health measure, 256, 263; obesity, 269–74; taxes, 281n50
welfare programs, 354
West Indies, in slave trade, 139, 140, 140*f*
West Nile virus, 68*t*
Western Europe: birth rate seasonality, 117; crude birth rates, 119, 120*f*, 122, 208, 208*t*, 209, 210*f*; crude death rates, 89, 90*f*, 208, 208*t*, 209, 210*f*; death seasonality, 82–3; divorce and laws, 237–8; education, 306, 308, 311n41; emigration, 138, 143–8, 147*f*, 162–4; fertility transition, 98, 118, 119, 120*f*, 126; illegitimacy rates, 115; Jewish populations, 164, 165*t*, 166; life expectancy/death information, 73, 76, 77*f*, 78, 86, 278; marriage age history, 106, 107*f*, 108*t*, 109*f*, 110, 110*f*, 112–13, 122, 227, 333; never-married, 112–13, 201; poverty, 243, 243*f*, 244, 245, 247; real wages across plague centuries, 332*f*; second demographic transition/modernity, 46–7, 48; sex ratios, 112, 118; third demographic transition, 48
westward expansion, North America, 108, 116, 125, 136, 148, 183–5, 202; advertisements, *184*; land scarcity, and psychological aspects, 187–8; Native American population effects, 319, 320
wetlands, 54
white Americans: birth weight data, 267; births by state, 193–4, 194*t*; child labor, 231; crude birth rates, 119, 121*f*, 211*f*; education, 309; female HIV infection, 334*f*; illegitimacy rates, 115; life expectancy, 92n28; marriage rates and never-married, 113, 114*f*; obesity, 272*t*;

seasonal birth patterns, 116, 116f; urban populations, 197, 197f
WHO see World Health Organization (WHO)
whooping cough, 66, 68t, 258
widowed individuals, 99, 113–14; financial arrangements, 240–241; poverty, 246, 248, 275
Wigglesworth, Edward, 78, 92n27
Wilberforce, William, 139, 140
William I (the Conqueror), 22
William III, King of England, 143
Williamson, Jeffrey G., 170, 290
wills see inheritances
Wilmoth, John, 80
Winegarden, Calman, 277
women: education, 49, 306, 308–9; farm labor, 124, 195, 223, 230; immigrant labor, 161; income potential, 221; informal labor force, 26, 45, 301, 302, 310n11; labor force entrance struggles, 49; labor force participation, 45–7, 46f, 47, 49, 56, 81, 124, 204, 223, 226, 242, 287–8, 301, 311n33, 331, 356; legal property rights, 224, 240–242; marriage attitudes, 44, 48, 224; see also maternal mortality; "missing" females
women-run businesses, 242, 250n62
women's suffrage, 238
wood products, 150, 151, 172n46
Woods, Robert, 83
work hours: housework, 302; manufacturing/offices, 230, 297–8, 297t
work-leisure choice, 286, 297–300
worker age: child labor acceptance, 229, 231, 249n29; child labor laws, 228, 229, 230, 233, 249n32; incomes compared, 22, 40, 134, 134f, 135, 170n2, 231
workhouses, 20, 230, 247
working class: Malthusian views, 17, 18; salaries vs. executives', 244
working poor, 246, 248, 274; see also poverty
workplace accidents and deaths, 66, 75, 230, 353

workplace courtship, 223
World Bank, 209; food supply data, 262; remittances data, 154, 155t; World Development Indicators, 39t
World Health Organization (WHO), 209; disability adjusted life years data, 259, 260t, 280n11; HIV data, 336f, 337; influenza data/policy, 339, 342; morbidity/death cause data, 65, 66, 67t, 261t
world population see global population estimates; population growth
World Trade Organization (WTO), 209
World War I: Chinese labor, 160–61; Civil War and, 28n5; deaths, 338; industrial jobs, 197; influenza outbreak/transmission, 339–40, 346n72; mortality rates and marriage effects, 113; mortality rates and sex ratio effects, 113, 118; postwar attitudes, 167
World War II: child safety, 132–3; deaths, 69, 112; famines during, 323–4; Holocaust, 69, 133, 164, 166; industrial jobs, 197–8, 287–8; post-war baby boom, 43, 45, 123, 239, 286, 287–8; post-war divorce, 239; post-war migration, 203
Wrigley, Edward, 21, 90f, 91f, 106, 107f, 119, 120f, 121f, 210f, 211

xenophobia, US, 157
Xenopsylla cheopis (rat flea), 68t, 326–7, 328

Y chromosome, 8
Yersinia pestis, 325–8, 344, 345n34, 345n40
Young, Alwyn, 337–8
young marriage see marriage age
youth migration: children, 144; young adults, 182, 183f, 209, 288
youth mortality, 70, 71, 74, 78, 80, 341
Yuan dynasty, 132

zero population growth, 31
zoonoses, 12, 51, 58, 66, 68, 68t, 82, 326–8, 339, 344